STOP WORRYING, START LIVING

A GUIDE FOR THE SPIRITUAL *warrior* ~~WORRIER~~

Cover Design:
Tree silhouette with roots © Kudryashka #1950502

The illustrations found on the following pages are in public domain or available for download from www.istockphoto.com. Three artists, however, contributed their work under licence:
Howard David Johnson, Terence John Cleary, Vanessa Ryan

Book Layout Inspired by: *The Writers Journey, Mythic Structure for Writers* by Christopher Vogler

Layout: Pageprint@pageprint.net

Copy-editing Team: Lois Braun and Elizabeth Falk.

Proof Readers:
Olivia Emma Ravenall and Vicki Neale

ISBN 978-0-473-22550-6

For copies of this book contact Caroline at:
info@carolineravenall.com

WITHOUT WHOM....

Until one has written a book, one has no idea about what's involved. It sounds easy. It isn't. Writing a book is a team effort, so there are a few people who should be mentioned:

Les Kletke, my book coach in Altona, Canada, whom I met by chance at a National Speakers Convention in Cape Town in 2009. Not only has he become a firm friend for life, he's the reason that this book exists today. He has given me the inspiration and guidance I've needed, and frequently talked me down from the ledge when the going got to be too much. Who'd have thought that one could have a coach on the other side of the world! But it works. (www.globalghostwriter.com)

Nick Williams (www.inspired-entrepreneur.com) who continuously encourages me to 'show up'.

My partner, Steve, who supported me throughout this process, allowing me to take eighteen months away from the grind to actually get the book finished. I don't think he knew what he was letting himself in for; he's put up with my highs and lows, and even though it's been difficult, he's also started on his own warrior's journey. This book wouldn't have happened without him.

Copy-editing team Lois Braun and Elizabeth Falk in Altona, Canada, who patiently edited, re-edited and edited again all the changes I made while striving for the perfect manuscript.

My friend Vicki Neale, who has been a rock throughout this process, and my mum, Olivia Emma Ravenall, who painstakingly proofread the final manuscript before it went to print and made some invaluable contributions to the end product.

Peter from Cafe Q in Warkworth, Natacha and Jonathan from the Dragonfly Cafe in Matakana, and Fenella and Bob from Matakana Market Kitchen, whose restaurants became my headquarters for many months before my home office became a reality.

My friends and family who have been a continuous support, and have badgered and cajoled me in their own inimitable ways, not to give up: my sister Suzanne, Bridget Edwards and Gavin Heimann, Peter Kramer and Annie

Heneke in Johannesburg; Adell Van Zyl in Cape Town; Vanessa Ryan in Nelson; Jo and Michael Hartley; Margot Minett; Vicki and Terry Neale in Auckland; and of course, my mum who has always been there, no matter what.

All those who have contributed to the book writing/publishing process but preferred to remain anonymous. You know who you are. I am very grateful for your thoughtfulness, insight and wisdom.

When I pick up a book for the first time, particularly one with over 400 pages (like this one) I tend to open it up and scan the contents before agreeing to buy it. I like to read in small chunks and find myself feeling a little overwhelmed when faced with oceans of solid text without natural breaks or illustrations. So when I set out to write this book, I had a very clear idea of how I wanted it to look. Whilst many of the illustrations you see on the following pages are in the public domain, there are three artists who contributed their work under licence and should be mentioned.

The first, the American illustrator Howard David Johnson (www.howarddavidjohnson.com) who has worked with many prestigious clients around the globe. His mythical art is simply out of this world. Those who wish to embroil themselves in myths will find his website makes for very interesting reading and viewing. I feel very privileged to be showcasing some of his work. The Grail Maiden (p.20), the Sleeping Beauty (p.62), the Dragon Slayer (p.133), Belleraphon and Pegasus (p.161,) Faerie Guardians (p.171), the Moon Goddess Diana (p.262), Pandora's Box (p.266), the Dragon Nidhoggr (p.280), the Protectors of the Earth (p.336), a Modern Semiramis (p.399), the Legendary King Arthur (p.403).

The second, Terence John Cleary (www.terencejohncleary.com) for the beautiful illustration of The Old Wagon Wheel on page 202.

And the third, my special friend Vanessa Ryan, whose artistic abilities are just amazing. Like Father, like daughter! The Tree of Life image you see at the beginning of each chapter and outlined in full on page 191, is her work.

For all those who are worrying and wandering

TABLE OF CONTENTS

INTRODUCTION

Come to the edge, he said.
They said, we are afraid.
Come to the edge, he said.
They came,
And he pushed them,
And they flew.

Guillaume Appollinaire (1880–1918)
French poet and playwright

'I am afraid,' he said. 'Nothing makes sense any more. Everything I am, everything I have worked for, everything I have believed is just so pointless. Where do I turn? I don't have a map, or a compass. I feel like I am going mad.'

My heart went out to him. This poor man, who babbled on almost incoherently, whose success on the surface was outwardly visible, had everything to live for. But yet his eyes were fearful. He was tired and burned out and utterly perturbed by the darkness and imbalance within himself. The desperation behind those eyes betrayed the inner feeling of absolute hopelessness that threatened to consume him totally from every angle; the terrible fear and the absolute terror of stepping into the unknown, to change, to look deeper.

I knew those feelings only too well. As an overly anxious individual who for over forty years unknowingly suppressed her creative spirit in an effort to fit in with the world, I spent most of my life worrying about pretty much everything. Did I live my life in the right way? Was I successful enough? What was I supposed to be doing? Was I too fat, too thin? Where was I going? I was only too familiar with the frequent stomach butterflies and gnawing restlessness eating away at my insides almost every moment of every day. The shortness of breath, the heart palpitations, the dizziness and queasiness that consumed me every time I tried to push against my own personal boundaries. I'd learned to live with the underlying fear that threatened to irrationally take over and override everything else in existence.

This excessive worry inevitably lead to frequent bouts of depression and anxiety – not all of them debilitating, but life became a real struggle and effort. The continuous striving was hard. I would find myself frequently suffering from fatigue and burnout. My weight fluctuated up and down along with the worry, which just added to the problem. I knew all the stress-busting techniques for my A-type, high-energy personality: exercise, stilling the mind, positive affirmations, meditation, relaxation, looking for the good and taking frequent breaks in nature. But this still did not quell the internal chaos. There were monsters within, scary ones, ones that I certainly didn't understand nor want to face.

At age 35, I had it all. As head of Sales and Marketing in Richard Branson's Virgin Atlantic Airways, I was a rising star. Focused and determined, I was seconded to South Africa at 29 years of age as part of a two-man team to set up the airline and launch the first Virgin brand on the African continent. I earned a great salary, travelled internationally and was destined to move around the globe from country to country working my way up in the Virgin hierarchy. I could regale listeners with wonderful stories of the time I spent with this renowned entrepreneur – mention the word *Virgin* or *Richard Branson* at any social occasion and people's eyes would light up. My diary was filled with business appointments. Parties? I was on the guest list of everyone who was anyone. I had amazing friends and acquaintances, lots of spare cash and many male admirers. What more could I ask for? If this was part of a successful life then I had arrived!

That was until the day that it all went horribly wrong. I can't remember when it started exactly, but the gnawing feeling of dissatisfaction and anxiety grew within me to fever pitch. One night I found myself sitting on the floor of my bedroom with my head in my hands sobbing uncontrollably – yet again. Months of depression had taken their toll. I was utterly exhausted. Overwork of course had contributed to this, along with my excessive drive, anxiety and constant striving for perfection. But deep down there was something more than this: a deep disillusionment with life, with the mundane routine that presented itself every day. I was stuck, physically, mentally and emotionally. A dichotomy raged within: I had a yearning for things to be different, but at the same time felt the impenetrable urge to keep them the same.

How do we make sense of our world when we suddenly wake up one day to realise that everything that we were convinced represented stability and security, is no longer? When everything we are striving for doesn't make sense? When the landscape is meaningless and we find ourselves fighting to regain control of the vision, hopes and dreams that motivated us for so long? Who do we turn to when we have deeper questions about life's issues – our boss? a psychologist? a life coach? I tried many avenues.

Talking to a psychologist helped, when I finally found the right one. Through the process of cognitive behaviour therapy I started to understand how to manage my moods and emotions, and think differently. The sessions were great in terms of getting my head around the issues that clouded my judgement. I put them neatly into boxes and filed them away. However, it didn't answer the questions that still burned so deeply.

For this I sought a coach to help me dig deep and find the answers. Coaches are great in terms of prompting and guiding you to find your own answers, providing that the coach is not stuck in the 'upping-your-game' mindset, and has the ability to help you transcend the issues of life. The coachees (clients) must also have a clear objective and know what they want to achieve. I didn't.

Friends and family were a wonderful support; that is, those who were close enough or astute enough to know what was really going on. Many have indeed given me insights and ah-ha moments over the years, but none of them were able to make any more sense of life and its meaning than I was. Their ideas and judgements were based on their own realities of life, their own ideas of what was right and wrong, ideas developed from religion, parental conditioning, confused teachers and the world around them.

In my humble experience, one of the only ways to overcome our own personal limitations and the resulting conditions they cause is to find *meaning*. Holocaust survivor Victor Frankl said, 'Those who have a "why" to live, can bear with almost any "how."' And I think he was right. This simple dynamic alone is worth more than a thousand anti-depressants or early-morning trips to the gym in an effort to release those magical endorphins. Meaning provides us with the motivation to move forward, to recover, and to rediscover life, even if we do need some help and support along the way. Without it, we cannot progress. It is the engine that drives us forward, giving us inspiration and hope.

A quest for meaning and the deeper answers to life's questions inevitably brings us to explore matters of the spirit. It's a quest that needs to transcend the rational considerations of the 'ordinary world' demanding that one enters the realms of the 'hidden and unseen' in an effort to find the anwers to life's deeper questions : Why am I here? What's my purpose? Who am I really? And how should I be living my life? But where does one start?

When one is trying to establish answers to questions that are not immediately forthcoming at a time in our life when one needs them quickly, it can be very discouraging, to say the least. (Not to mention time consuming and costly, particularly if you keep meeting up with the wrong people.) It is hard to find 'a truth' that makes sense in the plethora of today's modern religions and spiritual beliefs. As a self-confessed agnostic, I needed something substantial, a *framework* that made both logical and spiritual sense at the same time. Since childhood, I hadn't been able to find answers to a single one of my questions in Western orthodox religions. The orthodox systems of the East, although they seemed to hold more of what felt right, required me to lose myself in all consuming practices that the teachers themselves couldn't fully explain, at least not in a way that captured my heart and answered one fundamental question: Why? In the same way, self-appointed 'spiritual' gurus, with their unsubstantiated airy-fairy philosophies about life and God also made me sick with frustration. How come they had all got the plot and I hadn't? I felt as if I was really going around in circles.

That was, until I suddenly found myself in the middle of my own crazy spiritual adventure, my own 'warrior's journey' – moving from the world of day-to-day straight into the pages of Dan Brown's *Da Vinci Code*. It started when I met an extraordinary man who was to become my teacher, guide, and inspiration for many years. He led me on a journey that took me to places I couldn't have imagined. The journey, however, had its fallibilities. I learned, to my chagrin, that even the spiritual path is not paved with gold once the heavy gates guarding its secrets are set ajar. The path is treacherous and difficult to navigate. It requires discernment, courage and patience and it's certainly not for the faint hearted. But the upside is, as in all the 'hero myths' of the world, that there is a reward at the end, even though it may not be abundantly obvious to others or even to ourselves when we are in the throes of expedition.

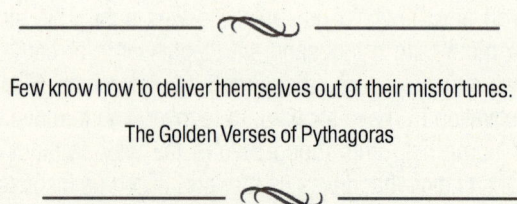

Few know how to deliver themselves out of their misfortunes.

The Golden Verses of Pythagoras

Life is difficult. To transcend it, each one of us needs a personal philosophy, one that we can cling to in times of difficulty. Without it, we are dragged through the streets by our emotions, inner conflicts and problems, lurching from one crisis to the next as life's worries and problems overtake us. Any personal philosophy needs to have a strong foundation, one whose roots run deep; a philosophy which becomes our own personal road map and compass, providing us with a platform of understanding upon which further knowledge and wisdom can be built and false doctrines discarded.

To find the answers to some of life's toughest questions, one needs to go on a journey, and this is fundamentally what this book is about. Ultimately, the journey is a quest for *personal liberation*, a way to stop worrying and start living to one's full potential. This book is intended for those who, amid the muddle of 'spiritual technobabble' out there in 2012, want to place their feet firmly on solid ground and not be gently swathed in cotton with mystique and mystery. I am assuming that by reading this, you have come far enough on your own journey in life to at least be intrigued by matters of the spirit, having found yourself searching for a different perspective. 'Adopt another's philosophy until you can find your own' were valuable words of advice once given to me. So my hope is that this book will perhaps serve as a stimulant, providing some *mental nuts to crack* or some *food for thought* in the form of questions, challenges, stories and ideas.

I don't profess to have all the answers; on the contrary, I continue to struggle with life issues daily. I just have the capacity to handle them a little better than I once did. However, the lessons I've learned have given me more energy, motivation and enthusiasm for life. I have more confidence to live authentically at my own pace with a greater degree of courage. Most of all, this journey has given me hope – even on my darkest days, when the world does its best to unseat me.

What you will find in these pages is by no means inclusive nor a universal panacea. I share my journey as a kind of 'road map', together with some of the lessons and weapons that I have found invaluable in shaping my understanding and sense of purpose. My wish is that you can find some truth within these pages that resonates with you, a truth that also gives you hope and supports you on your own path through life.

God speed.

A Practical Guide

GETTING THE BEST FROM THIS BOOK

This book has been written in three parts using excerpts from myth, fairy tales and legend throughout. (I'll explain the value of mythology below and in greater detail in the next chapter.)

Book One: Mapping the Journey tells of *my* journey; a journey of transformation from *worrier* to *warrior.* It's a tale from the trenches depicting the highlights and pitfalls that anyone sincerely searching for answers about life, the universe and everything may experience. It's been written as a *road map for change*, a sixteen-stage mythological compass of sorts to help readers navigate their own journey. (A graphical representation of the road map can be seen in Fig. 1 below.) It tells of an adventure, of going against the grain, of stepping into the unknown in an effort to live life more authentically. It also speaks of how I navigated my own spiritual journey without having to turn myself into a pretzel in some impossible yoga position or scour the monasteries and ashrams of India in search of a guru. And finally, it tells of the struggle to overcome my inner demons, which inevitably accompany any journey that leads us away from the beaten track.

Book Two: Lessons from the Special World contains a summary of 'things to understand', spiritual lessons and insights which, in my experience, are too often shrouded in spiritual hype and religious mystique making non-believers baulk and stick fervently to their agnostic ways. The lessons help to ground me during times of stress or personal difficulty, and substantiate my reason for being when I struggle for a perspective on life.

Book Three: Weapons and Tools is the self-help section of the book, containing some practical tools and insights that the modern-day spiritual warrior needs to use when navigating the white-water rapids of life.

A ROAD MAP FOR CHANGE

During times of great turmoil, when the answers to life's questions elude us and our old paradigms don't work anymore, we might want to have a more in-depth look at what's really going on. Mythology can serve as a good guide for taking action during times of change and transition because it doesn't wholly rely on one's personal belief system, nor on a world view that is no longer fully effective. As mythology doesn't favour any particular religion or system of belief, we are perhaps more accepting of the messages each tale brings forth, enabling us to consider our plight differently.

The road map in Book 1 is depicted as a *cycle of change*, one that has been loosely based on the work of Joseph Campbell (1904–1987), the American mythologist, writer and lecturer, whose book, *The Hero with a Thousand Faces*, may turn out to be one of the most influential works of the 20th century. Campbell dedicated his life to uncovering the symbolism and meaning behind many of the myths and legends of our time. His work runs parallel to that of the Swiss psychologist Carl G. Jung, who wrote of the *archetypes* which appeared frequently in the dreams of his patients and the myths of all cultures. (Archetypes are underlying mythic *themes* or *stereotypes* that exemplify different forms of behaviour. They often appear as universal personifications in myths, legends, fairy tales, Shakespearean dramas and Biblical stories.) Jung suggested that both myth and dream reflected different aspects of the human psyche, each potentially coming from a deeper source: the collective unconscious of mankind.

If you want to understand the mythological hero's journey, there is no

THE WARRIOR'S JOURNEY ROAD MAP

Figure 1

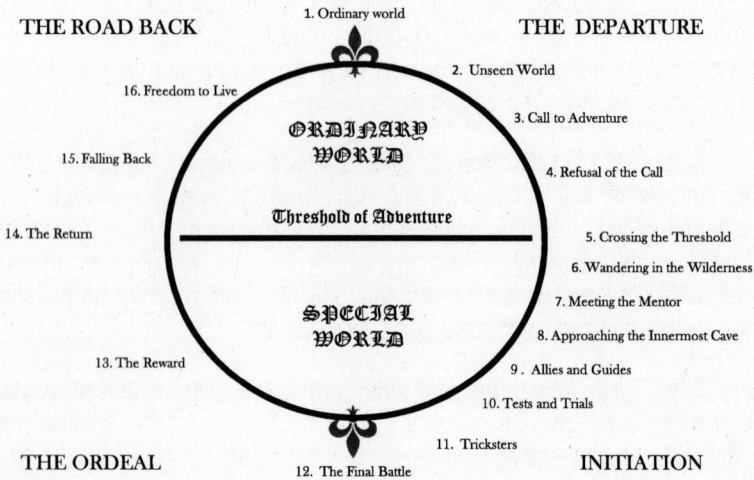

THE ROAD BACK

THE DEPARTURE

THE ORDEAL

INITIATION

1. Ordinary world
2. Unseen World
3. Call to Adventure
4. Refusal of the Call
5. Crossing the Threshold
6. Wandering in the Wilderness
7. Meeting the Mentor
8. Approaching the Innermost Cave
9. Allies and Guides
10. Tests and Trials
11. Tricksters
12. The Final Battle
13. The Reward
14. The Return
15. Falling Back
16. Freedom to Live

ORDINARY WORLD

Threshold of Adventure

SPECIAL WORLD

substitute for reading some of Campbell's works, which are listed in the bibliography. In Chapter IV of *The Hero with a Thousand Faces*, called 'The Keys', Campbell gives an outline of the *hero's journey*, which I have taken the liberty of adapting to reflect the journey of the spiritual warrior. You can compare the two outlines below. I am retelling the hero myth in my own way, and you might someday want to do the same. Every individual can change the mythical path to suit his or her own purpose.

COMPARISON OF OUTLINES

THE WARRIOR'S JOURNEY	**THE HERO'S JOURNEY**
	(from *The Hero with a Thousand Faces*)
The Departure	
The Ordinary World	World of Common Day
The Unseen World	
The Call to Adventure	Call to Adventure
Refusal of the Call	Refusal of the Call
Crossing the Threshold	Crossing the First Threshold
Initiation	
Wandering in the Wilderness	
Meeting the Mentor	Supernatural Aid
Approaching the Innermost Cave	Belly of the Whale
Allies and Guides	
Tests and Trials	Road of Trials
Tricksters	
The Ordeal	
The Final Battle	Meeting with the Goddess
	Woman as Temptress
	Atonement with the Father
	Apotheosis
The Reward	The Ultimate Boon
The Road Back	
The Return	Refusal of the Return
	The Magic Flight
	Rescue from Without
	Crossing the Return Threshold
Falling Back	
	Master of Two Worlds
Freedom to Live	Freedom to Live

THE WARRIOR'S JOURNEY ROAD MAP

The road map itself is a continuous journey, a cycle of change which takes the central character of the story from the '*ordinary world*' of everyday into a '*special world*' where life is vastly different from that with which the hero is familiar. Through a process of setting out (the departure), descent into the special world (initiation and ordeal), and a series of adventures, the hero eventually makes his way back (the road back) to begin the journey all over again with renewed zest and vigour, having learned much from his travels.

The road map depicted on page 8 is only a skeletal framework depicting the stages of my own personal journey. It does not have to be mirrored precisely should you decide to plot your own. Not all stages of the journey need to appear systematically at the point in which they are listed above. The order in which each stage appears here is only one of several possibilities. For example, one may meet the mentor before crossing the threshold, and as a result, the journey may turn out to be vastly different. In whichever way the journey is plotted, no two will be identical. The only thing that is really important is the journey itself.

The story of the mythological hero and the story of the spiritual warrior are the same. (The two words *warrior* and *hero* are used interchangeably throughout this book.) Despite the infinite variety of mythical stories in our global cultures, they all have one thing in common: There is always a journey. The journey may be an outward one to a strange and unfamiliar place – a forest, a city, a labyrinth or a cave – which sets the centre stage for many trials and challenges that the hero has to overcome. Yet the journey is also inward, into the depths of one's own heart or psyche, where one is irrevocably transformed in some way – sadness becomes joy, confusion becomes understanding, frustration becomes willing acceptance and anger becomes love.

The stages of the hero's journey can be found in every one of our lives, not just in the lives of mythological heroes. Maybe we are starting a new job, overcoming an illness, recovering from a divorce, moving to a new town or city, facing challenges in a relationship with a partner or a boss or writing a book; whatever situation we find ourselves in, there is always a journey to be undertaken and always a great degree of courage and tenacity (demonstrated by all mythological heroes) to complete it. The different stages of the journey emerge naturally, even when we're not aware of them; it's part of the mystery of dream and myth. I am convinced that the knowledge given to us by this most ancient guide will always be useful wherever we are, helping us to figure out where we are, and giving us the courage to again gather up the reins of our trusty steed and take the next brave step onward.

NOTE: It is also relevant to mention another book that has served as an inspiration in writing my own story, that being *The Writer's Journey* by Christopher Vogler, who is one of Hollywood's premier story consultants. For people wishing to write their own books or even simply plot their own 'hero's journey', his book is well worth a read.

The work of finding traces of hidden knowledge, or even hints of its existence, resembles the work of archaeologists looking for traces of some forgotten ancient civilisation, and finding them buried beneath several strata of cemeteries left by people who have since lived in that place, separated possibly by thousands of years, each unaware of the others existence....

Man is conscious of being surrounded by the 'wall of the unknown', but at the same time believes that he can get through the wall as others have gone through it. But he cannot imagine, or imagines very vaguely, what there may be behind this wall. He does not know what he would like to find there or what it means to posses such knowledge....

People clamour so loudly and so often about the unlimited possibilities of knowledge but in actual fact all the unlimited possibilities of knowledge are limited by the five senses: sight, hearing, smell, touch and taste, plus the capacity of reasoning and comparing beyond which a man can never go. We do not take stuffiest account of this circumstance and this is why we are at a loss to define the difference between ordinary knowledge, hidden knowledge and possible knowledge....

In this incapacity of man to imagine what exists beyond the wall of the known and the possible lies his chief tragedy, and in this is the reason why so much remains hidden from him and why there are so many questions to which he will never find the answer. In the history of human knowledge there are many attempts to define the history of 'possible' knowledge. But there is no attempt to find out what these limits would mean and where it would lead us....

In all myths and fairy tales of all times, we find the idea of 'magic, witchcraft and sorcery', which as we come nearer to our own period take the form of 'spirituality' and 'occultism'. But even people who believe in these words understand very little about what they really mean and in what respect the knowledge of a 'magician' or an 'occultist' differs from the knowledge of an ordinary man and therefore all attempts to create mystical knowledge end in failure.

P. D. Ouspensky (1878–1947)
The New Model of the Universe

THE VALUE OF THE MYTH

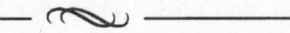

Myth is the secret opening through which the inexhaustible energies of the cosmos pour into human cultural manifestation. It provides the symbols that carry the human spirit forward in counteraction to those other common human fantasies that tie it back. It may be that the very high incidence of neuroticism among ourselves follows the decline of such effective spiritual aid.

Joseph Campbell (1904–1987)
The Hero with a Thousand Faces

yths and legends, regardless of their origin, may seem like childhood fantasies to some – a collection of weird and interesting stories that serve merely as good entertainment. To others, they open a fascinating doorway into a world of heroes and heroines, the triumph of good over evil and man's eternal struggle for identity and wisdom, telling tales of conflict, difficulty, sadness, confusion and the strength of the human spirit. If we learn to interpret their message, myths hold the power to help us uncover who we really are by connecting us authentically with our truest sense of identity and our deepest longings, each story stirring up something deep within us, sparking a sense of wonder and curiosity.

Whilst I agree that not all mythological heroes will be fighting with a Board of Directors, losing a small fortune in the stock market, or figuring out their next career move, their quests contain many symbolic representations of situations and events that stir up similar emotions of anxiety, fear, frustration, anger, humiliation, joy and passion. By interrogating these myths, we can uncover a valuable road map for change containing a deeper and more meaningful truth. The 21st century map makes the assumption that our careers will define us, and that material wealth, talent and hard work alone will help us overcome any obstacles in our path. Because we might at times win certain victories over the forces that conspire to derail us, we often naively believe that we can sail on unencumbered from one success to another, eventually arriving in the land where peace, recognition, and safety preside. Unfortunately, life's not like that. The obstacles we face are not outside of us, they lie within. Careers do not define us, neither do material wealth or our standing in society, and the Kingdom of Nirvana doesn't exist. So when we eventually realize that the current map is flawed in some way, we find ourselves floundering, confused, lost and afraid. At times like these, myths, fairy tales and legends can act as our own built-in navigation system, providing us with a more realistic and honest representation of what we are experiencing.

In the ancients' view, the mythic past was deeply rooted in historic times where oral tradition was combined with history concealing an ancient wisdom within. For example, many of the Celtic myths were integrated into the early versions of the Grail Legends, and carried across Europe by Anglo-Norman storytellers through the courts of France, England and Germany. Perhaps the Grail Legends themselves were written to protect this great spiritual and cultural heritage when sorely threatened by the Roman Empire and the Catholic Church. The 12th century in Europe was a turbulent time after the return of the Crusaders to the Holy Land, seeing a cross-fertilisation of Christian and Eastern/Islamic (Sufi) traditions, which the church fervently sought to eradicate. In its view, Europe had become 'infected' by the ways of the 'infidels' and it persecuted any 'heretical' system whose beliefs conflicted with its own, seeing the elimination of many pre-Christian traditions (for example, the Knights Templar, the Albigensa and Cathari) which maybe held more realistic and meaningful versions of truth.

However, the greatest of these myths have survived because the truths they tell span the ages. The heroic protagonists were seen as a link between the 'age of origins' and the every-day mortal world. Many of the stories were crucial to social stability, providing an explanation for the current state of affairs and driving many moral and personal decisions during times of great upheaval. Deep down within, we recognize that these stories are as relevant today as they have always been, reflecting situations faced by ordinary folk whose situations bear a striking resemblance to our own. Perhaps this is why we find ourselves inundated with so many movie remakes of myth-type stories: *The Chronicles of Narnia; Beowulf; The Clash of the Titans; Achilles; The Lord of the Rings; The Hobbit;* and *Alice in Wonderland*.

Is there any historical evidence to suppose there really was a Grail to be achieved? Or is the legend only a delightful literary device created by Troubadours and Conteurs to entertain the courts of Europe as they gently dozed off after stuffed aurochs and roasted boar? In searching for the answers to such mysteries we must step into an enchanted and mythical world which appears to endlessly expand in complexity and beauty wherever we look. Somewhere in the interwoven strands of this medieval tapestry there is a radical and compelling message which is as fresh and alive today as it was in the twelfth century.

Malcolm Godwin

The Holy Grail

From a very young age, I've always had a fascination with myths and fairy tales. From tales of kings, queens, enchanted castles, wizards and magicians, to gallant knights on a quest for the Holy Grail, each one captured my imagination and permeated my dreams, whipping up my optimism for a better life. Bedtime was always a rich and exciting prospect, particularly at my grandmother's house, which was awash with interesting trinkets and books, as I snuggled under the thick, quilted eiderdowns and begged her to read me another story of mystical places, fabulous creatures, the miraculous and unbelievable.

This fascination continued well into adult life. I grew up in the UK with a father who had a keen interest in history and historical architecture, so as a young adult, I often spent weekends and public holidays frequenting the historical sites of the British Isles. While my parents were wandering off somewhere with the guidebook, my imagination would run riot atop the towers of a ruined castle, as I fancied myself there in a long flowing dress, waiting for my brave knight to return on his black stallion to rescue me from my teenage suffering. I would imagine that I heard the clash of steel on steel, the thundering of hooves and the sounds of yesteryear as I stood quietly alone, with only the breeze for company. Soaking up the atmosphere in its entirety, I would painstakingly piece together in my mind the layout of the castle as it would have been in its time and fully picture myself there. I was certain that I must have known this kind of life, feeling so wild, carefree and untamed. I believed myself to be lost in time, a stranger in the 1970s. Times past were no doubt my true home.

I lost contact with mythology during my 'corporate episode', but rediscovered it during my own quest for identity and purpose, this time with a rekindled fascination and greater degree of appreciation as I started to understand why they resonated with me so deeply. This time I did not think of them merely as interesting tales or outdated beliefs from a defunct religion. I discovered that many of the poets and storytellers throughout history were not only wordsmiths but scientists and men of God. Like me, they strived hard to explore the nature of their inner world, to understand and devour the mysteries that have long since been lost to our Western civilisation. Many wrote their secrets in the myths, sagas, legends and fairy tales of our time, veiling them in secrecy, hiding them from the profane, but opening them up to those who have 'eyes to see'. This is why they resonate with us so deeply. There is truth hidden within, truth which can be seen in this allegorical Egyptian tale of the Seven Veils of Isis.

There was in Egyptian times in the Nile Valley a magnificent temple dedicated to the Goddess Isis at Sais. It was one of the most famous in all antiquity. In the vestibule was a statue of Isis, which was covered by seven veils, and an inscription which said, 'Isis am I, I am all that was, that is, and that shall be, and no one of mortals has ever lifted my veil.' In ancient times, these seven veils represented seven great mysteries that had to be penetrated by the sincere seeker. Only after one had successfully lifted all of the veils in the correct order, could he or she look upon the beauty of Isis. There is a tale told of one seeker, who crept into the temple alone late one night, impatient for a glimpse of the naked goddess. He lifted all seven veils, gazed at her beauty and instantly knew everything there was to know about creation. But he paid a heavy price, with his impatience; he wasn't ready to absorb the magnitude of what he discovered and immediately went blind.

The veils are symbolic of seven steps, or seven stages, that stood in the path of the seeker before he could fully realise truth. They served a twofold purpose: first, they hid the beauty of Isis – the truth – from the profane: but secondly, they exposed her beauty to the sincere seeker only if he penetrated the mysteries correctly and in the appropriate order. Not all are ready for truth and too much too soon can have a devastating effect.

These veils of truth can be found in the fables, fairy tales, myths, legends, sagas, allegories and parables we find in today's literature. When we take time to look more closely, we might be surprised to find that they are not just entertaining stories for children, they can enlighten those who have 'eyes to see' and serve a powerful purpose for young and old alike. When we take time to understand their hidden meaning, we can begin to unlock the secrets of our own true nature, which is so carefully concealed from us. The seven veils can be seen to represent seven *categories* of folklore, which I will refer to throughout this book to illustrate certain points or stages in the journey.

FABLES

We use the word *fabulous* all the time these days. However, the original use of the word came from a *fable* – a story containing a 'fabulous creature' – a unicorn, a phoenix, a sphinx, a lion or a griffin, who was the wise keeper of a deep secret. The mythical lion Aslan in *The Chronicles of Narnia* is one such creature. Fables are traditionally stories of animals that are endowed with human qualities. Such stories highlight human failings, weaknesses and limitations, which are portrayed as an interplay between animals instead of people. Many writers throughout history have adopted a fable to illustrate this principle. For example: the Greek slave, Aesop, wrote 'The Tortoise and the Hare' and 'The Fox and the Crow'; North American tales such as 'Uncle Remus' and 'Br'er Rabbit' are considered to be fables, together with the German tale of 'Reynard the Fox'. In the 1920s, Rupert Bear first appeared in the British tabloid *The Daily Express,* and his fantastic adventures became a hot children's favourite.

FAIRY TALES

Did you ever wonder why tales like 'Snow White', 'Jack and the Beanstalk', 'Cinderella' and 'Beauty and the Beast', just to mention a few, were so fascinating to you as a child? This is because fairy tales speak of the spiritual path and the different stages of the journey undertaken by the seeker. Each tale is steeped in symbolism, focusing on one single aspect of the journey, or gives details of the entire passage taken by the seeker towards enlightenment. 'Jack and the Beanstalk' is one such example. Whilst the storyteller speaks of fairies, gnomes, monsters, dragons, witches, magic and enchantment, these are depicted in veiled terms as the encounters that the 'initiate', or seeker, young or old, faces on his path. Perhaps this is why fairy tales are still read by so many children today.

MYTHOLOGY

Every culture has a form of mythology, whether it be the Greek, Roman, Celtic or Nordic myths (the Icelandic *eddas*), or the myths of China, Japan, Persia, India and Egypt. Myths tell of times past when gods, goddesses and humans dwelt together or were in contact with each other. They tell of rivalry, disputes, triumphs and failures. Again, these myths speak of the spiritual path in a veiled way. For example, the Greek hero myths speak of heroes like Hercules, Perseus, or Jason and his Argonauts who go in search of a Golden Fleece, or a Gorgons head, or some sort of magical talisman, symbolic of a quest for truth.

LEGENDS

These are based on *true* stories and events surrounding semi-historic figures that may once have actually lived. Their exploits are exaggerated to heroic levels to illustrate principles of the spiritual path. Examples are the legends of Charlemagne the Great, Samuel Taylor Coleridge's 'Kubla Khan', and the legends of Prester John, which tell the tale of a Christian patriarch, or king. Exaggeration gave the writers the opportunity to graft many principles relating to the spiritual path onto the story to illustrate a particular point. It is well known today that the Celtic oral traditions of King Artaius and Queen Gwenhwyvar were told through the historical figures of King Arthur and Queen Guinevere. Merlin was Myddrin, Mordred was Medrawt, Gallahad was Gwalchaved, Sir Kay was Kai.

EPIC POETRY

Epic poems depict 'tales of times past' which are told in prose, sometimes Pagan, sometimes Christian and sometimes Viking. They tell stories of humans and their trials and tribulations. The Völsunga sagas of Iceland and Norway, in the poetic and prose *eddas,* depict the tales of Viking families. Among the more notable adaptations of this text are Richard Wagner's *Der Ring des Nibelüngen*, more commonly known as Wagner's *Ring*, consisting of four epic operas.

The dozen or so versions of the Grail Legends, pagan, Christian and alchemical are also epic poems. The legends first appeared in the 12th century from the French poet, Chretien De Troyes, and were further embellished by the German *Minnesingers* (a poet or wandering minstrel) Wolfram von Eschenbach, and the British cleric, Geoffrey of Monmouth.

The 'Bhagavad Gita' is a 700-verse Hindu scripture, part of the epic poem, *The Mahabarrata*, depicting the tale of Lord Krishna and the Pandava prince, Arjuna.

The *Epic of Gilgamesh* from Mesopotamia is another, which originated from many Sumerian legends. The story revolves around a relationship between Gilgamesh and his close male companion, Enkidu, a 'wild man' created by the gods as Gilgamesh's equal to distract him from oppressing the citizens of Uruk. Within these tales, one will find a plethora of references to the spiritual journey.

ALLEGORIES

These are stories with a hidden meaning. They speak of one thing and mean another. *The Pilgrim's Progress* by John Bunyan, and Dante's *Divine Comedy* are examples.

In the allegorical romance, *The Chymical Wedding of Christian Rosenkreutz*, Christian is invited to a castle full of miracles in order to assist in the 'chymical wedding' of the king and the queen.

Goethe tells the complex story of Faust, who is a scientific empiricist forced to confront questions of good and evil, God and the devil, sexuality and mortality. 'The Green Snake and the Beautiful Lily' is another allegorical tale by the same author. *Alice in Wonderland* and *The Lord of the Rings* can be considered allegories because they each offer a concentrated depiction of the spiritual seeker's journey.

PARABLES

There are many examples of religious stories with a deeper meaning in the scriptures of the world. Jesus spoke in parables in the Bible. Rama Krishna, when asked by one of his followers what God was like, was purported to have told the parable of the 'little salt doll', a doll made of rock salt. She went through the country asking people what the sea was like, but nobody could explain. So eventually she went to find the sea herself. Upon walking into the sea, however, she melted completely and never came out again. Only then did she know what the sea was like. She had to give of herself to truly understand, as is the case with so many things in life. The meaning of the parable is that we can only truly understand God when we merge with him totally. One has to experience it.

For hundreds of years, Western civilization, although technologically advanced, has continued with little meaningful mystical or philosophical education. We have long forgotten how to think along abstract lines, and so mystical and mythical values are poorly understood. Shrewd in our economic dealings, we are completely out of touch in terms of who we are or why we are here. For those that are seeking wisdom and truth outside of Christianity and everyday materialism, this can pose a problem.

Those who study fairy tales, myths and fables, and their philosophical meaning, begin to close this gap, paying genuine attention to themselves and others, and to the world around them. Their curiosity awakens, they start to explore the underlying nature of things that they have, perhaps for many years, accepted without question. They read, they study, they ask more questions. If they continue this journey of discovery, they become increasingly adept at seeing their lives differently, seeing what *is*, rather than what they want to see or have been told to see. They begin to awaken to life.

Myths and folklore serve as a path to help us uncover that which is hidden from us. A Socrates resides deep inside each and every one of us, if we care to find him. If we know where to look and how to decipher his message, we can become richer for the experience and a step closer to truth.

MYTHOLOGICAL SYMBOLISM TO BE FOUND IN FOLKLORE

In each category of folklore, there are common threads and principles that can be found to a greater or lesser degree, each depicting the unfolding of the spiritual path and always depicted in a *veiled* way. I have listed some of them below. Each tale will be different, with perhaps only a few principles appearing in one story while each point may be fully covered in others.

1. The story often starts with a disadvantaged, unrecognised, poor, unfairly treated, or abused individual, one who does not fit with the norms of society. He becomes the central character, the spiritual warrior, the mythological hero or heroine. In the biblical story of David and Goliath, David is a poor shepherd. Jack in the fairy tale 'Jack and the Beanstalk' is poor; there is no food in the house. Perseus, in the Greek myths of the same name, is an orphan living under the rule of an evil tyrant. The hero protagonists of the Grail Legends often lacked the knowledge of 'worldly ways', or possessed a naive innocence which often earned them the name, 'great fool'.

2. The hero has a dream, or sees a vision, or experiences a revelation, or receives a visitation or a letter, informing him of a quest. Perseus had a dream of the Goddess Athena before his quest; Christian Rosenkreutz in the Chymical Wedding, received a letter from an Angel who carried a golden trumpet; Jack met a curious little man who gave him five magical beans. The Grail Legends speak of an initiation through the Court of King Arthur, and joining the fellowship of the Round Table. In other versions of the legends, the Grail appears to the knights in a sunbeam accompanied by a loud clap and the smell of beautiful spiced fragrances, and the knights then each swear they will go on a quest to look upon the Grail's mystery.

3. The hero, often unwillingly, sets out alone on his quest and undergoes many adventures, dangers, hardships or tests. He meets unusual people. He undertakes tests of strength and courage. He might have to solve a riddle or navigate a maze. In the Greek myth, Theseus had to work his way through a maze to find the Minotaur; in the epic poem of the 'Baghavad Gita', Arjuna was asked by Krishna to pull the magnificent bow, Gandiva. Arthur, the future and true-born king of England, must pull the sword from the stone. Oedipus had to solve the riddle of the sphinx. Perceval failed to answer questions correctly when he first set eyes on the Grail and was forced to go on an arduous adventure before he succeeded in his quest.

4. The quest takes a specific period of time – often seven days, or a year and day. Arthur was sent on a quest by Morgan le Fay, a quest that lasted a year and day. The allegorical tale of the 'Chymical wedding' is divided into seven days, or seven journeys.

5. The hero acquires gifts, weapons, abilities and skills along the way. In the Greek myth, Perseus was given winged sandals, a shield and a cloak of invisibility. Gallahad receives a shield that only he is worthy of bearing. Along the way, after they have travelled a certain distance, heroes often talk to animals, or learn to fly; in the case of the Greek hero, Bellerophon, he tames a winged steed with the help of the gods. It means that, after one has been on the spiritual path for some time, he can acquire special powers, *i.e.*, psychism, out of body travel, being invisible to onlookers.

6. Along the journey, the hero will see evidence of magic or enchantment, spells and other wonders. Arthur experiences the magical protection of Merlin and the magical trickery of Merlin's arch-enemy, the evil enchantress, Morgan le Fay. For indeed, anyone who embarks on a spiritual path and follows it to its ultimate conclusion, will indeed encounter the miraculous and the unusual.

Jesus' disciples saw the dead being raised, men walking on water and water being turned into wine.

7. The hero might meet allies or guides, people who have information that will help him on his quest. Perseus meets three grey crones, old ladies or sisters that have information about the Gorgon, the monster that he must slay before he can return home. Arthur meets an ugly woman who holds the answer to a riddle he has to solve. In another of the Grail Legends, he meets with three damsels – Grail messengers – in a cart driven by three white harts.

8. The hero meets a mentor, an older person, wise sage, guru, magician, or prophet who teaches him, or points him in the right direction, or offers magical help. Merlin was Arthur's protector and greatly assisted him in winning many battles. He also assisted many of the knights on their quests for the Grail. The seer Phineas assisted Jason and the Argonauts on their quest for the Golden Fleece. The Goddess Athena assisted Odysseus.

9. The hero is tempted along the way by maidens, tricksters, wicked queens, witches, pleasures, fame, gold or treasures. All of these are designed to sway them from the quest. Sir Gawain on his quest for the Grail goes straight to the nearest pub and gets sidetracked by pretty maidens, all thoughts of the quest forgotten. During his twelve labours, Hercules meets with the Hesperides nymphs who invite him to play, but he moves on. The Sirens sang a song so sweet that it lured men to their deaths. Life is full of ups and downs, but when we set out on a spiritual quest, there are a thousand and one more distractions that will tempt us away from it.

10. At some point along the journey the hero meets with a fair maiden, a princess, a beautiful woman, the fairest in the land. But she is in trouble, threatened by a monster, imprisoned in a castle, under an ugly spell or in a deep sleep. In the Greek myth of Perseus, Andromeda was chained to a rock and about to be sacrificed to the Kraken, a ferocious sea monster. Sir Gallahad rescues seven maidens held captive by seven knights in the Castle of Maidens.

11. The hero of the story uses unorthodox and seemingly ineffective means to make his way along the path. In 'Jack and the Beanstalk', Jack used five magic beans; the biblical character David used five small, white rocks to slay the giant Goliath. Each of these is symbolic of how the truth is hidden in the most unlikely places.

12. The seeker has to go into battle with a terrifying monster – a dragon, an ogre, a giant, a gorgon, a kraken – all of them large, ugly, strong and terrifying. This depicts the battle that the hero has within himself, with his dark side – his own ego.

13. The hero takes part in games or competitions, tests of strength or skills. Even though he may think that the journey is over, he continues to be tested. In the Greek myth of Perseus, it took five different competitions after his quest was over for him to win the prize. Failure could mean falling back or losing what he has gained.

14. The hero eats of special fruit from a special tree, perhaps a golden apple, which symbolises the fruit of The Tree of Life that grew in the middle of the Garden of Eden. Jack captured the goose that laid the golden eggs. Or the hero might drink magic mead, an elixir of life, an ambrosia or nectar, the 'dancing water' that prolongs his life here on earth. In the Grail Legends, Sir Gawain is lead into a hall with twelve ancient knights who were all over 100 years of age, yet they seemed no more than 40.

15. The hero will marry and be crowned king of a far-off land, along with his queen (twin soul). The far-off land is what we know as Heaven, or the Divine, where they live in perfect bliss forever. Or they are turned into constellations in the heavens – as were Perseus and Andromeda, immortalised as a star, comet, constellation or heavenly body.

16. The hero will often sail over the sea or a lake or cross over a bridge as he progresses. In the Arthurian legends, the bridge burnt behind Galahad as he raced across it and 'thrice above him, all the heavens burned.' In J. R. R. Tolkien's *The Lord of the Rings*, Bilbo Baggins sailed across the sea and was never seen again. In the same way, Ogier the Dane disappeared in a boat across the sea.

17. The rainbow is prevalent in many myths. In the Nordic myths, the Bifröst Bridge is a burning rainbow bridge that stretches between Midgard (the world of men) and Asgard, (the realm of the Gods.) The colours of the rainbow are the same as the colours seen in the inner vision of the mystic in various disciplines and exercises which raise consciousness. It also relates to the colour of the chakras in the human body. In the tale of Pandora's box, Hope was the fairy with the rainbow wings who came out of the box after all the ills of the world had been released.

Book 1

MAPPING THE JOURNEY

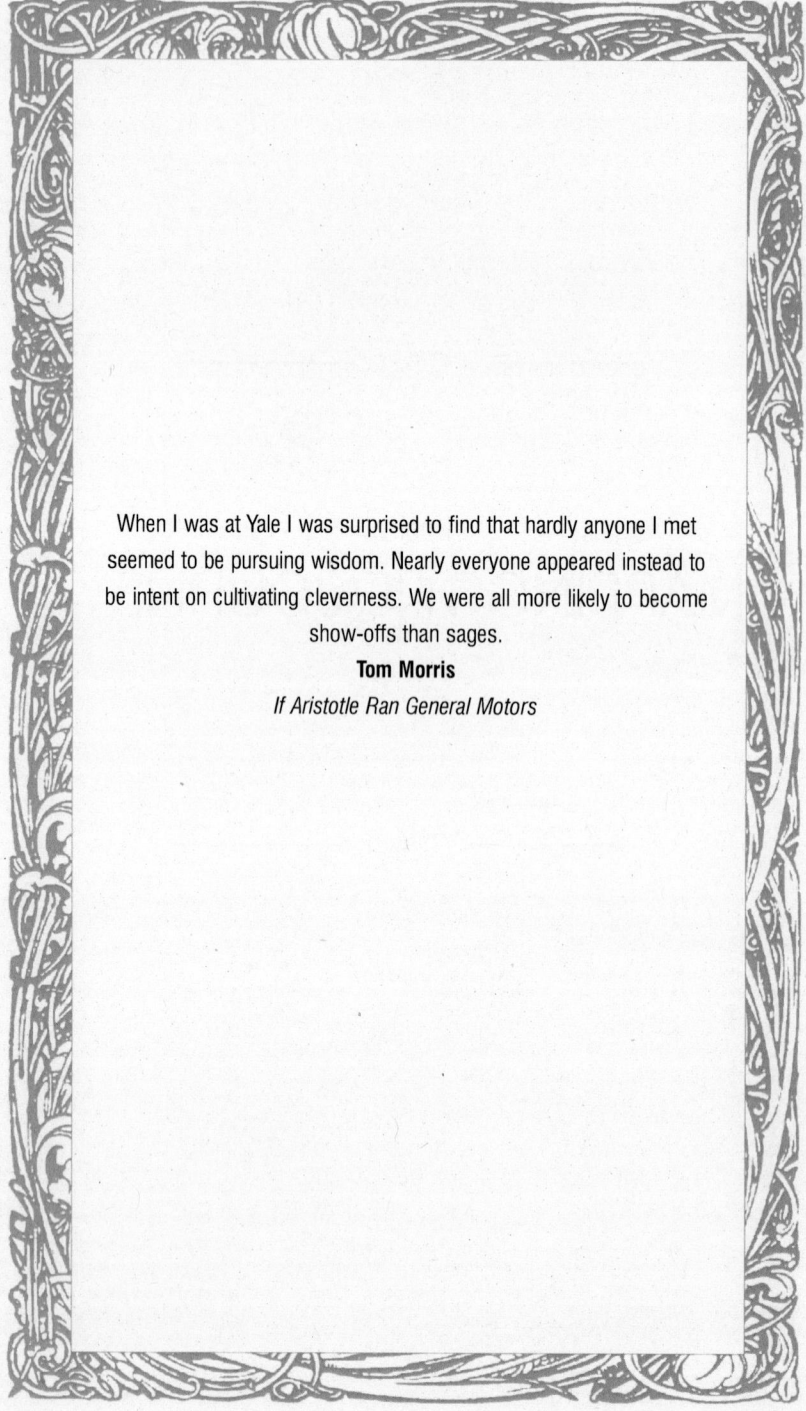

When I was at Yale I was surprised to find that hardly anyone I met seemed to be pursuing wisdom. Nearly everyone appeared instead to be intent on cultivating cleverness. We were all more likely to become show-offs than sages.

Tom Morris

If Aristotle Ran General Motors

STAGE 1

THE ORDINARY WORLD

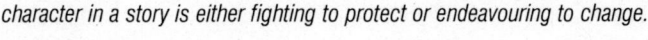

In all myths, there is a starting point where the central character moves from the ordinary into the world of fantasy and adventure – a severe contrast with the world of every-day affairs. The ordinary world may appear static and stable, enticing and exciting, the place where all desires can be fulfilled. But it is a tenuous condition. It's the place that any character in a story is either fighting to protect or endeavouring to change.

'Oh crikey,' I said to myself as I scanned through my diary for the following day. I'd forgotten about the important client lunch engagement at 11 Holland Park. How did I overlook that? Not too much of a problem under ordinary circumstances – I was used to doing most things on the fly, only right now it was Sunday night and I was on the other side of the Atlantic, at John F. Kennedy Airport, and had just boarded a flight for London. I'd have to get my skates on when I arrived at Heathrow and double-check that Sally, my assistant, had indeed made all the necessary catering arrangements with Richard Branson's office. I wasn't too perturbed – she was always on the ball and normally anticipated my needs. Thank goodness I'd had the sense to bring a clean change of clothes with me, as I wouldn't have time in London to go home and change first. I was relieved to be travelling in upper class for the return journey to Heathrow (not always guaranteed on a business trip), so that I could at least get a few hours sleep in comfort.

Lunch with Richard Branson (even though he was not yet *Sir* Richard) often carried a huge brag factor among the invited guests – high powered CEOs and executives from the cream of British business. An invitation to meet the man in person at an exclusive low-key lunch at his personal office was hardly ever refused. I smiled wryly as I thought how they might have nonchalantly dropped their imminent engagement into conversation over Sunday brunch in the local pub, telling all who would listen about their invitation to lunch with one of the world's most celebrated entrepreneurs, casually throwing it in as if it were an everyday occurrence, yet behind the scenes furiously rummaging through their wardrobes for something to wear to such an event, something smart-casual without a tie. Richard was renowned for never wearing a tie. However, one never quite knew what to expect with Richard; being the fun-loving entertainer that he was, he might turn up in a wedding dress, for all I knew.

As a co-host of some of these events with Richard – although nobody really cared too much about talking to me – I always found it amusing when these high-flying executives, who were legends in their own lunchtimes, would fumble and stumble over their words in the presence of this charismatic and influential personality whose Virgin empire spanned the globe. Conversation was always awkward in the early stages, as people unconsciously struggled to establish their own status and position among the small but diverse group of guests, made all the more difficult by their host, who was not a natural raconteur, preferring to cheekily pour an open bottle of champagne over someone than to sit pontificating with a bunch of investment bankers in suits. As a natural negotiator with a keen insight into human behaviour, I had the job of getting the conversation flowing, or steering it in the direction that would ensure that the PR event, designed to capture new business for Virgin Atlantic, was worthwhile. I personally felt at ease with Richard. I had done from the very first time I met him, not long after I joined Virgin in 1992. I have to admit, however, to feeling a sense of trepidation each time we met about being able to answer some of his unexpected and deeply probing questions regarding any one of Virgin's hundreds of clients, my thoughts on the strategic direction that Virgin might be taking or a pressing world problem in general. I always managed to scrape my way through. But on the whole, Richard was comfortable to be around and relaxed and I always looked forward to seeing him.

I was exhausted, the weekend in New York had been a long one, and I didn't

 cherish leaving Heathrow early the following morning to go straight into another Virgin PR event. I'd left London the previous Thursday evening with a group of senior managers from some of London's big investment banks – potential clients of Virgin – with the aim of showcasing the Virgin product. Three late nights, sightseeing trips and a Broadway show followed by dinner and dancing were taking their toll. I was, however, my own worst enemy, rarely taking time out. The previous weekend I had been in

Boston on a last minute shopping spree, grabbing some unbelievably cheap year-end bargains. (After all, a girl can never have too many shoes.) Six weeks earlier I had been in Los Angeles, at Disney Land and Universal Studios, hosting yet another business trip, and three months before that in Malaysia on a five-night whirlwind vacation. I seemed to spend more time in the air than I did with my feet planted firmly on the floor. But that didn't bother me. I adored the whole travel experience: the planning and dreaming as I wondered, after finishing one trip, where I might go next; the excitement I felt as the aircraft's wheels touched down on a well-worn runway in a country I hadn't yet experienced; and the *smell* of that country, particularly the US, when I set foot outside the terminal building with my over-sized suitcase (I never learned to pack light) to hail a taxi downtown. I had the travel bug. It was magnetic and I couldn't imagine myself doing anything else.

Flight VS010 arrived bang on schedule and I made my way with my clients to the Virgin upper class arrivals lounge in Heathrow's Terminal 3, where we each prepared for the work day ahead away from the noise and the bustle of one of the world's busiest airports. I quickly showered while my clothes got pressed, (part of the Virgin service), and said my goodbyes to my guests, grabbing a muffin and coffee to go. In no time at all I was in my car and on my way into central London. Thankfully, rush hour traffic had subsided somewhat and reaching Holland Park in West Central London was easier than I'd anticipated. Richard was in good spirits, and the lunch passed pleasantly without event. Now with time to spare, I made my way back to the small home in Surrey I shared with my partner Simon, and looked forward to a good night's sleep in my own bed. Tomorrow would be a busy day. I'd need to be in the office early to go through the final planning for a high level fee negotiation in central London with Virgin's largest travel industry supplier. I had the sense that it was going to be a long, drawn out and difficult debate. Even though negotiation was one of my strengths, and I'd been planning this very discussion for the last twelve months, I was still not looking forward to it.

The ordinary world of Caroline Ravenall was perhaps an enviable one for many onlookers. I lived the flamboyant lifestyle of the rich and famous on a comparatively meagre salary. As one of four national accounts managers responsible for Virgin's largest revenue-producing corporate clients in the city of London, I worked hard and I played hard. An endless stream of international travel and high-calibre social events filled my diary: client functions in central London at the Kensington Roof Garden, the Natural History Museum (a great venue for an event), or around the pool at Richard's house in Holland Park – exactly what one would expect from a wannabe high-flyer in the Virgin empire.

The 1980s and 90s were exciting times in the global travel and aviation industry. Flying was still fun in those days, even for those who did it frequently, as there was none of the post-9/11 security rigmarole which today quadruples the frustration of travellers and the amount of time spent at airports. The industry per se was growing at a rapid rate and experiencing some tumultuous but exciting changes. Competition was tough, particularly on the lucrative transatlantic routes in and out of London. Clients drove hard bargains and wanted good deals for delivering and directing large volumes of traffic Virgin's way. My role was to strategically maximise the airline's yield and revenue at every opportunity, so I needed to be on top of my game.

Growing up in middle-class England in the 1970s and 80s during Margaret Thatcher's premiership, with its strict conservative policies and tough stance against the trade unions, I was taught by my devout Tory-voting parents that getting a proper job and making an honest living is what life was all about. Yet I lacked imagination, inspiration and guidance from both family and teachers when it came to career choices, being very much left to find my own way. My natural tendency as an introverted child was artistic – I could sing, draw and write, was gifted with words, accents and a good sense of humour, but I was too shy to display any of these attributes in public. Neither did I have the raw natural talent to be any good at any of them as a first line career choice. Looking back, with a better insight into my temperament, I might have realised that I was more suited to a career in philosophy or journalism, but that would have required study. I didn't really have academic desires, although I was intelligent and loved learning new things. I simply wasn't motivated to study, I detested the public school I attended and at Eighteen years of age, couldn't picture my future behind a desk in some suburban office, or staring down a microscope at a disembowelled lab rat. Secretly, I would have liked to be an explorer, an adventurer, an Indiana Jones, crusading through the world on horseback searching for rare antiquities, but the job market in the farming community in Bedfordshire where I grew up was sparsely populated with that kind of work. So, inspired by a zany friend of my mother's, Heather, a talented artist who worked for Britannia Airways at Luton, I chose to join the travel industry instead.

Travel allowed me to incorporate adventure and international exploration into my job, and, more importantly, it allowed me to escape from the dreary British weather to sunnier climes. As I climbed the ladder, however, travel became less of an adventure and more about client meetings, strategies, negotiations, marketing presentation and international familiarization trips, where I occupied yet another hotel room which looked remarkably similar to the last. But still I couldn't imagine myself doing anything else.

My sales-and-marketing career began at the age of 22 with Continental Airlines and the now defunct TWA. I was tenacious and driven and dedicated to getting ahead in my career so I moved rapidly through the ranks from an office bound sales co-coordinator to an account executive who had the freedom of the road! My natural ability to get along with others and create an easy rapport worked for me in the sales-and-marketing environment. The American carriers were generous and I earned a really good salary until the tender age of 25, when I experienced my first ever career set back – retrenchment. As the competition for international dominance heated up, TWA sold its transatlantic routes to its rival American Airlines and I, along with all of the carrier's London-based employees, was forced to seek employment elsewhere. It couldn't have come at a worse time; I'd just got divorced and was left with hardly a cent to my name. In a knee-jerk reaction and to avoid joining the realms of the unemployed, I secured a job with Virgin as an Area Sales Manager, taking a substantial cut in pay to do so – the equivalent of a substantial down payment on a house or a brand new car! Yet I was determined to establish my own identity and become economically self-sufficient; and something told me the sacrifice was a good strategic move at this stage in my career.

I was right. Life in sales and marketing at Virgin was an unbelievable adventure. The airline was only eight years old when I joined, still in its entrepreneurial growth phase. Bureaucracy was nonexistent – ideas for new ventures and business strategies were scribbled liberally on the back of cigarette packets instead of being painstakingly mapped out on endless flip charts. The unstructured culture was perfect for my vivacious personality and go-getter drive. Virgin was the upstart, the rebel, the eccentric and the unconventional – a thorn in the side of British Airways. Everyone on the team was united by a powerful sense of purpose and shared Richard's enthusiasm for making air travel better and more accessible to everyone. Along with Syd Pennington, then the managing director of Virgin, Richard was a frequent visitor to the office and both men called on my clients. I got to spend to a lot of time with both of them and that just made the whole experience even more exciting. My learning curve was enormous, and the environment I worked in simply magical. Sometimes I didn't even want to go home at night.

Looking back, perhaps nothing represents the 'family feel' of Virgin's sales and marketing team, and my relationship with Richard, better than an incident which happened in October of 1993. I was 28. My father was killed suddenly at the age of 57 in a traffic accident. His untimely death devastated our family. I took time out of work to mourn with my mum Olivia and my sister Suzanne (who had flown to the UK from her home in South Africa), and also to deal with the entourage of family members and friends who came to pay their respects at our family home in Bedfordshire. It was on a particularly quiet and depressing Friday morning that the telephone rang.

'Caroline, it's Richard. I want to tell you how sorry I am to hear about your Dad,' he said. 'Is your family going to be all right? Does your mom need anything? Are you okay for money? Is there anything we can do to help?'

Shell-shocked by dad's death, I handled his call as I would have with any other friend calling to extend sympathies. I assured him that we would indeed be alright, that there was nothing we needed and promised to let him know personally if that changed. I thanked him for calling and hung up. Richard Branson had called to offer his sympathies to our family in the same way that neighbours would bring over warm plates of food in times of crisis. I guess this story goes a long way to demonstrate Richard's character and genuine and sincere concern for his employees; but looking back, although I was very touched by his thoughfulness, it also demonstrates the nature of my auspicious lifestyle at Virgin and the fact that I just accepted a call from this global celebrity as a normal every day occurrence.

In May of 1996, I was seconded to South Africa as part of a two-man team to set up Virgin's first operation on the African continent. After many years of government debate, Virgin had finally secured lucrative landing slots at Johannesburg's international airport and now needed a local operation in the country to support it. This would be a big job. Behind Virgin's first tender steps into any new country, there was always a bigger plan – the Airline's brand would be the first in Africa and would pave the way for other companies within the group to enter the market in years to come. Fifteen years on, there is a large Virgin presence in Africa – Virgin Atlantic, Virgin Nigeria, Virgin Mobile, Virgin Money and Virgin Active, to name a few. Despite the fact that I'd worked day and night to prepare for the interview process for this job, which I really wanted, I felt honoured to be recognized for my previous years of hard work and dedication. Virgin needed someone who had the reputation for getting things done, who embodied the entrepreneurial culture, and who had a strong sales and account management background. I fitted the profile perfectly! For me it was a dream come true. To be spearheading the launch of a brand such as Virgin on a new continent was more than I had ever imagined I was capable of. South Africa also held a special place in history after the end of apartheid and the release of Nelson Mandela eighteen months earlier. (Years later I was fortunate enough to meet Mandela as a guest of the Nelson Mandela Children's Fund.)

The transition was to be executed in true Virgin fashion – instantaneously, with little time to spare. Within days of accepting the position, I met my business partner and mentor-to-be, Mackenzie Grant, a seasoned veteran in the aviation business. I liked him immediately. He seemed to view *me* with some trepidation however. I was young, naïve and impossibly rebellious; he would have a lot to teach me. But inexperienced though I was, the enthusiasm, drive and willingness to learn more than made up for it. These qualities would certainly help us in our task, as we had only *six months* to build and launch a company from the ground up in preparation for the first flight in October.

Before leaving England for my new home in the Southern Hemisphere, I spent many weeks travelling back and forth between the UK and Africa, finalizing one role, handing it over to my successor and starting another. When it finally came time to leave the UK altogether, I almost didn't go. I felt incredibly guilty about leaving my widowed mum alone in the UK to fend for herself. My sister Suzanne already lived in South Africa and it seemed unfair for me to leave Mum too, despite the fact that she had many close friends and family members close by. It was a heart-rending parting for both of us.

Once I'd walked through the sorrow of parting and arrived in my new home, I couldn't fail to be excited about the enormous challenges ahead of me. Looking back, I am amazed at how easy it was for us to get so much done in such a short space of time. But perhaps I shouldn't have been surprised. This was Virgin, after all, and there wasn't the usual time-consuming bureaucracy that one finds in organisations around anything – including a company start up; Mackenzie and I were able to simply take a flip chart and list the tasks to be done, dividing them down the middle. I took sales, PR, marketing, call centre and distribution, whilst Mackenzie took on office setup, airport operations, the clubhouse and financial. And that is the way my role in South Africa evolved – on a single piece of flip chart paper! South Africa was my training ground and would be the first of many international posts for me. I was now in a rotating pool of senior managers who would move from country to country doing similar things as Virgin's international operations grew. I was literally flying.

A beginning is, indeed, a delicate time.

Christopher Vogler
The Writer's Journey

The six months preceding the official launch flew past in a blur. My learning curve was again enormous – I learned so much from so many, Mackenzie in particular; also from my leadership mentor, Terry Wiltshire; and from the UK marketing team, lead by global marketing director Alison Copus. The marketing PR lead-up to the official launch event in October, 1996, was an incredible affair lasting many weeks. I conducted numerous radio, magazine and TV interviews as the head of sales and marketing, becoming the cover girl of various topical business magazines. Richard arrived on the inaugural flight from London, with an entourage of British journalists and clients. Being the undisputed king of the publicity stunt, he rarely missed the opportunity to entertain, and as the first Virgin Airbus A340 to touch down on African soil taxied to the gate at the airport terminal, onlookers could see him in his Madiba shirt brandishing the South African flag from the small cockpit window. The passengers disembarked onto the tarmac beside the terminal building to a throng of waiting journalists and an assembly of African tribal dancers who helped to create a powerfully electric and moving atmosphere that was to remain imprinted on my memory for many years to come. Richard's arrival was followed by several days of high-calibre launch events, media interviews, client lunches, sales blitzes and PR stunts. Wherever we went, we attracted a crowd of bemused onlookers, as well as opportunists, each trying to attract Richards's attention with a new business proposal. Whatever your feelings about Richard Branson, he certainly knows how to win a crowd.

The launch of Virgin in South Africa was hailed by Richard himself as one of the most successful route launches in Virgin's history. The flights were full, the interest and expectations were high. Virgin had certainly arrived in style in Africa. For me, too, Africa had a style all of its own, one that had a huge appeal. I lived a wonderful lifestyle as one only can in Africa – a salary paid in English pounds, a large, fully furnished house with a swimming pool (standard issue in Johannesburg) paid for by the company, and a brand new Land Rover Discovery

every six months as a company car. With the strong British pound and weak South African rand, it was like getting a pay rise every month. I still got to travel to England every three months for an international sales meeting, which gave me the opportunity to see my mum. What could be more perfect? I could never have imagined this lifestyle living in my two-up-two-down in Earlswood, Surrey, where it rained most of the time. Now in this perfect climate, I embraced outdoor activities, taking an off-road driving course and learning to scuba dive, overcoming my fear of deep water.

I made quarterly long-weekend trips with my new found friends who also enjoyed the African outdoors, into Mozambique where the diving was absolutely magnificent. I also bought a beautiful black horse – a Friesian stallion called Dragon Heart whom I fell in love with the moment I clapped eyes on him. (I wish it was as easy to find a man that way!) He was a majestic creature and inspired great emotion within me. I often cried when I watched him work. When I wasn't

out riding in the country on the back of this magnificent animal, I was making frequent trips into the African bush, and to countries like Zimbabwe (before its real demise under President Mugabe), Zambia, and Mozambique. On other weekends I would visit the Cape wine farms and beaches. (Cape Town has to go down as the most beautiful city in the world for me.) I was now living the life of my childhood dreams – the life of an adventurer.

That lifestyle, however, did not come cheaply. My role as head of sales and marketing was a tough one. Tumultuous changes were taking place in travel distribution channels around the globe, driven by the airlines in an effort to reduce costs and change outdated distribution practices, which had been in place since air travel begain. Travel agents were facing a decrease or total elimination of the revenue streams they'd relied on for decades, which meant they had to totally remodel their business to survive. My role was to pave the way for the same transformation, from Virgin's perspective, in the African market. The travel industry was somewhat behind that of the US and Europe in its development, and it wasn't going to take these changes lying down. My commercially oriented approach was very different from that adopted by the other local airlines, and something that the industry was decidedly unfamiliar with. I was playing a difficult game: trying to build the Virgin brand and revenue streams in a new market, without paying through the nose to do it. I was used to this, however – I'd spent years in the city of London doing a similar thing. But in Africa, my approach often made me decidedly unpopular in an industry more comfortable conducting business with a handshake, a beer and a round of golf. I earned the reputation for being hard-driving and tough. I expected a lot of myself and consequently a lot from those who reported to me.

Meetings both internal and external were often battlegrounds – me against them – as I struggled to maximise Virgin's revenue growth (already weakened by the rand) without entertaining costly practices that threatened to dilute it even further with no additional benefit. It required courage, tenacity, planning and insight to go against the grain, employing commercially savvy account managers who had the capacity to think and negotiate like business people rather than like sales reps, who spent their time drinking tea with the CEO's secretary, having a cosy chat about life and leaving behind a brochure. The industry talent pool was limited and people were wary of working for this crazy redhead and unknown Virgin entity in a market littered with aviation failures. This was made even worse by Richard, who believed that people would work for substantially less than their competitors because of the power of the brand. After eighteen months, however, Virgin's sales team got the reputation of being the best in the business and was often head-hunted by other industry players. I realised then that I had a knack for developing people.

Mackenzie didn't stay in South Africa as I had hoped. He moved back to his home in Hong Kong several months after the launch was over, his work complete. I was sad when he left – I believed I would have developed well with his guidance. I missed his quiet and unassuming manner and his rock solid support, and the way in which we shared responsibility for South Africa's operation. Virgin HQ appointed another general manager from British Airways stock, who turned out to be the complete antithesis of Mackenzie and the Virgin culture. Unbeknownst to me at the time, this was to be my first lesson in how organisational culture, driven from the top down, can build or mutilate a brand. Although he was a personable man and well known in the industry, he was also reluctant to move from the *old way* to the *new way,* and we spent much time in opposition. He, too, was British, a great raconteur and a great golfer. But he was unaccustomed to the Virgin way of getting your hands dirty as a leader. Then my business mentor, Terry Wiltshire from the UK, died suddenly, and so I often felt adrift and alone, seemingly pushing and cajoling singlehandedly to bring change both within my own team and the industry itself.

The first two years I spent with Virgin in South Africa have to go down as the best in my career. I thrived on the challenge of starting a new business. I adored working in an environment that called for immediate action – perfectly suited for my sense of adventure and high levels of drive and energy. My learning curve, too, was enormous. I learned a whole new set of leadership and people skills to enable me to work in a better way with my team. I had finally found my groove, or so I thought.

Beneath the polished and successful exterior, however, I was concealing dragons, ones that I didn't particularly have the courage to face. They gnawed away at my insides and disturbed my sleep. But I suppressed them magnificently for fear that they would not be acceptable in the fast-paced world that I had chosen.

THE MYTH AND ITS MEANING:
King Minos and the Minotaur

All journeys have to have a starting point. The ordinary world provides the platform from which the protagonist can embark. It may seem like a world where everything appears to be normal on the surface, yet there may be repressive forces at play. Quite often in myth, these forces are depicted by a tyrant, one who bears a position of power, one who has control over others but does not truly understand himself. Myths often go to great lengths to describe the relationship between two opposing characters depicting the forces of good and evil; in reality they illustrate two warring aspects of the same character, the light and the darkness within. Thus, the oppressor may even be the hero himself.

Back in the distant past, when the ancient Minoan civilisation flourished on the island of Crete, there lived a mighty king known as Minos. According to legend, Minos was a great warrior, rumoured to be a son of the god Zeus and the mortal woman Europa. He had a wife, Pasiphae, and three children: Androgeus, Ariadne and Phaedra. They lived in a splendid labyrinthine palace at Knossos which was specifically built for him by the genius craftsman, Daedalus.

Minos was a strong character. As the ruler of one of the most powerful nations of the ancient world, he was greatly feared and healthily respected by all the neighbouring kingdoms. Although he was a great king, Minos was also flawed, often whimsical, irrational and insecure. He needed constant reinforcement that he was indeed the rightful king and so asked for a sign from the Gods to placate his gnawing anxiety. When a magnificent bull appeared out of the sea – a gift from Poseidon – the king was overjoyed. Poseidon demanded, however, that the bull be sacrificed to him in return, but Minos thought it was such a fine creature that he decided to deceive Poseidon and keep it for himself, sacrificing another animal in its place.

This angered Poseidon and as a punishment, he caused Minos' wife, Pasiphae, to fall in love with the bull. Crazy with desire, she sought the help of Daedalus, who created a mechanical cow in which she could copulate with the bull. As a result of her union, she gave birth to a monstrous creature with the head of a bull and the body of a man: the Minotaur. (*Minotauros* means 'the bull of Minos'.) Whilst the kingdom blamed Pasiphae for the creation of such a loathsome beast, Minos knew deep down that he truly bore the responsibility. As the creature grew into a terrifying monster, requiring human flesh to survive, Minos ordered Daedalus to construct a labyrinth deep below the palace to conceal his shame. Young men and women from conquered lands were imprisoned in the labyrinth by Minos until meeting their death.

Folklore is alive with many tyrants like King Minos, whose anxiety creates havoc in the kingdom. Yet the real monsters lurk within, deep deep down in the depths, in the 'labyrinth' of his subconscious. The labyrinth beneath the palace, deep into the earth, serves to remind us of the earthly and materialistic nature of the ordinary world. The deeper we climb into materialism, the deeper we move into darkness. Whilst the fantastic structure and palaces we build on the surface make us feel safe and secure, they are no match for the monsters that lurk below.

The Bull in any myth is often symbolic of man's earthy or animal nature – the dark side of us, the ego fuelled by desire – greed, power, recognition and control. Left unchecked it grows to hideous proportions and becomes a monster to be feared. The Minotaur is symbolic of King Minos' dark side – half man, half bull. He is at war within himself. It is a side he is ashamed of – a side that he needs to keep hidden deep, deep down.

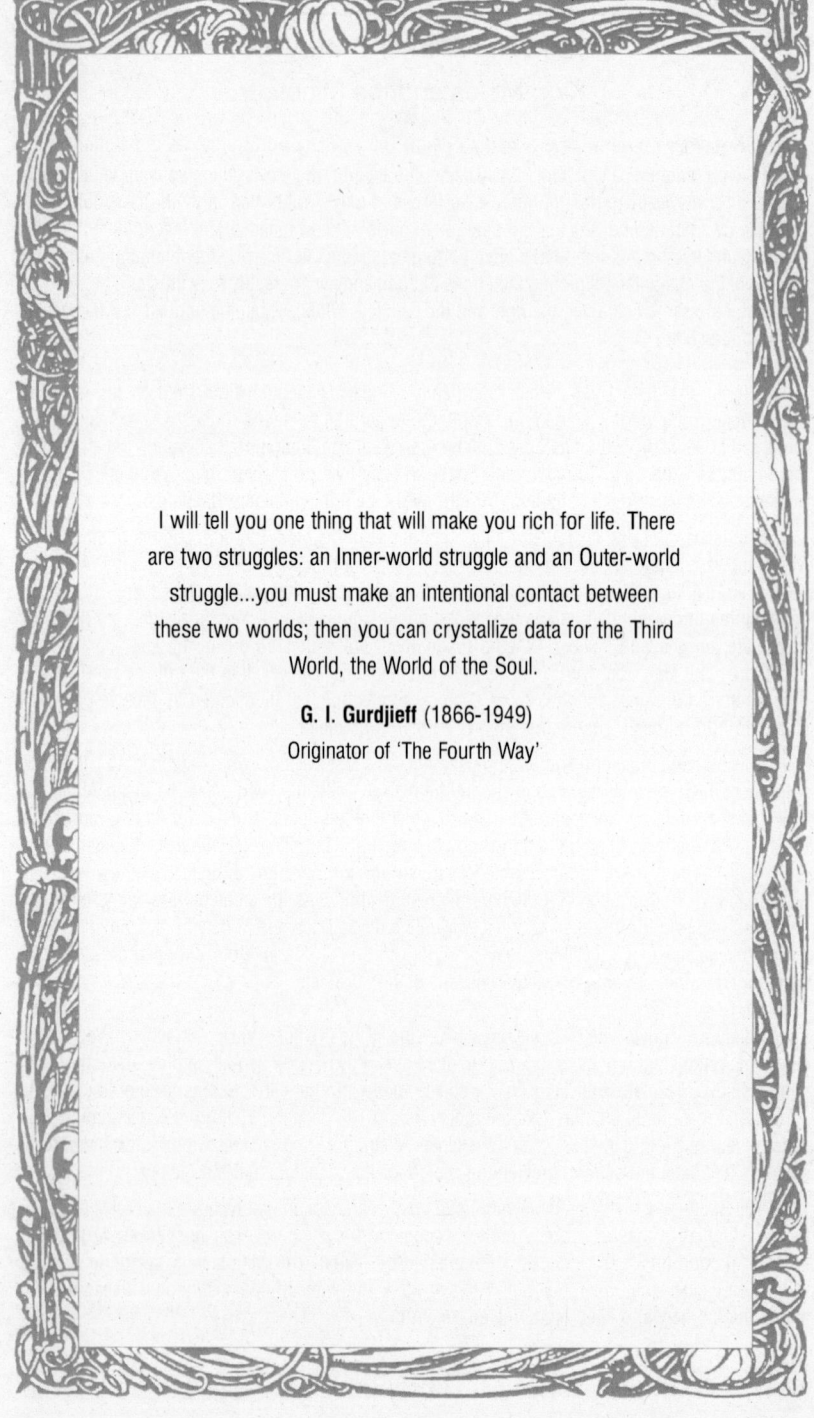

I will tell you one thing that will make you rich for life. There are two struggles: an Inner-world struggle and an Outer-world struggle...you must make an intentional contact between these two worlds; then you can crystallize data for the Third World, the World of the Soul.

G. I. Gurdjieff (1866-1949)
Originator of 'The Fourth Way'

STAGE 2

THE UNSEEN WORLD

The unconscious sends all sorts of vapors, odd beings, terrors and deluding images into the conscious mind, whether in dream, broad daylight or insanity; for the human kingdom, beneath the floor of the comparatively neat little dwelling that we call our consciousness, goes down into unsuspected Aladdin caves.

Joseph Campbell

The Hero with a Thousand Faces

he ordinary world of business demands a certain type of behaviour, a certain pace, a certain level of tenacity and drive if one wants to succeed. Whilst I strived hard to portray the image of 'warrior woman' to the outside world, I was nothing but a 'worrier woman' on the inside. Most of the time, I felt that I was just playing a part in a movie that might someday end and I'd watch the credits roll to discover that this wasn't actually me. Because it didn't feel like me. I expertly fooled myself into believing that the way I was living was indeed normal and that I was happy, contented and fulfilled – after all, this is what one does in life, isn't it? When I compared myself to everyone else out there who held a similar position, they seemed to be coping with life and enjoying the fruits of their labours. I rebuked myself for my continuous doubt and reassured myself that this was exactly what one did, and I should get over myself and get on with it. Yet deep down I felt like a fake. I worried about not being able to cope, not being good enough, clever enough or politically savvy enough to sustain my position. Whilst on the surface I was in a world of high-powered meetings and an overcommitted diary, underneath it was becoming a challenge for me to stay one step ahead.

These feelings, of course, were not new, when I looked back into childhood. In stark contrast to the vivacious personality I presented to the world today, I had been a very sensitive, self-conscious and withdrawn child. The serious business of life de-motivated me. As a teen, I preferred to isolate myself at home in my vivid imagination with a book instead of being out there in the world with friends at movies or nightclubs. I did venture out occasionally to *fit in,* to please people, but I couldn't wait to go home, back to the castle, my fortress and safe hiding place. I felt awkward around other people of my age. I needed isolation to be able to relax. I was a dorky looking kid, too, with a mop of thick dark hair not cut into any particular style, a squint and a big nose (until I had it fixed in my twenties). I didn't fit easily into any one group of friends at school. I dreaded break times, as I would often find myself alone and isolated, which made me a great target for the school bullies. I never succumbed to their demands, but the toll on my young psyche was immense. I couldn't concentrate or focus adequately on my school work and had to push hard to get even mediocre results.

Whilst home was my castle, it too was fraught with tension of its own kind. My father was a brilliant man, with an innate curiosity about life. He was clever, not just academically, but also in a practical way, with a great sense of humour. But we didn't see this side of him often. He was tormented by his own demons. Frequent bouts of anger and frustration permeated our lives. The family walked around on eggshells, never knowing who would be the next victim. Any number of things could set him off – a car parked in the wrong place in the driveway, the wrong TV channel played too loudly when he came home, too much noise, or a problem at work that he was unable to fix.

Raised voices, tears, slamming doors, the screeching of car tyres and stony silences were regular features. My mother did anything to keep the peace. She was, of course, fighting her own internal battles, often withdrawn and depressed herself. We were all like small boats adrift in a turbulent ocean, occasionally connecting because the wind blew us together, and then swiftly steering away from each other again to avoid a head-on collision. Conversations about our joys, achievements, strife and troubles were not encouraged. In fact, they were often ignored, or surreptitiously swept under the carpet, unseen, hidden, forgotten, pushed underground. The air was often heavy with silence and sadness.

As a child I was very sensitive to moods and vibes. Most children are, but it is made worse for the child who is hypersensitive to rejection, tension and conflict. I found the repressive environment so tense at times that I'd feel choked. I can clearly remember several vivid nightmares where I was sinking in quicksand or being chased through a forest by a cloaked figure on a large black horse. I couldn't run, my feet were mired in the earth, the dark stranger would leap from his horse and strangle me. I would struggle to wake up. These dreams added to my own heightened level of self-consciousness and anxiety about the environment I was in. I somehow felt responsible for the conflicts, taking on the emotions as my own. To escape, I spent a lot of time going inward, daydreaming and identifying with the characters in the books or fairy tales that I read. The prince and the princess were very real for me, not just characters in a story, and I would escape on a magical quest into their world. I later learned that *willed introversion* is one of the hallmarks of someone who is highly creative, providing that it can be employed deliberately. However, being so young, I felt like I was going completely stark, raving potty.

Outwardly, I was sullen and moody as the inner conflicts raged within. I found it difficult to handle the deep-seated anger that often welled up inside. I took most of this anger out on my younger sister Suzanne, who was totally different in temperament to me. I saw her as yet another pressure in my life, since my parents wanted me to be like her – normal, more sociable and industrious. Of course, no family is perfect, and I can't fault my parents for their efforts. They were both hard workers and good providers, ensuring that we had more than the average kids growing up. But they were too preoccupied with life and its strife and troubles to deal effectively with the psychological needs of a hyper-sensitive child who felt like the ugly duckling in a family full of swans. My father was the engineering director at a chauffeur drive company based in Luton, a career he entered at age 40 after a falling-out with his parents in the family business they'd owned which resulted in its sale. They never really forgave him. My mother split her time between raising us and working weekends and evenings as a waitress for an upmarket catering company where she mingled with the aristocracy at Buckingham Palace and other stately homes around southern England. Later as we grew up, she took on administrative roles to help pay the bills and build a better lifestyle for us. Like every family, they did the best they could with the knowledge they had.

Moving into adolescence, I swiftly boxed up my childhood emotions as *issues that every child experiences* and blocked them from my memory. As a teenager, I sought solace in one or two close friends who were like me and convinced myself that life would surely be easier when I could leave home, go to work, and find a man that would protect me from the cold, hard world. I did all of this by the age of 24, but the carefully suppressed anger and insecurity still pushed itself to the surface when I least expected it. Sudden furious outbursts of temper, just like those of my father, would distance me from society. I was constantly pushing my anger and fears back down inside by busying myself with other concerns, concocting my own never ending 'laundry list of things to do'. So life became a constant challenge: a search for greater excitement as a way to stave off boredom. The fanciful ideals that I believed carried no relevance in the real world; a new boyfriend, a new travel destination, a new drama, and, of course, possession of material things. I required more and more to keep me entertained, interested and focused.

One is harassed both day and night by the Divine being that is the image of the living self within the locked labyrinth of one's own disoriented psyche.

Joseph Campbell

The Hero with a Thousand Faces

The sensitivity and intuition from my childhood persisted into adulthood, becoming more acute, yet serving only to enhance my inner turmoil. At the time, I didn't know what being *clairsentient* or a *natural empath* meant. I didn't know that I was picking up on the vibrations and sensitivities around me, and that much of my tension and anxiety came from others and not myself. At times, I would walk into an office, a meeting or a restaurant, and suddenly become filled with anxiety, agitation or restlessness. As this happened infrequently, I believed that these feelings were of my own making. I chastised myself for being so overly sensitive and stupid and told myself to get a thicker skin and get on with it. I pushed the feelings away and focused on the task in front of me. Virgin's workforce in South Africa was dominated by women (real men didn't go into the travel industry in South Africa), and the environment was continuously filled with layers of *temperamental oestrogen* and it affected my mood. Working in London, I hadn't noticed it, as I spent a lot of time out of the office with clients, and the male/female ratio at HQ was more balanced. In South Africa, more aware in my leadership role, I often unknowingly took on the emotions of those around me, which drained me, made me irritable and added to the instability I already felt within.

As I climbed the career ladder and the pressure mounted, my bouts of frustration and anger became more frequent, seemingly coming from nowhere, rising up from the depths, usurping my entire being when I least expected them. Employees pay attention to how their leaders behave and act. I remember clearly the faces of some of the young reservations agents watching open-mouthed as this six-foot-tall redhead in her business suit and high heels marched down the corridor of Virgin's new offices in Hyde Park, Johannesburg, barking orders at the designers for a poor standard of work. For me it was perfectly justifiable. In less than forty-eight hours, the new office in Johannesburg was due to open. The furniture had still not arrived and Telkom (the SA national phone provider) had not yet switched on the lines to the call centre. I was under pressure.

Of course, I thought little of my outbursts. They were 'situation normal' for me. I had been able to release the mounting frustration in the only way I knew how. However, I noticed the effect that these emotions had on my energy levels. One minute I was upbeat, the next minute flat and lethargic. I rarely stopped to enjoy life in the moment as I raced around at break-neck speed, anticipating the next challenge. The days seemed to pass in a blur of activity. I was quickly acquiring the reputation as a whimsical Cleopatra who lorded it over her subjects, one who didn't care about anything other than herself. Yet I cared very deeply – too deeply. I just didn't know how to express it. The real me was hidden deep down below and it wasn't safe to let her out in public. Only when I was in the bush or diving below the surface of the ocean did I manage to actually relax and breathe without hyperventilating. Whilst the childhood nightmares did not return, they still haunted me; I was still that little girl being chased through the forest by the man on the black horse. I could not see his face , but then again, I didn't want to, because I didn't have the courage to face him.

The unseen world is the world of many unrecognised and disowned thoughts and emotions, dreams and nightmares, co-incidence and synchronicity, security and despair. As much as we may consciously or unconsciously ignore the presence of these internal dynamics, they are just as much a part of our life as the ordinary day-to-day world. My internal struggles were rooted in the search for self, a deep longing for meaning and understanding. Wherever I went, I felt like a misfit, trying desperately to belong, to find something or someone that I could identify with, adapting and changing my behaviour to suit the situation, to blend, to become one with my surroundings. I thought I'd found my place with Virgin, but day by day my sense of security slipped further away and the restless, gnawing desire to discover my reason for being returned. I couldn't articulate this, however; this desire to discover The Self at a meaningful level exhibited itself as a deeply rooted dissatisfaction and a feeling that I was living a life of falsehood, without integrity. For most, this is acceptable – people are often at odds with themselves. For me, I felt like I was living a total lie, that my life was a sham. I always felt at cross-purposes with others and with life itself, feeling as though I was just going through the motions. My sister told me once during an awful fight that I was the most messed-up person she knew. She was probably right. The cauldron of emotions that I'd expertly refused to acknowledge or pay much attention to throughout my life were desperately vying for attention. They had always been there, of course, lurking just below the surface, but I was a master of the mask, and suppressing emotions was what the Ravenall family did best. But my behaviour was becoming increasingly erratic, and this was impacting on my health and my ability to do my job.

Professor David Keirsey, in his book, *Please Understand Me,* describes the temperament of the INFP: (Introversion, Intuition, Feeling, Perception) – the *healer idealist* – as 'one who can never truly be himself, since the very act of reaching for the self immediately puts it out of reach'. Looking back, his words applied perfectly to me at that time and it seemed that Shakespeare's Hamlet wrestled with this same dilemma:

To be or not to be, that is the question:
Whether 'tis nobler in the mind to suffer
The slings and arrows of outrageous fortune,
Or to take up arms against a sea of troubles,
And by opposing end them....
And enterprises of great pith and moment
With this regard their currents turn awry
And lose the name of action....

However, at 34, without David Keirsey's insight into my true nature (which didn't come until almost ten years later), I didn't like who I'd become. I was self-centered, arrogant, angry and resentful a lot of the time. I felt completely out of balance and out of touch with the rest of the world. These were all symptoms of the chaos and turbulence I felt within. Whilst there were many days that I felt normal, the *off*-days were plentiful and it took enormous effort to keep body and soul together. The 'unseen world' was calling: my angry outbursts, dissatisfaction and erratic behaviour were all signals from the depths that something was very wrong. I didn't know who I was, what I stood for, what I cared about, what I loved or valued. I was just existing, surviving, getting on with life. After all, that's what life's about – isn't it?

THE MYTH AND ITS MEANING:
The Frog Prince (Part I)

Outside the world of our five senses lives another world, one that remains hidden from view. The unseen world is a stark contrast to the ordinary world. The hero knows that this labyrinth exists but strives to keep it hidden, to mask it even from himself. For there are ugly creatures lurking.

A long time ago, when wishing could still lead to something, there lived a king whose daughters were all beautiful. But the youngest was so beautiful that the sun itself, which has seen so much, was astonished whenever it shone in her face.

Close by the king's castle lay a great dark forest, and under an old lime tree in the forest was a well, and when the day was very warm, the king's child went out into the forest and sat down by the side of the cool fountain, and when she was bored she took a golden ball, and threw it up on high and caught it, and this ball was her favourite plaything.

Now it so happened that on one occasion the princess's golden ball did not fall into the little hand which she was holding up for it, but on to the ground beyond, and rolled straight into the water of the well. The king's daughter followed it with her eyes, but it vanished, and the well was deep, so deep that the bottom could not be seen. At this she began to cry, and cried louder and louder, and nothing could console her.

And as she thus lamented, someone said to her, 'What ails you, king's daughter? You weep so that even a stone would show pity.'

She looked round to the side from whence the voice came, and saw a frog stretching forth its big, ugly head from the water.

'Ah, old water-splasher, it is you,' she said, 'I am weeping for my golden ball, which has fallen into the well.'

'Be quiet, and do not weep,' answered the frog. 'I can help you, but what will you give me if I bring your plaything up again?'

'Whatever you will have, dear frog,' said she. 'My clothes, my pearls and jewels, and even the golden crown which I am wearing.'

The frog answered, 'I do not care for your clothes, your pearls and jewels, nor for your golden crown, but if you will love me and let me be your companion and play-fellow, and sit by you at your little table, and eat off your little golden plate, and drink out of your little cup, and sleep in your little bed – if you will promise me this I will go down below, and bring you your golden ball up again.'

'Oh yes,' said she. 'I promise you all you wish, if you will but bring my ball back again.' But she thought, 'How the silly frog does talk. All he does is to sit in the water with the other frogs, and croak. He can be no companion to any human being.'

But the frog when he had received this promise, put his head into the water and sank down; and in a short while came swimming up again with the ball in his mouth, and threw it on the grass.

The king's daughter was delighted to see her pretty plaything once more, and picked it up, and ran away with it. 'Wait, wait,' said the frog. 'Take me with you. I can't run as you can.' But to what did it avail him to scream his croak-croak after her, as loudly as he could? She did not listen to it, but ran home and soon forgot the poor frog, who was forced to go back into his well again.

From 'The Frog King' by the Brothers Grimm
The Complete Fairy Tales (Wordsworth Library Collection)

As with many characters in fairy tales, the princess walks through a deep dark forest symbolic of the unexplored depths of our own subconscious emotions, foreboding and dangerous. She sits at the base of a tree, as did the Buddha when he achieved enlightenment symbolic of the tree of life. The tree was next to a well that went deep, deep down, so deep, that the bottom could not be seen, again depicting the depths of the psyche. The frog is the 'herald' from the subconscious that something inside is not quite right. He is the bringer of bad tidings, showing up as the emotional turmoil that peppers our lives. The frog is judged as ugly by the world – all emotions are ugly and unwelcome – but his ugliness masks the ability he has to retrieve the jewel concealed within. His appearance on the surface symbolises a new period that has to be faced. He is the bringer of change. The seeds of change and growth are already planted in our subconscious and it takes only a little energy to germinate them. There is a part of us that may be fascinated, as was the princess, by his emergence, but there is a part of us that is scared half to death.

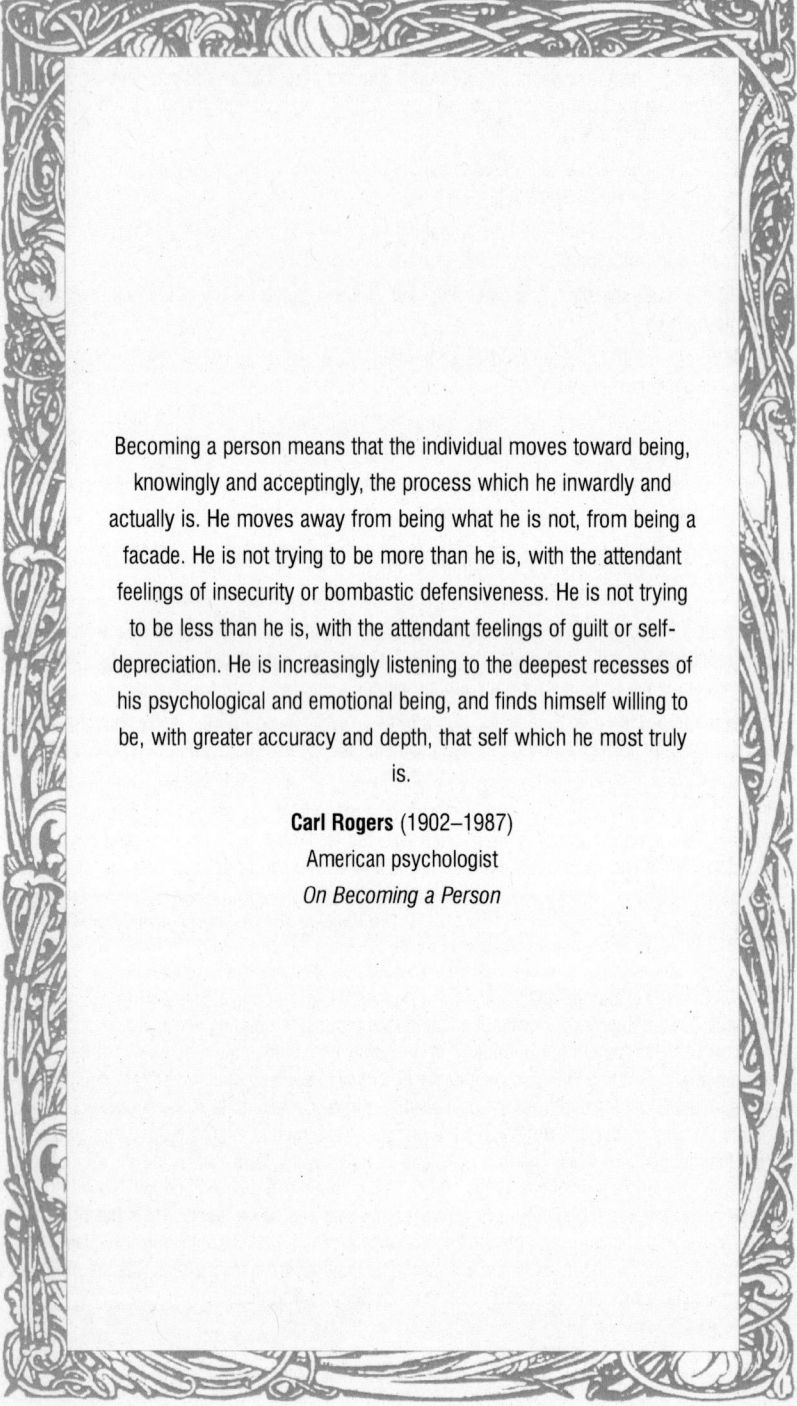

Becoming a person means that the individual moves toward being, knowingly and acceptingly, the process which he inwardly and actually is. He moves away from being what he is not, from being a facade. He is not trying to be more than he is, with the attendant feelings of insecurity or bombastic defensiveness. He is not trying to be less than he is, with the attendant feelings of guilt or self-depreciation. He is increasingly listening to the deepest recesses of his psychological and emotional being, and finds himself willing to be, with greater accuracy and depth, that self which he most truly is.

Carl Rogers (1902–1987)
American psychologist
On Becoming a Person

STAGE 3

THE CALL TO ADVENTURE

The ordinary world for most of us casts a veil of safety between this world and the next, but instability lurks just beneath the surface. We may become masters of disguise, keeping the unseen world hidden and controlled, but the seeds of change have been planted long, long ago. For years they lie dormant, undisturbed; waiting for an opportunity to flourish. Quite often the hero doesn't see that there is anything wrong with his everyday state of affairs, getting by on an arsenal of defence mechanisms which keep him fully occupied and oblivious to the turmoil within - outward achievements, sex, wealth, power, status, addictions to alcohol, drugs or adrenalin sports. When the call to adventure finally comes, a series of signals of increasing force and ferocity will continue to ring until the summons can no longer be denied. Eventually the hero is forced to kick away the crutches that he's relied on for many years and confront the cold hard truth.

The call to adventure rang with a resounding thump in November, 1999. Virgin was set to expand its South African operation in December of that year by adding Cape Town as a second destination from London. The launch event and Richard's packed itinerary in the Mother City had taken months to plan and promised to be a grand affair as always, executed in true Virgin fashion. As I stood beneath the canopy of a darkened marquee, erected especially for the evening's entertainment and filled to bursting point with people, I tried to absorb the events unfolding in front of me. Everything had slowed down, just as it does before one has a car accident; I felt somewhat removed from the scene, as if I wasn't really there, not fully in my body, but rather hovering above myself, watching from a distance. Richard was making a dramatic entrance, suspended on a rope, through the roof of the marquee – one of the usual daredevil-showman entrances that the world had come to love him for. The crowd, a mixture of local and international journalists, travel industry notaries and executives from the cream of Cape Town business, cheered as he emerged into the light. Our eyes met with mutual affection as always, and we greeted each other in the normal way – and that was the last time I saw Richard in the flesh for many years. The herald had sounded the call.

The event passed in a haze of loud music and conversations with many faceless people. I remember trying to be the charming, entertaining face of Virgin, the life and soul of the party. It was a Herculean task because I was running on empty – there was nothing left. Inside I felt dead and lifeless. All I remember is that the darkness in the marquee matched the darkness within my own soul. I couldn't wait to leave.

This is the threat to our lives. We all face it. We all operate in our society in relation to a system. Now is the system going to eat you up and relieve you of your humanity or are you going to be able to use the system to human purposes? ... If the person doesn't listen to the demands of his own spiritual and heart life and insists on a certain program, you're going to have a schizophrenic crack-up. The person has put himself off centre. He has aligned himself with a programmatic life and it's not the one the body's interested in at all. And the world's full of people who have stopped listening to themselves.

Joseph Campbell
The Power of Myth

I had woken that morning in my hotel room with the same fear and dread that I had experienced for several months previously. I had hardly slept the night before, even with a higher than normal dose of sleeping pills, and when the alarm sounded, I just wanted to sleep for another century. As I pulled the covers over my head, trying to shield myself from the brilliant Cape sunshine seeping through the curtains, I started to cry. I wanted the bed to engulf me in its softness and never let me go. I didn't want to face another day. I felt numb and heavy, and then that familiar sense of panic and dread started its daily ascent from the pit of my stomach into my chest and gently worked its way through my entire body, gnawing away at my insides, making me nauseous and light-headed. I wearily climbed out of bed, pulled on my jeans and a smile, and made my way downstairs to meet my team for breakfast and the mountain of promotional activity that we had planned in Cape Town for that day.

I didn't really know that I was severely depressed until months into the illness, when frequent and resurging thoughts of suicide started to grip my world. I wanted to be remembered, when I took my own life, as the woman who'd made a difference, one who always added something of value, even if I couldn't brighten my own. I wondered if I'd be missed. It was only then that a voice from somewhere deep down said, 'Get help.' It was the first time I'd experienced this kind of inner turmoil, and 'depression' wasn't a label I wanted to be identified with. It certainly wasn't something that I wanted to admit to family and friends. In my book, depression was for weak people and those who were not in control. Eventually, I took the plunge and confided in a business coach I'd employed to take the place of Terry, my mentor. He recommended that I see a psychologist.

All the signs of an imminent breakdown were right in front of me. I just hadn't paid much attention to them. I'd made several blunders in the year leading up to November when the call to adventure finally came. I'd had several car accidents, all of them my fault, as I was rushing around with my mind on the future. I would continuously forget things – important appointments, birthdays, and even the names and faces of people whom I had met on previous occasions, all of them key people in the industry who no doubt thought I was an arrogant fool. As life became harder to handle, I kept pushing back with equal ferocity, so much so that it took all my spare time to recover. I would spend weekends in isolation, not returning phone calls to friends or family. I didn't want to go out into the world; I was trying to conserve my energy and was becoming increasingly withdrawn from life.

However, it wasn't possible to hide for long. One Sunday afternoon, I was invited to a *braai* (a South Africanism for the British barbeque) at the home of my sister Suzanne and her famous Springbok rugby-playing boyfriend. I forced myself to go, preferring to stay at home alone rather than put energy into making polite conversation with the group of people who were going to be there. I should have listened to the guidance from within. At one point, out of the blue, and quite inappropriately when you are tucking into steak and corn on the cob, I started to cry, only this time the tears would not stop. I was so embarrassed that I'd let my guard down and tried hard to fight back the tears but my emotions were not listening to reason on this particular day. I continued to sob uncontrollably for what seemed like hours and nothing Suzanne or anyone said could console me. She was bereft at my condition and completely bewildered as to why I was so unhappy. 'But Caroline, why are you crying? You are beautiful, you have a lovely home, a great job, wonderful friends and family

– look at the good things you have.' Her words fell on deaf ears. I didn't care about my house, my job, my friends or family; in fact, I didn't care about anything.

What I did care about, however, was getting some sleep. If I could just sleep, I thought, I might be okay. Sleep had always been difficult for me, even as a child, with my frenetic, anxious and busy mind. But in the months leading up to the Cape Town launch sleep had become virtually impossible. I would sleep fitfully for a couple of hours each night and then wake up, unable to return to the world of my dreams as I usually did no matter how many nights I hadn't slept previously. So when sleep failed to return, I would find myself lying in bed staring at the ceiling, sobbing again. When the tears stopped, I would methodically get up, walk to the kitchen and flick on the kettle for some Sleepy Time Tea. It said on the label that it would help me drift off peacefully – but it didn't work. Oh, how I longed for daylight to come. Yet when it did, I would want so desperately to sleep again. Nevertheless, I would wearily trudge to the gym and religiously crank up my workout full blast in an effort to release those magical endorphins, which never seemed to show up, and then I would stand under the shower and find myself sobbing again.

Depression is a dark condition and totally misunderstood by those who have never suffered from it. The signs, symptoms and causes of depression are vast. We all get a bit down now and again, that's part of life, but getting so down that you cannot pull yourself up again is not just the occasional bad mood. Depression does not just descend upon us, it creeps up, slowly capturing us and luring us with its tendril like approach, anchoring itself in the suppressed emotions and conflicts within. The car accidents, the forgetfulness, the anger and the tears were all just ripples making their way to the surface, whilst seismic shifts very, very deep down rocked my world below.

Renee, the psychologist, exclaimed utter amazement at my strength and sheer determination to continue working under the circumstances, citing examples of men and women in similar positions who'd fallen apart completely, taking their own lives in the process. This was somewhat of a comforting thought – I was glad I hadn't ended up like them, although I didn't feel much better off. She diagnosed complete burnout, apparently a regular occurrence with high achieving A-type personalities who have an underlying propensity to anxiety and a history of depression in the family. She suggested that I meet with her regularly to ascertain the underlying dynamics behind my mental state and recommended I consult with my GP for medication in an effort to help me cope and restore my circadian rhythms.

Throughout the weeks of counselling, I realised that the pressure I'd put on myself to almost single-handedly implement a strategy for the future in a market that was on the brink of change, was futile, made worse by an unsupportive boss and the inevitable corporate politics that I had been blissfully unaware of in my role in the UK. Politics were a normal state of affairs for the world of business – even with a company like Virgin – and to this day, in any business, they baffle me. Politics, in my mind, are a pointless waste of time. However, with my naiveté and my propensity to take everything on my own shoulders, ignoring them was tantamount to disaster. To make change happen, you need a pistol in your pocket or a really good set of cards. I had neither, but what I had done was invest three-and-a-half years of focused effort and emotion, which had drained the life out of me.

I took Renee's advice and visited my GP, who happily dispensed the required sleeping pills as well as Eglonyl, a mild sedative and anti-depressant (usually prescribed to lactating mothers!). I disliked the idea of being a 'pill-taker' just as much as I disliked being a patient. I wanted to sleep, not to be dulled from life. However, the medication worked. I stopped crying and got some sleep, although a drugged sleep is never as refreshing as the real thing. I carried on working and I carried on exercising, although the latter was having no impact at all on my mood or my waistline. My weight had soared. I learned years later that stress and depression take their toll on the cortisol and adrenaline functions of the body. (GPs, however, don't advise you about this). Some people lose weight under stress, I put it on, which made me feel even worse about myself.

I spent many weeks consulting with Renee and got to the essence of some of my childhood issues and the reason behind my insatiable drive. I began a transcendental meditation (TM) programme to help me relax, and my life returned to some level of normality. Yet I still could not seem to uncover the source of my deep-seated frustration and discontent. Something inside me had changed dramatically; my life continued, but I felt only emptiness and a lack of fulfilment within. I went from being 'ten feet tall and bullet-proof' under the canopy of the Virgin brand to realizing my own fragility, my own humanity and my size-8 feet of clay.

Nothing was the same. Despite the counselling and the medication, I was still in turmoil inside, although the edginess had been removed somewhat. All the personality profiles I'd completed in an effort to help me uncover my place in life and my future career choices indicated that I had the required natural attributes of a leader, and with a little bit of work in certain areas, I could be successful in any high profile position. But they didn't provide answers for the more complex questions about life and its meaning that churned away inside, nor the reason behind my losing the ambition and drive that had once propelled me forward. I may be ideally suited for leadership, and Virgin might be the perfect environment for me to express this talent, but the herald had sounded his call and a new ambit had to be defined. It was time to move on, but to what? These questions concerned me deeply.

As the new Millennium dawned, I took a six-week holiday in an effort to improve my state of mind and motivation. Before I left, I spent some time talking to Mackenzie Grant, who had returned to South Africa for a while to surreptitiously oversee a part of the operation that head office had some concerns about. During his visit I cautiously shared with him some details of my emotional state, treading carefully so as not to overly concern him. I didn't want exaggerated reports finding their way back to head office about the crazy woman in Johannesburg who'd lost it after her first international assignment. He was sympathetic but a bit bewildered, and I knew intuitively from his reaction that he didn't understand, and that by sharing any emotional trauma beyond the confines of every-day work frustrations was making him uncomfortable and pushing the boundaries of our relationship. So I didn't share the cold, hard truth of my condition with him, or anyone in the company. I tried to make light of the situation, when what I really wanted was to break down and sob. I wondered then how many others there were like me, isolated and alone, plodding on and on, hiding their condition behind a mask of perfection for fear of judgement and ridicule, whilst others tiptoe around them, somehow knowing something is not quite right, but too afraid to be the one to point it out.

When I returned to work in the latter part of January of 2000, nothing had changed, apart from the depth of my tan. I carried on working, but with no clearer sign of meaning or purpose in my life. I was on auto-pilot, going through the motions. My international contract with Virgin was due to expire in less than a year. Part of me wanted to renew it, to maintain the façade, which in the absence of anything else, defined my existence. I was sure to be heading off to another international destination within the Virgin group, repeating more of the same, in a different culture, in a different country, facing different challenges. However, the deeper part of me dreaded travelling around the world, alone and feeling as brittle as I did. Virgin prided itself on a workforce of self-starters, not those going through their own personal hell. I'd be found out sooner or later. Besides, I wasn't sure if I was cut out for leadership, no matter what the assessments said. Leaders, after all, were grounded and comfortable in themselves, with a clear sense of vision and purpose. I had none of these qualities at that time, and besides, I was convinced that there was something far deeper going on here. I asked to be considered for a partial sponsorship to complete an MBA programme, believing at the time that it would help me with my leadership development and confidence. My request was politely declined with the assurance that once people obtained their degree, they always sought employment elsewhere, and MBA graduates were not Virgin's style anyway. Perhaps this was the final push I needed.

THE MYTH AND ITS MEANING:
Perseus & the Gorgon (Part I)

In myth, the call to adventure may come in many ways and not always of the hero's conscious reckoning. Circumstances may seem to conspire to bring time and space to a specific point where he has to make a difficult choice.

Acrisius was the King of Argos, but like many leaders throughout time, was full of self doubt, and needed continuous reassurance that life was indeed going as it should. Upon consulting the oracle of Apollo seeking answers to his questions of insecurity, he was given a prophecy that the son of his beautiful daughter Danae would one day kill him. Like many individuals faced with information that they don't really want to hear, he tried to conceal his demons, and make them go away. He ordered his loyal subjects to construct a bronze tower with no doors and only one small window and locked his daughter away so that she could never marry or have children.

One day, a bright shower of gold came through the window and the god Zeus appeared before Danae and told her that he'd like to make her his wife. In an instant, the prison became a beautiful field, filled with wonderful flowers and bright colours, almost as wonderful as the Elysian Fields themselves. But any light from a god shines brightly and attracts sometimes unwanted attention. Acrisius saw the light coming from the small window and instructed his men to tear down the walls. To his horror, he saw Danae with a baby on her lap. Smiling she said, 'I have named him Perseus.'

Acrisius was furious. He escorted Danae from what was left of the tower and forced her and her baby into a large chest and cast them out to sea, happy at last that he would no longer have to deal with the threat. But the gods smiled on Danae, and after many days, the chest washed up safely onto the island of Seriphos where it was discovered by a kindly fisherman called Dictys. He took pity on Danae and her son and gave them shelter for many years until Perseus grew up big and strong.

Dictys was the brother of the tyrannical King Polydectes who had cast his brother from the kingdom many years before. He was seldom spoken of and so it was years before Polydectes knew of the mother and child who had been brought to live in Dictys's hut. Reports had reached him about the incredible beauty of Danae and how she looked like one who had been favoured by the gods. So he made it his mission to meet with this beautiful creature and make her his wife. One day, when out hunting, Polydectes came to the hut of Dictys and upon setting eyes on Danae, knew immediately she was a king's daughter. But Danae detested this harsh and overbearing king and refused to wed him. However, not taking no for an answer, he continually pestered her, making her life unbearable and forcing her to take refuge in a temple where she became a priestess of the goddess.

Undeterred, King Polydectes continued his advances with even greater determination. Had Danae not been under the protection of the goddess he would have surely forced her to wed against her will. Perseus had also grown into a strong young man who was liked and admired by all who knew him and he was able to give some protection to this mother. Polydectes was a coward at heart and knew that if he stepped out of line, Perseus had the will and the power to seek revenge. He was afraid but instead of conceding defeat, he secretly developed a plan to remove Perseus from his kingdom so that he could force Danae to change her mind. Out of the blue one day, he announced before his princes and lords that he would marry someone else and invited everyone in the kingdom to join the celebrations, including Perseus. The day of the wedding feast came and everyone had brought great presents for the king. The princes and lords came forward with gifts of gold, jewellery and beautiful horses. When it came time for Perseus to present his gift, he stood with his head held in shame. The king smiled, but not as a good man smiles.

'What, no wedding present?' he yelled.

'I am a poor man, I don't have any money,' exclaimed Perseus.

'That's what you get for being a lazy good-for-nothing!' said Polydectes.

Perseus was furious. 'I can bring you any present in the world, anything,' he boasted.

'Then bring me the head of the monster Gorgon, Medusa!' replied Polydectes, knowing that he was setting an impossible task for Perseus. The Gorgon was a fearsome creature whose gaze alone was enough to turn any living creature to stone. Polydectes knew that this task would surely result in the death of this young hero. 'If you do not, then remain out of my kingdom forever, for in Seriphos we will have no lazy good-for-nothing young men.'

The lords and the princes applauded even though they deeply disagreed with the King. They were indeed sad for Perseus and his mother, but dared not do anything to help. And so Perseus had to leave Seriphos, in search of this legendary monster, to save his mother from the grasp of the evil king and to prove his bravery to the kingdom.

And this is exactly how the call to adventure can begin – a mistake, an unanticipated problem or a simple blunder that has unforeseen consequences. An idle boast from Perseus fell right into the hands of the conspiring king signalling that Perseus' world was to change forever.

The call to adventure may come suddenly out of the blue – a promotion, an illness or accident, the death of a loved one, a change in circumstances, retirement or the arrival of some good or bad news. It may also be a stirring from way down deep inside, one that has been suppressed for a long time. Whatever form the call may take, it symbolises the point in the journey where the world of the secure and familiar is no more. The current ambit has been outgrown. Old patterns, concepts and ideals no longer fit. It signals the death or destruction of one state and the creation or re-birth of another.

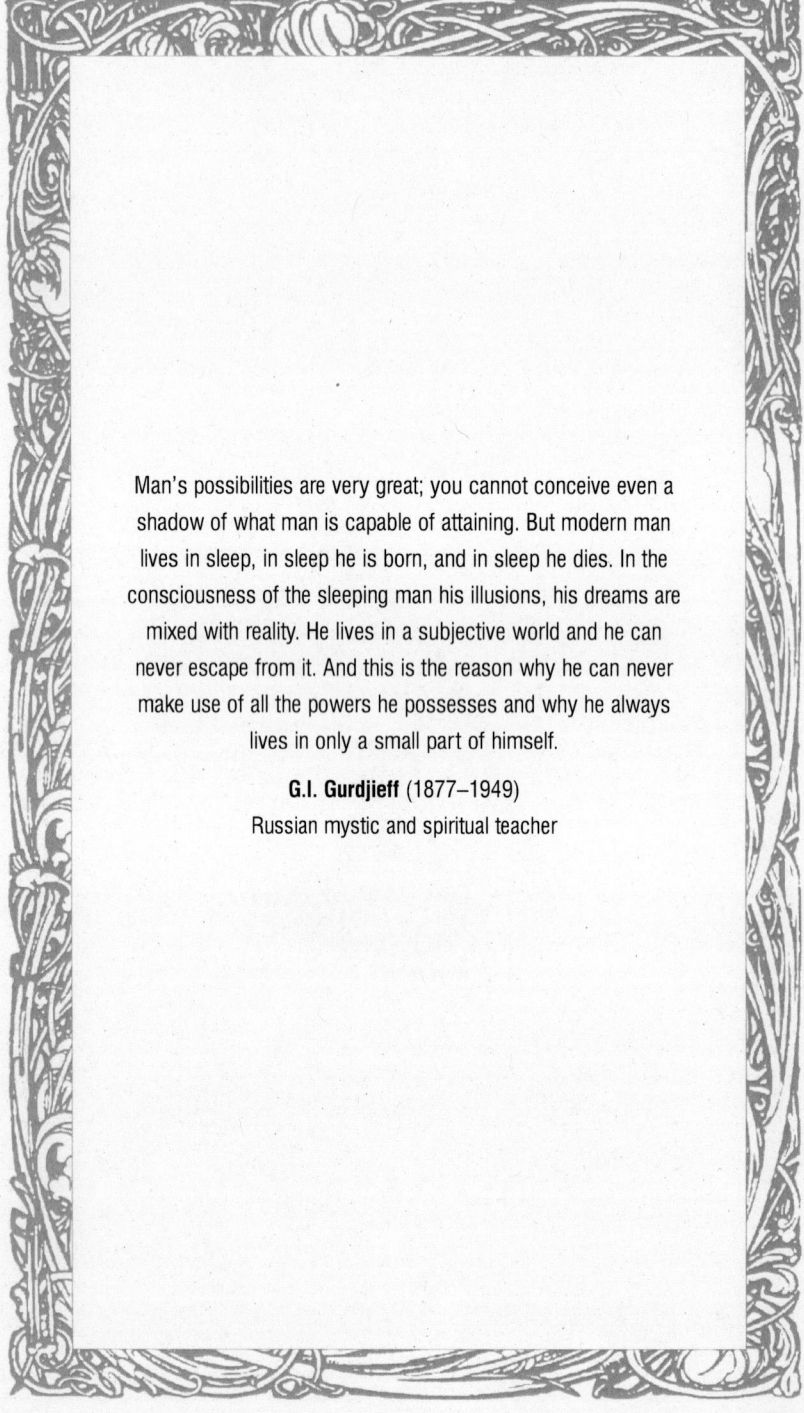

Man's possibilities are very great; you cannot conceive even a shadow of what man is capable of attaining. But modern man lives in sleep, in sleep he is born, and in sleep he dies. In the consciousness of the sleeping man his illusions, his dreams are mixed with reality. He lives in a subjective world and he can never escape from it. And this is the reason why he can never make use of all the powers he possesses and why he always lives in only a small part of himself.

G.I. Gurdjieff (1877–1949)
Russian mystic and spiritual teacher

STAGE 4

REFUSAL OF THE CALL

Often in actual life and not infrequently in the myths and popular tales, we encounter the dull case of the call unanswered; for it is always possible to turn the ear to other interests. Refusal of the summons converts the adventure into its negative. Walled in boredom, hard work or 'culture', the subject loses the power of significant affirmative action and becomes a victim to be saved. His flowering world becomes a wasteland of dry stones and his life feels meaningless – even though he may through titanic effort succeed in building an empire of renown. Whatever house he builds, it will be a house of death: a labyrinth of cyclopean walls to hide him from his Minotaur. All he can do is create new problems for himself and await the gradual approach of his disintegration.

Joseph Campbell

The Hero with a Thousand Faces

 he call to adventure may come more than once. It did with me and I ignored each one. When I was 12, our family moved to a different house in the county of Bedfordshire in South East England. My parents purchased a large, four-bed home in the upmarket country village of Langford. The house was beautifully situated next to a meandering river and overlooked open fields and woodland filled with grazing cattle and horses – your typical English country scene. I was ambivalent about the move; change was always hard for my sensitive demeanour. But I was happy to be moving away from the school I'd attended for some years, away from the school bullies and the ridicule from people who called themselves my friends but used every opportunity to mock the way I looked and dressed. I was not, however, looking forward to changing schools again. I was sure that I would encounter more of the same and, like before, not be in a position to defend myself.

However, the secondary-school experience turned out to be far less traumatic than I expected. I managed to fit in and blend surreptitiously with the background as much as I could. I eventually made new friends who didn't ridicule me, and although I still felt awkward and ill at ease, I reluctantly became more social. The bullying stopped, but the jibes continued about my oversized nose and my lankiness – I towered above others my age. Only now, a new dimension was added: I was known as the *posh kid* who lived in the big house on the high street. I hardened to the comments eventually, although the words still stung and I did what I could to avoid the purveyors of ridicule, alighting the school bus miles away from home, preferring to walk alone than ride with them. These times alone helped me to think and calm myself, and to try and make some sense of the harsh and critical world. I liked being alone and often sought my own company over that of others.

It was during these conversations with myself at this tender age that the call to adventure came. The event is as clear in my mind today as it was then, some thirty years ago. On a lazy Saturday morning in spring, I stood on a small footbridge over the river, gazing blankly at the resident swans and their signets as they undertook their morning ablutions in the shade of the big weeping willow tree. I had the usual feeling of irritable boredom that twelve-year-olds have, I suppose – only on this day I was also greatly unsettled by turbulent emotions that surged through my body with an intensity that I hadn't experienced before, making me edgy and restless. The only way I was going to get rid of this agitation that consumed me was to run and run until complete exhaustion overcame me. As I contemplated taking off along the footpath into the woodlands beyond, I heard a voice speak. It was loud, demanding and insistent. I turned to look about me, thinking that the voice had come from outside – but it hadn't. It was my own voice, but it didn't sound like me, and for a fleeting moment I thought that I was going mad, that maybe I was a crazy person.

'So is this it?' the voice asked. 'Is this all there is to life? You go to school, get a job, get married, have kids, buy a house and go on a couple of holidays a year, have grandkids, and then you die? What's the point? There has to be more to life than this.' The voice disappeared as quickly as it had arrived, leaving me feeling exhausted, empty and deflated. All the turbulent emotions were gone. I was scared, realizing that this kind of thinking was not the norm for one of my age – I hadn't heard anyone at school talk of such things. Yet as I felt the emotions dissipate I realised that the voice spoke of something that had been bothering me greatly for a long time. As I'd watched how my parents – the gods in my world – had behaved over the years, I really couldn't see the value behind the struggle, pain and heartache that they went through just to get on with life. There seemed to be little joy and pleasure, only a struggle for continued existence and a bigger and better house. Life was something to be survived, not enjoyed to the full. What was the reason for all this? Surely there had to be a purpose and a goal for which they were aiming.

I had no idea how long I stood on the footbridge lost in my world. Eventually I went home, my mind spinning, and went upstairs to my room so that I could continue to be alone. There I lay down on my bed and gazed at the ceiling for several hours until I fell into a deep sleep. Everything about the experience was still crystal clear in my mind – everything, that is, except the answer to the questions. Days later, I mumbled something to my mum, as teenagers do, about the experience and the questions posed by the voice. I asked her why life was as it was, why we seemed to be on this repetitive treadmill on the road to nowhere. 'That is what you do, love,' was her hurried reply as she busied herself with the ironing and the evening meal. I stared at her blankly, realising then that she had probably never given the question much thought because this was indeed *what you do*: You did the housework, raised the kids, cooked meals, earned as much money as possible to have a better standard of life. It seemed pointless to pursue the matter. I could have raised the issue with my father, but he was hard at work most of the time and rarely came home in the best of moods, so I didn't have the courage to confront him about my twelve-year-old existential angst. I would save his occasional good moods for more pressing discussions, like maths homework! Discussions with my friends were also out of the question, as I was convinced they already thought I was a bit 'cranky' and this would only result in more bus journey discomfort.

No matter what our age, we all need a sense of meaning and purpose to propel us forward, a mental map that makes sense. This is particularly true for teenagers who are desperately searching for an identity among their peers or family members. Such a quest is even worse in hyper-sensitive children whose perennial search for *self* becomes the single burning reason for existence. At twelve years old I was struggling to find somewhere that I could fit, and nothing felt right. The harder I tried, the more I felt like an outcast – like I wasn't meant to be here. Being so young, I didn't consider that these questions might be opening the door to another world and were perhaps a call to explore the spiritual side of my nature or my relationship with God.

Yet there was nothing about God that I liked. Christianity and the church failed to resonate with a single cell in my body. My parents weren't overly religious and went to church only for weddings and funerals, or to inspect the architecture whilst on one of Dad's historic quests. As kids, we went to Sunday school to save face in the village rather than to quench our desire to be holy. The

Bible seemed to comfort so many, but it made little sense to me and was seemingly full of threats. After being hauled out of bed by my father one morning at the age of 7 or 8 to attend Sunday school when one of the village busybodies came to enquire about my whereabouts, I'd made up my mind very firmly that I didn't want anything to do with God. As far as I was concerned, he was angry and judgemental and made my life more confusing than ever. When his representatives (the priests and the bishops) weren't threatening the congregation with God's wrath, they were telling us how, as children, we should be more like his son, gentle Jesus – humble, unassuming, tolerant and kind, always turning the other cheek. (I wondered if Jesus had ever been bullied at school?)

Religious education at school also bore no fruits. Whilst the teacher was extremely funny and very entertaining, she did nothing to convince me that there was something bigger for us out there. She just reinforced the message that we must be good people and get on with life. So when the door to another world opened up just slightly and offered the opportunity to explore my inner nature, the 'gatekeepers' were too fierce and foreboding. Bound in the repressed walls of childhood, I could not see that the pathway to *enlightenment* was actually illuminated in any way at all. The forest around was dark, and the path was totally in shadow, and I didn't know what terrors I may find there. I felt small and very alone. So I got up, and carefully and quietly closed the door and the opportunity it presented, and got on with life.

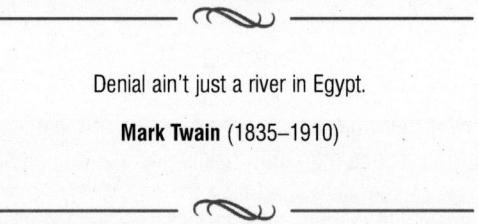

Denial ain't just a river in Egypt.

Mark Twain (1835–1910)

Over ten years later, in my early twenties, the call was to come again, this time with a slightly greater sense of urgency. Before joining Virgin in 1992 and working out of their head office at London's Gatwick Airport, I spent several years in London's fashionable Piccadilly Circus working for Continental Airlines and TWA. Their offices were almost next door to each other, separated only by St James Church, built in 1684 and designed by Sir Christopher Wren. Like many people I would use the church as a cut-through from Piccadilly to Jermyn Street. I wasn't a fan of churches, other than for their architecture, but there was something decidedly alternative about the atmosphere in this particular church – it was less foreboding than many of the other churches I'd frequented in my childhood, and I often found myself lingering, taking an interest in what was going on. I discovered that the evening seminars and events held frequently within those walls seemed – different. On occasion there were small markets and fairs that had a Celtic and pagan feel about them. I would casually browse, but didn't feel comfortable to explore each stall too deeply, in case I was cornered by some religious fanatic and couldn't escape. On one occasion, a guy noticed me and came up to talk to me about an upcoming event. To be polite, I expressed interest, but something terrified me and I didn't attend, although my curiosity had been sparked. I told myself that my days in London were too long as it was, particularly with the three-hour commute in and out of London every day; but in reality, my religious contempt was stronger than my curiosity.

Twenty years later, at the age of 43, whilst living in Johannesburg, I attended a seminar called 'The Work We Were Born To Do', facilitated by speaker and author Nick Williams. His life story was similar to my own and as I got talking with him I found out that about twenty years earlier, after leaving the corporate world, he became the director of a non-profit organisation called Alternatives, which ran seminars and workshops from... wait for it... St James Church in Piccadilly! Right under my very nose! Alternatives embraced a variety of spiritual traditions and diverse ways of living, and provided the platform for many leaders in alternative philosophies to share their views and opinions. Speakers like Deepak Chopra and Marianne Williamson had been invited guests. Yet again, the call had come, but yet again I ignored it. I was again standing on the threshold, but the guardians were too strong. I wasn't ready. It wasn't until much later in life that I made a connection between the two experiences. I spent a long time chastising myself about my ignorance and apparent blindness when I discovered my folly. At Alternatives I might have found some of the answers that I'd been subconsciously searching for since childhood, and my life may not have been so unfulfilled.

Over the years, I often felt the gnawing emptiness that I'd experienced at age 12 return. Tiny, distant voices from somewhere very deep, deep down insisted that there was something more that I should be doing, yet I pushed them aside, labelling them as extreme insecurity. Caught up in the river of life, I was carried along by the strong and enticing currents of fear and denial, turning my back on the still, small voice that cried out for adventures of a different kind. I smothered the spark of initial curiosity within, building the walls of my castle higher and higher in an effort to stave off what I somehow believed to be inevitable, keeping myself busy and turning my attention towards more acceptable, run-of-the-mill activities that promised greater outward acceptance. To follow my heart appeared selfish and risky and would attract the unwanted attention of parents and friends, who just didn't understand the extent of my 'madness'. To toe the line, to fit in, to appear normal became my resolution, even though the path I'd chosen required a herculean effort to sustain. I finally understood why the third call, when it came in 1999 in Cape Town, had to be so aggressive and insistent.

THE MYTH AND ITS MEANING:
The Sleeping Beauty

Folklore across the world describes the refusal of the call. The princess breaks her promise to the Frog, King Minos refuses to sacrifice the bull to Poseidon, and Sleeping Beauty slept for one hundred years:

A long time ago there were a king and queen who said every day, 'Ah, if only we had a child.' But a child did not come. One day when the queen was bathing, a frog crept out of the water onto the land, and said to her, 'Your wish shall be fulfilled – before a year has gone by, you shall have a daughter.' A year later, the frog's prophecy came true and the queen had a little girl who was so beautiful that the king could not contain his joy, and ordered a great feast to celebrate. He invited everyone in the kingdom, including the twelve wise women, so that they might be kind and well-disposed towards the child as she grew up. Even though he knew that there were thirteen wise women, he had only twelve golden plates and didn't think it would matter if one of them stayed at home.

The feast was held with all manner of splendour that one would expect, and when it came to an end, the wise women each bestowed a magic gift upon the baby: one gave virtue, another beauty, a third riches, and so on. When eleven of them had bestowed their promises, the thirteenth suddenly came in. She was angry at not being invited, and without greeting or even looking at anyone, she cried with a loud voice, 'The king's daughter shall in her fifteenth year prick herself with a spindle, and fall down dead.' And, without saying another word more, she turned and left the room. The congregation stood in shocked silence and the king and queen were speechless. Yet one gift remained, the one from the twelfth wise woman. She came forward to speak, saying that

62

whilst she could not undo the evil sentence, she could soften it. She said that the princess would not die, but would fall into a deep sleep for a hundred years.

The king gave orders that every spindle in the whole kingdom should be burnt so that the words of the wicked wise woman could not come true. Meanwhile, the gifts bestowed by the remaining wise women were plenteously fulfilled. The princess was beautiful, modest, good-natured and wise, so that everyone who saw her was bound to love her. But it happened that on the very day when she was fifteen years old, the king and queen were not at home, and the princess was left in the palace quite alone. So she went round into all sorts of places she hadn't been, looking into rooms and bed-chambers just as she liked, until at last she came upon an old tower. She climbed up the narrow, winding staircase, and reached a little door at the top. A rusty key was in the lock, and when she turned it the door sprang open, and there in a little room sat an old woman with a spindle, busily spinning her flax.

'Good day, old mother,' said the king's daughter. 'What are you doing there?'

'I am spinning,' said the old woman, smiling and nodding her head.

'What sort of thing is that, that rattles round so merrily?' asked the girl. 'I'd like to have a go.'

She took hold of the spindle, but as soon as she did so, the magic decree was fulfilled. She pricked her finger, and all at once fell down upon the bed in a deep, deep sleep.

And this sleep extended over the whole palace. The king and queen, who had just come home and had entered the great hall, began to sleep, and the whole of the court with them. The horses in the stables, too, went to sleep, as did the dogs in the yard, the pigeons upon the roof, the flies on the wall; even the fire that was flaming on the hearth became quiet and slept, the roast meat left off frizzling, and the cook, who was just going to pull the hair of the scullery boy because he had forgotten something, let him go and went to sleep. And the wind became still and on the trees around the castle, not a leaf moved again.

Folklore is resplendent with tales of sleep or hibernation depicting our lack of conscious awareness, or a desire to repress the unseen world. Sleeping Beauty slept under the spell of a jealous hag, The Bible tells the story of Adam who was put to sleep in the Garden of Eden, Rip Van Winkle slept to avoid the nagging of his wife. In the tale of Red Riding Hood, the grandmother was locked in a cupboard by the wolf, and the three little pigs refused to open the door to the big bad wolf.

It is natural for heroes to try and dodge the adventure. The journey towards truth is risky, dangerous and even life-threatening and the hero always feels that he needs to be better prepared. When standing at the threshold of a new world, where the road may be paved with thorns, fear is an understandable reaction. Stepping into the unknown is not a frivolous undertaking, but a gamble with life and death. It's no wonder that many refuse.

From wherever it comes, the call to adventure cannot be ignored. Even though the seeker may return for a while to his or her familiar occupation or way of life, he or she will find it meaningless, unfruitful and barren. Quite often it takes even more energy than before to sustain the effort of just getting by.

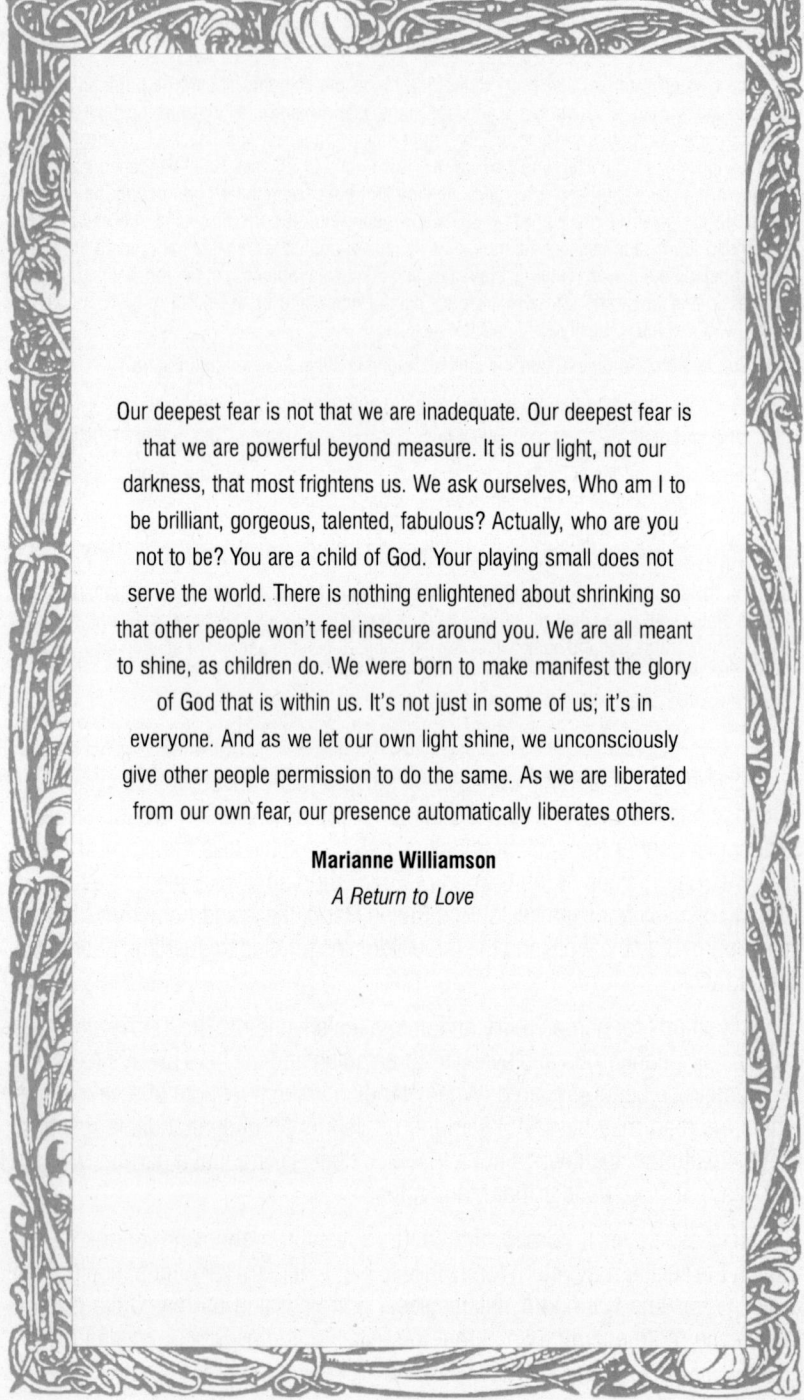

Our deepest fear is not that we are inadequate. Our deepest fear is that we are powerful beyond measure. It is our light, not our darkness, that most frightens us. We ask ourselves, Who am I to be brilliant, gorgeous, talented, fabulous? Actually, who are you not to be? You are a child of God. Your playing small does not serve the world. There is nothing enlightened about shrinking so that other people won't feel insecure around you. We are all meant to shine, as children do. We were born to make manifest the glory of God that is within us. It's not just in some of us; it's in everyone. And as we let our own light shine, we unconsciously give other people permission to do the same. As we are liberated from our own fear, our presence automatically liberates others.

Marianne Williamson
A Return to Love

STAGE 5

CROSSING THE THRESHOLD

Crossing the threshold signifies a turning point in the journey where the adventure begins in earnest. The call has been heard and fears and doubts are whipped up within as the hero stands on the edge of a precipice and at the threshold to a different world. Crossing the threshold is the point in the journey where a new path can be travelled, but its way is dark and poorly illuminated. Many are unprepared to retreat from the world of perceived safety and security which is why the majority continue to follow the well-trodden path of familiarity, even though it no longer carries the same lure of excitement as it once did. But those who have a deep sense of longing always take the road less travelled. They may linger and make excuses, they may delay what they deem to be inevitable, but eventually they will take the first step. Whilst others see a move from the ordinary world as the end, a premature retirement, the seeker sees it as just the beginning.

n March of 2000, I stood at the threshold, unsure of my future, confused about the many decisions I had to make, and concerned about why I was feeling so desolate and lost. Up to this point in my life, decisions had always been so easy, as though they'd already been made for me, laid out like railroad tracks that I seemingly just traversed with ease. I moved effortlessly from one career success to the next in an industry and company that I'd neatly slotted into, always finding myself in the right position at the right time, with a good salary and perks. I'd never really given much thought to the future, trusting that things would work out, as things always did in my life. I'd naturally assumed that I would climb my way up the career ladder, moving from country to country with Virgin or any other company that took my fancy, until it was time to retire. I didn't expect to have a near complete nervous breakdown before reaching mid-life that would force me to reconsider my entire existence.

During my 'condition', I'd realised, too, that money, power and success were not as motivating for me as they once were. At one time they were my sole focus, as they provided me the sense of freedom that I so craved. But I realised now that having the Midas touch was not all it was cracked up to be. I couldn't imagine myself chasing this goal for the rest of my life to the exclusion of all others. Living a life of significance was singularly the most important thing to me and for the first ten years of my career, significance meant an alignment of a strong and motivating purpose, money and recognition. Now I wasn't sure what it meant. The purposeful *crusade* that I'd embarked on with Virgin eight years ago didn't hold the same magic as it once did. My job was no longer the reason for getting out of bed in the morning. The allure had waned.

I'd also assumed when embarking on this journey of life that I would be happily married by my mid-thirties – after all, that's what one did, wasn't it? I'd given marriage a go in my early twenties whilst searching for love and security from the father figure I'd lacked in childhood, but found that I was completely hopeless in a run-of-the-mill relationship. I was too young, didn't fully understand myself, and found that being involved with a man whose sole goal in life *was* money became way too restrictive for this adventurous spirit. I assumed that I would find a soul mate in South Africa, now that I had matured, was outwardly successful and mixing with the 'who's who' of Johannesburg. I'd dated lots of men, but I still hadn't met The One.

So in my wildest dreams I never imagined being in a foreign country all by myself at 34 having to confront the rest of my existence. It just didn't fit the subconscious road map that I had for my life, and I felt utterly paralysed with indecision. Everything I'd sought to identify with seemed to have eluded me. Life seemed to have other plans for me, which I was blissfully unaware of, and I searched in vain for something to cling to which would help to take my internal crusade to another level. The strong feelings from childhood of being a misfit in society returned, mingling with terror and anxiety as a dichotomy raged within – the desire for safety and security coupled with the urge to be completely free. As Rudyard Kipling so eloquently put it, 'Never the twain shall meet.' And he was right in my case. I desperately wanted to find answers to the restlessness that churned and frothed away inside. Each night I would sleep a drugged and restless sleep, waking to face the same anxiety and indecision the following day. I didn't know what I wanted, and all the other driving motives no longer carried the same level of attraction.

When one is mired in the fabric of an organisation's culture as strong and purposeful as Virgin's, notions about leaving can seem entirely impossible. An organisation characterised by its strong sense of purpose creates the ruse of an extended family. And that is what Virgin was to me. I had identified so strongly with its cause – David vs Goliath (British Airways vs Virgin) – and its light-hearted approach to business, that I had become part of the very structure which made up the whole. One can easily lose one's identity in a powerful culture, and I'd certainly done that. The lines between where Virgin stopped and Caroline started were blurred. It was only years later as I worked with the concept of culture more intensely in other organisations that I began to understand how powerful Virgin's culture really was, lulling me into a false sense of security and delusion. Only then did I understand, with hindsight, why I was feeling so confused, lost and isolated at this particular point in my life. At the time, however, I yet again thought that I was going quite insane. [1]

All heroes encounter obstacles on the road to adventure. At each gateway to a new world there are powerful guardians at the threshold, placed to keep the unworthy from entering. They present a menacing face to the hero, but if properly understood, they can be overcome, bypassed or even turned into allies. Many heroes encounter Threshold Guardians, and understanding their nature can help determine how to handle them.

Christopher Vogler
The Writer's Journey

After over eight years with Virgin, the *family* I'd loved and cherished had lost its appeal and no longer inspired me as it once did. Perhaps I had outgrown it (or perhaps it had outgrown me?). Part of me was devastated that this was so, but another part of me no longer wanted to be constrained by its invisible bonds and the smokescreen of security it provided. My contract in South Africa was due to expire at the end of 2000, and opportunities to advance my leadership career within the company presented themselves – in Hong Kong, Shanghai, Athens, New York, and even back in London. From a purely material perspective, they made sense: If one is to make money as an employee in the airline business, which is a notoriously bad paying industry in comparison to others, travelling around the world on a rotating contract – spending two years in one country and two years in another – provides a great opportunity to save cash and a great opportunity for adventure. I'd worked really hard to get to this point, but now I didn't find any of the prospects facing me attractive. Besides, deep down, I didn't want to leave my beloved Africa, whose spirit had woven itself into every fibre of my being – something which is difficult to justify to outsiders who see only the crime and the violence and wonder how it's possible to survive in such situations and retain some modicum of sanity. There is a saying that once Africa gets into your blood, it stays with you forever. As far as I was concerned, never a truer word had been spoken. Africa was inside every cell in my body, and I often had vivid nightmares about returning to a damp, cold, dreary England, always waking with a sense of relief as the bright African sunshine streamed through my curtains and glistened off the swimming pool outside. I couldn't imagine living anywhere else, and certainly not in a big city like Shanghai or Hong Kong.

But I didn't have to leave Africa. Yet more career options were available. I had the opportunity to stay in Johannesburg with Virgin on a local rand-based package, although it was far less lucrative than the international package I was currently experiencing, and carried much less accountability. As the company had expanded and streamlined its operations, three-quarters of my initial area of responsibility had been assumed by full-time line managers, leaving only the sales and distribution under my wing. This role had become a hands-on, day-to-day management role, and certainly not challenging enough for this adventurous spirit whose sense of purpose and reason for being was aligned with the work she did. Besides, I'd probably achieved as much as I could in the four years I'd been there, and the team required a different leadership style to take it to another level. My relationship with the general manager was difficult, to say the least, and did nothing to enhance my fragile sense of self-worth. There was always the possibility that he wouldn't stay on, and in fact he did leave a short time later, but I was still young and relatively inexperienced as a leader, and to hang around waiting for a potential promotion was not an option. Even if the role of general manager was available in the future, Virgin frowned upon promoting leaders from within, preferring to select them from their rotating pool, which I was now supposed to be part of. I would have to leave Africa to perhaps one day come back – that was a chance I might have to take.

To top it all off, I had not one, but *two* competing job offers from two of the largest travel management companies in South Africa, both at board level – certainly a confidence booster and a testament to my skills and abilities. But at the time, they added to my confusion. The jobs were certainly more rewarding financially than the local Virgin package, and the opportunities each position presented would have rounded my leadership skills superbly. But in my fragile state of mind, I believed that, given the aggressive nature of the individual cultures of these companies and the personalities I would encounter, I would have probably ended up in a white hospital ward in a strait jacket if I'd accepted them. I didn't feel that I was coping well with corporate life, and believed that I wasn't tough enough, savvy enough or driven enough to assume another high-profile leadership role. After all, leaders are people you aspire to follow. I didn't know who I was or what I was about. Who in their right mind would follow me?

I wasn't sure if I could see a future for me as an MD or director of *any* organisation.

Of course, I could have got by, as most leaders do, and *coached* my way through my current state, adopting the old adage of *fake it until you make it*, putting the blinkers on and ignoring the source of my discontent and frustration. From an outsider's point of view, I'd managed to hold it together fairly well through all of this inner turmoil – why couldn't I just continue? But somewhere along the line, people would find out that I was a fraud, and besides, the salary benefits were not worth the enormous effort it would take on my part to be out of integrity. I would be hurting nobody but myself. I had achieved much in my years in the aviation industry and had certainly taken my first steps onto the rung of the highflying ladder. But the mere thought of accepting any one of these positions filled me with dread and fear, not joy and anticipation.

"The Adventure is always and everywhere a passage beyond the veil of the known into the unknown; the powers that watch at the boundary are dangerous; to deal with them is risky; yet for anyone with competence and courage the danger fades.

Joseph Campbell
The Hero with a Thousand Faces

The path of truth and adventure is littered with obstacles. At each gateway to a new world there are powerful gatekeepers that keep the unworthy from entering. In all myths of the world, dangerous presences can be found outside the safety of the village. In every desert, forest or deep ocean lurk ogres, monsters and wild creatures – hunters of men – who threaten to tear all those who stray limb from limb. Yet the danger that threatens from the realms of the unknown also weaves a magically enticing spell. In 2000, there were many opportunities that stood on the other side of the threshold, but fear, indecision and a longing for these opportunities to be more than 'just a job' prevented me from making a move in any one direction. Any job, of course, is what you make of it but right now, I felt as if I was mired in a peat bog. Unseen forces were pulling me down, holding me back, whilst others tempted me onwards, propelling me to change, to shape a different life.

So many choices and only one decision allowed. I would sleep one day with a decision made, and wake up the next in a total state of confusion again.

The forces of light and dark were at continuous odds within. And somewhere from deep, deep down, the same voice from twenty-three years ago spoke, only this time it whispered very quietly, with a sense of wonder and curiosity and a longing for freedom. It wanted the answer to one burning question: 'Who are you *really,* without the trappings of the corporate world – your title, your salary, the Virgin brand, your company car – and what is your *real* reason for being here?'

I didn't know. I'd defined myself by all of these external things – what I did for a living, financial success, the company I kept, the house I owned. I realised then that even though I might change my job, work for a different company or move to a different country, it would be just more of the same. I didn't have the slightest motivation to undertake any of the positions with gusto and I dreaded what might become of me if I wasn't honest with myself – maybe ending up like so many leaders I coached in my later years whose souls, lifeless and dull, stared out from behind the eyes of their pallid faces.

It was Mark Twain that said 'Action speaks louder than words but not nearly as often.' I wasn't going to resolve this dilemma by thinking about it and hoping that a solution would fall out of mid air. No matter how many times I meditated and waited for the answers to descend, all around me was silence. Many times, I seriously considered packing everything up and moving to Ponta D'Ouro in Mozambique to become a diving instructor. Nobody knew me in Mozambique. My title and achievements didn't matter and spending time on a beach and underwater in the silence of the deep blue ocean, I'd have freedom to really ponder the deeper questions about life. But ducking out wasn't my style, and besides, being mired in the class-conscious culture of Johannesburg, I had an image and reputation to maintain with friends and family. What would they say if I just upped and left to live barefoot in a dive camp in the war-torn country that Mozambique was at the time? This was something that you did in a gap year after leaving university, not in the middle of a career crisis, whilst paying off the mortgage on a luxury home and building a sustainable financial future. A move of that magnitude would clearly indicate that I'd lost the plot, particularly when those in my circle seemed to be coping admirably where I seemed to be falling apart. More importantly, such a move would ensure that I had realised my biggest fear: that I was indeed incapable of being anything worthwhile or valuable in life other than a beach bum. So that was completely out of the question, but a job that would allow me more freedom, flexibility and time to myself, wasn't.

In 1998, I'd co-founded the South African counterpart of an international travel educational body called ACTE (the Association of Corporate Travel Executives). It was designed to bring competing members of the industry together under one roof to discuss the complicated issue of travel distribution and the pending changes in the way in which air travel would be bought and sold over the next twelve to eighteen months. I became the local chair and spokesperson, which propelled me into the spotlight as a speaker – something I was good at. Strategic travel management as a practice within a corporation was nonexistent in 2000, This left a great, yawning chasm of opportunity in the market for a neutral and independent consultant, not linked to a specific agency body, who could advise and manage the process on behalf of a handful of clients on a full or part time basis. For many months, I investigated how a business of this nature might be constructed using international models as a guide. It was a concept that worked well overseas, and whilst the market in South Africa was small in comparison, there was no competition and I figured that with my insights, knowledge and solid reputation, I could make it work. More importantly, the idea enthused me greatly, providing me with the belief that I'd once more be making a difference, helping many bewildered organisations through the tumultuous changes due to take place in the industry in the next year.[2]

In March of 2000, the opportunity to put my idea into practice presented itself when, out of the blue, after a speaking engagement, I was offered a six-month contract with diamond giant De Beers as a consultant to help them with their travel management strategy. Money was no object. They offered to pay me a flat-rate salary, guaranteeing my income for six months, which just added to the additional twenty-four months of savings that I had behind me. If I was going to take the plunge – it would be now or never. Setting up a practice of my own would allow me to acquire the lifestyle change that I craved and still make a decent living at the same time, particularly if I could base my remuneration on a percentage of the savings I'd help to make. A year would surely be enough time for me to establish myself and determine if this would indeed be a lucrative business venture, financially *and* emotionally. By then, I felt sure that the airline commission cuts would have made their way into South Africa and companies might indeed be queuing at my door. Perhaps now was the opportunity I needed to help me find out. Naïve and foolish perhaps – this was a big risk. But then again, life is a risk, and Virgin had always prided itself on hiring individuals who would act and take those risks. I guess I was really no exception.

And so in May of 2000, with one contract and the comfort of an almost fully paid up house and some substantial savings behind me, I took one giant leap of faith and resigned from Virgin, stepping across the threshold into the unknown with only myself to rely on. I was either brave or utterly bonkers, perhaps a bit of both. But I'd discovered my new raison d'être and nothing else mattered. For the first time in over twelve months, I felt a sense of delirious happiness and relief as I set off on a new crusade – all thoughts of my 'condition' erased from memory. I felt absolutely free, courageous and fearless. I had no corporate responsibilities, no people to manage, no boss to please. I worked from home, I made my own hours and I absolutely loved it. Depression – pah! – I think someone had just put some of that *wacky baccy* in my cornflakes!

THE MYTH AND ITS MEANING:

Prince Five Weapons – A Buddhist Tale

Threshold Guardians are the Gatekeepers to a new world

At the start of any adventure, the hero has to confront deceitful and dangerous entities who cluster around the entrance to a new world, many of them nestling deeply in our own subconscious. Carved above the entrances to many churches and cathedrals in the UK and Europe are fearsome looking gargoyles often assuming a frightening and loathsome form. They are symbolic of the 'gatekeepers', whose role is to keep the unworthy from entering the sacred space beyond until they can figure out a way to circumvent the hostile forces or muster up the courage to tackle them head on. Often the threat is illusory and of the hero's own making, but nevertheless it signifies that he has reached the border between two worlds. At this point he must confront the 'monsters in the dark' and take a massive leap of faith into the unknown, even with his eyes squeezed tightly shut, or the adventure will never really begin.

Once upon a time, a young prince was born to the King and Queen of Benares. (He was the future Buddha.) When the prince turned 16, the king decided to send him to school, where he studied very hard. When he graduated, his teacher gave him a special award: a gift of five weapons and the title, 'Prince Five Weapons'. On his way home, the prince came to a dark, dark forest. The local people warned him: 'Young man, don't go through the forest. There is a monstrous demon ogre called Sticky-Hair living there. He kills everyone he sees!'

But the prince was self-confident and fearless, like a young lion. So he pushed on into the forest. When he reached the centre he came across the ogre who was as tall as a tree, with a head as big as a summer house and eyes as big as dinner plates. He had two big, yellow tusks sticking out of his gaping wide mouth filled with ugly brown teeth. He had a huge belly covered with white blotches, and his hands and feet were blue green. The monster roared and growled at the prince. 'Where are you going in my forest, little man? You look like a tasty morsel to me. I'm going to gobble you up!'

The prince had just graduated from college and had won the highest award from his teacher. So he thought he knew just about everything, and that he could do just about anything. He replied, 'Oh fierce demon, I am Prince Five Weapons, and I have come on purpose to find you. I dare you to attack me! I will kill you easily with my first two weapons – my bow and poison-tipped arrows.' Then he put a poison arrow in his bow and shot it straight at the monster.

But the arrow just stuck fast into his thick hair, without hurting him at all. The prince shot, all the remaining fifty poison-tipped arrows, one after another. But they also stuck fast to the one called Sticky-Hair. Prince Five Weapons threatened the Ogre a second time and drew a long sword and delivered a masterful blow. But, the sword stuck fast in the thick coat of sticky hair. He threw his fourth weapon, his spear, at the monster. But this, too, just stuck to his hair. Next he attacked with the last of his five weapons, his club. This also stuck fast onto Sticky-Hair.

Then the prince yelled at him, 'Hey you, monster – haven't you ever heard of me, Prince Five Weapons? I have more than just my five weapons. I have the strength of my young man's body. I will break you in pieces!' He hit Sticky-Hair with his right fist, just like a boxer. But his hand just stuck to the hairy coat, and he couldn't remove it. He hit him with his left fist, but this too just stuck fast to the gooey mess of hair. He kicked him with his right foot and then his left, just like a martial arts master. But they both stuck onto him like his fists. Finally he butted him as hard as he could with his head, just like a wrestler. But, lo and behold, his head got stuck as well.

Even whilst sticking to the hairy monster in five places and hanging down from his coat, the prince had no fear. Sticky-Hair thought, 'This is very strange indeed. He is more like a lion than a man. Even whilst in the grasp of a ferocious monster like me, he does not tremble with fear. In all the time I've been killing people in this forest, I've never met anyone as great as this prince. Why isn't he afraid of me?'

Since Prince Five-Weapons was not like ordinary men, Sticky-Hair was afraid to eat him right away. Instead, he asked him, 'Young man, why aren't you afraid of death?'

The prince replied, 'Why should I be afraid of death? There is no doubt that anyone who is born will definitely die! What's more, I have in my belly a secret weapon, a diamond weapon that you cannot digest. It will cut your intestines into pieces if you are foolish enough to swallow me. So if I die – you die! That's why I'm not afraid of you.'

Sticky-Hair thought. No doubt this fearless man is telling the truth. Even if I eat as much as a pea-sized tidbit of such a hero, I won't be able to digest it. So I will let him go.

Fearing his own death, he released Prince Five Weapons. He said, 'You are a great man. I will not eat your flesh. I let you go free.' And that is just what he did.

Adapted from *Buddhist Tales for Young and Old*
Translated by Kurunegoda Piyatissa Maha Thera
www.buddhanet.net

Sometimes, to progress, we have to step outside of what makes logical sense and call on weapons of a different variety which lie beyond our five senses and the reason of the ordinary world. Although Prince Five Weapons, was physically trapped, bound and unable to move, he remembered that he had a secret weapon buried deep within: the 'divine diamond of wisdom' – his intuition or sixth sense. Once he'd remembered this and learned to trust it, any fear he had dissipated. He was no longer a prisoner and found himself to be free.

When we learn to let go of those things that bind us, that keep us stuck, we too can become free and take the next tender steps in our journey. Sometimes we have to use unorthodox means to propel us forward, or make decisions which might at first seem illogical or irrational; ones which may bring ridicule from others. But if we are steadfast and know that we too carry the divine diamond of wisdom within, we begin to understand that there can never be a wrong decision. Any decision and course of action that allows us to traverse the threshold guardians within or without is a decision made for the right reason. What happens after that lies in the hands of the Gods.

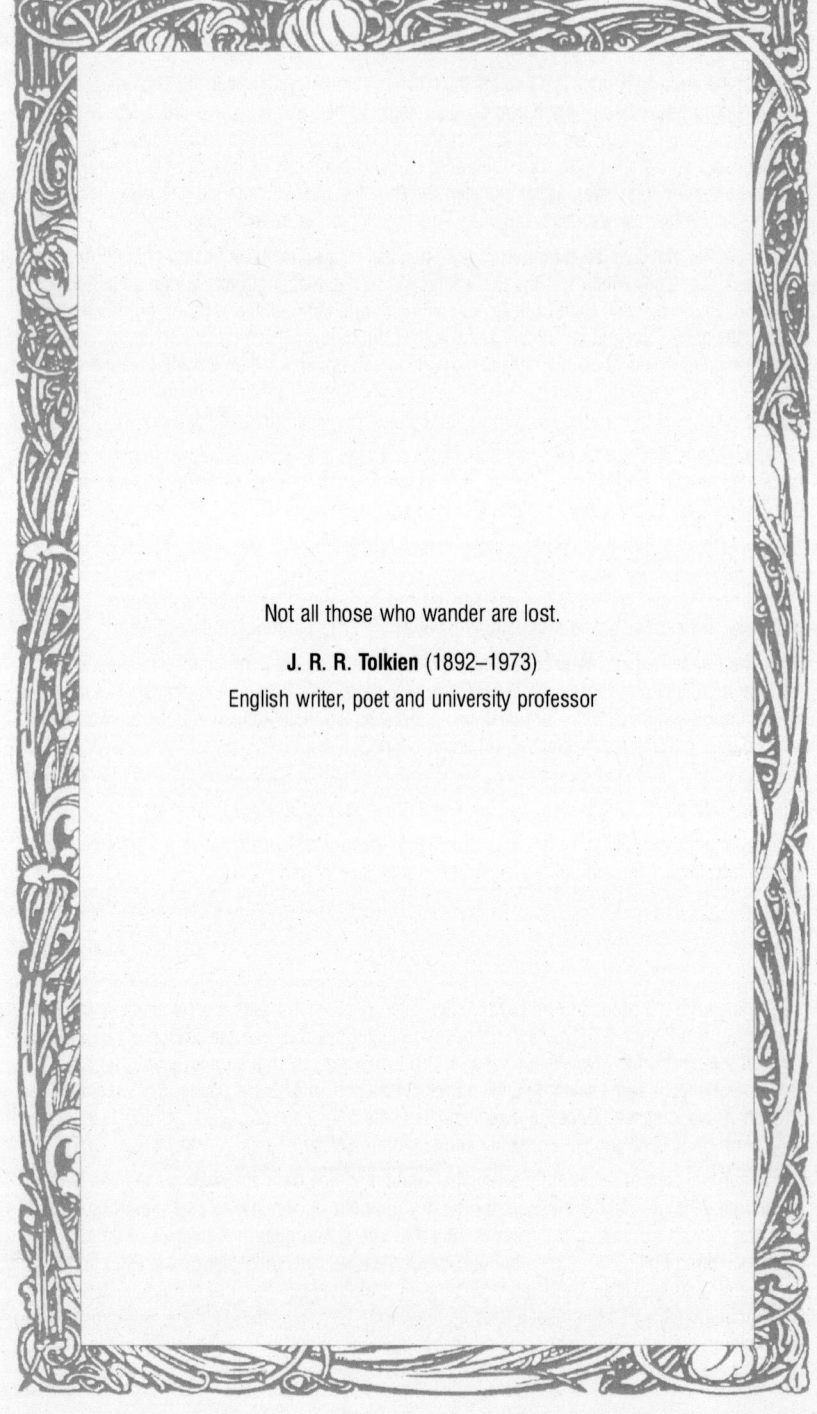

Not all those who wander are lost.

J. R. R. Tolkien (1892–1973)
English writer, poet and university professor

STAGE 6

WANDERING IN THE WILDERNESS

The dreamer is a distinguished operatic artist, and like all who have elected to follow, not the safely marked general highways of the day, but the adventure of the special, dimly audible call that comes to those whose ears are open within as well as without, she has to make her way alone, through difficulties not commonly encountered, 'through slummy, muddy streets;' she has known the dark night of the soul, Dante's 'dark wood' midway in the journey of her life, and the sorrows of the pits of hell…. And each who has dared to harken to and follow the secret call has known the perils of the dangerous solitary transit….

Joseph Campbell

The Hero with a Thousand Faces

ix months after leaving the safety of the Virgin empire, my small consulting practice was struggling. Whilst I'd gathered a handful of worthwhile projects about me and was enjoying my freelance capacity, I realised that this was not going to be as lucrative as I'd expected. The risks I'd taken hadn't paid off. The changes in airline distribution channels that I'd predicted would happen imminently were delayed for another two years as industry bodies fought tooth and nail to maintain the status quo. Without this external impetus, strategic travel management in companies was seen as a nice thing to have, but not a business imperative, so change happened rarely, if at all. My work with De Beers disintegrated into an administrative function, and the stream of proposals and presentations I delivered to potential clients were slow in coming forward, being placed on the back burner in favour of more pressing engagements. I had to concede defeat. Three years later, I was awash with requests to help, as strategic travel management became big business. My idea was perhaps ahead of its time, and before I knew it, I found myself back at square one facing the same dilemma I'd faced a year before, only this time, my anxiety was ramped up a notch because of what is engrained in the corporate psyche: that when you're 65, you're done – your time is up, your life is over, and if you haven't made it by then, you are toast. In South Africa, there is no state pension to speak of – you had to make your own luck financially, and at age 35, without a sustainable career in front of me, I started to panic.

I'd always told myself that if my business didn't work, I'd get a job again, never really expecting that I would have to. I'd crossed the threshold and didn't intend going back. To do so would mean living a lie. In a flat panic about my future, I took on a couple of short-term leadership contracts, which took my mind off my dilemma and gave me time to think. But they just reaffirmed my resolute belief that full-time employment was not for me. Whilst I missed the team spirit and camaraderie of working with others, I detested the political games and bureaucracy found across so many business cultures, and to this day it still amuses me to see how much valuable time is wasted on these activities. It went against everything I valued. I believed I was much better working from the outside in, rather than the inside out.

Yet I couldn't take just any old job simply to get by and pay the bills. Without a purpose to ignite me, inspire me to greater heights, my life took on a mundane and dull quality. I felt almost guilty that I couldn't be like others who just seemed to pick up the reins and carry on, whilst I still floundered around, wandering, searching for the illusive understanding of self that never fully materialised. Why couln't I be normal and just get on with things? What did it matter whether I had a purpose or not? Why was integrity in everything I did so damn important? But no matter how much I tried, I couldn't ignore the turmoil that raged away inside. Striving for financial success wasn't enough; I needed something to stimulate me, motivate me, capture my imagination and desire, and in the absence of a partner and children to add sparkle to my life, it was surely my work that had to compensate and help me discover that '*unique self*', the one that I'd been seemingly searching for my entire life. My work had to be more than just a way of earning a living. It had to have integrity so that I could live harmoniously with both my inner and outer experiences of life. Without integrity I was adrift, wandering aimlessly in a dark forest without direction, secretly dreading that I was insignificant – a copycat of someone else. I didn't want to live my life as a lie, maintaining a façade, faking a unity between head and heart just to survive. It took too much effort. I wondered again how everyone else managed to do it, to carry on with life as they did. Did they too have these internal struggles, the need to find 'the self' to find meaning and purpose? Did they have the answers that I so desperately sought? What had I missed along the way?

But where was this Self, this innermost? It was not flesh and bone; it was not thought or consciousness. That was what the wise men taught. Where then was it? To press towards the Self – was there another way that was worth seeking? Nobody showed the way, nobody knew it – neither his father, nor the teachers and wise men, nor the holy songs....They knew a tremendous number of things, but was it worthwhile knowing all these things if they did not know the one important thing, the only important thing?

Herman Hesse (1877–1962)
Siddhartha

Despite my angst and inner turmoil, I came to terms with the fact that the struggle for identity would have to wait for a while. I needed to work. I was single, and though I didn't have a family to support, I still had to pay the bills. My ideals and values would have to be placed on the back burner for the time being, and besides, there were many more people worse off in the world than I was. Perhaps I would need to make a series of stops and starts before I found my career comfort zone. So when a chance meeting occurred at a braai with a friend, Angela, who owned her own training business, I leapt at the opportunity to work as part of her team as a freelance leadership facilitator and coach.

Needing to up my game in terms of my public speaking and facilitation skills, now that I was to do it professionally, I undertook a series of qualifications to meet Angela's rigorous standards. Once again, I found myself on a steep learning curve as I researched, wrote and delivered a plethora of stress management, coaching and leadership programmes aimed at middle and senior management groups across a broad spectrum of business. (We teach what we most need to learn!) I discovered that I really enjoyed helping people learn and grow, and even though I say it myself, I was damn good at the work I did. I remembered how before, many of my employees and colleagues had complimented me on my ability to explain difficult subjects so clearly and simply. Perhaps there was more to this chance meeting than first met the eye? Pretty soon I became Angela's key facilitator and began running programmes to train other facilitators, too, as well as helping her with different aspects of her business from time to time.

This was to be a time of intense study, as I also undertook a 'Meta-Coach' training programme over a period of months (developed by Michael Hall, Ph.D, and Michelle Duval) through the University of Colorado. Some time later, I also embarked on a two-year mentorship programme in executive coaching, leadership development, organisational development and culture change. I used my new found coaching and facilitation skills to take on freelance projects with other organisations and one-on-one coaching assignments for executives.

In hindsight, I don't think anything really happens by chance. When we learn to let go, to drop the intensity, we allow another power to intervene in our lives which can push us in a direction that we might never have considered for ourselves at all. By allowing myself to let go, I'd found a place to rest my head, albeit for now. I was busy but could make my own hours, and with my new-found freedom and flexibility, I was able to continue my search in completely unexpected ways for the deeper answers that concerned me about life, the universe and everything.

It was whilst I was wandering, lost and trying to find my footing again, that on the recommendation of a friend I attended an 'Alpha Mind' techniques workshop facilitated by a well-respected hypnotherapist and Buddhist teacher, Terry Winchester. During the two-day workshop, I learned some invaluable techniques for 'cycling down' brain wave frequencies and entering the 'alpha mind' at will, which helped me tremendously in dealing with the ongoing stress and anxiety that seemed to be part of my make-up. In later years, I qualified as a hypnotherapist myself, as it is probably the most useful tool that I've encountered for changing deeply held negative emotional states and belief systems. Terry also ran mid-week meditation classes, where he read from *A Course in Miracles*, a metaphysical thought system developed by academics which uses forgiveness as a foundation for truth. I went along with it for a few weeks, but after a while, the familiar knot of irritation which occurred when anything 'religious' crossed my path returned. Yet, I was keen for a spiritual essence in my life, so instead of dismissing the concepts out of hand as I usually did, I persisted. I bought a copy of the book in an effort to uncover some of my own miracles and integrate them with some of the Buddhist philosophies I was researching at the time. But to no avail. As with so many philosophies I'd endeavoured to understand in the past, the book irritated me, Terry irritated me, Buddhism irritated me, and in fact, life irritated me all together. And so *A Course in Miracles* was relegated to the bottom shelf to gather dust, and once again I felt at odds with the world that seemed unwilling to give up its secrets.

It seemed that reaching a dead end had always been my experience with spirituality and religion. Perhaps I had to resign myself to remaining a self-confessed agnostic, suffering with feelings of frustration and disillusionment for the remainder of my days. Since childhood, I'd been deeply drawn to matters of the psyche, the mysterious, the metaphysical, the historical and all things Egyptian. I read widely on a variety of topics and always considered myself to be somewhat spiritual, but not religious (although I couldn't clearly articulate what being 'spiritual' actually meant). Organised religions of any kind didn't interest me. I'd always found it hard to conform to group-think, silently rebelling against authority, particularly when it was dogmatic, uncorroborated or abused. Since my early Sunday school experiences, Christianity had appalled me with its unsubstantiated doctrinaire preachings, which seemed archaic and hypocritical and totally unsuited for modern day life. A few hundred years ago, I probably would have been branded a heretic and burnt at the stake. The Eastern systems of Buddhism and yoga seemed to hold more of what felt right, but they appeared too soft and flaky for this uptight, stressed out, career-oriented Western woman, who couldn't see herself chanting the Om mantra, cleaning temples or turning herself into a pretzel to try and find 'The Way'. Whilst I had a deep longing to understand life's meaning and purpose, a religious system which required complete dedication or devotion, hours of meditative practice and the study of scriptures that I couldn't even read, let alone understand, was more than I could bear. All so that I could become one with …errr… what, exactly?

It wasn't the concept of God that I had a problem with, it was the concept of religion itself. There seemed to be no middle ground for one searching deeply within. Western Christianity seemed to promote an every-man-for-himself mentality, forcing the *self* into greater isolation, whilst in the Eastern practices the individual self was seemingly lost in the identity of 'the all'. The number of new age alternatives around at the time – theosophy, neo-theosophy, Thelema, the Gaia hypothesis, the Seven Rays, the Peace Alliance, Neale Donald Walsh and his Conversations with God, the Rudolf Steiner's Anthroposophical Society and Edgar Cayce's Association for Research – all proposed so many different theories, from self-help, psychology, holistic health, metaphysics, parapsychology, consciousness research, to quantum theory, that I didn't know where to start. But more importantly, I didn't see myself joining some caftan-sandal wearing, pot-smoking cult whose members were vegetarian, danced naked in the moonlight and hugged bunnies and trees, seemingly swapping one overbearing school of dogmatic thought for another. Perhaps I was just too hard to please.

In South Africa I was flabbergasted at how frequently mystical and spiritual concepts were bandied around in conversation in the same way my mother and her friends discussed the price of a joint of beef. Everywhere I turned I seemed to meet another 'spiritual authority' who would lecture me on astrology, tarot cards, psychic phenomena, auras, crystals, chakras, energetic healing and a whole host of other topics. Others would claim to be privy to secret information from behind the veil, channelled by various 'enlightened' spiritualists who spoke directly with the Pleidians, Cleopatra, Lord Kutumi, Saint Germaine, Jesus and sometimes God directly. I was referred to psychics, numerologists, tarot card readers, palm readers, chakra tuners and aura cleansers, who told me my energy was scattered and I needed greater focus. Well, I didn't need a psychic to tell me that! I watched amused, and sometimes irritated, as these esoteric wizards would grasp any opportunity to parade their knowledge, gifts and talents at social gatherings, each one competing for air time by speaking louder and with greater insistence that their way was indeed the right way. When I asked them how their claims related to God and what was going on in my life right now, I was told that it was 'karmic' and that I just needed to learn my lessons. Yet, none of *them* seemed to be asking the tough questions I had about life: Why are we here, what's our purpose, who am I really and how should I be living my life? It wasn't long before I discovered that they were just as confused and perplexed about life as I was, each one struggling to translate all their well-researched rhetoric into a practical hands-on 'system'. I guess everyone is looking for his own personal life boat, something to hang onto in times of crisis. They'd perhaps found theirs in an ability or talent, but I hadn't, and I was still looking. To my way of thinking, spirituality in the new millennium seemed to be just another designer label, like a Gucci handbag or a pair of Prada shoes, and seemed to serve no better purpose than to provide the mystical entertainment at dinner parties.

George Gurdjieff, a Russian mystic and developer of the system known as the 'Fourth Way', taught that traditional paths to spiritual enlightenment followed one of three separate ways: the way of the fakir, the way of the monk or the way of the yogi. The fakir focused on mastery of the physical body to achieve wisdom; the monk (or nun) did the same through affections of the heart, or faith, and religious feeling (emphasized in the West); and the yogi concentrated on developing the mind. Gurdjieff notes that even though these paths were aimed at achieving the same result, they tended to cultivate certain faculties at the expense of others. He stated that a *fourth way* was needed, one that required the awakening of another intelligence – knowing and understanding. I couldn't have agreed with him more. In my mid-thirties, my journey of self-discovery seemed to be a minefield of confusion and stomach-churning disappointment. I was wandering and lost in a deep dark forest of bewilderment, and I, for one, certainly needed a new way.

THE MYTH AND ITS MEANING

Crossing the threshold is the first real step in the adventure, however, as with all voyages into the unknown that lure us into a dark wood, the path is seldom clearly marked and we may find ourselves roving aimlessly, feeling lost and isolated and terribly alone.

Many mythological heroes are voluntarily or involuntarily exiled from their kingdoms and are forced to navigate a different terrain. Before finding their footing, they often find themselves alone and drifting in strange and unfamiliar surroundings with the burden of seemingly impossible tasks to achieve. In the Greek myths, Perseus was sent from the kingdom of Seriphos by Polydectes to retrieve the head of the Gorgon, and he spent a lot of time wandering before being aided by the goddess Athena. Hercules wandered in the woods and wild places after the Oracle at Delphi prophesied the labours he was to perform for Eurystheus, the High King of Mycenae, whom Hercules despised. For several weeks he lived completely alone, angry and frustrated at his penance until his brother, Iphicles found him and his Twelve Labours began.

In Dante's allegorical poem, *Divine Comedy*, 35-year old Dante is lost in a dark wood, assailed by beasts he cannot evade, unable to find the 'straight way' until he is rescued by Virgil and the two of them begin their journey into the underworld.

Christian Rosenkreutz on his way to the Chymical wedding of the King and Queen, wandered in a dark forest before finding a tablet fastened to a cedar tree which bade him to select one of four ways to reach the castle. He did not know which way to take and made his decision quite by accident when pursuing a black raven who had mischievously stolen a piece of bread that he shared with a white dove (a symbol of divine intervention).

The Grail Legends tell us that anyone searching for the Grail castle will never discover its whereabouts. Percival wandered and searched in vain for many years for the castle and only when he forgot his search for a moment, did he discover it quite by accident. Percival had surrendered to the grace of existence, the rivers of life, relaxing the reins so that his horse might carry its own bridle freely, with no restraint, and so he found what he sought unexpectedly. The Grail cannot be won; it is not a goal one can attain by striving. It can be achieved only as the result of a journey and learning the arts of love, compassion and trust.

Stepping over the first threshold with a leap of blind faith is simple compared with the difficult tasks which lie ahead. It is only when silence descends and the reality of the situation becomes apparent that the hero begins to doubt and falter, furiously clinging to anything familiar to stop himself from falling completely. He knows that he cannot return to his old ways or return home without his boon; he has to move forward, but is sometimes at a complete loss to know which way to turn next.

Wandering is an important and natural part of the journey. When we are at our lowest ebb, our most vulnerable, we are ironically making the most progress. Sometimes we need to learn to give up the struggle and let providence take its course. Mystics say that the 'gold brick falls when least expected.' Quite often, where there is continuous effort, nothing happens but when we relax our grip on the reins, we provide space for the next stage of our journey to unfold. And here lies a paradox: Enlightenment and truth cannot always be forced by effort and diligent action, yet the seeker still has to make an effort in order to prepare himself to receive what he seeks. Once again, learning to let go is a valuable tool in the arsenal of the spiritual warrior.

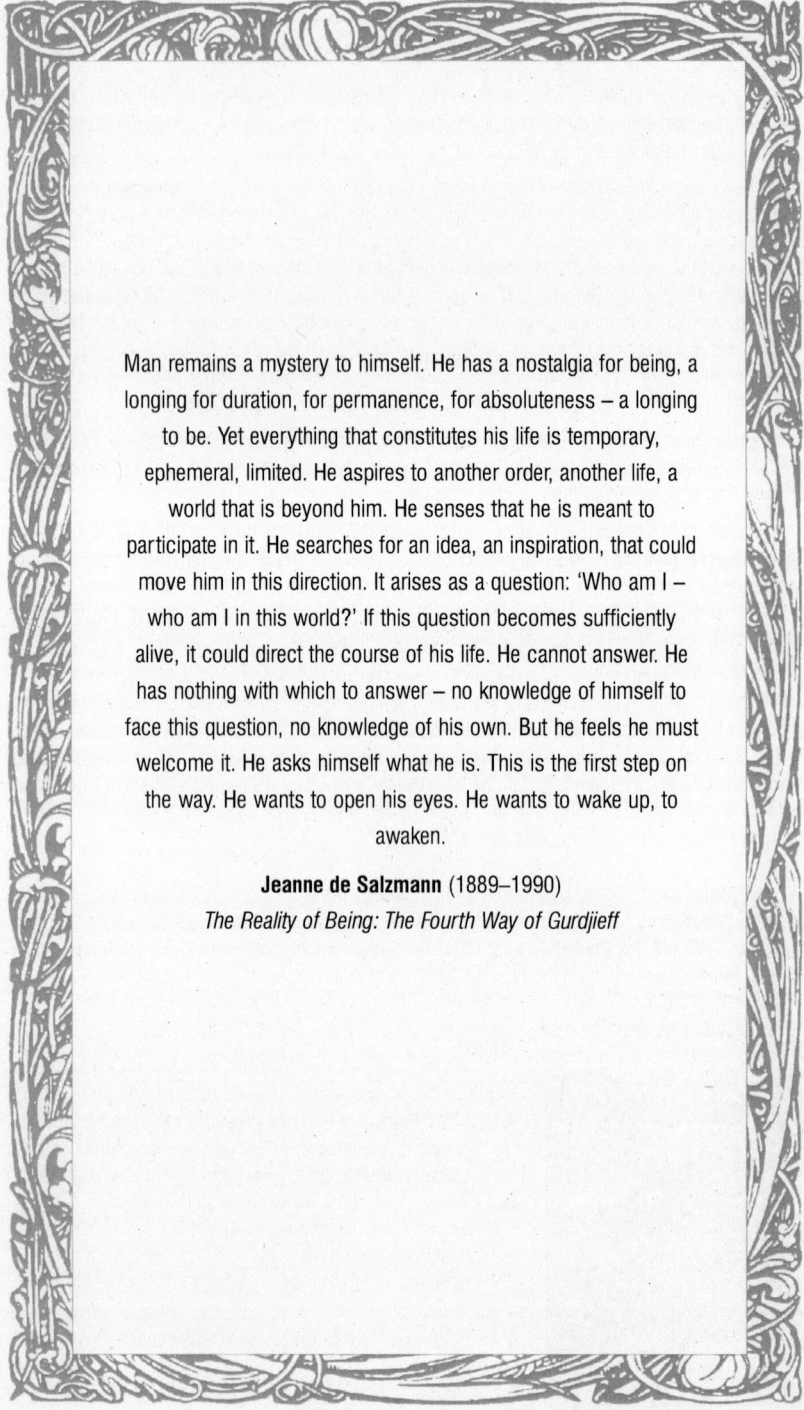

Man remains a mystery to himself. He has a nostalgia for being, a longing for duration, for permanence, for absoluteness – a longing to be. Yet everything that constitutes his life is temporary, ephemeral, limited. He aspires to another order, another life, a world that is beyond him. He senses that he is meant to participate in it. He searches for an idea, an inspiration, that could move him in this direction. It arises as a question: 'Who am I – who am I in this world?' If this question becomes sufficiently alive, it could direct the course of his life. He cannot answer. He has nothing with which to answer – no knowledge of himself to face this question, no knowledge of his own. But he feels he must welcome it. He asks himself what he is. This is the first step on the way. He wants to open his eyes. He wants to wake up, to awaken.

Jeanne de Salzmann (1889–1990)
The Reality of Being: The Fourth Way of Gurdjieff

STAGE 7

MEETING THE MENTOR

For those who have not refused the call, the first encounter of the hero-journey is with a protective figure (often a little old crone or old man) who provides the adventurer with amulets or against the dragon forces he is about to pass.

Joseph Campbell

The Hero with a Thousand Faces

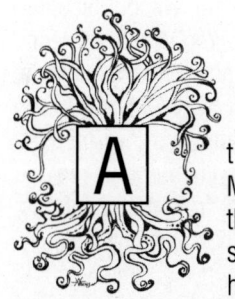

At the weekend Alpha Mind gatherings, I met a man called Michael who, like many of the individuals I'd met, knew a thing or two about spirituality, although he was much more subtle in his approach. He recommended a course that he'd attended some time ago, called 'The Bridge', run by a crowd out in Benoni, about an hour's drive from home. I went home and stuck the yellow Post-it note with the organiser's contact details to my fridge door, and there it stayed for seven months. I guess I was disillusioned with all the spiritual stuff and couldn't see the benefit in attending a workshop that ran from Wednesday to Sunday and went on into the wee small hours of the morning. What on earth could they be talking about for five days? What if it was another *Course in Miracles,* and this time I couldn't escape? But, seven months later on a Thursday evening I found myself sitting among a group of about fifteen people in a small room with wooden floors in a little back street house in Benoni, watching this strange Scottish woman bouncing around. She was one of the lead facilitators of 'The Bridge' and I couldn't understand a single word she was saying. As I sat there listening to her gibberish (which in later years I was to discover made absolute sense), surrounded by all these slogans on the wall that also made no sense to me whatsoever, I started to feel irritable again and began to figure out an excuse for not coming back the following day. That was, of course, until I met Marcos.

When he walked into the room to run the next session, my world seemed to stand still. He was an average-looking man of a slight build – actually he was quite skinny – with a shock of red curly hair and glasses. He wore a long, black leather coat like the Keanu Reeves' character, Neo, in the movie *The Matrix*. It seemed to swamp his small frame, which was clothed in a simple pair of jeans and a t-shirt. But there was something oh, so different about him. He carried an air of authority and calm. His eyes twinkled and his face shone, and whilst I had never before seen an aura, I swear that I saw a golden hue around his head. I blinked a few times to make sure I wasn't imagining things, but it didn't go away. I just sat there, mouth open, gaping, with a sense that this man somehow knew a hell of a lot of things that I didn't. I was sure that he knew God. The room was silent and the air heavy with anticipation. He took a seat on a wooden bar stool at the front of the room, and with no notes or microphone to support him, he took a deep breath and started to talk.

For over three hours he spoke eloquently about the 'scheme of things', answering questions that I hadn't even thought of asking about life and its meaning, and he did so without preaching, without dictating, without faltering. Not a contradiction nor an 'um' nor an 'er' passed his lips. When someone challenged him, he responded calmly and factually, not by ridiculing the question, interrupting or shouting down a particular point of view, or by providing his own unsubstantiated philosophies; he simply explained the answers in a focused and sometimes grave way, peppering his responses with humour, real-life stories, metaphors, parables and axioms from the myths, from the scriptures, and from his own personal experience. When elucidated so simply and logically, the answers became blindingly obvious, and even I in my ignorance could understand them. His knowledge was vast, spanning relationships, nature, auras, chakras, different religious and new age philosophies. He answered simply and effortlessly the many questions posed by each individual about their existential angst, life challenges and reason for being. His answers combined the heart and the head, and very slowly, I felt a flood of absolute relief descend upon me as I started to make sense out of all the metaphysical phenomena that I'd wondered about for so long. I felt as if I was starting to see a chink of light in the darkness, and wondered if this was how Saint Francis of Assisi had felt after he had his vision that prompted him to move away from his worldly life.

Spirituality (if this is what it was) became a lot less confusing when it was explained by this ordinary looking bloke on a bar stool who certainly didn't fit the image of your average guru or teacher of wisdom. He was white, for a start, without a long, white beard, sandals or a long flowing caftan. I just knew with every fibre of my being that the words that came out of his mouth rang true within. My spirit was quickened, my mind flew and my heart raced as he linked one abstract concept to another, and I was even more delighted to find that I wasn't feeling the same familiar ball of irritation churning away inside as I usually did when listening to the philosophic musings of various gurus and self appointed bringers of light. I sat motionless, stunned and amazed, and didn't want the day to end.

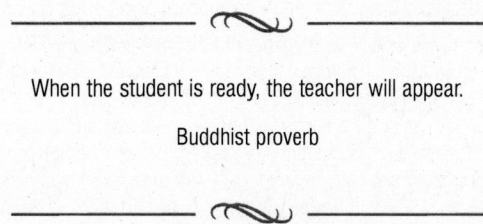

When the student is ready, the teacher will appear.

Buddhist proverb

Marcos stopped every forty-five minutes for a break and a cigarette. People swarmed around him, hanging on his every word, sitting on the floor at his feet where there were no chairs, yearning for knowledge, desperate to understand. I was irritated with my puny little mind that seemed to be unable to fully process the information I'd just heard. I felt an intense buzzing in my ears and my entire body was alive with electric energy. I had so many jumbled thoughts in my head that I didn't know how to start formulating them into even one intelligent question. I was impatient, hungry for knowledge, and finally I had found someone who I believed could actually help me. After over thirty-five years of searching, wandering, lost and at absolute odds with the world, I felt that at last I was facing in the right direction.

THE MYTH AND ITS MEANING:
Jack and the Beanstalk

Folklore is full of descriptions of heroes who meet with magical guardians or protectors who seem extraordinary in some way – a wise old man, a fairy godmother, a wizard or a helpful old crone. Frodo finds Gandalf in Tolkien's *The Lord of the Rings*, C. S. Lewis writes of Aslan, the wise magical authority who becomes the mentor of Peter, Susan, Edmund and Lucy Pevensie as they fulfil their destiny to rule Narnia. Harry Potter finds Dumbledore, Cinderella meets her fairy godmother. Virgil finds Dante in *Divine Comedy,* and in the Bhagavad Gita the mighty warrior Arjuna finds a mentor in Krishna.

The mentor is the bringer of wisdom, the provider of knowledge and information and the bestower of gifts. His purpose is to assist and inspire the hero on his quest. Sometimes mentors are difficult to find – they don't just appear out of the blue like the magical genie from Aladdin's lamp. In Greek mythology, Perseus had to call on the goddess Athena three times before she would assist him. Meeting the mentor heralds a time of great change for the hero, even though he or she may not recognise it at first.

In the fairy tale, 'Jack and the Beanstalk', the young Jack is on his way to market to sell the last of his poor family's worthwhile possessions, a prime milking cow. On his way he meets an odd-looking little man he's never seen before who somehow already knows Jack's name. Jack swaps the cow for five magical beans, which the old man promises will bring him good fortune. His mother is disgusted with her son's decision and throws the beans into the garden, chastising Jack for his stupidity and sending him to bed after boxing his ears. Overnight the beans grow into a giant beanstalk which is so large that it grows beyond the clouds. When Jack climbs the beanstalk, he finds his way into another world, where he steals the goose that lays the golden eggs, and the magical harp, killing the ogre in the process as he gives chase.

Jack is symbolic of the seeker, searching for truth. The mentor provides him with the seeds from which truth can grow, which, if followed to its ultimate conclusion, will result in enlightenment (symbolised by the golden goose) and the destruction of our 'dark side' (symbolised by the slaying of the ogre). If we can find the seeds of enlightenment, we have a platform from which we can gain wisdom and learn. Jack is courageous, willing to take risks, and in order to find truth seeks somewhat unconventional ways that are largely misunderstood by others. His mother, who is mired in materialism, stress and anxiety, is only concerned with her troubles and does not believe that any ordinary bean will rescue them from their plight. Even when the beanstalk grows beyond the clouds overnight, she still ridicules her son for his seeming stupidity; that is, of course, until he returns with enough riches for them both to live happily ever after. It takes tremendous courage for Jack to go against the grain, to step into danger and the unknown, eventually emerging victorious. At some point in our search for identity, we might want to do the same.

Dante and his mentor in the dark wood. Dantes Divine Comedy.

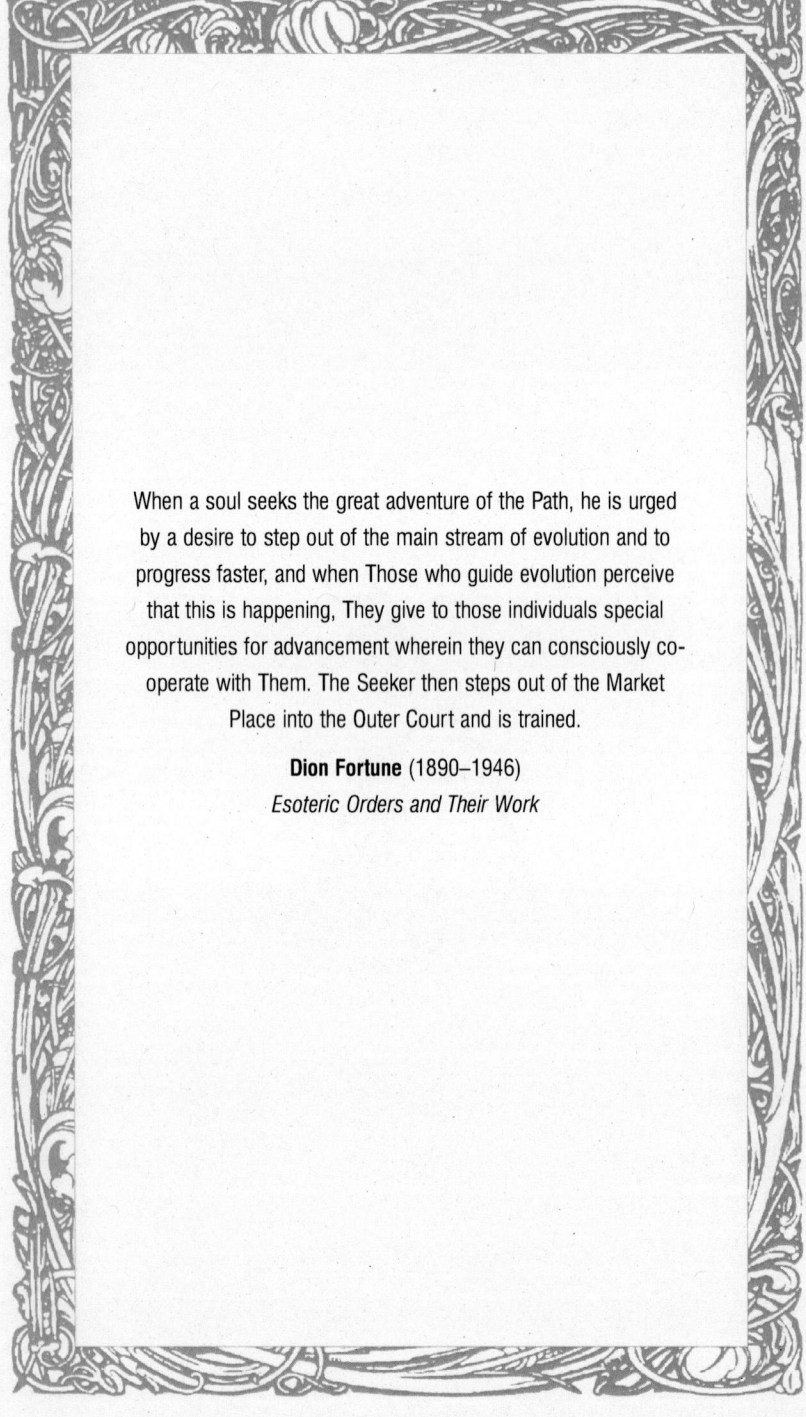

When a soul seeks the great adventure of the Path, he is urged
by a desire to step out of the main stream of evolution and to
progress faster, and when Those who guide evolution perceive
that this is happening, They give to those individuals special
opportunities for advancement wherein they can consciously co-
operate with Them. The Seeker then steps out of the Market
Place into the Outer Court and is trained.

Dion Fortune (1890–1946)
Esoteric Orders and Their Work

STAGE 8

APPROACHING THE INNERMOST CAVE

Heroes having made the adjustment to the Special World, now go on to seek its heart. They pass into an intermediate region between the border and the very centre of the hero's journey. On the way they find another mysterious zone with its own threshold guardians, agendas and tests. This is the approach to the innermost cave, where soon they will encounter supreme wonder and terror. It's time to make the final preparations for the central ordeal of the adventure. Heroes at this point are like mountaineers who have raised themselves to a base camp by the labour of testing and are about to make the final assault on the highest peak.

Christopher Vogler
The Writer's Journey

ate on Sunday afternoon, after the completion of the five-day Bridge programme, the little room with the wooden floors was transformed into a lecture hall. By around 6.30 p.m., many people who I didn't know were cramming their cars into the small carpark outside the house and spilling out onto the street. Queues began to form at the makeshift reception desk where people duly paid their R20 (US $2) entrance fee. At 7 p.m. the room was full with about thirty people and the lecture began. It was delivered by a man I knew to be called Lance – a middle aged man who was quiet-spoken with a dry sense of humour. It was on the topic of the Illuminati, a subject that I had more than a passing interest in. Once again, I was mesmerized, as time after time I felt little seeds of inspiration and recognition ignite within. I certainly got way more value than I bargained for, as historical facts and abstract spiritual concepts were linked to this often controversial topic. After many questions from the audience, questions the lecturer answered with ease, the lecture ended at 8.30 sharp.

For the next two-and-a-half years, twice weekly, I attended almost every lecture that I could, only missing them when work commitments or inflexible social activities conflicted. On a Sunday and Tuesday evening I made the 100 km round-trip journey from my home to that little house with the wooden floors. Each lecture ran in exactly the same format as the first, starting at 7 p.m., running for exactly ninety minutes. The topics were vast, and different every time; each one relating to a plethora of esoteric and exoteric concepts covering more subject material than I could ever have imagined – Mysticism, natural magic, Leonardo Da Vinci, Sir Richard Burton, Nikola Tesla, mystical orders of the past, field theory, quantum mechanics, pre-Christian sects, creation and the Bible, myths and legends, divination, astrology, alchemy, ancient mystery schools, Egyptian pyramids and their role, the golden section, the solar system, dreams, astral travel, reincarnation, karma, the Bermuda Triangle, Pythagorus, Paramahansa Yogananda, meditation, ancient monuments…. The list was endless. There were literally hundreds of well-researched lecture topics, each supported by a CD which one could purchase for a minimal fee after the event – all for only $2! How can one put a value on such knowledge?

I was astonished – I could never imagine that there was so much to learn, but even more dumbfounded that there was an esoteric connection linking every topic together in a kind of 'mental web' that, over the weeks, gradually started to form a bigger picture. I was amazed to discover, too, that not once was a religion or the belief of other cultures scoffed at; instead, entire lectures or weekend workshops were dedicated to explaining them, including their history and how they fitted in the vast mental framework of knowledge that I was starting to form in my mind. The same courtesy was applied to the variety of New Age movements around – theosophy, neo-Platonism, anthroposophy and scientology, among others. I started to see the common threads and principles that underpinned each system of belief. Over the two-and-a-half years I attended, the pieces of the puzzle began to come together, helping me make sense of the plethora of seemingly abstract concepts and the deep body of esoteric knowledge and understanding that somewhere deep down I felt that I'd always known. Truth resides within the depths of the often disoriented psyche, just waiting to be discovered, waiting for the keys or the right combination to bring it into waking consciousness. When we recognise truth, something inside whispers quietly or sings out with laughter and joy. I left every lecture as if I was walking on air – inspired, lifted, challenged, and always with so many questions. Perhaps this was what I had been so desperately searching for all along.

Having responded to his own call and continuing to follow courageously as the consequences unfold, the hero finds all the forces of the unconscious at his side.

Joseph Campbell
The Hero with a Thousand Faces

The organisation that facilitated the lectures was extraordinary, calling itself the 'Aquarian Dawn'. Unlike many other *groups* I had encountered, it didn't advertise or conscript people in an effort to increase membership, or try in any way to convert people to a particular system of belief. Those who attended the lectures came via word of mouth, attending of their own volition and because of a genuine interest in the subject matter. They took nothing away with them as proof of their months or years of dedication – no certificate of attendance or certified Master's degree, even though there was enough material imparted over the years to make up a sort of metaphysical MBA or doctorate. People just came and went – if they liked what they heard, they came back; if they didn't, they'd stay away. The entrance fee was minimal so it didn't pose a barrier to attendance, and in some cases, if someone was really struggling financially, the fee was waived completely. This was not an organisation looking for recruits. Regardless of how many people attended, the lectures continued, week after week after week.

Aquarian Dawn, a non-profit organisation, had been running for many years, back into the 80s, long before I arrived in South Africa. Its purpose was to impart knowledge to those who were sincerely looking for an alternative and more comprehensive spiritual system. People who showed a keen interest in the lectures and finding a spiritual path were considered for another level of teachings. (This wasn't an unusual practice, as far as spiritual organisations are concerned. They seek to collaborate with like-minded individuals who take their spiritual path seriously, and not with those who consider it idle amusement.) I guess one could liken it to any other New Age movement, such as the Theosophical Society, although I had nothing to compare it to. By all accounts, Marcos seemed to play a senior role in the process, together with two other people: Martin and Pierre. I made sure that I never missed a lecture or course delivered by these individuals, as their knowledge and insights were profound. Not much was mentioned about the organisation during lectures, and nobody seemed to ask any questions. There was undoubtedly much more to this establishment than first met the eye, and I was curious to find out what it was.

Being somewhat of a self-confessed agnostic with a dislike for groups, I was, at first sceptical of any organised activity that might have a subliminal agenda. But I was struck by how 'normal' everything seemed. The audiences were white Caucasian, a mix of male and female, largely professional people – a diverse group that included everything from lawyers, doctors, CEOs and insurance brokers to artists, scientists, hairdressers, school teachers, and mothers of small children. As I'd already met Michael and his wife Phillippa who were themselves, very grounded and down to earth and both regular attendees at lectures, I was quickly accepted into a new circle of friends who were as hungry of knowledge and understanding as I was. It completely dispelled the myth that I'd held about New Age organisations being full of wistful vegetarian weirdos (although I'm sure there was probably a vegetarian or two in the audience somewhere). I had never challenged this attitude which was largely aquired during my childhood in rural England. Movies or TV programmes often portrayed New Age thinkers as some sort of sex-crazed, devil-worshipping cult.

As I began to get to know the organisers and lecturers, which included spending as much time as I could with Marcos, I realized what a welcoming and non-judgemental bunch of people they were, as twee as that might sound. If one didn't attend a lecture or want to participate in some of the social gatherings, no questions were asked. There was absolute respect for free will. Nobody came knocking at my door demanding to know where I'd been, as they had in my Christian Sunday School days. The ten or so lecturers were also regular individuals holding down steady day jobs. They rotated the delivery of their well researched topics as and when the need arose, each expounding on his chosen subject with the same comfort and ease. Each lecturer followed an identical format to the last, and each gave his own logical, factual and honest interpretations of the vast array of principles discussed without confusion, mystique, dogmatism, distortion or fuss. More importantly, there were no oversized egos preaching from the pulpit. I soaked up the information like a sponge, approaching each lecture with an almost childlike sense of wonder. Yet again, I was on another steep learning curve; the knowledge and practical experience I gained during the lectures was outstanding. My sense of identity was no longer linked to my work and the relationships I had, or didn't have, but to something much bigger – perhaps as it always should have been. I started regular 'spiritual psychological' counselling with Marcos, and always left each encounter feeling more lifted and enlightened than ever. He frequently alluded to the fact that I was on the right path, and doing okay, and that I should continue as I was and more doors would be open to me. I didn't need any extra encouragement.

Gradually, as the answers to some of my deeply probing questions became clear, I believed that I had indeed found what Gurdjieff had termed the 'Fourth Way', a way of knowing and understanding that combined a path of faith and belief in a loving Supreme Being with the path of the yogi and fakir, requiring the mental discipline and control of mind and body to help us begin to realise what we could truly become. The logical structure and delivery of the lectures had dispelled many myths and misunderstandings that I'd held about spirituality, misunderstandings that had made me stick fervently to my agnostic ways. The anxiety, loneliness and angst from my childhood started to disappear as the meaning and purpose of life became crystal clear, regardless of what I did to earn an income. No wonder psychology as a solitary practice hadn't been able to reach the root of my discontent! The usual dull feelings that permeated my days gave way to a sense of joy. I became quieter and still within and far more confident and self-assured. The obstacles of life didn't faze me as they once had. I looked at them differently, able to approach each issue with greater presence and insight. The mystique around the 'self' was starting to lift and I started to remove the blinkers and shutters that I'd pulled down to protect myself from the world. For the first time in my life I felt a consistent sense of lightness and balance, and I woke in the morning with a feeling of glee and anticipation rather than dull dread. To top it all, I started dating again – a six-foot-four gentle giant of a man called Peter, a friend of Michael's, a businessman, artist and a musician, who, like me, was in regular attendance at the workshops and lectures. It was the start of a new relationship, and yet another phase in my life. I felt as if I was finally at home.

The idea that the passage of the magical threshold is a transit into a sphere of rebirth is symbolised in the worldwide womb image of the belly of the whale. The Hero, instead of conquering or conciliating the power of the threshold, is swallowed into the unknown and would appear to have died.

Joseph Campbell
The Hero with a Thousand Faces

But all of this came with a price, the first of many trials I was to face. With my intense studies and desire to fully integrate into my life the concepts I was learning, I found myself moving further and further away from the company of my sister and a wide circle of friends who'd been my constant companions since arriving in South Africa. In the beginning, I tried desperately to balance both – the inner world of self-discovery and contemplation, and the outer world of evening dinners, weekend parties and crazy wildlife adventures. With my new-found enthusiasm for the 'special world', I encouraged a few friends who had an interest in spiritual matters to try out the lectures for themselves. Some of them found the content informative and 'nice' but had no intention of immersing themselves in the studies completely. Others, who deemed themselves to be spiritual gurus, were downright irritated to discover contradictions to their existing framework of beliefs, and sometimes vehemently argued with the lecturer. Yet others – those with a strong commercial orientation – regarded me with suspicion, asking awkward questions about my whereabouts and the nature of my fascination with the *occult,* a word which sends shivers down the spine of many people, but which actually means 'secret', or 'hidden away from view' and 'not overtly obvious'. Some of them even started to ridicule my intensity and dedication and assumed I was selfishly abandoning them in favour of my relationship with Pete.

In an effort to be understood, I tried at first to explain, but it served only to alienate me even more. They'd perhaps always believed me to be a little eccentric and odd (nothing new) but I don't think any of them had any idea how deep the internal struggles for identity and meaning really went. I was embarking on a journey of deep transformation and didn't feel obliged to justify or debate the choices I made in life with anyone. I no longer relished a weekend packed with social activities, attending a Sunday braai, drinking large quantities of alcohol, playing the fool, listening to jokes, discussing rugby or the latest version of *East Enders*. Socializing that way had its place, and I'd loved every moment of it, but that particular stage of my journey was over, at least for the time being. I somehow wished that the little house with the wooden floors was on the other side of the world, so that I would have a reason to move away, to temporarily desert and abandon those whom I cared about deeply. I envied the people who had rushed to India in search of a guru. But I had to make some painful choices, and so I silently started refusing invitations to events and gatherings, sending myself into a self-imposed exile from the ordinary world and hoping, somewhat naively, that they wouldn't even notice I was gone.

THE MYTH AND ITS MEANING:
The Phoenix

'No creature,' writes the late art historian Ananda Coomaraswamy, 'can attain a higher grade of nature without ceasing to exist. Change in life is a constant feature – to grow, to develop, to move on, to reach our highest potential, we have to experience a form of self-destruction or annihilation; death of the old to make way for the new.'

'It's a bit like swimming,' says Sufi master Bhai Sahib. 'With the act of swimming we are always pushing the water away, behind us, which is how we propel ourselves forward. Spiritual life is the same, you keep throwing everything behind you as you go on. This is the only way.'

This rebirth – this letting go of the past – is depicted in the myths of the world by heroes that are swallowed by large creatures. Joseph Campbell writes of the Irish hero Finn MacCumhail, or Finn MacCool, the pupil of a Druid priest who was swallowed by a *peist*, a monster of indefinite form. Red Riding-Hood was swallowed by the wolf, and Jonah was swallowed by the whale. In the Greek myths, Hesione was the daughter of King Laomedon of Troy, a city in a state of crisis. The king had cheated Poseidon and Apollo, and to punish him, Poseidon sent a large sea monster, whose only appeasement would be to devour the princess. The Greek hero Hercules, on his way homeward from one of his twelve labours, bravely killed the beast by allowing himself to be swallowed whole by the monster and killing it from the inside.

The mythological Phoenix, with its rainbow-coloured plumage, is symbolic of this reincarnation, or rebirth. The firebird lived for 500 years, and upon nearing its end, would build a nest of sweet twigs and wood, which it ignited. When both the nest and the bird were reduced to ashes, a new, young Phoenix would arise, reborn to live again. In some stories, the new Phoenix embalms the ashes of its old self in an egg made of myrrh, and flies to Heliopolis, the 'City of the Sun', where it would deposit the ashes on the altar of Ra, the Sun God. In Greek legend, the Phoenix lived in Arabia near a cool well. Every morning as the Sun rose and dawn broke, it would immerse itself in the cool clear water of the well and sing a delightful and sweet song so that the Sun God would stop his chariot to listen.

The Roman poet Ovid writes: 'Most beings spring from other individuals; but there is a certain kind which reproduces itself. The Assyrians call it the Phoenix. It does not live on fruit or flowers, but on frankincense and odoriferous gums. When it has lived 500 years, it builds itself a nest in the branches of an oak, or on the top of a palm tree. In this it collects cinnamon, and spikenard, and myrrh, and of these materials builds a pile on which it deposits itself, and dying, breathes out its last breath amidst odours. From the body of the parent bird, a young Phoenix issues forth, destined to live as long a life as its predecessor. When this has grown up and gained sufficient strength, it lifts its nest from the tree (its own cradle and its parent's sepulchre), and carries it to the city of Heliopolis in Egypt, and deposits it in the temple of the Sun.'

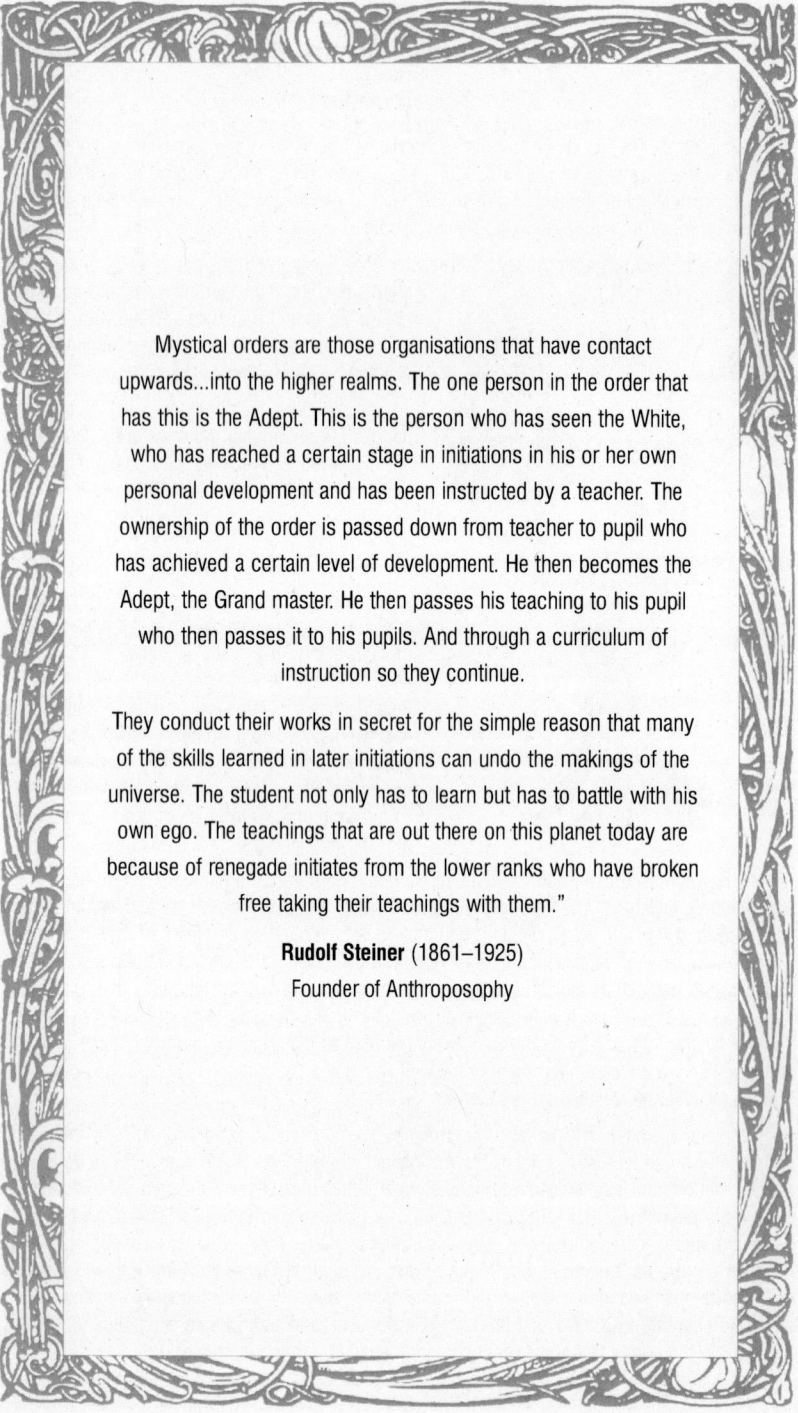

Mystical orders are those organisations that have contact upwards...into the higher realms. The one person in the order that has this is the Adept. This is the person who has seen the White, who has reached a certain stage in initiations in his or her own personal development and has been instructed by a teacher. The ownership of the order is passed down from teacher to pupil who has achieved a certain level of development. He then becomes the Adept, the Grand master. He then passes his teaching to his pupil who then passes it to his pupils. And through a curriculum of instruction so they continue.

They conduct their works in secret for the simple reason that many of the skills learned in later initiations can undo the makings of the universe. The student not only has to learn but has to battle with his own ego. The teachings that are out there on this planet today are because of renegade initiates from the lower ranks who have broken free taking their teachings with them."

Rudolf Steiner (1861–1925)
Founder of Anthroposophy

STAGE 9
ALLIES AND GUIDES

Once having traversed the threshold, the hero moves in a dream landscape of curiously fluid ambiguous forms, where he must survive a succession of trials. The hero is covertly aided by the advice, amulets, and secret agents of the supernatural helper whom he met before his entrance into this region. Or it may be that he here discovers for the first time that there is a benign power everywhere supporting him in his superhuman passage.

Joseph Campbell

The Hero with a Thousand Faces

 n January of 2002 I was invited by Marcos into the outer circle of a mystical order whose lineage ostensibly stretched back into 15th century Rosicrucian dynasty (not to be confused with AMORC, the American Society of Rosicrucians). Mystical orders are different from New Age movements in that they have, as Rudolph Steiner comments, contact upwards into the higher realms via the head of the order, the Adept, who has reached a certain level of development himself and who has been officially instructed to open a branch of the order in a particular country. The Adept in this particular order was Martin, whom I'd met on several occasions at lectures and weekend workshops, and if I thought Marcos knew a thing or two about life, then he paled into insignificance in comparison. Martin seemed to me to be a kindly, wise but stern grandfather, perhaps even a bit pedantic at times. Marcos treated him with the utmost dignity and respect and I suspected he saw him as a father figure, as he seemed to be estranged from his own family. The contact into the 'higher realms' was with Martin's teacher, who had passed on some years ago, a man fondly referred to as Father Rolfe, the twelfth Celestine of the Rosicrucian dynasty. The organisation I was to be involved in apparently had its foundation throughout history in the Knights Templar, the

French Albigenses, the Cathars, the Gaelic Bards and the Hermetic Order of the Golden Dawn. Its mission was to promulgate the teachings throughout Africa. Marcos was to become my official teacher, and the other initiates – my partner Pete (who had already been a member for two years) and my fellow classmates, many of whom I attended lectures with – became my new allies.

At first I was somewhat sceptical, although again, I was mightily curious. I knew that mysterious orders had existed throughout history, but I didn't expect to find one right on my doorstep! A far as I was concerned, the only way to enlightenment was through Eastern practices like Buddhism, Sufism and yoga which, with my little understanding of eastern esotericism didn't appeal to me. I'd learned from my lectures and from reading *Autobiography of a Yogi* that Paramahansa Yogananda was the Adept who brought yoga to the west, and that the legacy of Sufi mystic Hazrat Inayat Khan had been carried through The Golden Sufi order into Europe and North America for many years. However, I didn't realise that there was a 'Western way', other than orthodox Christianity. But since my last two years had been spent sumptuously devouring what I now understood to be 'preliminary teachings' and since I'd found a greater sense of purpose and meaning within, wild horses couldn't have dragged me away. More than anything in the world, I wanted to master the techniques that would result in complete freedom from the stress, pain and suffering that I'd experienced since childhood. I'd always said to myself that if Dr Who landed his Tardis in my back garden, opened the door and said, 'Come with me,' I would have been off like a shot! Why would this be any different?

With Marcos as my teacher, I felt that this was an opportunity to grow and learn and break free from the illusions and limitations of my life in a *Western* way, without having to isolate myself in a cave or an ashram for the next twenty years to do so. How would I know whether this was a true path of wisdom or a dead end unless I discovered it for myself? I had nothing to compare it with – after all, it's not every day that one gets invited into a mystery school. I could walk away full of fear and doubt, only to regret it. I'd had enough internal pain and suffering in this life, and I wanted my future to be different. Perhaps the Greek hero Hercules felt the same way. He was born with both a blessing and a curse from the gods, persecuted from birth by the vengeful Hera. In his youth he was visited by two nymphs called Pleasure and Virtue. It was then that he had to make a choice on the direction his life would take, the choice between a pleasant and easy life or a severe but glorious one. He chose the latter. Faced with the same choice – although I didn't notice any nymphs around – I did the same and grasped this opportunity with both hands. Turning back was not an option.

The gloom and depression represented is the spiritual soul unable to express itself because it has accepted the limitations and illusion of the world. Man is neither better or wiser after death than during life if he does not rise above ignorance during his sojourn here.

Manly Palmer Hall (1901–1990)
The Spiritual Teachings of All Ages

There are perhaps thousands of organised religious denominations on our planet, catering to all cultures, temperaments and creeds, that can be whittled down into a handful of orthodox systems: Buddhism, Taoism, Hinduism, Christianity, Islam and Judaism. Behind the ritual and dogma of every orthodox religion lies a *mystery school* whose secret doctrines about the inner mysteries of life have been preserved among small groups of people since the dawning of time – through Ancient Egypt, Sumeria, Chaldea, Assyria, India, China, Europe and right up to the present day. Unlike orthodox religions, which are often beset with false dogmas, man-made laws, misinterpretations, commercialism and fear-instilling tactics, the mystery schools practice *religion* in its simplest form, as a system of guidance and teaching, assisting its members to make their way back to the Divine Realms. Yoga is probably the best known of all of these, sitting behind the millions of deities revered in the orthodox Hindu belief system. Although yoga has been greatly watered down in many areas of the West, its secrets are held by only a few obscure yogis, whose locations are undisclosed. Behind Islam sit the Sufi and the Dervishes. Behind Buddhism – Tantra, and Lamaism – Zen (in China) and Shinto (in Japan). Behind Judaism sit the Essenes, and behind Christianity sit the Gnostics (founded by Pythagoras) and what I came to know as the Masons (not the Freemasons, which are entirely different). There is a mystery school for every temperament, Eastern or Western. One does not need to travel far and wide to find it, but one does need to search.

Some of the wisest and most creative men in history have been advocates of these mysterious organisations, their lives and works enthused by inspiration from the unseen – classical composers, illuminated philosophers, artists, poets, prolific writers and political leaders. They each passed down their secret traditions, formulae and principles to those they instructed, from mouth to ear only when the *neophyte*, *abhyasi* or *shishya* (spiritual seeker or student), was deemed ready to receive them. They taught man to conquer fear of death, falsehood and darkness, and to increase love, light and truth. In order to protect themselves from the persecution of the church, many of these organisations became secret. The mysteries were often conveyed in symbols, allegories or myths, which could only be understood by those who had the keys. The tarot cards are one such form of instruction. When unlocked, the individual would find a treasure house of scientific and religious truth known only to the few who took vows of silence and secrecy in order to keep the secrets hidden. Admission to these schools was through initiation, where the individual had to undergo an apprenticeship – a long and arduous series of tests and trials over many years to prove his worth and sincerity. Only then was the wisdom revealed to him in stages via various levels of initiation. The head of the order was known as the Grand Master, the Adept or Highest Initiate.

I had always been used to the idea that spiritual teachings were given freely, without secrecy, and wondered why the next level following the lectures would be shrouded in such mystery. Dion Fortune, in her book *Esoteric Orders and Their Work* explains: 'The reason lies in the fact, which cannot be too clearly understood by its would-be neophytes, that occult science is a mental, not a spiritual thing, and is neither good nor bad in itself, but only as it is used. It is potent for good or for evil; it can save souls which no other means could approach, and it can, ever without evil intention, destroy them. It is no child's play, and few there be who are suited to that path to the heights.' (A full translation of this piece can be found in the appendix.) I now understood the truth behind tales from the East of dedication and abstinence, why the sincere seeker had to undergo much hardship in an effort to gain insight, as the protectors of the mysteries sought to only impart them to the few who had proved themselves worthy.

The word *religion* has its origins in Latin, from *religio*, which, when broken down, means two things: *re* means 'again', and *legio* means 'the way' (which came from the Roman legionnaires, who were always on their way somewhere). Alternatively, *religion* comes from the word *legare*, meaning to reconnect. Religion, therefore, technically means, 'the way back'. The goal of all mystery schools and its teachers is to help all pupils find their way back, through reaching Adepthood. An Adept, according to mystical writer Dion Fortune, is 'one who by intensive training has raised himself or herself beyond the average development of humanity, and is dedicated to the service of God'. Adepthood was achieved through a strict curriculum of initiations, thirteen in total. The entire path could take upwards of thirty years to complete, with no guarantees that any particular individual would see it through to its ultimate conclusion. Success depended on a number of factors and was entirely down to the individual.

Each stage in the curriculum involves the attainment of knowledge and understanding of the *true self*; what man *may* become with development and deliberate focus, together with all aspects of divine law, history, mythology, psychology, ethics, aesthetics, nature and natural laws, the sciences, philosophy and mathematics. It involved the study of many different concepts found in all the mystery schools from different cultures and what is referred to as the *Hermetic sciences*. Ultimately, to understand God meant to understand the manifest world – His creation. The training during each initiation involved two key things: firstly, the senses of the neophyte being opened so that he may receive the teachings, which went into greater and greater depth and complexity as one progressed. Secondly, the continual development of *character* so that the initiate (seeker) did not abuse the knowledge conveyed to him. One's teacher had already gained the power of insight into each pupil to guide them along this path and would dispense a series of mental exercises and disciplines for each student designed to still and focus the mind and balance the body. The exercises took the form of breath work, visualisation, concentration, meditation and contemplation. Thus the seeker was provided with a complete system of spiritual and psychological growth which greatly increased the individual's speed of development beyond that which he or she could achieve alone.

There is no point in blindly believing that after I touch you, you will be saved, or that a chariot from Heaven will be waiting for you. Because of the guru's attainment, the sanctifying touch becomes a helper in the blossoming of Knowledge, and being respectful towards having acquired this blessing, you must yourself become a sage, and proceed on the path to elevate your soul by applying the techniques of sadhana given by the guru.

Sri Yukteswar (1855–1936)
Teacher of Paramahansa Yogananda

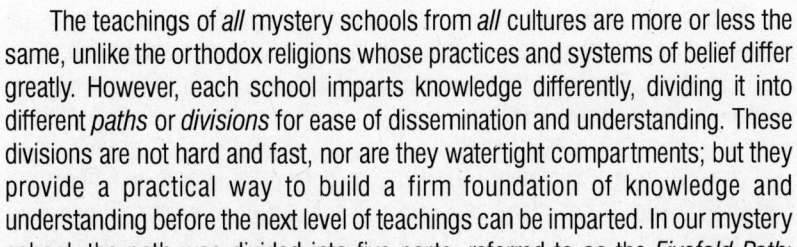

The teachings of *all* mystery schools from *all* cultures are more or less the same, unlike the orthodox religions whose practices and systems of belief differ greatly. However, each school imparts knowledge differently, dividing it into different *paths* or *divisions* for ease of dissemination and understanding. These divisions are not hard and fast, nor are they watertight compartments; but they provide a practical way to build a firm foundation of knowledge and understanding before the next level of teachings can be imparted. In our mystery school, the path was divided into five parts, referred to as the *Fivefold Path*:

mysticism, thaumaturgy (magic), alchemy, cosmic astrology and mystical kabbalah – one path, but with five separate divisions that interacted continuously with each other. One could not be studied without the other.

Mysticism: Designed to build awareness and character. The word *mystic* is derived from the Greek *mu* and *estic*, meaning 'with closed eyes'. People who achieve the status of the mystic have developed inner vision and skilfully apply the mind towards a spiritual goal. It involved the gradual release of the kundalini energy latent in the subtle body of all human beings. One who has contact with higher powers, higher beings and divine knowledge can use it to break ties with this life in favour of another life in the Divine. It is known by different names in different cultures – in yoga and Buddhism it is known as *sâdhana*, or *abhyâsa*, or *kriyâ*. The ultimate goal of mysticism is enlightenment – *satori, unio mystica, moksha* and *nirvana*, each meaning a 'union with God'. Mysticism had to be mastered before any of the other disciplines.

Thaumaturgy (Magic): In its simplest form, magic is the use of the mind, imagination and willpower and 'od' (chi), combined with an understanding of divine laws, to facilitate the mastery of matter beyond the usual restrictions of the physical world. There are various different types of magic: natural, ritualistic, talismanic, etc. Teachings involved the study and experimentation with subtle energies (od or chi,), hypnosis, healing and the use of willpower and imagination.

Alchemy is known as the 'science of life', designed to speed up nature's processes. It brings the body into a natural state of perfection which results in an understanding of divine consciousness and nature. Known as the 'great work', it is the synthesis of many of the separate sciences – bioecology, chemistry, crystallography, metallurgy, biology, microbiology, physics, zoology and so on.

Cosmic astrology is the study of the universe – how the galaxies, solar systems, stars and planets came into being, together with the chemical processes and the physics and mathematics involved. It also involved the study of alien civilisations.

Mystical Kabbalah: The word comes from the Egyptian *ka,* meaning 'astral body', and *ba,* meaning mental body. It is the study of the science of creation, the kabbalistic Tree of Life, the tarot, and creative hierarchies – angels, intelligences and nature spirits.

There were approximately 150 members in the order in both Johannesburg and Cape Town. Order members were not *enlisted* or *recruited.* Those who were ready and earnestly seeking were given the opportunity to find the door, but they had to be *invited* through it. There is an old Chinese proverb that says, 'Teachers open the door, but you must enter yourself.' The lectures and public workshops had been the path to the door, but my own dedication had turned the key. Many of the high initiates were lecturers I'd met before, some of them healers and clairvoyants. As I got to know them at social gatherings, and listened to them speak about their respect for Martin and the order, any trepidation that I had about being in the right place were allayed. The initiates were ordinary people like me, each with a desire for wisdom, only they had perhaps progressed a little further than I. They, too, became my inspiration, particularly one man called Pierre, a teacher who, like Marcos, was one of the three highest initiates in the order. He was level-headed and grounded, perhaps more than Marcos and the Grand Master himself.

Outer circle lectures were held weekly on a Monday at a different venue from the house with the wooden floors and were facilitated by Marcos. They combined teachings from both the East and West, each lecture forming part of a strict curriculum that was to take approximately two to three years to complete. Its objective was to provide us with the *weapons* and *tools* that would enable us to develop 'a clear understanding', what Buddhism describes as 'right knowledge'. With this we could start loosening the bonds of illusion that bound us tightly to the physical world. Our system of belief creates our reality. If we are not able to see the world differently, then we cannot progress. Some of the exercises we were required to do as part of the curriculum were designed to prove certain things to us about an *alternative* reality, where we could start to recognise the presence of different planes of existence. In the same way that quantum scientists crash invisible subatomic particles together to enable them to measure the fields of energy they produce, so we played with fields of energy in a different way, using latent talents and abilities that lie in all human beings. This practice introduced a hypothesis of living beyond the pale of materialistic theology, and built naturally onto the previous two years of learning.

Lectures were given orally and we were required to make handwritten notes as we went along, which we had to keep in a file. I still have the mountain of files today and remind myself of the knowledge continuously. Marcos referred us to specific books and scriptures from varying ancient and modern belief systems, to enhance our insight and understanding. The teacher's role was to provide us with a framework, but we had to fill in the blank spaces with our own insights and knowledge taken from our meditations, exercises and observations. At each session, each of us had to ask at least one question based on our review of the material, which Marcos would answer freely, often rebuking us for our lack of insight and preparation!

It was tough going. Whilst I adored my lectures and my teacher, I always silently dreaded that someone would ask the same question that I'd prepared, forcing me to think of another that proved that I'd meditated deeply on the subject. Sometimes the questions came thick and fast, at other times not at all. There was so much to take in, so much to learn, and at times I never believed that I would succeed. But looking back, it is easy to see how my own insight and understanding grew rapidly, something that would not have happened had I stayed in the 'ordinary world'. Marcos never ceased to amaze me with his own insight. His ability to explain complex and obscure subjects easily and in a language we could understand was remarkable. He was my constant inspiration to keep plugging away. In retrospect, I believe I owe most of my knowledge and insight to him and the hard work and dedication he had put in those fifteen or so years before I came on the scene.

Whoever believes he can reach God by his own efforts, toils in vain. Whoever believes he can reach God without effort is merely a traveller on the road of intent.

Abu Sa'id al-Kharraz (d. 890 or 899)
Sufi mystic

Swami Vivekananda, the chief disciple of the 19th century mystical Adept Ramakrishna Paramahansa, says, 'The soul can only receive impulses from another soul, and from nothing else. We may study books all our lives, we may become very intellectual, but in the end we find that we have not developed at all spiritually. This inadequacy of books to quicken spiritual growth is the reason why, although almost every one of us can *speak* most wonderfully on spiritual matters, when it comes to action and the living of a truly spiritual life, we find ourselves so awfully deficient. To quicken the spirit, the impulse must come from another soul.' As much as I had studied and read before, I realised now how inadequate my insights were. I was nothing more than a 'book intellectual', able to quote wonderfully on spiritual matters but at complete odds as to how to incorporate them into my life. To grow spiritually, one needs three things: a curriculum of instruction, a teacher, and a like-minded community of 'allies' with whom to share and grow and learn. When we let-go of the shackles of the ordinary world, we can find these allies in every realm of existence, waiting and willing to help. But we have to take the first step.

THE MYTH AND ITS MEANING

Gods and goddesses, angels, allies and guides are commonplace in all myths and systems of belief, each helping the seeker to find his way through often dangerous and treacherous terrain. Frodo had Sam in Tolkien's *The Lord of the Rings*, Jason had his Argonauts and Hercules in one of his twelve labours was aided by the goddess Athena and the charioteer, Iphicles, who helped him conquer the Lernean Hydra by providing advice on how to cauterize each of its nine heads. In the Mesopotamian *Epic of Gilgamesh* the gods send Enkidu, a wild man to befriend the wayward king Gilgamesh and help him on his way. In Grimm's fairy tale, 'The White Snake', a faithful servant is sent on many impossible errands by the beautiful princess before he can claim her hand in marriage. He is assisted by many *animal* friends – fish, ants and ravens whom he'd shown great kindness and compassion along his journey. They assist him when he is most in need, helping him with tasks that he would not have accomplished alone. He is finally able to present the princess with an apple from the Tree of Life, thus taking her hand in marriage.

The hero on his journey turns away from traditional support, from the ways of the ordinary world, from people mired in the day-to-day who cannot understand the nature of his quest, befriending allies in different realms – spirit protectors, ancestors, goddesses and guardian angels – who have trodden this path before him. It is only they who can guide and assist him after he's crossed the threshold into the unknown, even if like Iphicles, they just offer suggestions for how to overcome the many dangers he may face. In Roman mythology, it was believed that a man has a 'genius' at birth who protected him and his family. The genius would bestow success and intellectual powers on its devotees. Women had their own genius, which was called a 'juno', who was the protector of women, marriage and birth. Psyche calls on Ceres and her temple juno to help her in her search for her lost lover, Cupid.

Perhaps some of the best loved allies in folklore can be found in the children's story, *The Wizard of Oz,* where Dorothy and her companions are each searching for the mythical wizard in their quest to recover what they've lost or believed they never had. Dorothy wants to find her way back home to Kansas, the Cowardly Lion is looking for courage, the Tin Man is searching for a heart, the Scarecrow is looking for a brain. The story is an allegorical tale of finding truth. It is the collective faith in the wizard that each of them holds which eventually sees them successful.

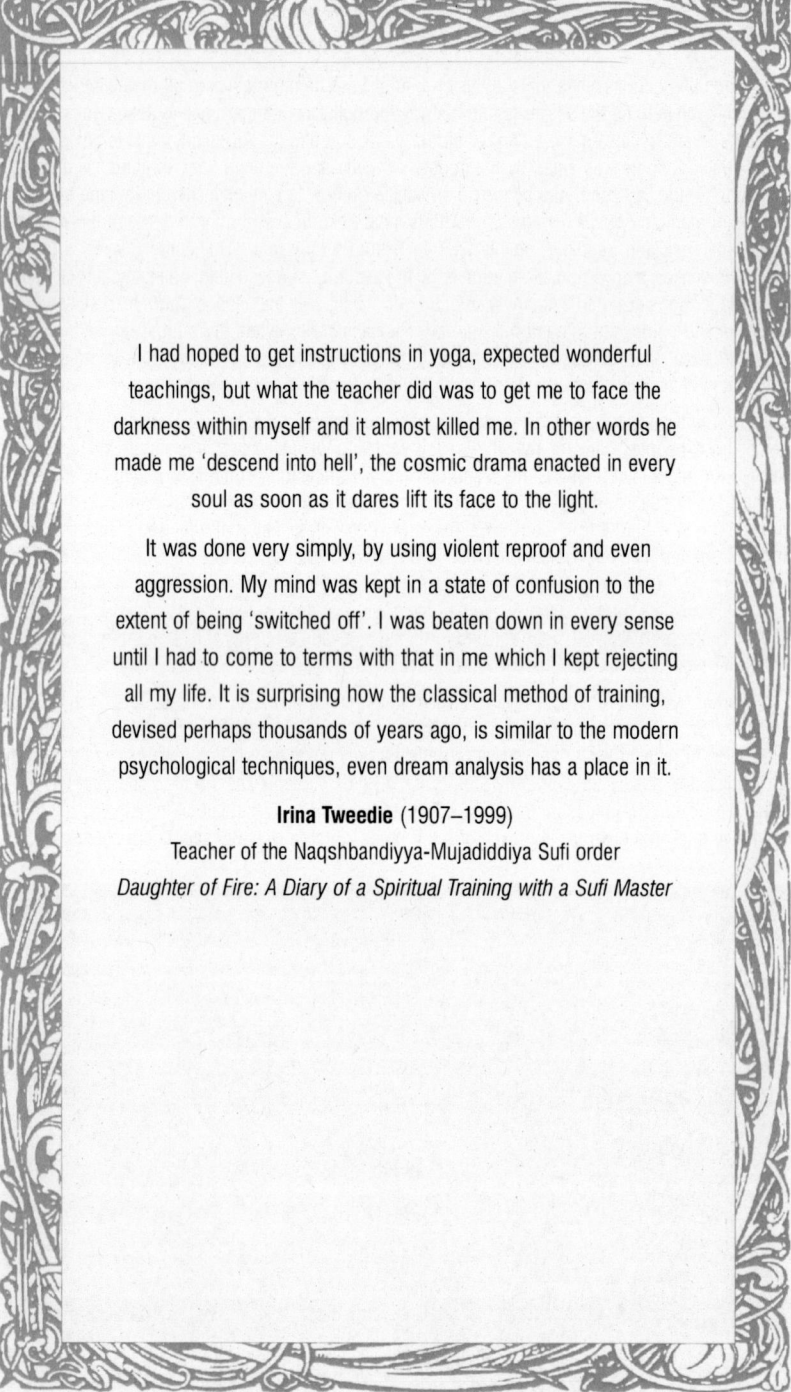

I had hoped to get instructions in yoga, expected wonderful teachings, but what the teacher did was to get me to face the darkness within myself and it almost killed me. In other words he made me 'descend into hell', the cosmic drama enacted in every soul as soon as it dares lift its face to the light.

It was done very simply, by using violent reproof and even aggression. My mind was kept in a state of confusion to the extent of being 'switched off'. I was beaten down in every sense until I had to come to terms with that in me which I kept rejecting all my life. It is surprising how the classical method of training, devised perhaps thousands of years ago, is similar to the modern psychological techniques, even dream analysis has a place in it.

Irina Tweedie (1907–1999)
Teacher of the Naqshbandiyya-Mujadiddiya Sufi order
Daughter of Fire: A Diary of a Spiritual Training with a Sufi Master

STAGE 10
TESTS AND TRIALS

Once the warriors have entered the special world, they must undergo a series of tests, or trials, to prove their worth, their desire and their sincerity. They will need to draw on vast resources of courage, tenacity and sometimes physical strength to overcome the obstacles that may seem frightening and perhaps seemingly impossible to achieve. As Joseph Campbell states: 'And so it happens that if anyone – in whatever society – undertakes for himself the perilous journey into the darkness by descending, either intentionally or unintentionally, into the crooked lanes of his own spiritual landscape, he soon finds himself in a landscape of symbolic figures (any one of which may swallow him). In the vocabulary of the mystics, this is the second stage of The Way, that of the purification of the self, when the senses are 'cleansed and humbled' and the energies and interests concentrated upon transcendental things'.

he objective of the outer circle was to prepare the neophyte for a fully fledged initiation into higher degrees of the order by testing the sincerity and aptitude of its pupils. The process was designed as a form of 'self purification' – a journey of trials involving the building of a disciplined intellect, cultivating balance of mind, body and emotion, and the controlling of the 'lower self', or the ego. Without this, the greater tests and responsibilities which came with the higher degrees of initiation would be impossible. At the fourth initiation, a specific exercise, known as the frame exercise,[3] was given to certain initiates to help them release the kundalini energy (latent in all human beings). The process could take many years and could only be carried out with help from your teacher, who himself had undertaken the process. All mystical systems have a version of this (known as *sâdhanâ* in yoga and Buddhism). However, the material nature had to be first subdued and the required exercises undertaken in earlier initiations to prepare the mind and body.

During some of our first lectures in the outer circle, we were encouraged to think seriously about life and our future, what we wanted and where we were going. Marcos cautioned us, 'Do not think that you can take vows of secrecy as you have just done, and that you won't be severely tested. Many people say that they want to follow a spiritual path but are fooling themselves. Be honest! If you would rather be at home watching *The Bold and the Beautiful* instead of attending lectures, hanging out with your mates instead of studying, or you just want some information to make you look good at dinner parties, then this path is *not* for you.' This last statement brought a slight smile to my lips as I fondly remembered a female friend of mine who loved to show-case her spiritual knowledge in front of a group, often talking over others to command centre stage, or chastising them harshly if they disagreed with her. I made a silent vow to myself that I would walk this path to its ultimate conclusion. I wanted nothing but this.

Marcos continued, 'But if you stick with this path, then I guarantee you one thing: you will not be the same person at the end of the this journey as the one that is sitting here today. You will have changed beyond recognition. But beware, the attrition rate is high. Only a handful of people in this class will make it through the outer circle curriculum, and even fewer through to fourth initiation. There will be one reason and one reason alone that you will leave this order...and that is your ego!'

I silently made another vow, that no matter what, this ego would not get the better of me.

A strict code of conduct, entitled 'The Life and Conduct of an Initiate', was outlined at the very first lecture. It formed the foundation of our relationship with the order, our teacher and the world. (I wished that I could have used this with some of the companies I consulted with, to replace their bland statements of intent, which served no other purpose than a pointless marketing exercise.)

THE LIFE AND CONDUCT OF AN INITIATE

1. **Silence.** Never let a good opportunity to keep quiet pass you by. Become still. Let the system move around you. Hide your enthusiasm. It is easy when starting on this path to want to tell all and sundry where they are going wrong because you think you know a thing or two. Or you may feel that you now have the answer to all the world's problems. But question yourself. What is your motive? To be seen? To be noticed? To score victories over others? Keep quiet

until someone asks you a question and then answer, but only enough to satisfy the enquirer and that is it.

2. **Fanaticism.** There is no room for fanatics on this path. It is a path of evolution, not revolution. Fanaticism means we are imbalanced. Everything on this path is about moderation and balance. This path takes years, not days. It requires dedication and commitment.

3. **Respect.** Respect the people, the culture, the creeds and religion of the country in which we live. Adepts and initiates do not look like Adepts and initiates. Afford people proper respect, whoever they are. Look into not at. Don't judge by appearances. Realise that the teachers, temple masters and initiates, and the leaders of our order and all other orders are human. They have many faults, limitations, weaknesses and fallibilities. They are also striving to better themselves and to become more conscious. Do not confuse the teachings with the teacher.

4. **Helpfulness, sacrifice and willingness**. We have a duty to support our order. Use every situation to grow and to your spiritual advantage. From now on you will pay your karma in an accelerated way. Life will become more difficult. Many tests and trials will be ahead of you. Remember where the rose grows it blooms. Elevate every mundane situation to divine levels. Use sacrifice as a way to learn and grow.

5. **Contentment.** Detach from the things of this world. Look around you at the pain and suffering it causes and the striving will stop. Materiality is not in line with the priorities of an initiate. Stop complaining. Be content with what you have and learn to pay your karma with dignity and fortitude.

6. **Study.** Research, learn, understand. Do revision, meditation, discussion, read, read and re-read.

7. **Reverence the oath**. Keep your word. Learn to say NO unless you are sure you can meet it! You will be tested on this again and again.

8. **Discipline.** Punctuality, consistency, reliability, regularity, trust-worthiness, dependability. In all things. As a mystic, this has to be so.

9. **Respect free will**. This will help you to attain freedom. Master this and you will gain more free will.

10. **Secrecy.** We seek to elevate ourselves. Remember that the truth is not for everyone. Do not advertise your faith. This includes not talking about your

powers to your classmates and spreading stories about others if you do hear them, whether actively or passively.

11. **Sense of humour**. Learn one quickly. Enlightenment means to be light-hearted.

12. **Be law-abiding and patriotic**. We deserve the laws and government we have. Similarly we must respect the coat of arms, the anthem and the laws.

13. **Courage**. We are not doormats. There is no room for cowards on this path. Fight if you must but do not initiate fights.

Just as in any business, country or culture, the order had a hierarchical structure which was respected by all. Only in a mystery school, it was the *wisest* who ruled, not the one with the most money, power or political expediency as it is in every day life. The Grand Master and the high initiates who had achieved certain levels of moral, ethical and spiritual development called the shots. I laughed when Marcos related a story of when he first joined the order fifteen years earlier and found that there was a renegade group, like there are in all groups or gatherings, who started underground rumblings about the things they didn't like in the order. He likened it to finally reaching the Divine, after lifetimes of struggle, pain and sacrifice, finally crawling to the pearly gates on bended knee, bruised and battered but rejoicing that you'd at last made it back home, when someone comes over and taps you on the shoulder and says, 'Pssssst – just a word, be careful what you say around here. A few people are not happy with the way that God is running the Universe, we think he's smoking something right now.'

The 'rules of the game' seem so easy when written on paper and when you're sitting in a classroom alongside twenty or so other hopeful neophytes, but putting them into practice was another matter entirely. Trying to live the life of a mystic while balancing the demands of the everyday world is difficult and sometimes seemingly impossible – staying centred, remaining silent, keeping your word, maintaining integrity, and battling with the constant whims of the ego, which always wants to push the mind into the past or the future, and always has an opinion that needs to be expressed. Again I envied those who exiled themselves completely from the material world, seeking enlightenment in the refuge of an ashram or monastery, although I'm sure that, too, presented its own set of problems. However, we need relationships with others as our 'mirror', and we need deadlines, obstacles and difficulties to help us develop. Life is a constant striving for balance: finding time to do breathing and concentration exercises every morning at the same time, without fail, summer or winter, rain or shine, whilst teenage step-children (whom I'd 'inherited' as part of my relationship with Pete) were in need of care and attention; struggling to make the ninety-minute drive in gridlocked traffic to attend lectures sometimes two or three times a week; prioritising important work meetings with responsibilities within the order. Moment by moment, I always seemed to be in contravention of one tenet or another – a broken promise, a slip of the tongue, a harsh word spoken in judgement of another, or an errant complaint about my lot in life. Several years ago in my 'other life', I would do these things without thinking, but with the principles being outlined so blatantly, actions that are in conflict create a sudden prick of the conscience, a rush of guilt. Every moment, I seemed to be questioning myself. I watched the numbers in my outer circle class dwindle as people found the going too tough. At the end of the two-year curriculum, less than 30% of my class remained.

As I tried to stay resolute to my goals of growth and inner knowledge, so my views of the world changed drastically and I now understood more fully why I'd been so at odds with the world for the last thirty something years. Everything I knew started to gently become obsolete as a different world view took its place. I sometimes felt as if I were on a another planet in my day to day interactions, but then again I felt that somewhere deep down, I'd always known these things that I was learning now, and that I was just revisiting knowledge perhaps gained centuries ago. In the tarot cards, an ancient system of mystical instruction, card number twelve in the major arcana is 'the hanged man' – the seeker is turned upside down, his perspective having changed completely. He hangs dangling between the mundane world and the spiritual world with everything seemingly inverted.

THE HANGED MAN

What made sense one moment doesn't the next, as new levels of consciousness and understanding start to unfold. In some cases, the hanged man is referred to as 'a traitor'. Indeed, he is a traitor as far as the world sees him – what is right to him is not right to others and vice versa. He sacrifices himself for a cause. I seemingly had one foot in the ordinary world and one in the unseen world, unable to navigate my way with any certainty through either of them. Life took on a dreamlike quality as I struggled to be in the world but not of it. This is symbolised by the lily – the symbol of spiritual growth – whose roots are embedded firmly in the mud of the riverbank, yet it has its flower turned upwards towards the light. It was much harder than I imagined it ever could be, and this was just the beginning.

The road to truth is littered with tests of the individual's sincerity. Again and again the seeker will be tempted to give up as each trial takes on an almost relentless assertion. Whatever goal or aspiration captures our minds and hearts, there will always be tests of our sincerity, and also guides and helpers when we least expect them to help us find the way. It is only if we are strong and resolute that we will gain the wisdom we seek to pass onto the next level.

THE MYTH AND ITS MEANING:
Oedipus and the Sphinx

Extracts from mythology describe the path of the initiate and the tests and trials that each one must complete in order to prove his worth. In Greek mythology, Hercules had his twelve labours, and Jason and the crew of the Argonaut, had many trials to overcome in the search for the Golden Fleece. In the Greek myth, *Cupid and Psyche,* a tale of a female seeker, the beautiful mortal woman Psyche goes on a quest to find her lost lover Cupid (Eros), overcoming many obstacles deliberately put in her way by Cupid's jealous mother, the goddess Venus. Eventually, with the help of Ceres, her temple Juno, a speaking tower and an army of ants, she receives the ambrosia of the gods and achieves immortality whereupon she can at last be with her lover and make her peace with Venus.

Tests, too, are not always of a *physical* nature. In Grimm's fairy tale, 'The Riddle', the king's son had to pose a riddle to the fair princess that she could not solve, before she could entertain marriage. Nine suitors had already perished in the task as the princess had always solved the riddles they posed. The prince asked her, 'One slew none, and yet slew twelve. What is this?' It proved to be the one riddle she was unable to solve. (See appendix for full fairy tale and answer to the riddle.)

In the Egyptian/Greek myth, Oedipus had to solve the riddle of the sphinx before he was allowed to proceed on his journey to Thebes.

Oedipus, was abandoned at birth after his parents, King Laius and Queen Jocasta received a prophecy that any son born to them would kill the king. His ankles were pinned together to stop him from crawling and he was given to a servant to abandon on a nearby mountain. (Oedipus means 'swollen foot'.) The sympathetic servant, however, passed the baby on to a shepherd from Corinth, and eventually, after being passed from shepherd to shepherd, Oedipus came to the house of Polybus and Merope, king and queen of Corinth, who, being without children of their own, adopted him.

Some years later, Oedipus got to find out that he was adopted, and when it was denied by his parents, he consulted the Oracle of Delphi, who told him nothing of his adoption, but prophesied that he would murder his father and marry his mother. Believing his parents to be those who raised him, he decided not to return to Corinth, but to go to Thebes. On his way, he came to Davlia, where three roads crossed, and he encountered a chariot driven by his birth father, King Laius. They fought over who had right of way, and Oedipus killed Laius in self-defence. Thus the prophecy was partly fulfilled. Continuing on his journey, Oedipus encountered a Sphinx who stopped all travellers and asked them a riddle. If the travellers were unable to answer correctly, they were killed and eaten. The riddle was: 'What walks on four feet in the morning, two in the afternoon, and three at night?' Oedipus answered correctly: man, as he crawls on all fours as a child, walks on two legs as an adult, and in old age uses a walking stick. The Sphinx was astonished that the riddle had been solved and threw herself into the sea, freeing Thebes from her harsh rule. The people of Thebes gratefully appointed Oedipus as their king and gave him the recently widowed Queen Jocasta's hand in marriage, which fulfilled the rest of the prophecy. (See appendix for remainder of the myth.)

Each test poses great dangers for the seeker and requires the summons of much insight, courage and discipline, symbolising that the spiritual path, the journey of the initiate is not for everyone. Not all seekers are worthy to occupy the 'Siege Perilous', the seat reserved by Merlin at King Arthur's Round Table for the one who was fit to see the Holy Grail. Only Lancelot, Sir Galahad and Perceval (depending on which Grail Legend one reads) were worthy enough to go in search of the Grail, but in the end it was only Lancelot's son, Sir Galahad, who was 'pure' enough to set eyes upon it. He, too, was the only one to be able to pull the sword from the stone with ease, which all other knights, including Arthur, had been unable to budge. Lancelot made it to Corbenic, the mythical Grail castle, but was refused entry by the Grail kings, as his life was deemed to have been less than wholesome. Perceval sets eyes on the Grail at the castle of the Fisher King, but fails to ask the questions that would heal the Grail kings' wounds, for fear of offending his host. When he discovers his mistake, he wanders for years, defeating dark forces, overcoming temptations and coming to terms with his own past, until he eventually achieves his aim. Seeing the Grail in all its glory, he dies in peace. The story is beautifully depicted in Wagner's operatic version of *Parsifal*.

Before divinity can be attained, the seeker has to go through the whole experience of human evolution in the 'school of life'. Mysticism and mystery schools speed up that experience. Mankind is completely unself-conscious, living in a waking sleep, a state of divine ignorance, untouched by things of the spirit. At some point in his evolution, he will desire to leave this state, descending into the pits of Hell, experiencing all the conflicts and obstacles that this particular type of advancement entails. Each one of us is a precious stone, which, through suffering, pain, discomfort and development, can be transformed.

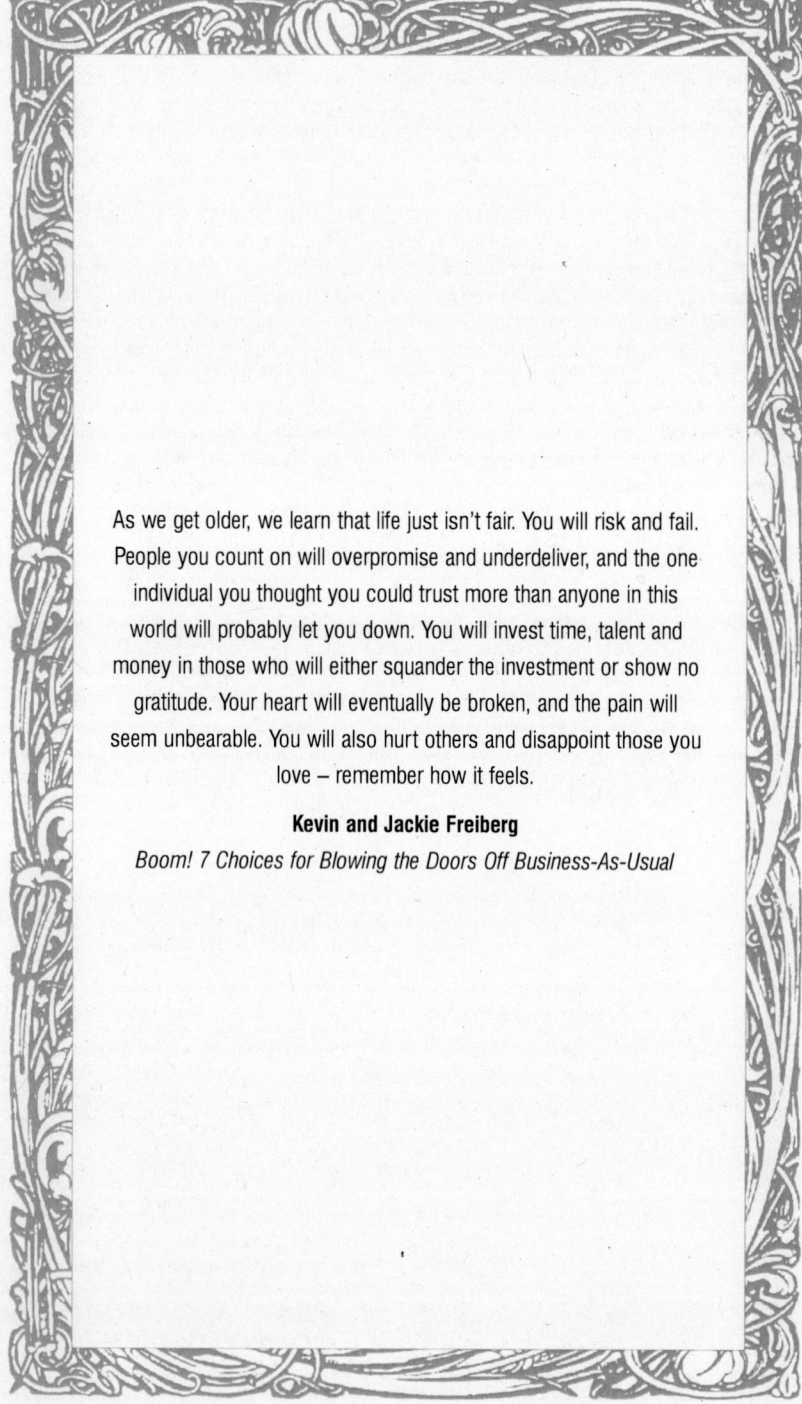

As we get older, we learn that life just isn't fair. You will risk and fail. People you count on will overpromise and underdeliver, and the one individual you thought you could trust more than anyone in this world will probably let you down. You will invest time, talent and money in those who will either squander the investment or show no gratitude. Your heart will eventually be broken, and the pain will seem unbearable. You will also hurt others and disappoint those you love — remember how it feels.

Kevin and Jackie Freiberg

Boom! 7 Choices for Blowing the Doors Off Business-As-Usual

STAGE 11

TRICKSTERS

There comes a point in one's spiritual journey when the seeker has to put his faith and trust in someone completely, despite any doubts that he may have. Doubts are a natural part of the journey and come frequently to all who sincerely want to find their way home. The seeker knows that the path towards truth will become more difficult and harder to navigate with every step. He is aware that he can easily become disillusioned or lost, becoming a victim to be saved from a lonely wilderness between this world and the next. Greater guidance and training is needed – always. Developing consciousness requires long, hard work, as the methods used to achieve it cannot be described in books or taught in ordinary schools for the simple reason that every person is different and no universal method will apply equally to all.

I adored my teacher. In fact, I loved Marcos dearly – not the kind of love one has for a lover or friend, but the deep love and respect for a guru, for the one who carries the secrets to an inner world. From the moment I met him, I felt as if I were rekindling a relationship that I'd known for centuries, for lifetimes. Outside of formal lectures, I spent as much time with him as I could, in one-on-one consultations and in accompanying him to lectures and seminars that he'd facilitate for business. I watched bemused as the audience clung to his every word, as I had when I first met him, mesmerised by this charismatic man who had a deep understanding of the scheme of things, and by his ability to connect the most abstract concepts and answer the most difficult of questions. He held a special kind of power, a magnetic and potent unseen energy, and I was convinced that he could see deep into my soul, that he knew my thoughts, my deepest desires. It was unnerving to be so exposed, and I always seemed to be making puny efforts to withdraw into myself as much as my neophyte skills would allow, so that he could not see how clumsy I really was.

My dreams, too, took on an alive quality, instead of always being about nonsense. I would dream of being with my teacher, he would show me wonderful places. I distinctly remember one dream where his face shone with a golden hue as he took me to a canyon, a place so vast and huge that it would put the Grand Canyon to shame. The colours on the canyon walls were bright and vivid. He shared with me some great secret, though I couldn't remember afterwards what it was. Whilst I looked forward to our meetings, I dreaded them at the same time, as he would use different tactics to shape the rough edges from his pupils. Sometimes he was caring and helpful when I consulted him about my existential angst, at other times he appeared irritated at my ignorance, and sometimes even aggressive. I was convinced it was deliberate, a way of helping me control the 'lower' part of myself, a tactic deployed by many teachers on many paths towards truth. Some of his other students, I learned, simply found him ruthless and cruel. I, however, took the blows in my stride, assuming that these were lessons that I needed to knock me into shape. Harsh as they were, they always extended my awareness, lifting me from my self pity, drawing my attention away from my problems to a higher and more noble focus, penetrating far deeper than any traditional psychological practice I'd ever experienced. I began to experience myself more fully – gaining glimpses of a truer essence within, hidden deep beneath layers of personality and self-imposed falsehoods developed since birth. I always left even the harshest meetings with my spirits quickened.

There is a vast difference between *spiritual* psychology and the psychology of many modern day therapists which, while it has its place, keeps the seeker somewhat stuck in the problem of life. Spiritual psychology is designed to lift the seeker from the mire, allowing him to gain glimpses of his greatest possible potential, his divine heritage and the truth of his glorious nature, one that can never be dreamed of or imagined when starting out on this path. As one progresses, these insights and periods of self-awareness become more frequent. But the path is difficult; there is no road map to help one find the way. The journey for each person is different and each step is taken blindly with only intuition and desire as a compass, together with the guidance of one's teacher. I was very grateful that Pete and I were both travelling this path together. We would stay up until the wee small hours discussing our journey, our learning, the joys and the sorrows. We laughed together at our own foolishness, our lack of awareness and stupidity, and we cried when we experienced painful lessons and serious doubts about the path we were travelling. Any concerns we had were simply washed away by our desires to see this path to its ultimate conclusion. We wanted nothing more than this. We were tired of repeating the same old mistakes, lifetime after lifetime. We wanted to make this life different, to focus on our spiritual journey above everything else. If we were wrong, it didn't matter. We wanted nothing more than this.

There is a kind of power at his place – it is a fact, I am quite sure, not just imagination. Very disturbing. I keep away, waiting for L. She must help me to clear some points. And if she cannot...then I will go to Madras, have a look at South India and Ceylon, and then forget the whole affair. If I can. But it will not be so easy, if at all possible. Only at the idea of going away, something in me keeps crying. It is so deep that I am hardly conscious of it, it is just on the threshold of comprehension. It is like a homesickness. A great yearning homesickness for our real home. The home of all of us, human beings, and the home of everything else, as well, in the Universe.

Irina Tweedie, expressing her concerns about her teacher, Bhai Sahib
Daughter of Fire: A Diary of Training with a Sufi Master

The physical property inhabited by Marcos and Martin and the others was called Viewpoint.[4] The place had a potent energy, and Pete and I spent most of our spare time there, involved in many different pursuits which added to our skills and development – art classes, musical pursuits, healing workshops, astrology workshops, dream-circle investigations, and other weekend activities. It was a little oasis of calm in a sea of chaos. The philosophy was that we have a limited time here in life, so we should use every opportunity to learn and grow. And indeed, our learning soared and the order and its members became like a second family.

Many members, including those who did not live at Viewpoint, donated cash and/or worked tirelessly on order-owned projects and businesses (overseen by Marcos) to bring funds into the organisation and to support its vision and goals for expansion. As members, we paid a minimal amount for our monthly lectures (approximately $15 US a month) which, when added together, hardly even covered the cost of the electricity bills, so initiates found ways to support the order in any way they could, setting up *projects,* or businesses, which the order benefitted from financially in some way. Any spiritual organisation requires service and sacrifice from its members, and this organisation was no exception. One might work in the rose gardens or vegetable gardens or set up a website, record lectures, assist in the temple or deliver a presentation to a board of directors in a large company. The order also supported several charities: children's homes, animal shelters and seniors' residences, providing care where they could for those less fortunate. I always found the work that I did for charity so rewarding, particularly working with the old people, who were so grateful for the opportunity just to have a conversation with someone different. With knowledge comes the responsibility of sharing it and giving back to others, and so growth and expansion of the order to fulfil this aim seemed a natural thing to do.

To the outside world, it would have appeared an odd setup, perhaps completely out of step with a society that has an every-man-for-himself mentality. But to me and many others, it made perfect sense. What value does one place on knowledge, wisdom and guidance that has the capacity to transform a person entirely, propelling him to heights he cannot even conceive of, lifting him from the drudgery of life and its miseries? I could now understand why people dedicated themselves wholeheartedly to service in an ashram or travelled across the globe, experiencing the harshest of conditions to receive deeper insights and wisdom from a revered guru or teacher. When one sincerely embarks on this journey, there is no turning back.

Time spent at Viewpoint was in vast contrast to living in the crime-ridden city of Johannesburg, where burglaries, car-jackings, rapes and murders were commonplace. In the city, there was little community spirit and one didn't get to know the neighbours, as they barricaded themselves into their elegant homes clustered in secure complexes behind high walls and electric fencing, state-of-the-art alarm systems, razor wire, twenty-four-hour armed response and bars on every door and window. It was rare to see a white person walking along the street. People travelled everywhere in their cars, even for the shortest of distances, with the doors firmly locked and windows tightly shut. I was the victim of three burglaries in a short space of time when I first moved to Johannesburg, and now with children in my life, I became fanatical about security. Although we lived in one of the most sought-after suburbs, it was only a few kilometres away from the black township of Diepsloot, where violent crime was rampant and seemingly encroaching more and more into white areas.

Both of my neighbours had been the victims of serious crime – an armed robbery in broad daylight on one side, and a break-in and rape on the other. While out walking her dogs, my close friend Sue was hijacked at gunpoint, driven around for hours as her armed black abductors took her from cash-point to cash-point in an effort to drain her bank account, then dumped her on the side of the street, miles from anywhere, taking off in her vehicle. She left the encounter with her life intact, but was an emotional wreck, not knowing if she would live or die. Unless one has lived in Africa, it is hard to imagine the class divide between those who have and those who don't have, and the lengths that some will go to in an effort to obtain even the smallest of prizes, often with extreme brutality and complete disregard for human life. Ten years after the first elections in 1994, the country was fast deteriorating. Viewpoint always provided a welcome respite from the harsh reality of staying alive in Africa.

Dedicating time to the order in some way was expected and I'd been involved for some time in giving my time to helping out at the weekly public lectures and workshops as I enjoyed the learning. However, when Marcos called me to a meeting in 2003, while I was still in the outer circle, and asked me to head up one of the order's businesses, I knew the time had come to get more involved. He wanted my help in a personal and organisational transformation business called Perspective, that was floundering in its current guise. He wanted my business acumen, speaking skills and experience with organisational start-up to help move forward. He took me into his confidence, sharing with me the vision for the order held by Martin and the high initiates, to fulfil the mission of its founder, Father Rolfe. I knew little of Father Rolfe, other than the fact that he was greatly respected and revered by everyone who'd known him. A birthday celebration was held in his honour on July 1st every year, where Martin shared fond memories of his teacher, together with many of his illustrious incarnations. Whilst I hadn't known Father Rolfe personally, I lived his mission vicariously through my teacher and Martin. He was an inspiration to all of us, as all gurus and masters in all spiritual disciplines have been throughout history, having trodden this difficult path ahead of us, proving that it can be done.

Without a doubt, I was flattered when Marcos approached me. Only fully fledged initiates were appointed to run order projects, not beginners on the path. Perhaps he had already identified me as one who would be fully initiated, something I deeply desired. Yet I also felt a subtle sense of pressure from my teacher, like saying no wasn't really an option. I wondered what would happen if I did refuse, and how it would affect my standing with my teacher. I quickly pushed these doubts aside as it was deemed to be an honour to serve my teacher and the order through which I was receiving so much. So I cautiously agreed, telling him that it would take some time, as I had to give some thought to how I would find the time to fulfil my promise.

Pete and I were struggling financially. Eighteen months earlier, we'd sold our respective properties and bought a family home in the upmarket suburb of Lone Hill to accommodate us and his two children, who lived with us at the time. A month after we moved in, there was a downturn in Pete's business resulting in a downturn in his income. This was to be the start of a very long period of financial difficulty in my life. Not one to give up easily, I threw myself into my new role as 'initiate stepmother', working tirelessly to keep my newly acquired family afloat. Taking on this extra responsibility of Perspective made me deeply concerned as to how I'd balance family life, work and studies, together with the added pressure of starting yet another business. And sure enough, with the extra responsibility, I found myself working harder than ever, slogging away evenings and weekends in an effort to keep it all together. I was exhausted, but in a few months, with the assistance of an organisational development expert (also an order member), I'd secured Perspective's first large contract with an international hotel chain to change the organisation's culture under a new leadership regime.

Marcos was absolutely delighted with my efforts and the subsequent profits that would come of it and asked me to take on a larger role of working alongside him on other projects and order businesses, as he was drowning under the pressure and needed some assistance. We discussed the finanaical ramifications of my pulling back on some of my consulting work and dedicating more time to the order. He agreed to the proposal of my taking a salary from the business to help support the needs of my family and gave me carte blanche to run Perspective as any managing director would. So now it seemed I would be working for God in a way that I could never have conceived possible! I was doing the work I loved with people and businesses and doing it for a good cause. Marcos also began to mentor me on how to present his lectures, the ones that amazed so many people, so that I could deliver these too and perhaps train others to do the same. With the opportunity to learn even more from him, I felt I had died and gone to Heaven.

There were times that I deeply regretted taking on the responsibility of a bigger house and a family that wasn't technically mine. I was completely overcommitted, often irritable and exhausted. My health and studies were suffering, and so was the relationship. Time and again, I considered walking away so that I could get my life back to some degree of debt-free normality, chastising myself for selling my modest home, which I'd paid for outright in order to upscale. But my teachings as an initiate were deeply engrained. I couldn't leave my partner when he was down and out. If I was in his shoes, I'd be grateful for someone supporting me in the same way, and besides, I wasn't sure that I wanted to walk this path alone. One needs allies on a spiritual journey that one can trust. Pete and I had started this path together and would see it through to its ultimate conclusion. So when I consulted Marcos about my dilemma, and the financial burden it was placing on us, he offered a solution: 'Move to Viewpoint,' he said, 'like others are doing. We are setting up an investment portfolio for those who wish to participate in the community. We have advocates, lawyers and brokers looking at it right now. You will need to build a house because the existing properties here are taken, but it will solve your problem and achieve many objectives of your spiritual growth and supporting me. Your money will grow in line with investment and property growth, if we do it correctly, and will add to the overall value of the land when we come to sell it.'

Pete and I deliberated for weeks and had many discussions with Marcos, with the appointed house-builder (an order member) and with the legal team. It all seemed feasible, albeit risky, but I trusted Marcos and he'd given me no reason to doubt him. Here was a solution that would solve many issues and alleviate the mounting pressure. Our costs would be reduced, allowing us to contribute to a greater cause and allowing me to be closer to Marcos to help him with Perspective and the other businesses. More importantly, we would be part of a spiritual path that we both envisaged being involved in for the rest of our natural lives. The cost of property in South Africa is low in comparison to international standards. Building costs were even less. If we sold the house and built a downscaled version at Viewpoint, we would even have money left over. We could be liquid again. After yet more discussions, we decided to proceed. We borrowed money against the house from my mum in the UK so that we could immediately start with the building project, and put our property on the market, anticipating a quick sale.

Pete was an engineer, and with the help of the builder and architects, quickly designed the house. We made our first payment to the order via the investment fund so that an audit trail of our outlay could be tracked, and building got underway. Pretty soon the walls were up and the roof was due to go on and everything was seemingly racing ahead of schedule.

Then, suddenly, everything came to a grinding halt. The builder left the order under a cloud, apparently taking with him money that Marcos had paid him from our investment to buy materials. Marcos was furious. I'd never seen him so angry at being betrayed by this renegade initiate. He took full responsibility, ensuring us our investment was safe. But now, of course, the costs of the project would increase and we'd have to put more money in to complete it. Marcos vowed to oversee every part of the project himself. Very loud alarm bells started to ring in my head.

For many long weeks, the building project was stalled as we waited for our other house to sell, facilitating access to funds. Thoughts of scrapping the Viewpoint dream plagued me frequently. There was a constant nagging feeling in the pit of my stomach that something was deeply wrong, but we had almost gone too far to turn back. I held Marcos and Martin in such high regard that I pushed negative thoughts away. When Martin, the Grand Master, chastised us for the 'unsightly building site' we'd left on the order's property, I knew we had to finish what we started. I went back to my mother, cap in hand, and asked her for a second advance. She agreed, and in December of 2004, after many months' hard work from both Pete and I, the new house was complete. But our house in Lone Hill was still not sold, and I got the distinct feeling that it wasn't going to. My days were filled with worry and dread as I wrestled with this state of affairs in my head and tried to allay my own fears. Pete in his casual laid-back way thought I was just overreacting, but I was panic-stricken.

In an effort to improve our financial situation and achieve our dreams, I'd now sunk deeper into debt than ever, with not one but two properties, one that wasn't selling and an investment property at Viewpoint for which the paperwork was still not forthcoming, despite continued assurances from my teacher. I felt as if I was getting myself into a real unholy mess with no light at the end of the tunnel.

However, a stroke of luck occurred just before the Viewpoint property was completed. We had an offer to rent our property in Lone Hill, which we accepted, and in January we moved to the house at Viewpoint, no longer with the same excitement we'd originally anticipated for our spiritual future. Marcos had been acting strangely in the weeks prior to our move. He was often sick and irritable and he'd lost a lot of weight. Our classes, too, were frequently cancelled, and the weekend musical and artistic activities were now non-existent. He was also becoming almost dictatorial about the businesses and how they were to be run. After soliciting my help and encouraging me to move closer to him, he was now excluding me completely from any project.

I was beside myself with worry and indecision and a fear of challenging my teacher. I couldn't understand what was happening. I'd just uprooted my life and moved to the other side of the city, miles away from what I knew, and it now seemed to be of little import or consequence. I tried to tell myself that this was a test of my sincerity, so I persisted, trying to push negative thoughts aside. But since moving to Viewpoint, the deep sense of foreboding that began some months ago and permeated my every waking moment was growing stronger. Towards the end of 2004, yet more people had left the order, and without warning, Pierre, Marcos' contemporary, had also moved to Cape Town to set up another branch of the order and a community, leaving a great big gaping hole of instability in the higher ranks. The feelings of anxiety I'd suppressed for months now ballooned into feelings of nauseating dread and mistrust.

Beware of false prophets, which come to you in sheep's clothing, but inwardly they are ravenous wolves.

Matthew 7:15

My worst fears were realised when two weeks after moving, Marcos called me to his office and fired me from the business projects, telling me that he'd found someone else in the order to do the work, someone who wouldn't require payment. Then he dropped another bombshell: Viewpoint was to be sold and the investment portfolio had been scrapped. No paperwork was going to be provided for the investment and I had to take my teacher's word that my money would be returned. I sat dumbfounded. I'd worked tirelessly for the order and had just uprooted my life, turned down a full time CEO's position at a training company (offered to me by Angela) so that I could work more closely with the order, and now my teacher was dispassionately casting me aside like a used tissue, without a second thought. I knew this path was going to be tough, but this was ridiculous. I felt betrayed and sick to my core. I left his office in a daze and walked back to my house, stumbling across the neglected and sad-looking gardens, once so beautifully kept, tears streaming down my face. I felt as if I'd just stumbled into some horrible nightmare.

THE GREAT JESUS SWINDLE

In religion and mythology, the trickster character embodies all the energies of mischief and deceit. The *Judas principle* exists as an archetypal function in the system, one that any character in life can assume, even those who we might consider spiritually advanced. The trickster can be the seeker or even the mentor himself.

The Bible is full of stories of betrayal. Perhaps the best known is that of Judas Iscariot, who betrayed Jesus for thirty pieces of silver. Sampson is betrayed by Delilah, Joseph the prophet by his jealous brothers, and Esau by his brother Jacob. But perhaps the biggest mythical religious trickster of all time was the 4th century Roman emperor, Constantine the Great, who oversaw the creation of a falsely created belief system, the *Katholikos*, a Latin word meaning 'general' or 'universal', which gave rise to the Catholic Church, Christianity, its canon of scripture – the Bible – which is still around today.

Around 325 AD, there was great dissention in Constantine's vast realm due to religious differences. There were many mystical sects and systems of belief around at the time: Hinduism, Judaism, Buddhism, Mithraism, Gnosticism, coupled with Egyptian, Greek and Roman beliefs stemming from times long past. Just as we see today, a conflict in religious beliefs creates infighting and competition. It was the same in Constantine's day and it was interfering with his ability to govern. So for political expediency, he ordered the formation of a general religion, one to which everyone could belong and which would bring peace and harmony to his realm. Over 300 religious leaders were gathered together from across the empire, tasked with developing the parameters of this new religion. They became known as the First Council of Nicea. Many principles from each of the different mystical orders and religious and spiritual systems were subtly moulded and grafted into the Katholikos, forming a general system of belief.

If you, like me, wonder why Western churches are emptying and why Christianity doesn't make much sense, here's some food for thought:

The general religion needed a central character upon which to base its principles. Jesus of Nazareth was a historical personage who lived in the 1st Century. He was an avatar,[5] a special man sent on a divine mission, like the Buddah and Zoroaster. He founded the mystical order of the Nazarenes from which the Essenes grew. As this was the strongest and most recent religion around at the time, the *Katholikos* was based around him.

The concept of 'Jesus' and 'Christ' are two different things. The term 'Jesus Christ' was developed only when Christianity came into being. The term *christ* originated with the Egyptians and Greeks. Egyptian orthodox religions believed that when one passes on, they are resurrected in the land of light. The body had to be preserved through mummification to help this process. The embalmed body was called the *krs* and the resurrected body was the *krst*. The Greek word *christós*, meaning 'the anointed one', or 'messiah', was based on the Egyptian word. This is how the concept of Christ and the resurrection came into the Bible.

The Hindus believed in a trinity of three Gods: Brahma the Creator, Vishnu the Preserver and Shiva the Destroyer. They became The Father, Son and Holy Spirit.

Buddhism had been around since approximately 490 BC, and stories of the Buddha's unusual birth developed through the centuries. The Buddha was, like Jesus, an avatar, descended from the Divine Realms, appearing in his mother's womb as a 'shining gem'. In essence, the Buddhists believed that Buddha was sent straight from the Divine and born of a virgin, so unless Jesus was born of a virgin in this new religion, it would be difficult for the Buddhists to accept. So they took Mary, the mother of Jesus, to be a virgin and the immaculate conception was conceived.

The Greeks believed in their Olympian gods and could not accept this 'Christ' character unless he was a god. So Jesus became the 'Son of God'.

One of the biggest mystical religions in Europe and the middle East at the time was Mithraism. The religion was centred around the god Mithra who was believed to have been born on 25th December, risen from a rock. Before the development of the Katholikos, there were no popes, so 400 years of Christian popes had to be created, based on historical personages around that time, to support the new religion. The first pope was therefore named Petre, which means 'rock', meaning that the Catholic church, too, would then have risen from a rock.

In the times of Constantine, there were many mystery schools, none of which had a canon of scripture. But they held many eye-witness accounts relating to the life of Jesus, his birth, life, and the crucifixion. As they have been throughout history; these mystery schools were persecuted, and their letters and private accounts confiscated. Some of them were amended and made into the 'new testament of the Bible'. Many eye-witness accounts were not included, such as the Gospel of St Thomas and the Gospels of Mary Magdalene. The aptly named 'Lost Books of the Bible' (the Dead Sea Scrolls and Nag Hammadi Library), discovered in 1945 and 1947 in the caves and foothills of Qumran and Nag Hammadi, perhaps hold the keys to the truth behind Christianity. The discovery also included multiple copies of the Hebrew Bible untouched from as early as 300 BC.

The Essenes, a mystical sect believed to have been founded by Jesus, contributed the story of Jesus' baptism. John the Baptist baptised Jesus in the River Jordan but he did not baptise Christ. The Dead Sea Scrolls are believed to have been attributed to the Essenes. They are also known as the Essenes' Library.

There is much debate about the actual birth date of Jesus. Some reports indicate a birth on the 4th of January, others any time between March and September. It is widely disputed that he was born on 25th of December itself. That was the birth date of the god Mithra, and it was also the day on which the Romans held their solstice festival in honour of the god Bacchus – a day devoted to wine, merry-making and feasting. And so, that date became Jesus' birthday and to this day it has remained unchanged.

Judaism, the orthodox religion that Moses founded, still existed at the time and had a big following. So the Jewish rabbis who sat on the Nicene Council wanted the Torah to be kept in. It became the 'old testament'.

So, the first *Christian* was not actually Jesus, but Constantine the Great. The compilation of the Bible was a complicated project involving churchmen of varying beliefs in an atmosphere of dissension, persecution and bigotry. Upon its completion, Christianity was passed as a law and has for centuries been the plunderer of all that is real and true in our belief system in the name of political control. Following the First Council of Nicea, many other amendments to the Bible were made to promulgate control, including the removal of references to reincarnation in 553 AD during an Ecumenical Council meeting of the Catholic Church in Constantinople.

Yet each man kills the thing he loves,
By each let this be heard,
Some do it with a bitter look,
Some with a flattering word,
The coward does it with a kiss,
The brave man with a sword!

Oscar Wilde (1854–1900)
The Ballad of Reading Gaol

STAGE 12

THE FINAL BATTLE

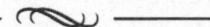

Seeker, enter the Inmost Cave and look for that which will restore life to the Home Tribe. The way grows narrow and dark. You must go alone on hands and knees and you feel the earth press close around you. You can hardly breathe. Suddenly you come out into the deepest chamber and find yourself face-to-face with a towering figure, a menacing Shadow composed of all your doubts and fears and well armed to defend a treasure. Here in this moment, is the chance to win all or die. No matter what you came for, it's Death that now stares back at you. Whatever the outcome of the battle, you are about to taste death and it will change you.

Christopher Vogler
The Writer's Journey

or two weeks after the incident with Marcos, I couldn't think, sleep or eat. I was devastated as the realisation dawned on me that the teacher I loved had seemingly no compassion at all. I'd walked through fire to get to him and now wanted to be as far away as possible. Exercises designed to balance my mind and emotion that had previously produced some wonderful results had no effect and frequently disintegrated into body-wracking sobs of self-pity. My entire being was awash with sadness at being so deceived. I needed to think to get away from him and Viewpoint. Each day I left at dawn to sit in a coffee shop to avoid being in his presence. I tried to find a rational answer. Perhaps this was a test of my sincerity just before my initiation. But no matter how much I tried to convince myself, I knew this was no test. My guru was a big problem and I was facing the greatest challenge of my life with my most loved and feared opponent.

I had to pull myself together, I couldn't stay fearful and lost forever. I was here in the dragon's den, the physical centre of my spiritual universe, and there was danger afoot. Withering and dying was not an option. I had an obligation to my mother to return the money I'd borrowed. I was an initiate and initiates had responsibilities. I reminded myself of the 'Life and Conduct' given to us in our first lectures. (I still use it today.) Initiates had courage, a sense of humour and the ability to separate the teachings from the teacher. 'There is no room for cowards on this path,' it said. 'Fight if you must, but don't initiate fights.' With trepidation, I started to prepare myself for battle.

In March, I was formally initiated into the order along with the remainder of my classmates. It was a powerfully moving but solemn affair, and for a while I completely forgot about the Viewpoint ordeal. We had several exams before the initiation and also had to complete a panel interview. I was sure one of the panel members would be Marcos and I worried that he may hold a deep dark secret about me that would reveal his reason for firing me from the project, and that he'd now use it to fire me from the order. But I needn't have worried. No deep dark secrets were revealed, and he and the other high initiates welcomed me into their midst with open arms. I breathed a sigh of relief. Perhaps the whole affair had nothing to do with me after all?

The enthusiasm I had for my lessons had not waned; after all, they were the main reason for my move to Viewpoint and I tried to push all other concerns aside. I was glad to learn that my new teacher would not be Marcos. Although I missed the depth of his insight and the way in which my spirits were quickened in his presence, I felt sure that my mistrust of him would betray me. I couldn't afford to leave the order: firstly, because I valued what I was learning so much; but secondly, because there was a lot of money at stake that didn't belong to me.

First initiation classes were held weekly at a venue a few kilometres from Viewpoint. The curriculum became harder and more intense. Additional exercises and disciplines were added to those we already practised. To my absolute joy, we started an in-depth study of the myths and their hidden meanings. It was here that I realised that what I was experiencing was perhaps experienced by all mythological heroes as they moved closer to the centre of their *ordeal*. Ironically, it provided me with some valuable insight in terms of how to handle Marcos and protect my money and my spiritual path. I started to observe the goings-on at Viewpoint very carefully. It was easier now that I was at the very heart of the organisation instead of being on the periphery. I spent a lot of time chastising myself for my foolishness in moving to Viewpoint, but there were advantages. On the outside, one cannot see what is going on. Moving to the source, I was able to study my enemy more closely, getting to know the 'dragon' and its weaknesses. I got to see firsthand how others reacted and behaved around Marcos and realised that I was not alone in my fears.

Despite his brilliance as a teacher, there was no doubt about it, Marcos was a ruthless bully and tyrant. People avoided him, particularly the veterans of the order. As he was one of the three highest initiates, he was rarely challenged. People seemed afraid to confront him as he carried the power to instantaneously destroy their spiritual journey, seemingly on a whim. He was also very well versed in the magical arts. I wasn't one to startle easily, but this man was powerful and had developed the ability to use his will and imagination (the properties of magic) to get others to do his bidding. He was powerful in more ways than one. His brash manner didn't concern me as much as it concerned others; even though he'd been very harsh with me on several occasions, I figured that I probably deserved the feedback. Even the greatest gurus get angry with their pupils. He had certainly helped me to shift, toughen up and change, and our exchanges always ended positively. But it wasn't the same for others. Many walked on eggshells around him, terrified of what he might do next. I was starting to feel the same way.

I'd made allowances for Marcos's erratic or sometimes out-of-character behaviour by trying to put myself in his shoes. He worked tirelessly for the order, taking on perhaps too many responsibilities. (I was a victim of that trait myself). He was dedicated to his exercises and disciplines and the proof could be seen in his magical and healing abilities. He wasn't able to heal himself, though. He suffered from recurring bouts of pancreatitis, which debilitated him and even hospitalised him. It certainly explained the sudden and dramatic weight loss. But I made allowances for that, too. He was human, like everyone else, an initiate treading this path in the same way as me. But with his knowledge, insights, powerful abilities, charisma and the adoration of his neophyte pupils, power had gone to this guru's head. He was arrogant and often downright cruel. In my opinion, he was fast losing the plot, demonstrating the same power-crazed paranoia typical of all tyrants in the Greek myths I was studying – King Minos, Polydectes, Accrisius and King Aeetes.

Looking back on this, it's hard not to chuckle at the experience, but at the time, it unsettled me greatly. Whopping cash donations were pouring into the order from sensible, professional people, members and non members alike. CEOs, doctors, lawyers were draining their savings and cash reserves and ploughing it into the nonexistent investment fund without receiving any supporting paperwork or guarantees. I wondered where it was going and what kind of hypnotic power Marcos had over others to keep the cash pouring in as it did. I understood that the order needed cash to survive and grow like any Section 21, not-for-profit organisation, but this was ridiculous. Annual general meetings were held, open for all members to attend, where official announcements were made about donations and expenditures, but no tough questions were asked by the membership, and if they were, the querant didn't seem to be around for long. A conspiracy of silence abounded. Marcos held the purse strings and that was the way it was.

There were a total of fifty or so different projects, businesses and charities underway, ranging from one-man craft businesses to those with a much larger potential for employment, like Perspective. Every one of them had a connection with the order and every one of them was overseen by Marcos. In an ideal world, it was a brilliant concept, a community of people united around one common purpose using their God-given talents and abilities to work for the greater good; yet not one of the businesses seemed to be succeeding. Marcos put it down to the fact that the people in charge had no business acumen, but that was not so. The businesses were stripped of their cash by Marcos as soon as it came in, leaving nothing in reserve for future growth and expansion. As the first sprouts of these seedling businesses started to poke their heads above the earth, they were snatched out by their roots, leaving the landscape barren and dry. Although Marcos was a great teacher, he was without doubt a lousy businessman and refused to accept the advice of the wealth of business and financial talent around him. Meetings with order members were always held one-on-one, never as a group. Divide and rule. My guess was that he had inspired them with the same stories that he'd shared with me, instilling the initiates with a sense of obligation and duty. He appointed board directors for the Section 21 company based on their ability to agree and comply, rather than question and challenge. I now understood why I was fired from the project. I'd protested against his excessive demands for proceeds from the business I'd started, which through back-breaking hard work was beginning to produce fruits. He didn't take kindly to my remarks. Like many others before me, I had become a threat. I was sure that I too was branded as one of the 'selfish and uncommitted' order members that I'd heard so much about in my own discussions with him.

At Viewpoint itself there was an unhealthy conspiracy of silence among all ranks of initiates, creating an atmosphere which had an almost Machiavellian feel. Everyone was wafting around like puffs of smoke, trying to look all mystical, contemplative and busy, but underneath I guessed that they were just as worried and concerned about the state of affairs and their spiritual future as I was. People were mistrustful of each other, nobody said a word against Marcos or Martin for fear of retribution or expulsion. Some, particularly fledgling initiates, would stop at nothing to betray their colleagues to curry favour with their teacher. Many watched from the sidelines as young neophytes, unfamiliar with the system, became fanatical, changing their lives, draining their savings, donating money, time and effort, which they could ill afford, to further the order's cause. No one dared to discourage them or point out the error of their ways. My guess was that everyone operated under the threat of expulsion if they interfered with the so called free will of another.

I expressed my concern to one teacher, a psychologist, whom I consulted when the situation got too much for me. She was deeply concerned about the state of affairs and promised to speak to the Grand Master, who was strangely conspicuous by his absence. However, the next time I saw her, she refused to look me in the eye, denied all knowledge of our discussion and suggested that I keep my mouth shut and support Marcos as best I could. It seemed that someone had bullied her, too. I'd spent a lot of time working with dysfunctional organisational cultures that emulate exactly these same behaviours under the rule of a tyrannical leader. This organisation, despite its mystical goals and aspirations, was one of the most toxic cultures I'd ever experienced. One could find people with more compassion and integrity at the checkout of the local Pick 'n' Pay supermarket than in this holy brotherhood.

It was a heartbreaking time for me. I'd learned so much from my teacher and from the lectures that I'd attended and couldn't deny how much I had changed as an individual. But the sudden dramatic focus on cash and expansion marred the spiritual focus of the organisation and my commitment to it. There is a fine line when it comes to spirituality and business and the line had well and truly been crossed. At first I had believed that the combination was possible with the amount of dedication and willingness I'd seen from so many. It proved to me just how powerful a strong vision and purpose can be as a motivator of hearts and minds. However, the two cannot mix when the reconciling factor, my teacher, was seemingly off his trolley. People carried out his bidding without question, all in the name of duty and a higher cause, or they conveniently turned a blind eye to his abusive and paranoid behaviour. Initiates, whom Marcos didn't much care for, particularly ones without cash, were being fired from the order for simple misdemeanours, like late payment of their membership fees. When I joined the outer circle in 2002, people were making reasonable donations to help support their teacher and the existing infrastructure. But today, the demand for cash had gone nuclear. I realised with great sadness that despite my unquenchable thirst for knowledge, this was no longer a path that I could follow. One learns to separate the teachings from the teacher, but one has to also listen to one's conscience and intuition. Both had been screaming at me for many months and I'd completely ignored them.

It was with these insights, gathered over some months, that I decided to take action. Marcos was now running the order as a business, so I had to deal with him in a business-oriented way. I couldn't tackle the dragon in this small, enclosed space head-on; I had to apply cunning, as I didn't have a legal leg to stand on as far as my money was concerned. If he suspected that I was trying to outsmart him in any way he would undoubtedly expel me, as he'd done with others. The journey would be over. I would lose both my money and my spiritual journey. So, with the help of my accountant, I drafted a loan agreement citing that the money I'd put into Viewpoint would be paid in full when the property was sold. I wouldn't make the returns I'd been promised, but I might at least protect the capital I'd invested. I then went to him with all the confidence I could muster, warning him I was under investigation by SARS (the South African Revenue Service) owing to the large cash sums I'd imported from the UK and invested at Viewpoint. I expressed great concern for the order and how I didn't want to be the one responsible for leading an audit trail to his door. It was almost true. SARS did investigate me two years down the line for the very same thing. He hastily signed the agreement together with two witnesses, and my heart leapt for joy at this small victory. Little did I know that this was to be my only saving grace in the future.

It wasn't long after getting my contract signed that this crazy situation at Viewpoint came to an abrupt end. With much uproar and fuss, Marcos was expelled from the order by the Grand Master, along with several of his 'henchmen'. The whole affair was more akin to the 'Gunfight at the OK Corral' than a mystical brotherhood. He was unceremoniously escorted from the premises, his belongings on the back of a truck. As I watched with great sadness from a distance, I wondered what he might be feeling. He had dedicated twenty years of his life to this organisation and to his teacher, Martin. Viewpoint was his home and he was ousted like a scalded cat caught stealing milk from the kitchen. His immortal words imparted at our first lecture rang in my ears: 'It is your ego that will take you out of this order and nothing else.'

THE MYTH AND ITS MEANING:
Perseus and the Gorgon (Part II)

At some point in his journey, the hero goes into a life-or-death battle with a fearsome creature. In all myths, it is symbolic of the seeker's battle with his dark side, the 'ego monster'.

Perseus is exiled from the kingdom of Seriphos by the tyrant King Polydectes, who demands that he retrieve the head of Medusa, a Gorgon, whose gaze alone turns men to stone. After wandering lost for a long time, not knowing which way to turn, Perseus is visited by the goddess Athena (who previously appeared to him in a dream prophesying the journey he would embark upon) and the messenger god Hermes, symbolic of the invisible allies and guides who help seekers on their journeys. They provided him with guidance, weapons and gifts to help him on his way. In the myths, when gifts are bestowed they are symbolic of certain mystical powers and abilities which are unleashed in the seeker at a certain point in his spiritual development. For Perseus, winged sandals depict his ability to astral-travel, a sword depicts his state of balance, and a highly polished shield depicts his ability to reflect darkness back on itself.

To find the Gorgon's lair he had to seek the Nymphs of the North, holders of many secrets, who were to provide him with a cap of darkness (invisibility) and directions for how to get to the Gorgon's lair. However, to find the Nymphs of the North, he sought help from the Grannae: three strange women sharing only one eye among them, which they constantly fought over. The Grannae symbolize the balance between mind, emotions and body. One single eye depicts the 'third eye', or the 'brow chakra' which, when opened, can lead to states of higher consciousness, clairvoyance, precognition and out of body experiences. Perseus watched the Grannae from the cover of a thick bush. When one took out the eye to give to another, Perseus sprang from his hiding place and snatched the eye from them (depicting that he had achieved this higher state of consciousness), threatening not to give it back unless they provided him with the information he needed to advance on his quest. Different powers are unleashed in the seeker at different stages of the journey. Not all power can be given at once. Only when the seeker is ready, or has completed another stage in the journey, is he ready to face his biggest test.

When Perseus reached the Gorgon's lair, he put on the cap of darkness given to him by the nymphs and flew down. He crept up on the sleeping monster by viewing her reflection in the highly polished shield. When the Gorgon awoke and opened her eyes, he lifted the shield directly in front of her and reflected her gaze back on herself. She immediately turned to stone and he was able to cut off her head and take flight with Medusa's sisters in pursuit.

At some point on his journey, the seeker must overcome the most fearsome and darkest of beasts, ones who reside deep within himself. The darkness is depicted in myths as a specific creature or monster which the hero has to overcome but in reality lies within. It cannot be fought head-on; cunning and wits and the passing of many tests are required if he is to tackle it successfully. The monster is always symbolic of the seeker's ego.

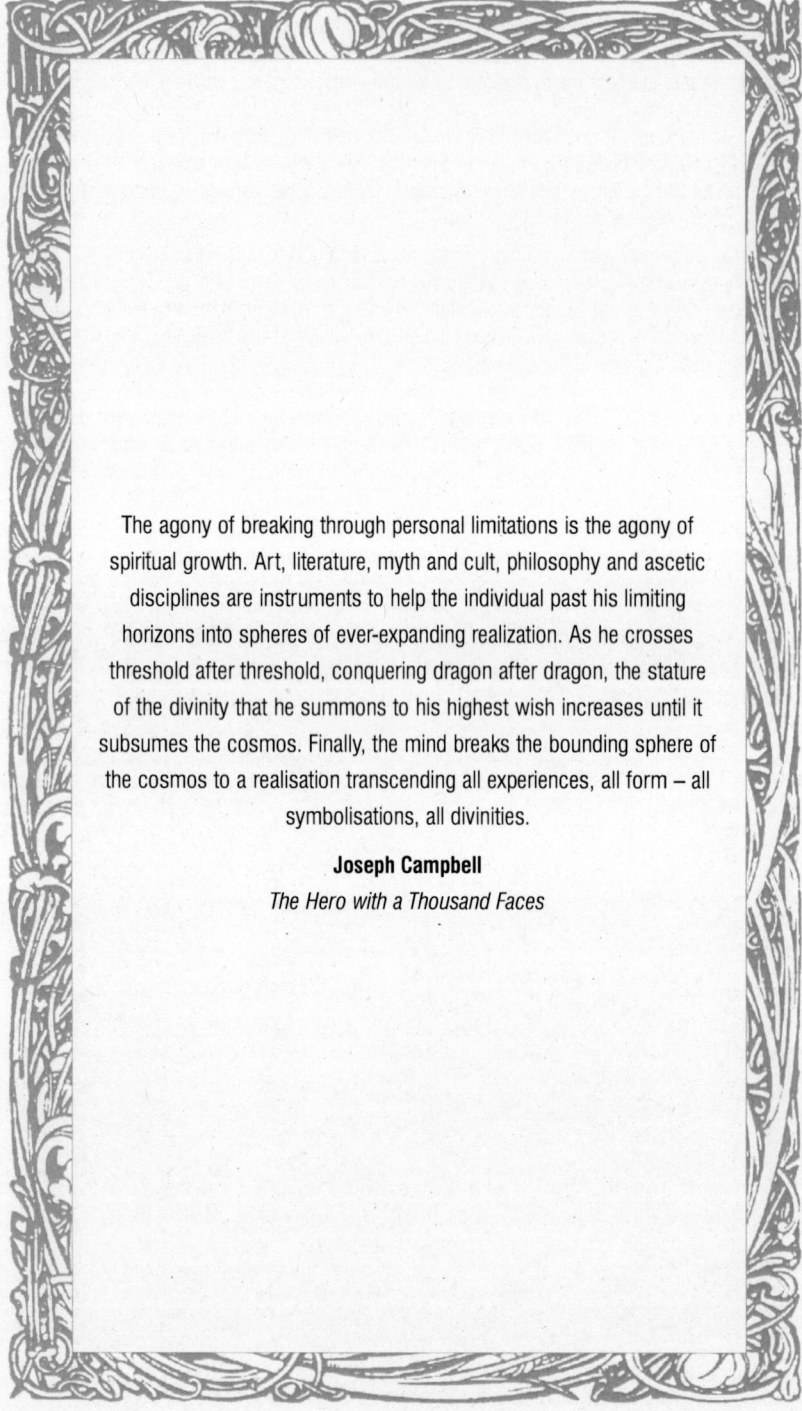

The agony of breaking through personal limitations is the agony of spiritual growth. Art, literature, myth and cult, philosophy and ascetic disciplines are instruments to help the individual past his limiting horizons into spheres of ever-expanding realization. As he crosses threshold after threshold, conquering dragon after dragon, the stature of the divinity that he summons to his highest wish increases until it subsumes the cosmos. Finally, the mind breaks the bounding sphere of the cosmos to a realisation transcending all experiences, all form – all symbolisations, all divinities.

Joseph Campbell
The Hero with a Thousand Faces

STAGE 13

THE REWARD

Once the battle is over, the hero has time to consider the consequences of his near-death experience. With the dragon now slain, the tyrant vanquished, the hero can rescue the maiden, steal the elixir or grasp the grail cup and make his way homeward. It is the point in the journey where the hero, who has risked life and limb, now gets something in return. Emerging from the dark cave into the light, he can take in deep breaths of fresh air and rejoice, bathe his wounds and share his stories around the campfire. The final battle is a critical stage in the journey towards truth. From here on, the hero is changed forever.

eroes and seekers always emerge from their ordeals radically different and ineradicably changed. They possess insights, perceptions and inner wisdom that they didn't have at the outset. After five years with Marcos as my teacher, I was indelibly changed. The outer circle curriculum and my initiation into the order provided me with an understanding and inner knowledge that I couldn't possibly have found in a book or an on-line degree course. Had I managed to find disparate pieces of the information elsewhere, I wouldn't have understood how to connect them together to form a complete picture, and even if I had a bigger picture, I wouldn't be able to understand what it meant. I wouldn't have known which discipline was right and true, which teachers to trust, where to look to find one, or which questions to ask when I did. Without my teacher and the strict curriculum of instruction, my enthusiasm would have waned considerably and I would no doubt have lost interest. It may have taken me a lifetime, perhaps more, to reach this point in my journey. I needed a 'trial of fire', a complete immersion in the spiritual experience, and that's exactly what I got. The discipline, the exercise, the constant battle with the ego, coupled with the lectures, workshops, study groups and advice and rebukes from my teacher had softened some of my rough edges. More than that, they had given me a glimpse of the truer side of my nature, and what I might become if I persisted with this journey. More than anything, I'd stopped worrying. I'd found meaning beyond my material surroundings, one that I'd craved since childhood. I now had a valuable platform from which I could take bigger and braver steps onwards, one that would help me separate the wheat from the chaff in any future spiritual adventures. I was no longer a *worrier* in life, trying to keep the flimsy fabric of my reality together, but a *warrior* on the path of truth. I'd ventured into the realms of the unknown – a place where most fear to tread.

As the dust settled after Marcos' departure, and Viewpoint became still and quiet once again, I tried to make sense of the last five years. It hadn't been as I'd expected, but then again, I couldn't really remember having an expectation at the outset, anyway. I'd seemingly stumbled across this path, having little insight or understanding of anything esoteric or hidden. I was like a machine, on automatic pilot, governed by my five senses, reacting and overreacting time and again. The order had helped me overcome all of that, and once I'd started to uncover the secrets it held, I believed that this path would take me all the way home, and that Marcos and Martin somehow held the keys to my destiny. But that was not so.

The spiritual path, the road of truth, the path of self-discovery is the hardest path that any person can undertake. The Divine realms, like the summit of any mountain, are shrouded in mist and mystery and no one man holds the keys to eternity. We have to get there alone, by ourselves, for ourselves. When we set out, we quickly begin to realise that there are no definitive signposts marking our path onward, no well trodden paths to follow, no map, guidebook or compass to consult when we get lost. The seeker does not find his way paved with gold when finally deciding to turn his face towards the light. The journey is long and arduous, full of disappointments, ambiguity, false starts, twists, turns and dead ends. It can be a maze of contradictions and misunderstandings. Seekers meet allies and tricksters on their spiritual journeys just as we all do in every walk of life. We may have set out with good intentions but somehow got lost along the way. Part of the journey is learning how to navigate these muddy waters, endeavouring to apply the insights and wisdom learned, to separate the true from the false and to develop the wisdom, love and compassion to deal with ourselves and others who will disappoint us, perhaps time and again. In fact, we learn not to have expectations, because we cannot know with certainty what they should be. Having too many expectations only leads to disappointment, but that does not stop us from having aspirations – aspirations of a different nature – no longer material possessions, recognition and success, but to discover ourselves, our greatness and all that we can possibly become.

Wherever we are on our journey, there is always danger. No matter how far we have progressed, we can regress almost to the very beginning and further, having to claw and clamour our way back to the point where we stumbled. Our progress is often painfully slow one moment and at warp speed the next. But, if one is sincere about the quest, if one persists even in the face of darkness, one can traverse any terrain, no matter how difficult. Then the insights become greater, the wisdom enhanced and the courage and tenacity inherent in all seekers indelibly increased. Martin Luther King said, 'Even if I knew that tomorrow the world would go to pieces, I would still plant my apple tree.' Nothing is ever lost. The effort that we put into our growth today will serve us tomorrow, no matter what's in store for us.

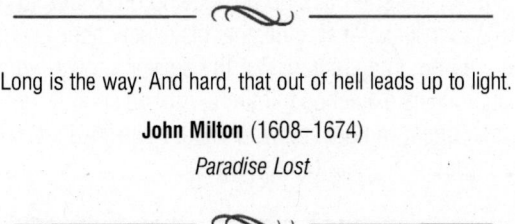

Long is the way; And hard, that out of hell leads up to light.

John Milton (1608–1674)

Paradise Lost

I had achieved my reward. I was transformed on the inside – calmer, more together, less erratic, more intuitive, connected and whole within. I'd experienced the miraculous – seeing mystical and magical abilities demonstrated that I would never have dreamed possible. I'd met allies and guides who would now become lifelong friends. I had confidence and utter belief in the higher realms, and knew that never again would I be alone. The ordinary world and the unseen world had been somewhat reconciled within. But most of all, I now had a system of belief that allowed me to make sense of life, one that spanned the globe, across all cultures and beliefs and wasn't aligned with any dogmatic school of orthodox thought. Regardless of my spiritual future, I knew one thing: that I wanted, above all else, to know God, and that somehow, at some time in the distant future, that I would most certainly find my way home.

I hadn't given much thought to what would happen when Viewpoint was sold, what I would do or where I would go. Pete and I had become estranged through this whole affair and our relationship had become one of respect rather than love, a deep respect for a fellow initiate who had the courage to walk this path. We would inevitably go our separate ways. Perhaps it was divine providence that we hadn't sold our house after all. The lease agreement on our property in Lone Hill was coming to an end and I had mixed feelings about returning. I was looking forward to having my space and privacy back, but I dreaded returning to the *ordinary* world, facing people who I hadn't seen for two or three years, putting on a brave face and pretending that everything was as it should be when I still had so many unanswered questions about the order, its founder, its mission, Martin's sincerity and whether or not I'd been part of some god-awful cult for the last five years. How could I justify why I was returning so soon? How could I explain what I'd experienced, what I'd learned and how much I'd changed? I couldn't exactly bring back any souvenirs from my five-year journey – no golden nuggets, magical rings or golden-egg-laying geese. I looked the same; there were no outward signs that anything was different. I remembered reading in many fairy tales of those who endeavour to bring the 'fairy gold' back from the land of the little people only to find its magic evaporating as they moved further away from the forest. A heavy sack of gold coins taken from the wee folk would be found to contain nothing but wet leaves when opened in the light of the sun back home, leading onlookers to believe that the seeker was perhaps delusional after all, that his experiences lay only in his vivid, and somewhat warped, imagination. But the seeker knows the treasure is real – he just cannot prove its existence to others. And as spiritual growth is such an intensely personal quest, onlookers would just have to undertake the journey for themselves if they really wanted to know.

THE MYTH AND ITS MEANING:
Seizing the Sword

The ultimate goal of spiritual growth is a union of consciousness with God – *unio mystica*, *nirvana*, enlightenment; or what alchemists call the completion of the 'Great Work'. It is depicted in all the hero myths of the world and symbolised by the retrieval of certain objects of value – a golden fleece, a golden ring, golden eggs or nuggets, grail cups, or the drinking of a magical elixir said to heal every ill, restore life to the kingdom or transmute metals into gold.

To achieve the ultimate boon, the hero has to undergo many trials and tests, proving his worth again and again, expanding his consciousness and developing special talents and abilities along the way to capture what he seeks, permitting him to proceed to the next stage of the journey. Each test involves greater hardship, requiring the use of every fragment of insight gained along the way. At the end of the journey, after much suffering and sacrifice, it is only the most perfect knight who achieves his aim, and he always does so alone. Only those mortals who have been 'favoured by the gods' can take their place among them. In the Grail Legends, Sir Galahad is the only knight in Arthur's court who is fit to see the Grail. In Grimm's fairy tales, Cinderella is the only maiden in the kingdom whose foot is delicate enough to fit into the glass slipper. In the Persian tales of the Arabian nights, Scheherazade, the Vizier's daughter, is the only Virgin able to enrapture King Shahryar with an entertaining story each night, thus postponing her inevitable execution the following morning; this goes on for 1,001 nights, until he makes her his wife.

In the Nordic myths, Odin sacrifices an eye in an exchange for a drink from Mimir's well, which bestows upon him great wisdom and the ability to read the sacred runes. Sometimes the sacrifice is so great that the seeker must lose a sense to gain a sense.

Folklore also depicts stories of seekers who are not successful in their quest. In the Mesopotamian *Epic of Gilgamesh*, a distraught Gilgamesh goes in search of the plant 'never grow old' – a quest for immortality - after the death of his beloved friend Enkidu. The goddess Ishtar tries to dissuade him. He ignores her advice and searches for many long years for the plant, finally retrieving it from the bottom of the deepest ocean. He lays down to rest after his ordeal and while he sleeps, a serpent enchanted by the plant's wonderful perfumes, carries it away, later eating it and gaining the power of sloughing its skin – the symbol of renewed youth and eternal life. Gilgamesh weeps with disappointment when he wakes to find the plant gone. For some people, the time is not right and the magical elixir is just out of reach.

So great is the reward that seekers may go to any lengths to retrieve it. Many myths depict tales of theft, a stealing of the elixir by those who are not yet worthy. However, there is always a price to be paid for this folly. Prometheus stole fire (the symbol of knowledge) from the gods to bring it back to humankind. Zeus, angry at his impudence, chained him to Mt. Caucuses as a punishment, where an eagle would eat daily from his liver. The Welsh tell the tale of Gwion Bach, who steals the elixir from the evil sorceress, Caridwen. She chases him night and day, eventually catching him and swallowing him whole. He is not successful in his first attempt, but is reborn again as a child with great wisdom and insight.

The effort we put into our spiritual growth and personal development in one life bears fruits, but perhaps not when we expect it. One has to deliberately focus on a spiritual path to get results, and this can take many years and perhaps many lifetimes of work. However, the rewards will always come, perhaps not in the time or way we initially imagine. Those who achieve enlightenment, the ultimate boon, quickly and easily have perhaps unknowingly worked hard on themselves for many lifetimes. All men are indeed *not* equal. But *all* psychological and self-development work, to whatever depth, is valuable. Nothing is ever lost.

After the battle is over, the boon won, the hero, and his princess make their journey home.

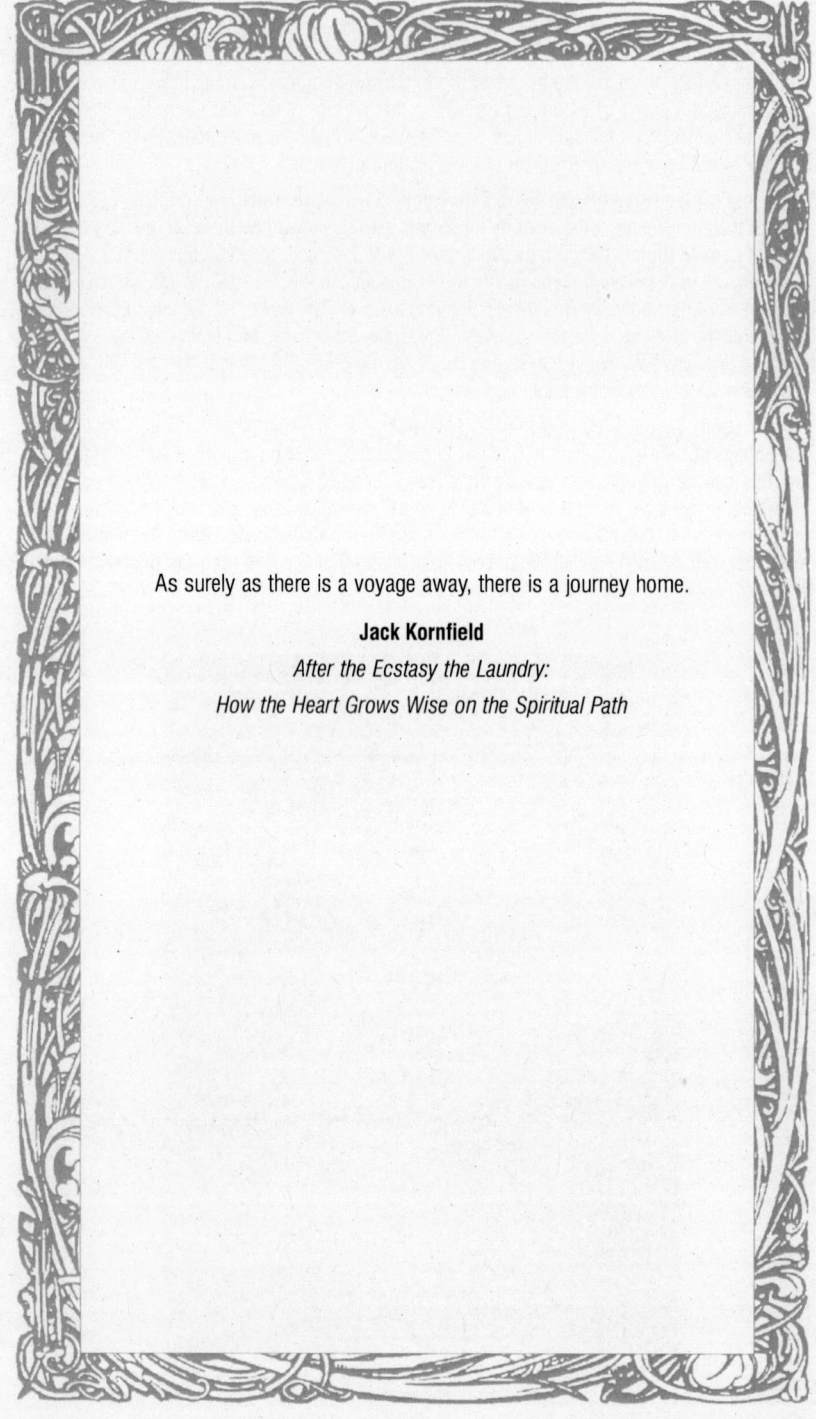

As surely as there is a voyage away, there is a journey home.

Jack Kornfield

After the Ecstasy the Laundry:
How the Heart Grows Wise on the Spiritual Path

STAGE 14
THE RETURN

When the hero-quest had been accomplished, through penetration to the source, or through the grace of some male or female, human or animal, personification, the adventurer still must return with his life-transmuting trophy. The full round, the norm of the monomyth, requires that the hero shall now begin the labour of bringing the runes of wisdom, the Golden Fleece, or his sleeping princess back into the kingdom of humanity where the boon may rebound to the renewing of the community, the nation, the planet, or the ten thousand worlds.

Joseph Campbell
The Hero with a Thousand Faces

he road back to my old neighbourhood of Lone Hill was an emotional journey mixed with confusion and sadness. After Marcos left, life in the order carried on pretty much as it had done before. Official announcements were made about his departure, how he had deceived the Grand Master who had implicitly trusted his pupil. High initiates jumped vehemently to Martin's defence, portraying him as a victim of circumstance and Marcos as a cruel and vicious man who had simply gone too far. No announcements were made about the large cash donations. The same conspiracy of silence abounded much as it had in Marcos' day; in fact, it got worse. People were actively dissuaded from discussing the whole affair with other members or contacting any ex-order members again. I found it odd that Martin didn't face the entire membership himself, comforting them, reassuring them and helping them to understand why his star pupil had gone off the rails. His behaviour fuelled my now deeply entrenched suspicions about the authenticity of this organisation and added to my concerns about the money I'd invested. There were without doubt some dark secrets being harboured here, and it broke my heart that something so beautiful had turned so ugly. But when a fish rots, it rots from the head.

Many questions remained unanswered. I needed to reconcile the events of the last eighteen months and make sense out of what I'd been involved in. How did this mystery school, with all its insights and wisdom, its connection into the highest of subtle realms, and a self-realised Adept at the helm, a god incarnate, fall into such a state of decay and wretched disillusionment? With the gift of clairvoyance bestowed on all Adepts who have 'seen the white', reaching an advanced stage in their spiritual development, why was Marcos not stopped? Who was this character Father Rolfe, the mysterious founder of the order, on whose authority the plans for expansion were founded? Did he really exist or was he a figment of someone's imagination? The whole affair was shrouded in mystery.

Viewpoint was sold. In December of 2005 the new owners moved in and began flattening every building in sight to make way for a new hotel. In January, 2006, I moved back to the house in Lone Hill, alone and delighted to be away from the noise and the intense sadness and tension. Crime-ridden Johannesburg seemed like a better option than a mystical order with dark and unpleasant secrets to conceal. The petty and violent crime in Lone Hill had dropped radically since I'd been away, as the management of the armed-response company had changed hands. In a national poll, Lone Hill was voted the safest suburb in South Africa, another little oasis in a sea of chaos. It provided me with the perfect platform to try and rebuild my life and reconcile the events of the last few years.

Like anyone who'd had the rug ripped from under them in such a vehement way, I, along with many others who had been affected by the whole affair, needed to heal. But healing can really only take place when the tragedy is over. I still needed to get my money back and for the next few months, it would be life as normal as far as the order was concerned. I wanted to give Martin no excuse to find fault with my behaviour or my commitment and so I continued to toe the line as I had before, pretending that I was as deeply committed to this path as I'd always been. Part of me was; I really didn't want to lose my teachings, but I knew I couldn't pursue them in a place such as this.

After a long wait of ten months or more the money was reluctantly returned by the order. Marcos' former colleague Pierre played a big role in this, using his influence and senior position, fighting tooth and nail from Cape Town to bring the order to justice before himself resigning in disgust. He knew what Martin was all about and it was the indicator, as if I needed any more, that this was a desperate organisation. 2006 was a year of great tension, always touch-and-go as to whether the funds would be recovered, and several attempts, fair and foul, were made by senior order members in Johannesburg, acting on Martin's behalf, to persuade me to relinquish them to the 'greater good'. Marcos was certainly not alone in his bullying tactics.

With my money returned, I didn't care what these people thought of me, and I began blatantly investigating the order and its history, flagrantly disregarding the rules laid down by Martin and his cohorts not to contact Pierre or previous members of the order. What did he have to hide? Eventually, like many others before me, I was falsely accused of a minor misdemeanour and expelled. I was perhaps too close to uncovering the secret that the order was trying hard to protect. So much for the clairvoyant Adept, I thought. My journey with this organisation, whatever it was, was now finally over.

I put on a brave face, but I was devastated inside, despite the catastrophic events of the last two years. The search for identity and meaning is so cavernous and all encompassing. One cannot just walk away from any journey of this depth and magnitude without feeling empty and lost. At the time of my departure, I still didn't understand what was going on, and the complete picture only emerged after many months of searching. I was grateful that I'd surfaced from the ordeal bruised and beaten, but otherwise relatively unscathed. But Martin clearly had a lot more to lose if whatever secrets he was hiding became public.

Gradually over the months and years to come, the veils of secrecy were lifted, as more people left the order, disappointed and mistrustful, and began to seek answers to the same questions. I spent some time after my departure looking for clues, re-researching the history of the Golden Dawn as I'd done so many times before. The Golden Dawn was a mystical brotherhood that began around the late 19th and early 20th Centuries that also purported a history of Adepts, stemming back to the 12th century Rosicrucians. Members allegedly included characters like Dion Fortune, Wynn Westcott, McGregor Mathers, Pamela Coleman Smith and William Butler Yeats, to name a few. They, too, appeared to have the same issues and bitter disputes over legitimacy and supremacy as our order had. What was one to believe?

As the pieces of the puzzle started to crystallize, I experienced a rollercoaster of wild emotions which would descend on me without warning, from feelings of stupidity, foolishness, anger, sadness, bitter disappointment and disbelief at my utter gullibility on the one hand, to absolute gratitude, elation, and jubilation on the other, over the depth and clarity of the teachings I'd received. Without doubt, I had benefited from the whole experience and learned lessons both good and bad. However, the whole affair may always be shrouded in mystery, like any myth, and never be solved entirely.

As in any story, this one contains elements of truth and falsehood. By all accounts, Father Rolfe was not a myth, and after many conversations with his pupils (those who were still alive), I ascertained that he was indeed a very special man – an Adept, a hierarch (a man sent from the Divine), a man with special powers and qualities. Many who knew him recount experiences of being totally uplifted in the presence of this holy man and having their abilities greatly enhanced, as if he were working on them at a much deeper level. He was loved, adored and respected by everyone who knew him. Originally from Austria, Father Rolfe came to South Africa in the 1960s, in the middle of the apartheid era, when books were not readily available. He came with a simple mission: to find *one* pupil he could train to Adepthood, a pupil that would take his teachings to others. So upon hand-selecting a few individuals around him, he began to teach and continued to do so for many years.

Martin, who was not regarded highly by his fellow students, was indeed a pupil of Father Rolfe's, but their relationship was not a happy one. A big rift finally occurred between teacher and pupil a few years before Father Rolfe's death, when he set a test for Martin, as he did with all of his apprentices, and caught him red-handed. Martin had a reputation for exaggerating Father Rolfe's history and status, to embellish his own standing as a teacher, something he had apparently been guilty of for lifetimes. (Martin fabricated the story of Father Rolfe's link to the Rosicrucians.) It was this among other factors that lead Father Rolfe to stop teaching completely, disappointed that the pupils he'd selected to continue his work had lost their way. He did, however, continue to privately teach two other members, who stayed with him until the time of his death. (One of those private students, a healer, I am pleased to say, became a firm friend and helped me to recuperate after my experience.)

When Father Rolfe died he handed his properties and notebooks and the authority to continue the order to a pupil in Cape Town named Steve, who declined the responsibility. The order was disbanded. But Martin couldn't accept this. In the same way that the power-hungry Pelias in the Greek myth of Jason and the Argonauts overthrew the rightful King Aeson and laid claim to the kingdom of Thessaly, Martin declared himself to be Father Rolfe's sole successor. Hungry for supremacy and hoards of adoring followers, he carefully eliminated all those who could contest his legitimacy, sending them into exile in the same way that Pelias sent Jason, the rightful heir to the throne, in search of the Golden Fleece, hoping he'd never return. With potential detractors out the way, Martin started to wield his power as 'King' and 'High Priest'. He continued to exaggerate stories about Father Rolfe's illustrious incarnations and the nature of his mission.

So part of the story was true: Father Rolfe did exist, and was a special man who no doubt imparted some valuable knowledge and information to Martin and his other pupils. Martin himself was quite unique, although his morals and ethics left a lot to be desired. He had a prodigious spectrum of knowledge on an extraordinary variety of topics; some believed that he perhaps knew more than Father Rolfe himself. He was a powerful healer and hypnotist (magic) and a good teacher, able to amalgamate the teachings from a variety of spiritual disciplines in such a way that made sense to all those searching for answers in a sea of confusion. By the late 1990s, the order, under Martin's leadership, had grown to approximately 400-plus members.

It's easy for any guru, self-styled or not, to lose the plot when he has the adoration of so many followers. The pressure on him is huge and unless his humility and strength of character is developed enough through the practice of mysticism and the guidance of a wise teacher to withstand it, he can easily fall from grace. Looking back, the order placed a big focus on magic and alchemy, mystical practices (which I'd spent a lot of time focusing on) that were small in comparison to others, unless facilitated by Pierre. When a person realises how powerful he can become after years of practice and dedication to specific exercises, he starts to believe himself to be omnipotent. I discovered that Martin had always had a propensity towards power, greed and control, and when his wife Sheila died, there was nobody around to keep him in check. As people believed he had contact with his teacher in the Divine, not many questions were asked until he started to contradict himself. This ultimately became his downfall, as it would later do with his pupil Marcos, who took his lead from the man he idolised and adored. They were, for all intents and purposes, two peas from the same pod. But, we can never truly know what drives another.

However, Martin's reign was short-lived. In the late 1990s when his 'kingdom' was at its peak, there was a major split in the order, which occurred after a no-confidence motion was brought against Martin as a teacher and healer. Many of his pupils were starting to see through him, and rumours abounded about his inappropriate behaviour with some of the female members, and an abuse of power, something he tried hard to cover up. But Martin's true identity was coming to the fore. The situation got so bad that in a heated confrontation, 80% of the membership base resigned almost overnight, and the order collapsed. Martin, like all tyrannical leaders in myth, was a coward at heart and went into hiding, something he apparently did often when the going got too tough.

Enter Pierre and Marcos, the heroes of the hour, themselves fledgling initiates, with no knowledge of Martin's history. They didn't care about the rumours and disagreements. They wanted to learn. So they rallied the troops, cajoled Martin into returning to the lecture hall, and restored him to his former glory with a judicious spin. Pierre and Marcos themselves became teachers and Martin's closest allies and star pupils. With all the troublemakers out of the way, Martin continued to portray Father Rolfe and his mission in an exalted light, and thus the order began to grow once more, as new members like myself joined up, desperately seeking in the same way as those who had gone before. This was when the idea of building businesses and starting order projects came into being to fund the organisation's expansion, which Marcos took control of.

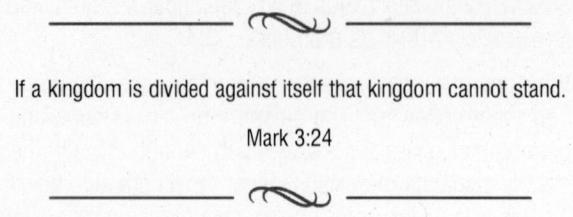

If a kingdom is divided against itself that kingdom cannot stand.

Mark 3:24

The order continued growing in strength until March of 2004, when Pierre challenged Marcos and Martin about the direction it was taking. Knowing Marcos better than anyone, Pierre was aware of the litany of business failures in Marcos' past. He was concerned that members like me were giving up their homes and making large, unsubstantiated donations to the order to sustain this business and community idea. He was also concerned about Marcos' failing health. Marcos was taking on too much, pushing himself to the limit and making bad decisions without any apparent support or guidance from his teacher. This challenge created rifts among the order's leaders. Martin sided with Marcos and refused to teach Pierre any longer. Like so many others who had gone against Martin in the past, Pierre too, was now discarded and left to his own devices. He moved to Cape Town to take over the order there, believing he might be able to do some good and at least help the poor souls in that part of the world. He began to deeply regret the part he played in revitalising the organisation so many years ago, realising for the first time that something was dreadfully wrong and Martin was not all he appeared to be. His departure was a sad time for all, as he was the one person out of the three who had his feet on the ground and who subtly maintained the balance of power at Viewpoint.

With Pierre gone, the desire for cash went nuclear, but Marcos wasn't coping at all. His health was suffering badly, and his girlfriend of fifteen years – who, like Pierre, had calmed his erratic behaviour – walked out. He began relationships with several neophyte members who couldn't wait to be bedded by their charismatic and powerful guru. These were the same behaviours that his own guru had been accused of a few years earlier. With all the stress, his painful pancreatitis flared with a vengeance. He became addicted to Pethadine (a high-dosage pain killer), which contributed to his decline, his erratic and out-of-character behaviour and a drastic increase in the volume of donations required to sustain the order. I eventually understood why the cost of building our house had doubled overnight!

A year after Pierre left, Marcos, too, had his own falling-out with Martin, a man whom he'd idolised as a father for many years. I suspect that he, too, had discovered that the order did not carry the legacy that Martin professed and that Martin himself was just like the Wizard of Oz – nothing more than a frail and elderly professor, himself lost and alone, hiding behind a giant curtain, using smokescreens and loud booming voices to create the illusion of power, until Toto the dog inadvertently revealed the truth.

In what must have been great disappointment and anger, which would explain his erratic behaviour, Marcos began to orchestrate another split in the order. Using funds donated by a wealthy member, he bought a farm in the Natal Midlands and started rallying his loyal subjects around him, with plans to create a new community far from Johannesburg. Realising that Marcos had rumbled him, and that his own pupil was in fact more powerful than he was in terms of magical abilities, Martin was scared. He sent in the 'heavies' to forcibly remove Marcos from the property – a task that many were willing to undertake, as Marcos was not well-respected by many of his comrades. Several were glad to see the back of him, particularly those who'd been waiting in the sidelines for an opportunity to prove themselves.

And so the deception continued. Under the instructions of Martin, Marcos' replacement quickly smoothed over the whole affair, again rallying the troops as their predecessors had done before them, proclaiming Martin's innocence, now that Marcos was not there to defend himself and Pierre was in Cape Town. And so began a new reign of tyranny designed to maintain fear and control among the membership base. Many members who didn't toe the line (some who had been there for many years), were gradually pushed aside. Martin once again welcomed new members who wouldn't ask any difficult questions, who would be more than willing to donate cash and to work themselves to the bone on projects and businesses for Martin and his order. The shape-shifter guru archetype was alive and well in the system.

When one is searching for the answers to perennial questions of existence, one will go to extraordinary lengths to hold onto a system or teaching that makes sense, even if it means putting oneself in great danger or turning a blind eye to the suffering of others. It is easy to ignore the inner voice that protests loudly from deep within. In his book, *The Tipping Point*, Malcolm Gladwell cites how Catholic priests in training, their eyes firmly fixed on God, blindly stepped over homeless people in the street as they rushed to achieve last-minute academic deadlines that would secure their future. In the same way, fledgling initiates, mightily serious about their spiritual journey, wanted to make their way to the revered 4th Initiation, to get to the *meat* of the teachings, turning a blind eye to the sacrifice and suffering of others. Caught up in a spiritual culture inspired by a great purpose and vision, it is hard, perhaps impossible to go against the grain, particularly when there is so much at stake. Had I not been at the heart of the organisation, after throwing myself headlong into this journey, I, too, would still perhaps be holding on for dear life, oblivious to what was really going on, ignoring my intuition, just to get a glimpse of the wisdom and magic that lay just out of reach.

Then there arises the question of how to find the real guru. Very often people are in doubt. They do not know if the guru they see is a true or false guru. Frequently a person comes in contact with a false guru in a world where there is so much falsehood. But at the same time, a real seeker, one who is not false to himself, will always meet with the truth, with the real, because it is his own real faith, his own sincerity in earnest seeking that will be his torch. The real teacher is within, the lover of reality is one's own sincere self, and if one is really seeking truth, sooner or later, one will certainly find a true teacher. And supposing one came into contact with a false teacher, what then? Then the real one will turn the false teacher into a real teacher because REALITY is greater than falsehood.

Inayat Khan (1882–1927)
Sufi mystic

Martin died of a heart attack in June, 2011. One will never truly understand why he felt it necessary to fabricate elaborate stories about the order's heritage and his own guru status. Perhaps his propensity for power and greed became magnified on his own spiritual journey when he, too, embarked on a version of the frame exercise.[3] Playing with subtle energies like kundalini is not child's play, and exercises like Kundalini yoga and Hatha yoga should be undertaken with the guidance of an experienced teacher who has walked the path himself. Unless one is totally balanced in all three bodies, mental, emotional and physical and has a strong grip on his desires and the ego, unleashing the kundalini energy by even a fraction creates havoc in the life of the pupil, sometimes sending him completely off the rails. Without a true guru as a guide, one is literally playing with fire. I wondered if the same fate had also befallen Marcos, who was undertaking Martin's version of the frame exercise. As Martin was not a true guru and had certainly not 'seen the light' himself, even though he consistently claimed he had, Marcos was literally on his own.

However, it was the mystique that Martin had created around his 'school' that kept people coming back, together with the subtle promise that they too might one day uncover the secret exercises that would propel their own spiritual development. Martin vehemently protected these for many years until certain pupils proved themselves 'worthy' in his eyes. Without doubt, the mystery he created, coupled with the opportunity to uncover 'secret knowledge' that couldn't be found elsewhere, laid out in a neatly structured system of instruction had a huge sense of appeal.[6] Perhaps nothing is more powerfully motivating than a rallying purpose and a worthy cause with a noble heritage – one that allows people for once in their life to truly believe they are indeed part of something special and that the miraculous does indeed exist. In today's world where many people are disillusioned and jaded by life, possibly there would be few who are not at least a little curious.

The teachings at Viewpoint bridged the spiritual gap between East and West in a way that I have never since experienced. Perhaps I never will again. Eventually, I came to terms with the fact that, in any search for truth, we will always encounter the false, no matter how much we might like to believe that the spiritual path we are travelling is indeed the path of righteousness. Part of our 'pilgrimage through matter' is to develop the ability to discriminate between truth and falsehood, to separate the wheat from the chaff. To do this effectively, we have to traverse a number of dangerous terrains, learning from experiences and becoming a little wiser each time.

I was again reminded of the powerful and destructive influence of the guru in October of 2009, when James Arthur Ray, a self-appointed spiritual teacher and motivational speaker, was arrested in connection with the deaths of three disciples in Sedona, USA, after a sweat lodge exercise he'd facilitated went horribly wrong. Eighteen other pupils were hospitalised, suffering from burns, breathing problems and kidney failure. People had pushed themselves to the limits to fit in with the crowd, to be accepted, ignoring the messages that their failing bodies were sending to them, each one desperately searching for the wisdom that this man seemingly possessed and might be available to them if they could withstand the discomfort for just another minute. James Ray was later tried for manslaughter.

THE MYTH AND ITS MEANING:
Perseus and the Gorgon (Part III)

After the ordeal is over, the seeker makes his return to the everyday world. However, the road back has its own set of trials and challenges, as Perseus discovered. The journey home is almost as important as the ordeal itself.

On his way back to Seriphos with the head of the Gorgon, he stops in the kingdom of Ethiopia ruled by King Cepheus and Queen Cassiopeia. The kingdom was in trouble. The queen's vanity had angered Poseidon, who sent an inundation to the land, as well as a sea serpent, Cetus, which persecuted Ethiopia, destroying man and beast. The oracle of Ammon announced that no relief would be found until the king sacrificed his own daughter Andromeda to the monster. Andromeda is chained to a rock awaiting her destiny when Perseus arrives. Full of pity and indignation at the barbarity of the situation, he leaps to save the princess. With his special skills and weapons, gained along his journey to the Gorgon's lair, he slays the monster and claims the hand of Andromeda in marriage. But Andromeda had already been promised to another, an Ethiopian Prince called Phineas, who had stood back in fear, watching his bride-to-be being led to her fate, and who had now come to claim her with an army of one thousand men. When they tried to set upon Perseus, he brought the head of the Gorgon from its satchel, and holding it high by the writhing serpents that leapt from its scalp, turned it to face the army of men, turning them all to stone.

Leaving Ethiopia and taking the fair Andromeda with him, Perseus returned to Seriphos arriving in the nick of time. The tyrant King Polydectus had forcibly removed his mother Danae from her refuge in the temple and was about to marry her against her will. Perseus arrived at the wedding, mocked by the king and all his lords and princes (who were feasting and merrymaking), for daring to show his face again in Seriphos without completing his task. When the taunts subsided, Perseus sprang to protect his mother, saying, 'I have brought you a present at last, O King, one for you and each of your mocking friends.' And with his words, he pulled the Gorgon's head from his satchel, holding it up for all – except his mother – to see, and the king and his wedding guests met the same fate as Phineas and his army.

Upon leaving Seriphos with his bride, his mother and the kindly fisherman Dictys, Perseus returned to Argos where he wished to make peace with his grandfather, Acrisius, who had imprisoned his mother in a tower so many years before. However Acrisius had fled to Larissa after his wicked brother Proteus had waged war against him and captured Argos. The people of the land pleaded with Perseus to help them.

After defeating Proteus, Perseus was made king of Argos. But he still sought to make peace with his grandfather and so made his way to Larissa to find him. When he arrived, there was feasting and all kinds of games taking place in honour of Acrisius. Perseus was asked to take part, which he agreed to do, but he did not tell them his name, thinking that if he carried away the prize, his grandfather might soften towards him and he could be reunited with his kin once more. He was the best man of all in the running, leaping, wrestling and javelin-throwing competitions, and won four crowns. But there was a fifth crown to be won in a discus-throwing competition. As before, Perseus put out all his strength and hurled it five fathoms beyond all the rest. But a sudden gust of wind came from the sea and took one discus way off course, striking the elderly king dead. The prophecy Acrisius had tried so hard to avoid had at last come true.

Perseus wept and told everyone of the prophecy and his journey to seek the Gorgon. A great mourning took place and Perseus went to the temple where he was purified from the guilt of his grandfather's death, for he had done it unknowingly.

Then he went home to Argos, and reigned there well with the fair Andromeda. They had four sons and three daughters and died in a good old age.

And when they died, the ancients say, Athene took them up into the sky with Cepheus and Cassipoeia, and there on a starlit night you may see them shining still.

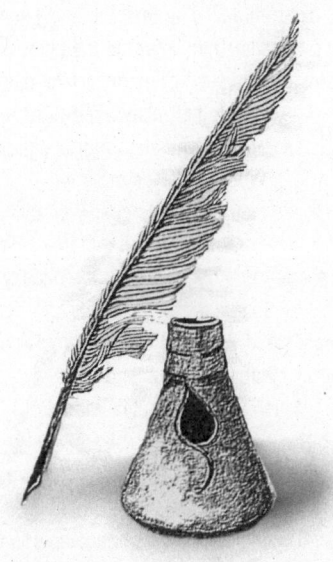

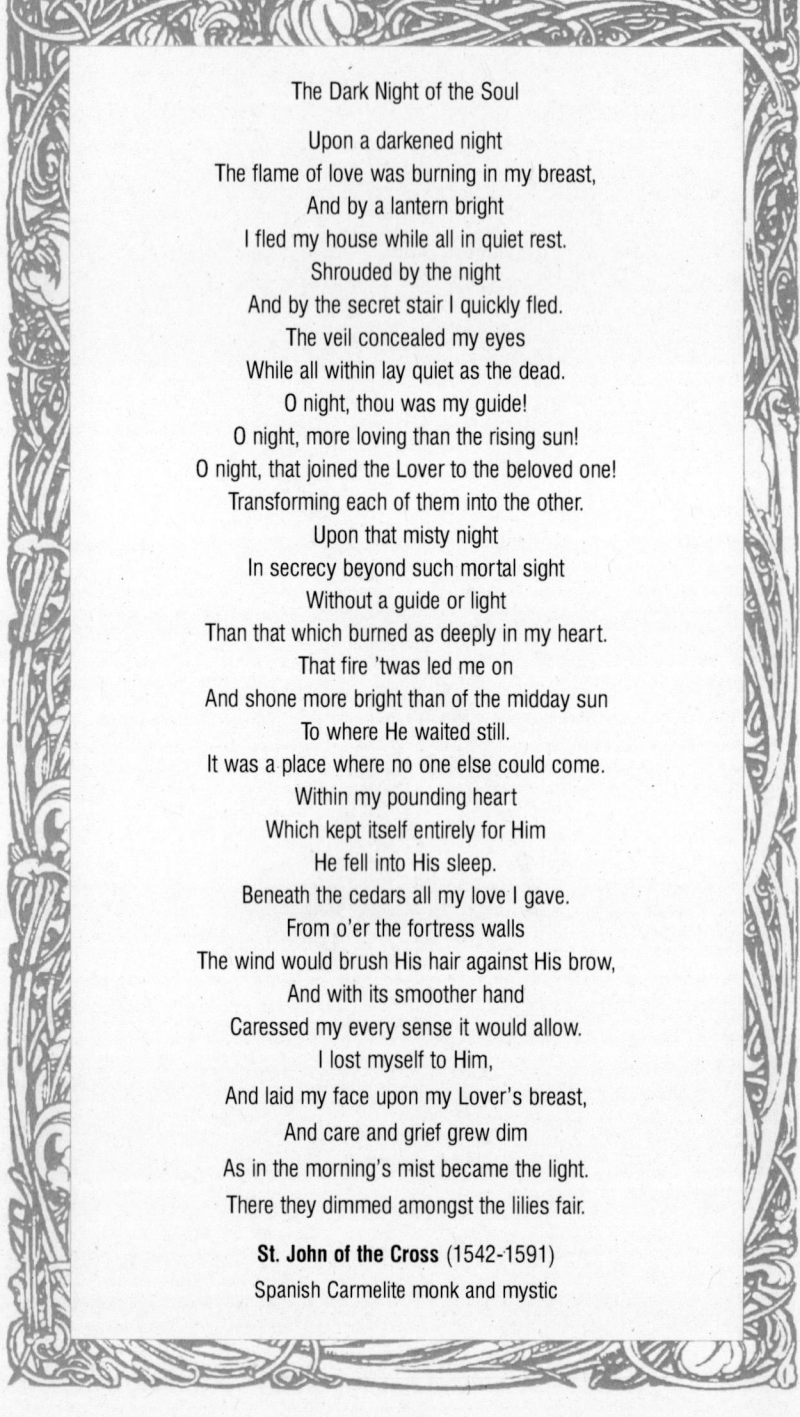

The Dark Night of the Soul

Upon a darkened night
The flame of love was burning in my breast,
And by a lantern bright
I fled my house while all in quiet rest.
Shrouded by the night
And by the secret stair I quickly fled.
The veil concealed my eyes
While all within lay quiet as the dead.
O night, thou was my guide!
O night, more loving than the rising sun!
O night, that joined the Lover to the beloved one!
Transforming each of them into the other.
Upon that misty night
In secrecy beyond such mortal sight
Without a guide or light
Than that which burned as deeply in my heart.
That fire 'twas led me on
And shone more bright than of the midday sun
To where He waited still.
It was a place where no one else could come.
Within my pounding heart
Which kept itself entirely for Him
He fell into His sleep.
Beneath the cedars all my love I gave.
From o'er the fortress walls
The wind would brush His hair against His brow,
And with its smoother hand
Caressed my every sense it would allow.
I lost myself to Him,
And laid my face upon my Lover's breast,
And care and grief grew dim
As in the morning's mist became the light.
There they dimmed amongst the lilies fair.

St. John of the Cross (1542-1591)
Spanish Carmelite monk and mystic

STAGE 15

FALLING BACK

In myth, as in life, would-be heroes forever face the possibility of losing their way. Those who have progressed some way along the path towards truth, who have gained some knowledge and insight, are continually tested – tempted by wealth, power or material desires. Those who become careless, overly confident or renege on their promises, ignoring the helpful advice from a wise crone or ally, often meet a difficult and sometimes painful end.

During my ordeal at Viewpoint, I had lost focus on my career. I sought various coaching and facilitation contracts to keep me busy and to keep cash rolling in, but work came sporadically and was fraught with its own difficulties. My heart wasn't in it anyway. I'd set my sights on working for God and completing a spiritual journey which I figured would take the rest of my natural life and when it was cut short, I couldn't muster up the enthusiasm to do anything else with gusto. The motivation for anything to do with life in general had virtually disappeared.

As much as I was relieved to get away from the intensity and claustrophobia at Viewpoint, returning to the ordinary world, alone, now in greater debt than ever, was a daunting prospect. In his book, *A Path with Heart,* Jack Kornfield explains how, after spending many years in Thailand, Burma and India, training as a Buddhist monk, he returned to the shores of North America once more with only his monk's robes, having to start his life in the ordinary world over again. I began to deeply understand how he must have felt.

But I realised when I got back that the time for sentimentality and emotion was over. There was work to be done. With my savings almost depleted and bills to pay, I had to earn some serious money. The most logical course of action was to head back into the world of business and find a place to 'fit' where

I might benefit from the company of like-minded individuals and perhaps forget about the events of the last few years. With the help of an old acquaintance, I secured a three-month contract with a company to turn their marketing department around. It was going to be a tough assignment – I was going to be clearing up the mess that the organisation's entrepreneurial founders had ignored for years, sweeping issues under the carpet in the hope that someone, anyone, might magically fix them overnight. It was an initiation of fire back into the ordinary world, taking every ounce of my strength to keep my own fragile psyche together while I struggled to deal with maverick leaders who fought against everything they'd asked me to do. The contrast between the two worlds was enormous, but somehow – I don't know how – I managed to pull it off. At the end of the contract, the company was delighted with what I'd achieved and offered me a full time position as a director, which I politely declined. I was the wrong fit for that organisation – the wrong fit for *any* organisation – and I knew beyond any shadow of a doubt that I couldn't go back into a corporate world. Yet again, the same old question returned to haunt me: So what now?

Although I soldiered on, as one does when one has only oneself to rely on, I was vulnerable and traumatised by the events of the last two years and I should have sought help in fully integrating myself with the world again. But how could I explain my ordeal to anyone? I understood the theory, 'Be in the world but not of it', but trying to live it was another matter. At the time, I was still floundering, searching for anwers, endeavouring to make sense out of the last few years, trying to figure out if I'd just been gullible and stupid for seeking something more, for finding myself in some god-awful cult, or if there was indeed a higher purpose that had taken me there in the first place. I didn't believe that I could confide in anyone. Psychologists would surely have me committed.

Caught between the dread of returning to a full-time executive role and the unreachable realms of higher consciousness that I so desperately desired, I began to understand what St John of the Cross meant when he wrote of the 'dark night of the soul' – the distractions and entanglements of the world when travelling along the 'narrow way' that Jesus spoke of. (Matthew 7:13-14).

The dark night is a very private matter, not something that one can readily share with others. After throwing myself head-first into my spiritual journey for many years, and being so disillusioned by my guru and his guru in turn, it was hard not to feel bitter and frustrated. As a sincere seeker, I had progressed through many significant stages of spiritual growth and expanded my consciousness in all directions. Although I still had a long way to go, I wasn't the same person that arrived in South Africa all those years ago. From being an agnostic, perhaps even a complete atheist, I now yearned to be more deeply in touch with the higher realms, to have greater wisdom and understanding; but the journey I'd sacrificed so much for had been cut short. I felt painfully lost and alone. On the outside I presented to the world the perfect picture of togetherness, the face that I believed everyone else wanted to see. I was light and dismissive about my experience when I spoke to others. But inside, I suffered greatly. Where I could, I avoided those individuals I knew would ask difficult questions. I spent many lonely nights in tears as I tried to rationalise my experience, focusing on what I'd gained instead of what I'd lost. But deep inside, the disappointment gnawed away, accompanied by a profound sense of hopelessness and despair. Once again I felt like I didn't fit anywhere, that I was inadequate, not knowing what to do next. I was an exile from both worlds, alienated and confused.

However, things were about to change. A CEO friend of mine, whom I'd recently supported through a tough divorce, introduced me to a company called Blu-prints, which she'd just engaged to 'unify the culture' of her securities business. I met with the company's unconventional but brilliant founder, Guy Martin, an ex-fighter pilot in the British RAF, who walked me through his unique 'formula concept' using mathematics and art, one which he'd initially developed for his own logistics business, but after having spent much time in commercialising the product, was now rolling it out into large, multinational corporations as a tool for change. Since leaving Virgin, I'd been fascinated with the concept of culture and its power to build and destroy any group. Coupled with my coaching and organisational development experience and newly acquired metaphysical understanding of archetypes and the power of the 'collective unconscious', I instantly connected with Guy and his company. He was looking for another partner who would be the right cultural fit, someone with exactly my background who could work with clients alongside him and his colleague, Craig, to take the business international. When he offered me the position, I had to pinch myself. I had at long last found a place in which I could be myself, express myself and undertake work that I was completely passionate about.

Blu-prints was blissfully un-corporate and attracted entrepreneurial individuals who, like me, didn't easily fit into bureaucratic business structures and who quite simply wanted to make businesses a *better place to be*. The office itself was like an oversized, brightly lit toy cupboard, more akin to an off-the-wall advertising agency than a serious cultural transformation business: But then again, that was part of its appeal to clients: artwork, quirky models, antiques, photographs and paintings adorned the small space, abuzz with activity as the multi-talented staff engaged in operational and artistic pursuits and the contracts poured in. However, its clients were very much the opposite: large, multinational corporations facing all the issues that big companies face with strategy and culture. I watched bemused as board directors from a plethora of industries sat through meetings and presentations in the boardroom, mesmerised by their surroundings, the ingenuity of the concept and the possibilities that now came to light for their own organisation. There was a sense of magic and enchantment within Blu-prints that is so rarely found in business today, and I am convinced that many leaders believed that if they bought just a little piece of this magic, their organisations, too, would be enthused with the same.

As far as my job was concerned, closing deals was a breeze. In the first eighteen months I worked on six large projects, each spanning many months, getting to know the intricate nature of each organisation: the boardroom dynamics, the highs and lows, the strengths and weaknesses and the nature of each client's business. But most of all, I delighted in the success that each of these brave organisations achieved after many months of hard effort using Blu-prints as the catalyst for transformation.

For the first time in years, I started to have a lot of fun at work again. My zest for life returned. I felt that my occupation mattered, that I was making a difference. I had the freedom to come and go as I pleased, a great team of people to work with, and most of all, in this 'delicate' time, a place to belong.

But more importantly, as I closed deal after deal, and the contracts continued to roll in, I started to earn a lot of money. With the trend set to continue into the distant future as the business started to take small steps into the global markets, I was ecstatic. Over the course of two years, I paid my debts, invested money, purchased Peter's share of the property in Lone Hill, and started to live life to the full yet again. I even bought myself a new car, a Mercedes SLK. I'd never before owned a sports car, and I loved the feeling of freedom, the wind in my hair, the speed and the looks I got from male admirers. The gods were indeed smiling on me.

With my new-found success and financial stability, the pendulum was making a full swing in the opposite direction. The ordeal at Viewpoint was still ever present in my mind, and with many of the questions about what I'd been involved in still unanswered, I started to feel irritated with talk of spiritual things. I initially tried to sustain my exercises and studies, determined that I would not let my spiritual practices drop, but the demands of the ordinary world became more pressing and more appealing. Working with rich and powerful individuals, many of whom became my friends, and without the continuous guidance of my teacher, the regular lectures and disciplined regime of exercises, my spiritual journey became a distant memory.

If all you have is a few copper coins in one pocket, those coins are of great value to you. But if someone places a thousand gold pieces in your other pocket , those few copper coins are no longer important.

Bhai Sahib (d. 1966)
Sufi adept and teacher of Sufi mystic Irina Tweedie.

However, my exciting sojourn in the ordinary world was to be short lived. At the beginning of 2008 the great global financial crisis hit South Africa. My sales pipeline dried up almost overnight as clients reined in their expenditure, cut costs and bolted down the hatches to weather the storm. When times are hard, the last thing companies will consider investing in is culture, clinging to the one they have like limpets to a rock, even though it may be dysfunctional.

At first, I wasn't concerned, as I had enough savings in reserve to last for a while and I was sure that it would be situation normal again in a few months. So I changed my sales tactics and looked further afield for contracts. For over twelve months, I travelled, networked, cold-called, presented, formed alliances, wrote articles for magazines and joined professional associations. I tried everything I knew to convince, cajole and entice, but to no avail. By March of 2009, I was at the end of my tether. I hadn't been successful in securing one piece of new business, and with only a few months of money left, I was once more staring into the abyss. I found myself driving home from yet another unfruitful meeting, scared and alone, watching as more and more white people took to the streets to beg, alongside their black brethren. Perhaps they had always been there, I had just been too caught up in my own world to even notice them. I wondered how soon it might be before I would be joining them.

The strange thing was that nothing in my life seemed to be working, as though there were some divine plan afoot to topple me from my success. Business alliances I'd formed proved wholly unsatisfactory, many of them downright abusive. Everywhere I turned for professional help and comfort, I would find sharks with several layers of teeth ready to take advantage of the situation. Cruelty, disinterest, greed and the survival instinct seemed to outweigh any love and compassion. I suddenly became acutely aware of how pitiless humanity can be in times of crisis. It really was a case of every man for himself. All the new-found friends and acquaintances I'd made were conspicuous by their absence as they, too, struggled with their own battles for survival. My world, just like the entire world, was in chaos. I started to panic, making many stupid judgement calls and decisions as I tried to fire-fight or rectify situations that seemed to be escalating out of control. I found myself slipping further and further downwards in this increasing spiral of doom. To top it all, in the space of a few weeks my entire support system fell away as if years of unresolved tension had suddenly burst to the surface. My mum sided with my sister in a family dispute and disowned me, and I fell out with two of my closest friends, one of whom I'd walked through fire with at Viewpoint.

I tried to convince myself that there were people struggling far more than I out there, that the path of the spiritual warrior required overcoming many hardships and battles, but it did nothing to stave off the turbulent emotions of loneliness, fear and worry that raged within. Like the mythological hero Bellerophon, I had perhaps flown too high and was now rushing headlong towards earth.

The final blow came in March of 2009 when I discovered with horror that an investment I'd been relying on to see me through the next few years had hit the wall. I'd lost a lot of money, as had several hundred other people around the globe. I'd fought hard to keep my head above water, dreading slipping back into the same feelings of despair I'd had so many years before. I found myself going around in circles, paralysed with fear, unable to make a decision. This was the final straw. I had to face facts. I had to sell my car (which had somehow defined my success), and started to make plans to put my house on the market, hoping against all odds that I might recoup at least some money.

I struggled to put on a brave face around my remaining friends and acquaintances, fearful of letting them see I was an emotional wreck. But I wasn't succeeding. The betrayals and traumas of the last few years gradually pushed their way to the surface and I began to fall apart. I felt overwhelmed with pain, sadness, disorientation and confusion, with all emotions, one not distinguishable from the next, converging into an ocean of nausea and panic. There seemed to be no release; the tears just wouldn't come. Daybreak was the worst time. As the effects of sleeping pills subsided I would open my eyes at dawn to the bright African sunshine and wish I could end it all. As I took my firearm from under my pillow to its day-time abode in the gun safe in my bedroom, I felt as if I were sitting on the threshold of life and death, suspended on an invisible thread, one which could break at any moment. Without the understanding gained from my spiritual studies as to what happens to those who take their own lives, I doubt I would be here today.

Somewhere from deep within I knew that I had to go on, that this pain was only making me stronger, more powerful, that perhaps I was paying my 'karmic debts', from which there is no escape; and that if we give in to the darkness, we receive but a temporary respite, only to have to face the same trials again with a greater intensity next time around. In Hindu mythology, *Lila* is the great cosmic game or play – an illusion in which we become lost. Nothing is really real. Pondering this, I decided that I needed to get help instead of watching like a silent observer from the sidelines as my world fell apart.

Reluctantly, I once again visited my GP, who this time prescribed Paroxetene (Paxil), an SSRI anti-depressant. Whether they really helped or were just a placebo, I didn't really care at this point. I needed to function. I also sought the help of a psychologist recommended by my colleague, Craig, who had recently been through his own trauma, having been gagged, bound and beaten in his own home at gunpoint while his attackers ransacked his house – par for the course in Johannesburg!

I spent several weeks of counselling with a lady called Wendy Hay from the Bellavida Centre. She helped me piece together the events of the last few years and the reasons behind my insatiable drive for meaning and purpose. It was exactly the kind of support that I needed, and uncovered more than I'd bargained for.

Since embarking on my spiritual path, I had tried hard to rationalise the betrayals, the pain and the events of my life from an almost super-human spiritual perspective, in perhaps the same way as a *warrior* or *initiate* would – in the same way that Marcos would. I found it easy to elevate a situation to its 'divine level' (or so I thought), which would give it meaning and significance and provide me with the courage and motivation to keep going. But in my desire to find an identity 'beyond the veil', I'd lost sight of the fact that I was also a human being with endless flaws, foibles and limitations. I was vulnerable and alone, at my lowest ebb and probably facing some of the toughest years of my life. Perhaps I had to be pushed to the brink to find some love and compassion for myself. For the first time, perhaps ever, I began to accept myself as being human.

St John of the Cross taught that if you seek God you will eventually cast off all attachments to the material world, but to do so, you must first pass through a period, perhaps many periods, of great disillusionment, fear and doubt. The dark night is a time of testing, a time of great suffering and pain and agony, accompanied by uncertainty, confusion and fear. You find yourself in a space where you don't know where you are *spiritually*, separated from both God and man, not knowing which way to turn. But on the other side of the darkness, should you be determined and strong enough to make your way through, a mystical union with God awaits, and perhaps the answers to the questions that you have fervently sought become clear.

Over the last few years, I had so often doubted whether the spiritual path I'd embarked on was right and true, whether I shouldn't just forget the whole affair when it proved to be just as full of disappointments as the world of everyday things. For long periods, I mistrusted anything 'spiritual', and as a result, I experienced the deepest misery and pain. The outer world was unable to heal me. No material possessions could make me whole, and not even my closest friends could bring me peace. When we set out in earnest on a spiritual path, we cannot turn back; the gates into the ordinary world are closed forever.

THE MYTH AND ITS MEANING:
Bellerophon and Pegasus

Individuals who lose their way in the myths are often depicted as being turned into salt or stone. In the biblical tale of Sodom and Gomorrah, Lot's wife was turned into a pillar of salt as she turned and looked longingly back on the corrupt kingdom of Sodom, failing to heed the warning of the angels of deliverance.

In the Nordic tale of 'The Giant Who Had No Heart in his Body', six brothers sent on a quest by their father, the king, forgot a promise they'd made to their younger brother and for their foolishness were each turned into stone by a giant. Their younger brother had to go in search of the giant's heart, which held the key to their misfortune, and with the help of a beautiful princess he was able to restore them to life. The Catalans tell a similar tale of brothers who set out on a quest for the 'water of life'. They meet with a giant who tells them they will have to walk past a *wall of stones* that would chide and mock them furiously. If they did not respond, if they did not forget their quest, they could continue unencumbered on their journey. But if they allowed the taunts to get the better of them, if they turned to look at the wall, they, too, would be turned to stone. Each brother failed, turning in anger and humiliation to hurl a rock at the wall when the taunts became too much. They could only be saved by a few drops from the magical waters of life, which was eventually retrieved by their younger sister, whose innocence and steadfastness enabled her to ignore the taunts and walk past unencumbered.

In Greek mythology, Bellerophon was the son of King Glaucus of Corinth and the grandson of Sisyphus. He was exiled from the kingdom after accidentally killing his own brother and sought protection in a neighbouring kingdom, ruled by King Proteus of Tiryns. Proteus' wife, Anteia, took a shine to the handsome young hero, and tried to seduce him, but Bellerophon resisted her. Angry at being rejected, Anteia told her husband that Bellerophon had instead tried to ravish her. Proteus was furious but did not want to seek revenge on his guest, so he sent Bellerophon to Anteia's father, King Iobates of Lycia, asking him to dispose of the presumptuous man. Not willing to undertake the task of killing Bellerophon himself, Iobates sent him on a dangerous mission from which he would surely never return – a mission to slay the Chimaera, a fire-breathing monster with the head of a lion, the body of a goat, and the tail of a serpent. With the help of the gods, Bellerophon tamed the winged horse Pegasus, who helped him in his task. When Bellerophon returned unscathed, the frustrated Iobates sent him on another task to defeat the warlike Solymi and the Amazons, a race of women who fought like men. Upon returning from that also, the exasperated king set the palace guards against him. With the help of Poseidon, Bellerophon caused a great flood to strike Lycia, and Iobates finally realized that with such a sign from the

Gods, Bellerophon must be innocent of all charges laid against him. Upon discovering the truth, Iobates gave Bellerophon one of his daughters as a bride and made him heir to the throne of Lycía.

Proud of his success, Bellerophon felt that because of his victories he deserved to fly to Mount Olympus, the realm of the gods. However, his conjecture angered Zeus and he sent a gadfly to sting Pegasus, causing the horse to buck, sending Bellerophon falling headlong back to earth. He lived the rest of his life in misery, a blinded, crippled hermit, shunning the haunts of men until he died.

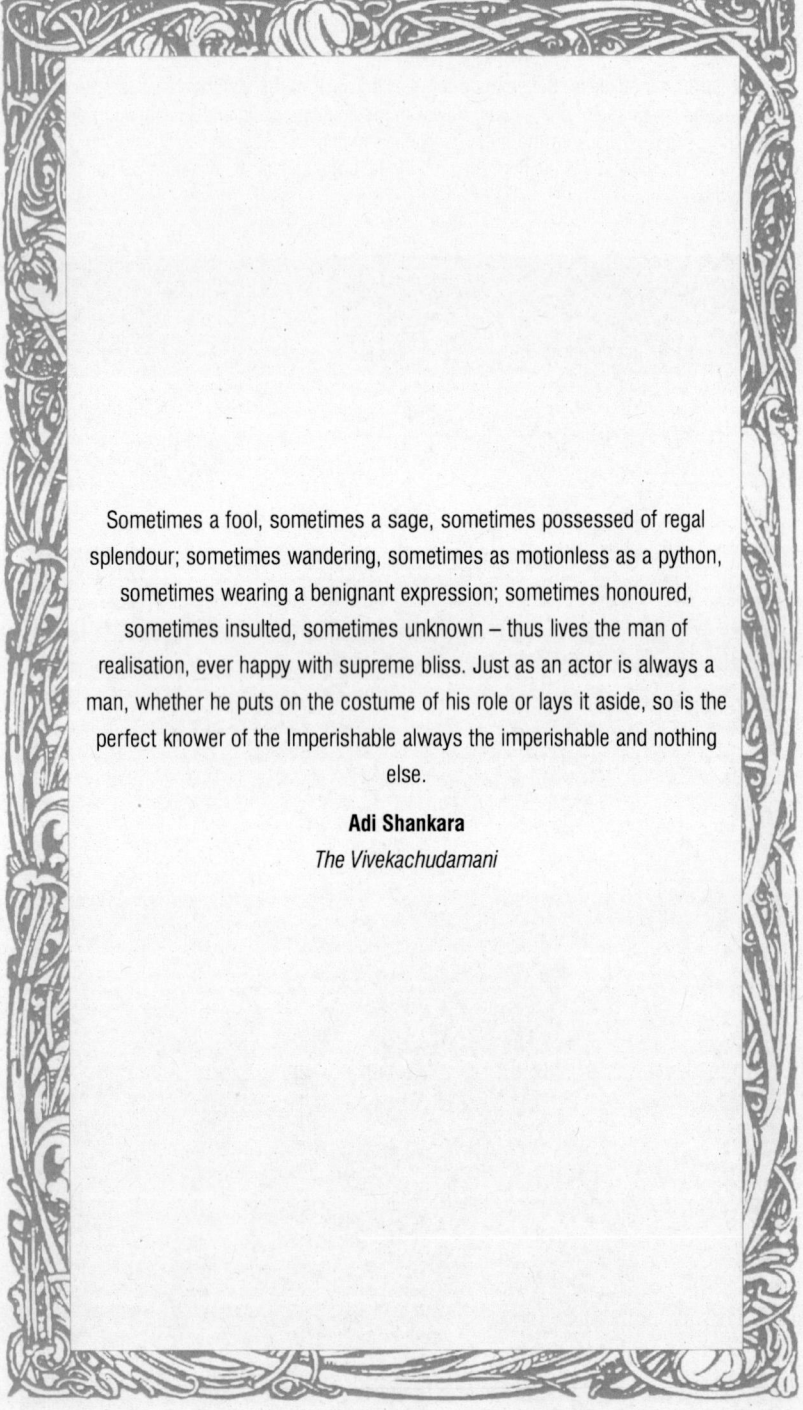

Sometimes a fool, sometimes a sage, sometimes possessed of regal splendour; sometimes wandering, sometimes as motionless as a python, sometimes wearing a benignant expression; sometimes honoured, sometimes insulted, sometimes unknown – thus lives the man of realisation, ever happy with supreme bliss. Just as an actor is always a man, whether he puts on the costume of his role or lays it aside, so is the perfect knower of the Imperishable always the imperishable and nothing else.

Adi Shankara
The Vivekachudamani

STAGE 16

FREEDOM TO LIVE

The two worlds, the divine and the human, can be pictured only as distinct from each other, different as life and death, as day and night. The hero adventures out of the land we know into darkness, there he accomplishes his adventure, or again is simply lost to us, imprisoned or in danger; and his return is described as coming back out of that yonder zone. Nevertheless – and here is a great key to the understanding of myth and symbol – the two kingdoms are actually one. The realm of the gods is a forgotten dimension of the world we know.

Joseph Campbell
The Hero with a Thousand Faces

ounselling with Wendy helped me in more ways than I imagined. Since childhood, I'd believed myself to be an oddball, one that didn't fit easily with the rest of the world. Overly sensitive, always searching, looking, never satisfied with life, and especially since I'd left Virgin and the regularity of fulltime employment, I believed myself to be fickle and hopeless. I didn't seem to be able to make it alone, nor fit into the corporate world either. It was this desire to find a *home* that drove me towards a spiritual solution – a search for identity and meaning in a world that just didn't make a lot of sense. It became my driving purpose, my reason for being. It answered all my questions. But when my path was cut short once again, I found myself floundering and lost in the 'dark night of the soul'.

Over the last twenty years, I'd undertaken a number of 'personality profiling' assignments, designed to test ones aptitude for a specific career or organisational culture fit. They each served a purpose, but not one of them really provided the much needed insight into my somewhat eccentric nature, other than to highlight specific tendencies and character flaws. But Wendy was about to change all of that. She introduced me to the Keirsey Temperament Test, developed by Prof. David Keirsey and outlined in his book, *Please Understand*

163

Me. It was the missing piece of the puzzle. Combining the work of the ancients (Hippocrates and Galen), Carl Jung and his theory of archetype, the Myers-Brigg type indicator, and many other professionals in the field of the behavioural sciences, Prof. Keirsey had placed a modern day spin on the ancient study of one's true nature – temperament, character and personality, taking into consideration that one is already highly formed at birth.

I found myself to be (as Wendy had rightly assumed) an INFP: an 'idealist healer', the temperament displayed by many artists, writers, musicians, playwrights, character actors, ministers, philosophers and counsellors of the world. According to David Keirsey, 'Plato was the quintessential idealist – seeing the inspiring idealists as the philosopher kings of his ideal Republic, destined to serve a philosophical function in society, their job no less than to divine moral principles and the full meaning of life.'

INFPs make up less than 1% of the total population (no wonder I felt like an oddball), and the hardest place for them to fit is in the harsh world of business. The realisation suddenly dawned on me that for my entire life I'd been forcing myself into a career space in which I could never possibly fully succeed. Whilst I had become adept at taking centre stage during my roles in sales, leadership and facilitation, to sustain it, continuously, day after day required an enormous effort, which took its toll on my well-being. I often needed to retreat into privacy and isolation, sometimes for days on end, to contemplate the mysteries of life and regain my sense of wholeness. My natural drive and tenacity had seen that I would make a success out of anything that I turned my attention to, but I was being unrealistic. No wonder I was tired, jaded, stressed out, depressed and seeking a way out. This insight was the first powerful stage in my healing process, although deep down I felt as if I'd always known it; I just needed to make sense of it. For the first time in a long time, I felt a tremendous sense of relief.

To understand Healers, we must understand their idealism as almost boundless and selfless, inspiring them to make extraordinary sacrifices for someone or something they believe in. The Healer is the Prince or Princess of fairy tale, the King's Champion or Defender of the Faith....

David Keirsey
'The Portrait of a Healer Idealist'

It was with this realisation that things started to take a turn for the better – almost as if the dam had burst and all the impurities were now leaving my system. Around the same time there were a lot of water problems in my life: my car radiator sprang a leak; my house was flooded during a tumultuous Highveld storm; a water main burst outside my front gate and spewed litres of precious water through my garden for seven days before Johannesburg City Council did anything to fix it. Water is deeply symbolic of emotion. I guess there had been a lot of pent up emotion for many years in that place, and now it was to come flooding out. With the understanding that pursuing a business career was the wrong avenue for me, I needed to find another way to earn a living, one that might not be as lucrative financially but would allow me to be myself, whilst honouring my highest sense of purpose and integrity. At the age of 44, I was going to be starting my career all over again and I needed to find a way to do it. I was getting used to turbulent change in my life by now, but first I had to fully heal.

To overcome my sleep disorder, depression and chronic fatigue after years of stress, I used hypnotherapy, natural remedies and energy medicine, with the aid of the SCIO biofeedback machine. (SCIO stands for The Scientific Consciousness Interface Operating System, a device that treats the entire body system, developed by Prof. Bill Nelson for stress detection and stress reduction. See appendix.) It really helped my body to heal. I realised then how much I was drawn to the field of spiritual and emotional wellness, to health and healing. After all, this seemed to be what my own life's work had been about. So I purchased a SCIO machine and embarked on a diploma in hypnotherapy, naturopathy and energy medicine, a journey that would perhaps take me many years to complete, but would doubtless be my focus for the future. It seemed like a natural adjunct to the skills I'd developed over the last few years – NLP coaching,[7] leadership facilitation and the mental and emotional well-being of people within organisations. So perhaps the step was not too large after all.

But there was another dimension in my career to be considered, one that came from out of the blue. I never cease to be amazed at how well the universe, the divine scheme of things, life – whatever we want to call it – has a funny way of bringing us to a certain point, never in a way that we imagine. Over the previous twelve months I'd become involved with the Professional Speakers Organisation in South Africa, as public speaking was a large part of my work. I met a small group of kindred spirits who, like me, were trying to find different ways to promote their businesses during tough times. One of the ideas was to jointly write a business book, each contributing three chapters about our chosen subject. The thought of writing a book had never occurred to me. I didn't believe myself to be particularly creative or to have anything worthwhile to say that hadn't already been said. Yet when the suggestion was made, I received a powerful flash of insight that seemed to jerk my entire body into realisation.

I remembered how my junior school teacher, Mr Richards, had encouraged my parents to persuade me into a writing career at the age of seven. I'd always had a vivid imagination and an ability to conjure up entertaining short stories, even at that tender age – all the hallmarks of an unrecognised INFP child. For a number of reasons, the writing career didn't materialise then, but several decades later, I felt that I was onto something.

Like many of the relationships I'd founded during the turbulent 2009 recession, my relationship with this speaking group was fraught with disappointment and betrayals and it didn't survive, but my desire to write a book did. Only I didn't want to write a business book. The world has enough business books, most written by seasoned business veterans and MBA graduates – something that I wasn't. But there was a book churning around inside me vying for attention and dying to get out. I spent many nights at odd hours in front of the computer, writing down abstract ideas that came to mind. I also started to meet book coaches, writers, artists and poets everywhere I went, seemingly quite by accident. No doubt synchronicity was at play, but the structure for the book still didn't present itself; that is, until one Saturday morning during a marathon spinning class. I wasn't particularly paying attention to anything, other than trying to breathe, when the entire book downloaded in my head in an instant– the composition, the outline, the chapters, the links to mythology. It's the book you are reading today.

Under this deluge of self-realisations, my life seemed to be changing dramatically in a short space of time. I decided that if I was serious about writing a book, I'd need to focus on it wholeheartedly, not dabble with it over a period of several years, perhaps never completing it, as is the case with so many people. So I decided to actively sell my house and move out of Johannesburg. I was tired of living in my prison cell, as beautiful and tranquil as it was, not able to fully enjoy the outdoors for fear of crime. Besides, nothing was really working for me in this city, a sure indication that it was time to move onto something different. For over two years, I'd wanted to move to the ocean so that I could enjoy the outdoors. I'd toyed with the idea of living in Cape Town, which was trying to secede from the rest of Africa and the ANC, calling for a return to independence. I had several close friends there, some who'd made the move from Johannesburg and were enjoying life. I figured that I could live off the proceeds from the sale of my house for about two years, *if* I could sell it for my asking price. Maybe I'd also find a part-time job, something simple, to help pay the rental on a small garden cottage. I started to feel so free at the thought of not being tied to my large four-bedroom home, which I rattled around in alone, of no longer having a mortgage to pay, security and maintenance to worry about, and a whole heap of furniture and possessions to tie me down. I could at long last start to simplify my life and focus on what was really important.

Only I didn't end up in Cape Town. I'd just put my house on the market when I received an unexpected email from an old flame whom I'd dated almost twenty years earlier while living in the UK. His name was Steve and he now lived in New Zealand. We started having long daily conversations over the phone, sometimes lasting six or seven hours, and found that we had many things in common. Our lives seemed to carry some strange parallels and coincidences. After almost giving up on the idea of love, perhaps now at 45 years old I had at last found The One. Several months of dialogue passed, after which Steve sent me a ticket to visit him. I spent six weeks in the country deciding if I could make New Zealand my home and if Steve and I could get along. It wasn't Africa, and it wasn't Cape Town. But it was beautiful, and I could see a stable future in New Zealand, a successful Western country, that I couldn't picture in Africa under the control of the ANC.

As with any move of this magnitude – in my case to a tiny island at the bottom of the world, in a completely different time zone, away from everything familiar – there were the usual reservations, shared by my friends. Steve and I were vastly different; in fact, we were almost polar opposites and there would no doubt be some challenges. Yet there also seemed to be a strong pull to New Zealand, as if something wasn't quite finished between Steve and myself. We had a path to walk together – perhaps another path of fire. I didn't quite know where it would take us, but I was willing to find out. Stepping into the unknown had become almost a constant feature in my life and I figured that I may as well get used to it. The call to adventure was happening all over again. After all, how on earth can you change unless you're prepared to break your well-laid plans? I'd moved to a different continent before, leaving behind everything that was familiar, surely this couldn't be too different.

I also felt deep down that I had some important lessons to learn here, about relationships, compassion and tolerance. The only way we can become fully human is through our relationships with others, and this would no doubt be another difficult path for me to follow. I was getting used to that, too. So, I made the decision that the Pacific region would be my new home, albeit just for now. I reasoned that I could always come back if things didn't work out. If I didn't try, how would I know?

With the decision made, everything started to slot into place. Within weeks of putting my house up for sale, it sold for the asking price, in a downturned market. The agent was flabbergasted. I sold my car, furniture and half a wardrobe of clothing almost overnight, seemingly finding the perfect home for everything in the right way, at the right time – including a loving home for my two cats. Just before I left the country, the broken relationships with family and friends healed effortlessly, as if divine intervention was yet again playing its part.

I'd like to be able to write that the move to New Zealand had a fairy-tale ending, but life's not like that. This is not a fairy tale and I'm not a princess. Starting life on a new continent, somewhat isolated from the rest of the world, was tough. Dealing with a different culture, a dramatic change in climate, and embracing a new relationship after I'd been single for over five years brought way more challenges than I'd expected. Often I've lost my way and considered packing my bags and moving back to Africa, my *spiritual* home. But when I falter I am reminded of the many lessons I've learned over the last five years, which keep me balanced and focused on what really matters. It's at times like these that I remember two lines in a poem written by the Persian poet and Sufi mystic, Rumi:

> Love isn't the work of the tender and the gentle;
>
> Love is the work of wrestlers.

The relationship between Steve and myself has brought its challenges, but also its benefits. We are learning to work with each other. Steve provided the grounding that I needed and the ability for me to take time out to write my book, start my SCIO/hypnotherapy and coaching practice and continue with my healing studies – something that, in hindsight, I wouldn't have completed successfully in Cape Town, living alone in my head, worrying about my future, distracted by friends, family and life. I've also made some really good, new friends in a short space of time. In return, I enabled Steve to lighten up and open up, to believe in himself and a higher power. Just as I was fifteen years ago, he, too, was a fervent agnostic, a 'rational mastermind' (Keirsey) who had erected as a coping mechanism severe mental and emotional barriers between himself and the rest of the world. Today, he is starting to marvel at the number of seemingly synchronistic, unexplainable and wonderful occurrences that happen to him, things that he can't logically explain with his 'scientific' mind. The more he opens up, the more the gifts of the universe seem to support him. For the first time in his life, I think he is learning to fly! Perhaps there was a reason for me being here after all.

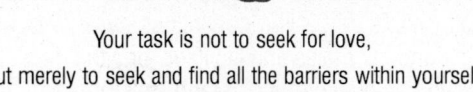

Your task is not to seek for love,
but merely to seek and find all the barriers within yourself
that you have built against it.
Rumi (1207–1273)
13th century Muslim poet

Having spent so many years with Marcos as my teacher, the person who stripped the fanfare and mystique from spirituality, I am able to explain ethereal and spiritual concepts to Steve in a way an agnostic understands. It's important for our relationship, as my spiritual practices are now a fixed part of my life and something that I won't again ignore. The ordinary world and the unseen world are becoming one. 'Special world' experiences tend to fade away if we do not integrate them into our daily lives, so in New Zealand, I resumed my spiritual studies with a greater but more balanced intensity. The foundation I'd built in Africa proved significant in helping me make informed choices about which path to follow during the next stage of my journey, one that will hopefully lead me to a greater discovery of who I *really* am, now that I'm open enough to find out. I am far from being self-realised – I still have a long way to go. I've made the return to the ordinary world, but the return to my *true* home is still to be fulfilled. However, I am more accepting of my life's path. Once we courageously allow ourselves to surrender, to listen to our hearts, we discover that we actually have more freedom than we could ever possibly imagine.

Perhaps there really are no coincidences in life and things do indeed happen for a reason. Looking back, I can see that the challenges I faced, the pain and turmoil I experienced, the indecision and uncertainty, the anxiety, depression, courage, foolhardiness and unquenchable desire to learn, drove me along the road less travelled to this point. Had I embraced my INFP qualities earlier on, perhaps there would be no story to tell. Perhaps I would have stayed in the UK floundering around, stressed out, uptight, wondering who I really was, where I was going and trying to figure out this thing called life. In later years, I may have looked back with regret and a sense that I'd missed out on life in some way if I'd ignored the beautiful music from deep in the forest.

Aspiring authors are, I guess, like all mythological heroes. They can only prepare for their work after being crushed by life in some way, enduring great pain and hardship and surviving terrifying ordeals. One almost needs to die in order to be reborn, to stand with one foot in this world and the other in the next. The warrior has to shed off his old self to enter the 'special world'. But the self is resurrected in some way – different, changed, transformed – before he returns. Every one of us no doubt has a heroic story to tell. The elegance of the mythological road map is that it is a continuous cycle, a blueprint for change found in the myths and fairy tales and life itself, one that must be courageously traversed before we can begin to understand life's meaning, to reveal our true purpose and discover what we can one day become.

THE FROG PRINCE (PART II)

by the Brothers Grimm

After running away from the frog who had kindly retrieved her golden ball from the deep well, the princess thought no more of the old water splasher. But that very evening, just as the princess had sat down to dinner, she heard a strange noise: tap-tap, plash-plash, as if something was coming up the marble staircase to the castle; and soon afterwards there was a gentle knock at the door, and a little voice cried out and said:

Open the door, my princess dear,

Open the door to thy true love here!

And mind the words that thou and I said

By the fountain cool, in the greenwood shade.

The princess ran to the door and opened it, and there she saw the frog, whom she had quite forgotten. At this sight she was sadly frightened, and shutting the door as fast as she could came back to her seat. The king, her father, asked her what was the matter. 'There is a nasty frog,' said she, 'at the door, that lifted my ball for me out of the spring this morning. I told him that he should live with me here, thinking that he could never get out of the spring; but there he is at the door, and he wants to come in.'

Then the king said to the young princess, 'As you have given your word, you must keep it; so go and let him in.'

She reluctantly did so, and the frog hopped into the room till he came up close to the table where the princess sat. She was embarrassed and set up a little place for him under the table, but he was having none of it. 'Pray lift me upon chair,' said he to the princess, 'and let me eat off of your golden plate.' When he had eaten as much as he could, he said, 'Now I am tired; carry me upstairs, and put me into your bed.' And the princess, though very unwilling, took him up in her hand, and put him upon the pillow of her own bed, where he slept all night long.

As soon as it was light he jumped up, hopped downstairs, and went out of the house. 'Now, then,' thought the princess, 'at last he is gone, and I shall be troubled with him no more.'

But she was mistaken; for when night came again she heard the same tapping at the door and the frog came in once more and slept upon her pillow as before, till the morning broke. But when he came for a third night, it was more than the princess could bear.

Now, there are many ways that this fairy tale could end: The first could be that she kisses him and he transforms into a handsome prince; or she allows him to sleep on her pillow for yet another night. But I prefer the solution proposed by Joseph Campbell (*Pathways to Bliss*), where the princess throws the frog against the wall in frustration and the frog shell cracks open and out steps this beautiful prince with eyelashes like a camel!

170

The prince was in trouble – he had been cursed by a spiteful fairy, to abide as a frog until a princess took pity on him. The prince is symbolic of the little boy who has not dared move into adulthood, sheltering himself from the world with everything familiar. She is the little girl, also on the brink of transformation into a new life, and now each one helps the other out of their respective childhood states.

'You,' said the prince, 'have broken this cruel charm, and now I have nothing to wish for but that you should go with me into my father's kingdom, where I will marry you, and love you as long as you live.'

They then took leave of the king, and got into a coach driven by the prince's faithful servant, Heinrich; pulled by eight beautiful horses decked with plumes of feathers and a golden harness, they set out for the prince's kingdom, where they lived happily for a great many years.

Book 2

LESSONS FROM THE
SPECIAL WORLD

INTRODUCTION

The pioneering anthropologist Louis Leakey said, 'Without an understanding of who we are, we cannot truly advance.' I believe there is a lot of truth to that statement. We cannot open ourselves up to a different way of living if we are stuck in our views of the past. So in the next few chapters, I'll share with you a few of the lessons, insights and philosophical musings wrapped up in myth that I discovered on my own hero's journey and which helped me find a deeper understanding of life and its meaning.

To be able to understand some of these concepts, we need to begin at the beginning – from the time when all things began, the time when the Universe was created. Whether we believe religion's version of creation or the scientific version (the Big Bang), it's clear that there is definitely something *out there* which we don't fully understand – a force, a field, a presence, a great net or web that links us and our world together and probably to a higher intelligence, too. Whether we refer to this intelligence or presence as a Supreme Being, God, the Almighty, Allah, Jahweh, Brahma, Vishnu, Shiva, Buddha or Universal Consciousness, these terms of reference describe a very private and personal relationship that each one of us has with something greater than ourselves. So, for the sake of simplicity throughout this section, I will refer to this power as the Supreme Being, or sometimes God when it's appropriate, although the reference to *God* always seemed to grate on me somehow, probably because I associated it with religion itself and not a universal force. You of course, can replace it with whichever term feels comfortable. I also refer to him in the masculine.

We all have different styles of learning new information. I have found in life that I've often rejected worthwhile information because of my own prejudices, usually because it's communicated in a way that conflicts with my own natural style, either by someone I didn't respect or in a manner I didn't much care for. This is particularly the case when it comes to spiritual and religious beliefs.

There are three core systems of teaching and learning: The first is a *dogmatic system,* the system I grew up with. In this system, we are told what to do, how to think and how to behave. The Church, its religious leaders, our parents, high school teachers – who also took their instructions from the Church – told us it was so and we should just accept it. We weren't really permitted to ask the adults intelligent questions about God, as they didn't really have the answers themselves. Heaven was a place you went to when you died, only if you were good. Hell was the place that you went if you weren't. Where are Heaven and Hell? Nobody knew. 'You'll find out when you pass on,' they would say. I am still waiting for an answer on that one.

The second system is the *empirical system*, one that is used by science and academia. Something has to be first proven beyond reasonable doubt for it to be accepted as fact, tried and tested by a handful of individuals with lots of letters after their names. Science says that it requires a huge *leap of faith* to believe in the existence of God. Yet science has experienced several leaps of faith of its own. Stephen Hawking, the prominent cosmologist, said that the Big Bang theory cannot be proven, and that believing it requires a leap of faith. Darwin's theory of evolution is still that – a theory. It's not been proven. Yet it's taught to children in schools as if it were a science and a matter of fact. If science cannot prove the Big Bang, then how can it disprove God? Until a theory has been proven, it isn't physics and it's not a fact; it remains a matter of myth. Science is supposed to be the best knowledge we have for figuring out our existence; yet it's incomplete, always growing and sometimes very much mistaken. Scientists may explain their beliefs as facts, but we down here in the trenches are required to accept them on blind faith alone. Is science then not another form of religious doctrine? Either way, we can never hope for science to prove anything to us sufficiently enough (in the short term at least) to provide us with meaning or purpose, certainly not in a way that captures our heart and imagination.

The third system of learning is known as an *axiomatic system*. An axiom is something that is self-evidently true. Water is wet. We know that. It's a fact. We can experience it for ourselves. An axiom is understood through the observation of life, its repeating cycles and patterns and the resulting connections we make. For example, by observing the behaviour of the electrons in an atom we can understand the workings of a solar system. That's what Einstein did. He took one part of the picture and applied it to another and so by studying one part of the system, we can learn about another. There are a few idioms that illustrate how an axiom works: the big picture is always in the little picture; the microcosm and the macrocosm; history always repeats itself; everything in nature is cyclical; as above, so below; the subtle influences the gross; the Universe is holographic.

Understanding the way of axioms requires effort on our part, which is perhaps why many of us haven't even heard of the term (unless we've studied mathematics). We had enough learning in school or at university and prefer to leave the thinking about the deeper matters of life to science or the clergy. It's easier to follow the herd than it is to go against it, and besides, where do we even start to find these axioms from which we can begin to form our own ideas and opinions? We can't easily see them unless someone points them out to us, and we haven't been taught to think in this way.

Eventually however, as with any skill, the more we practice, the more we see. The more we see, the more we look. The insights start to come thick and fast. Myths, if interpreted with insight, are axiomatic. They speak of principles in times past which can be applied to our own lives today. By applying this thinking to any principle, we can, with the right amount of conscious insight, understand our own nature and the nature of the Universe. It was through this system that I started to accept the concept of a Supreme Being, not because someone told me it was so, or proved it to me scientifically (although each of these systems also validated my own findings); I came to the realisation myself. And when we achieve understanding in this way, it is firmly cemented in our entire being forever.

The 'warrior's journey' – the cycle of change that we just experienced in Book I, (see Fig. 1 below), is axiomatic. It's a small fragment of a larger picture, part of a grand cycle that we are each experiencing, whether we know it or not, as we travel through life.

Just as I've used a mythological road map to illustrate my own personal experiences of life and spirituality, I've also highlighted a second 'map', or

THE WARRIOR'S JOURNEY ROAD MAP

Figure 1

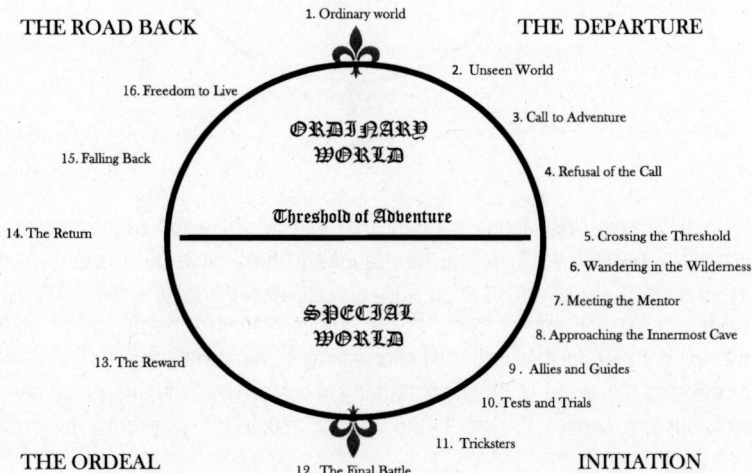

cycle, of sorts, in Fig. 2 below, that relates to the greater scheme of things or universal scheme of things. Of course, it's only my interpretation of the way things might be and not an absolute truth, and you may wish to combine this concept with your own thoughts and ideas about creation and how it works. Please do not try and follow the map in this section in a linear fashion, in the way you might have done in the first. It is intended as an illustration of the bigger picture from which I have compiled key points that I believe are relevant if we wish to get a better sense of our own identity. Its purpose is to portray the bigger picture in an axiomatic way rather than to enable you to pinpoint where you are in the journey. The illustration is intended as a starting point in accepting that each one of our lives is part of a much bigger picture or cycle, one that is continuous, without beginning nor end, and one that we may never fully understand entirely, no matter how enlightened we become.

THE ROAD MAP OF CREATION

Figure 2

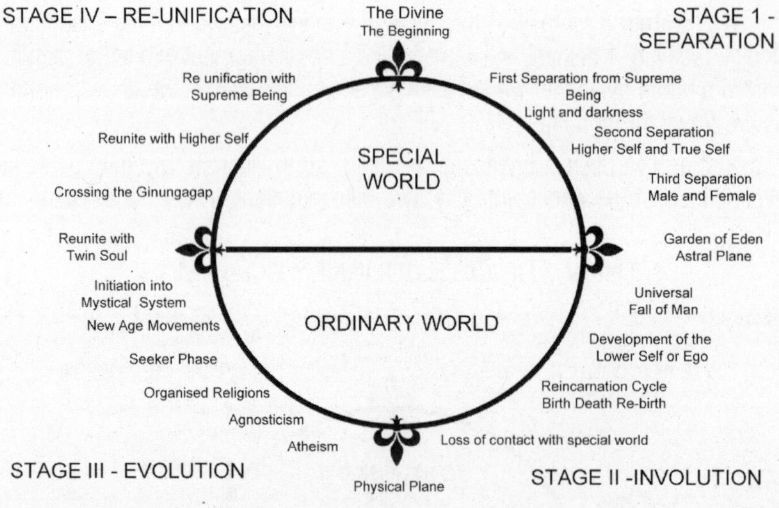

STAGE IV – RE-UNIFICATION

STAGE 1 - SEPARATION

The Divine
The Beginning

Re unification with Supreme Being

First Separation from Supreme Being
Light and darkness

Reunite with Higher Self

Second Separation
Higher Self and True Self

SPECIAL WORLD

Crossing the Ginungagap

Third Separation
Male and Female

Reunite with Twin Soul

Garden of Eden
Astral Plane

Initiation into Mystical System

Universal Fall of Man

New Age Movements

ORDINARY WORLD

Development of the Lower Self or Ego

Seeker Phase

Reincarnation Cycle
Birth Death Re-birth

Organised Religions

Agnosticism

Atheism

Loss of contact with special world

STAGE III - EVOLUTION

Physical Plane

STAGE II -INVOLUTION

The above illustrations suggest that just as there are four stages to the warrior's journey, so there are four stages to the 'cycle of creation'. As with the warrior's journey road map, the 'special world' remains the realm of the hidden or unseen and consists of the 'subtle planes of existence' (a concept we will discuss further in this section of the book), while the 'ordinary world' represents the world of physical matter – a reality which we primarily perceive with our five senses. In Fig. 1, the warrior makes his way from the ordinary

178

world into the special world in a series of journeys, or cycles, until he becomes master of the two worlds. Fig. 2 depicts the 'universal special world' as 'the source' – the centre or location of our origin. It depicts life as part of a far greater existence – a voyage or descent into the ordinary world – a journey (we will discover) that has a significant purpose and one that began perhaps billions of years ago. Our journey back to the universal special world as indicated in the cycle in Fig. 2, is enabled through mastery of our own personal warrior's journey.

The next twelve chapters in Book II focus on Stages I and II of this universal cycle: the *Separation* and the *Involution* – why we are here and some thoughts about the laws that govern this system. Each chapter builds on the last to bring us to a certain point in the cycle. I have used ideas from myth, science and spirituality in an effort to elucidate the main points. Of course, I have only scratched the surface in terms of an explanation, so to fully integrate this knowledge and make sense of it in *your* life will require some thought and study of your own.

Stage III, *Evolution,* is a very personal journey. It illustrates the stages that one might go through to 'make his way back to the source.' My own journey of evolution is described in Books I and III, including some of the 'weapons' that I've found useful in helping me reach the point where I am today. However, your own journey will no doubt be entirely different. When it comes to Stage IV of the journey, *Re-Unification* – well, it will take a far more enlightened individual than I to pontificate on these matters. However, there is a recommended reading list in the appendix which may help to enlighten you if you wish to explore some of these ideas further and form your own opinions.

The word human contains at its core the idea expressed in Genesis. That God formed man from the dust of the ground and then breathed breath into him. The word human is from the Latin homo, derived from the Indo-European root dhghem, meaning 'soil' or 'Earth'. This word is the basis of the word human, meaning man of the ground, dust or earth.

We infer that because man is created in the image of God, God breathed into him the breath of life, and Earthly man is carrying around some sort of divine substance. A fragment of God. The consciousness we have is the substance of God's own breath. This divine component within us is crucial to our identity. Before anything else we are fragments of God, by virtue of our humanity.

So by virtue of the fact that we are human, we are little gods. But a strange thing has happened. These divine sparks have been trapped in a body which is formed from the dust of the ground, which is in itself trapped in a physical universe where we no longer walk with God or talk with God or communicate with higher realms. We cannot see God. We cannot hear God. And we are trapped to the extent that there are those who even deny the existence of God and write him off as mere superstition.

Even so we sense we separated from God to the point of denying God. We are driven to seek God by this fundamental divinity that is so well concealed within us. But how did we get to be so separate and distanced from God? God indeed must have been a curious being because he would not have bothered with a creation. Consequently we who are made in the image of God, are also curious. This curiosity causes us to wonder about our own origins and speculate about our ultimate destination. It is because we are inherently divine that we are seekers of enlightenment.

CHAPTER 1

ACCEPT YOUR OWN DIVINITY

A Myth of Creation

You do not have to struggle to reach God,
but you do have to struggle to tear away
the self-created veil that hides him from you.

Paramahansa Yogananda (1893–1952)

Bhagavad Gita

It is hard to believe today that we are part of God. Almost universally there is a feeling that runs through each of us that we are alone, abandoned and adrift in this pointless ocean of life. We feel separated from whoever is responsible for our existence in the greater scheme of things. And these feelings are understandable. As a Western society we have advanced tremendously over the decades. We can map the human genome, unleash the power of an atom, read and engineer the DNA of life, and store a library the size of a small town or village on a computer chip. Yet we still have little clue as to who we are, how we got here, and where we are going. We make a definite distinction between our place here on Earth and our place in Heaven, Heaven being 'up there somewhere'. And I believe this is what lies at the root of why we spend so much time worrying.

Who or what is God? We know so little about him. He is the supreme mystery. We understand him to be the highest of the high, the all-knowing, the almighty, the greatest, the wisest, without beginning or end. But that doesn't really explain anything.

When it comes to accepting our own divinity, nobody can prove the existence of a God to us, no matter what scientific evidence they might present us with. We grow into the idea somehow. It may be as the result of an event, a sudden epiphany or by gradually developing an acceptance over the course of many years. Although I was raised with the concept of a God, I needed a lot of cajoling to even entertain him as part of my everyday life. Western Christianity and its scriptures proclaimed a God concept that distanced me from any Supreme Being. The picture the church painted through religion was of an angry and judgemental God who would sentence me to eternal damnation if I didn't toe the line. On the other hand, the Eastern belief systems of Buddhism and yoga meant that I was to lose my own personal identity in an all encompassing *existence* before I was really ready to let go. That frightened me. I liked it here on Earth sometimes, even though I moaned about it a lot. I understood that 'unity' might be an 'end result' (of what I wasn't sure); but I certainly didn't want to lose myself just yet. When I found a system that bridged East and West I began to understand the God concept differently, but first the scheme of things had to be explained to me in a different way.

The idea of religion (which we discovered earlier has its origins in Latin, meaning 'the way back' or to 'reconnect') is to provide man with a set of practices, beliefs, systems and rituals to help us find our way back to the source. Sadly, many of the orthodox religions have been so distorted over the centuries that the path, the way back, has been obliterated, lost in religious dogma, doctrines and practices that require a huge leap of faith to fully accept, its true meaning long forgotten. Many of the scriptures have been translated and re-written so many times that their original meaning or intent has been dramatically warped, even lost completely. Religion, however, is only a preliminary stage, a stage which prepares a man for his journey on the path to freedom, a path that can only be found in spirituality. God is not to be found within the folds of a particular religion or New Age movement, and neither can he be traced from within the scriptures. We have to seek him in the core of our hearts. If we are serious about finding meaning, we have to start re-tracing our steps in a different way. The myths are a good place to start. However, none of this bears any relevance unless we can understand why we are here in the first place, what brought us here, and how we get out. (Soon please!)

Stories of creation span our history in the scriptures and myths of the world. In each narrative, one will notice that there are common themes that run throughout, regardless of their culture of origin. In essence, they are all saying the same thing in a different way. Many of them talk of a great flood, of Heaven and Earth being separated, of the Garden of Eden and man's fall from Paradise (found in the biblical tale of Adam and Eve, the Greek tale of Pandora's Box, and the Hindu Vedas – the story of Adamoh and Hevah.) Many of them talk of our separation from God and the separation of the sexes. And many of them refer to trees – the two trees in Paradise, the Tree of Knowledge of Good and Evil, and the Tree of Life – the *Axis Mundi* or world navel; in fact, at the core of many religious beliefs and mythologies lies The Tree. It is deeply symbolic of our spiritual centre and our journey back to the source.

Without doubt, creation myths have many interpretations depending on whose translation we read and which religious system we belong to. In the remainder of this chapter (and again in some of the following chapters) I am going to briefly share different versions and interpretations of these myths as they were explained to me, using axiomatic principles, starting with the Bible myth of creation.

A BRIEF HISTORY OF CREATION

We don't know how long ago – perhaps billions of years – God caused a creation to be. We know from the scriptures, whether we study the Hindu Vedas, the Old Testament, the Sefer Yetzirah (book of creation), the Zohar, (Book of Splendour), the Chaldean (Sumerian scriptures), or even Egyptian hieroglyphics, that at some point in time God said, 'Let there be light.'

We also read in scriptures that on the First Day, God separated 'the light from the darkness.' I'd always believed this to mean he separated 'night from day'. But *light* used in this context doesn't mean the physical light particles that carry reflected images from the pages of a book to our eye, but rather a concept that represents 'illumination' or 'brightness', knowledge and awareness learned through conscious experience. (We refer to light of this nature in our everyday conversation when attributing it to the characteristics of different people, using phrases like, 'He has seen the light,' or she is 'very bright' – each relating to insights or degrees of intelligence that a specific individual has.)

At some point in his existence, the Supreme Being, who was the all and the everything, must have taken a good hard look at himself and saw that there were parts of him that were not as 'light' or equally bright as others, parts that were not as knowledgeable, conscious or intelligent, or as filled with love and compassion. He found that he himself consisted of both light and darkness. And so he separated those dark parts from himself by casting them out. And this is where creation began. The light was separated from the darkness. In the myths it was known as the 'first separation from God'.

So one has to ask, why would God do this? Did he get out of bed on the wrong side? Was he just having a bad-hair day? Why did he suddenly decide to create a universe? We need to look at our own nature to understand this. Deep down, it is the desire of all human beings to become greater, to experience, to expand, to learn to extend and have greater skills and abilities. This is why we create, build companies, start families and embark on expeditions to the summit of Everest or the North Pole. Creation and discovery lies at the core of our existence. If we apply this to the Supreme Being, at a single point in time he realised that, contrary to many religious doctrines or popular systems of belief, he was *not perfect*; there was a *lack of light* within and he needed to do something about it.

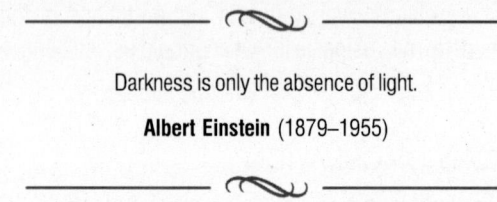

Darkness is only the absence of light.

Albert Einstein (1879–1955)

The act of creation signifies a change in his attitude, a change in his belief, a change in his own spiritual development. Being God, he couldn't go to the nearest psychotherapist to discuss his existential angst about the darkness within. He was alone, he was by himself and so being the most powerful, he was able to cast out the darkness which became creation.

As mere mortals, it is hard for us to conceptualise what life is like in the Divine. A place filled with light, a place where nothing ever goes wrong, where there are no problems, where everything is harmonious and completely balanced – the 'perfect place' where God resides. But what learning can possibly take place in an environment where everything is pleasant, where there are no hardships and difficulties? A different environment was necessary for this learning to take place.

And this perhaps brings us back to a point of contention which we touched on earlier. God realised that he was not perfect, for if he was, surely there would be no need to learn, to create. He could have just continued basking in his own glory, sipping piña coladas all day long (or whatever God does in Heaven). Therefore, the being that had the most free will, the greatest intellect and the greatest wisdom, decided by himself, on his own, for himself, to brighten himself. This was a very freeing concept for me. So, *God is not perfect*. He is not flawless; he is in the process of learning, of brightening himself, of striving to be greater. Just like me. Perfection does not exist anywhere in the Universe. If we had a concept or an idea of perfection, then it would be God and if he too wasn't perfect and needed to brighten himself, why was I worrying so much about always getting it right.

The darkness which he separated from himself became what we know as the *manifested* universe consisting of what we will call, for the sake of clarity, 'divine sparks,' which are you and I and all other beings that share this universe with us. Every subatomic particle, every atom, every cell, every molecule, every rock or mineral, every plant, every animal, every person, every planet, every solar system, every galaxy, even space itself is all alive. Everything has consciousness (even though it's hard to think of a rock as being conscious;) everything consists of energy and matter, varying in degrees of subtlety, density, knowledge, brightness and intelligence. By calling creation to be, God created a physical manifestation of himself. The *Rigveda*, an ancient collection of Sanskrit texts dating back over 7000 years, describes a force that underlies all of creation from which all things are formed, a force that existed before the beginning. This force – namely, Brahma – is described as 'the unborn in whom all existing things abide'. Before creation, Brahma was formless. Now he had form – in the Universe and everything in it. By creating the Universe he was able to observe the workings and interactions of the parts of himself, the divine sparks that he placed there with one sole objective: to learn and brighten himself. The Supreme Being remained in the Divine, brighter than he was, as the darkness had been cast out. Only light remained.

A funny picture came to mind when I heard this; I wondered if casting out the darkness was like getting rid of a toxic relationship – with a lover or partner – that's just not going anywhere; you know – the ones that drag you down, making you feel lethargic and low. When they're not around or out of your life you feel light again, happy, joyous and free. You spend your time skipping around your house basking in your freedom and space, reconnecting with yourself. I wondered if God did that....

MADE IN THE IMAGE OF GOD

We read in the scriptures that we are 'made in the image of God', but this doesn't mean in his *physical* image. God is pure spirit. He is formless. Being made in the 'image of God' means in the image of *his very nature*. Every quality or characteristic we have is found in the Supreme Being in greater measure. (As above, so below.) He is spirit, and so are we. He has consciousness and intelligence, and so we have consciousness and intelligence (albeit confined temporarily to a physical body). He has the capacity to create a universe; we have the capacity to create in smaller measure – to draw, to paint, to write books, to build organisations. The Supreme Being has free will and we, too, have free will in smaller measure, in accordance with the level of 'light' – consciousness and intelligence – we each have. So it was by our *free will* that we *chose* to take part in this creation, the cosmic game or play referred to as 'Shiva's Lila' in Hindu mythology. By accepting a 'tour of duty' here we subjected ourselves to divine laws and principles, laid down by the Creator. But most of us don't like what we experience, which is why we spend so much time worrying and cursing ourselves for agreeing to come here in the first place.

Let's use an analogy to explain this: I'm sure that you will agree that any lawyer who spends many years studying his profession, practicing, making mistakes and finally getting to the top of his game, winning many cases and perhaps receiving notoriety, no doubt has a much greater understanding of legal matters and loopholes in the law than his clients do. Understanding the law has become a power he possesses. He is no longer caught out by aspects of the system that he doesn't understand. It's the same way with creation. Our job is to learn the rules and laws of the system, so that we too have power over them and not the other way around. We can only do that after a long tour of duty.

According to the scriptures, when you and I, by the use of our own free will, realised that we were now separated from God, each one of us looked within ourselves in the same way the Supreme Being did, to see that we also contained both light and darkness. We, too, separated the light and darkness from within ourselves – a re-enactment of the creation cycle all over again. (This is known in mythical terms as the 'second separation'.) The brightest part of each one of us remained in the Divine. This part is known as the 'higher self'. The darker part of that divine spark descended further down the 'ladder' (symbolised by the tree) into the manifest universe. This part is known as the 'true self'. It is that part of you that is reading this sentence (the part of you that lost the argument with the higher self as to who should actually come here). The true self consists of both male and female aspects. There was eventually a 'third separation', which we will cover a little later on. So we are indeed a small fragment of God, a part of him resides within each of us. It's that part within that seeks enlightenment.

THE SEVEN DAYS OF CREATION

We read in Genesis that the Universe was created in six days, and on the seventh day God rested. What does this mean? When Moses wrote the *Old Testament*, he was not referring to a day or a week being a twenty-four-hour, seven-day period as we understand it today. When the Bible was translated from its original Hebrew, the word *yom* (day) had over fifty meanings. In terms of creation, it means a '*solar day*' – an unimaginably long period of time, not twenty-four hours. (In his book, *The Complete Ascension Manual*, Dr Joshua David Stone describes one 'cosmic' day and night in the life of Brahma as being equal to eight billion, six hundred and forty million years. In this book, I refer to a *day* as being a 'cosmic day', to distinguish it from a twenty-four-hour day.) By using this idea, we can begin to rationalise Darwin's theory of evolution with the mythical concept of creation. It also ties in with science's belief that the Universe was created some fifteen to twenty billion years ago by a massive release of energy that was the size of a pea! It's interesting to point out that the great thinkers in our history – Aristotle, Galileo, Isaac Newton and Einstein – saw no separation between God and science in the way science does today.

So creation took place over billions of years and is still happening today. It was not over and done with in the blink of an eye, or a Big Bang. It is ongoing. Scientists believe that the Universe is still expanding, growing, and there will be a point where it will reach its maximum potential, and will then contract again. In fact, there is a growing body of research which says that we are actually creating the Universe as we go. We are the very energy that is making the Universe what it is today, as well as the beings that experience what we are creating. This concept is also reflected in Hindu mythology as the 'In Breath' and 'Out Breath' of Brahma, and in the Nordic myths as Ragnarok: 'the twilight of the Gods,' relating to the submersion of the world in water, after which it will resurface renewed and fertile.

All divine sparks did not come into the Universe at the same time. Those who were simple, *crude,* less refined, and possessed the least amount of light and free will came first, during the first five days of creation. They became the planets, the stars, the rocks, the plants, the animals. Those who were more refined, with the most amount of light, came out later, in successive cosmic days. (I guess if I were running the Universe, I wouldn't send a well educated and refined child, with delicate white skin, spectacles and good breeding to break in a planet, he wouldn't last five minutes. Instead, I would send dinosaurs and primitive men with long arms and short foreheads, who carried clubs and grunted 'Ugg.') We read that Man was created in the latter part of the sixth day. So creation will continue for as long as the Universe exists. There are still divine sparks who are destined to be human waiting in the Divine to come into this physical universe for the first time. They will come when the overall *consciousness* of the planet has increased.

The light that each divine spark has gathered has been the product of its progress in earlier creations. The process of creation never had a beginning or an end. It is a continuous cycle of expansion and contraction, the in-breath and out-breath of Brahma. The whole act of creation never stops. It's one continuous cycle of learning and growth. It's hard to conceive of that. Eventually we will gather enough light to make our return much brighter than it was before. Today, we are supposedly in the seventh day of creation. And the reasoning behind that is a whole different story.

Whether one sees the world as God's creation or as a secular mystery that science is on the way to figuring out, there is no denying the beauty and majesty of everything from mountain ranges, deserts, and rain forests to the exquisite details in the design of an ordinary mosquito.

Robert C. Solomon

Professor of business and philosophy,

author of *Spirituality for the Skeptic*

So God is indeed everywhere as an energy or force that science is now discovering. He is linearly distributed throughout the Universe. We *are* fragments of God even though we don't remember being so. In the same way that you are God to the individual cells in your body, the Supreme Being is God to us. The cells in our body are living creatures – they think, they breathe, they multiply, they make decisions, they act, absorb food, excrete – the same functions, on a smaller scale, as human beings perform (the big picture in the little picture). Each cell in our body has intelligence. Let's take the white blood cells, for example. They swim in the blood stream with a mission to seek out and destroy foreign particles and germs that don't belong in the body. How do they know if something is friend or foe? Does this not indicate intelligence, an ability to reason, albeit on a small scale?

No matter how small its IQ, each cell is responsible for a different function in the body that contributes to the whole in some way. There are cells in the brain, in the blood, in the heart, in the liver, the bones, the lungs, the digestive system, each one a mini 'solar system' responsible for its part in the bigger picture. If we take the IQ of every cell of our body and add them all together, we will arrive at our total IQ. When you add the consciousness of everything in the Universe together, you get God's IQ. Every cell in your body is your representative, just as we are representatives of the Supreme Being. If you accidentally burn yourself on the stove, you feel pain. The cells in your body cry out. It's a form of lamentation, a form of prayer to you. In the same way, we cry out in pain to God when we are suffering.

As we take in information every day through our five senses (six, if you include intuition as the sixth sense,) God learns through us in exactly the same way. We are his *senses*, or *extensions*. As we brighten ourselves, so we brighten the Supreme Being and the whole 'scheme of things'. God is the captain of the ship. He can't come into this universe himself – he needs to be there, steering the ship. And so he learns through those parts of himself that he placed here. Just as we learn through our children, and by observing others, observing nature, observing animals, the Supreme Being learns by observing us. The Universe was created so the Supreme Being could brighten himself as we in turn brighten ourselves. Through the process of two 'separations', we find a part of our *self* here in the manifested universe. Our higher self is in the Divine; it's the part of us that we can contact, when we learn how, that can help us and guide us on our journey through life and back to the source.

By learning to accept my own divinity, I started to look at life differently. My dog Loki (the name for the Norse god of mischief), for example, is also a little being, a fragment of God with perhaps not as much consciousness, intelligence or brightness as I have, but he is still here learning and growing. He has four legs and fur; I have two legs and a lot of hair (on my head). I communicate with him with touch, words and tone of voice. He communicates with me with little grunts, snorts, growls of varying intensity and depth, chewing, licking and wagging his tail. We are both part of the whole, whether we know it or not, here on this planet with this same mission in life: to gather light.

THE SYMBOLISM OF THE TREE

The tree in all mythologies is symbolic of our journey into the manifest universe. It is also a symbol of the way back to the source. In many myths it is depicted as a physical tree, a connection between Heaven and Earth and forms the basis of many religious schools of thought.

In the Book of Genesis in the Old Testament of the Bible, we read of the Tree of Life in the Garden of Eden, or Paradise, which stood next to the Tree of Knowledge of Good and Evil.

In Nordic mythology the Tree of Life is known as *Yggdrasil*, or the upside-down tree. It has its roots in Heaven and its branches on Earth. A large dragon or serpent-like creature, Níðhöggr, constantly gnaws at the roots of the Tree in an effort to destroy it.

In the Maori creation myth, Tâne is the son of Ranginui the Sky Father and Papatuanuku the Earth Mother. Tâne forces the separation of his parents from their marital embrace. He pushes his father, the Sky, high above his mother, the Earth. Tâne then sets about clothing his mother with vegetation. The birds and the trees of the forest are regarded as Tâne's children. In New Zealand's northern region stands Tâne Mahuta, Lord of the Forest, a giant kauri tree symbolic of this myth.

In the fairy tale 'Jack and the Beanstalk', Jack climbs the beanstalk (a form of tree) to reach the Kingdom of the Giants beyond the clouds, where he captures the goose that lays the golden eggs.

In Greek mythology, in the Garden of the Hesperides, the orchard of the goddess Hera, grows a tree which bears golden apples, said to bring immortality. The tree was given to Hera by her mother Gaia as a wedding present upon Hera's marriage to Zeus. The garden is difficult to find, and the tree is closely guarded by the nymphs of the Hesperides and by Ladon, a monster with 100 heads.

In Egyptian mythology, the Egyptians have a celestial sycamore tree given to them by Ra, which stands on the threshold of life and death, connecting the two worlds of Isis and Osiris. They were said to have emerged from the acacia tree of Iusaaset, which the Egyptians considered to be the Tree of Life, referring to it as the 'tree in which life and death are enclosed'.

The Bodhi tree was a large and very old sacred fig tree with heart-shaped leaves under which Siddhartha Gautama, the spiritual teacher and founder of Buddhism, later known as Gautama Buddha, is said to have achieved enlightenment.

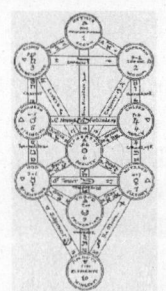

The ancient Babylonians depicted the tree as a tower that stretched from earth into Heaven. The Tower of Babel, known as the Gate of God, is the tower from which man fell.

The Jewish system of Kabbalah, the Divine science of creation, originated in Egypt. In this practice, the tree is symbolised by a geometric glyph known as the Sephiroth, the *Otz Chim* in Hebrew. Also known as the Tree of Life, it is symbolic of the Universe and man, and maps out the path the mystic has to make back to the source. It depicts different stations and paths (branches of the tree) that the mystic may use as a gateway to greater knowledge and personal development. The system is intrinsically linked to the tarot cards, which are not, as I once believed, just a system for foretelling the future, but an ancient system of mystical instruction.

The Brahmanic version of the tree is depicted as the spine of man. It is through the spine that the *kundalini* energy, which resides in every human being, is released during mystical practices. The energy travels up the spine, through the seven *chakras* (force centres) until it reaches the crown chakra, the thousand-petalled lotus – union with God.

In Genesis Chapter 28, verses 11-13,16 and 17, we read the story of Jacob, who had a dream of a ladder which spanned from Earth to Heaven. On the rungs of the ladder were different celestial beings, ascending and descending. Jacob described it as a Gateway to Heaven. The ladder is a depiction of the tree and the hierarchical structure of the Universe. All beings occupy a station in creation. The further down the ladder they are, the further and higher they have to climb. This ladder analogy is also depicted in the Kabbalistic Tree of Life.

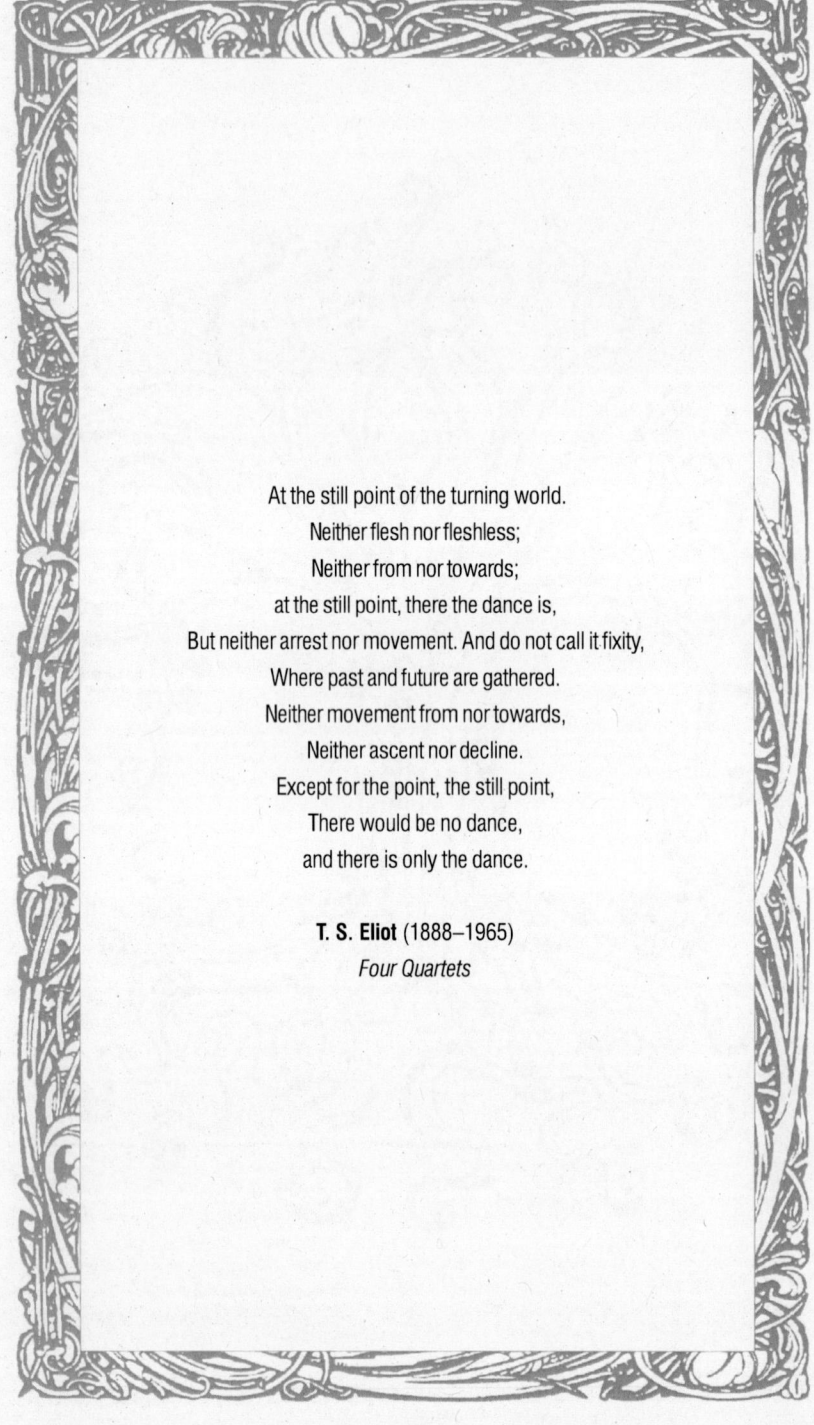

At the still point of the turning world.

Neither flesh nor fleshless;

Neither from nor towards;

at the still point, there the dance is,

But neither arrest nor movement. And do not call it fixity,

Where past and future are gathered.

Neither movement from nor towards,

Neither ascent nor decline.

Except for the point, the still point,

There would be no dance,

and there is only the dance.

T. S. Eliot (1888–1965)
Four Quartets

CHAPTER 2

THE DIVINE MATRIX
The Nature of the Special World

When we look at our lives from the viewpoint that everything is everywhere all the time, the implications are so vast that for many they're hard to grasp. It's precisely because of our universal connection that we're empowered to support, share and participate in life's joys and tragedies anywhere, anytime.

Gregg Braden
The Divine Matrix

During my journey, I discovered many theories about the nature of the *special world*; from science, mythology, and well-meaning individuals who each had their own ideas about the scheme of things. It was hard to accept myself as part of something bigger when I. met so many contradictions that I couldn't understand. This chapter is designed to bring the two worlds, the ordinary world and the special world (fig. 2, page 178) into a single coherent analogy, which I will be referring to throughout this section.

The new science of quantum mechanics likens the Universe to one great big ocean of oscillating energy, matter and consciousness. Everything is alive, moving, vibrating, circulating, pulsing, learning, growing and expanding. Gregg Braden in his book *The Divine Matrix* describes it as a 'cosmic blanket that begins and ends in the realms of the unknown'.

At the beginning of the 1900s, respected physicists and Nobel Prize-winners Niels Bohr, Max Planck, Albert Einstein, Werner Heisenberg, and Erwin Schrödinger, among others, developed a new type of physics – a body of scientific principles which attempted to explain the behaviour of matter and energy on an atomic and subatomic level. Their discoveries rocked the scientific world, uncovering fascinating ideas and theories that classical physics has so far been unable to explain. It gave rise to the understanding that space is no longer just the boring bit between planets, it is in fact teeming with life – different invisible non-material influences, forces and fields of energy that connect all of creation, forming the basic tapestry, or building blocks, of the Universe. Max Planck stated that the existence of this field suggests that a great intelligence was responsible for the physical world. He said, 'We must assume behind this force is the existence of a conscious and intelligent mind and that this mind is the matrix of all matter.'

Experiments with these tiny parts of creation take place in giant, underground particle accelerators, like the Hadron Collider at CERN in Switzerland, where scientists spend their days clashing subatomic particles together in vast electromagnetic fields and observing the effects. These particles are so small that they are invisible, even with the most powerful microscopes, but scientists can still observe the energy left in their wake. Through these experiments, they have come to the conclusion that even at this minute level, subatomic particles have intelligence. It's fundamentally changed the way science views creation and the structure of the Universe itself, giving rise to the following conclusions:

- That there is a field or matrix of energy that connects any one thing with everything in the Universe.

- The DNA in our bodies gives us access to this field, and our thoughts and emotions are the key to tapping into it.

- The Divine matrix is holographic, meaning that any one part of the field contains everything in the field.

- The past, present and future are intimately joined; time does not exist in the way that we have come to understand it.

These discoveries have opened the door to a whole new way of thinking about how we live our lives, and have given rise to a plethora of personal transformation books and DVDs, like *The Secret* and *What the Bleep Do We Know*, which are based on manipulating the new laws of physics to gain the life of our dreams. Through the presence of these subtle *planes* and *forces*, we are to understand that we are in fact creating our own reality, our own state of awareness, our own happiness and problems in life. The Universe is one holistic, intelligent web of matter and energy, with various interplays and dynamics that cross-reference and interact with each other. Our thoughts, emotions and state of wellbeing have a definite influence on us and what is going on around us.

As mere mortals, we cannot observe these forces, but we can understand their effects if we compare them to the invisible fields of energy that we interact with every day without thinking. Every time we use our mobile phone or turn on the TV or radio, we are using some part of the *electromagnetic spectrum*. (See figure 3.) Only the smallest fraction of the entire spectrum is comprised of visible light, the remainder – gamma rays, x-rays, ultraviolet rays, infrared, radar and radio waves – are invisible, yet we accept their presence without much thought or consideration.

Figure 3

The Electromagnetic Spectrum

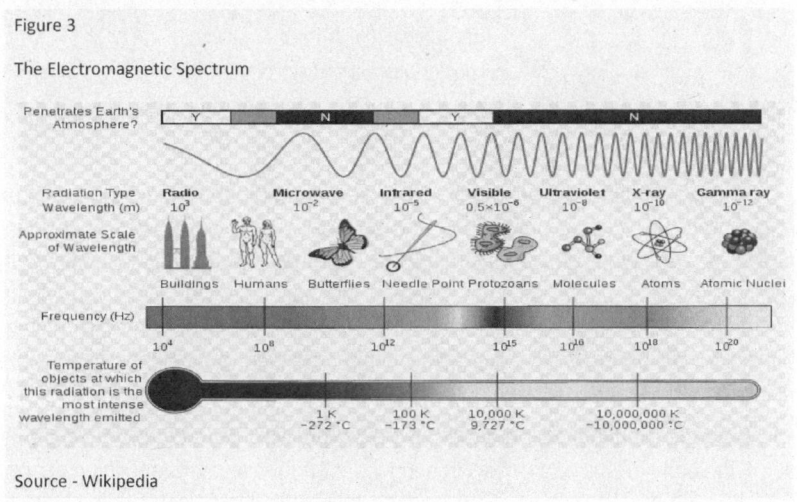

Source - Wikipedia

In the same way we are continually interacting with the special world, with this Divine matrix. Only a fraction of what we believe we know about ourselves is visible or apparent to us, because we generally only experience that which we can perceive with our five senses. Yet we have glimpses of this unseen world on odd occasions – at night in our dreams, or when synchronicity shows up in our lives. For example, we bump into someone in a café who we have been thinking about for days, only to find that they were thinking exactly the same thing. Or maybe we have one of those déjà vu experiences where for one fleeting moment, with every fibre of our being, we simply *know*, beyond any shadow of doubt, that what we are experiencing now is a repetition of something we did long ago. For a split second, two points in time and space seem to suddenly collide and we feel an overwhelming sense of familiarity with something or someone that should not be familiar at all. At such moments, we find ourselves spontaneously transcending the limits of the laws of physics as we know them today. In these brief instances we are reminded there is probably more to us and our Universe than we consciously acknowledge.

One of the motives for spiritual development is to allow us to become more familiar with these different states of awareness at will, so that we can ourselves start to experience the nature of the special world and all its profundity. As we do, we begin to understand ourselves more fully and eventually learn to master the fundamental laws of existence.

Quantum physics has found that there is no empty space in the human cell, but it is a teeming, electric-magnetic field of possibility or potential.

Dr. Deepak Chopra

Medical doctor, speaker and author

The new science of quantum theory is perhaps just the beginning of the realignment of science, philosophy and spirituality in a way that it once was centuries ago, where the great minds of our time saw no division between science and God. But what is the nature of this special world? We always look to the sky when we think of Heaven and God, as if we might find him hiding behind a cloud somewhere. But these different planes of existence cannot be discovered by looking outward. They can only be discovered within.

In the first chapter we read about the symbolism of the tree, prevalent in all mythologies of the world. The tree is also symbolic of a ladder, which Jacob saw in a dream, stretching from Heaven to Earth where many beings were ascending and descending to and from the Divine, some going higher than others and some descending lower. It is this ladder that we need to climb to make our way back to the source.

In Figure 4, Jacob's Ladder describes a possible graphical representation of the divine matrix – different 'planes of existence' or 'consciousnesses' prevalent in the Universe, stretching from earth (the physical world) to the Divine. It's a kind of bridge between imagination and reality. In our everyday lives, we are preoccupied with the lowest 'rung' of the ladder – the physical plane; but when we experience the strange and unexplained, we are beginning to interact with invisible and more subtle rungs on the ladder –the astral plane and mental plane.

Energy, matter and consciousness are the composition of the Universe and exist in one *unified field*. As we move down the ladder towards the physical plane, energy slows down to become a more condensed form of matter. As we move upwards, matter becomes a more subtle form of energy. Energy and matter are also two polar opposites of the same spectrum. When energy slows down it condenses and solidifies to become matter. We see this when

JACOB'S LADDER
The Nature of the Special World

The illustration below depicts the Divine matrix as a 'universal ladder of consciousness' stretching from the Divine into the physical plane of existence. It also depicts the Tree of Life or World Tree which alludes to the interconnectedness of all life. The Divine matrix touches everything in existence. It acts as a metaphor for the descent of the Divine into the manifested universe and depicts the degrees of illusory separation from the source. It can also be viewed as a map of the human psyche both visible and invisible; manifested and un-manifested. As one ascends the ladder (moving in the direction of the upward arrow) physical matter converts to a more subtle form of energy; the degree of centeredness, balance and 'light' increases and time ceases to exist as a linear concept. The more we identify with the lower rungs of the ladder, the greater the degree of imbalance and personal suffering we experience. The spiritual warrior realises his Divine nature by transcending all three planes of existence - mental, emotional and physical – gradually ascending the ladder and finding his way back to the source.

Figure 4

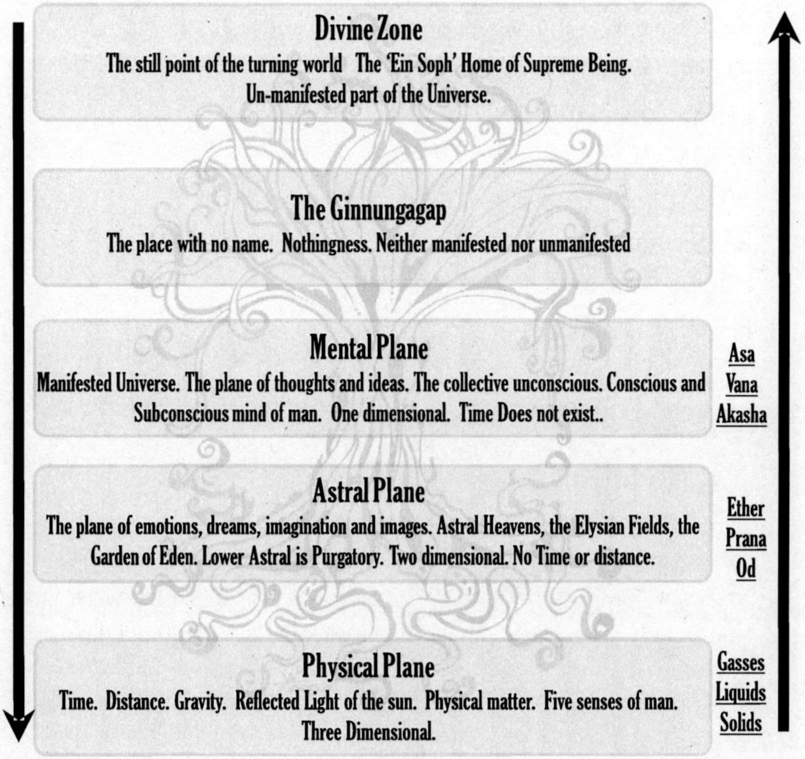

Divine Zone
The still point of the turning world The 'Ein Soph' Home of Supreme Being.
Un-manifested part of the Universe.

The Ginnungagap
The place with no name. Nothingness. Neither manifested nor unmanifested

Mental Plane
Manifested Universe. The plane of thoughts and ideas. The collective unconscious. Conscious and Subconscious mind of man. One dimensional. Time Does not exist..

Asa
Vana
Akasha

Astral Plane
The plane of emotions, dreams, imagination and images. Astral Heavens, the Elysian Fields, the Garden of Eden. Lower Astral is Purgatory. Two dimensional. No Time or distance.

Ether
Prana
Od

Physical Plane
Time. Distance. Gravity. Reflected Light of the sun. Physical matter. Five senses of man. Three Dimensional.

Gasses
Liquids
Solids

we boil a kettle of water. Water when heated beyond a certain temperature changes its state, becoming gaseous in the form of steam or vapour. When we cool it down it freezes, condenses and becomes ice. We also see this in the electromagnetic spectrum (Figure 3). Gamma rays oscillate at a higher frequency than radio waves which means that they too occupy a higher 'rung on the ladder'. So the energy of the mental plane, when slowed down, becomes astral matter. Astral matter slowed down becomes physical matter.

On each rung, there are again various sub-divisions, comprising of different levels of subtle energy. This subtle energy permeates everything in existence. It originates in the Divine as a form of light, an intelligent and conscious force which comprises all of creation. We interact with this subtle energy all the time and our own subtle bodies emanate forms of this subtle energy. The higher up the rungs of the ladder, the more subtle this energy becomes, the lower down the ladder we go, the grosser and denser it becomes. Asa is the highest form of this subtle energy and it vibrates at the highest frequency. By using the Sanskrit terminology for these different energies (for there is no English equivalent) we can see that:

ASA when slowed down becomes

VANA when slowed down becomes

AKASHA when slowed down becomes

ETHER when slowed down becomes

PRANA when slowed down becomes

OD (also known as CHI) when slowed down becomes

GASSES when slowed down become

LIQUIDS when slowed down become

PHYSICAL SOLIDS.

All physically manifested things exist only by virtue of a more subtle or finer matrix within. An example of this can be seen in ice and snow. Even before the tiny globules of rain freeze into the beautiful hexagonal snow crystal, within the water is an invisible but very real form-determining matrix of subtle lines or patterns along which the individual atoms of oxygen and hydrogen align themselves in preparation for the final crystallization process. Every snowflake is said to be unique. In the same way, our physical body only exists because there is an astral matrix, the astral matrix can only exist because there is a mental matrix and the mental matrix can only exist because of the existence of a divine spark. (We explore this in more detail in the next chapter.) We are clothed in different layers of potential – layers of consciousness that we can access through personal and spiritual growth.

THE NATURE OF THE SUBTLE PLANES

The physical plane is the grossest, dullest and slowest of all of the three planes. It is where energy has slowed down to its densest form of matter in the form of solids, liquids and gases. The physical plane is three-dimensional. Objects have physical height, width and depth. It is where the concept of time exists. The light on the physical world is provided by the sun which reflects light from the objects to our eyes. Without the sun, there would be no light, only darkness. Things on this plane move very slowly in comparison to the other planes. They take time because they require physical effort and exertion.

The astral plane is more subtle than the physical plane, but less subtle than the mental plane. The word *astral* comes from the Greek word *astrum*, which means star. So the astral is often referred to as the 'starry plane'. Objects on the physical world reflect light. Even moonlight is a reflection of the sun's rays. However in the astral world, objects have their own light.

When we are physically knocked unconscious, we talk about 'seeing stars'. Many cartoon characters are depicted with stars floating around their head when they've received a bop on the noggin. This relates to the astral plane. When we sleep and dream our consciousness is on the astral plane, which is why dreams seem so real. In our dreams, moving around is easy. We seem to effortlessly move from place to place, from situation to situation, from one dream to the next. That is the nature of the astral plane. Movement does not require the physical effort as it does on the physical plane; we can think about a place we would like to be and we are there.

Time does not exist on the astral plane the way we understand it in the physical world. It was Einstein who asked us to consider time as another dimension. When so-called spiritually attuned people talk of another dimension – the fourth or fifth dimension – they are referring to the astral plane. I have asked the question many times when I hear reference to these different dimensions being chucked around in conversation: 'What do you mean by the fourth dimension?' and I haven't yet got an answer that makes sense. The astral *is* another dimension, but it is only *two-dimensional*, much simpler than that of the physical plane. It has height and width, no depth, like the images on a TV screen. I can only imagine that a fourth or fifth dimension must be inextricably more complicated than the physical plane.

The language of the astral plane is emotion – feelings, pictures, visual images. There is no need for words as we can just visualise a picture and instantly communicate our message. When we sympathise or empathise with someone we are using the astral plane. The astral plane relates to the astral body of man, which we will explore in the next chapter. It is also the home of 'chi' energy (alternatively referred to as *od*, or *prana*) which many healers draw on in the practice of *reiki* and other methods requiring the laying on of hands. The higher the level of consciousness of the healer, the higher and more powerful the energy they draw becomes.

When the different religions or myths refer to 'Heaven', they are referring to the astral. It is the place where we go when we pass on, depending on our belief system in life. (This is addressed in a later chapter). The Italian allegorical tale of Dante's *Divine Comedy* refers to the different levels of consciousness on the astral plane, when he talks of Inferno, Purgatorio and Paradiso: Hell, Purgatory and Paradise. Homer's *Odyssey* speaks of the 'Elysian fields'. The mythical Garden of Eden can also be found on the astral plane. It is where man fell from paradise. Before we fell, to the physical world, we resided in the upper part of the astral plane, where the universal language of communication is symbols and pictures. After the universal *Fall of Man*, depicted in the myths, we no longer had this communication ability, necessitating that we 'speak in tongues,' using only language and sound projected by the vocal chords.

There is also a second concept of Heaven, the one that mystics refer to: the Divine, which is transcendental, beyond human understanding.

The mental plane is the highest and subtlest of the three planes in creation. It is also the brightest and the most dazzling, as it is the plane of mind, of mental thought processes, both within man and universally. (I often imagine all these thoughts as cartoon characters like little beams of light with different personalities: some are really busy, whizzing from place to place with no time to spare, some slow and lethargic, some thin, some fat, some high-powered and magnanimous with briefcases and a cigar and others lounging with a cigarette and a cup of tea on the couch in front of the TV.)

The mental plane is the home of what the eminent psychologist Carl Jung described as the 'collective unconscious', the universal mind that is shared by all people, the collective memory of the human experience, which is known, too, as the 'chronicles of man', or the Akashic records. When we have developed spiritually to a point when we are able to *access* the Akashic records, we can accurately obtain a picture of all of our past lives (which the Buddha did when he achieved enlightenment.) Like the other divisions, the mental plane has three levels: Asa, Vana and Akasha. It is the simplest of the three planes, being only one-dimensional.

The **Ginnungagap**, as it is known in Nordic mythology, is the 'seeming emptiness', the great yawning abyss from which creation sprang. It is the primordial void separating Niflheim, the land of eternal ice and snow, and Muspell, the land of eternal heat and flame.

In religious terms it is referred to as the 'place with no name'. In some mythologies it is believed to represent Hell – the bottomless pit, or the Underworld. In mystical terms it is the place where all the divine sparks who used their free will to decide that they did not want to participate in creation reside until the end of this 'cosmic week'. The Ginnungagap is benign, a place of nothingness. It is across this abyss that the seeker must travel on his way back to the Divine. The Ginnungagap falls outside the scope of this book. However, you may find references to it in its various names in myths and legends and religious scriptures, so it's worthwhile mentioning at this point.

The Divine Zone is the home of the Supreme Being and is the divine origin of all created existence, what T.S. Eliot called 'the still point of the turning world'. It is where our higher self resides.

The divine zone is also known as the *Ain Soph Ohr* (Hebrew): the *limitless light*, 'the most hidden of all things'. In Kabbalah it is referred to as *Kether*, or crown. The nature of the Divine is completely incomprehensible to man. The Divine is also referred to as Heaven, although this is a different Heaven to the one we find on the astral plane. The astral heavens are like holding cells in which we reside before we reincarnate again in the physical world.

It is from the Divine that we began our journey into the manifest universe, and it is to here we must return. It is the place with the most light, the most consciousness, the most subtlety, refinement and brightness. We came from light into darkness so that we could be 'enlightened.'

AT THE STILL POINT OF THE TURNING WORLD

To understand the ladder in a different way, think of the different planes of existence not as a linear concept but in the form of a wheel.

At the centre of the wheel is the axel, rotating very slowly, hardly moving. This is the Divine, the still point of the turning world. The outer rim is the physical plane. The Mental and Astral planes would sit in between the outer rim and the centre.

The further we move away from the centre of the wheel, the greater the rotation or spin. If we were a bug on this wheel that was attached to a cart, pulled along by a horse, we would want to be at the centre where the ride would be a lot more pleasant. If we were on the outside, we would be holding on for dear life as this wheel careers over rough ground at break-neck speed, jarring our little body into oblivion. The Universe can be likened to one big rotating wheel. The further away from the centre we are the greater the difficulty, the greater the hardship, the greater the imbalance and the more tightly we have to cling.

If there is anything in life that we are absolutely sure about, it is that the world we experience is real. We can see it. Smell it. Feel it. Hear it. When we fall down and hurt ourselves, it feels real. When we drive to work in the morning in rush hour traffic, it feels real. When we put our back out by lifting a heavy piece of furniture, it seems undeniable that out there, around us, independent and apart from us, stands a physical world, utterly real, solid and tangible.

But is it?

I have held much to be true, which I now discover to be false. I have no reason to suppose anything to be more certain. Possibly everything that I conceive and believe is false. What then is true; what is certain?

René Descartes (1596–1650)

French philosopher and mathematician

In the ancient language of Sanskrit, the word *maya* means illusion, the great 'veiling power that binds the mind'. This whole universe is often likened to an illusion, an idea in the mind of God, a cosmic game, or a play. Yet, it is only the beliefs *we* hold about the system that bind us here. Quantum theory is now starting to challenge those beliefs; there is now a very large grey area around what we might consider to be really, really real – and what isn't.

People quite often begin their journey on the spiritual path because they are disillusioned by life in some way. They are tired, jaded and have had enough. They desire to break the bonds of 'illusion' that are holding them so tightly, so that they can begin their journey towards the centre of the wheel, through the special world back to the source. The purpose of spiritual growth is to transcend the illusion which is depicted in all the myths of the world. When the hero has reached a certain stage in his journey, he starts to experience the miraculous – visions, insights or visitations from allies in the form of gods or goddesses, angels and nymphs who reside on the subtle planes. And when we get our first glimpses of *life beyond the veil,* we begin to realise that the laws of the Universe have actually not been created with much integrity, and that cracks easily appear in the very fabric of creation itself. If we persist, then we too, can begin to gently scrape away layers of the great cosmic oyster, uncovering its pearls of wisdom. And when we eventually find our way back to the centre of the wheel, we may find that this journey we've been on was just a long ride in a giant flight simulator, and we actually never really left the Divine at all.

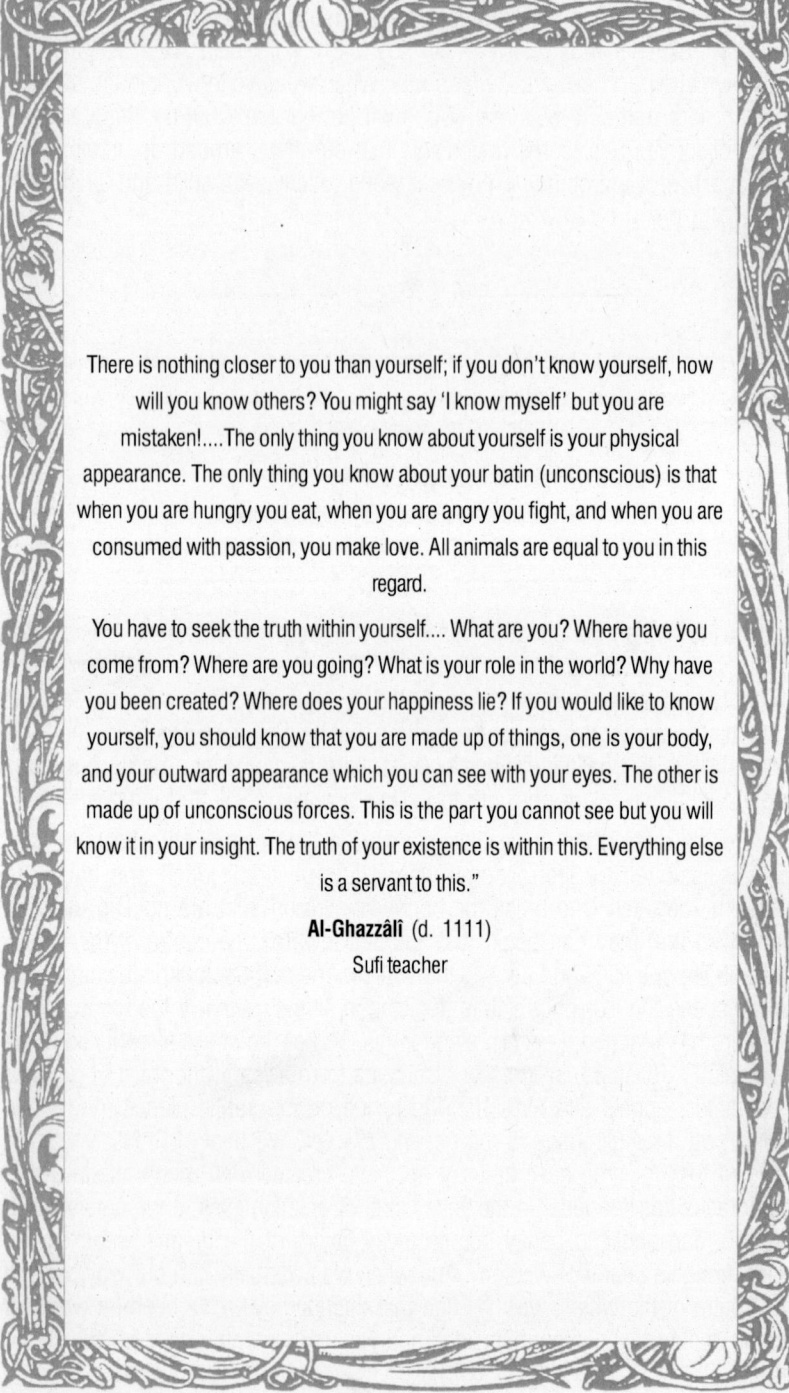

There is nothing closer to you than yourself; if you don't know yourself, how will you know others? You might say 'I know myself' but you are mistaken!....The only thing you know about yourself is your physical appearance. The only thing you know about your batin (unconscious) is that when you are hungry you eat, when you are angry you fight, and when you are consumed with passion, you make love. All animals are equal to you in this regard.

You have to seek the truth within yourself.... What are you? Where have you come from? Where are you going? What is your role in the world? Why have you been created? Where does your happiness lie? If you would like to know yourself, you should know that you are made up of things, one is your body, and your outward appearance which you can see with your eyes. The other is made up of unconscious forces. This is the part you cannot see but you will know it in your insight. The truth of your existence is within this. Everything else is a servant to this."

Al-Ghazzâlî (d. 1111)
Sufi teacher

CHAPTER 3

NOTHING IS EVER LOST
The Subtle Bodies of Man

All is impermanent in Man except the pure bright essence of Alaya, the Universal Self. Man is its crystal ray, a beam of light, immaculate within, a form of clay material upon the lower surface. Thy shadows [or bodies] live and vanish, that which in thee shall live forever, that which in thee knows, for it is knowledge, is not of fleeting life; it is the Man that was, that is, and will be, for whom the hour shall never strike.

The Voice of the Silence
Tibetan Buddhist scripture

As you will no doubt have gathered if you read the first part of this book, I spent a lot of my life worrying. One of the major sources of my concern was my apparent de-motivation about life when everyone else seemed to be just getting on with things and striving away for goodness knows what. I couldn't see the point in struggling bravely onwards just to accumulate vast amounts of wealth or power so that I could retire comfortably and leave a legacy for my children. I wondered if I would ever 'make it' before retirement age and before society relegated me to the scrap heap, used up and thoroughly worn out, regretting the things that I never had time to do because I was too busy making money. And finally, what was the point in all of this anyway, because at some point I was going to die and that would be it, all over and done with. If I'd been good enough in my seventy or so years on earth, I could join God in Heaven for the rest of eternity. How dull. So life became a very worrying thing for me, quite simply because I didn't understand it and I was sure that I should be doing something more with it than I'd planned. It wasn't long before I realised that I wasn't alone in my concerns, although few people ever express them openly.

So what is this thing called life? It seems to be the one thing that we take most for granted, but at the same time the one thing that we least understand.

From a medical point of view, there is hardly a doctor or scientist that can agree at what point we cease to exist. Some say it's when we stop breathing, others say it's when our heart stops beating, or we no longer exhibit brain wave patterns. Yet we have developed machines that can take over almost every function of our body if one of our vital organs ceases to operate. But is that life? It seems that the last thing we can actually do in an intensive care unit is die, because there are machines that can take over every function of our body and keep it going for decades. So according to science, if our body is not reproducing, breathing, moving, exhibiting brain wave patterns or a DNA structure, then it's not actually a life form. It's dead. And this I believe is what lives at the core of the biggest worry that we have as human beings: the fear of death. Because death, in this equation, means 'non-life', a cessation of life as we know it and the end of everything that we have worked so hard to achieve.

It might be a comforting thought to know that there is more to us than just our physical body, and that we *don't* die when our physical body ceases to exist. New Age thought has made reference to this point for decades, so this concept is not new, but I didn't really understand it or how it fitted in with the whole idea of creation and eternal life.

We do, in fact, have three bodies or three 'vehicles' which correspond with the three *planes of existence* in the Universe: one for each of the *terrains* we have to navigate in life. As we have to do physical things, we have a **physical body.** We also have emotions and feelings and so we have an **emotional body** and we have mental processes, thoughts and ideas which involves a **mental body**. Each of these bodies clothes a 'divine spark' – our true self, a fragment of God which has been around since the creation began.

The physical body is the vehicle that we use on the physical plane. It is the least subtle of all three bodies, containing the physical organs, vessels, cells, veins, arteries, bones and tissues that make up our physical structure and help us to function. From birth it is subject to the ravages of time, a concept we are only familiar with on the physical plane. Eventually, after about seventy or eighty years, it wears out. It is a temporary vehicle and the least enduring of the three bodies. The physical body has an aura which extends about one centimetre from the physical body which is made from a subtle energy called *od* (or chi energy.) The aura, if it can be seen clairvoyantly, indicates the state, vitality or health of the physical body.

The emotional body is often called the soul, the etheric body or vital body. As it corresponds with the astral plane of existence, it is also known as the astral body. We will refer to it as such from this point forward. When we feel emotions, we talk of the heart but in reality, emotions are experienced everywhere in our body which is why they seem to engulf us on occasions. For example, love is an intense and powerful emotion and the phrase; 'love hurts' seems to be particularly apt at certain times in our life, particularly when we are young and in love. I remember in my teens being entirely consumed with emotions that I didn't understand; aching, yearning and desiring to be with someone, not able to concentrate or think of anything else other than the object of my affection, only to find after a while that I felt tainted by the very same person. I believed my *heart to be broken*, because I felt pain; I was emotionally sore. My heart was, of course, still intact; I was feeling the emotions through my astral body, but the only way I could explain them was through the heart.

The emotional body is the part of us that is associated with dreams, lucid dreams and astral projection. At night when we dream, our astral body leaves the physical body and moves onto the astral plane. The kind of dreams we experience depends on our mood, and our emotional and mental state just before sleep. We all dream, whether we know it or not. The emotions, images and experiences we remember from our dreams can often be quite intense and may sometimes affect us for many hours after we wake. This is because we experience dreams during a much higher state of consciousness, when we are more alert and sensitive. The astral body, during life, is attached to the physical body with a 'silver cord'. It remains with the physical body until we pass on.

Regarding the soul, when it is separated from the body in sleep or at the moment of death it assumes its true nature and foresees the future, as we see in Homer.

Aristotle (384 BC–322 BC)
Greek philosopher

The astral body, like the physical body, has an anatomy. But it is totally different from that of the physical body. It has no digestive organs or organs of excretion, as it draws its energy from the astral plane itself. It doesn't need to eat or digest food for energy. The most important organs in the astral body are the *chakras*, the energy centres, which are roughly located along the spine, and one above and outside the head. The chakras are like bright spinning wheels or vortices of energy. The astral body also contains three streams of energy called *nadis* that connect the seven chakras. In Sanskrit, they are called Ida, Pingala and Shushumna. There is no English equivalent. One is on the left side of the spine, one is on the right and the other is in the centre. It is the spinning of the chakras that creates the astral *aura,* which is in approximately the same shape as the physical body, but extends outward by several centimetres from the physical body. It is the aura that the psychic sees as swirling colours of light. The colours portray the emotional state of the individual. The chakras also emanate od, sometimes called an odic force, subtle energy, chi, prana or vital force.

The Chakras and the Three Nadis

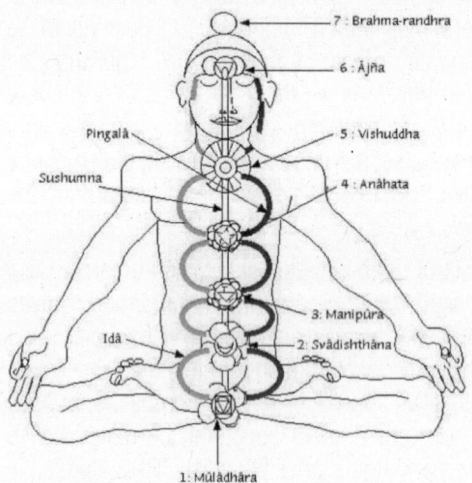

7 : Brahma-randhra
6 : Ájña
5 : Vishuddha
4 : Anáhata
3: Manipúra
2 : Svádishthána
1: Múládhára
Pingalá
Sushumna
Idá

When we die, we don't cease to exist, as many think. We cast off the physical body like a raincoat and our consciousness transfers to our astral body. But the gates to the five senses of the physical body are closed. Otherwise we remain unchanged. The astral body lasts longer than the physical body. But after a period of time, it too wears out. When it comes time for us to reincarnate again in this world, we have a new astral and physical body.

The mental body is also referred to as 'the 'spirit'. It is the *mind* of man and it, too, has an aura, in the shape of an egg which extends about one to two metres away from the physical body.

The mind and the brain, contrary to commonly held beliefs, are two separate things. The brain does not think. It is the mind that thinks and there is a vast degree of difference between the two. Often we hear people say that so-and-so 'has a good brain', indicating an admiration of someone's intelligence. Yet the brain is a physical organ inside our head. Its function is to convert glucose into electrical impulses within the body, enabling the mind to access and control various organs and speech centres. The brain is merely the telephone exchange through which the mind functions. The mind exists outside of the physical body, in the mental body of man.

Anyone who has been in contact with departed loved ones on the 'other side', via a medium or a psychic, might wonder how it is that these disembodied spirits can speak to us with so much clarity and coherence when they don't have a brain. It is the *mind* that is facilitating the dialogue, the mental body of the spirit communicating with us via the mental body of the medium who has the psychic abilities to communicate readily with those who have moved on. (Developing psychic abilities is one of the talents that unfold within us as we grow spiritually.)

So, when we are thinking, remembering, analyzing, reasoning, making judgements and drawing logical conclusions, we are using our mental body. The amount of intelligence we have relates to the amount of mental flow that is coming through the brain. (The intelligence someone has, however, does not just mean academic intelligence; it also relates to the natural, or common sense intelligence. Common sense is the amount of information we have gathered and stored about life itself. So intelligence is not just the ability to do mathematical calculations.) If the 'telephone exchange' is damaged, or small and impaired, then the communication naturally won't be great; but if its capacity is bigger there will generally be a much greater interplay.

The mental body houses both the conscious and subconscious mind. The subconscious mind or intuition operates through the solar plexus. Known as the 'stomach brain,' it's where we have those 'gut feelings', that uncomfortable feeling in the pit of our stomach when something is not quite right. We sometimes refer to it as intuition. The subconscious mind in the mental body of man is the part of us that is the most enduring of all the three bodies. It lasts for the entire 'cosmic week' – the entire period of creation.

When we pass on, we discard our physical body and eventually our astral body. But our mental body remains, storing all experiences from birth to death. *Nothing is forgotten*. No matter how joyous or

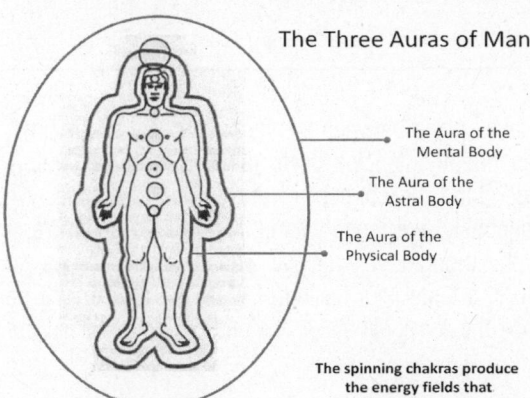

The Three Auras of Man

The Aura of the
Mental Body

The Aura of the
Astral Body

The Aura of the
Physical Body

The spinning chakras produce
the energy fields that
form the auras

pointless we might find life, everything we have learned or strived to achieve, is remembered, in the smallest of detail even though we might not be aware of it today. Deep down in our subconscious, we know all things from all time. This is why some people can clearly remember aspects of their birth, early childhood dreams and, in some cases, aspects of their previous lives – the memories are stored in the subconscious.

THE POST BOX ANALOGY

To understand the interplay between the different bodies, we can use the analogy of a post box. When we decide to write a letter or a card and post it to a friend, we are re-enacting the interplay between the three bodies of man during his various incarnations:

- The ink and the writing on the card can be likened to the divine spark

- The card can be likened to the mental body

- The envelope can be likened to the astral body

- The post box can be seen as the physical body

When we write on the card, the ink (the divine spark), and the card (the mental body), become united. It is hard, if not impossible, to separate the ink from the card. In the same way it is hard to separate the divine spark from the mental body. If we put this card in an envelope, it is the same as the mental body moving into the astral body – the card can be taken in and out of the envelope, just in the same way that the mental body can move in and out of the astral body. The post box represents the physical body. The envelope containing the card can be taken in and out of the post box just in the same way as astral body and the mental body can move in and out of the physical body. But the envelope, the card, and the writing on the card exist whether the post box is there or not.

There is interplay that takes place between the various bodies all the time. They do not function independently. It helps us to think of them separately when we are trying to understand the concept of our eternal existence. We use all three bodies simultaneously, every day without thinking. For example, if we want to cook a meal, the thought of what we want to cook comes 'to mind', together with a picture, a taste or a feeling of what the food might be like. Then we physically cook the meal. Whatever the end result, it started out with a thought.

Sometimes the interplay is so quick we believe we experience an emotion before a thought. Indeed, many emotions have automatic thoughts attached to them. Thoughts have automatic emotions attached to them, too. This is why we can find ourselves caught in a negative downward emotional spiral before we know it, particularly if we are not aware of our thinking. The two happen almost simultaneously. But the thought *always* comes first. For this reason, much focus in psychological circles is placed on positive affirmations – if we can change the thinking, we can change the emotion and ultimately our behaviour.

I think it would be marvellous if more and more people would become aware of the fact that there are many lives we have to live in order to learn all the lessons.

Elizabeth Kübler-Ross (1926–2004)

Swiss-American psychiatrist, pioneer in near-death studies,

author of *On Death and Dying*

I became decidedly more motivated about life when I began to understand that not one thing I've thought, felt or experienced in any lifetime is lost or wasted, and that there is indeed a point to our existence. All the effort we put in, all the knowledge and wisdom we gain together with the learning from each of the mistakes we've made, is stored in our mental body and the mental plane of the divine matrix. This wisdom ultimately accrues to the Supreme Being, re-enforcing the whole purpose of creation in the first place. As we push against boundaries and overcome obstacles we grow stronger, our consciousness expands and greater wisdom ensues. Along the way we gain a greater and greater capacity to use our mental body more industriously, eventually reaching the point where we can remember everything we have learned since the beginning of time. Spiritual development helps to speed up this process.

So eternal life does indeed exist. As divine sparks, we are immortal; it's just our physical and emotional bodies that can't withstand the ravages of time. We have perhaps had thousands of incarnations here on this earth to get to the point where we are today. The three bodies of man are vital to this, our continued existence. We use each of them interchangeably every moment of every day as we progress through each lifetime, gradually making our way back home.

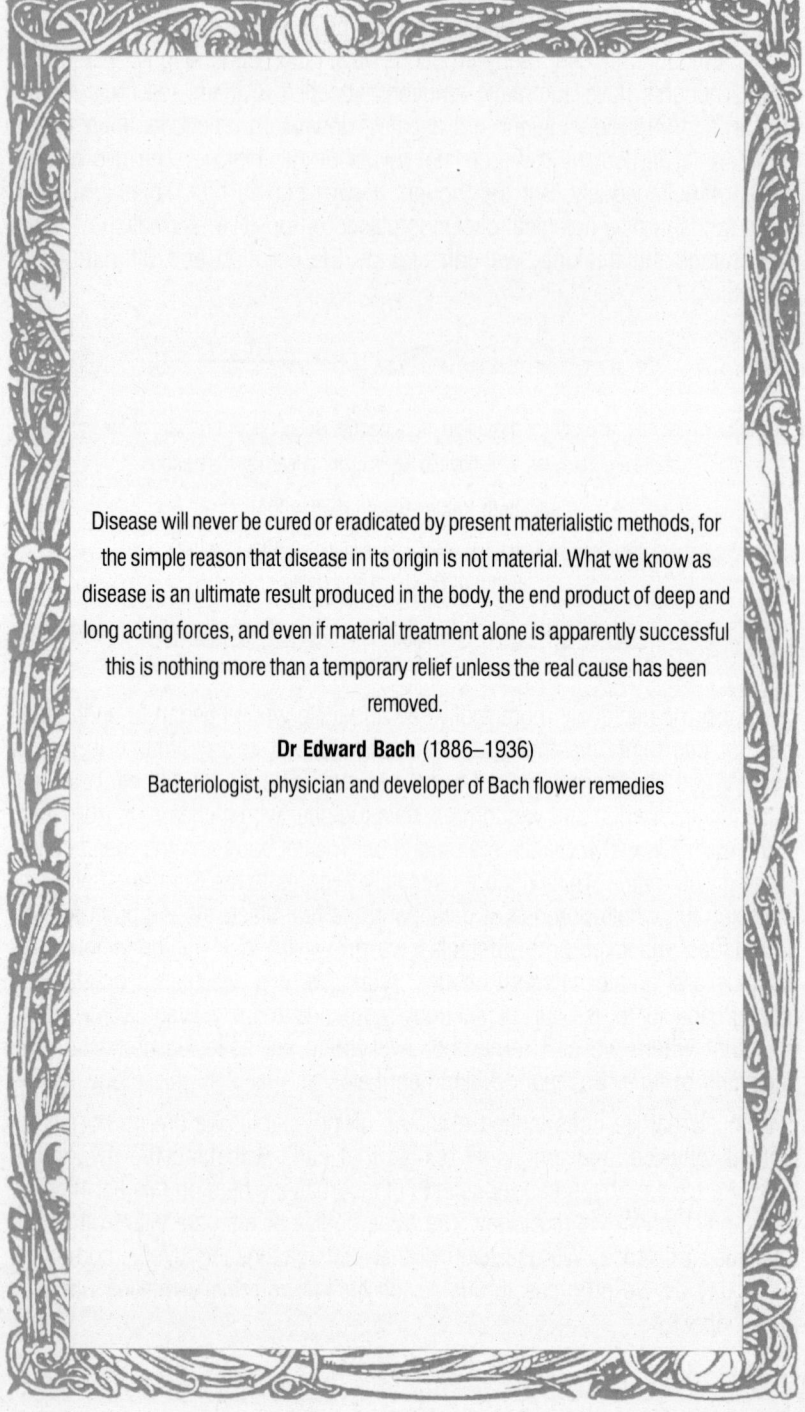

Disease will never be cured or eradicated by present materialistic methods, for the simple reason that disease in its origin is not material. What we know as disease is an ultimate result produced in the body, the end product of deep and long acting forces, and even if material treatment alone is apparently successful this is nothing more than a temporary relief unless the real cause has been removed.

Dr Edward Bach (1886–1936)
Bacteriologist, physician and developer of Bach flower remedies

CHAPTER 4

WHEN YOU'RE A 'HANDEL' IN A 'BON JOVI'

Od, Vibration and Resonance

He who understands the principles of vibration has grasped the sceptre of power.

Ancient Hermetic teaching

I'd always been very sensitive to moods and environments since childhood. More times than I can remember I found myself in a situation or environment that just didn't *feel* right, only to find my moods and sense of well-being fluctuating in response. This was particularly the case in the business world, which is often fraught with stress and tension. I would often walk into a room or office and feel waves of nausea or anxiety hitting me. For many years, I blamed myself for the irrational moods and emotions that would sometimes consume me. It took me a long time to figure out that it wasn't actually all my fault. I was picking up on cues from the environment that are beyond the capacity of the five senses to grasp.

'Tuning in' is an ability we all have, some of us to a greater degree than others. Have you ever walked into a room where people have been arguing, to find the atmosphere heavy with indignation and emotion? Metaphorically speaking, you can cut it with a knife. Even though we haven't witnessed the nature of the disagreement, and the individuals concerned show no outward sign of discomfort, the atmosphere is heavily laden with antagonism and resentment. Or perhaps you meet someone you've never clapped eyes on before and find yourself agitated and uncomfortable for no apparent reason. The hairs may stand up on the back of your neck and you feel cold shivers running up and down your spine. Or on the flip side, you meet someone for the first time and feel yourself instantly connected; a certain magic occurs between you, even though no words have been exchanged. If these things happen to you, then you are tuning in.

For the badly informed intuitive, these experiences can make life very stressful. Our own private heaven or hell can be recreated at any moment if we have a well developed 'sixth sense' which we don't fully understand. (After all, they don't teach us about this stuff in school.) So, if you, like me, were concerned that you were a victim of your own vivid imagination or just completely bonkers because your mood seemed to change so frequently, then stop worrying. What you experienced was the force of vibration and resonance carried by a subtle energy, (od or chi) which is emanated by every living thing – a notion that most of us are blissfully unaware of.

As we read earlier, we are more than our physical body. We have three bodies which operate in harmony. We don't just experience life through our physical body; we experience emotions through our emotional body and thoughts through our mental body, although it seems like it's one body. When we tune in, we are picking up on the subtle energies emanating from another person with one of our subtle bodies. Everything in the universe contains a form of subtle energy – people, animals, plants, minerals, cells and atoms. We find it distributed throughout the cosmos. From the largest to the smallest, our subtle bodies, via the chakras, emanate *od* or *chi*. The word *od* comes from the Scandinavian word 'oden', after the Norse god Odin, the principle god of the Æsir who was omnipresent and everywhere. Baron Karl von Reichenbach (1788–1869), who spent many years investigating the complexities of this subtle energy, coined the term od because it was to be found everywhere in existence. He wrote a book about many of his findings entitled, *Odic Force – Letters on Od and Magnetism.* German physician Franz Anton Mesmer (1734-1815) called it 'mesmerism'. The degeneration of Mesmer's ideas and practices led Scottish surgeon James Braid to develop hypnosis in 1842.

As we discovered earlier, od is a form of astral matter and the subtlest form of physical matter. It emanates from the cosmos and every living thing, and can be found in our physical, astral and mental auras as swirling colours that depict our physical, emotional and mental state. The food we eat, be it vegetable, plant or animal, contains od. We are continually transmitting od via our chakras. The chakras act as energy vortices which transmute and emanate energy in and out of the body. (See illustration on page 215) This is why we experience hunches, impulses, feelings and emotions which we cannot always logically explain. People's moods and emotions are carried by od, which is why when someone yawns in a group, the entire group does the same. It is through od that a dog tracks the spoor of a thief or animal, and not just through smell. The od will remain on any plant, mineral or bacteria it touches, as each, being alive, retains quantities of od. When we walk into a room and feel negative

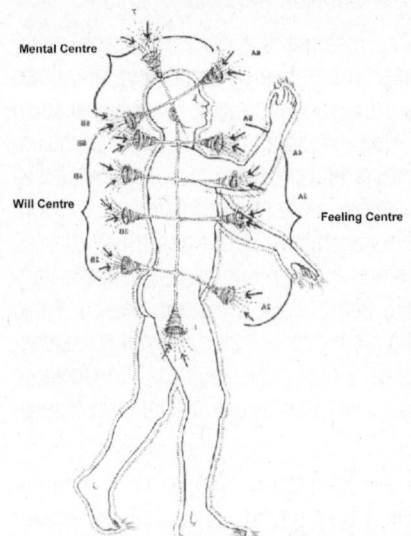

Mental Centre

Will Centre

Feeling Centre

vibes, we are picking up on the odic force which has emanated during the heated exchange between two people. Od doesn't dissipate. It stays in the room and eventually infiltrates the walls. This is also why certain places have a horrible vibe about them, even without people present. Od is an intelligent force; it carries the anger generated from one person and we absorb it. The food we eat in a restaurant can be contaminated by the od of the chef – a good reason for not eating in restaurants where the chef is always angry! (The real significance of saying grace around a table comes from the original practice of blessing the food to remove negative vibrations.) We emanate od from all parts of our body, particularly our eyes, hands and solar plexus. If you've ever felt someone staring at you, their eyes metaphorically burning into the back of your head, it's the od from their eyes that you are sensing. Od, vibration and resonance are synonymous. When we speak of od, we are speaking of vibration and vice versa. Od *is* a vibration.

The words *vibration* and *resonance* come from two Latin sources: *vib*, which means *to tremble*; and *resonare,* which means *to return to sound.* Upon investigating the etymology and meaning of the words, we discover metaphors like shake, tremble, pulsate, beat, oscillate harmony, reverberation, and rhythm, words that we freely associate with sound, music and movement, but not with everyday life. 'Vibration and resonance' is, however, a phrase used in psychology to denote empathy and compassion in relationships. *Empathy* literally means 'into feeling.' Many of us can identify with this concept when we meet someone that we instantly connect with. Through an exchange of od, we tune into someone's vibrational *essence.* When we are 'in empathy,' we feel connected with that person, even if we've only just met them. Distance literally disappears. The opposite of resonance is dissonance. When we consciously or unconsciously lack empathy with another, we don't resonate with them. Thus the 'gap' between two people can be enormous, even though they may share the same household or work space. Eventually however, the subtle energy emanated by each individual will rub off on the other and the gap will close somewhat. If someone is of a high vibration, the essence will raise the vibration of another person. In the same way, if someone is of a low vibration, their essence will also lower the vibration of another person.

We read in an earlier chapter that the Universe is a combination of matter and energy and exists on three planes: mental, emotional and physical. Everything in the Universe is alive, has consciousness and emanates a form of energy, whether we can see it or not – sound, light, space, atomic particles, earthworms, pot plants, mountains, bacteria and viruses, and every living cell in the human body. This energy and matter is in constant motion and we, too, are in constant motion within it, not just in the rhythm of our heartbeat, the rise and fall of our breath or the coursing of blood through our veins, but in the very energy particles that makes up our entire being – all swirling in unison. From the emperor to the atom, nothing in the Universe is still. Everything moves, circulates, oscillates and vibrates. It has its own unique rhythm. The Universe is one ocean of vibration, of continuous movement. It creates its own kind of music.

Every day, without knowing it, we are subject to thousands of different vibrations coming at us from every angle. Every sound, colour, shape, action, thought or emotion has its own unique vibrational 'frequency' and finds its home on the cosmic ladder of existence. In terms of music, classical music has a higher vibration than heavy metal. A church or place of worship has a higher vibration than a hospital or mortuary. Newly picked fruit has a higher vibration than three-day-old meat. A healthy blood cell has a higher vibration than a cancerous cell. The emotions of love, acceptance, trust and compassion have higher vibrations than anger, jealousy, fear, guilt and shame.

At one end of the scale, on the higher rungs of Jacob's Ladder, we find high vibrations that are closer to the Divine, closer to the source, towards the centre of the wheel of creation. If we could see these vibrations we may find them to be operating at such an infinite rate of intensity that they may appear not to be moving at all, just as a rapidly spinning wheel appears to be motionless when rotating at high speed. At the other end of the scale, lower down the ladder, vibrations, or grosser forms of matter, might be vibrating so slowly that they, too, seem to be at rest. Between these poles, there are millions upon millions of varying degrees and permutations of vibration. From corpuscles and electrons, atoms and molecules, to entire worlds and galaxies, everything is in motion.

Each one of us has a specific vibration: the combination of our mental, emotional and physical essence, which is the culmination of perhaps thousands of lifetimes. There are as many different vibrations as there are people on this planet. It is this *essence* that we tune into when we meet someone for the first time or enter an unfamiliar environment. It is this vibration that allows us to be either resonant or dissonant with our surroundings. It takes a difference of only a few percentage points to feel comfortable or uncomfortable, in harmony or not. For example, have you ever come across certain individuals who are continually telling you how moral and ethical they are? Yet the whole sense you get just by being around them speaks of something entirely different. Despite their continued assurance to the contrary, you still feel agitated, low or out of sorts when you are in their company. They seem to dampen your spirits and you certainly don't get the good feeling that you might expect when hanging out with ethical, moral people. Your answers come a few weeks later, when you discover that they've been knifing you in the back, or running a cocaine syndicate from their garage. With vibration, there is nowhere to hide.

Our entire body is like a giant antenna or tuning fork, which is continuously tuning into subtle energies: specific mental, emotional and physical wavelengths and frequencies. In the same way we press the 'seek' button on our radio to tune into a specific station – classical or rock – we unknowingly tune into the different vibrations around us being given off by everyone and everything we come into contact with. By throwing a pebble into a still pond, we can create the same effect. As the pebble disturbs the equilibrium of the water's surface, it creates ripples which move outward towards the shore. The nature of our own vibrational state, driven by our own moods and emotions, changes from moment to moment, depending on the vibrations we tune into and the environment we've been exposed to. Every day we are caught up in an ocean of odic waves and ripples which we tune in and out of without thinking. These waves eventually take their toll on our bodies, particularly if we don't focus on keeping our vibrations high, which is why we get sick.

There are no diseases, only sick people.

Dr Edward Bach

Vibration and od form the basis of all forms of natural healing – energy healing, naturopathy and homeopathy. Od is not confined by time, space or distance, hence we have the concept of distance healing. All diseases, viruses, infections are, in fact living creatures, divine sparks and vibrations in their own right. They simply find a host in whose vibration they feel comfortable, one with which they resonate and set up shop. If the host's vibration is low, the conditions become more favourable for the virus to multiply or grow. This is when colonies, or cancers, are formed. It's a well-known fact in the natural healing profession that cancers are caused by lifestyles and negative emotions and, some physicians believe, from fungus, which already exists in all human bodies and has been allowed to multiply because of the vibration and lifestyle of the individual. Synthetic drugs and medications like anti-depressants and sleeping tablets alter the body's vibration enormously – for the worse, not better, which is why some people end up feeling more depressed when taking anti-depressants.

MUSIC, VIBRATION AND WORK

The very essence of vibration and resonance lies in music. When we listen to music, we don't just hear the rhythm through our physical ears, we feel it in our subtle bodies. The rhythms and pulses we experience in music resonate with the combined vibration of our mental, emotional and physical bodies. This is why music has the ability to stir up such deep emotions within us, sometimes filling our bodies with ecstasy, healing our hearts of sadness and making us forget about our problems as we embrace the beauty of life's simplest moments. Yet, as much as music has the power to heal and inspire, music also has the power to destroy. When I first met Steve, he liked to listen to the heavy metal band Motörhead. He used to play it in his car at full volume to help his driving ability. Yet, when I listen to Motörhead for only a few seconds it gives me a headache. Even when it's played quietly (if that's possible with a band like Motörhead), it makes me nauseous, irritable and anxious. In the same way, my meditative and classical music often irritates Steve, particularly when he's not in the right frame of mind. The type of music someone listens to can tell you a lot about their emotional or vibrational state.

In his research with water and water crystallisation over many years, Dr Masaru Emoto, a Japanese biologist and author of *The Hidden Messages in Water,* provides us with proof as to how the human body is affected by words, music, sound, light and colours. In one experiment, he exposes drops of water, taken from an identical source, to different kinds of music – one to classical compositions from the likes of Handel, Vivaldi and Bach, and the other to rock and heavy metal bands like Bon Jovi and Motörhead. The water crystals from each experiment were then frozen and photographed, in the same way that one photographs the crystalline patterns formed in snowflakes. The water crystals exposed to classical music displayed beautiful, intricate patterns, while the ones exposed to rock and heavy metal music were malformed, discoloured, dull, and in some cases, failed to crystallise at all. It's an interesting concept, when you think that 70% of the mature adult body is comprised of water. The vibrations of our environment can have a devastating effect on our body.

When we become sensitive to vibrations, particularly as we start to develop an interest in spiritual things, we become much more sensitive to our environment. Space is not empty but is filled with different fields and energies. Therefore, buildings and places where people gather retain the vibrational energy of its inhabitants long after people have vacated. The energy is held in the physical structure of the walls and fixtures. Compare the feeling you get when you walk into the house of an elderly person who has been terminally ill with walking into an art gallery or a temple. The environments will feel totally different. Physical objects attract and store energy, which is why when some psychics who are extremely sensitive hold a specific object in their hand, they can accurately explain where it's been and what it's been used for.

In the same way, working in a toxic environment or culture can impact negatively on your vibration, making you depressed, stressed and physically ill. The real danger of continuing to work in a negative culture is that eventually we become immune to the vibes around us, but wonder why we leave work feeling drained and exhausted, tired, frustrated and angry. Take a few days off from work and then go back into the environment again. Notice how you feel, how your body reacts, what thoughts and emotions you experience. Sometimes the negative vibes can hit you like a wall or a slap in the face, and you can suddenly find yourself becoming uptight or irritable for seemingly no reason at all. Very often, when walking into the main reception area of a company that I was to consult with, I would find myself almost

Molecular structure of water.
Photographs courtesy of Dr. Masaru Emoto.

Top Left: Water before prayer
Top Right: Water after prayer
Middle Left: Water exposed to the word 'Love'
Middle Right: Water exposed to the word 'Gratitude'
Bottom Left: Water exposed to heavy metal music
Bottom Right: Water exposed to light classical music

wading through a thick fog the moment I entered the building. It was a good indication of the kind of issues and problems I would find within, which always came out through the various processes I facilitated later.

If you get that sinking feeling in your solar plexus on a Sunday night before you have to go to work on Monday morning, that's a good indication that you are working in a toxic culture and it's taking its toll on your body. The more sensitive we become, the higher we move on the spiritual ladder, the more difficult it is to sustain our equilibrium in tough and harsh working conditions. So when you're a 'Handel' in a culture more akin with 'Bon Jovi,' it's probably time to get out!

Our vibration changes all the time, depending on our mood, our thinking pattern, our life circumstances and the physical environment. In the last couple of years in Johannesburg, when I was going through physiological hell in so many respects, lurching from one crisis to the next, my vibration was very erratic. Our physical body in its healthy state has a specific vibration. However, when we are sick, angry or depressed, our vibration lowers and we feel out of sorts. Just walk into a doctor's waiting room or a hospital filled with sick people when you are full of the joys of spring and notice how you feel. If you are sensitive, you will immediately feel uncomfortable (which is why so many people say they don't like hospitals). However, spend a little time there and you won't have the same spring in your step – you'll come out feeling a whole lot worse than when you went in. The ambient vibration of sickness will have an effect on every cell in your body.

The spiritual warrior is acutely aware of vibration and does whatever he can to raise it and keep it high. He burns incense, he listens to light, classical, meditative music, he reads things that will uplift him, he is careful about what he eats and drinks, selecting only those things that will nourish and sustain the healthy vibration of his body. He spends time in nature or places of learning and hangs out with people who are interested in these things. He actively cultivates around him a sense of well-being and peace. We need to raise our vibration in all of our three bodies – physical, emotional and mental. Becoming aware of vibration in your life and becoming sensitive to vibration enables you to make better choices and decisions about the places you go and the company you keep, decisions that impact your level of stress and anxiety and help or hinder personal and spiritual growth.

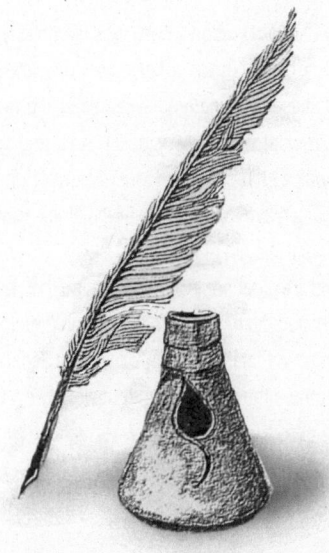

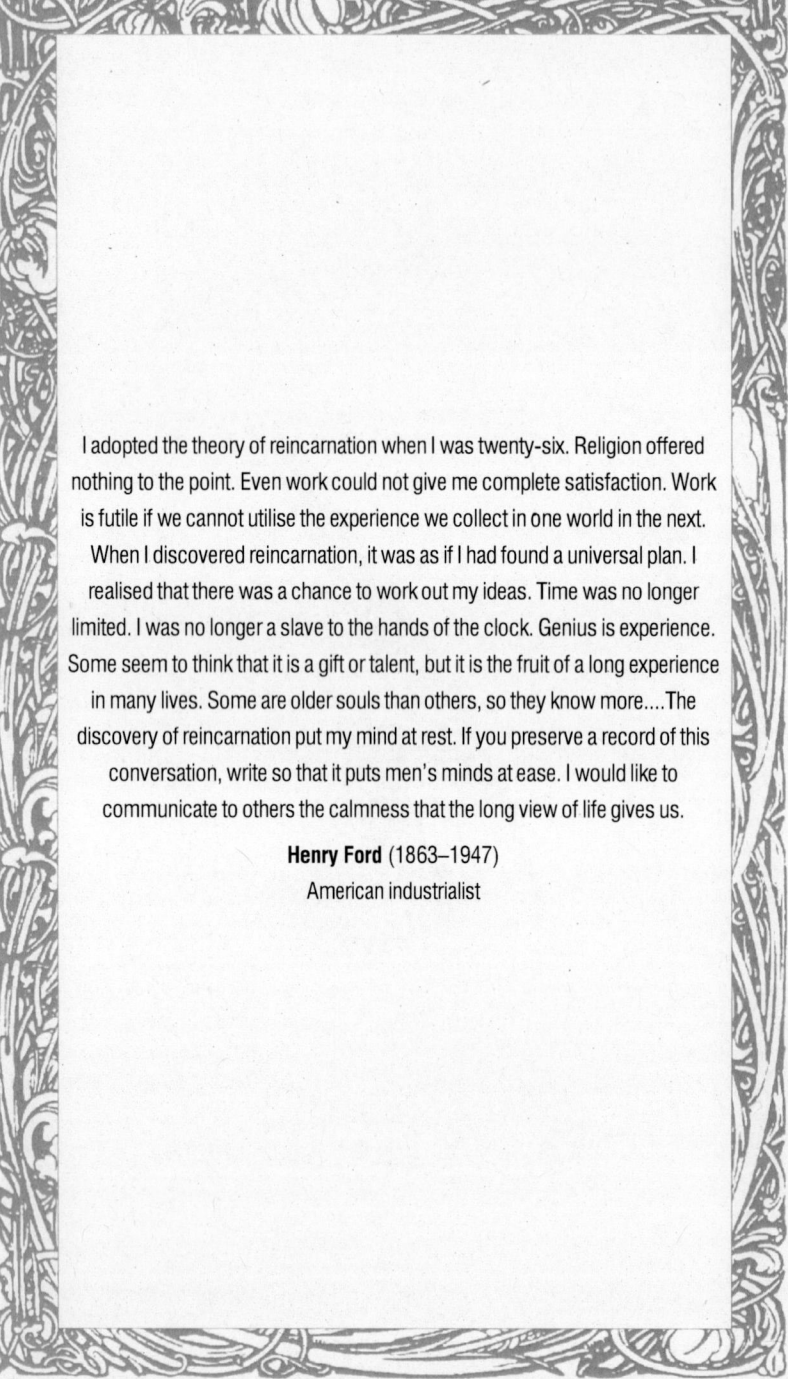

I adopted the theory of reincarnation when I was twenty-six. Religion offered nothing to the point. Even work could not give me complete satisfaction. Work is futile if we cannot utilise the experience we collect in one world in the next. When I discovered reincarnation, it was as if I had found a universal plan. I realised that there was a chance to work out my ideas. Time was no longer limited. I was no longer a slave to the hands of the clock. Genius is experience. Some seem to think that it is a gift or talent, but it is the fruit of a long experience in many lives. Some are older souls than others, so they know more....The discovery of reincarnation put my mind at rest. If you preserve a record of this conversation, write so that it puts men's minds at ease. I would like to communicate to others the calmness that the long view of life gives us.

Henry Ford (1863–1947)
American industrialist

CHAPTER 5

STOP THE WORLD, I WANT TO GET OFF
Reincarnation

It seems to me that I have always lived. And I possess memories which go back to the Pharaohs. I see myself very clearly in different professions and in many sorts of fortune. My present personality is the result of my lost personalities. Many things would be explained if we could know our real genealogy. Thus heredity is just a principle which has been badly applied.

Gustave Flaubert (1821–1880)
French novelist

n the Greek myths we find the story of Ixion, the King of Lapithae, who angered the gods with his rudeness, disrespect and vulgarity. As a punishment they tied him to a winged, fiery wheel that kept turning and turning for all eternity and from which he couldn't escape. The wheel is symbolic of reincarnation.

Although we might be blissfully unaware, we are all tied to an endless metaphorical wheel of birth, death and rebirth that goes on for millennia. We've had perhaps thousands of lifetimes before this one. For many years, before I understood this, I felt as if I was on this endless treadmill of dull drudgery – toiling away, going nowhere. All I wanted to do was reach down and hit the large red stop button with as much force as I could muster and climb off. Perhaps I subconsciously remembered being here before, going through the same old motions, doing the same old thing. Understanding the concept of reincarnation helped me to consciously start working towards a solution.

The word reincarnation comes from the Latin *re,* which means 'again', and *karos,* which means 'flesh'. Thus incarnation means to be *enfleshed,* or to have a body of flesh and blood. Reincarnation literally means to be re-enfleshed. The word itself seems to indicate a cycle of sorts, signifying that we have lived in a physical body before.

Everything in the Universe is cyclic: A year is a cycle of weeks, minutes, hours, days and months. There are seasonal cycles, the annual, perennial or biennial birth and death cycle of plants and trees. There are cycles to be found in spectral colours, musical notes, animal migration and weather patterns. We have the water cycle, carbon cycle and the nitrogen cycle. Planets orbit in cycles around the sun. Our solar system orbits around the centre of the Milky Way. The Milky Way orbits around the galaxy. The whole Universe itself is rotating. Electrons orbit around a nucleus in an atom – one single scheme, one single planet, endless cycles and orbits. Reincarnation is just another cycle in the greater scheme of things.

Before I embarked on my spiritual journey, I had a number of questions about reincarnation. Some of the beliefs I'd encountered seemed inconsistent and totally bizarre, littered with contradictions and contentions that seemed to bear no relevance in the world of anyone who had even half a brain – like the belief that humans reincarnated as plants, spiders or cockroaches; hence, in many of the Eastern traditions, people would avoid stepping on anything vaguely insect like, in case it was a brother from a previous life. I couldn't bring myself to believe that. How would all this hair fit into that one tiny little body, anyway?

My first question was: Is reincarnation fantasy or fact? It seemed that many world religions from India to Tibet hold reincarnation as part of the very fabric of their belief system. But Christianity does not. Many even had specific words in their language to describe this *mystical state,* which originated in the ancient Upanishad texts. In the Indian belief systems, *sansāra* means 'continuous flow', relating to the cycle of birth, life, death and rebirth. In Tibet, the word *bardo* means literally 'intermediate state', referring to the state of existence between two lives on Earth. Even some of the best known thinkers throughout history – Pythagoras, Socrates, Plato, Albert Einstein, Sir Isaac Newton, Sir Francis Bacon and Carl Jung, for example – accepted the philosophy, along with many renowned artists and composers – Leonardo da Vinci, Mozart and Wagner. Many esoteric works written in the last century also suggested a link to reincarnation like the writings of Helena Blavatsky, Alice Bailey and Rudolph Steiner. Yet despite this, Christianity makes no mention of it anywhere. Every devout Christian whom I've had the temerity to discuss religion with – those, that is, who had even considered the notion of death – believe that when you die, you die, and that's it. Your number is up. You lie rotting in the ground and your 'soul' goes to heaven. But nobody knew where Heaven was. I found this somewhat perplexing, so final, so harsh. One life. That's it. What's the point?

A vast transformation will take place in life when the ideas of reincarnation and karma are no longer held by a few people.... The whole configuration of the plane, as well as the social life of men in their future, depends upon how men have lived in earlier incarnations....

Rudolf Steiner (1861–1925)
Austrian philosopher

However, one of the first books I read on the subject – *Many Lives, Many Masters,* by Dr Brian Weiss – shifted my thinking considerably. Brian Weiss was a traditional psychiatrist, a sceptic, who was completely stumped when one of his patients began recalling past-life experiences and traumas while under hypnosis. The experiences she recounted held the key to her recurring nightmares and anxiety attacks. When she began to channel messages from 'the space between lives', containing remarkable revelations about his own family and the death of his firstborn son, it changed his life completely.

With this as an inspiration, I deepened my search for information that would provide proof and found that there were indeed thousands of documented cases of reincarnation, where children in particular demonstrated language, knowledge, or musical abilities at a very young age that could not be explained by any other means. Wolfgang Mozart was one of these mysteries; he displayed extraordinary musical abilities from the age of three, and went on to compose music from the age of five. A Canadian biochemist and psychiatrist, Professor Ian Stevenson (1918–2007), dedicated an entire lifetime to documenting cases of reincarnation (largely funded, incidentally, by Chester Carlson, the developer of the Xerox machine!), adding fuel to his theory that reincarnation offers 'a third possibility' in the development of character, along with hereditary and environmental influences (nature and nurture). I conceded that reincarnation had to have *some* credibility.

So why does Christianity not mention this concept in its Canon of Scripture, when it seemed so glaringly obvious that there was some foundation here? The concept of reincarnation pre-dates Christianity. In fact, it goes back to Egyptian times, perhaps even before. Early priests and scholars taught reincarnation as a 'truth beyond question' until the Dark Ages, when the Catholic church persecuted any individual or sect who held views and opinions different from its own. The philosophy of reincarnation was apparently actively removed from the Bible in 553 AD during an Ecumenical Council meeting of the Catholic

Church in Constantinople, which was of the opinion that if common folk knew they would come back again, it would be difficult to frighten them into paying large sums of money to the Church as recompense for their sins. You have to admit that it's a good scam.

As long as you are not aware of the continual law of Die and Be Again, you are merely a vague guest on a dark earth.

Goethe (1749–1832)
German writer and physicist

My second question was: Why do we reincarnate? There seem to be three predominant reasons: The first brings us right back to the purpose of creation: Our purpose here on earth is to learn and brighten ourselves as a divine fragment of the Supreme Being, and, in short, one lifetime is not enough for us to do that. We can't learn enough in seventy years or so, even to make the smallest of dents in the Universe. We are creatures of habit, we don't like to change, we like that which is comfortable, and so have a tendency to stick to the familiar and well known. In some of the pretty English villages close to where I grew up, many people died in the same village that they were born into. They married their childhood sweethearts, lived close to the parents and grandparents, who could help to take care of the kids, and perhaps ventured into a neighbouring town or city to work. If we do this self-same thing life after life, it may take thousands of incarnations before we start to break through our many limitations. Perhaps we need to wear out many bodies before we can become enlightened. Seventy or so years is not enough time for us to learn, especially if we consider that the Universe has been around for billions of years. So reincarnation is a continuous cycle that every divine spark, human or not, participates in as a continuous development process for the soul.

The second reason we reincarnate is to fulfil our desires and wishes. As the Supreme Being is a creator, so we are creators, as we are made in his image. (Even science is now saying that we are in fact creators and not just passing observers of life on our planet.) If we wish for things or have strong desires in life, or if we are ambitious, want to marry a prince or win the lottery or buy that big mansion on the hill overlooking the sea, we can indeed have it all – just like Rhonda Byrnes' book, *The Secret,* tells us. The Universe corresponds to our thoughts and desires. However, it may mean that these desires can't be fulfilled in the time frame that we've set for ourselves and may only materialise a few lifetimes down the line. There is no time or space on the subtle planes; each life is seen as another chapter in the soul's journey, so the Universe doesn't conform to time frames in the way we understand them. If we can't marry our prince in this life because our karma dictates we are ugly with big feet, then we will have to come back again, perhaps many times, before we can achieve the object of our desire. It may be that the life you are living today is a result of the desires you had many lifetimes ago.

There is nothing wrong with having aspirations on a spiritual journey. One doesn't have to give up everything to live the life of an aesthete. Part of the spiritual journey is learning to balance our lives, incorporating both the material and spiritual. But our problems arise when we become attached to things, which is why many spiritual systems practice non-attachment to *anything* – people, places, things or events. In the system of *Sahaj Marg*, derived from the ancient Indian system of Raja Yoga, there is a belief that all our experiences, actions, reactions, thoughts and emotions leave impressions. These impressions, called *samskaras,* accumulate over time (lifetimes), wrapping themselves around us like a thick sludge or web, influencing our view of reality and consequently our behaviour. As habit patterns emerge and solidify we continue to react in the present as we have in the past, setting the blueprint for future action. In this way, we become in a real sense slaves to our past experience and have to keep reincarnating as a result.

The third reason for reincarnation is found in the law of karma, which is intrinsically interwoven between our journey of development and the fulfilment of desires and wishes. The next chapter is dedicated to this subject.

There is also a fourth reason for reincarnation, which falls outside the scope of this book, simply because I wouldn't know where to begin in terms of explaining it. Throughout history we have seen individuals who have reincarnated for a specific purpose or mission for the greater good of humanity; Jesus of Nazareth, the Buddha, the prophet Zoroaster come to mind. I've also met many 'ordinary' people, too, who believe that they have been sent here on a special mission. Who am I to doubt them? I will never know. God doesn't confide in me on these matters. The proof will only be in the fruits of their labours.

However, this point leads me to another point: Why is it that the majority of us don't remember our previous lives? Surely that would make reincarnation so much easier to accept as a 'global belief'. I guess the answer is a simple one: The majority of us are not strong enough to be burdened with the extra emotions and mental images of things we've experienced in our past lives. It's hard enough dealing with the guilt and remorse we feel about the mistakes we have made in this life. We may have been guilty of horrible acts over thousands of years, things that we just can't bear to witness or we would spend our lives in a deep depression, not being able to stand the pain.

Another reason we don't remember is because our current life would be chaos if we did. Imagine lying in your bed one night, just dropping off to sleep when someone holding a very large shovel and a pickaxe taps you on the shoulder and asks you if you wouldn't mind if he digs here under your bed because he remembers that he buried gold there 200 years ago. Or perhaps 200 years ago you robbed a house, holding the residents hostage with a carving knife. If you remembered doing that and understood the law of cause and effect (karma), then your days would be spent in terror – you would be living behind a barbed-wire fence, with an alarm system, Rottweiler dogs, sandbags, tin hats and gun turrets to guard against the same thing happening to *you*. (Maybe all the residents of Johannesburg were burglars in their previous lives?)

If we consciously remembered our previous lives, then we wouldn't progress or move forward at all. If I remember myself to be the Queen of Sheba (which so many people seem to think they were in a previous life), where I had loyal subjects catering for my every whim, why would I be content with being a street sweeper, or someone's personal assistant in this life? Our memories of what we once were wouldn't allow us to do a scrap of work or make any progress at all.

Our ability to remember these lives depends on how far up the cosmic ladder of evolution we have progressed. One of the ultimate benefits of *enlightenment* is to accurately remember each one of our past lives when we reach a certain point in our spiritual development (as the Buddha did when he achieved enlightenment). Past-life regression has, no doubt, proved a beneficial therapy time and again in helping people overcome serious anxiety, depression and trauma. However, I am not a great fan of those who want to know about their past lives for entertainment value and trawl from one hypnotherapist or psychic to the next, just so they can look good at dinner parties. 'Oh, you know Mary? She was my mother in a past life – a psychic told us.' Even under hypnosis it is virtually impossible to separate genuine past-life memories from unconscious fantasies. Childhood experiences or totally imaginary episodes can be mistaken for past lives, as can any thought or experience. If we want to know what we did in our past life we can do so by looking at the trends and patterns taking place in this life. We will talk about that more in the following chapters.

Of course you don't die, nobody dies, death doesn't exist, you only reach a new level of vision, a new realm of consciousness, a new unknown world. Just as you don't know where you came from, so you don't know where you're going. But there is something there, before and after, I firmly believe.

Henry Miller (1891–1980)
American novelist and painter

Life is like a gigantic, ongoing movie. Each life is another scene or act. When the director screams 'action,' off we go again. We are the constant feature – the princess in one scene and a poor street sweeper in the next. Each time, the scenery, the backdrop, the costumes, the other characters and the overall plot change. But we remain the central character. We may forget our lines, lose the plot and get some bad reviews in one life, but in another we will excel in every act. Each time we become a teensy tiny bit wiser and change just a little. This lifetime is the culmination of every single lifetime we've had to date. The sum total of all the acts, all the curtain calls, all our good and bad choices and deeds. The question is, how long do we want to keep playing the starring role? Surely we are well-rehearsed by now?

Through the thousands of lifetimes we've had, we have all been rich, we have all been poor, we have given birth to and fathered children, and we have gone through a plethora of professions and emotional, socio-political experiences. It takes hundreds, perhaps thousands of lives for us to become all that we can be.

The *spell* we are under in life is very powerful and for many incarnations it dupes us. We are convinced in our mind that we are the victims of difficulties and limitations but we are in a temporary state. Physical life as we know it forms a very small part of our existence. Even if we've had thousands of incarnations, if we compare the totality of time spent in a physical body with the totality of time that we have been here, going way back into the past and stretching far forward into the future, it is a mere drop in the ocean.

So if we are tired and jaded by life, that is a good thing, because the time is approaching when we will wake up and say, 'Stop the world, I want to get off,' and start taking deliberate steps to seek our salvation. The only way to get off this revolving wheel, or slow it down just enough so we can catch our breath is to embark on a spiritual journey. But there is no rush, no deadline to achieve. Every experience in every life contributes to our brightness as a spiritual being. Nothing is ever lost. As Henry Ford said, 'Life gives us the opportunity to work out our ideas instead of being a slave to the clock.' By understanding the law of reincarnation we can begin to embrace life as a glorious pageant, and use every opportunity to enjoy being fully human.

HEAVEN AND HELL

Just as we don't remember details of our previous lives, we don't remember what it's like to die, either. Not many of us like to think about death or what happens to us when we die. It seems too morose to have such a conversation around the dinner table in polite company. Perhaps this is why so many of us fear death and spend so much time in mourning when someone does pass on. Yet in certain traditions, death is seen as an inevitable part of life and is often considered a time of joy and celebration. They recognise that the person now had a brief respite from the hard rigours of existence perhaps after many years of suffering. Death is a holiday, a time when the departed can relax. Some even believe that spending too long in mourning and sorrow, holds back the development of the spirit on his journey into 'special world'. And I have to say that I agree with them.

What we call *death* is simply the transition of one state of consciousness to another. When we die, in whatever circumstances, we are temporarily separated from a physical body and move onto the astral plane in our astral body, as we have done thousands of times before, every night during sleep. When we sleep at night our astral body leaves our physical body, only to return to it again before we wake. We experience dreams on the astral plane. In the mind of the mystic, sleep is like a mini-death.

The astral plane is governed by laws completely different from the physical plane. There is no concept of time as we know it. There is no inertia, no gravity and no mass. Moving around is simple. We only have to think of a place or a person and we are with them immediately. On the astral plane we are free from the rigours of life, we no longer have to work for a living and we can live a very peaceful existence indeed. We call this state or place 'heaven.'

All mythologies, religions and spiritual ideologies have a concept of heaven of one kind or another – an ultimate sanctuary, a spiritual haven for those who have been saved. The book of Revelations describes the Christian heaven as awesome and magnificent – filled with gold and precious gemstones, saints and celestial beings. The Supreme Being sits on a throne with Christ on his one side and the Holy Spirit on another.

The Muslims conceive of seven heavens, each being more glorious than the other, as one proceeds upwards. The topmost is the seat of Allah and the Muslem saints and where the dark-eyed Huris entertain the Muslem martyrs.

The Hindu idea of heaven is a place occupied by all the devas, minor gods, demigods, and Brahma the Supreme Being; it was achieved through the state of *moksha*, a final release. The devotee is said to enter into this state when 'Samadhi' is reached.

Buddhists conceive of a heaven as a state called 'Nirvana' reached after achieving the condition of 'Satori'.

Heaven to the ancient Greeks was to be found either in the fields of Elysium or in the clouds over Mount Olympus, both of these states or locations thought to be glorious. In the Nordic myths, heaven is not just one place, but several. Asgard was the dwelling place of the higher gods of the

Asas. Vanaheim was the heaven or dwelling of the lower gods, or the Vana gods. There were also Helheim, Nifleheim, Elfheim, Midgard, Valhalla. The Tree of Life, Yggdrasil, connected all these places or states together.

Myths and all systems of belief can of course be interpreted in many ways, depending on the insight of the interpreter. In the eyes of the mystic, both Heaven and Hell are *states of consciousness*, not actual places. The various Heavens, however, do exist because of the belief systems of the hundreds of thousands of people who have followed these specific spiritual or religious paths over the centuries. The web of the matrix captures these thoughts as beliefs. They are located on the middle astral plane. Every soul has its own personal symbolism – a symbolism we find in myths and dreams. The symbolism is the same throughout all members of the same faith. So the Heaven of the Christian will differ in many ways from the Heaven of the Muslim. Whether we are a Presbyterian, Catholic or Baptist, whatever our idea of Heaven is in life, so we will experience it when we pass on. The biblical concept *'As a man thinketh in his heart'* applies to the physical plane *and* the astral plane, whether we are incarnate or discarnate.

Many of us might be familiar with the concept of Purgatory as the place after death where we first 'burn' our desires before moving into the 'Heaven World'. Purgatory is also associated with what we know as the 'triple review': the state in which our life plays out in front of us, backwards, from the moment of our death to the moment of our birth. People who have encountered near-death experiences describe this. British mystic and author Dion Fortune describes Purgatory as a 'hospital where sick souls are operated on,' a place where some of our desires are purged or burnt from us after death, before we return again to the physical world. The depths of despair we sink to in physical life determine the experience we have in Purgatory. Our state of mind at the time of our death also has an impact, which is why so many of the Eastern traditions, such as those in Tibet, place such importance on helping people die peacefully, passing from the physical plane to the astral plane with a minimal amount of fuss and trauma.

In the eyes of the mystic, Hell doesn't exist as a place. Hell is the physical world to which our desires keep us reincarnating. It, too is described in the myths. *Divine Comedy (Divina Commedia)* is an allegorical poem written by Dante Alighieri. It is divided into three parts: the Inferno, Purgatorio and Paradiso – Hell, Purgatory and Paradise. Paradise is a depiction of Heaven. Hell and Purgatory are represented by different circles, ten in all, representing different layers of sin. The deeper one goes into Hell and Purgatory, the more each soul is suffering, and so it joins with other souls, which makes the experience worse. Misery loves company. Each layer can be deemed to be a certain mood or vibration which attracts all other similar moods through the concept of resonance. Thus all the murderers cluster together, as do the thieves, and the suicide victims. The different layers depict the different levels of psychological hell experienced by the so called sinners and non-believers after death. I guess we can liken it to our prison system today, where all wrongdoers in the eyes of the law are required to reside together. Atheists don't believe in Heaven or an afterlife, so when they die they find themselves in a kind of limbo, 'a nothing space' which is also depicted as a form of Hell.

Hell is also described in the Greek myth of Sisyphus: The gods condemned King Sisyphus to be chained up in Tartarus, the deepest part of the Underworld reserved for the punishment of evildoers. He had seduced his niece and killed many of his house guests. However, he did not want to face his wrongdoings. He tricked his way out of the chains and convinced Persephone to allow him to return to the world of men to chastise his wife for failing to bury him correctly. But when he had again seen the face of this world, enjoyed the water and the sun, warm stones and the sea, he no longer wanted to go back to the 'infernal darkness'. For many years more he lived facing the curve of the gulf, the sparkling sea and the smiles of earth. It was by a decree from the Gods that Hermes came to seize the impudent man, snatching him from his joys, leading him forcibly back to the Underworld, where his punishment was to be tied to a rock and forced to roll the large boulder up a mountainside. But always, when he reached the crest, the boulder rolled away from him, back to the base of the mountain below, binding Sisyphus to an eternity of frustration. This is symbolic of reincarnation and our continual return to the physical world.

Another myth describes Purgatory – a place where our desires are burnt from us before we move into the Heaven World: Tantalus (the source of the English word *tantalise*) was also accused of many wrongdoings – human sacrifice, cannibalism and the killing of newborn babies; it is also said that he tried to steal the Ambrosia of the Gods. His punishment was to stand in a pool of water in Tartarus, beneath a fruit tree with very low branches. Whenever he reached for the fruit, the branches raised the intended meal from his grasp. Whenever he bent down to get a drink, the water receded before he could get any. His fate has cursed him with eternal deprivation of nourishment.

The experience of Purgatory can be likened to a dream of remorse and cleansing. The mystic does not believe in the Christian doctrine of eternal punishment. Hell does not exist as a permanent place. No psychic who has the ability to access the astral plane has ever confirmed this belief. No individual who has ever had a near-death experience has reported it. Yet those who have experienced Purgatory profess to having a healthy respect for it. Once the cleansing is over, we move into the Heaven World for a holiday, of sorts, until it comes time to reincarnate again. The more work we do on ourselves spiritually here in the physical world, the more control we can have over the subtle planes.

The Law

The sun may be clouded, yet ever the sun
Will sweep on its course till the cycle is run.
And when into chaos the systems are hurled,
Again shall the Builder reshape a new world.
Your path may be clouded, uncertain your goal;
Move on, for the orbit is fixed for your soul.
And though it may lead into darkness of night,
The torch of the Builder shall give it new light.
You were, and you will be: know this while you are.
Your spirit has travelled both long and afar.
It came from the Source, to the Source it returns;
The spark that was lighted, eternally burns.
It slept in the jewel, it leaped in the wave,
It roamed in the forest, it rose in the grave,
It took on strange garbs for long aeons of years,
And now in the soul of yourself it appears.
From body to body your spirit speeds on;
It seeks a new form when the old one is gone;
And the form that it finds is the fabric you wrought
On the loom of the mind, with the fibre of thought.
As dew is drawn upward, in rain to descend,
Your thoughts drift away and in destiny blend.
You cannot escape them; or petty, or great,
Or evil, or noble, they fashion your fate.
Somewhere on some planet, sometime and somehow,
Your life will reflect all the thoughts of your now.
The law is unerring; no blood can atone;
The structure you rear you must live in alone.
From cycle to cycle, through time and through space,
Your lives with your longings will ever keep pace.
And all that you ask for, and all you desire,
Must come at your bidding, as flames out of fire.
Once list to that voice and all tumult is done,
Your life is the life of the Infinite One;
In the hurrying race you are conscious of pause,
With love for the purpose and love for the cause.
You are your own devil, you are your own God,
You fashioned the paths that your footsteps have trod;
And no one can save you from error or sin,
Until you shall hark to the Spirit within.

Ella Wheeler Wilcox

From *Poems of Sentiment*

CHAPTER 6
SNAKES AND LADDERS
The Law of Karma

O youth or young man who fancy that you are neglected by the Gods, know that if you become worse you shall go to worse souls, or if better, to better, and in every succession of life and death you will do and suffer what like may fitly suffer at the hands of like. This is the justice of heaven, which neither you nor any other unfortunate will ever glory in escaping.

Plato
Student of the philosopher Socrates and teacher of Aristotle

ave you ever wondered why some people seem to have continuous bad luck in life, whilst others sail seemingly from one success to the next, without batting an eyelid? You know – the ones who seem to have the Midas touch: whatever they touch turns to gold without any real effort at all. Whether these people are millionaires or regular, everyday folk, they seem to have got the plot about life, while you find yourself floundering with even the most simple of things.

The questions about the justice of life really started to come thick and fast when my dad died suddenly at the age of 57 in a car crash. At his funeral there was standing room only. I never realised how many lives he'd touched. His death left our family feeling robbed and cheated by life, which had ripped our rock from us. We don't expect that our parents will die so soon. Why is life just so unfair? I spent a long time being desperately angry at people I deemed to be worthless, people who dared to still be alive in this world when he wasn't, people who couldn't articulate properly, who whinged and moaned about their own sorry state of affairs, life's dropouts – single mothers, hobos, alcoholics, drug addicts, convicts, the milkman, the neighbour's cat and anyone or anything that seemed to get in my way. In my book they were nothing more than oxygen thieves. How come they deserved to live, when a good man like my father didn't?

Once I calmed down, Dad's death prompted me to ask deeper questions about life than I had seriously considered before, questions that were more than casual musings ambling aimlessly through my head on a hot summer's day. They really troubled me. Why did I have to be without a father at 27 years of age? Why couldn't I enjoy his retirement with him? Why did God take him so soon? (I hated God even more at this point.) But more importantly, here I was, closeted nicely in middle-class England, banging on about losing my father, when there were people out there who were born into single-parent families who had never even known their fathers, or who had fathers who spent their lives in the pub, coming home at all hours, drunk and abusive. What about those who suffered years of abuse? What about those living in abject poverty whose fathers couldn't or woudn't provide at all?

At this point in my grief, I could totally understand why people gave up their lives to become missionaries in Africa or counsellors supporting the victims of rape, violence or abuse. I wasn't inclined that way, although it would have helped to alleviate my guilt for being alive when my father wasn't. Our own difficulties in life do indeed lead us to express greater compassion towards others, enabling us to take off the rose-coloured spectacles that don't permit us to see others' misfortunes.

But that was not my journey. Helping others might make me feel better, ease my conscience, but it wasn't going to give me the answers I sought which only came years later when I started to understand the system of Divine justice through the concept of karma and reincarnation. It was only then that I started to make peace with my father's death and become more accepting of life and my place within it. This one teaching, probably more than any other, has helped me to stop worrying and start living. But it's not for the faint hearted. For those who think that life has served them up a raw deal, that life should be lovely, cuddly, compassionate and beautiful all the time, then this chapter might be a little tough to take.

The word *karma* comes from the Sanskrit word *krma*, meaning 'action and reaction', or 'cause and effect'. What you sow in this life, you reap in the next. It is one of the fundamental laws of existence, as are the laws of reincarnation, gravity, duality, and the cyclic nature of the Universe. Karma is also referred to as *fate* and *destiny*. In a conventional sense, it means the law of recompense, the law of retribution, the law that sees that justice will be done – an eye for an eye, a tooth for a tooth, tit for tat.

Karma runs from life to life. It does not 'pay you back' in this life, as so many people think. Karma could not exist without reincarnation. We read earlier that we keep reincarnating for a number of reasons, but one of them is because of karma. We often hear people say that we are here 'to learn lessons'. That is true, and some of the lessons we learn in life are very harsh. The lessons however, come in many ways, and one of them is through the law of karma.

All of us, in everything that we do, create karma. It doesn't just happen in India or Tibet. We can't avoid it. It is a fact of life. No matter how high or low we are on the cosmic ladder of existence, the law applies to us. I have met people who believe they are exempt – 'Oh, this is my last life here; I don't have to come back any more, so karma doesn't apply to me.' Well, I wish I'd found the same spiritual guru as they did, then perhaps I wouldn't still be here in this world, either.

There are three types of karma: good, bad and indifferent. In its simplest form, it works this way: If you do a good deed in this life, you have to come back to this world to have a good deed done to you. If you do a bad deed, then you have to come back and experience the effects of that bad deed. So karma can be both positive and negative depending on our attitude towards it. All the good things that we do, all the kind thoughts that we think, all the positive emotions that we experience will lead to positive karma. All the negative things we do, all the dissension we sow, all the people we lash out at will revisit us. It is the only way we can truly learn.

Here's an illustration to explain this: If I slap you around the face in anger and frustration, I have learned what it is like to be the 'slapper'. But I don't know what it is like to be on the receiving end of the slap, to be the slapped, or the 'slappee'. I can imagine what it's like to be slapped, and I may feel some remorse immediately after dishing out the slap. I may apologise profusely to my victim, but for me to truly learn the 'slapping' lesson I need to experience being slapped myself. It is not until I am on the receiving end that I can experience the pain, the discomfort, the anger or humiliation of receiving a slap. If we only experience one side of the lesson, then this is unbalanced. The Universe cannot tolerate imbalance of any kind.

Not everything that happens in life is karma. To understand karma and how it plays out in our lives, we need to look at the major *trends,* the repetitive patterns, the obstacles that seem to continually litter our path. For example: We step out of our car and twist our ankle in a hole that we did not see. If this only happens once and does not happen again, this is not karma, it's an accident. We weren't looking where we were going. But if we have twisted our ankle twenty-five times in the same way, that is a trend in our life. We did someone wrong in the last life and now we are paying for it with equal pain or discomfort.

So the trends in our life are the things that are repetitive, that keep happening or are longstanding. Relationships with our parents, siblings, children and romantic partners are all longstanding and are karmic. So is our physical appearance, the strengths and weaknesses of our body, the congenital deformities we have, *i.e.* bad eyesight, or one leg shorter than the other, a heart condition, the psychoses and psychological imbalances. These are all trends – long lasting and repetitive – and are a result of karma that *we*, by the wise or unwise use of our free will, created in our previous life. How many times have you heard children say to their parents, 'I didn't ask to be born.' They blame their parents for the fact that they are here. This attitude often continues way into adult life, unless they develop an understanding of karma and reincarnation. They *did*, in fact, ask to be born, because by their very actions, nothing else but birth could come from it.

How do we create karma? When do we make the decision about the kind of life we will have next time around? Many think that we make the decisions when we pass on. As we sit on a cloud in an exalted state, thoughtfully sipping on our piña coladas, we look down on earth after reviewing our life and nobly decide, 'These are the lessons I need to learn next time around.' But when we pass on into the Heaven World, we are in an exalted state; why would we choose to live in a slum, or be the victim of constant abuse, or be poor or disabled? Surely we would all choose to have perfect childhoods, big houses with swimming pools, and fast cars. Who in their right mind would choose a life of pain and suffering?

When we pass on, we do become aware of the folly of our way as we pass through the lower part of the astral, Purgatory and the triple review, but all the choices about our next life have already been made. The options have already been taken. We make the decisions about our next life *right here and right now* in our very existence, not when we are sitting on a cloud. Every moment of every day, by the wise or unwise use of our free will, by our actions, words and deeds, we are choosing the type of parents, children, romantic partners and friends we will have in our next life. If we are abusive, disrespectful and disinterested parents, we will have abusive, disrespectful and disinterested parents in our next life. If we are angry partners, continually lashing out at those we love dearly in this life because we ourselves are upset and emotionally unbalanced, we will experience anger from our partners in our next life. If we are two-faced as friends, or always judging others and talking behind their backs, we will experience the same with our friendships in the next life.

KARMA IN ACTION
When Your Number's Up
Reported by Aislinn Simpson of *The Telegraph*

A married, middle aged couple from Zagreb, named Mirna and Stipe Cavlovic, got caught up in a row between two men over a debt. One of them pulled out a gun and shot at the couple at point blank range.

'He was so close you'd think that one or both of them would have died instantly,' said a police source.

The bullet grazed the cheekbone of Mr Cavlovic's terrified blonde wife and slammed into Mr Cavlovic's mouth. But instead of killing him, the bullet got caught in his dentures and fell harmlessly to the ground.

'I thought I was dead for sure,' Mr Cavlovic told police. 'I didn't even see the bullet hit my wife. I just saw the flash of the gun's barrel. The next thing I knew was something hit my false tooth and I spat out the hot lead. It hurt like hell but we're both still alive.'

Police ballistics experts believe Mr Cavlovic survived the bullet because it had lost so much speed when it first skimmed his wife's cheek. The would-be hit-man fled the scene but was arrested soon afterwards. Zagreb police confirmed a 58-year-old man is in custody on firearms charges.

Source: Osrail Morendis
The Art of Staying Alive http://osrail.blogspot.com/

We read in the Bible that 'The sins of the fathers will be visited upon the children in the third and fourth generation.' (Exodus 20.5.) I didn't get this. How can a child be punished for something his great-grandfather did? Yet if we bring karma and reincarnation into it, then we *are* our great-grandfather and therefore it is only divine justice that we should come and pay for what we ourselves have done. It's hard to conceive that all newborn babies born on this planet are not completely innocent. They are ancient beings that have had thousands of lives before this one. Our children in fact are one lifetime ahead of us. Sometimes newborn babies suffer and the law of karma helps to explain this.

The problem with being human, however, is that when we suffer we lash out and hurt others around us. We have a philosophy of, 'Why must I be unhappy on my own? If I am miserable, in a deep depression, hungry and cold, you're gonna know about it. I won't allow you to forget I'm miserable.' And so instead of suffering in silence for the things we have brought upon ourselves, and for which nobody bears any blame, we lash out at those around us, hurting them in the process, as though it is their fault. We pay off our karma, but we make fresh karma, which we have to pay next time around. And this is how we go on, life after life after life.

I came to the conclusion that I was responsible for my whole life, whatever had happened. I used to blame my family, society, my wife... and that day I saw so clearly that I had nobody to blame but myself. I put everything on my own shoulders and I felt so relieved. Now I'm free, no one else is responsible.

Henry Miller (1891–1980)
American novelist and painter

When we pass on we go to the astral plane and, perhaps for the first time in this particular incarnation, we become aware of the nature of the spirit world. We make all these wonderful promises to ourselves that in our next life we will be different, that we will become aware of the spirit world at a much younger age; in fact, we wish we had died earlier, as the spirit world is much more peaceful than the life we had on the physical plane. But when it comes time for us to reincarnate, we are born again into forgetfulness. If we are born into a poor family, we want to be rich, to avenge our father, to help our mother, to prove ourselves, to make money. All thoughts of the promises we made to ourselves before birth are gone. In the same way, if we are born to rich parents, have access to a lot of money, a good life, why would we want to seek boring old spiritual things? We are having way too much fun here. And so, we meander from life to life making good progress in some, and very little in others. Hence we change very little overall. The progress we make in one life is undone in the next and so our progress up the ladder is really slow.

Our disposition in life always drives the decisions and choices we make and how we handle ourselves in this world. But what better way to learn than through our mistakes? These choices, good and bad – lashing out when we are in pain, or putting on a brave face and suffering in silence – will determine what karma we create and what we have to pay for when we come back in the next life. Through this process of life after life, which may take thousands of incarnations, we eventually get to the point where we are so fed up that no amount of money or good times can appease us, and so we want nothing more than to seek spiritual things as a way out of this mess. Until that point, we are involved in a futile game of existence.

In each lifetime, we lay down the railroad tracks for our next life, except in our next life we are the train having to traverse the tracks that we have laid. So if we botched the job in our previous life, we can expect a bit of trouble this time around. We are setting the course for our next incarnation right now where we will either enjoy many windfalls, or we will suffer many obstructions. But always in this mix is the choice we make as to how we handle them. We can choose our attitude as we have been given the divine gift of free will. If we use our free will wisely we will come back to experience fruitful and positive karma. If we use it unwisely then we come back to this world and face a number of very difficult and painful impediments. And so, the way we conduct ourselves in this life is very important, because we are busy drawing a blueprint for our next life, laying out the foundations. We are determining our own future, fate and destiny.

RUBBER DINGHY OR OCEAN LINER?

Karma can be likened to a boat on the ocean. If you find yourself in a rubber dinghy that keeps springing a leak so that you need to keep baling it out and patching the hole, while the ocean around you is rough and turbulent, then you probably have some pretty heavy karma. All our energy goes into survival, keeping the boat afloat as one obstacle after another is put in our path.

On the flip side, if your karma is good, you may find yourself in a large ocean liner that seemingly sails effortlessly from port to port on a calm flat ocean. The sun always shines and the fishing is good. The liner has lots of plush staterooms, entertainment, sundecks and a mountain of waiters to cater to your every need.

And so we carry on in this way for thousands of lifetimes. Doing good deeds in some lifetimes, and bad deeds in others, until we can find a way to break free. I guess you can liken it to running up a credit card bill: We make many purchases until we reach our credit limit, then save for months to pay off our debt. And just as the last instalment is paid, we go out on another spending spree and make fresh debts. Until we decide to cut up the credit card. The reincarnation cycle is designed to purge us of these desires whilst helping us learn through our mistakes. In that way we can get to a point where we truly want things to be different.

I have often heard people refute the law of karma as something that 'God wouldn't do', as it lacks compassion. Or people insist that the perpetrator in any act should be caught and punished. These are normally people who have been on the receiving end of some harsh lessons that never seem to stop. I know, because I have been on the receiving end of many myself. So who am

I to disagree – we live in a culture of blame, where everyone likes to point fingers and find the culprit. Convict the perpetrator, prove them wrong. Let justice be served. Blame is the very nature of our social, commercial and political world. We spend a lot of energy ranting and raving, finger-pointing and seeking out a fall guy. Finding a guilty culprit helps us make sense of the world. It makes us feel better inside. But it also stops us from being accountable. How else do you explain why some people get such a raw deal in life and others don't? Did all the wealthy, beautiful, well mannered, moralistic people get some divine dispensation that I was not privy too? That would make God an unfair God – a God who has favourites. Having us learn through our mistakes is probably the most compassionate thing God could do. Isn't that what we encourage in our own children when we prepare them for life?

Karma and reincarnation are far-reaching laws with many, many implications, way too many to cover succinctly in this simple chapter. It is because of karma that we must be reborn in this world. The mystic does not desire to be reborn and therefore is careful about the amount and type of karma that he or she makes. The purpose of life is for us to learn, to grow and develop, to expand our consciousness, to raise up our vibration, and to eventually be acceptable in the divine by becoming better human beings. With karmic debts to pay, we are stuck here.

This seemingly simple yet profound lesson has taught me more than anything else to stop worrying and start living, helping me to get a grip on life and stopping me from feeling sorry for myself. That doesn't mean that I don't have pain, that I don't suffer. I do. With understanding comes compassion, both for myself and others. We are all caught up in the cycle of life, no matter what our station or standing is – today the prince, tomorrow the pauper. Each of us plays the perfect role in assisting others to fulfil their karmic debt, as well as learning the valuable lessons ourselves that help us to become better human beings.

SNAKES AND LADDERS

Who would have known when we were children playing the board game of snakes-and-ladders that we were actually playing the game of karma? With a mere roll of the dice, we slide down the snake or climb up the ladder. The ladder is the Tree of Life, the snake is the symbol of the mistakes we make during life. This is how life is and how easily karma can be created.

The serpent is one of the oldest and most widespread mythological symbols in the world, with many seemingly contradictory meanings. It is often depicted with its tail in its mouth, forming a ring or a circle. The Greeks called it the *ouroboros*. It is a symbol of infinity and the cyclic nature of the cosmos. Many times, it is portrayed as the 'deceitful one', or a trickster. In the Nordic myths, the serpent dragon, Níðhöggr is continually gnawing at the roots of Yggdrasil, the Tree of Life, in an effort to topple it permanently. In the Garden of Eden, Eve was encouraged by the Serpent to eat the apple of the Tree of Knowledge of Good and Evil. Christian mythology brands the snake as a form of evil, responsible for destroying Paradise, for bringing about the fall of man. Yet in the Gnostic philosophy, the snake is praised for the same act. Without the snake encouraging Eve to stretch, to wake up, to seek knowledge, to make her first big mistake, the fall of man may never have happened and we may still, in our ignorance, be stuck in the garden of Eden, bored out of our minds eating figs, and learning very little.

In the Hindu myths, we find the Holy Trinity of Brahma, Vishnu and Shiva. Brahma is the creator of the Universe. His work now being done, he rests like an old grandfather. Vishnu is the preserver of cosmic order. Shiva is the destroyer of illusion. He dances to bring about the destruction of *Maya* (illusion.) For centuries he has been associated with *Naga,* the Sanskrit word for 'giant snake', as the Naga is wound around his neck. It represents rebirth, death and mortality, due to its ability to shed its skin and be symbolically reborn. In the tales of the Brahman, Vishnu lies sleeping on a coiled serpent, Shiva. He is dreaming of life. It is the dream of Vishnu we experience in this world. Shiva, however, keeps wriggling, trying to wake Vishnu from his dream. It is the dream that we need to wake from to find our way off the wheel of birth and death.

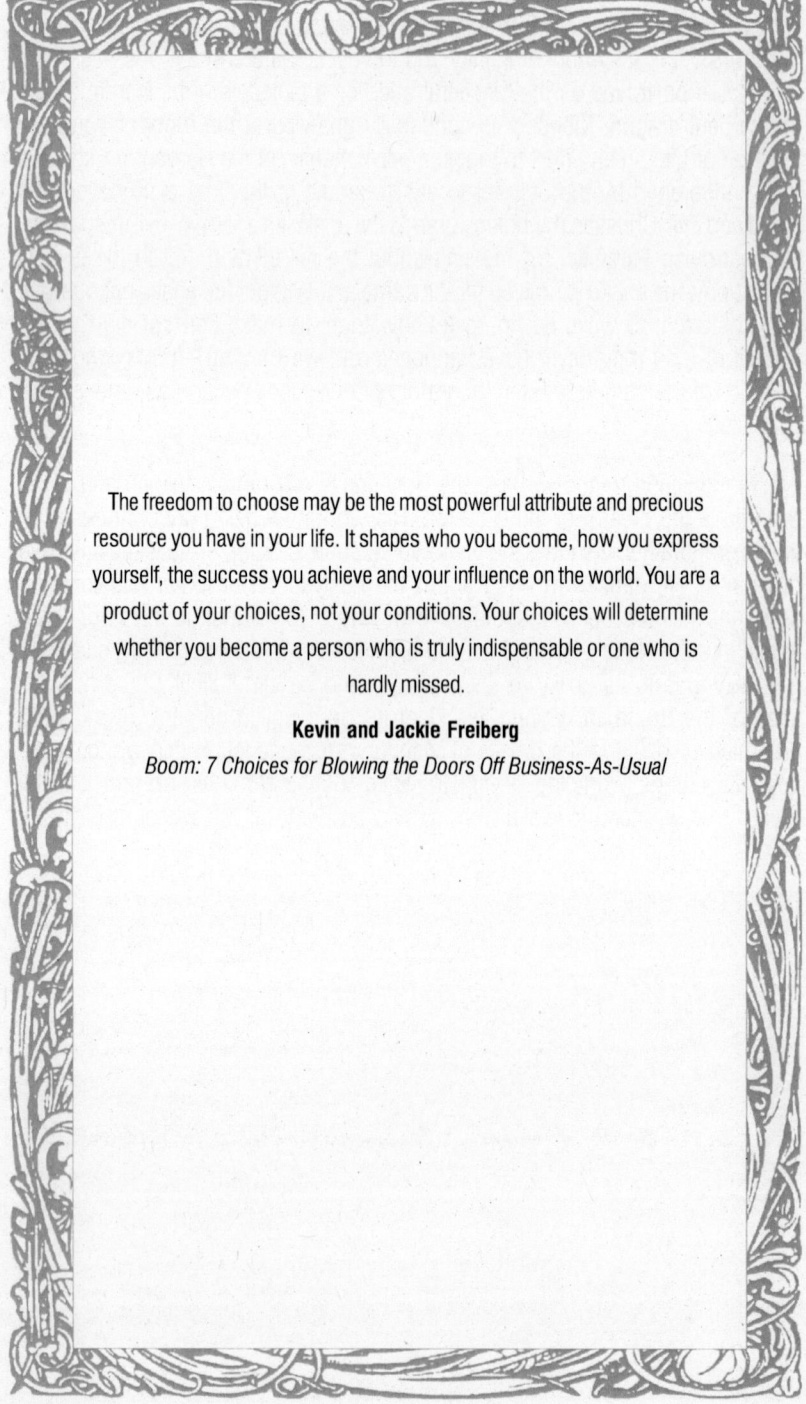

The freedom to choose may be the most powerful attribute and precious resource you have in your life. It shapes who you become, how you express yourself, the success you achieve and your influence on the world. You are a product of your choices, not your conditions. Your choices will determine whether you become a person who is truly indispensable or one who is hardly missed.

Kevin and Jackie Freiberg

Boom: 7 Choices for Blowing the Doors Off Business-As-Usual

CHAPTER 7

THE ANGEL WITH THE BIG BOOK

Free Will, Conscience and Karma

We are punished by our sins and not for them.

Elbert Hubbard (1856–1915)
American writer, publisher, artist and philosopher

 s a child, I always imagined that when it came time to pass on and finally make my way to the pearly gates of Heaven, Saint Peter would be there peering at me over his half-moon spectacles with a rather disapproving look on his face as he reviewed the long, long list of my evil deeds on an even longer ream of parchment that trailed off into the distance behind him. I believed that Judgement Day for me would no doubt result in eternal damnation to the Underworld because I hadn't embraced God as every good Christian should.

As adults, we might believe this idea of damnation to be a fallacy, even if we haven't found another belief system to replace it. But this belief, instilled in us from a very early age causes us great problems. Deep down, the fear of being *judged* resides in the cultural psyche of all Western thought. And it causes us to worry a lot. I'd spend a lot of my life, consciously and subconsciously, fretting about being judged not only by God but by almost anyone I came into contact with. It stopped me from living my life to the full. I worried about getting it wrong, being a failure, being a success, of not doing enough, having enough, being enough, caring enough, saying or doing the right thing. Looking back I guess it was really a bit of a pointless pastime for a self-confessed idealist who was always chasing a cause and not a stable career. There are those who will always think you are odd, flighty, or unfocused, in comparison to what they understand to be 'normal'. I am convinced that this subliminal fear of judgement, perpetuated by Christianity and held in the collective consciousness of the human race, prevents us from living a full and fruitful life.

I was somewhat relieved to discover that we are not judged by God or any being greater than we are. There is no angel with a big book making notes about how we live our lives. (I have this funny picture in my mind of this dishevelled and exasperated angel, whose wings and halo hang at half-mast, sitting behind mountains of paperwork trying to convince God that Caroline Ravenall, case number 65,765,876, actually did good this week and should be pardoned for all the wrong she did in the previous week because it kind of balances out). There is no special entity whose task it is to try us, to act as our judge and juror. There is no special path that we are made to walk by the Supreme Being. He sits in an impartial way and observes all the divine sparks in creation, watching how each of us learns and reacts, whatever situation we find ourselves in. He does not judge us. We *alone* are responsible for all the good or bad things that happen to us. We are our own judge, juror and jailor. For many people this responsibility is quite hard to accept.

So if we are not judged by God, how do we create karma? There are two aspects to this answer: through the wise or unwise use of our free will, and through the development of our conscience.

Being made in the image of God, we have been given the gift of free will, which ultimately gives us the ability to make choices and decisions. Free will is something that we take for granted, assuming that everyone has the same ability to choose as we do; but that's not so. The amount of free will we have depends on many factors, particularly the way we've used it in previous incarnations and the amount of wisdom or consciousness we have gained as a result. Free will is like a precursor to choice: a combination of all the mental, emotional and physical experiences we have had to date, which remain within our three bodies. We can liken it to a power or talent we've developed.

At the bottom of the hill close to where I live, along a quiet road which runs from Sandspit harbour up over the peninsula, lives a goat that's tied by a rope to a stake in the ground. The amount of grass she has access to depends on what she's done with her rope. Sometimes it's flowing freely so the size of the grass patch on the menu is expansive. At other times, it's wrapped around the stake several times or caught up on the little 'bad weather' hut, restricting the choices on the menu. Then she can only eat on the same patch of grass she has eaten on before, where the grass is shorter, earthy and not so sweet. Yet, even though the rope may be short, the goat stretches and pushes as hard as possible, pulling against the rope and the collar around her neck, extending her neck, head and lips and every muscle in her body to get at those super-green shoots of grass that lie just out of reach.

Think of the goat on a rope as an analogy for the concept of free will. Sometimes the rope is long and flowing and sometimes it's short. In the same way, some people have greater amounts of free will than others. We all come from different backgrounds and upbringings, and different circumstances, with different levels of parental conditioning, karmic loads, gifts and attributes. The amount of free will we have depends not only on these factors but also on how much we have struggled to overcome the obstacles in our path, both in this life and previous lives. The amount of free will we have depends on how much effort we have put in, how much we have pushed our limits, practised and developed ourselves – how much we've stretched against the rope. For example, someone with musical or artistic abilities in one life may decide to develop these abilities to their fullest extent from a very early age, choosing to dedicate many hours to the practice and perfection of his craft until it becomes a real talent. After many years, he achieves much success and notoriety with his music and it brings joy to many people. Alternatively, he may choose to ignore these abilities, instead turning his hand to a different pastime or occupation that provides a greater financial reward to support his family. Eventually, he forgets all about his music and art as life gets in the way. In his next life, he still has his talents, but lacks the motivation to use them. He has to work harder and longer to make anything of them and even when he does, he finds that he doesn't achieve much success and eventually, after many years, he gives up completely. In his next life, his artistic abilities may be nonexistent and he spends his life complaining about how he wishes he had artistic and musical talents so that he could leave his job as an accountant. What you don't use, you lose. Free will isn't the same for every person and not all men are equal. Like any talent, we can work with it to develop it and put it to good use, or we can ignore it completely.

Every single human being, or divine spark, also has a conscience; it's the voice that screams at us from the pit of our stomach when we make decisions that aren't quite right. We often talk about the 'prick of our conscience' – the little summons from inside that fills us with regret or anxiety when we go against it. Our conscience dictates to us what is right and what is wrong regardless of the rules of any system we find our self in. Our subconscious mind speaks to us through our conscience. It's that part of us that has recorded everything since the beginning of time. The part of us that has stored information from this life and previous lives. When we make bad choices in life, take rash actions to protect ourselves or those we love we feel the prick of our conscience but in many instances we ignore it. We smother it – put ear plugs in, and sometimes, if we are angry, overly anxious, stressed, busy or uptight, we don't hear it at all. This is why so many spiritual philosophies encourage us to go within, become still and quiet so that we can begin to hear that small voice from within and under the layers of life that surround it. When we ignore our conscience, we start to make mistakes, mistakes that are wrong for us alone, not for anyone else. And this is how we make bad karma for ourselves.

But how is our conscience formed. How does it determine what is right and wrong? Each time we pass on – when we blow out our last breath – we review our life backwards from the moment of our death to the moment of our birth. This happens in the lower part of the astral plane. People who have had near-death experiences tell of this. They say that after they lost consciousness their life started playing out in front of them, backwards. This review happens not once but three times – one for each of our three bodies – physical, emotional and mental. First, we look at all the good and bad things we physically did in our lives – the joy and the happiness, the pain and discomfort we brought both to ourselves and others. When we finally reach the point in the review when we see our own birth, we go back again for a second time. This time we review all the emotional pain we experienced and the pain we caused others – the anger, the jealousy, the vindictiveness, the negativity, the unconscious mistakes, the laughter and the tears. And again, when we are back at our birth, we review our lives for a third time. This time we look at all the mental issues, the bad thoughts, the anguish, the suffering and psychological pain we caused for ourselves and others – all the thoughts that brought us into disharmony with the divine scheme of things. So we don't just have one conscience, but a triple conscience that we are responsible for.

At the time of our review, we are in a very sensitive state – we are the observer, not the participator. If you remember having awakened from a dream crying or laughing, you are in a hyper-sensitive state then. Multiply that sensation by 1000! Being in such a sensitive state, we are filled with remorse at our bad actions (and there are normally more bad ones than good), so much so that our conscience is deeply engraved. All our wrongdoings are chiselled indelibly into our subconscious mind. We are forced to face the cold hard truth of our actions only this time we cannot turn our heads. This is the so-called purgatory that the Catholics talk about, the Inferno and Purgatorio of Dante's *Divine Comedy*. It is the forced realisation of the significance of our own transgressions in this life, communicated to us in signs and symbols, which are in line with our own spiritual beliefs (or lack of them).

The triple review is the most effective system to cure our sins and make us aware, as we are judged by our own standards and not the standards of a greater Supreme Being, who has a much deeper insight and understanding than ourselves. The amount of time we spend in Purgatory depends largely on our ability to rise above our weaknesses and desires during life. None of us, however, escape the opportunity to review our life in this way, and none of us can escape the law of karma. Once the triple review is completed, we move on to a higher plane in the astral, where in line with our beliefs we will experience the 'Heaven' we always imagined, until we are reborn. Whilst we don't remember existing in this world before, we now have a 'soul memory' of our actions in the form of our conscience. Although it doesn't remind us of all the gory details of our misdoings in our previous life, it will remind us with a little prick or a large clout when something is not quite right. You may repeat all the wrong doings you were blissfully unaware of in a previous life, but this time, you will know that it's wrong because it's been deeply and indelibly ingrained within.

… the dross of an evolution cannot be burnt away in the purgation of a single death. Few souls are so pure and strong that they could endure so severe a trial without their fibres being disintegrated. Therefore we are shown no more at a single purgation that we can well bear and profit by (from one lifetime only). We are permitted to wipe out a certain proportion of our karma and then come back to earth with the rest still bound around our neck, and it is this un-expiated karma that causes our suffering in the next life. And so gradually, with what we realise while in purgatory and with what we make amends for while on earth, we compensate our karma and adjust the balance. Thus, does the soul make its growth.

Dion Fortune (1890–1946)
The Book of the Dead

All spirits are not of equal age or experience. We have not all come from the Divine at the same time. Some have to go further and deeper into the depths of Hell before they learn, whilst others may learn quickly. Therefore, we do not all have the same degree of conscience or free will when it comes to overcoming life's obstacles. For example, you may be more organised or better with money than your friends or siblings. This is because over lifetimes, organisation has become a skill that you've developed, something that you have practised and perfected. Your friends may be better at other things that don't hold an interest for you. Looking at life in this way, we can perhaps learn not to judge others so harshly for their faults, for if we judge others, we are placing ourselves higher than God, who judges no man, and all we are doing is making our own triple review more painful.

We are not punished *for* our sins, we are punished *by* them. Karma, the use of our free will and the state of our conscience, ensures that we keep coming back to this world in an endless cycle of reincarnation until we decide we have had enough. (See fig. 5) By the use of our free will we create karma and so have to be reborn again to pay the karma. In our triple review we develop our conscience, which helps to guide our thoughts and deeds. In our next incarnation we pay off the karma we've created, but make fresh karma in the process. Gradually, as our conscience becomes more exacting, we make less and less karma until eventually we can pay it off completely. Spiritual development speeds up this process.

Figure 5

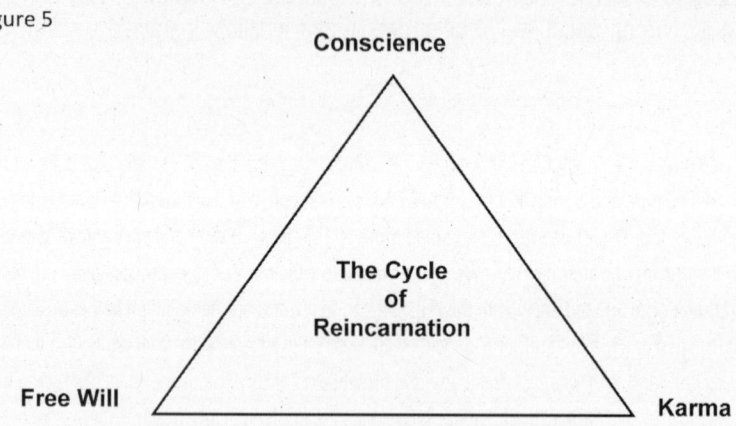

Conscience

The Cycle
of
Reincarnation

Free Will

Karma

So, we cannot explain life in terms of fate or karma alone. Neither can we explain life in terms of free will alone. There is a case for both. Life is a mixture of fate and free will. The decisions we make today have ramifications tomorrow. We always reap what we sow. Our environment, our features, the language we speak, the religion or country in which we were born, our parents and siblings – these are all products of our own free will, which becomes our karmic destiny. Life is nothing other than an amalgamation of decisions and choices. We are the sum total of every choice we have made in this life and previous lives. If we make wise choices, the path will be smooth; if we make foolish choices, it won't. The very things we do take their full course in the grand cycle of life, and come back to us. As a result we come back to the physical world again and again, to be rewarded for the good things we have done and be punished by the bad things. So doing good deeds does not, in fact, get you a passport into Heaven, it just makes your karma easier to bear the next time around. However, in the greater picture, there are fundamentally no really good and bad choices because only one thing can come of it – *learning* and *light-gathering*.

We can't conquer the problems of life by withdrawing from life. Unless we find our way in the school of life, we are not going to develop at all. Knowledge is power; therefore, our free will increases as our knowledge increases. But this means that as we grow and develop, we have a greater responsibility to listen to our conscience. As more things come into our awareness, our conscience becomes more exacting. As we go higher on the rungs of the ladder of conscience and consciousness, so we go higher on the rungs of authority. As we go higher on the rungs of authority, so we go higher on the rungs of responsibility. The higher we go, the easier it is to make bad karma. Ignorance is indeed bliss. The highest authority in your personal philosophy is *you* and your conscience. It is not a fixed, static thing. It is dynamic, ever growing and always changing. What was right yesterday may well be wrong today. So we are our own angel with the big book, our own judge, juror and jailer. It is the only way that true justice can take place. It is the only way we can learn.

THE CASE OF THE HOLY SPIRIT

In the New Testament we are told that if you 'sin against man it shall be forgiven you but if you sin against the Holy Spirit it shall not be forgiven.' I didn't understand that. Does it mean that I can go around causing as much damage as I like, unless I come across this Holy Spirit chap, when I have to start thinking about watching my P's and Q's? If I intentionally and deliberately hurt someone, if I do something that I know is going to bring pain and discomfort to their lives, knowing full well that it is wrong, then understandably my victims certainly might not forgive me. If it's really bad, a transgression of the law of the land, then the law might not forgive me, either, tossing me in jail and throwing away the key. But the law of karma forgives me – not through undertaking a thousand 'Hail Marys' and making a large donation to the church, but through experience of the same pain and discomfort delivered in similar circumstances, that I have to pay next time around.

However, if I *accidentally* upset someone, I will not have to pay the karma for it, even if the person I hurt doesn't decide to forgive me. I won't pay karma because I didn't go against my conscience. But come the time for my triple review, I will deeply understand how much pain I caused and develop a conscience about it for my next incarnation. Sinning against the Holy Spirit means that we sin against our conscience and better judgment. By going out of my way to hurt someone, I may have disobeyed that still small voice within and therefore, that will not be forgiven me, I will have to come back again to this world to pay the debt and face the obstacle I caused for someone else.

We don't have a court of justice on this world. We have a court of law. True justice cannot exist. How is it possible to have a different law for every person on this planet? Each one of us comes from a different background, has different learning experiences, has different values and tastes gleaned on this long 'pilgrimage through matter'. No man-made law could possibly serve us, and if it could, at best it would be a compromise of the average person. We would find it too harsh in some instances and too lenient in others. But Divine Law – karma – takes all of this into account. This is the only law that is just and fair. Life is a system whereby we can convert our foolishness into wisdom. We are foolish, we do things to hurt others, we can be callous, unthinking and cruel. Our foolishness manifests in other people as pain. In the fullness of time, the things we have done come back to haunt us through karma. In trying to circumvent the pain, we find ways of eliminating it. By bumping our head, we learn not to make the same mistakes again. When learning dawns on us, it becomes wisdom. Through the process of life, through hurting ourselves, our foolishness is converted. So the prerequisite of wisdom is foolishness, and I, for one, have a hell of a lot of that.

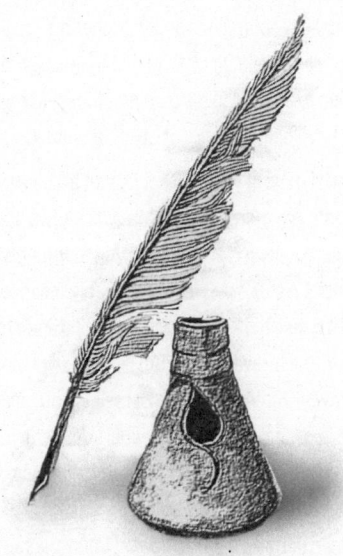

I have a history of making decisions very quickly about men. I have always fallen in love fast and without measuring risks. I have a tendency not only to see the best in everyone, but to assume that everyone is emotionally capable of reaching his highest potential. I have fallen in love more times than I care to count with the highest potential of a man, rather than with the man himself, and I have hung on to the relationship for a long time (sometimes far too long) waiting for the man to ascend to his own greatness. Many times in romance I have been a victim of my own optimism....

"People think a soul mate is your perfect fit, and that's what everyone wants. But a true soul mate is a mirror, the person who shows you everything that is holding you back, the person who brings you to your own attention so you can change your life. A true soul mate is probably the most important person you'll ever meet, because they tear down your walls and smack you awake. But to live with a soul mate forever? Nah. Too painful. Soul mates, they come into your life just to reveal another layer of yourself to you, and then leave. A soul mate's purpose is to shake you up, tear apart your ego a little bit, show you your obstacles and addictions, break your heart open so new light can get in, make you so desperate and out of control that you have to transform your life, then introduce you to your spiritual master....

Elizabeth Gilbert
Eat, Pray, Love

CHAPTER 8

A LID FOR EVERY POT
Twin Souls and Soul Mates

Spiritual relationship is far more precious than physical. Physical relationship divorced from spiritual is body without soul.

Mohandas Gandhi (1869–1948)

here is a lid for every pot, my mother used to say, when I would moan about not being able to find the right mate. 'So where the hell is mine then?' I would think. Where was The One who would make my life complete, The One with whom I could dovetail perfectly, The One who could lift me from my misery and make everything okay, just like in the fairy tales?

Like many women across the globe, I always seemed to be searching for the perfect soul mate to walk this journey with me; one who would just 'get me' at a deeper level, so that I wouldn't have to constantly explain myself; someone whom I could be completely at ease with; someone who was comfortable in his own skin without trying to mould me into some logical, practical sidekick trained to bring him his slippers and the *TV Magazine*; and most of all, someone who was tuned into his own needs. Emotional cripples looking for a surrogate mother were really not my style. Accepting anything less wasn't just compromise in my book, it was a downright lie, one that I couldn't fake. So naturally, whomever I got together with was never really quite right. These men loved the inspiration that this Celtic woman with the red hair added to the mix, but she didn't quite measure up to the ideal that they held as to what a partner should be in the 'real world'. Even when I did meet someone special, whom I believed I could map a future with, one who lifted my soul and my spirit, he didn't quite feel the same way about me, or the timing and circumstances of our liaison were stacked against us. I always seemed to be unlucky in love.

I totally related to Elizabeth Gilbert's sentiments. Looking back, I always fell in love too quickly, only to be disappointed when the object of my desire didn't quite live up to my expectation of what his highest potential could be. Even though I became more adept at seeing the flaws in my thinking and became more discerning in my relationship choices, I was still a victim of my own optimism. Time and again, as I was continually disappointed, I resigned myself to simply believing that it was easier to be alone than to waste time and energy constantly searching for the perfect mate. Besides, I adored my own company. I was my own best friend and needed a lot of space in a relationship, perhaps too much. Yet, a few months down the line, I would find the longing return and I'd start my search all over again, only to find that when I did find a compatible partner, the same old issues resurfaced, and I wanted nothing more than to be on my own again, just to get some peace.

My singledom was even more perplexing to my friends, who seemed to feel my lack of success in relationships more acutely than I did. They constantly worried that I didn't have anyone in my life, that I was 'messed up', from the man perspective. Many of them strived tirelessly to fix me up, to fill the void they felt existed in my life. At times I was really touched by their concern, at others downright irritated. Some of my friends understood where I was coming from, others got it completely wrong. Internet dating, which I ventured into at the behest of a friend, was a disaster, and so were the high-end professional dating agencies. In both I found the same little boys who weren't quite ready to leave the sweetshop. It was just easier for me to get a cat. This relationship thing was truly karmic for me.

The drive to find the perfect love has consumed men and women throughout history. Music, art, literature and movies have been dedicated to passions of the heart – ardent reflections of love and romance and fairy tale endings. But where does this drive which consumes so much of our time and emotion come from? The roots of this conundrum reach back into the beginning of time, which once again requires a different interpretation of the creation myths.

We read in the first chapter, 'Accepting Your Own Divinity', that during the process of creation we were separated from God. Our higher counterpart (the higher self) stayed in the Divine, and the true self (us) came down the ladder, or Tree of Life, into creation. The Bible refers to Adam[8] being the first race of mankind who was placed in the mythical Garden of Eden, or *Paradise,* which is located on the upper part of the astral plane.[9]At this point in our existence, we were androgynous beings, or hermaphrodites, both male and female in the same body. The term *hermaphrodite* comes from the myths: Hermaphroditus was the child from the union of the goddess Aphrodite and the god Hermes; that is, until the separation of the sexes took place, which is depicted in many of the myths and religious tales – Adam and Eve (Judeo-Christian), Adamoh and Hevah (Indian Vedas), Epimethius and Pandora (Greek), and Enki and Adapa, or Ninti (Sumerian.) In Greek and Roman creation mythology, the separation was brought about by Zeus (Jupiter), who was angry at the Androgynes, as their strength had made them arrogant. So he separated them into 'hemi-people', and since then they have each sought their other half in members of the opposite sex. The Greek philosopher Plato also writes of this separation:

Anciently...the androgynous sex existed...coupled back to back...till jealous Jupiter divided them vertically...as people cut eggs with hairs...after then, these divided and imperfect folk ran about over the earth ever seeking their lost halves to be joined to them again...and the reason being that human nature was originally one, and the desire and pursuit of the whole is called love....

From this brief interpretation, we can see that desire for a partner and mate is subconsciously engraved within us and has been since the beginning of time. We seek that which we have lost, the other part of ourselves without which we are incomplete. Perhaps this is why the preoccupation with finding the perfect love is so all-consuming and leads us into so many dead ends.

This separation into male and female did, however, serve a purpose in the greater scheme of things. The Supreme Being created the Universe with one sole aim: *to gather light.* As a fragment of God we came here to fulfil the same purpose. The way that we gather this light is by overcoming obstacles and difficulties. When we are balanced emotionally and mentally, we can take many things in our stride and withstand the hardships of life. But if we are unbalanced, sometimes even the simplest of tasks can seem incredibly difficult. The final separation of the sexes created a deliberate imbalance within us, which added a dimension of difficulty to our lives, but ultimately ensures that a greater degree of learning and development takes place to fulfil the objective of creation.

Being both male and female in one body made us strong, not just physically but mentally and emotionally. If we look at our own lives we can see this is so. As a rule, women are largely more emotional, empathetic and compassionate than men. Men, on the other hand, have lots of logic but often lack empathy. Neither finds it easy to make a completely balanced decision on his or her own. Women often allow their strong emotions to cloud their judgement in the same way that men overrule emotional considerations in favour of more logical, common-sense approaches. When males and females work together in a relationship or team, their decisions are more reasonable – providing, of course, they are willing to listen to each other!

Part of the reason for undertaking this journey through life is so that we can become balanced. Through thousands of successive incarnations, one life as a male and one life as a female, we learn to aquire those characteristics we don't have. Females learn to acquire some of the male characteristics and males learn to acquire female characteristics. Ultimately, after many incarnations we become stronger.

THE BIG RIB MISTAKE

In Genesis 2:20-24, we read of the separation of the sexes:

The Lord God caused a deep sleep to fall upon Adam, and He took one of his ribs, and closed up the flesh instead thereof; And the rib which the Lord God had taken from man, made He a woman, and brought her to the man.

One has to question: Why didn't God just make woman from the dust of the ground as he had made Adam and all the other animals? As we read before, the Bible has undergone many translations over the centuries from its original Hebrew, Aramaic, or Greek, so one might expect a few discrepancies. One occurred right here: The words *rib* and *side* in Hebrew are spelt almost identically. *Tsela* means 'rib' and *tseda* means 'side'. God took an *aspect* of Adam, not a rib. He took a *side* of Adam away, the *female* aspect. Woman was not created merely from one rib, but from one *side*.

Who would have thought that one piddly little letter could be responsible for many centuries of pain and heartache and atrocities committed against women across the planet?

Our twin soul is the exact other half of us, someone with whom we will dovetail completely. Somewhere deep down, we know that he or she exists out there, which is why we often feel compelled to seek a relationship. Part of the purpose of the School of Life is to find our matching half so we can become completely balanced once again. So we search among the members of the opposite sex, go on numerous dates, trawl the Internet and frequent pointless parties in the hope that we might meet The One.

Sometimes in this search, we may find a good match, a soul mate, a marriage that may last for sixty or seventy years. But there is still no complete dovetailing, because we were not united before; we can only meet our twin soul when we have progressed further along the spiritual path, developed a greater degree of balance, strength and light, and have retraced our steps up the ladder to the same position on the astral plane that we were on when our twin soul was separated. At that point, we will then become one again, and together retrace our steps into the Divine to unite with our higher self and ultimately God.

We might believe that the person that we are with right now is our twin soul. In fact, we may feel that we have met more than one twin soul. But soul mates are *not* twin souls. All twin souls *are* soul mates but not *all* soul mates are twin souls.

But what is a soul mate? I am not sure that I agree with Liz Gilbert's interpretation. Soul mates in my world have always been much easier to be around. A soul mate doesn't have to be a member of the opposite sex or even a sexual partner; you can have any kind of relationship with a soul mate, and you can have more than one. With soul mates, their age, gender and background are not important – you immediately like them and enjoy spending time with them. You share the same ideologies, philosophies or views about life. You enthuse each other and charge each other's batteries. A soul mate makes your life complete. Soul mates are people who lift and inspire you. When you meet, the connection may feel so strong that you may believe that you have been looking for this person your whole life.

Soul mates may meet in this life for the first time, and through affinity or resonance, they connect. Or, it may be that they meet again because they have been together in earlier lives. Maybe they have gone through hard times together. Perhaps they sat in prison together for several years during the French Revolution. They may have been burned at the stake together, or one may have saved the other's life, or one may have persecuted the other and now feels tremendous guilt. Whatever it is, a strange bond is built up between these people on the mental plane and the astral plane, a bond so powerful it may persist for lifetimes. This is why soul mates have been found between pupil and teacher, between friends, between brothers and sisters, people who work together or even between complete strangers.

It is a wonderful thing to meet a soul mate. The simple concept of knowing that we are there for each other means that words are unnecessary. Soul mates can engender a wonderful feeling of respect and caring. If your soul mate is your husband or wife, then life can seem blissful. But the danger is that you can become obsessed with each other, become reliant on each other, and lose that sense of independence that we all need to maintain for our own purpose in this world.

Even if you haven't met your soul mate, *any* relationship you find yourself in adds to your light, whether the relationship is sexual or not – it just won't be as comfortable as a relationship with a soul mate. The spiritual warrior, however, always takes the road less travelled because he or she realises it will be the greatest path of learning. Relationships of any kind serve as our mirror, and they are some of the best ways for us to experience ourselves, the good the bad and the ugly. I have come to learn that you can make any relationship work, with time, effort and understanding, providing this understanding comes from both sides. *Love is not a feeling, it's a choice.* When both parties recognise this, each can embrace the relationship in a more philosophical way, helping them achieve their ultimate aim, which is to balance themselves and improve the chance of once again meeting with their twin soul.

When I understood this, I stopped worrying about finding the perfect soul mate to 'fix' me and my existential angst. I started to take more responsibility for myself, my foibles and issues. I tried to look for qualities in someone through which I could learn, qualities that would help to balance out those parts of me that were not so well developed, and qualities that would enhance my life path in ways that I couldn't. I realised that the path may be painful, and I would whinge and moan and cry a lot – but we never transcend life by lounging on a beach sipping cocktails. When both parties understand this concept, a relationship can become very freeing. It provides the opportunity for mutual love and respect to blossom through the development of a deeper understanding about who we are and why we are here. When we focus on this, instead of being forever upset about the fact that he leaves the toilet seat up or she leaves the lid off the toothpaste tube, life becomes a lot easier.

Relationships of any kind are always temporary, whether they are for a reason, a season, a lifetime, fleeting moments or years. Whether it be a relationship between husband and wife, parents, grandparents and children, friends or co-workers – it is always temporary. We come into this world alone – we leave it alone. The relationships we have along the way add the zest, the colour, the sparkle and wonderment that makes up this glorious pageant of life.

LOVE AND THE FAIRY TALE

The most popular fairy tales of our time are the ones where a handsome prince meets a beautiful maiden or princess who is the *fairest in the land*. (She is the fairest in the land because she is his twin soul.) However, their meeting is not without problems. One of them is suffering – turned into a frog or a toad by an evil sorceress, or under an ugly spell or a sleeping spell (which is indicative of the 'sleep' or 'illusion' that we are all in). The spell can only be broken with the kiss of 'true love', and sometimes the hero or heroine has to prove sincerity over and over again, often travelling far and wide, making many sacrifices, or undergoing great difficulty before being able to win the object of their affection. (The journey is, of course, symbolic of the seeker's journey.) But always in the end, the couple marry and are crowned king and queen in a far-off land (the Divine), and live happily ever after.

In the story of Briar Rose, the princess pricked her finger on a spindle and fell into a deep sleep for over 100 years. The spell is symbolic of her state of consciousness: a deep sleep, a state of ignorance, one that was experienced by the whole kingdom. A huge thorn bush sprang up around the kingdom hiding it from sight (symbolic of the mental shutters that we erect around ourselves to protect ourselves from truth). The story of the sleeping princess rang through the kingdom and many suitors set out to find the fabled castle, but never succeeded, as it was so well concealed (depicting that a true spiritual path is often difficult to find – the truth is hidden from the profane). That is, until a handsome prince (wealth and status are often significant in the myths and fairy tales of one who is spiritually elevated from the rest of society) came upon the thorn bush and found that its barbed tendrils parted with ease. He entered the castle and found the beautiful Briar Rose asleep in the highest chamber, and after gazing at her beauty for a while, he woke her with a kiss. The 100-year-old spell was finally broken.

Snow White, the fairest in the land, ate a poisoned apple given to her by the jealous queen who disguised herself as a witch. Even though the bite took her life, she looked so beautiful in death that the seven dwarfs who loved her dearly laid her in a crystal coffin with rose petals. One day the dwarfs found a handsome prince peering at her through the coffin. He opened the coffin lid and kissed her. The spell was broken and she woke up.

Cinderella was downtrodden by her wicked stepmother and ugly stepsisters. They refused to allow her to go to the ball at the castle, forcing her to stay home and scrub floors. Yet with the help of her Fairy Godmother, Cinderella used magic to conjure up a beautiful dress, glass slippers and a stagecoach pulled by magnificent horses that took her to the castle. Her beauty captivated the prince and he danced with nobody else for the whole evening. However, she had promised to leave the ball on the stroke of midnight before the magic spell could be broken. As the clock began to strike, she rushed to leave, and in so doing, lost her glass slipper (a symbol of purity) on the steps of the palace. The prince travelled far and wide, visiting every household in the land to find the maiden whose delicate foot would fit the slipper perfectly. The final house he called upon was the house of Cinderella and her sisters. The ugly sisters all pushed and strained to squeeze their large feet into the tiny slipper and failed. But Cinderella slipped her foot into the slipper with ease. Naturally, it was the perfect fit. And thus she found true love.

In the story of 'Beauty and the Beast,' Beauty is forced to live in the castle of the Beast to make amends for the mistakes made by her father. The Beast is rude and insufferable, but Beauty, through her kindness, love and integrity, breaks the spell that has been placed upon him. He turns into a handsome prince and they eventually marry.

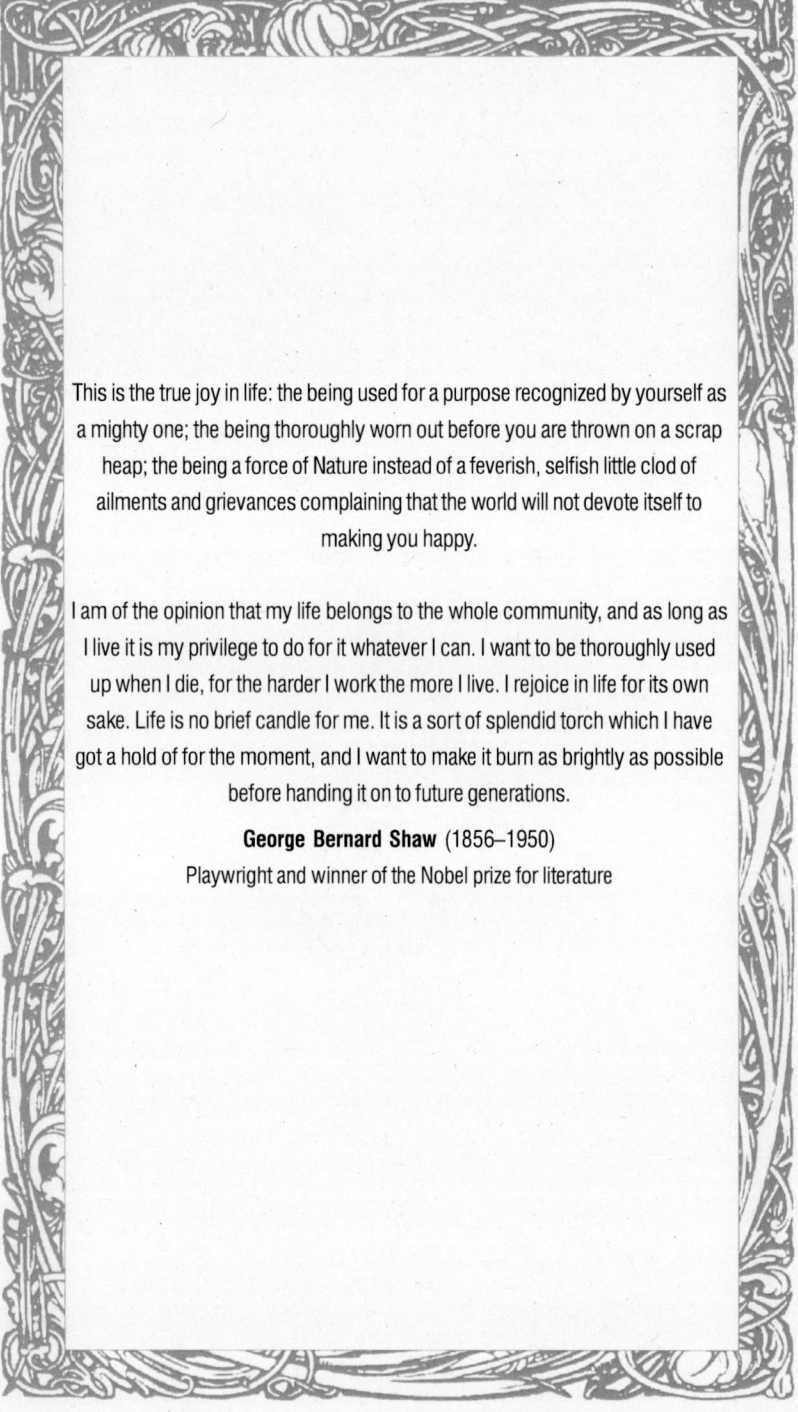

This is the true joy in life: the being used for a purpose recognized by yourself as a mighty one; the being thoroughly worn out before you are thrown on a scrap heap; the being a force of Nature instead of a feverish, selfish little clod of ailments and grievances complaining that the world will not devote itself to making you happy.

I am of the opinion that my life belongs to the whole community, and as long as I live it is my privilege to do for it whatever I can. I want to be thoroughly used up when I die, for the harder I work the more I live. I rejoice in life for its own sake. Life is no brief candle for me. It is a sort of splendid torch which I have got a hold of for the moment, and I want to make it burn as brightly as possible before handing it on to future generations.

George Bernard Shaw (1856–1950)
Playwright and winner of the Nobel prize for literature

CHAPTER 9

A PILGRIMAGE THROUGH MATTER

The Curriculum of the School of Life

Do not be too timid and squeamish about your action. All life is an experiment. The more experiments you make the better.

Ralph Waldo Emerson (1803–1882)
American essayist, lecturer and poet

ife is not a fairy tale. We all know that to be true. But somehow we keep living our lives as if it were. We find it hard to accept that life is not smooth sailing, and that obstacles, burdens and difficulties often litter our path. We moan, either deafeningly or under our breath, about our problems as if life *should* be easy, and somehow we've been dealt a wicked blow of misfortune. We lash out at others in anger and frustration when life doesn't quite go our way, as if it's someone else's fault, somehow. And many of us avoid confronting the issues that we face, preferring to turn a blind eye in the hope that they might go away and bother someone else.

After spending many years endeavouring to understand my divine heritage, I was pleased to say that I no longer had a fear of dying (although I didn't want to bring my death forward), but I still had a problem with the living part. Trying to live a *wholehearted* life – overcoming difficulties, finding the courage to face fears, the compassion to forgive others and the self discipline to keep muddling through – is not easy, no matter how much knowledge or spiritual understanding we might have gained. We can't just think, 'Great – I'm a spiritual warrior,' and charge off into the sunset with these lofty ideals. Compassion, courage, self-discipline and establishing a connection with something higher than ourselves require daily practice, and we very often get it wrong. The process of spiritual development is a difficult one because it involves changing almost everything about ourselves. This is because it is conducted against a natural resistance to keep things as they are, to take the easy way out and avoid the pain of facing up to our difficulties. And this resistance to life which plagues every one of us started a very, very long time ago.

THE TALE OF PANDORA

Long ago, when this old world was in its tender infancy, there was a child called Epimetheus who had no mother or father, and so that he might not be lonely, a playmate was sent to him from a far-off country. Her name was Pandora. The world then was a very different place than that of today. Then everyone was a child, and there were no mothers or fathers necessary to take care of the children because there was no danger or trouble of any kind. There were no clothes to mend and there was always plenty to eat and drink, and life was very pleasant indeed.

The first thing that Pandora saw when she entered the cottage where Epimetheus dwelt was a great box. And almost the first question she asked after crossing the threshold was, 'Epimetheus, what have you in that box?'

Epimetheus replied that it was a secret. The box had been entrusted to him by Quicksilver (the god Hermes) and that she should not ask any more questions about it and instead come outside and play.

It was probably the greatest disquietude a child could ever experience. Pandora was extremely vexed at not being able to discover the secret of the mysterious box. This was at first only a faint shadow of a trouble, but every day it grew more and more substantial until the world of Pandora was less sunshiny than those of the other children. She didn't care about having a merry time with her

playmate and talked of nothing else but the big old box. It seemed to have bewitched her. It might have been better for Pandora if she had a little work to do or anything to occupy her mind, so as not to be constantly thinking of this one subject. But life was very easy, and there was really nothing to employ her attention. Epimetheus grew very tired of her nagging and obsession with the box and went out to play with the other children on his own.

However, life wasn't as much fun without Pandora, and after only a short while Epimetheus returned to the cottage to find that she had unknotted the large golden cord that fastened the lid to the great box. But instead of crying out to her to stop, Epimetheus' curiosity had also been sparked, and he walked over to where she sat to help her lift the heavy lid.

All at once, the cottage grew very dark and dismal and black clouds began covering the sun. Heavy peals of thunder started to rage across the heavens. But Pandora and Epimetheus heard nothing of this for they were peering inside the big dark box. Suddenly a swarm of winged creatures brushed past them, taking flight out of the box and filling the already darkened cottage with a loud buzzing sound.

As her eyes grew more accustomed to the imperfect light, Pandora saw a crowd of ugly little shapes with bat's wings looking abominably spiteful. They were armed with terribly long stings for tails. An odious little monster settled on her forehead and would have stung her if Epimetheus had not brushed it away, getting stung himself in the process.

The creatures were a whole family of earthly troubles, diseases of all kinds, evil passions and a great many species of cares and sorrows. Everything that has since afflicted the souls and bodies of mankind had been shut up in the mysterious box and given to Epimetheus and Pandora to keep safe in order that the happy children of the world might never be molested by them.

Scared and alone inside the cottage, the playmates didn't know what to do. The creatures had stung Epimetheus quite badly, so there was no choice but to open the door so that the creatures could get out. And so the Troubles gained a firm foothold over the children of the world and could not be driven away in a hurry. The children then no longer played, they grew older day by day, becoming youths and maidens, men and women and aged people, who soon forgot about the peaceful places where they once played.

Meanwhile, Epimetheus and Pandora stayed in the cottage, as they had been grievously stung and were in a good deal of pain – the first pain they had ever experienced. Epimetheus sat down sullenly in a corner with his back to Pandora and Pandora flung herself upon the floor, sobbing as if her heart would break.

Suddenly there was a gentle little tap in the inside of the lid and a cheery little voice called out to them. When they lifted the lid with some trepidation as to what they might find, out flew a sunny, smiling little fairy with rainbow-coloured wings, who hovered about the room, throwing a light wherever she went. She told them her name was 'Hope' and her job was to make amends to the human race for the swarm of ugly Troubles which were destined to be let loose among them.

Hope said she would be around just as long as they needed her and promised never to desert them. And even though there came a time and a season when they thought she had utterly vanished, she came back again and again when they least dreamt of it.

Hope is always made anew, and even in the Earth's best and brightest aspect, Hope shows it to be only the shadow of an infinite bliss hereafter.

The tale of Pandora depicts the universal myth of the Fall of Man from Paradise, which is also depicted in the biblical story of Adam and Eve, who ate from the Tree of Knowledge of Good and Evil, and in the Babylonian myth of the Tower of Babel.[10] For misdemeanours in Heaven, we were exiled from Paradise (on the astral plane) to the lowest part of creation on the physical plane, which is depicted in the tale of Pandora by the troubles of the world. The physical world is difficult in comparison to the astral plane. We found ourselves in a world of gravity and matter, grovelling around in the dust with the animals, where even the simplest of tasks were complicated in comparison. We now had to work for a living and fight for food and shelter. It was the start of a 'pilgrimage' of a different sort, one where we faced an enormous amount of difficulty and hardship. And we are still complaining about it to this day.

Life here on the physical plane can be likened to a pilgrimage. A pilgrimage is a long, arduous, physical journey with a perceived spiritual reward at the end. Before the pilgrim sets out on his journey, he enjoys many facets of his life; he is settled, happy and comfortable. Yet, for some spiritual purpose, he sets out on a journey. Along the way he encounters great difficulties and hardships and finds a vast degree of difference between the conditions that he meets on the pilgrimage and the pleasurable circumstances he had at home. He may struggle, he may weep, he may regret ever starting out on the journey. But eventually he reaches his goal and, looking back, he realises that it was worthwhile. He has learned from his experiences, expanding and extending himself in many different directions.

As with all journeys, it's not the end result that's important, but what happens *during* the journey itself. By overcoming adversity and conquering life's problems, the pilgrim matures and develops, becoming a very different person along the way. If not for the pilgrimage, he would perhaps remain naive and immature.

In the same way, we left the comfort of the Divine and the Garden of Eden to come down into the physical world on a pilgrimage through matter. We have come out of the very place where there were no limitations, no hardships. As we descended the Tree of Life, or Jacob's Ladder, into the creation, we found that the restrictions were greater. The lessons were harder. We have been forced to make changes and adapt in every possible way. In each life we set out on another stage of the pilgrimage – each incarnation is a continuation of the journey in the 'curriculum of the school of life'.

In the same way that we send our children to school to get an education to prepare them for what they will experience in life, so life is a school where we prepare for a higher life in the Divine. When children finish the school curriculum at the age of 18 or so, they have gained a certain amount of pre-life experience to help them deal with the challenges they may face during adulthood. We would not think of sending our children to a school where the curriculum is easy, where they would sail through each of their grades without blinking. We spend a lot of time searching for the right school with the right curriculum that will push them, stretch them, and encourage them to learn as much as possible. Children go from year to year in a particular grade or class structure, and at the end of it they are tested with exams. Then they go on their summer vacation to rest, to recuperate and do different things. When they return in the new year, they either repeat the same grade or are promoted to a higher one. This they do until they pass the highest grade examination in school, so that they can move up to a university of higher education.

In the same way, the curriculum of the school of life has to be hard, because without it we wouldn't learn very much. We need problems to solve, boundaries to push against and obstacles to overcome, ones that evoke feelings of frustration, grief, sadness, anger, guilt, fear or anxiety within. These are uncomfortable feelings, often as uncomfortable as physical pain itself. Yet, it's through the pain of resolving and confronting these problems that we learn. At the end of each school term after seventy years or so, we too go on holiday, onto the astral plane, and come back through the laws of reincarnation and karma to repeat the mistakes we made, or move on to a higher grade.

Just as we don't send our children to school to make them happy, to make their fellow pupils happy, or to engage in carefree and pleasurable activities, we didn't volunteer for a tour of duty in creation because we thought it was going to be a fun thing to do. We also don't send our children to school so they can become famous or make lots of money, or to meet boys and girls. In the same way, we didn't come here to enrich ourselves in a monetary sense or gain fame, notoriety and power. Yet fame, wealth, power and members of the opposite sex are what we continually pursue, which is what keeps us stuck here life after life.

As we read earlier, we can't conquer the problems of life by trying to get out of life. Bunking school, running away, trying to get out of the curriculum isn't going to get us the certificate. We have to continue with the grade system until it comes to its natural conclusion. Unless we find our way in the school of life, we are not going to develop at all. In every lifetime, we go through different experiences in different bodies with different levels of karma. It's a way of passing through the grades of the curriculum. In the end, the culmination of all the experiences we have is made clear to us. The harder the path, the greater the learning and the more valuable we become in the greater scheme of things.

If you, like me, often find life's lessons tough, then rejoice, because in so doing, we are developing an immunity to hardship. It is in this whole process of meeting and solving problems that greater depth and significance is added to our lives. Problems call forth our courage and our wisdom, enhancing our free will and increasing our capacity to change and transform. Benjamin Franklin said, 'Those things that hurt, instruct.' And it's for this reason that we can learn not to dread but actually welcome problems and difficulties, because either way, they are an inevitable part of the journey.

The good news is, this is as bad as it's going to get! Life is but an illusion of separation. When Adam and Eve were cast out of the Garden of Eden, they forgot about Paradise. We have forgotten what kind of beings we truly are. And when our journey becomes too much, there is always Hope, and each of us needs a little of that every now and again.

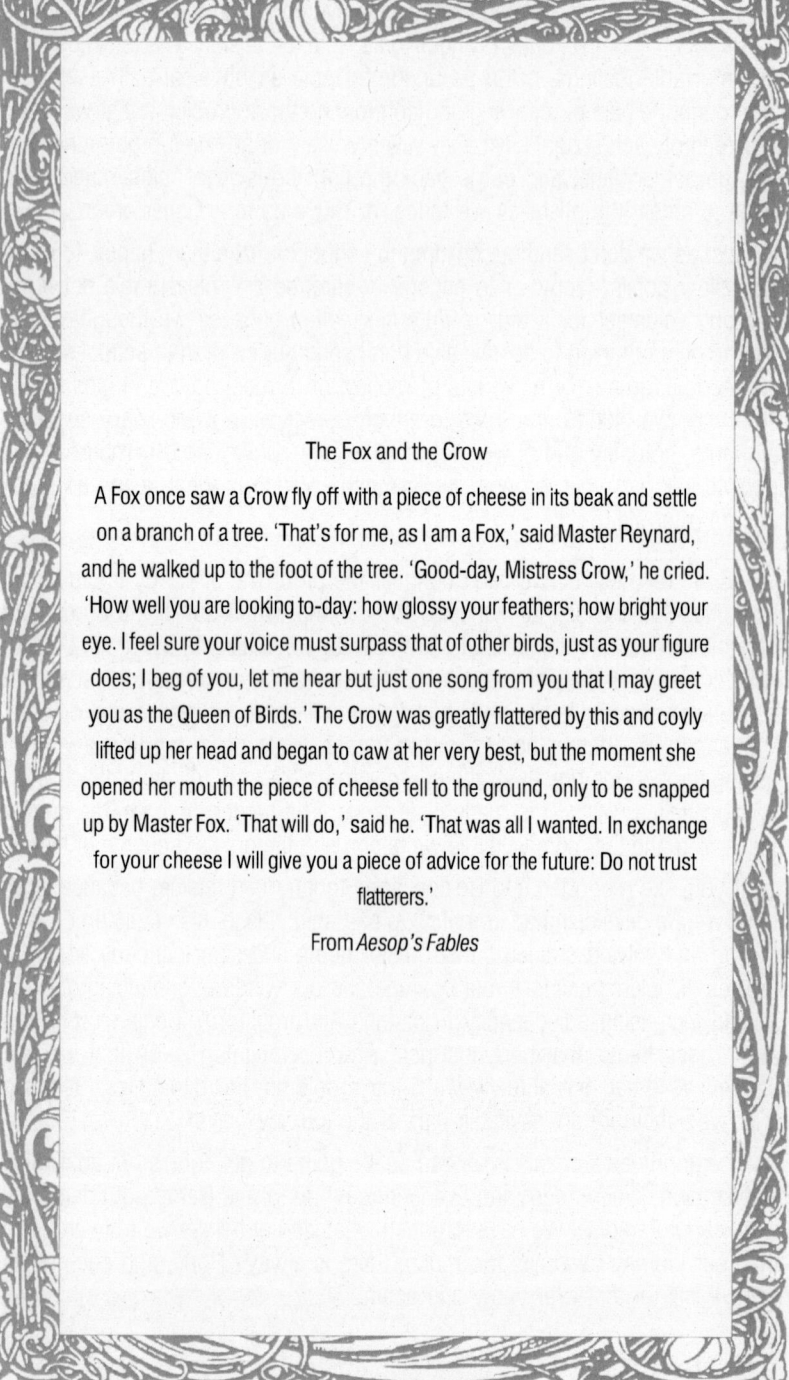

The Fox and the Crow

A Fox once saw a Crow fly off with a piece of cheese in its beak and settle on a branch of a tree. 'That's for me, as I am a Fox,' said Master Reynard, and he walked up to the foot of the tree. 'Good-day, Mistress Crow,' he cried. 'How well you are looking to-day: how glossy your feathers; how bright your eye. I feel sure your voice must surpass that of other birds, just as your figure does; I beg of you, let me hear but just one song from you that I may greet you as the Queen of Birds.' The Crow was greatly flattered by this and coyly lifted up her head and began to caw at her very best, but the moment she opened her mouth the piece of cheese fell to the ground, only to be snapped up by Master Fox. 'That will do,' said he. 'That was all I wanted. In exchange for your cheese I will give you a piece of advice for the future: Do not trust flatterers.'

From *Aesop's Fables*

CHAPTER 10

SLAYING THE DRAGON
The Ego Monster

Unfortunately there can be no doubt that man is, on the whole, less good than he imagines himself or wants to be. Everyone carries a shadow, and the less it is embodied in the individual's conscious life, the blacker and denser it is. If an inferiority is conscious, one always has a chance to correct it. Furthermore, it is constantly in contact with other interests, so that it is continually subjected to modifications. But if it is repressed and isolated from consciousness, it never gets corrected.

Carl Jung (1875–1961)
Psychology and Religion

vercoming problems and difficulties in life might seem like a simple thing when we talk about it on paper. But we are complex beings and there are many hidden aspects within us that hamper our voyage and serve to make our journey through life all the more convoluted. One of these aspects is known as *the ego*. The word *ego* comes from the Latin and means 'I: the personal identity'.

The ego is the dark part of us. Carl Jung referred to it as our 'shadow', saying, 'It is a frightening thought that man also has a shadow side to him, consisting not just of little weaknesses and foibles, but of a positively demonic dynamism.'

The ego shows up as the *resistance* we experience in our lives in a thousand different ways. It is the part of us that seeks only pleasure and gratification and goes out of its way to avoid pain and hardship. It is the part of us that is cynical, negative, and wretched. The part of us that takes offence gives offence and gets upset. It is both the victim and the aggressor. The part of us that wants revenge, wants to get even, wants to prove that it's right, showing up as restlessness, irritability and impatience when we try to go against it. The ego is also at the root of our internal suffering, causing all our doubts, worries and fears. It is the ego monster within that drives us to seek counselling for our existential angst that stops us from achieving our noble dreams and ambitions.

The ego despises discipline, routine and hard work. Those of us who have tried to study for an exam, write a book or dedicate ourselves to any worthwhile goal that requires long term effort will testify to this. The ego chastises us for working when the sun is shining and the beach is only a few minutes away. It tempts us to phone our friends and go out and have some fun; after all, nobody is going to actually read the book we are writing, most of what we have written is lousy anyway. Who are we to think we can become an author or obtain a degree? For months it will plague us, never ceasing, yet when we finally obtain our degree or get our book published, it will have no qualms in standing up there as proud as punch taking the credit for all the hard work we put in.

The simple fable from Aesop that we read at the beginning of this chapter illustrates one of the most fundamental problems with human beings who are governed by the ego: the love of flattery. Because we don't have the humility of our true self, we thrive on flattery. We love to be complimented. People have hot buttons. If you can find and press the right button you can get almost anything out of them, as all the hot buttons are wired into the ego. Aesop's fable shows us an aspect of human frailty. It shows us up for what we are and illustrates one of the many stumbling blocks for all spiritual seekers: the need to be accepted by another. Any time we feel fear and anxiety or stress in our lives, we can guarantee that the ego has something to do with it.

There are two predominant views of the ego: The first is the view adopted by certain schools of psychology and says that the ego should be developed because it's responsible for our ambition and drive and getting us places in life. The second view is that of the mystic, which says that the ego is the *false self*, the *lower self*, the dark half of us that is arrogant, intolerant, self-important, impatient and deceitful; left unchecked it can usurp our true nature entirely. In the view of the mystic, the ego is likened to a separate entity occupying the same body alongside the true self and should be destroyed so that the true self can shine forth. Although there is probably much justification for using the word as psychologists use it, because we do need our ego to a certain extent during the school of life, the devastating effects that the false self has on our being perhaps justifies a completely different use of this word, and some investigation into what this ego monster actually is.

With the disappearance of God, the Ego moves forward
to become the sole divinity.

Dorothee Steffensky-Sölle (1929–2003)
German theologian and author

The ego is created at birth, and its development continues throughout life, depending on many factors, including our conditioning and the environment. We read in earlier chapters that we are only a fragment of our former selves. Even though our *true self*, the part that is here, still contains a pure fragment of the Supreme Being within, we have forgotten our divine heritage. Because we subconsciously recognise that we are incomplete in some way, we make attempts to fill the void and emptiness within us. (We have seen how this desire to feel *whole* manifests itself in our continuous search for a partner or mate.) Being made in the image of God, in terms of his skills and attributes, we are creators, so we created for ourselves another 'self'. A lower self. A false self. An ego.

We came into this world ego-less. The reincarnating spirit enters the foetus when it takes its first breath. At that time it is pure. Only the true self exists in the tiny body of the baby. Seconds after it's born it starts the process of ego-building. It's hard to remember, when we hold this little tiny baby in our arms, that the spirit inside of the child is not new. It is an ancient being which once more occupies a physical body. Although it is born in forgetfulness, deep down it knows very well that this life is going to be painful. No human being is born laughing. All babies cry bitterly when they are born. The spirit is entering a new body that has never been used before. The lungs need to be worn in a bit, like a brand new pair of shoes, so the first breath is painful. As the baby cries, the mother holds the child close to her, keeping it within her aura. The baby enjoys the attention, the feeling of being close to its mother and feels comforted and nurtured once more. So when she tries to put it down, it cries again. It's tasted the attention and desires it once again. And so the ego is born. From then on, every time the infant cries, has a tantrum, or screams and shouts, sometimes even when there is nothing wrong at all, it gets the same attention from doting parents and grandparents. Parents who are wise can easily detect the ego's development in their children, but those who aren't and who cater to its every whim find that even in early childhood, the ego is already well developed.

So the ego is not a divine creation. It is homemade and totally different from the true self. The true self is an immortal being which has never had a beginning nor an end. The ego comes into the body only minutes after birth. It exists as long as the astral body exists; therefore, it follows us even after death, like a little dog, onto the astral plane. The true self knows that it is an immortal being. It wants for nothing and needs nothing. But the ego is only temporary. Being created by us out of ignorance, its philosophy is, 'Let's eat, drink and be merry, for tomorrow we die.' The true self is the one that realises that 'we will never die, so let's set store in lasting values.' But as time goes on, the ego usurps the position of the true self completely.

Its strength and voracity depends on how aware we (and our parents) are of this 'other self', and how much we control it as we grow through childhood into adulthood.

Whenever I climb I am followed by a dog called 'Ego'.

Friedrich Nietzsche (1844-1900)
German classical scholar and philosopher

We are particularly vulnerable to the effects of the ego during our first seven years as children. I could see it in my own development. Growing up in the 70s, like so many others of my era, I went to Sunday school (more through coercion than choice), where the priest told us all about the life of gentle Jesus and how, as young children, we should follow in his example. 'Be gentle. Be humble. Be tolerant and kind,' he would say, 'and turn the other cheek.' At home, this message was also supported by my parents, who frequently repeated, 'Be quiet, don't make a noise, don't talk back, get along with your sister, be seen and not heard.'

However, when I was old enough to go to school, I was a little perplexed to find that the rhetoric had changed completely. I was now expected to get good grades and be the top of my class. I was encouraged to become competitive, to be good at athletics, to win in sports, to be an achiever, be a go-getter – completely the opposite kind of behaviour that was originally expected of me.

This situation breeds a great feeling of inferiority in the mind of any child, and in the mind of the adult after the child matures. There is a part of us that wants to be humble and unassuming, patient and tolerant, kind and considerate; but there is this other part that wants to achieve, that wants its own outward show, wants to be the centre of attention, wants to be entertained, wants to be recognised and regarded with esteem. Even in the course of a single day we witness these two seemingly opposing parts of our self. We may work hard at being tolerant, understanding, patient and kind in the morning, only to find that by the afternoon we have completely destroyed everything that we've built in an effort to prove ourselves, score points over another or achieve a pressing deadline or goal. But if we are humble in the morning, and then intolerant, arrogant and selfish in the afternoon, surely there is some sort of identity crisis going on here? How can we be assertive, confident and self-esteemed, yet humble and unassuming, without actually becoming completely schizophrenic?

And schizophrenic is exactly what we are. There is more than one of us living in this body. If there wasn't, why else would we talk to ourselves? Have you ever found yourself in a disagreement with your partner or a friend or colleague that has caught you completely off guard? You know the kind of argument – where the other person, whoever he is, manages to succinctly and swiftly wipe the floor with you, lambasting you time and again whilst you stand there agog, open-mouthed, surprised and utterly speechless. No matter how hard you try, you can't think of even the simplest retort, or the easiest justification for your actions; that is, until he's left. After a few moments, when you've had a chance to pick yourself up off the floor, brush yourself down, and gather your thoughts, you start to have a conversation with yourself which might go something like this:

'You idiot, he has just completely slaughtered you. Why didn't you say this?'

'It's easy for you to talk – he came upon me so quickly, I didn't have time to think.'

'That's what you always say. He wiped the floor with you, just like he always does.'

'I feel so stupid.'

'Well, damn well think about it for the next time!'

'I know, I will, I will, you're right, I'll get him next time around.'

Now, who is talking and who is listening? How is it possible to have this conversation in this way if you are utterly alone and there's nobody else in the room? But this is how we carry on. People have been known to chastise themselves, reprimand themselves, praise themselves, apologise to themselves, make vows to themselves and break those vows and get into trouble with themselves all over again! Situations such as these would be totally impossible if there was only one of us. We often talk of wrestling with our own inner demons, and indeed, that is what we are doing. The wiles of the ego are positively demonic and can be so extreme that without great understanding, cunning and strength we may never be free from its grasp.

As the ego shares the same body with us, it too has access to the same aspects of consciousness that we do. Every single one of us has both a conscious and subconscious mind, a mental body. In reality it's one mind with two functions that operate at different levels. At a subconscious level, the mind controls the involuntary functions and processes of the body – those functions that happen automatically, whether we are conscious of them or not: the heartbeat, the regulation of our body temperature, and the digestive process. Our thoughts, decisions, movements and speech are a product of the conscious mind. The ego has access to both and uses them to its own advantage, which is why we find ourselves being caught out by little Freudian slips of the tongue. Perhaps you have found yourself in the following situation:

We have all had those friends who come to visit and never seem to want to leave. The evening is drawing to a close, the festivities are over, all the other guests have left, but there is one couple who still keeps talking. At midnight, you feel yourself yawning and your eyes drooping. You are worried, because you have to be up for work the following day. You avoid pouring them another drink, hoping that they get the subtle hint, but that has no impact. Eventually at two a.m., they get up and slowly move to the door – and find yet another story to tell you in the hallway. Eventually, you eagerly show them to the front door. As they step out into the cold night air, you intend saying, 'I'm glad you came' – but out of nowhere you hear this voice saying, 'I'm glad you're going!' Immediately you try and apologise, but it's too late – they know what you meant. The ego, who has access to both our conscious and subconscious mind, got its dig in when your guard was down. What you intended to say was overridden. You are terribly embarrassed. The evening is ruined and you certainly don't get much sleep because you keep chastising yourself over and over for your stupidity.

Socrates, the wise teacher of Plato, was the first one to isolate the various 'selves of man', the different personae and faces of the ego, which create such imbalance and conflict within us:

1. The person we truly are – the true self, a divine fragment of the Supreme Being whose purpose is to learn in this illusion of physical things. The true self is not encumbered by likes and dislikes, pleasure or pain. It is the pure and incorruptible part of us that is often swathed in so many layers of self-deception.

2. The person we want others to believe we are – This is the 'mask' we put on for others and ultimately come to believe ourselves. It says to the world,

'I am successful. I'm in control. I have it all together. I'm perfect. I don't hurt, I don't make mistakes, and I know exactly what I am doing. I have mastered life.'

3. The person we think we are – As we don't understand our true identity, we define ourselves by external attributes – our name, our gender, our job title, our body, our credit cards, financial status, where we live, possessions, relationships, our personality and achievements – all those things that we can put a label on to justify that we exist.

4. The person we want to be – Every time I open the *Hello Magazine* and see how the rich and famous live, I find myself longing for a different life. I could win the lottery so I could buy a Georgian manor house on twenty acres of parkland in Oxfordshire, own a summerhouse at a beach resort, and never have to worry about money ever again. I'd also like to be a skinny size-eight catwalk model and be able to eat what I like, travel the world and drink champagne all day. Oh, and I'd also like to have a mind like Einstein. Am I asking for too much?

5. The person we can be – Karmic implications may mean that I will never be a millionaire, have Einstein's IQ, or be a catwalk model. I wouldn't even get one of my thighs into a size-eight skirt. But if I set my desire to be this, at some point in this journey it will be so. This desire will keep me coming back to this world again and again until it is fulfilled. We can choose the life we want to live and our goals and aspirations within the realms of our karma. What I can do in this life is work with what I have and perfect it as much as I can, make the best of what I have.

In the beginning, before one develops spiritually, these five selves are totally opposing and different, one from the other. If we become self aware, we can constantly observe the conflicting dialogue within, driven by the needs of the ego. But as we progress along the spiritual path, becoming more balanced, these identities slowly merge, where eventually they are all exactly the same. If there is a great difference between these five, then we are very likely at the lower end of spiritual development and the ego has more control. If they are identical, then we are higher up. The purpose of spiritual development is not just to merge the conscious and subconscious mind, but to unite these five different views. We do this by living life, incarnation through incarnation. The more we focus on building our knowledge and understanding, the quicker we can progress.

If you want to reach a state of bliss, then go beyond your ego and the internal dialogue. Make a decision to relinquish the need to control, the need to be approved, and the need to judge. Those are three things the ego is doing all the time. It's very important to be aware of them every time they come up.

Dr Deepak Chopra
Medical doctor, speaker and writer

The spiritual warrior works hard to get to know the ego because eventually he must destroy it. The enemy is not out there in the material world, as the ego would have us believe. It is right here within. It is the ego that causes us pain and suffering in this life and the next. It is the ego that makes karma for us, yet the true self has to keep coming back to this world to pay it off. By learning to control the ego we can eventually turn it against itself and use it as a force for good. The first step in this process is conscious awareness: paying attention to our thoughts and emotions and what's happening in our bodies.

As Sun Tzu says: 'Know thyself and know thy enemy.' Once we understand the ego, we can stop worrying and start living a less stressful existence.

SLAYING THE DRAGON
The Ego in Mythology

In all hero myths and fairy tales of the world, the hero at some stage in his journey has to prepare for and engage in a battle with a fearsome creature: a Gorgon (Perseus), an ogre ('Jack and the Beanstalk'), a basilisk (Harry Potter), a Kraken (Perseus) or a dragon ('Jason and the Golden Fleece'). The monsters are a depiction of the ego – a creature so fierce and of such strength and proportion, that failure to win the battle will mean certain death for the hero.

The ego is cunning and deceitful. It knows everything about us, and so its destruction is often difficult and takes a long time. In the Danish fairy tale of 'Nils in the Forest', the ego is depicted as an enormous troll wife who chases Nils this way and that through a dark forest. Everywhere he tries to hide – in the trees, in the reeds and the river – she finds him and tries to capture him for her cooking pot. The ego is deceitful and cunning; it knows everything about us and sometimes we need special help to overcome its wiles.

In many myths, the ego monster can only be appeased by the sacrifice of human flesh. In Nordic mythology, Níðhöggr was the name of the serpent dragon who continuously gnawed at the roots of Yggdrasil, the Tree of Life. His name means 'tearer of corpses'.

In the Middle Eastern myth of Saint George and Dragon, a dragon was terrorising the inhabitants of a small village settlement. The villagers, afraid of the creature, tried to quench its insatiable appetite by supplying it with sheep to eat. However, as it became more demanding, they decided to sacrifice their own children, one by one, drawn from a lottery. Even the king's daughter was not to be spared until Saint George saved the day. The simple villagers, victims of their own egos, would rather sacrifice their own children than go into battle. In the same way, we are often willing to sacrifice our very *soul* to appease the whims of the ego as it drives our desire for material things, wealth, fame and power, even if it sometimes means riding roughshod over others.

In Celtic mythology, Myrddin, who became the legendary Merlin, was selected as the special 'fatherless boy' to be sacrificed to the red and the white dragons who continually fought in a lake beneath the mountain fortress of Dinas Emrys, preventing the kingdom from becoming a stronghold. Through his prophetic insights, Merlin was spared from his fate and went on to become one of the greatest dragon masters of the Celtic legends. His visions of the Red Dragon eventually foretold of the coming of King Arthur.

Those who slayed dragons and monsters in folklore were not ordinary folk, they were depicted as magicians, knights or heroes or the sons of a god. They are symbolic of those who have realised their divine nature. It is this that makes them powerful. The hero, however, could not hope to kill the monster in one fell swoop. Sometimes he had to engage in many battles before the final blow could be dealt. The Greek mythological hero Hercules had twelve labours to perform before he was finally free, many of them resulting in a battle with a different creature each time: the Nemean lion, the Lernean hydra, the Ceryneian hind and the Erymanthian boar. His labours also depict different stages of initiation on the spiritual path, together with his ability to unite the imbalance within himself.

Sometimes the hero has to apply cunning and wisdom to overcome his enemy. Jason, in his quest for the Golden Fleece, lulled the dragon that guarded the fleece to sleep with a few drops of a powerful magic potion provided by the goddess Medea.

Perseus used a highly polished shield, given to him by the goddess Athena, as a mirror and was able to reflect the gaze of the Medusa back on herself. The ego cannot reflect against itself unless it has a mirror to know where it's at. The external world is its mirror, and this is one of the reasons that it drives us to seek approval and acceptance in society.

But when it comes down to it, the ego is quite stupid and with a certain level of understanding can be fooled. In Grimm's fairy tale, 'The Crystal Ball', Richard, the youngest of three sons, ran away from home and the clutches of his mother – an enchantress. On his way through a forest he saw two giants and they were quarrelling over which one of them should have the wishing cap. When giants quarrel it is very hard not to notice them. The earth shook and the trees shivered. They depict the wild imbalance that we experience within when the ego takes hold.

One of them saw Richard and called to him. 'Hey there,' he said. 'I've heard small men are more clever than giants. You must settle this argument for us.'

Richard agreed. He took the wishing cap from them and said, 'I will walk a short distance, and when I call, whoever reaches me first shall have it.'

It seemed reasonable and the two giants agreed that way at least one of them would have the wishing cap; if they carried on quarrelling, the cap would be torn in two. The ego will continue its battles until a futile end; it is so obsessed with itself that it fails to notice when it's being tricked.

Richard put the cap on his head, (depicting his ability to overcome the ego through internal balance and control of his thoughts and emotions). He began to walk, but he was so busy thinking of higher things that he forgot to call out to the giants and kept the wishing cap for himself, using it to save the king's daughter, who was imprisoned in the dungeon of the Castle of the Golden Sun.

Small men who set out on the road less travelled can indeed overcome giants. The battle with the ego monster is something that we mere mortals face every day, in every aspect of life. Eventually we will be involved in a battle to the death. Slaying the dragon is the goal of every spiritual warrior.

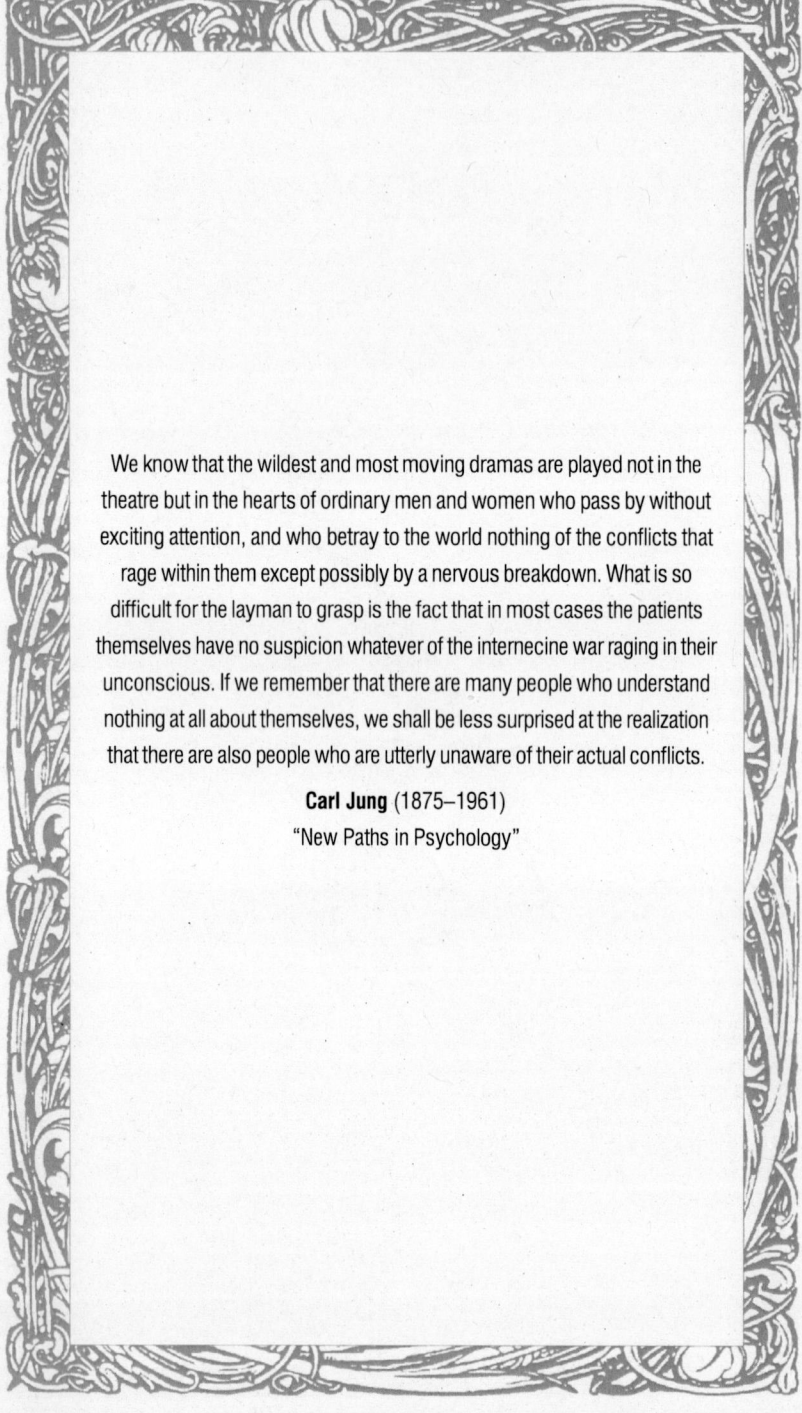

We know that the wildest and most moving dramas are played not in the theatre but in the hearts of ordinary men and women who pass by without exciting attention, and who betray to the world nothing of the conflicts that rage within them except possibly by a nervous breakdown. What is so difficult for the layman to grasp is the fact that in most cases the patients themselves have no suspicion whatever of the internecine war raging in their unconscious. If we remember that there are many people who understand nothing at all about themselves, we shall be less surprised at the realization that there are also people who are utterly unaware of their actual conflicts.

Carl Jung (1875–1961)
"New Paths in Psychology"

CHAPTER 11

ANGELS AND DEMONS
The Law of Opposites

From the moment of birth to the surrender of the last breath, man has to fight in each incarnation innumerable battles – biological, hereditary, bacteriological, physiological, climatic, social, ethical, political, sociological, psychological, metaphysical, so many varieties of inner and outer conflicts. Competing for victory in every encounter are the forces of Good and Evil.

Paramahansa Yogananda (1893–1952)

Bhagavad Gita

 ne of the main reasons for using folklore as an illustration of life's issues is that we can readily identify with many of the traits and behaviours displayed by the characters of each story; traits we see in ourselves or in our nearest and dearest.

For most of my adult life, until I 'saw the light', I likened myself to a fictional character in Lewis Carrol's *Alice in Wonderland:* the capricious Queen of Hearts, who was sweetness and light one day, and yelling, 'Off with her head!' the next. I would be up one moment and down the next, one day at war with myself and the world, and the next day at peace. On some days I felt lethargic and bored, moping around like a wet rag; on other days I was driven, determined and impossibly rebellious. Some days I took the high road, making decisions out of compassion, wisdom and understanding. On other days I would act out of ignorance and discontent, becoming hard and unbending just because I could.

I was exhausted with this continual imbalance within, which I seemed to have so little control over, blissfully unaware at the time that I was driven of course by the needs of the ego. Some days, I believed I was completely bonkers as the mood swings seemed so extreme. I always knew I was a little eccentric in my ways, but this continual turmoil unsettled me greatly, not to mention the chaos, pain and discomfort that I caused others. To them I was indeed like a whimsical Queen of Hearts, lording it over her subjects. No one ever really knew what to expect. I was just grateful that I wasn't like the jealous queen in 'Snow White' who actually poisoned her subjects, or the wicked stepmother in 'Cinderella' who spent her life putting other people down just so she could take the limelight. In my book, whimsical was okay – although it wouldn't actually get me very far in life and I would have probably ended up old, miserable and alone unless I did something about it.

It was during my initiation into Hermetics and the spiritual sciences that I started to understand that I, along with the majority of the planet's population, was emulating a principle that is built into the very fabric of creation itself: *imbalance*, the continuous movement between two pairs of opposites. The big picture and the little picture.

The ancients envisioned their world in two halves – masculine and feminine. Their gods and goddesses worked to keep a balance of power, Yin and Yang. When male and female were balanced, there was harmony in the world. When they were unbalanced there was chaos.

Dan Brown
The Da Vinci Code

There is nothing that we know in this world that we have not arrived at without comparison with its polar opposite. We only know light because we compare it with darkness. We know heat because we have experienced cold. And we know what it's like to be happy because we've spent a lot of time being sad. All of us have good and bad days as the battles rage within, but for some, the battles are extreme. All forms of psychosis, bipolar disorder, depression and borderline personality disorder are born out of imbalance. But even if we're not suffering to this extreme, we all become a little crazy as we struggle to overcome the forces of light and darkness within us.

Does this cosmic principle of polarity really have such an impact on our lives and the way we view the world? The answer is, of course, *yes*; but we are probably unaware of it. The principle ultimately impacts on the way in which we *perceive* the world and our place within it. If we consider the law of opposites at its definitive level, then good and evil don't actually exist – they are constructs born of mankind's limited understanding of the scheme of things. Einstein said, 'Darkness is only the absence of light, and evil is only the absence of God.' A person is not an *evil* person but they may do *evil* deeds. In the same way, a person who we deem to do *good* deeds is not necessarily a *good* person. People are not all they appear to be. An individual's propensity towards good and evil is based on the 'light' and 'balance' they each have within. Not all men are equal.

The law of opposites is essential in helping us learn and grow and it's what makes life interesting. In any myth, movie or novel, it is only the tension between the forces of good and evil or between contrasting characters that keeps the story compelling. If the characters didn't falter, didn't make mistakes, didn't subject themselves to ridicule or danger, the story would be decidedly dull. Life's the same way. The problems and difficulties we face, whether without or within, cause us to push against boundaries and limitations and to overcome them. In every good story there is always a reconciling factor – the central character learns to overcome the difficulties he faces, or he overcomes his demons, or is reconciled with his loved ones, and becomes a better human being as a result. Opposites exist so that we can strive, push and drive against them, and in the process become conscious. They are built into the very scheme of things to help us learn. We can never regret anything or feel guilty about anything or learn from anything unless we have two behaviours against which we can compare: one that is good in our perception, and one that is bad; one that we like, one that we dislike. We can never define *anything* unless we have two co-ordinates of comparison.

Everything is dual; everything has poles; everything has pairs of opposites; like and dislike are the same, so are love and hate, courage and fear. Opposites are identical in nature but different in degrees of vibration. Everything has a natural rhythm; everything flows out and in; everything has its tides; all things rise and fall; the pendulum swing manifests in everything. The measure of the swing to the right is the measure of the swing to the left.

The Kybalion: *Hermetic Philosophy (Anon.)*

A simple example can illustrate this: If we were running in a marathon, we would need to know where the start and the finish points were, otherwise how would we know whether or not we were making any progress? Without an understanding of these two points, a beginning and an end, we wouldn't be able to determine if the person that just overtook us was doing so because we were trailing way behind and he was in fact lapping us, or because we were actually leading the field and *he* had to run like crazy to catch up. To determine our position, we need two co-ordinates: a beginning and an end, a start and a finish. If one is taken away we have nothing against which to compare our position. Without two co-ordinates, either internal or external, we are lost.

Paradoxically, we need the law of opposites to help us learn; yet it is the law of opposites that lies at the root of so much pain and unhappiness in life. Our internal imbalance, driven entirely by the whims of the ego, is made worse through the *comparison* of these opposites.

We are a funny race, human beings, most of us never happy with what we have, no matter how much we have. Few of us are able to look fondly at life and count our blessings. No matter how many times we are reminded about how we should be grateful for those things we already have, we are always comparing our situation with another. When I moved to New Zealand in 2010, I thought it would be an easy-peasy transition. I had, after all, moved to a different continent once before, when I left UK/Europe for Africa. Only this time, I spent months deliberating my decision logically and intuitively, instead of just packing up and moving out, as I had done fifteen years before. I wanted a new adventure. I was excited about the opportunity of an old/new relationship, of sharing my life with someone who seemed to tick most of the boxes in terms of what I wanted in a man. I wanted to write my book, start my healing business and give love a chance to blossom. The only way I was going to make change happen was to step into the unknown, again. And so it was to be that on 20th September, 2010, I found myself at Auckland International Airport, ready to start my new life in a new relationship with a new country. I was blissfully happy.

Six months later, such was not the case. I found myself longing for South Africa again. Being in this new relationship was difficult. I missed my family and my friends. I felt so isolated on this little island on the backside of the world. I missed being an overnight flight away from my mum in the UK. Forty-eight hours to fly back to SA or the UK was a long time. I missed being single and the freedom to be myself, doing what I wanted, when I wanted, as I had been doing for the last five years. I missed Cape Town, the wine farms, Table Mountain, the wild ocean, diving in Mozambique and the spirit that is just Africa. I missed the dry climate, the continuous sunshine and the continuous good health I had in such a climate. I found myself constantly sick in New Zealand, as my body adjusted to a more temperate climate. I missed the living-on-the-edge-of-your-seat mentality that I was once keen to leave. I found New Zealand dull by comparison. In spite of my absolute certainty about leaving Africa and stepping into a new life, I now wanted nothing more than to get back on a plane and go home.

What had I done? With the help of my ego, I had allowed my consciousness to slip back into the past. Of course, going through such a massive change was bound to have its effect on my emotional state, but it was made all the worse with the concept of *comparison;* I was comparing where I was right now, with all its beauty and benefits, to where I once was. I was comparing my likes and dislikes of one country with my likes and dislikes of another. I felt the familiar feeling of anxiety gnawing away at my insides.

The ego drives the imbalance in us through the comparison of things outside of us. Its demands are always relentless. No more is this so than when we compare ourselves to others. I have always been able to expertly beat up on myself because I always compared my situation to that of other people who I believed were better or more successful. I was never thin enough or pretty enough compared to my size-8 girlfriends or the celebs in *Hello Magazine*, never smart enough compared to my mates with MBAs. I didn't earn enough money compared to my sister or my friends who ran their own businesses and drove Porsches and lived in multi-million-dollar houses. I didn't make the right career choices after I had ducked out too soon compared to those people who were surging up the corporate ranks. I didn't drive the right car for the upmarket Sandton neighbourhood where BMW and Mercedes were commonplace.

This kind of situation is made worse by those who sit in judgement of you with little or no understanding of what is driving you or the journey you are on. Have you noticed how people love giving you their ideas and opinions about your mistakes, even when you don't ask, yet all of their comments are still grounded in this universal law of comparison? They are comparing where you are to where they are, or comparing what they believe is right for you in relation to their picture of success, what they would do in your situation. But you can understand why people do it – this comparison thing helps us feel good about ourselves.

Have you noticed how when we find someone who is down on his luck and sharing his story with us that we somehow feel better about ourselves and our situation, even a little smug? If someone else's relationship is lousy, we feel better about ours. If someone is having a hard time with the boss, we feel good about working for ourselves. If someone is going through a hard time financially, we don't feel so bad about all the money we lost in a stupid investment. We feel that our life is okay in comparison to theirs. I am convinced this is why women in particular spend so much time talking about other people – they feel better about themselves as a result.

The ego is forever caught up in defining itself through comparison. It measures life in terms of loss and gain, success and failure, like and dislike, better or worse, possessing and being dispossessed. This is how it exists. I am doing okay because I am comparing myself to all the other guys who are not doing okay. I can do better because I am comparing myself to all the guys I can see are doing better. I am a success because I am comparing myself to all the failures that I've had or others have had. And this lies at the root of what makes our lives a very worrying thing. All of our worries and concerns are linked to comparison and driven by the ego. If you think about any counselling, coaching or development you've been through, the source of your angst can probably be summed up in this one little lament: *If I could just be somewhere else, with someone else, in some other body, in some other time or some other place, doing something else, I'd be happy.* While the ego is in control, our life will be one continuous blur of endless desire and unhappiness. We are continually seeking answers for happiness with something that lies outside of ourselves. We have lost our capacity to draw the distinction between the needs of the ego and who we really are, and so we need more and more things outside of ourselves to define ourselves. Our definition of success is decidedly flawed. We have lost the capacity to define what success is, other than by comparison with something else. The *unrealised* man or woman cannot define himself by anything other than definitions outside of himself. The *self-realised* man or woman does not need this external definition.

Material force moves and flows in all directions and in all manners. Its two elements unite and give rise to the concrete. Thus the multiplicity of things and human beings is produced. In their ceaseless successions the two elements of yin and yang constitute the great principles of the universe.

Chang Tsai (1020-1078)
Philosopher – Confucianism, Neo-Confucianism

The Universe is in perpetual motion, continually sliding between two polar opposites. It is what keeps it alive, moving, vibrating, for it is only the opposing forces of gravity that keep the planets in orbits around the sun. When the pendulum swings one way, it has to, by law, swing the other way. The whole system is designed with opposites as a template for learning. We even have polar opposites built within ourselves – left and right hemispheres of our brain, a conscious and subconscious mind, an astral body and a physical body, a true self and a false self, a left side of our body (symbolised by water) and a right side to our body (symbolised by fire.) For us to enjoy a beautiful sunny day, we must first have some really dark nights, and so our experience is enhanced. Therefore, ignorance has just as important a role to play in the scheme of things as enlightenment, for we cannot achieve enlightenment unless we have ignorance that we must overcome.

So here's the rub: We are never going to be successful enough, rich enough, handsome enough, beautiful enough, clever enough, have big enough boobs or thin enough thighs. The appeasement of the ego is a bottomless pit. It will never be satisfied and neither will we. No matter how much we've got, if we rely on the wiles of the ego through comparison, we will always believe that we never have enough, we will always feel lower than some people and higher than others. This is why the ego is the part of us we must destroy.

There is no such thing as success and failure or good and evil. It is part of the 'illusion of opposites'. The purpose of spiritual growth is to overcome this illusion and become balanced, to take the middle path straight between two opposing points. To stop worrying and start living, we must learn to be *indifferent* to both success and failure, happiness and sadness, joy and pain. They are products of the ego and comparison. One is not better than the other, it just is what it is. The Supreme Being learns from every single part of creation, from the atom to the emperor. There is not one part of creation that is more worthy than another. *All* light is relevant, whether it is the light from a butterfly breaking free from a chrysalis, a predator stalking its prey or the mistakes that you and I make every moment of the day. *All* light accrues not just to ourselves but to that which we are part of: the Supreme Being. There are no definitions about which is the better light or worse light – it's just light.

POLARITY IN CREATION AND MYTH

The law of opposites has existed since the dawning of creation. In the beginning, only the Supreme Being existed. Then he separated the light from the darkness, and with that the Universe came into existence, together with the law of duality. Creation is the Supreme Being's ego, his dark shadow. Just as we seek to balance the darkness and the light within us, so the entire Universe is a balance seeking mechanism. Sufi Mystic, Bhai Sabib describes it beautifully:

"In the whole of the universe there are only Two: the Lover and the Beloved. God loves his Creation, and the soul loves God. In order to be able to create, the one being had to become two, and logically there had to be a difference between the two. The creation was only possible because of two opposites; everything in creation responds either to positive or negative forces, or vibrations. There is the sound and the echo, the call and the response to it, light and darkness; without the opposing forces how could the world exist. Even in the Angelic kingdom there are Angels of Power and Angels of Beauty. As soon as the Creative Ray of God touches the plane of manifestation, these two forces come into play inevitably. On the physical plane those two forces will manifest either as masculine or feminine, as male or female. Both forces are inherent in everything and either one or the other will predominate. Upon the predominance of the one or the other, sex is determined. Even some plants are either male or female. Every living thing has this procreative, or sexual energy, in its very make up for it is the creative energy of God manifesting on the dense, physical plane of creation."

There are billions of permutations of this law throughout the Universe. Wherever we find one aspect, we will always find its polar opposite in any aspect of life we care to consider:

Water & Fire	Fear & Courage	Repulsion & Attraction
Female & Male	Acid & Alkaline	Reflective & Projective
Magnetism & Electricity	Passive & Active	Beauty & Ugliness
Cold & Hot	Coccus & Bacillus	Love & Hate
Sedative & Stimulant	Contraction & Expansion	Fidelity & Promiscuity
Inferior & Superior	Synthesis & Analysis	Yin & Yang
Matter & Spirit	Ignorance & Enlightenment	Intuitive & Logical
Ego & True Self	Humility & Arrogance	Controlling & Impulsive
Astral & Mental	Subconscious & Conscious	Manifestation & God

In myth, we see the law of opposites playing out in Homer's *Odyssey*. The ultimate goal of the spiritual warrior is to become balanced and in myth, the state of balance is often symbolised by the hero overcoming a difficulty or an obstacle in some way. In the tale of Jason and the Argonauts, we encounter the Symplegades, the Cyanean Rocks found at the Bosphorus (the Istanbul Strait), that moved randomly about in the ocean crashing together and crushing any ship that tried to pass between them. They are symbolic of the illusion of duality.

No normal human being had ever sailed between these rocks safely, but it was through the Symplegades that Jason and his Argonauts had to pass to enter the Hellespont on their quest for the Golden Fleece. Acting on the advice of the seer Phineas, Jason first let a white dove fly through the rocks to ensure the passage was safe; the dove (a symbol of divine intervention) passed through, losing only its tail feathers as the rocks crashed together behind it. Jason and his Argonauts then rowed mightily through the passage behind the dove as the rocks opened once more, making the hazardous trip safely and losing only a stern ornament from the ship in the process. The rocks would no doubt have crushed any man who was unworthy, but Jason, a mythological hero, a warrior who had travelled some way down the spiritual path, was balanced enough to make it through unscathed. After the Argo's successful journey, the Symplegades stopped moving and stood apart forever.

The soul can only receive impulses from another soul, and from nothing else. We may study books all our lives, we may become very intellectual, but in the end we find that we have not developed at all spiritually. This inadequacy of books to quicken spiritual growth is the reason why, although almost every one of us can speak most wonderfully on spiritual matters, when it comes to action and the living of a truly spiritual life, we find ourselves so awfully deficient. To quicken the spirit, the impulse must come from another soul.

The person from whose soul such impulse comes is called the Guru – the teacher; and the person to whose soul the impulse is conveyed is called the Shishya – the student. To convey such an impulse to any soul, the soul from which it proceeds must in the first place possess the power of transmitting it, as it were, to another; and in the second place, the soul to which it is transmitted must be fit to receive it. The seed must be a living seed, and the field must be already ploughed; and when both these conditions are fulfilled, a wonderful growth of genuine religion takes place. The true preacher of religion has to be of wonderful capabilities, and clever shall his hearer be.

There are great dangers in regard to the Guru. There are many who, though immersed in ignorance, in the pride of their hearts, fancy they know everything, and not only do not stop there, but offer to take others on their shoulders; and thus the blind leading the blind, both fall into the ditch. Fools dwelling in darkness, wise in their own conceit, and puffed up with vain knowledge, go round and round staggering to and fro, like blind men led by the blind. The world is full of these. Everyone wants to be a teacher, every beggar wants to make a gift of a million dollars. Just as these beggars are ridiculous, so are these teachers.

Swami Vivikenanda (1863–1902)
Chief disciple of the 19th century saint Ramakrishna

CHAPTER 12

THE QUICKENING OF THE SPIRIT

The Dangers of the Guru

The real seeker, one who is not false to himself, will always meet with the true, with the real, because it is his own real faith, his own sincerity in earnest seeking that will become his torch. The real teacher is within, the lover of reality is one's own sincere self, and if the one is really seeking truth, sooner or later one will certainly find a true teacher.

Inayat Khan (1882–1927)
Founder of the 'Sufi Order in the West'

he desire within us to seek truth and the answers to the perennial questions about life drives us down many roads and avenues. To seek God eventually becomes more of a need than a desire. From the primal venerators of tribal gods to the most enlightened professor of physics, all of us, without exception, are seeking God, even though we may not know it. Sooner or later we feel the stirring of our own internal divinity and are prompted to seek answers to questions of existence.

The tribesman may make sacrifices to his ancestors, the professor may study the birth of stars, but each in his own way is trying to make sense of this world and his position in the scheme of things. Because all people are unique, we seek truth in different ways, with different levels of commitment and motivation, with varying degrees of success, and with different emotions and responses. We seek with varying ratios of reason to faith.

Sooner or later in this quest, we all come across individuals whom we perceive as ahead of the game in the spiritual journey – priests and pastors, bishops and cardinals, sheiks and llamas, ascetics and monks. And if we are discerning in this quest, we are able to separate the wheat from the chaff and penetrate beyond the outward appearance of these people to infiltrate their inner workings and motivations. We are then able to discover the truth – or not – of what they are saying. Eventually we are able to know beyond all doubt that these spiritually advanced people can provide us with the keys to Heaven.

If you have been agreeing with everything you have read here thus far, then you are living in a different world from mine. In my world it is not easy to discern real truth. It is not easy to know whether all mentors, gurus and priests are everything they're cracked up to be. The spiritual journey is a minefield of fact and fiction. It is a road that is littered with cul-de-sacs, confusion and uncertainty. It is a quest that treads the blurry line between saints and charlatans, God-realised Adepts and cult leaders who cynically exploit people for their own ends.

Yet time after time, people fall prey to the charlatans and their personality cults. The seeker is desperate, desperate to give substance to the compulsion within for a meaningful spiritual life. When we eventually discover someone who appears to know what he is talking about – someone who has gathered a bunch of disciples or individuals about him, someone who delivers his philosophy coherently and without any apparent self-serving motive, someone who consistently teaches a spiritual way that resonates with what we feel to be the truth – then we feel that it is too good to be true. We grab on with both hands, determined never to let go, because we have found the one person that can help us make sense of it all, help us to make our way back. It is our desperate need for meaning and God that makes us vulnerable to charlatans.

The spiritual path is full of gurus and teachers with abilities way beyond the ordinary. Many can inspire us to extraordinary levels, but sooner or later we may discover that they too have feet of clay and are just as susceptible to human failing and fallibility as we are. This in itself is not problematic, if we are wise and discerning and do not confuse the message with the messenger. It is important to consider that no teacher can be truly equal to what he teaches, otherwise he would not be a teacher in this world.

So in our great need to express our spirituality and in our search for enlightenment, we try not to judge these messengers, if we are wise, for their weaknesses. We simply continue to eagerly devour the message and make a mental note not to make the same mistakes. This is okay, we learn to live with these things. But still, we are no closer to knowing if we are on the right track. The doubts about what we are doing and the path we have chosen to tread continue to flood in. The spiritual journey is difficult, it is painstaking, and the fruits of the journey in one lifetime can be very few and far between. So onward we plod, never knowing where it is we are going, or even if we are going anywhere at all. And always in this picture is the teacher or the guru we seem to imagine knows a great deal about this process we are engaged in.

Here is a simple guide of do's and don'ts gained from my experience, for those attempting to discern the messengers of truth:

Do not confuse the teachings with the teacher.

Your teacher is a human being, just as you are, not a god (even though he might like to think he is). He is also treading the weary path of enlightenment, albeit a few life experiences ahead of you. He is also just as susceptible to human failings and the wiles of the ego as you are.

Do not be impressed by vast amounts of knowledge.

Just because someone is able to pontificate knowledgeably on a wide variety of spiritual subjects does not make him a saint. As Swami Vivikenanda said in the quote at the beginning of this chapter, learning from books and courses creates intellectuals. It does not make anyone spiritual. To be able to speak wonderfully on spiritual matters does not necessarily mean that someone is living a meritorious and spiritual life.

Be careful of those who need to adopt the mantle of guru and take on disciples.

If there is such a personal need for recognition, then there is a problem. True teachers are reluctant teachers, they are called to teach or they are instructed to teach. They don't simply wake up one day and decide to share their revelations with the world. Self-appointed gurus are often victims of their own ego and they are dangerous. Do not undertake exercises and disciplines that involve the manipulation of your subtle energies, particularly the kundalini, unless your guru knows what he is doing. Watch carefully how the guru conducts himself in life before agreeing to undertake any exercises that you don't understand. Let your conscience be your guide.

Do not be impressed by the authority of teachers who claim (or imply) that they are in communication with higher beings.

If such communication exists, there will be no need to make this claim. The imagination and the ego can play all sorts of tricks on ones psyche. The ability to communicate with or channel higher beings who can impart worthy advice and knowledge depends on the vibration of the individual who claims to have the contact. Again, watch how the individual lives his life. The consistency and spiritual fruits of such a communication will be self-evident.

Be wary of those who claim to *channel* communications with high beings on 'the other side', calling themselves Jesus, Abraham, Thoth, Melchizedek, Saint Germaine, or any other name they can think of. Dying does not make you wise. Anyone can do it. It does not require a special skill – it's living that's the hard part. Dying does not give you the keys to Heaven. If the being on 'the other side' was devious and stupid in life, he will also be devious and stupid in death. The only difference is, that now that he's passed on, there are thousands of people on the physical plane who want to listen to him. The ego stays with you for some time when you pass on, until you are re-born again in this world, at which time you have a few seconds of respite before you start to create another one. So, a spirit on the other side can masquerade as anyone he wishes. Channelling can also be very dangerous – the uneducated channeller who willingly opens himself up for possession or communication from a discarnate spirit can be exposing himself to all kinds of mischief if he doesn't know what he's doing.

This is not to dismiss respectable mediums or psychics who have a clear and sentient gift in this area. Gordon Smith, the psychic barber from Glasgow, Scotland, is a good example – he brings much comfort and peace to those whose loved ones have passed on. In my experience of his work, he does not claim to channel high beings for his own notoriety and gratification. But he does demonstrate time and time again a clear ability to communicate with the other side at will and makes no outlandish claims of being in contact with any big brand name in spirituality. He has also developed his psychic skills and abilities to 'tune in' when *he* decides, not at the whim of a discarnate being in search of a physical body, which is always the danger with those who dabble in channelling practices.

Do not be impressed with someone just because he's been to India or lived in a monastery.

Because Christianity lacks so much of what we feel to be true in a religious context, we flock towards Eastern religions like moths to a flame, assuming that enlightenment is ten a penny. We seek gurus and teachers in the ashrams and the mystical centres of Sufism, yoga, Buddhism and Hinduism, who expound principles and doctrines that make more mystical sense to us than those of our often wayward bishops and cardinals. Not everyone from the East is 'enlightened'. In his book, *The Evolutionary Energy in Man*, Gopi Krishna describes his painful experiences with kundalini energy. Through the practice of daily yoga meditation, disciplines and exercise, *without* the aid of a guru, he unleashed this powerful force; yet the experience almost killed him. For many years, he and his family travelled far and wide, seeking the guidance of knowledgeable gurus and seers whose insight and study of this ancient practice might help him in his plight. Yet every seer he engaged, some of whom had a large following and discipleship, was more baffled and perplexed by his condition than he was. He describes the disappointment he felt in those who were able to profess wise words from the scriptures but had no hands-on experience of what they taught. If you can't do it, you don't know it, no matter where you live in the world.

Again, with this statement, I do not wish to denigrate those worthy individuals who have dedicated their lives to a spiritual practice and are clearly able to give help and guidance to many people. However, it is wise to point out that a guru can only take you as far along the path as he or she has travelled himself and no further. Beyond that, he may have a number of theories or scriptures from which he can quote, but this does not mean he is enlightened. We must apply discernment.

Do not be impressed with special powers and abilities.

Special powers and abilities do not denote that someone is spiritually enlightened or that he has integrity. I personally experienced a couple of con artists, a male and female partnership, who purported to be healers from a South American monastery. They used their incredible psychic gifts to extract money, food and lodging from unsuspecting individuals. They were also responsible for the untimely death of one elderly woman in particular whom they claimed to be 'healing'.

An estate agent friend of mine was charged the equivalent of $3500 US by a psychic who claimed she could clear her house and business of the negative energies impacting her current sorry state of affairs. In desperation to rid herself of these ills, my friend paid the healer a 50% deposit to do the work. After ten days there was not the slightest change in her circumstances; in fact, her plight worsened. When questioned, the psychic claimed to be 'still working on it – matters of this nature take time.' I introduced my friend to a reputable psychic healer whom I had experienced to have incredible insight, ability and integrity. He did the job for her in thirty minutes and charged her a mere $50. Her life changed immediately.

Special powers do not make you spiritual in intention. Approximately one in five people is born with a psychic 'gift' of some sort – clairvoyance (seeing), clairaudience (hearing), clairsentience (feeling and sensing). You and I can also develop these powers through leading a balanced life and learning and practicing certain spiritual and practical techniques and disciplines. As we journey along this path these skills come alive within us.

Do not swear allegiance to a guru or organisation or anything that you don't understand.

No matter how powerful the guru or the legacy that he has behind him, know this and don't forget it: your word is your bond – in this lifetime and the next and the next. A girlfriend of mine was required to swear allegiance to a well-known Indian guru for *all of eternity* to gain access to the next level of teachings. Eternity is a very, very, very long time. Needless to say, she didn't do it.

Do be impressed by the capacity of your teacher to respect all people.

Divine love and genuine compassion for others are the hallmarks of souls that have travelled the path of God-realisation.

Do be impressed by humility and service.

The God-realised person lives only to serve and uplift fellow human beings. A true teacher will clean the toilets himself before he directs his disciples to do it.

Do be impressed by insight and clear understanding.

If your teacher consistently demonstrates the ability to accurately assess people and situations with startling penetration, accuracy and perceptiveness that sometimes defies logic, then he is demonstrating a power that is associated with spiritually advanced souls. Be very impressed with this.

What Swami Vivekananda refers to as a 'quickening of the spirit' in the quote at the beginning of this chapter is the hallmark of a true messenger of truth. The true teacher has the ability to tangibly enrich the experience of your own spiritual nature and provides an impulse at a *soul level* that elevates you in some way. Perhaps you enter a mystical or ecstatic state while you are in the presence of your teacher. Perhaps you receive insight and inspiration in a manner, scale or frequency way beyond what you have experienced before, leaving you open-mouthed in awe. Perhaps you see the unfolding of some remarkable ability through the intervention of your teacher. Perhaps you have a dream that seems strangely real, where you and your teacher are together. Perhaps, perhaps, perhaps....

Always, this experience with a guru is extraordinary and enormously meaningful, and is what's meant by the 'quickening of the spirit'. It is one of the great advantages of being taken on as a pupil by a true teacher. The quickening of the spirit produced in *you* is one of the unmistakable signs of being in the presence of a true teacher. If in your association with your teacher or guru you cannot recall any occasions where your spirit has been quickened, or where the experience has been tangible and unforgettable, then do not be impressed with that. If you clearly and unmistakably can look back on numerous occasions where your teacher has been directly responsible for the 'quickening of your spirit', then rejoice, because in today's world that is a very rare thing indeed.

Book 3

WEAPONS AND TOOLS: WAKING UP

INTRODUCTION

According to Vedanta, there are only two symptoms of enlightenment, just two indications that a transformation is taking place within you toward a higher consciousness. The first symptom is that you stop worrying. Things don't bother you anymore. You become light-hearted and full of joy. The second symptom is that you encounter more and more meaningful coincidences in your life, more and more synchronicities. And this accelerates to the point where you actually experience the miraculous.

Deepak Chopra
Ayurvedic medical doctor

In Hindu mythology, there is a story of creation, of *Pralaya,* a stage of 'non-existence' between the destruction of one universe and the creation of another, where Brahma (God) was planning the next cosmic stage of existence known as *Lila,* the cosmic game or dance. Man, it was decided, would be the *crown* of this creation, the wisest and noblest of all creatures in the universe. In this story, Brahma asks his advisers where he should hide man's true identity, his spirit. Brahma wanted to prolong *Lila,* so that man would have the maximum opportunity to enlighten himself, to learn and grow, so adding to the brightness of the whole.

Should they hide the spirit in the deepest ocean, upon the highest mountain? His advisers suggested neither, as during man's quest for adventure, he would develop ways to dive deep into the ocean and scale the highest mountains. The truth would be found too quickly and the game would be over. Brahma suggested that this spirit, or truth, should be hidden on the moon, and he was again advised against this. Man will develop ways to land on the moon and the truth will be found too quickly. We need to find a place that man will not think of looking.

And that was when Brahma had an idea: 'What if we hide truth deep within man? He won't think of looking there. He will seek himself through material possessions, riches, fame and power. Someday, when all other things have been exhausted, he may wish to find his true nature.'

And so it was. The truth was hidden deep within man and he is today still searching.

Life is indeed a game with its own set of rules, a game that we often take way too seriously. The rules of the game serve us until we outgrow them in some way and a new set of rules has to be found. This is illustrated in another Hindu myth, known as 'Shiva's Lila'. In the tale, Shiva and Parvati are playing a game of dice. As they play, they quarrel and gradually become separated from their androgynous condition into male and female. With each game there is a wager and the stakes get higher and higher as the tension between them mounts and their separation becomes greater and greater. In one game Shiva loses everything but refuses to admit he's been beaten. Humiliated by his defeat, he heads off into the cedar forest where he meets Vishnu, who feels sorry for him. 'Play another game,' says Vishnu. 'This time I promise that you'll win.' And that is exactly what happened. Shiva won back all that he had lost in his earlier games, but now Parvati was suspicious of Shiva's sudden success and another quarrel ensued. To pacify them both, Vishnu appeared on the scene and told them that the game was a deception, their quarrels a product of delusion. On hearing this, Parvati and Shiva realized that life was like their game of dice – totally unpredictable and beyond their control until they decided to do something about it, which ultimately brought them back together as one, stronger than they were before.

It occurred to me the other day that life and the game of snooker actually have a lot in common. I am not a good snooker player and don't think I ever will be. When I pick up a cue in an effort to play a game, I freely admit that I have about as much finesse as the 'Dirty Yellows' rhino at the *Bedknobs and Broomsticks* football match. There really isn't much style to my game. I don't have the practical skills and I couldn't really be bothered to acquire them. I'm quite pleased with myself if I manage to pot the ball, any ball, just so long as it's not white. But I often do that, too, in my chaos – that is, until it comes to family gatherings at Christmas in Johannesburg, when I have to play against my sister, who is actually quite good. She always beats me hands down. Only then do I wish I'd spent a little bit more time in snooker halls and vow silently to myself that I will dedicate a little more time to learning this craft in preparation for next year. Of course, I never do.

In the same way, if we pick up the snooker cue of life and just strike out at anything in the hope of sinking something, we aren't going to get very far. We may sink the right ball into a few pockets if we're lucky, but if we keep on missing our intended target, potting the balls out of sequence, we will find that the game is over before we know it and the same coloured balls are still on the table. In each life we may vow to ourselves that things will be different, but we still carry on in the same way, playing by the same rules, repeating the same mistakes, becoming more and more frustrated, until eventually we want to learn the rules of a different game.

It had long since come to my attention that people of accomplishment rarely sat back and let things happen to them. They went out and happened to things.

Leonardo da Vinci (1452 – 1519)

Italian Renaissance polymath: painter, sculptor, architect, musician, scientist, mathematician, engineer, inventor, anatomist, geologist, cartographer, botanist and *writer*

Spiritual growth comes only by deliberately focusing on it. In a game of snooker, a veteran player will line up the balls for several shots in advance, ensuring that each ball is perfectly placed after each cue strike to make its way into a pocket. In the same way, we can learn to set up the shots in this life to facilitate a better state of play in the next. Each life is a continuous unfolding of chapters and scenes in the great cosmic play. To progress, we have to keep playing the game, but by mastering a different set of rules, by getting deliberate about our intention in life, we have a better chance of becoming seasoned veterans and improving our lot the next time around.

The spiritual journey is a very personal journey and each path or system, organised or not, will have its own set of rules and practices. This section of the book is not dedicated to explaining a plethora of spiritual practices. *Ascension* is not solely about finding the right meditation practice or spiritual group; it's a process of *constant remembrance and deliberate intention* so that we can awaken from our sleep and begin to make our way back up the ladder, step by step.

The transition between our outer and inner search for truth can be a painful one. We are often unsure how to live our lives in a more meaningful way when caught between this world and the next. We founder and fluctuate until we can place our feet firmly on solid ground in a system that makes sense. In the next seven chapters, I have highlighted some weapons, skills, observations and practices that serve a twofold purpose: The first is to help us gain a firm footing during our transition; and the second is to help us take baby-steps to awaken from the illusion and the deep sleep we are in. They are practices that any spiritual warrior can observe, regardless of the spiritual or religious system he belongs to, and each one links back to the lessons we discussed in the previous chapter: the law of karma, reincarnation, and the ongoing battle with our ego. In fact, most of our worries and woes in life are as a result of the ego. I have found them useful in my own life to help me learn and grow, plan ahead, remain focused on my goal and live life more contentedly and meaningfully in the process.

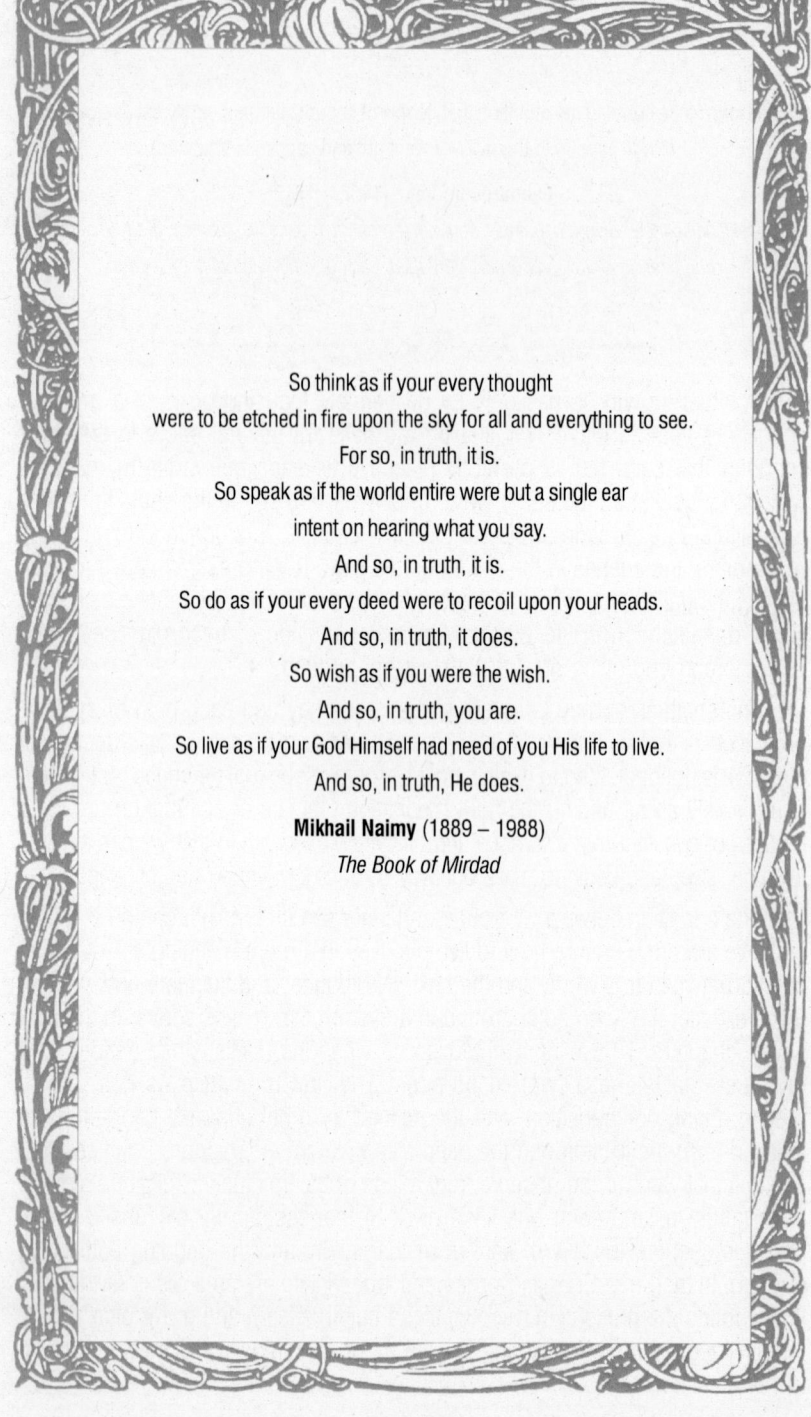

So think as if your every thought
were to be etched in fire upon the sky for all and everything to see.
For so, in truth, it is.
So speak as if the world entire were but a single ear
intent on hearing what you say.
And so, in truth, it is.
So do as if your every deed were to recoil upon your heads.
And so, in truth, it does.
So wish as if you were the wish.
And so, in truth, you are.
So live as if your God Himself had need of you His life to live.
And so, in truth, He does.

Mikhail Naimy (1889 – 1988)
The Book of Mirdad

Chapter 1

WAKING UP

...we are really asleep. We only imagine that we are awake. So when we try to remember ourselves it means only one thing – we try to awake. And we do awake for a second, but then we fall asleep again. This is our state of being, so actually we are asleep. We can awake only if we correct many things in the machine and if we work very persistently on this idea of awaking....

P.D. Ouspensky (1878–1947)
'The Fourth Way'

ussian mystic, George Gurdjieff, described all men as machines that live their lives solely under the power of external influences. 'All man's deeds, actions, words, thoughts, feelings, convictions and habits are the result of external influences and external impressions,' he says.

At first I found this hard to accept; we believe we are conscious, that we make deliberate choices about where we want to go and what we want to do. We believe we know a thing or two about life, and for someone to suggest that we aren't conscious of any of it seemed absurd. But the reality is that we spend most of our lives in a waking slumber. I can't remember the number of times that I've driven my car to a particular destination, sometimes hours away, only to wonder once I'd arrived how I actually got there. I was on autopilot, a state of hypnosis, a waking sleep. In the same way, certain things would happen in my life and I would find myself reacting in the same way that I did in childhood when my buttons were pressed. Although I hated to admit it, I realised that Gurdjieff was right. As a typical representative of the human race, I lived most of my life as a machine. My reactions, my thoughts, my impressions about certain things were mainly automatic and repetitive. I was conscious of my actions for only a few moments every day before slipping back into my comfort zone. We are born as machines and we

307

die as machines unless we can awaken to our *true mind* and begin consciously organising our own lives.

The mystic is acutely aware that every thought, emotion, action and deed will reverberate back to him through the various laws of existence. As we've had thousands of lives prior to this one, we carry the *impressions* within us of every thought, action, deed, judgement that we've ever had. These *samskaras* (the Sanskrit word for impressions in the mind that create our beliefs, attitudes and persona) build up over time and cling to us like glue. Samskaras are like grooves on a vinyl record that become a permanent record of all that we think, say and do. Each time we think or do the same thing, these impressions become more engrained. Over time, if we keep repeating the same patterns, the grooves become deeper. If we don't clear samskaras before we die, we carry them forward into our future life as karma. Samskaras are the seeds of karma. We may be creating our destiny, not by something that we've done today, but by unconscious reactions that we've allowed to build up over centuries. Hence, trying to change our lives for the better can be a difficult and painful process.

Man is a microcosm of God. God is the greatest mystery. As microcosms of God we are also a mystery. Our true natures are hidden, not just from other people, but from ourselves. We are complex beings with multiple facets. We read in the last section that there is not just one being that inhabits this physical body of ours, there are several. One of them is called an ego. This ego and its complexities are what the mystic studies, as the ego is responsible for creating samskaras and karma. In everything we do, we are in mortal combat with this ego and fighting for balance within. By becoming more aware and more conscious, we gain an intimate knowledge of our greatest enemy, which is actually our 'self'.

There are four ways that I have found help to serve me when I am floundering. If we can deliberately focus on these four things, we are well on the way to waking up, and ultimately, to enlightenment. And if enlightenment is not your thing, then just know that even by being aware of these principles and practicing them whenever you can makes you a lot easier to be around.

GUARD YOUR THOUGHTS

It is impossible to stop thinking. The mind never stops, no matter what the books tell you. Try having no thoughts. It's impossible. Even those who have been meditating for years report that they still have errant thoughts running through their head. The whole universe is one giant mental plane, and we can tune into thoughts from anywhere, particularly those with the same vibrational frequency as our own. Mahatma Gandhi described this perfectly when he said, 'I will not let anyone walk through my mind with their dirty feet.' The mind cannot focus for more than a second on one thing before it flits off somewhere else. It is always in 'search mode'. The first step in awakening is learning to control the mind which ultimately controls our emotional state, the impressions we build and our state of vibration. By controlling the mind we are also controlling the ego as we teach it to do *our* bidding instead of what *it* wants.

There are two types of thoughts: *voluntary* and *involuntary*. Voluntary thoughts are thoughts that we ourselves have created. Involuntary thoughts are products of our impressions, childhood conditioning, the environment and our own vibration. They are often automatic thoughts or reactive thoughts. Our partner or work colleague behaves in a certain way that reminds us of our abusive father. We think the same thoughts, feel the same feelings and respond in exactly the same way we did thirty years ago. Again, the process is so quick we don't identify our reaction with a thought. The more we repeat a particular pattern of thinking and behaving, the more automatic it becomes. This is because the neural pathways in the brain – the telephone exchange for the mind – have already been created through repetition. Thoughts travel more easily along well worn paths, filtering quickly into the body and affecting our vibrational state in exactly the same way they did when the experience first happened.

Repeated thoughts create emotions and emotions eventually become beliefs. The subconscious mind is like the fertile soil in a garden – whatever you plant will grow. The subconscious does not differentiate between good or bad thoughts. They are just thoughts. The more they are repeated, the stronger the emotion around them, the deeper their roots go and the harder they are to change.

Approximately 98% of our thoughts are *involuntary*. Very few of us have original thoughts, although we tend to dispute that. Our vibrational state, created by repetitive thoughts, also attracts similar 'gypsy thoughts' that are looking for a place to pitch their tent. They arrive when we least expect them, and like all vagrants, they can be difficult to evict once they've set up camp. Sudden bouts of moodiness and irritability are often the result of gypsy thoughts that have found a home in our minds through the process of *sympathetic resonance,* or vibrational affinity. If we are aware, we will notice how these thoughts start to trickle through into our consciousness, particularly when we are unfocused, daydreaming, tired, feeling sick or down. It takes identification with only one thought for a whole convoy to arrive and our vibration to ultimately drop.

This type of repetitive thought fuels anxiety and depression. Those who have considered ending it all often believe themselves to be in an enormous pit of despair, a pit that is so deep that it is impossible to climb out of. Through 'ignorance', we have allowed our vibration to drop so low that we begin to resonate with the 'suicide crowd' – all the thoughts and emotions that depressed and suicidal people have had, are having and will have. When our vibration is so low, it's very, very hard to raise it up again, particularly if we are sick or in a toxic environment. A low vibration consumes every fibre of our being and contaminates every cell in our body. The lower we go, the more we attract negative thoughts and the more we carve the grooves of our impressions. To change our thinking, we need to slow life down a little, instead of instantly reacting. We need to stop, look, and consider whether there is any truth in the thoughts or emotions that threaten to drown us. Are they real? Where did they come from? Are they really our own thoughts? Does it really matter?

Voluntary thoughts, on the other hand, arrive when we stretch against the invisible ropes that are binding us, expanding our awareness and consciousness and pushing against the self-imposed boundaries and limitations in our thinking, feeling and behaving. Affirmations are a form of voluntary thinking providing we perform them consciously. Voluntary thoughts are hard work and require a lot of effort, which is why the voluntary thought percentage is so low. Many of us don't want to work hard on ourselves. We are prepared to work hard at our careers and our financial success, but not on ourselves. We need noise, we need entertainment, we need people around us, we can't be by ourselves. When we are alone, when all is quiet, then all the automatic thoughts about our troubles in life start to plague us. So we put on some music, turn up the volume and crack open a bottle of wine to drown out the noise in our head. Yet it is only in the silence that progress can be made. If we persist in controlling our thoughts, we can build a bridge between the conscious and subconscious minds, one of the goals of spiritual growth. With practice we can increase our voluntary thought percentage to 98% instead of 2%. People who have achieved Nirvana have gone beyond thought.

So when you find yourself permanently thinking a particular thought, recognize that it might not be your own. If you find yourself starting to feel low and depressed, look at what you have been thinking lately, where you have been hanging out, what you've been eating or drinking. Repeated thoughts supported by strong emotions form the basis of magic. Thoughts are things. They last for eternity. They are permanent and they are powerful and we are *totally responsible* for them.

The spiritual warrior *chooses* the thoughts that occupy his mind. This is why the suit of armour worn by the knight going into battle carries such symbolism. He spends time raising his vibration so that he can tune into higher ideals and higher levels of thinking. He learns to recognise the patterns in his thinking and consciously changes them before his vibration is lowered to the extent that it affects his entire wellbeing.

BE CAREFUL WHAT YOU WISH FOR

As we read earlier, the bestselling book and DVD, *The Secret* by Rhonda Byrne, was a worldwide phenomenon in 2006, telling us that we can indeed have the life of our dreams through the application of a natural law that determines the complete order of the scheme of things: the law of attraction. But what she didn't tell us is that our desires are the things that keep us stuck here in this world. If we are unable to fulfil our desires in this lifetime because of the law of karma, we need to come back again. The mental plane lasts for a whole cosmic week (a cosmic week being a succession of cosmic or solar days), which is an extraordinarily long period of time, beyond our intellect to fathom. Our physical body dies after about seventy years, our emotional (astral) body eventually dissipates too, but thoughts last. They are real; they occupy space in the mental matrix of the universe. Desires come from thoughts and they don't go away when we pass on, particularly if they are intense, repetitive, and supported by strong emotion and visualisation techniques. This is also the process of magic.

We may say who cares? I want my big house and ten cars, a holiday home and servants. But consider this: if in the future, we reach a point in one lifetime where we can develop our skills enough to achieve Nirvana, to make it back to the Divine, we will still have a whole chocolate box full of unfulfilled wishes and desires that we have to come back and fulfil. They don't just go away because we don't want them anymore. They occupy a space in the scheme of things. Our desires attract samskaras, which stick to us like glue, forming unconscious patterns and beliefs that also work with the law of attraction.

Sufi mystic Al Ghazzali says, 'Only that which cannot be lost in a shipwreck is yours.' So if we are to desire anything, perhaps we should desire peace, desire balance, desire freedom, desire wisdom. For how important is that brand new yacht anyway?

GETTING THE EGO ON THE RUN

When we start to pay more attention to how we act and react in life, we begin to notice how much control the ego has over us. We can find ourselves acting up without even being consciously aware of it. I know how, when writing this book and being extremely tired after putting in many long hours, particularly towards the end of the process, I stopped paying attention to this demon within and relaxed my guard. Even though I was meditating regularly and breathing and trying to stay calm, if I gave it some rope it would immediately rise up and try to assume command. Immediately I'd be hungry when I'd just eaten, immediately tired and restless after just taking a nap, and irritable at the slightest interruption, blaming others for daring to interject in my sacred writing space. I noticed how I became defensive with even the slightest provocation, and overly critical of myself and my work.

Controlling the ego requires constant awareness and attention. One of the quickest ways to take it in hand is to deliberately seek ways to weaken it by imposing rigid disciplines and routines in our lives. The ego despises routine and discipline and anything that is unpleasant. Disciplines, routines and the deprivation of certain pleasures get the ego on the run, gradually badgering it into submission until it hides away. When our ego is weak, our vibration is high and we are open to higher things, allowing us to become more focused on what's really important.

The easiest way to get into a routine or to create a discipline is to do the same thing at exactly the same time every day, even at weekends. For example, get out of bed at exactly 6 a.m. every day; have breakfast at exactly the same time every morning; get into an exercise regimen and stick to it, no matter what the weather; if you eat a lot of chocolate buttons, like I do, stop eating them. Also, start to deprive yourself of pleasures in a calculated way. Let's say you look forward to watching a TV programme each Thursday evening. You mentally set aside the time to watch the programme, you wonder what the content will be about, you prepare yourself for the event; you make the popcorn, you buy the chocolates, you find your slippers and you get nice and comfy; but try this: just as the credits roll, you get up and lock yourself in your bedroom and don't come out until the show is over. The ego will hate it. You will find yourself feeling all sorts of misplaced emotions, but you have started to get the ego on the run.

Or, if you are a shopaholic, like me, plan a shopping expedition. Pencil in a day's leave from work and meticulously plan where you are going to go. Imagine the clothes and shoes you might find; make sure that your credit card bill is paid off so that you have the money to spend. When the day arrives, go to the mall and try on outfit after outfit. But as soon as you find the perfect one, hand it back to the assistant and get in your car and go home. That's discipline. The ego runs away, plus you save yourself a lot of money on impulse purchases.

THE TRIPLE REVIEW

We read earlier that we make karma by the wise or unwise use of our free will. We can only use our free will wisely if we are conscious of *how* we are using it and the patterns within us that create incorrect thinking and emotion. One way to enhance our awareness is through a triple review. Pythagoras, in his *Golden Verses*, says: 'Never suffer sleep to close thine eyelids when going to bed until thou has thrice reviewed all thy actions of the day.' This means, don't fall asleep at night without reviewing three times everything that you have done during the day, three times for the three planes of existence – mental, emotional and physical.

In the evening, before the day ends, sit in a comfortable position for ten to twenty minutes, and replay the events of the day in your head. Work backwards from the moment you sat down or climbed into bed until the moment you wake up. Look at everything you did in the day physically, emotionally and mentally. For example, a specific event may have caused a specific train of thought to emerge or specific emotions to surface, which may in turn have caused you to react in a certain way. Don't judge yourself or others during this process, but observe as if you were an impartial witness how your day unfolded, how the ego played out and the impact it had. The exercise itself is a discipline.

We read earlier that when we pass on we do a triple review of our life. The purpose of the triple review at death is to heal the soul, to show us all the bad things that we have done in life and to engrave our conscience, so that in our next life, we will be more sensitive and won't repeat the same mistakes. Sleep is the microcosm of death, the big picture in the little picture. When we sleep at night, the astral body leaves the physical body, as it does in death. By repeating this practice, we enhance our consciousness so that the following day we don't repeat the errors that we made the previous day. Gradually, as we do this more and more, our conscience becomes more exacting and we make fewer and fewer mistakes.

SYMBOLISM OF THE KNIGHT

We read earlier that those who slay dragons (the ego) are not ordinary men and women. They are knights or warriors or the sons of gods. There is great symbolism in the weaponry worn and carried by the warrior knights of times past, in the path of the seeker and his journey to ascension.

The helmet with the visor symbolises the ever vigilant attitude of the sincere seeker who never for a moment relaxes his guard. It is symbolic of a defensive weapon against unruly thoughts and temptations. The visor was raised in the company of friends and lowered in the face of the enemy.

The gauntlets, or metal clad gloves, were not only protective covering for the hands but they were symbolic of guarding the hand from the bad deeds that the ego tempts us into doing. We are judged by our actions, good and bad, and it is from this judgement that we will rise or fall.

The shield is the most important weapon in the arsenal of the knight, protecting the seeker from his lower self, or ego, during the journey for reunification with his higher self.

The breast plate is symbolic of a defence against attacks to the heart. The heart is the symbol of the emotions. It represents the extreme caution that the seeker has to exercise with respect to undisciplined emotions. Too much sadness or emotion is an indicator of the internal imbalance on which the ego thrives.

The broadsword is held with two hands and represents balance, equilibrium, moderation, evenness and steadiness. The sword is in the form of a cross and symbolises the balance between fire and water, passive and active, male and female, and indeed all forms of opposites in the polarity of the scheme of things. The seeker who is balanced has a much greater chance of successfully defending himself against the onslaught of the ego as well as the ability to wage war against it.

The spear is the biggest defensive weapon in the arsenal of the knight and symbolically associated with a frontal attack from a distance. A direct thrust at the lower self with this symbolic weapon does and can considerably weaken the monster that shares with us the same body soul and mind.

The axe is the second largest symbolic weapon of the knight initiate and is used to hack pieces from the giant ego so as to reduce it in size and strength. In order to do this, one must get closer to the enemy and therefore know the monster better. If and when the lower self has been sufficiently reduced in size and strength it makes the final death blow easier.

The mace is a round ball with spikes and attached to a chain. It is smaller than the axe and has a shorter reach. It can only be used for very close-in fighting, which in turn can only be done by the knight who has completed a great deal of introspection and self study. The seeker is cautioned that in this kind of combat, unless the enemy is intimately understood, it can predict a potential blow and avoid it and thus the mace misses its mark and will sweep around to strike the seeker.

The dagger is the ninth weapon and the smallest, and can only be used at very close range – so close, in fact, that only when the knight is very familiar with the dragon can it be used. Detailed knowledge of its exact weaknesses and vulnerable spots close to the heart must be known before the dagger can be used.

When I think of 'myself,' I am thinking of the part of me which I am conscious of. That is my ego (Latin for 'I'). But there is more to me than that ...

There is also my persona (Greek for 'mask') which hides my ego from the outer world. I actively maintain that mask, according to the conventions of family, society, profession, etc.

There is also my personal unconscious, which contains forgotten or never-conscious experiences of various kinds, but which is uniquely my own. And then, there is the collective unconscious which connects me with the whole human experience.

Within this unconscious realm there are several different 'structures'. Though the Self is the whole person, conscious and unconscious together; it also acts as center, seeking to organize the whole.

Each of us has both masculine and feminine elements in the psyche. Though the appropriate one becomes incorporated into the conscious ego, the other expresses itself as an unconscious focus of creative energy, serving the balance of ego and Self. Jung gave the name anima *to the feminine center of a man, and* animus *to the masculine center of a woman.*

But there is also my Shadow. In a sense, the Shadow is all of that which is 'dark' (unconscious) to me; but in a more special sense, it can be an activated center ('complex') energized by repressed feelings, anger, old hurts, etc. If not recognized as such (made conscious), its energy can be projected onto others. Then the faults I see in other people are really the mirror image of my own. My first task of individuation is to 'own my own shadow'.

Carl Jung's model of the psyche
Source: http://www.socionics.com

Chapter 2
KNOW THYSELF

I have ransacked the mysteries of creation for 5000 years and I still do not understand what goes on in the heart of the common peasant.

The fictional Russian avatar Mejnour
from the book *Zanoni*
Sir Edgar Bulver Lytton (1803 – 1873)

ho am I really? This question plagues the spiritual warrior when all around is quiet and still – for those of us, that is, who are brave enough for stillness and quiet. We have a need to know, to define ourselves. If we have fallen so far down the ladder of existence to have lost sight of our true nature, how do we begin to understand what we might become? We are indeed complex beings consisting of many different aspects that are way beyond our comprehension. It's easy to recognize how almost every facet of our life is mechanical when we understand that our thoughts and desires (which lead us to believe we know a thing or two about life) are mainly the construct of an imposter: the ego. It's even more disheartening to learn that this imposter masquerades as our personality, using a different *self* or *mask* when interacting with the world. How do we begin to have a modicum of understanding about whether we are valuable or not if we cannot compare it to something or someone else? If we don't have any idea about ourselves without an external definition – our careers, a title on a business card, our relationships, our children, our money, possessions or accomplishments – we need to establish some kind of basic understanding, a foundation from which we can begin to recognise the shadow and nurture the truth. Once again, the myths are a good place to start.

When Renaissance sculptor Michelangelo carved his two greatest masterpieces, the statue of David and the Pietà, he used the best Carrara marble. He knew that qualities of the raw material he used would allow him to chisel and shape the stone into the beautiful finished works of art he'd initially imagined. No two works he created were ever the same. No matter which raw materials he used, the quality of the rock or granite he chose would ultimately determine how much shaping, chiselling and moulding he could do before the piece was completed. He could change the shape of the stone with all his hard work and efforts, but he could not change the ingredients or make-up of the stone.

In the same way, when the Supreme Being moulded us from 'the dust of the ground' (the raw materials of the earth), the basic ingredients he used were not all the same. Some of us were granite, some marble, some alabaster, some sandstone, some rubies and diamonds, others pieces of copper. Each one of us is composed of a certain mixture of raw materials that make up our basic temperament. (The word *temperament* comes from Latin *temperare* – 'to mix'). It's these raw materials that determine our basic nature and the potential that each of us has to become a unique masterpiece in our own right.

Through various incarnations, we have been chiselled, chipped, hammered, sanded and buffed, and a few of our rough edges have been removed, but the raw material from which we were created remains the same and remains consistent life after life. It constitutes our total potential. No matter how much we sculpt and mould a piece of granite, it can never become marble. No matter how much we buff copper, it can never become gold, and neither can a diamond become a ruby. But each can be moulded and shaped into something beautiful in line with the potential of its raw material.

Our *temperament* is the real us. Our *personality* is the dress that we put on in the morning to cover up all the bulges and fat bits. It's only a mask, the face that we show to the world. (The word *personality* comes from the Latin *persona*, which means 'mask'.) Through various incarnations, our temperament is moulded, chiselled and shaped by all the hardships and difficulties and external influences we experience in life to become the brightest possible piece of alabaster or gold it can be. The composition of the raw materials doesn't change, but our *shape* can be altered. We start with our own set of inborn traits, and gradually they are moulded, embellished or perhaps obliterated as we continue on our journey though life. The darkness gradually becomes light, and ignorance is converted to wisdom. However, like the pearl in the oyster, we are covered deeply in layers of gloop, or false personality that has to be removed if the pearl (our true self) is to shine. Our true identity remains hidden. It may take lifetimes for us to understand ourselves fully, but we have to start somewhere and creation seems a good place to begin again.

In many of the creation myths of the world we find reference to the four elements that sustain all life. In the Bible we find them in the book of Genesis as the Four Rivers *(Pi-son, Gi-hon, Hid-de-kel, Eu-phra-tes)* that flowed through the garden of Eden. In Nordic mythology, they are referred to as four streams of milk from a great Celestial Cow. The Sphinx in Egypt is also symbolic of the four elements: It has the front paws of a lion (fire); the head and chest of a man/woman (water); the hindquarters of an ox (earth); and according to Greek and Egyptian legend, the Sphinx also had wings, symbolising the element of air. The myths depict that the entire universe is constructed of these four elements, which exist in every part of creation and underpin the very fabric of our existence. The four elements were well known to the ancient Egyptians, Babylonians and Greeks. They are mentioned here in the Greek text called the 'Kore Kosmou' or 'Virgin of the World', ascribed to Hermes Trismegistus, the name given by the Greeks to the Egyptian God, Thoth:

And Isis answer made: Of living things, my son, some are made friends with fire, and some with water, some with air, and some with earth, and some with two or three of these, and some with all. And, on the contrary, again some are made enemies of fire, and some of water, some of earth, and some of air, and some of two of them, and some of three, and some of all. For instance, son, the locust and all flies flee fire; the eagle and the hawk and all high-flying birds flee water; fish, air and earth; the snake avoids the open air. Whereas snakes and all creeping things love earth; all swimming things – love – water; winged things, air, of which they are the citizens; while those that fly still higher – love — the fire and have the habitat near it. Not that some of the animals as well do not love fire; for instance salamanders, for they even have their homes in it. It is because one or another of the elements doth form their bodies' outer envelope. Each soul, accordingly, while it is in its body is weighted and constricted by these four.

Everything is connected to everything else, and when we look beneath the surface of anything we can begin to unearth a plethora of insights that help us figure out other things, including some clues about our identity. The Greek philosopher Hippocrates was one of the first to formally recognise this and to attribute the four elements to existing conditions in the body, mind and emotions with the introduction of his 'four humours', which were later classified by the Roman physician and philosopher Galen into four temperaments: choleric, sanguine, melancholic and phlegmatic (see the summary of the four temperaments below). He mapped them to a matrix of hot/cold and dry/wet, and said that when there was a balance among these qualities, the ideal personality was formed. In less ideal personalities, one of the four qualities was believed to be lacking, or else dominant over all the others.

An imbalance of these humours in the human body was thought to cause disease – a theory of imbalance which is also courted by today's modern-day natural medicine. It is the four elements that form the basis of Ayurvedic medicine, known as the Hindu and Buddhist *tattvas,* and is also referred to in Japanese and Chinese methods of healing. The four elements have, throughout history, permeated literature, philosophy and the sciences of alchemy, astrology, numerology and psychology. Nearly six hundred years before Galen, Plato referred to them in *The Republic.* Aristotle defined them in terms of different *virtues.* Paracelsus, a mid-sixteenth century Viennese physician, proposed four *totem* or *nature spirits* that symbolised four personality styles: sylphs, salamanders, nymphs and gnomes. Even some of the early 20th century writers demonstrated knowledge of temperament theory. D. H. Lawrence, for example, saw human nature as organised around 'four poles of dynamic consciousness'. Psychologists and philosophers through the ages, such as Immanuel Kant, Rudolf Steiner, Erich Adickes, Eduard Spranger, Ernst Kretschmer, Carl Jung, Isabel Briggs Meyers and Prof. David Keirsey, have all theorized on the four temperaments and developed systems from which many modern day psychometric tests, profiling and assessment tools have been developed, some with greater degrees of accuracy than others. We speak of these four elements in relation to psychology, perhaps without thinking, when we describe someone's character or personality traits. When someone is quick to anger or extremely ambitious we consider them to be very 'fiery'. We talk of someone 'going with the flow' (water), depicting an easy-going person, or someone as being 'wet' when he has no backbone and seemingly lacks courage. We call someone an 'airhead' when they appear to have their head in the clouds, or 'grounded' and 'earthy' if they appear to be practical and well-rounded.

THE FOUR ELEMENTS AND THE FOUR TEMPERAMENTS

A brief overview of each of the four temperaments: Sanguine, Choleric, Melancholic and Phlegmatic and their personality characteristics is outlined below. For a more in depth insight into the positive and negative temperament traits see the Bibliography.

Sanguine Temperament

Key descriptors: Excitable, impulsive, impactful, stimulating, generous, virtuoso, talkative, humorous, demonstrative, expressive, changeable, child-like, colourful, energetic, enthusiastic

The sanguine temperament is fundamentally impulsive and pleasure-seeking; sanguine people are sociable and charismatic. They tend to enjoy social gatherings, making new friends and tend to be boisterous. They are usually quite creative and often daydream. However, some alone time is crucial for those of this temperament. Sanguine can also mean sensitive, compassionate and thoughtful. Sanguine personalities generally struggle with following tasks all the way through, are chronically late, and tend to be forgetful and sometimes a little sarcastic. Often, when they pursue a new hobby, they

THE FOUR ELEMENTS – ANCIENT AND MODERN.

The illustration below provides a brief summary of the four elements and the way in which they feature in different aspects of psychology, history and natural science. The four elements comprise the entire universe and can be found in all things. My own experience of life tells me that you can reasonably interpret both life and experience through the energies of earth, air, fire and water and observe how almost anything can be broken down into four-ness.

Every one of the four elements exists within us in varying quantities, although it is likely that one or two will be dominant. Identifying our temperament helps us to understand the influences that play out in our life and make the appropriate corrections. By learning to balance the mental, emotional, physical and spiritual qualities of the elements, we can achieve a greater level of personal equilibrium and positive momentum. If any of these energies are out of proportion we can become unbalanced.

Element	Humour	Season	Organ	Qualities	Ancient Name	Astrological Sign	Paracelsus Four Totems	Plato	Carl Jung	Keirsey Temperament	MBTI
Air	Blood	Spring	Liver	Mental (Insight)	Sanguine	Aquarius, Gemini, Libra	Sylphs (Changeable)	Artisan	Thinking	Artisan (Dionysus)	SP
Fire	Yellow Bile	Summer	Gall Bladder	Spiritual (Drive)	Choleric	Aries, Leo, Sagittarius	Salamanders (Inspired)	Idealist	Intuition	Idealist (Apollo)	NF
Earth	Black Bile	Autumn	Spleen	Physical (Expression)	Melancholic	Capricorn, Taurus, Virgo	Gnomes (Industrious)	Guardian	Sensation	Guardian (Epimetheus)	SJ
Water	Phlegm	Winter	Brain/ Lungs	Emotional (Flow)	Phlegmatic	Cancer, Pisces, Scorpio	Nymphs (Curious)	Rational	Feeling	Rational (Prometheus)	NT

MBTI = Myers Briggs Type Indicator

321

lose interest as soon as it ceases to be engaging or fun. They are very much 'people persons'. They are talkative and not shy. Sanguines generally have an almost shameless nature, certain that what they are doing is right. They have no lack of confidence.

Choleric Temperament

Key descriptors: enthusiastic, taking leadership, intuitive, romantic, identity, recognition, sagacious, dynamic, active, motivating, stimulating, need to change, isolated, organising.

The choleric temperament is fundamentally ambitious and leader-like. They have a lot of aggression, energy, and/or passion, and try to instil it in others. They can dominate people of other temperaments, especially phlegmatic types. Many great charismatic military and political figures were choleric. They like to be in charge of everything. However, cholerics also tend to be either highly disorganized or highly organized. They do not have in-between setups, only one extreme or another. As well as being leader-like and assertive, cholerics also fall into deep and sudden depression. Essentially, they are very much prone to mood swings.

Melancholic Temperament

Key descriptors: concerned, authoritative, belonging, security, grateful, executive, sensitive, philosophical, poetic, conscientious, talented, creative, purposeful, analytical, perfectionist.

The melancholic temperament is fundamentally introverted and thoughtful. Melancholic people often were perceived as very (or overly) pondering and considerate, getting rather worried when they could not be on time for events. Melancholics can be highly creative in activities such as poetry and art, and can become preoccupied with the tragedy and cruelty in the world. Often they are perfectionists. They are self-reliant and independent; one negative part of being a melancholic is that they can get so involved in what they are doing that they forget to think of others.

Phlegmatic Temperament

Key descriptors: calm, reasoning, achieving, knowledgeable, deferent, wizard-like, low-key, easy-going, relaxed, patient, listener, steadfast, agreeable, mediator, consistent, witty.

The phlegmatic temperament is fundamentally relaxed and quiet, ranging from warmly attentive to lazily sluggish. Phlegmatics tend to be content with themselves and are kind. They are accepting and affectionate. They may be receptive and shy and often prefer stability to uncertainty and change. They are consistent, relaxed, calm, rational, curious, and observant, qualities that make them good administrators.

Sources: Wikipedia: *Please Understand Me* – David Keirsey; *Personality Plus* – Florence Littauer

---

We are already greatly formed at birth, with fundamentally different temperaments and dispositions already deeply embedded within us. Our temperament is the *real us* made up of a combination of the elements above. The four elements combine to make us what we are, and play out in a combination of characteristics and traits that make each and every one of us different from the other. It's not possible to know every aspect of our self because the ego masquerades as our true self for most of our life; but with practice, we can begin to uncover those traits within us which we believe to be false, part of the personality or mask, and those which we believe to be true. In the dialogue below, I share with you two weapons that I have used as a way to become conscious of my 'machine nature' and to begin to understand the influences that affect my life.

THE KEIRSEY TEMPERAMENT TEST

There are many personality profiling/testing instruments on the market designed to assess how people perceive the world and make decisions. Their usefulness depends on the situation for which they are being utilised – career development, culture fit, assessment of leadership abilities etc. and in my experience, provide only a snapshot of how someone will behave in a given situation based on the frame of mind they were in when taking the test.

However, the ones that I have found to be the most accurate and beneficial from a personal perspective are based on the work of Carl Jung, taken from his work *Psychological Types,* which categorized people into types of psychological function. He proposed four main functions of consciousness (relating to the four elements): two perceiving functions – sensation and intuition; and two judging functions – thinking and feeling. The functions were modified by two main attitude types: extraversion and introversion. Jung theorized that the dominant function characterizes consciousness, while its opposite, being repressed, characterizes unconscious behaviour. The Myers-Briggs type indicator (MBTI) is based on this system, together with its more modern equivalent, the Keirsey temperament test, developed by Professor David Keirsey, who adapted his thorough system of research around psychology, the work of the ancients, and even mythology. The four temperament types relate to Greek deities: Apollo, Dionysus, Epimetheus and Prometheus. Perhaps that's why it appealed to me.

As you would have read earlier, I only discovered this profiling instrument, together with David Keirsey's book, *Please Understand Me,* when I was 44. I naively assumed that it would be readily utilised by psychologists and psychometrists in all forms of therapy, but I was wrong. Understanding my INFP profile literally helped to change the way I related to the world. I really cannot do it justice in this short chapter. I suggest that anyone serious about getting a better understanding of himself should spend some time undertaking the online assessment or perhaps even buying the book.

My reason for mentioning it again here is twofold: firstly, to illustrate its importance as a way of helping us establish a fragment of our identity during this life. When we have a picture of what we are, even if it's not perfect, we have a platform in which we can begin to accept ourselves and the differences in others more readily, and the defined boundaries that we can push against. I am acutely aware that temperament assessments don't paint the entire picture in terms of our identity and purpose, but it's a start. We just have to figure out which parts are our true self and which parts are false and part of our personality, or egoic nature.

The second reason is to again illustrate the axiomatic tenets which permeate everything in existence. The Universe is a hologram; the patterns and connections to be found in philosophy, mythology and the beginning of creation can even be found in the construction of our own temperament. As I always approach life from a philosophical standpoint (it's part of my INFP healer profile) I begin to experience myself as part of something bigger, which prevents me from feeling alone and isolated from the rest of the world. No matter what our spiritual beliefs, when we can see axioms play out in our own lives, we can begin to marvel at the incredible mind that put all of this together.

The assessment helped me discover a dramatic sense of peace and inner acceptance. I began to acknowledge myself more readily – my introverted nature in childhood, my drive to succeed in an impossible business environment, the good and bad choices I'd made in a tumultuous path through life. But most of all, it stopped me from worrying that I was a misfit in the world. I started to embrace my differences, now that I could clearly understand them by putting myself in some form of box (which my temperament type dislikes intently).

Discovering the temperament sorter hasn't just helped *me*. Two years after taking the test, I presented my 'INFP Healer' profile to Steve during a really difficult patch in our relationship. It was a last-ditch attempt to get him to 'please understand me' rather than judge me as a second-rate, inferior version of himself. It changed our way of relating to each other overnight, and helped him immeasurably in his own development. His 'INTJ Mastermind' profile was also a rarity (only about 1% of the entire population demonstrate this profile) and he, too, had felt at odds with the world for many years. We all need a place to begin our healing and develop an acceptance of ourselves. Once we can find a degree of acceptance of ourselves, we can begin to accept where we are, accept others for their differences and stop fighting to prove our rightness and sanity.

We are all different from one another and no amount of cajoling, sculpting or moulding is going to change that. Marble is marble, coal is coal. We each have different lessons we must learn, different purposes for being here, motives, aims, values, needs, drives, impulses and urges. We each think, perceive, conceptualise, understand and comprehend things differently based on diverse beliefs, drives and motives. Differences abound and they are not difficult to spot if one takes the time to look deeper. What we once believed to be the madness, badness, stupidity, sickness, flaws or afflictions in others are simply manifestations of this difference.

When we realise this, we can start to embrace life and one another with childlike curiosity instead of endeavouring to fit in or sculpt others into a form which we find more acceptable. Improvement and change is always possible, but a piece of sandstone will not become a piece of alabaster, no matter how much we might wish it to. A cello cannot become a violin, nor a lily a rose. And if we remove the fangs of a lion, behold, we still have a toothless lion and not a domestic cat (Keirsey). Acceptance of who we are and what we might become allows us to find peace.

ASTROLOGY

What's your star sign? Most people know the answer to that question. It's one of the greatest chat-up lines of all time. But the depth of discussion never extends much beyond that. For many years, astrology meant little more to me than the snippets of so-called 'prophecy' that I read in a magazine or newspaper. I had to admit that I never really understood how a bunch of planets could determine how my life would pan out on earth, so I dismissed it, as many do, as mere fantasy and interesting entertainment. I was satisfied that I knew my star sign to be Aries with an Aquarian /Capricorn ascendant, and that was enough.

That was until I discovered that the planets do *not* determine or influence what takes place in our lives and neither do they influence global events; they are, in fact, a map in the heavens of historical patterns and cycles that have taken place on earth throughout history since time began. (As above so below.) Everything in life, as we read earlier, is cyclic, and thus astrology is a map of these macro- and micro-cycles in which our individual lives play a part.

Throughout most of its history, astrology was considered a scholarly tradition (and not just a source of entertainment as it often is today), being accepted in political, scientific and academic contexts. It was also built into the fabric of astronomy, alchemy, meteorology and medicine. Over thousands of years, scientific and mathematical observations of these patterns and cycles have correlated the various planetary positions with a huge array of human-related, individual and global conditions, and mapped them scientifically and mathematically. (The dependability of these astrological maps have been proven time and again, in a rigorous, scientific way, by the mathematician-astrologer Michel Gauquelin, using complex statistical techniques.)

The snippets we read in the newspapers and magazines are at best a poor and often very inaccurate assessment of just one element of our astrological chart, the sun. To gain an accurate picture about the trends, influences and potential in our life, we need to consult an astrologer. An astrologer is one who looks at the birth horoscope and uses the established wisdom from centuries to make inferences about an individual, a business, a tennis club or a country. Astrology is a system of correspondences that links the positions and configurations of celestial bodies (planets, stars, sun, moon, etc.) at the moment of birth, to the personality, character, temperament, strengths, weaknesses, talents, quirks, and the passage of unfolding destiny of the enquirer. The birth chart, or natal horoscope, is a symbolic map of what the heavens looked like at the location of birth, erected for the precise moment, and at the precise latitude and longitude.

Whilst astrology is about influences, impulsions and cycles, nothing is cast in stone. One hopes that a person with a musical talent written into his star map at birth will exploit this. By contrast, one hopes that someone with violent tendencies in his chart will avoid them, or repress them, or find some other outlet for them, such as the sports field. The extent to which we incorporate or exploit the gifts, or deny the debilities and bad qualities, is entirely a matter of choice. Therefore, what an astrologer sees in your chart is not necessarily how you are (although it certainly could be you, if you allow it to be). A chart pattern which indicates difficulties and challenges may well incubate into a startling and astonishing ability as a result of the individual's will to work at it. The negative qualities need never become manifest unless we so choose. Everything in astrology has an upside and a downside. It is up to the person to exploit the positives and transcend the negatives.

An astrology chart also indicates karmic trends. In astrology, there are two types of karma: The first, innate karma, shapes our persona and environment; in other words, things that we're born with – body type, health profile, emotional constitution, intelligence and intellectual style, the circumstances of our birth, and so on; all the little things that, when perceived as a whole, contribute to our lot in life – the rubber dingy or the ocean liner. The second type is the karma of unfolding destiny and is what happens as one goes through life. This is the kind of karma the astrologer considers when using astrology as a predictive tool.

Astrology can be a powerful tool to help identify challenges in our life. We all have our issues in life, things that we find difficult to deal with – relationships; money; addictions; weight problems; employment, self esteem, parenting; etc. That is, after all, why we are here in physical bodies to help us overcome them. When my natal chart was initially constructed, I uncovered certain negative influences in terms of close personal relationships – partners, business associates and friends, an influence that my INFP temperament profile, together with my 'choleric loner' traits, indicated would cause difficulty for me. So relationships are heavily karmic for me and I have seen that in the patterns that have unfolded in my life. The temperament that I have is designed to help me fulfil my karmic path, being perfectly designed to encourage me not to be too reliant on others for my happiness. Astrology and profiling helped me to understand and work with the influences without getting too bent out of shape about it.

THE ARCHETYPES

It was during my time working with organisational culture that I first came into contact with Archetypes, or 'Forms', to use Plato's word, which also relate to the four elements, the tarot deck and the kabbalistic Tree of Life. The term *Archetype* has its origins in ancient Greece, stemming from *archein*, which means 'original' or 'old'; and *typos*, which means 'pattern', 'model' or 'type'. Together, the words refer to the 'original pattern' from which all similar persons, objects or concepts are derived. The concept of Archetypes was first developed by Carl Jung. 'Along with our individual unconscious, which is unique to each of us,' Jung asserted, 'there exists a second psychic system of a collective, universal, and impersonal nature that is identical in all individuals.' This collective unconscious, he believed, was inherited rather than developed, and was composed mainly of Archetypes.

As you may remember from the introduction, archetypes are underlying mythic themes that can be found in all races, countries, cultures and groups throughout history. They are universal personifications of patterns of behaviour or forms of expression that reside in the collective unconscious. We unconsciously plug into these different archetypes every moment of the day via the chakras, depending on our vibration and the situation we find ourselves in. The positive and shadow aspects of each archetype can be easily recognised in myths and fairy tales – the 'Hero/Warrior' archetype, the 'Herald', the 'Trickster', and the 'Threshold Guardian', to name a few. (Joseph Campbell and Christopher Vogler give great descriptions of these archetypes in their written works, details of which can be found in the bibliography.)

The number of archetypes are, in fact, limitless; but there are a few basic ones from which many others emerge (a few of which can be found in the following pages, together with certain sub-archetypes). Although they are ancient and universal, we begin to own them when they become part of our own psyche and when they begin to unconsciously form the foundation of our drives, motives, feelings, thoughts, beliefs and actions. Every one of us will be born with a particular preferential archetypal behaviour, perhaps more than one. At birth, we may come into this world as one or another of the archetypes, or a mixture of several. This is because we may have lived a particular archetypal theme in many of our previous lives, and past-life experiences often manifest as pre-programmed sub-personalities in our subconscious (which holds the memories from all our incarnations). Medical Intuitive, Caroline Myss says 'The energy that surrounds you, which is created by the chakras, contains all the data of your biology and your biography, so it makes sense that this energy would manifest in patterns of archetypes that affect your life.'

I was fascinated by the way in which these archetypes played out in individual or group behaviours within organisations or teams as people would plug into the collective unconscious and the archetypal behaviours that existed. For example, in a particular situation an individual would take on a certain mode of behaviour that was in many cases completely foreign to his usual behaviour. I would observe strong and intelligent Warrior Archetypes, who were legends in their own lunchtimes, being reduced to silent, scatterbrained fools when confronted by a Destroyer Archetype; or quiet and submissive Innocents behaving like aristocratic rulers, lording it over their subjects when faced with trying or testing circumstances, just because they could (and I knew all about that!).

When running workshops to determine the specific archetypes that play out in the group dynamics of specific organisations or teams, it was enlightening to witness the frequency with which the same archetypal behaviours would pop up again and again, regardless of the situation or the nature of the business itself. One would expect the dynamics in a bank, for example, to be very different from those in a primary school; yet time and again I would see the same archetypes in both. A large business can operate in diverse industry segments, have completely different strategies, values and mission statements; yet the archetypal behaviours in group interactions are often virtually identical to those of a kindergarten class!

Archetypal influences also help us to understand why we are not succeeding in particular relationships or professions – primarily because we are pursuing

The Archetypes

The table below indicates not only the twelve Archetypes, but also some of the sub-archetypes from which hundreds of others are derived. Their link to the Four Elements is also indicated. Each Archetype has higher and lower aspects, light and dark shadows. Medical Intuitive, Caroline Myss in her book *Sacred Contracts* asserts that each of the four primary archetypes - Child, Victim, Prostitute and Saboteur – exist within the psyche of every individual indicating the majority life challenges and/or strengths.

The Twelve Archetypes/Sub-Archetypes

Hero/Warrior (Fire)	Magician (Fire)	Wise One/Sage (Fire)	Child/Innocent (Water)
Fighter	Fairy Godmother	Guru	Artist
Gladiator	Merlin	Mentor	Child
Hunter	Priestess	Holy One	Harmless One
Knight	Shaman	Master	Romantic Dreamer
Rescuer	Sorcerer	Truth Seeker	Trusted One
Rival	Warlock	Oracle	Wonderer
Soldier	Witch/Wizard	Philosopher	Naïve Youth
Survivor	Inventor	Prophet	
Struggler	Transformer	Sage	
		Teacher	
		Thinker	
Martyr/Victim (Water)	**Seducer/Lover (Water)**	**Seeker/Explorer (Air)**	**Jester/Fool (Air)**
Great Soul	Enchanter	Adventurer	Risk Taker
Saint	'Sales Person'	Hermit	Clown
Saviour	Tempter/Temptress	Hunter	Flake
Loser	Philanderer	Monk	Lunatic
Struggler	Prostitute	Pursuer	Madman
	Deceiver	Wanderer	Philanderer
	Trickster	Wonderer	Scatterbrain
		Pioneer	
Rebel/Saboteur (Air)	**Patriarch/Matriarch (Earth)**	**Ruler (Earth)**	**Servant (Earth)**
Change Maker	Ancestor	Aristocrat	Assistant
Destroyer	Father	Emperor	Attendant
Herald	Mother	Empress	Right-Hand Person
Enemy	Old One	Judge	Slave
Betrayer	Great Father/Mother	Prince/Princess	Subject
Evildoer		King/Queen	Subordinate
Mischief Maker		Superior	Worker
Devil			
Rascal			

Chart adapted from the work of Dr. JD Stone in his book Soul Psychology.

a life that we are not meant to be living. All the workshops in the world will not bring about the success that we want if the archetypal influences are not in our favour. As with astrology, if we can understand the influences of the archetypes, we can learn not to over-identify with any particular one of them, but to integrate them all within us, eradicating the negative points (which are part of the negative ego) and growing the positives. Our challenge is to integrate all of the archetypes within our *self* to enable us to consciously choose the role we want to play in a particular situation, rather than being a victim of a particular archetype. We have probably lived out many of these archetypes in the past, anyway.

To fully cover the concept of archetypes in this book would be an impossible task. One could write volumes about it. However, to help identify our own particular archetypes there is no substitute for reading the book *Sacred Contracts* by Caroline Myss. Understanding archetypes and their influence on behaviour is a process of being overwhelmingly honest with ourselves and exploring every motive behind our behaviour to see whether it's coming from the true self or the lower self. Indian sage Sai Baba said that seventy percent of the spiritual path is about self-enquiry, and so, as with all psycho-spiritual development, the key to understanding the archetypes is to be aware that we are manifesting one or more of them every moment of our lives. Left to their own devices, the archetypes, through the ego, will monopolise us entirely. They don't reason, rationalise or work with us co-operatively; we have to observe them and work with them consciously by becoming the master of two worlds – the ordinary and the special worlds – ensuring that we are the cause, not the effect.

THE ENNEAGRAM

From the spiritual warrior's road map in Book I, we will have seen that the mythological hero is continually tested during his journey. As spiritual warriors on the 'road to ascension', we face the same tests – primarily from the ego. Time and again, we see the 'dragon' emerge from hiding when we least expect it and suddenly find our *self* falling afoul of this 'monster' just when we thought we were coming to grips with it. In my experience as a coach and counsellor, the ego tends to tighten its grip when we are faced with tests in one or more of the following aspects: anger, attachment, desire, false pride, fame, fear, jealousy, power, money, greed, sexuality, selfishness and vanity. Unless we are vigilant, time and again we will fall prey to the whims of the ego and continue to make the same mistakes. So understanding how this ego can manifest in each of us, catching us off guard, is a distinct advantage. One of the ways I have found to help us with this is the *Enneagram*.

The Enneagram, from the Greek words *ennea* (nine) and *grammos* (something written or drawn), takes the concept of some of the main Archetypes one step further: The Enneagram is a model of human personality, or a method for self-understanding and development, and uses a typology of nine interconnected personalities that are based on the archetypes.

Principally developed by Oscar Ichazo (the Bolivian-born founder of the Arica Institute of personal development in Chile) and psychologist Claudio Naranjo, it has roots in antiquity and can be traced at least as far back as the works of Pythagoras. The Enneagram symbol was reintroduced to the west by George Gurdjieff, who founded a highly influential 'inner work' school that still exists today. Using the Sufi tradition to convey his messages, Gurdjieff taught the symbol to his pupils through a series of sacred dances or movements, designed to give the participant a direct 'feeling' or sense of the meaning of Enneagram. Although the philosophy behind the Enneagram contains components from the Sufi, many mystical traditions are believed to have contributed to its formation – Judaism, Christianity, Islam, Taoism, Buddhism, and the teachings of ancient Greek philosophers, particularly Socrates, Plato, and the Neo-Platonists. The ideas from these ancient traditions gradually found their way from Greece and Asia Minor into Syria and Egypt and were embraced by early Christian mystics who focused on studying the *loss* of the Divine Essence during 'ego consciousness'. The particular ways in which these Divine essences in man became distorted came to be known as the Seven Deadly Sins: anger, pride, envy, avarice, gluttony, lust, and sloth. How the original *nine* forms became reduced to *seven* deadly sins, in the course of their travels from Greece to Egypt over the span of a century, remains, however, a mystery.

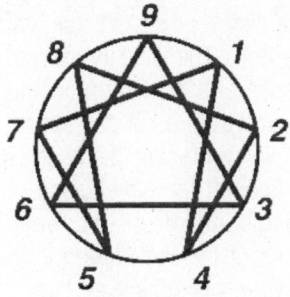

Courtesy of The Enneagram Institute

Another key influence in the development of these nine forms comes from mystical Judaism, and particularly from the teachings of the Kabbalah. Central to kabbalistic teaching is the Tree of Life, or *Sephiroth,* comprised of ten stations and twenty-two paths connected in particular ways (which also relate to the chakras, the four elements and the tarot system.) Kabbalistic teachings indicate that all human 'divine sparks' arise out of these ten spheres. In the traditional teachings of the Kabbalah, for instance, each of the great patriarchs of the Bible was said to be an embodiment (archetype) of the different spheres of the Tree. The Enneagram is a way of examining specifics about the structure of the true self and the way in which actual soul qualities, or 'essences', become distorted, or contracted into 'states of ego'. In developing his Enneagram theories, Ichazo drew upon the recurrent theme in Western and mystical tradition, of nine divine forms. (This concept was originally discussed by Plato as *Divine Forms* or *Platonic Solids,* qualities of existence that are essential and cannot be broken down into constituent parts.) In Ichazo's own words:

We have to distinguish between a man as he is in essence, and as he is in ego or personality. In essence, every person is perfect, fearless, and in a loving unity with the entire cosmos; there is no conflict within the person between head, heart, and stomach or between the person and others. Then something happens: the ego begins to develop, karma accumulates, there is a transition from objectivity to subjectivity; man falls from essence into personality.

As used today, the Enneagram is a '9-point' personality typology that indicates the link between 'psyche' and 'spirit', or the true self and the ego.

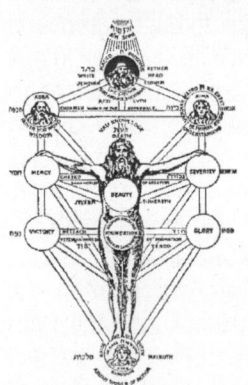

The nine points represent nine different Enneagram archetypes and depicts how each defends its realities, either taking the high road of the true self or the low road of the ego. The nine types are distinguished by unconscious motivations and preoccupations that produce patterns of perception, feeling, and behaviour, which present themselves as gifts or obstacles. Although the psychology of the types is fascinating, and often uncannily accurate, the real purpose of the Enneagram is to help us discover a dimension of ourselves that is infinitely more interesting, more rewarding and more real – a part of us that is grounded, connected and free from the whims of the ego. For example, during my own work with the Enneagram, I discovered that I am a 'Type 6' – the *Loyalist*. Fear and worry are recurring components of my ego, which keep me stuck in indecision and doubt if I allow them to dominate. However, *Courage* is one of the highest aspects of the Loyalist, and indeed, it's something that I have tried to master on my journey through life. Under stress I resort to a 'Type 3' – the *Achiever* – and burn myself out; when I am relaxed I move into 'Type 9' – the *Peacemaker*. The chart on the following page – *The Nine Enneagram Types* – gives you a brief overview of each type, together with its high-road/low-road tendencies. One of the purposes of understanding the archetypes using the Enneagram is to make us more aware when a negative-ego archetype begins to take over. We can then use our will to halt it in its tracks, counteracting the negative traits with positive ones.

Like the archetypes, the wisdom of the Enneagram contains an exhaustive supply of material, so the only way to work with it is to take the test yourself. The bibliography contains links and reading material for those who feel drawn to it.

The Enneagram

The table below gives the principal characteristics of the nine Enneagram types, along with their basic relationships and connections. The illustration has been adapted from the book, *Understanding the Enneagram: The Practical Guide to Personality Types* (revised edition) by Don Richard Riso and Russ Hudson. The types are normally referred to by their numbers, but sometimes by their 'characteristic roles,' which refer to their distinctive archetypal characteristics. The 'Stress' and 'Security' points are the types, connected by the lines of the Enneagram figure. It is believed that a person's behaviours may be particularly influenced in certain adverse or relaxed circumstances. For example, a Type 6 person will resort to Type 3 behaviours when under stress, and to Type 9 when feeling relaxed.

Type	Characteristic Role	Ego Fixation	Holy Idea	Basic Fear	Basic Desire	Temptation	Vice/Passion	Virtue	Stress	Security
1	Reformer	Judging	Perfection	Corruptness, imbalance, being bad	Goodness, integrity, balance	Hypocrisy, hypercriticism	Anger Resentment	Serenity	4	7
2	Helper	Flattery (Ingratiation)	Freedom Will	Being unloved	To feel love	Deny own needs, manipulation	Pride	Humility	8	4
3	Achiever	Vanity	Hope Harmony Law	Worthlessness	To feel valuable	Pushing self to always be 'the best'	Deceit	Truthfulness Authenticity	9	6
4	Individualist	Melancholy (Fantasizing)	Origin	Having no identity or significance	To be uniquely oneself	To overuse imagination in search of self	Envy	Equanimity (Emotional balance)	2	1
5	Investigator	Stinginess (Retention)	Omniscience Transparency	Helplessness Incapable Incompetent	Mastery	Replacing direct experience with concepts	Avarice	Non-attachment	7	8
6	Loyalist	Worrying	Faith Strength	Being without support or guidance	To have support and guidance	Indecision Doubt Seeking reassurance	Fear	Courage	3	9
7	Enthusiast	Planning (Anticipation)	Work Wisdom Plan	Being trapped in pain and deprivation	To be satisfied and content	Thinking fulfillment is somewhere else	Gluttony	Sobriety	1	5
8	Challenger	Vengeance (Objectification)	Truth	Being harmed Being controlled Being violated	Self-protection	Thinking they are completely self-sufficient	Lust	Innocence	5	2
9	Peacemaker	Indolence (Day-dreaming)	Love	Loss Fragmentation Separation	Wholeness Peace of Mind	Avoiding conflicts Avoiding self-assertion	Sloth Disengagement	Action	6	3

In his book, *Soul Psychology*, Dr Joshua Stone describes the science of 'psycho-epistemology' which is a long but very apt word for describing how our unconscious perception filters the way we see the world. Every one of us has a different filter or lens through which we experience life. For example, anyone who has been involved in any type of counselling or personal development work will likely have developed certain filters or psychological lens in terms of their worldview, depending on the type of counselling they've received or what makes intuitive sense. For those who have not undertaken this work or who are not on a spiritual path, the lens will be primarily formed by the ego and held in the subconscious mind – reacting time and again to the mishmash of beliefs collected from past lives, childhood trauma, family conditioning, schooling, society, the media, archetypal influences, etc. A person with this world view will do whatever the ego and the whimsical mind dictates. As I am sure you have gathered, this state is not a very evolved state, spiritually speaking.

We cannot develop spiritually until we destroy the negative ego. If we learn to let go of our lower self, our true self can begin to be 'reborn'. However, it requires an enormous amount of effort and work to both understand and change our self. We are in a perpetual battle with the dragon. Yet, it is only by undertaking this work that we can progress. Whilst I have simply scratched the surface of 'what's out there' in terms of mechanisms for personal awareness and change, from experience I have found the tools indicated above, with their roots originating in antiquity, to be incredibly valuable in terms of helping me interrogate the light and dark aspects of my own nature. Used with integrity and absolute honesty, they can help us unravel the bigger picture relating to our unfolding destiny, providing us with valuable insights into what we might expect if we continue with a particular course of action. I don't by any means believe that any of these weapons can help us to establish who we are intrinsically. We are mired in so many layers of confusion and illusion it's difficult to know where our true self starts and the false self, or machine, stops. It requires much deep meditation and insight to help us really understand our true essence.

In each lifetime, we experience different manifestations of the four elements in our make-up. The star sign we are born under continually changes, as do the archetypal persuasions and the circumstances we are born into, together with the influences we experience from samskaras and karma. This is why the path to understanding your self is indeed a 'warrior's journey', and probably *the* most difficult path a person can ever undertake. And where you are in your journey is not a question I can answer, it's a matter between you and God.

HOW ALL THINGS BEGAN

This is the tale the Northmen tell concerning the Beginning of Things.

Once upon a time, before ever this world was made, there was neither earth nor sea, nor air, nor light, but only a great yawning gulf, full of twilight, where these things should be.

To the north of this gulf lay the Home of Mist, a dark and dreary land, out of which flowed a river of water from a spring that never ran dry. As the water in its onward course met the bitter blasts of wind from the yawning gulf, it hardened into great blocks of ice, which rolled far down into the abyss with a thunderous roar and piled themselves one on another until they formed mountains of glistening ice.

South of this gulf lay the Home of Fire, a land of burning heat, guarded by a giant with a flaming sword which, as he flashed it to and fro before the entrance, sent forth showers of sparks. And these sparks fell upon the ice-blocks and partly melted them, so that they sent up clouds of steam; and these again were frozen into hoar-frost, which filled all the space that was left in the midst of the mountains of ice.

Then one day, when the gulf was full to the very top, this great mass of frosty rime, warmed by the flames from the Home of Fire and frozen by the cold airs from the Home of Mist, came to life and became the Giant Ymir, with a living, moving body and cruel heart of ice.

Now there was as yet no tree, nor grass, nor anything that would serve for food, in this gloomy abyss. But when the Giant Ymir began to grope around for something to satisfy his hunger, he heard a sound as of some animal chewing the cud; and there among the ice-hills he saw a gigantic cow, from whose udder flowed four great streams of milk (the four elements), and with this his craving was easily stilled.

But the cow was hungry also, and began to lick the salt off the blocks of ice by which she was

Audumla suckles Ymir.
Painting by Nicolai Abraham Abildgaard

surrounded. And presently, as she went on licking with her strong, rough tongue, a head of hair pushed itself through the melting ice. Still the cow went on licking, until she had at last melted all the icy covering and there stood fully revealed the frame of a mighty man.

Ymir looked with eyes of hatred at this being, born of snow and ice, for somehow he knew that his heart was warm and kind, and that he and his sons would always be the enemies of the evil race of the Frost Giants.

So, indeed, it came to pass. For from the sons of Ymir came a race of giants whose pleasure was to work evil on the earth (the beginning of the existence of opposites – good and evil); and from the Sons of the Iceman sprang the race of the gods, chief of whom was Odin, Father of All Things That Ever Were Made; and Odin and his brothers began at once to war against the wicked Frost Giants, and most of all against the cold-hearted Ymir, whom in the end they slew.

Now when, after a hard fight, the Giant Ymir was slain, such a river of blood flowed forth from his wounds that it drowned all the rest of the Frost Giants save one, who escaped in a boat, with only his wife on board, and sailed away to the edge of the world. And from him sprang all the new race of Frost Giants, who at every opportunity issued from their land of twilight and desolation to harm the gods in their abode of bliss.

Now when the giants had been thus driven out, All-Father Odin set to work with his brothers to make the earth, the sea, and the sky; and these they fashioned out of the great body of the Giant Ymir.

Out of his flesh they formed Midgard, the earth, which lay in the centre of the gulf; and all round it they planted his eyebrows to make a high fence which should defend it from the race of giants.

With his bones they made the lofty hills, with his teeth the cliffs, and his thick curly hair took root and became trees, bushes, and the green grass.

With his blood they made the ocean, and his great skull, poised aloft, became the arching sky. Just below this they scattered his brains, and made of them the heavy grey clouds that lie between earth and heaven.

The sky itself was held in place by four strong dwarfs, who support it on their broad shoulders as they stand east and west and south and north.

The next thing was to give light to the new-made world. So the gods caught sparks from the Home of Fire and set them in the sky for stars; and they took the living flame and made of it the sun

and moon, which they placed in chariots of gold, and harnessed to them beautiful horses, with flowing manes of gold and silver. Before the horses of the sun, they placed a mighty shield to protect them from its hot rays; but the swift moon steeds needed no such protection from its gentle heat.

And now all was ready save that there was no one to drive the horses of the sun and moon. This task was given to Mani and Sol, the beautiful son and daughter of a giant; and these fair charioteers drive their fleet steeds along the paths marked out by the gods, and not only give light to the earth but mark out months and days for the sons of men.

Then All-Father Odin called forth Night, the gloomy daughter of the cold-hearted giant folk, and set her to drive the dark chariot drawn by the black horse, Frosty-Mane, from whose long wavy hair the drops of dew and hoar-frost fall upon the earth below. After her drove her radiant son, Day, with his white steed Shining-Mane, from whom the bright beams of daylight shine forth to gladden the hearts of men.

But the wicked giants were very angry when they saw all these good things; and they set in the sky two hungry wolves, that the fierce, grey creatures might for ever pursue the sun and moon, and devour them, and so bring all things to an end. Sometimes, indeed, or so say the men of the North, the grey wolves almost succeed in swallowing sun or moon; and then the earth children make such an uproar that the fierce beasts drop their prey in fear. And the sun and moon flee more rapidly than before, still pursued by the hungry monsters.

One day, so runs the tale, as Mani, the Man in the Moon, was hastening on his course, he gazed upon the earth and saw two beautiful little children, a boy and a girl, carrying between them a pail of water. They looked very tired and sleepy, and indeed they were, for a cruel giant made them fetch and carry water all night long, when they should have been in bed. So Mani put out a long, long arm and snatched up the children and set them in the moon, pail and all; and there you can see them on any moonlit night for yourself.

But that happened a long time after the beginning of things; for as yet there was no man or woman or child upon the earth.

And now that this pleasant Midgard was made, the gods determined to satisfy their desire for an abode where they might rest and enjoy themselves in their hours of ease.

They chose a suitable place far above the earth, on the other side of the great river which flowed from the Home of Mist where the giants dwelt, and here they made for their abode Asgard, wherein they dwelt in peace and happiness, and from whence they could look down upon the sons of men.

From Asgard to Midgard they built a beautiful bridge of many colours, to which men gave the name of Rainbow Bridge, and up and down which the gods could pass on their journeys to and from the earth.

Here in Asgard stood the mighty forge where the gods fashioned their weapons wherewith they fought the giants, and the tools wherewith they built their palaces of gold and silver.

Meantime, no human creature lived upon the earth, and the giants dared not cross its borders for fear of the gods. But one of them, clad in eagles' plumes, always sat at the north side of Midgard, and, whenever he raised his arms and let them fall again, an icy blast rushed forth from the Mist Home and nipped all the pleasant things of earth with its cruel breath. In due time the earth was no longer without life, for the ground brought forth thousands of tiny creatures, which crawled about and showed signs of great intelligence. And when the gods examined these little people closely, they found that they were of two kinds.

Some were ugly, misshapen, and cunning-faced, with great heads, small bodies, long arms and feet. These they called Trolls or Dwarfs or Gnomes, and sent them to live underground, threatening to turn them into stone should they appear in the daytime. And this is why the trolls spend all their time in the hidden parts of the earth, digging for gold and silver and precious stones, and hiding their spoil away in secret holes and corners. Sometimes they blow their tiny fires and set to work to make all kinds of wonderful things from this buried treasure; and that is what they are doing when, if one listens very hard on the mountains and hills of the Northland, a sound of tap-tap-tapping is heard far underneath the ground.

The other small earth creatures were very fair and light and slender, kindly of heart, and full of goodwill. These the gods called Fairies or Elves, and gave to them a charming place called Elfland in which to dwell. Elfland lies between Asgard and Midgard, and since all fairies have wings they can easily flit down to the earth to play with the butterflies, teach the young birds to sing, water the flowers, or dance in the moonlight round a fairy ring.

Last of all, the gods made a man and woman to dwell in fair Midgard; and this is the manner of their creation.

All-Father Odin was walking with his brothers in Midgard where, by the seashore, they found growing two trees, an ash and an elm. Odin took these trees and breathed on them, whereupon a wonderful transformation took place. Where the trees had stood, there were a living man and woman, but they were stupid, pale, and speechless, until Hœnir, the god of Light, touched their foreheads and gave them sense and wisdom; and Loki, the Fire-god, smoothed their faces, giving them bright colour and warm blood, and the power to speak and see and hear. It only remained that they should be named, and they were called Ask and Embla, the names of the trees from which they had been formed. From these two people sprang all the race of men which lives upon this earth.

And now All-Father Odin completed his work by planting the Tree of Life.

This immense tree had its roots in Asgard and Midgard and the Mist Land; and it grew to such a marvellous height that the highest bough, the Bough of Peace, hung over the Hall of Odin on the heights of Asgard; and the other branches overshadowed both Midgard and the Mist Land. On the top of the Peace Bough was perched a mighty eagle, and ever a falcon sat between his eyes, and kept watch on all that happened in the world below, that he might tell to Odin what he saw.

Heidrun, the goat of Odin, who supplied the heavenly mead, browsed on the leaves of this wonderful tree, and from them fed also the four mighty stags from whose horns honey-dew dropped on to the earth beneath and supplied water for all the rivers of Midgard.

The leaves of the Tree of Life were ever green and fair, despite the dragon which, aided by countless serpents, gnawed perpetually at its roots, in order that they might kill the Tree of Life and thus bring about the destruction of the gods.

Up and down the branches of the tree scampered the squirrel, Ratatosk, a malicious little creature, whose one amusement it was to make mischief by repeating to the eagle the rude remarks of the dragon, and to the dragon those of the eagle, in the hope that one day he might see them in actual conflict.

Near the roots of the Tree of life is a sacred well of sweet water from which the three Weird Sisters, who know all that shall come to pass, sprinkle the tree and keep it fresh and green. And the water, as it trickles down from the leaves, falls as drops of honey on the earth, and the bees take it for their food.

Close to this sacred well is the Council Hall of the gods, to which every morning they rode, over the Rainbow Bridge, to hold converse together.

And this is the end of the tale of How All Things began.

SOURCE: TOLD BY THE NORTHMEN:
Stories from the Eddas and Sagas
By E. M. WILMOT-BUXTON

A busy executive father was trying to relax after a long, hard, demanding day at the office. Yet his young daughter had other plans.

'Read me a story, Dad,' the little girl requested.

'Give Daddy a few minutes to relax and unwind. Then I'll be happy to read you a story,' pleaded the father.

The little girl was insistent. 'Daddy please read a story to me, I'm bored.'

Frustrated and keen for some peace, he tore off the back page of the magazine that he was reading. It contained a full-page colour picture of a map of the world.

He tore the picture into several small pieces and gave it to his daughter, telling her it was a puzzle game and she must put all the pieces together. He promised to read her a story when she had done that. He was convinced that this would take her some time and settled back into his comfy chair with what remained of his magazine.

In under five minutes, the little girl announced the completion of her puzzle project. To her father's utter astonishment, the world picture was completely assembled.

When he asked his daughter how she managed to do it so quickly, the little girl explained that on the reverse side of the page was the picture of a man.

'You see, Daddy,' she said, 'when I put the man together, the whole world came together!'

Author unknown

Chapter 3

SEEK GUIDANCE

No man is great enough or wise enough for any of us to surrender our destiny to. The only way
in which anyone can lead us is to restore to us the belief in our own guidance.

Henry Miller (1891–1980)
American novelist and artist

n his play, *Man and Superman*, George Bernard Shaw
provides us with a great metaphor for life, turning classical
images of Heaven and Hell upside down. He describes
Hell as a place of complete satisfaction, where all desires
are freely fulfilled. Personal responsibility has no place in
Hell, although it does in Heaven, which is a place for the
'masters of reality', and, curiously enough, the place where souls are free to
go when they finally get sick of Hell.

We are spiritual beings on a human journey. Only one-third of us reside
here in the physical world. The remaining two-thirds of us are hidden in the
'subtle planes' of the Divine Matrix. It is in the unseen world that we find our
true nature, but uncovering this true nature involves a journey into a deep, dark
forest. Those of us who have the courage to step off the well-worn path of
familiarity, away from societal norm, can find ourselves in deep water. Just
when we believe we've made some headway in our journey of discovery,
when we think we are beginning to get a grip on things with our new perspective
of life, we are faced with another challenge or situation, whereupon we uncover
yet more layers of stuff, obstacles we haven't foreseen and people who just
don't see life in the same way we do. It can at times be quite disheartening,
when we believe we have travelled so far and made such progress, only to
realise that we don't really know ourselves at all. At times we may feel ourselves

341

floundering, taking one step forward and two steps back. Understanding ourselves takes many lifetimes of work. The road to enlightenment is hard, and whilst it's a journey we must undertake alone, sometimes we need a little help and guidance from others.

In many myths and fairy tales, the seeker gets help and guidance from a wise mentor – a god or goddess, an ally or guide, or a strange little man with a handful of magic beans. Sometimes the hero meets with one mentor who guides him every step of the way, as Krishna guided Prince Arjuna in the Bhagavad Gita. Sometimes this aide is there only for a short time, prompting the hero in a different direction, one that he might not have considered but for the influence of another. In the ancient Sumerian story, *Epic of Gilgamesh*, Enkidu was sent by the gods to rid Gilgamesh, the King of Uruk, of his arrogance. Enkidu becomes the king's constant companion and deeply beloved friend, accompanying him on many adventures until he dies suddenly after a serious illness. The tragic loss of Enkidu inspires Gilgamesh on a quest of his own to seek the answers to life's questions and his own immortality.

When life overwhelms us, we can become blind to our foolishness and stuckness. It is then that we need help and guidance. Each step we take towards lifting the veil may uncover another layer of illusion, but it also takes us a step higher on the ladder of consciousness. Eventually we begin to understand that the journey towards self-discovery is a never-ending journey, without beginning nor end.

Here are some ways, external and internal, some conventional and others not, that I have found useful not only in peeling away layers but curbing anxiety, regaining balance, and taking sometimes uncertain steps into the unknown.

PERSONAL DEVELOPMENT PROGRAMMES

Any revolution has to start with the transformation of the individual, otherwise individuals are corrupted by the power they get if their revolution succeeds.

Wes Nisker

Author, radio commentator, comedian and Buddhist meditation instructor

I have never really been one to bare my soul to a group of people I don't know; worse still, to look vulnerable and foolish in front of a group of people that I *do* know (the influence of the ego). I would rather work through my stuff alone. But without the mirror that others provide, we cannot see ourselves – the ego is too powerful. It is in relationships with others – family, partners, friends, colleagues and even casual acquaintances – that we can get to know our greatest weaknesses and realise our greatest strengths.

I have attended several personal development programmes over the years in an effort to find myself. Only one of them was really worthwhile: a trilogy of programmes delivered by Life Dynamics Training in Johannesburg – 'Gateway', 'Genesis' and 'The Revelation'. They were delivered over a period of six months. You had to complete one part of the curriculum to qualify for the next. Each programme was four to six days long, plus many hours of preparation and homework before, during and after the course. The programmes were tough, really tough, involving much introspection and feedback, which I often wasn't prepared for. The whole process hurt, and forced me to confront my ego and uncover the parts of myself that I didn't even know existed.

So many times during the programmes I wanted to leave. I didn't feel capable of facing the next challenge. But I did. Full of fear and trepidation, I went back to the next exercise as I realised that I would not be able to look at myself in the mirror again if I chose to walk away. What I was observing was my ego in action, detesting the pain that I put it through. Each programme became progressively more difficult as the trilogy progressed, forcing me to confront a number of aspects about myself (and my ego) that I really didn't want to see – how I failed to show up in life, vote for myself, take responsibility; how I blamed others for my sorry state of affairs. Eventually, after much fighting, snot and trauma, as my sister is fond of saying, I learned that fighting wasn't going to get me anywhere, so I learned to become the 'watcher', observing how my ego behaved – catching me completely unaware, standing up to be counted one moment and hiding away the next. The ego has so many facets that it is impossible to detect, unless we deliberately place obstacles in its path, and unless we deliberately place it in a situation that's uncomfortable or stressful.

The trilogy presented me with a microcosm of life condensed into a few short weeks. Unlike many other programmes of this nature, one was not left reeling and broken from the experience. Each segment carefully took you into the depths but also carefully brought you out the other side, highlighting your unique potential and talents. After attending the programmes, I continued to go back as a co-facilitator/supporter, helping others in their journey. But more importantly, I continued to learn about myself, too, from those courageous souls who, like me, had the fortitude to confront themselves full on. This one programme was responsible for helping me tangibly *shift,* and peel away some of the layers of self-destruction that were clearly holding me back.

Other programmes I've attended have been little more than background noise in comparison. Many of them contained re-hashes of the same old rhetoric, stuff that I already knew I should be working on; it was just packaged differently. Quite often, I found them too flakey, too nice, too wishy-washy and bland to make a real difference. On many occasions, I found that the facilitators or programme developers had just found a way to capitalise on the personal transformation market and weren't really any more clued up than certain members of their audience.

Every personal journey towards truth is different. If you like attending classes and workshops and being part of a group, I believe there are many programmes out there that can add meaningful input and provide worthy tools. You just need to find the programmes and tools that work for *you*. Don't follow the crowd and don't be impressed by programme facilitators who have developed a clever Internet marketing strategy and written a book. It doesn't necessarily mean they are enlightened. Some of the practices they encourage can also be dangerous.

The real danger of a personal transformation programme is that we become overly reliant on it as our saviour and begin to use it as a crutch. I have met many personal development junkies who, like recovering alcoholics, attend programme after programme in an effort to find the one 'ray of light' that will show them the way. Quite often they fool themselves into believing they are working on themselves, when in reality, they are hiding, waiting for that one illuminating piece of evidence that will force them to change, but which never fully materialises. In addition to a personal transformation programme, consider the relationships you are in and your interactions with the world in general, to be your mirror and a place of learning.

COACHING & COUNSELLING

In Greek mythology, Sirens were beautiful seductresses; creatures with the head of a female and the body of a bird, who with the irresistible charm of their song and the promise of ripe wisdom, lured mariners to death and destruction on the rocks surrounding their island. The Argonauts narrowly escaped them when Orpheus, realizing the peril they were in, took out his lyre and sang a song so loud and clear that it drowned out their enticing melodies. On another adventure, Odysseus wanted to hear the Sirens' beautiful voices, so he had his shipmates fill their own ears with wax before tying him to the mast of his ship. Although his heart rang with longing, the ropes held him tightly and the ship sailed uneventfully into safer waters.

When the Sirens sing their sweetest song, we often need someone to play the lyre and tie us to the mast to prevent us jumping off the edge. We lack the ability to introspect accurately because of the ego. The ego will *always* provide us with answers and justifications that make sense to us, tricking us into taking the easiest route, the path of least resistance, in any situation, which can quite often lead to our demise. This is why we need counselling or guidance from someone who has a different point of view or deeper insights.

In a time of great need in South Africa, when I was feeling particularly vulnerable, alone and down, I decided in a fit of ruthless anticipation that I needed someone to help me take action. Nothing was working in my life – I was stuck, emotionally and financially, and for many months I'd made little progress. The global financial crisis hadn't helped, but I needed to find a way to get myself out of the pit that I was in. At the time, I didn't believe I needed a psychologist to help me figure out what was wrong with me, I needed to make big changes and I wanted someone who could help me get to the nub of my stuckness and walk with me as I decided to take action. So I hired a person who branded herself as a 'coach's coach', who had touched a deeper part of me during some introductory breakfast seminars that she'd previously facilitated for busy executives. We spent a couple of emotional hours discussing my issues and where I needed help. We agreed on a course of action to take place over the next three to six months. I paid in advance for her coaching, as the type of interaction I needed extended beyond a weekly two-hour chat.

My coach portrayed a professional picture. She was on the board of the Professional Speakers Association, a psychometrist, and seemingly a great *empath* who, from the interactions I had with her prior to our appointment, assured me she was on top of her game. She looked the part, spoke the part and I believed she would deliver. I was expecting great things and believed this process might be the answer to my prayers. I was sadly mistaken.

In my vulnerable state, I'd allowed emotion to take over. I could no longer hear the intuition and inner guidance that I relied on so heavily in the past. What I hadn't realised, until we started our sessions, was that her life was a bigger mess than mine. After the initial discussion and assessment, our time together disintegrated into pointless consultations about time management and her own personal problems. Looking into not at, I realised her intention was not to deceive; she simply didn't have the skills to help me to the level of my expectation. She was also going through her own private hell emotionally and financially. She needed cash, so willingly took my large down payment without due consideration of whether or not she could deliver. When I tried to discuss my dissatisfaction regarding her services, she had a screaming hissy fit and threw me out of her office. I apparently reminded her too much of her sister. Needless to say, I didn't get my money back and I didn't have the emotional strength at that time to fight her legally or through professional channels. What goes around comes around. Besides, I felt partly responsible for my mistake, being a coach trained in cognitive behavioural science and Neuro-Linguistic Programming, I believed my lack of shrewdness played a role. It was a dumb move to appoint her in the first place.

When we are feeling vulnerable, it's easy to fall into the trap of handing over the responsibility for our life to others. We hope against all odds that some coach or counsellor or healer with the magical touch will be the answer to our problems, having insight into our situation that we don't have. Psychologists and coaches occupy a valuable rung on the ladder in terms of helping us unpack life's issues, providing us with skills and strategies for sorting out our heads and assisting us in regaining balance. However, we have to be clear about our expectations and be honest with ourselves when the type of therapy they utilise is not working. Sometimes, however, we don't know what we want – we just want the pain to go away. It's sad to see people drifting from therapist to therapist looking for answers that can only be found by going deeper into the forest. A good therapist or coach will help you determine what outcomes you want and how you will recognise them, before you start the coaching process.

I was amazed to discover that there are over fifty different branches of psychology, including cognitive psychology, systems and family of origin psychology, humanistic and integrative psychology, behavioural psychology, neuropsychology, moral psychology, transpersonal psychology and many others. There are also many systems of coach training. It's important to remember that certificates adorning the walls of therapists' offices don't denote the level of their own personal enlightenment. The same applies to healers and practitioners of certain therapies and techniques. A qualification in naturopathy, reiki, body talk, hypnotherapy or any other therapy does not make the counsellor wiser than you. So beware – look into not at. You are the ultimate authority in your life.

In my experience, the practice of psychology is the prelude to spiritual understanding and finding a deeper meaning. The issues we face in life are not outside of us, they lie within. And the more issues we have, the more questions we ask, the deeper we go. Whilst certain forms of traditional psychology contain 'slivers of truth', in my experience they have only been roughly twenty to thirty percent effective, overall, in helping me to reach a point of centeredness, primarily because they don't address the negative effects of the ego. When we are wandering lost in the forest of life we don't need someone to coach us to perform better, psychoanalyse us or provide us with medication to dull us from life. We need someone to show us the way (like the poet Virgil did for Dante when he was wandering lost in a forest) and remind us who we truly are (as Krishna did for Arjuna when faced with the moral dilemma of war, reminding him of his duties as a warrior and prince). Sometimes, we need someone who has been there before us, who can take us by the hand and steer us out of this mess, something that goes beyond intellectual reasoning, someone whose philosophy we can adopt until we find our own. Marcos was that person for me. As much as I was disappointed that my teacher wasn't all I expected him to be, I can't deny that I always came away from our interactions feeling uplifted and in greater control of my being. When I presented him with my life issues, he would throw a completely different point of view into the mix that related to the purpose of life, transcending it and not analysing the problem or the reason why I believed I was stuck. Albert Einstein said, 'No problem can be solved with the same consciousness that created it.' The reason that we remain stuck in our problems for so long is that we are surrounded by people who have the same consciousness as ourselves. That's the law of resonance. Few people think deeply or philosophically about the dynamics of life. When you find someone who does, it is a very, very rare thing indeed.

Undertaking self-correction is extremely hard work. It needs a fresh point of view. Teachers who have travelled some way along the path of self-realisation will have the greatest respect for your free will. They are generally not out there making a name for themselves, and generally won't advertise their beliefs unless you ask. This makes them difficult to find. In fact, a *true* teacher will find *you*, not the other way around. But if you are lucky to find someone along the way and give him the opportunity to help, he will climb in boots and all to steer you in the right direction.

LISTEN TO YOUR INTUITION

I feel there are two people inside me – me and my intuition. If I go against her she'll screw me every time, and if I follow her, we get along quite nicely.

Kim Basinger

Hollywood actress

Whether we call it a *gut feeling, vibes, sixth sense* or *psychic sense*, intuition is something we all have. We just need to understand it and learn to distinguish its *true* message from the false communications of the ego. Intuition is not experienced in the mind; it is *felt* in the solar plexus, which is why we speak of intuition as a feeling – a *gut* feeling. Intuition is closely linked with vibration and our ability to tune in to different frequencies. Intuition is our ability to understand the subtle cause-and-effect relationships behind many events, which goes way beyond the understanding of the intellect. Our intuition is our greatest gift and can be, if we interpret it correctly, our wisest source of guidance. It is our subconscious mind talking to us, communicating with us in feelings or emotions. Deep inside we know all things but we are often unable to bring this subconscious information into the conscious realms. The subconscious part of our mind is tuned into the subtle realms of the Divine Matrix. It's the connection we have with our astral and mental bodies and thus defies logic and time. When we experience our intuition we are connecting into the hidden realms, albeit briefly. Intuition, if developed, becomes a psychic ability.

We have become so conditioned by the ego, the mind and our thoughts, that we no longer listen to that little voice within. The price I've paid in life for ignoring my intuition is high. I've ended up feeling more stressed and anxious than ever, feeling powerless, inadequate, confused and trampled on by life.

Ignoring it has also resulted in me making some daft decisions that led into situations that I didn't really want to be in, ones that I've paid a high price for – losing money, being falsely accused of something I didn't do, or wasting time that I could have spent better elsewhere. Every hiring mistake I made in the business world happened when I applied logic over intuition. Each time, the little voice rang – sometimes only faintly, and I ignored it.

However, for the most part, listening to my intuition has brought great joy to me and others. Recently, I purchased a set of oracle cards for Steve developed by Sonia Choquette, called 'Trust your Vibes'. People who know Steve would have laughed their heads off if I'd mentioned my intention to buy him anything of the 'woo-woo' nature. He was a firm non-believer in anything subtle and often brushed off my sentiments on intuition. He, too, has a strong sense of intuition, however, that he rarely paid attention to, passing it off as nonsense in his logical, left-brained world. On one particular day I had a strong sense that the oracle cards were indeed the right gift to buy him, so I ignored thoughts of the potential ridicule I'd get when I presented him with his gift and followed my heart. When he opened it, he became instantly overwhelmed with emotion – something that he wasn't used to, and neither was I. He immediately started to use the cards, and to this day, every morning before he gets up, he selects one card and pays attention to the message each one brings. Every evening, too, he tells me how relevant the message has been during his day, as if he's guided in some way. Everything is connected to everything else. Even those things that appear unconnected are intimately associated with each other. Divination of any sort works on this principle. (The word divination comes from the Latin word *divinus*, which means 'deity' or 'god'. 'To divine' meant to obtain information through divine means. When we are not always able to bring unconscious information into conscious awareness through our intuition, we can use other means. Oracle cards, pendulums, dowsing, among others, are all forms of communication with the subtle realms of the Divine Matrix.)

I have found that people who listen to their intuition have several things in common: They have a heightened sense of awareness about themselves and what is going on in their mind body system. They respect what they feel at times, even when it doesn't make obvious sense to others, and they follow the message without hesitation. People who are guided by their intuition let their 'psychic' energy lead them day by day and are, generally speaking, lighter, easier to be around, more creative, resourceful and quicker to act than the typical five-sensory people. People who listen to their intuition have a greater sense of security, confidence and courage, going with their feelings instead of struggling against them. They often don't concern themselves with whether they are making sense to others – because invariably they aren't. People who listen to their intuition pay attention to life differently; in fact, they seemingly enjoy life more freely than those who rely on their five senses alone. Intuitive people have the ability to switch tactics or make changes *before* the pressing need is upon them, anticipating in advance, what to do and how to behave.

I often feel my intuition as an immediate apprehension that has no logical reasoning – a simple knowing beyond all doubt that something is about to happen, good or bad. Sometimes it comes as a feeling of dread, sometimes as a moment of fleeting joy or a sense of elation, sometimes a sinking feeling, like the bottom has just dropped out of my world. On other occasions, I have experienced it as a loud voice in my head. Suddenly the answer to a particular problem or solution is found and with it a deep sense of familiarity or recognition, as if I'd known the answer all along. Often I have found myself moved to tears as a rush of insight or intense feeling wells up inside me. Carl Jung in his *Memoirs* describes the experience of his intuition during an altercation with Sigmund Freud:

> While Freud was going on this way, I had a curious sensation. It was as if my diaphragm were made of iron and were becoming red-hot – a glowing vault. And at that moment there was such a loud report in the bookcase, which stood right next to us, that we both started up in alarm, fearing the thing was going to topple over on us. I said to Freud: 'There, that is an example of a so-called catalytic exteriorization phenomenon.'
>
> 'Oh come,' he exclaimed. 'That is sheer bosh.'
>
> 'It is not,' I replied. 'You are mistaken, Herr Professor. And to prove my point I now predict that in a moment there will be another such loud report!'
>
> Sure enough, no sooner had I said the words than the same detonation went off in the bookcase. To this day I do not know what gave me this certainty. But I knew beyond all doubt that the report would come again. Freud only stared aghast at me. I do not know what was in his mind, or what his look meant. In any case, this incident aroused his distrust of me, and I had the feeling that I had done something against him. I never afterward discussed the incident with him.

When I am unsure or unbalanced, and can't quite get clarity on the message presented by my intuition or any other means of divination, I seek guidance from others whose intuition has developed to a point of a psychic sense. I found a really good intuitive psychic in Germany: Sue Schoning of the Soul Lighthouse, with whom I converse via Skype when I get desperate. She isn't one of those psychics who tells you that you will be married by Friday and heading off into the sunset with a new lover. (I've been to several of those kind of psychics and I am still waiting for that to happen!) She has a unique ability to succinctly clarify the 'wooliness' in my head and help me make sense out of it. Invariably I find that my intuition was right all the time.

We all have the ability to become psychic with some work and effort. Some people just need to work on it more than others. Whilst many people are born with a psychic gift, not all people who call themselves 'psychic' have clear insight. Quite often their timing, observations and insights are incorrect and can be a result of their own internal imbalance, the ego, or misinterpretation of the messages they receive. Good ones take some finding. From experience I have found that it is ultimately better to develop your own intuition as a guide in your life and not rely wholly on others to predict your path. We are ultimately all psychic on the astral plane during dreams and when we pass on.

Working with our intuition takes time and each of us will experience it in a different way. I've personally found that the more I listen to my intuition, act on its guidance, pay attention to my dreams and stimulate my subconscious, the more my intuition works for me.

WORK WITH YOUR SUBCONSCIOUS

Imagination is the beginning of creation. You imagine what you desire, you will what you imagine and at last you create what you will.

George Bernard Shaw (1856–1950)
Irish playwright

Hypnosis has been the greatest contributor in changing some of the long-held, dysfunctional beliefs about life I learned in childhood. It has also been the most effective way of dealing with stress, anxiety and depression, as it works directly with the subconscious mind. Hypnosis can be used to change and eradicate deeply held fears, phobias, suppressed emotions, negative beliefs, bad habits and behaviour patterns. It's the *only* therapy I've found that's had lasting and permanent results, particularly if it's combined with cognitive coaching or psychotherapy. The effects of some of the other stand-alone counselling methodologies I've experienced diminish within hours, sometimes minutes, as the conscious mind and ego take over as soon as the stressor reoccurs.

Contrary to popular belief, hypnosis is not a state of deep sleep, nor does it involve the induction of a trance. We induce our own states of hypnosis every day when we daydream, drive somewhere without thinking, listen to music, watch a movie or become seduced by the dulcet tones of someone's voice. During hypnosis, we are in an advanced state of awareness and totally in control. In this state, the conscious mind is suppressed and the subconscious mind comes to the fore. During hypnosis, the breathing becomes slower and deeper, the pulse rate drops and the metabolic rate falls. The subconscious mind in this state is far more receptive to suggestion and change than it is during a waking state.

When you are in a state of hypnosis – a state of deep relaxation – your astral body moves slightly out of your physical body, as it does in sleep. We enter a state of heightened awareness by using our imagination and will power. (In my experience of hypnotherapy, if a therapist has suggested something to me that jars me, I still have the capacity to change it in my imagination.) Hypnosis and subtle energy work together – the subtle energies of the hypnotist and the subject. Hence, an experience with a real, live therapist, instead of with a guided meditation or hypnotherapy CD, is more powerful.

It is possible to record your own 'guided meditations', if you are so inclined; however, I don't like the sound of my own voice. I prefer to listen to that of a therapist. John Dutton, from GMTI (Guided Meditation Therapy Institute) in Durban, Johannesburg, who first formally instructed me in the science of hypnosis, is the man whose voice my subconscious seems to like.

It's important, for treatment to be effective, to find a therapist that you are 100% comfortable with. Let your intuition be your guide. Whilst I have personally found that we can't be made to do anything against our will during hypnotherapy, the influences that certain people have over others can be powerful if we are unaware of them. However, these influences, as a result of subtle energy (od), affect us during our waking state, too, particularly when we are unaware of our surroundings. We are just more susceptible to them when we are in a state of hypnosis. All forms of energy healing involve the transfer of od and subtle energy. The vibrations, thoughts and emotions of the healer are transported into the subtle body of the patient, either by the laying on of hands, imagination or both. Choose your therapist with care.

PAY ATTENTION TO YOUR DREAMS

The spirit of man has two dwelling places, both this world and the other world. The borderline between them is the third, the land of dreams.

The Upanishads
Early philosophical Hindu texts

The ancients regarded dreams as prophetic messengers, or guidance from the gods. In Greek mythology, both the *Iliad* and the *Odyssey* speak of the gods who frequently sent dreams to individuals or appeared themselves in dreams. Before we can pay attention to our dreams, we first need to accept that we actually have dreams. We all dream, most of us just don't remember them. At night when we sleep, our astral body leaves our physical body. It is through our astral body that we experience dreams. They can be a huge source of guidance and, once we have learned to gain some measure of control over them, a way of dealing with life's worries and strife. Dreams are a product of our subconscious mind and the closest direct experiences that we can have of the subtle planes and higher stages of consciousness.

The myth is the public dream and the dream is the private myth. If your private myth, your dream, happens to coincide with that of the society, you are in good accord with your group. If it isn't, you've got an adventure in the dark forest ahead of you.

Joseph Campbell (1904–1987)
American mythologist, writer and lecturer

The subconscious communicates with us in pictures and symbols that don't always make immediate sense. But with practice, we can start to identify the specific symbolism relevant to our dreams, something we won't find in a 'dream book' bought from a shop. The symbolism we find in books is someone else's myth, and often only symbolic to the author – a product of someone else's subconscious experience. It often bears little relevance to our own lives.

Since childhood, I have always been able to remember my dreams. In fact, even today I can remember a specific dream I had at the age of three as clearly as if it happened only yesterday. With practice I have been able to gain better control over my dreams and their lucidity. During lucid dreaming, one has the capacity to actually become conscious, to wake up whilst in the dream and deploy some measure of control over what's actually happening. I dreamed one night that as I was driving along a narrow road, my car began to slide off the road into a deep lake. One moment I was struggling for control of the vehicle in a state of fear and shock, and the next I suddenly realised that I was dreaming and that in a dream I could do anything I liked. As I became lucid, I took off in the car, flying and circling above the lake like Dick van Dyke in the movie *Chitty-Chitty-Bang-Bang*. I remember laughing loudly as I flew into the air, realising that in any dream I couldn't get wet or be afraid of water. This was the prelude to many dreams where I have been able to fly and consciously control situations that are unpleasant.

Dreams are greatly affected by our vibration. When I am angry, sick, anxious or depressed, my dreams can become nightmarish and terrifying. I find myself being chased, hemmed into a corner, threatened, verbally or physically fighting with someone. Before I learned to establish some degree of control, I would wake forcibly, feeling exhausted, drenched in sweat and scared to close my eyes again lest I go back into the same situation. I gradually learned to recognise that these activities are all symbolic of the unconscious internal struggles I had within.

As I progressed in my dream control, I noticed how I am no longer a victim of circumstances. Sometimes when I feel like fleeing in a dream, I quite unexpectedly stand my ground and take control. I have found, too, that controlling my dreams helps me to control what is going on in my life in the physical world. I don't always get it right – if I am unbalanced or stressed, it's much harder, if not impossible. Sleeping pills can also destroy any real ability to dream. When my vibration is high, when I feel peaceful and balanced, I can have the most uplifting dreams, in which the colours are bright, vivid and clear. Once again, I often find myself physically flying, swooping over treetops like a bird and meeting amazing people who ooze love, whose skin is always illuminated by a golden light. I always feel totally at peace or elated, and waking up from these dreams is such a disappointment. With practice, though, I have learned to go back into the same dream again.

We can find out many things about ourselves in dreams. They contain a valuable source of guidance, as we again access the subconscious mind and the subliminal messages it sends to us. We also have access to the collective unconscious in dreams. Carl Jung recognized that the archetypical images that recurred in many of his patients' dreams could also be found in myths and legends as well as in contemporary literature, religion and art of the same period. Archetypes, which are original patterns or models, exist in the collective unconscious on the mental plane. Sometimes dreams can be prophetic, containing archetypal images of future events.

I know that if we meditate on a dream sufficiently long and thoroughly – if we take it about with us and turn it over and over – something almost always comes of it.

Carl Jung (1875–1961)
Psychologist

We can start working with our dreams by paying attention to them and practicing dream recall techniques. Start a dream diary, keeping notes of all the dreams you experience. If you cross-reference your dreams with a journal detailing specific events in your life, quite often you can begin to see that many of your dreams have prophetic qualities. Perhaps you remember a conversation you had in your dream or remember a specific symbol which warns you about a specific event or situation, or gives you advice on how to handle it. In this way, we can start to become familiar with the individual symbolism of our dreams and use it to greater effect. Get into the habit of setting the intention before you sleep that you will remember your dreams; when you wake up; keep a note pad and pen by your bed so that you can write down fragments of your dreams. Even if you wake in the middle of the night, by writing down only one or two key words in the dark, you will find when you review these words in the morning that the contents of the entire dream unfurl and come flooding back in full colour. When I review my old dream diaries, I can re-experience the content of my dreams from ten years previously; yet I have a hard time remembering the actual events that took place at work three days ago during waking consciousness. There is no time and space on the astral plane. Dreams, particularly lucid dreams, are a prelude to conscious astral travel or out-of-body experiences where life can take on a whole new dimension.

Our state of consciousness before we sleep is vitally important to the type of dreams we have. Although a triple review at the end of the day is a recommended practice for raising our consciousness, I personally find that it can't be the *very* last thing I do at night before falling asleep. Since rediscovering the value of fairy tales and myths, I find myself instead re-living my childhood by immersing myself in a story or two before dropping off. As these tales are full of symbolism, subconsciously meditating on the hidden meaning of the myths when we are in a relaxed state is a great way to ensure that our dreams take on a magical quality.

PRAYER AND GUIDANCE FROM THE HIGHER REALMS

A man can no more diminish God's glory by refusing to worship Him than a lunatic can put out the sun by scribbling the word 'darkness' on the walls of his cell.

C. S. Lewis (1898–1963)
Novelist, poet, academic

For most of my life, I couldn't bring myself to pray. I felt stupid and awkward. And besides, prayer was something that only the orthodox religions practised on a Sunday in church, which was hypocritical, in my book. As far as I was concerned, God wouldn't listen to me because he was too big, too busy and too complex, and I didn't go to church. I also could not bring myself to get down on my knees and look earnestly up at the sky and feel *Him* in my soul. Initially, like many of us, I only prayed when I was acutely desperate because I'd run out of money, or found myself in an impossible situation and there was nobody else in the physical world to turn to. I could imagine God raising his eyes to the heavens while thinking, 'Here she goes again! Why is it that I only seem to hear from this chick when she wants something?' Perhaps this was why the answers to my prayers never seemed to come, and if they did, I was too busy, too naive and too arrogant to attribute them to God's work.

Gradually, as my journey through life continued, as I grew in humility, became more balanced and reframed my beliefs about existence, I realised that the answers I sought about life were not to be found here amongst my friends and colleagues, but in higher realms. I gradually came to accept prayer as a form of two-way communication. If we are asking for help, and we believe in the existence of higher realms, we have to do two things: firstly, we have to humble ourselves enough to pray; and secondly, we have to ready ourselves to receive the answers from the Universe in obscure ways. (When I learned this, I imagined that God had probably sent thousands of solutions to my requests over the years, but I was too wrapped up in my own misery to really pay attention.) So when I did open a channel with the higher realms and became still and quiet enough to receive the guidance, the answers came thick and fast. Not with a lightning bolt or a thunder clap, or with a pair of winged sandals, but in less obvious ways in the little things that happened in my life. A book would just happen to fall from a shelf in a bookstore as I ambled past, springing open at the right page. Synchronistic events would occur – someone I hardly knew, perhaps a complete stranger, would utter comforting words that related to the problem I was experiencing. Or I would meet with someone who connected me to the right person or situation, streamlining my path or helping me find the answers that had previously eluded me. One day, during a particularly difficult time in my life when I felt alone and afraid, I sat in the garden of my home in Lone Hill sobbing and sobbing and begging for help. When I had no more energy to cry any longer, I walked back into my office, still feeling an immense bleakness and emptiness, only to find a beautiful, large, speckled, grey and white feather neatly placed on the floor beside the desk in my office. Still today, I don't know how it got there. It was impossible for the feather to have been casually dropped by a stray bird that happened to be nonchalantly passing by. Besides, the feather was too large and too perfect to be casually discarded – from a large bird's wing, no doubt. I immediately felt a sense of warmth fill my entire body, as if angels were wrapping their tender wings around me, healing me of my sadness and pain. I felt as if my prayers had at last been heard, and whoever was listening had used any means at their disposal to let me know they were listening. When I started to consciously pay attention to prayer as a form of guidance, every one of these little signs I received helped me to realise that I was not alone. Whatever form they took, each one provided me with the courage and strength to take the next step.

The question you may ask is, how did I know the answers I received were right? I just knew – intuition again. We always recognise truth within us, and that's really all we have to go on. There has to come a time when we stop doubting and looking for proof and just accept the gifts of the Universe. The words I read in the errant book that slipped from the shelf would make my heart sing, or I'd feel a sense of inner peace and comfort which eased the flow of tears, or perhaps a sudden surge of inspiration would propel me into action, even though I might have been tired and exhausted. I learned that these moments of connection with the higher realms may be fleeting and brief, but their effects are long-lasting, acting as a source of constant reassurance and hope.

Prayer is a very personal thing. Whom we pray to is also a very personal thing. In the various beliefs systems of the world, God takes so many forms, both physical and transcendental. But how do we pray to something that is so big, so immense, totally incomprehensible and utterly invisible? I for one felt so tiny in the face of this vastness that I didn't understand. To get on my knees and face this emptiness was a difficult act to get my head around. I needed structure and form, something to offer my prayers to, that I might be able to understand. Although I began to comprehend why so many religious and spiritual systems have a need to identify with a physical form of their God or guru – Jesus, Mary, Buddha, Vishnu and Shiva, Ganesha, a goddess, the sun or a saint – I couldn't see myself praying to a photograph, a statue or an elephant deity with a large belly and sixteen arms, no matter what the symbolism might be. That just didn't do it for me (although I later learned that Ganesha is the Hindu deity deemed to be the Remover of Obstacles, so maybe I should have got my act together sooner!),

So when I did finally get over myself and decided to pray more sincerely, whom did I pray to? I didn't pray to God directly. I prayed to the high ones, the ascended masters. The order referred to them as the 'holy hierarchy of men'; the ones who were once here on earth, treading this weary path before me, those who had broken free from this wheel of birth and death and could help me do the same thing. (Tarot cards are an ancient system of mystical instruction, not a divination system. Card number 1 in the tarot pack is the Magician. He holds one hand up seeking guidance from above, and one hand down in an effort to help those beneath him raise themselves. He symbolises a chain of assistance, based on vibration, that stretches from here in the physical world back into the Divine.) Whether we call them angels, spirit guides or helpers, it doesn't matter. What their real name is, I don't know. In my book, I prayed to those beings who could show me the way, not those who were waiting for their turn to reincarnate. I prayed to those whose duty it is to help us break free from the reincarnation cycle as they themselves had broken free and as they themselves were helped on their journey by those further along the way. Praying in this way felt more real to me than praying to God directly.

All prayers are worthy, whether they are offered to our ancestors, the moon, the wind, a Mother God, or one of the million deities in a specific religion.

Each one of us has something that we believe in, something that we worship, whether it has a physical form or not.

Prayer is only one form of veneration or worship. When we light an incense stick with thoughts of the higher realms, when we sacrifice something of importance for a greater cause, give thanks to those who have helped us, or live in constant remembrance of our divine heritage, we are praying. Prayer is

THE MAGICIAN.

also a form of meditation. It is an activity that contributes to raising our vibration and increasing balance. When we pray, we grow in humility, create space for new information to come to us, and admonish the ego. When we humble ourselves in prayer, we find that extraordinary things can happen. Solutions present themselves that are unexplained by science and can perhaps only be relegated to the world of magic and myth.

The way we pray and who we pray to relates to our vibration and our understanding of the scheme of things. As I became more accustomed to praying (and it requires deliberate effort to do so), prayer became a daily dialogue, a conversation that I had with the high ones – not just to ask for something, like a needy child, but to thank the high ones for all they do for me and those that I care about in my world. I didn't feel as if I had to get down on my knees to be worthy of their attention. I just had to be sincere in my dialogue.

When I am impatient, really struggling, or need extra-special guidance and a feeling of being connected with the 'high ones,' I consult the I Ching, the *Book of Changes*. Over many years, it has gently guided me step by step in the right direction and helped me pay attention to my intuition, stay steadfast and humble, and avoid many perilous situations. I do this using a very experienced interpreter by the name of Annie Heneke, a wonderful 80-year-old lady who is my inspiration for when I reach that age. She is a little dynamo, has just taught her 17-year-old grandson to drive, travels all over Africa, and is more advanced with technology than I am. She is an absolute joy to be around.

The I Ching is a book of wisdom in the ancient Chinese tradition, and for centuries it has been consulted on questions of state, warfare and personal decision making. Carl Jung regarded the I Ching as the clearest expression of synchronicity. According to R. L. Wing, who wrote the I Ching *Workbook*, it may be the oldest book on the planet.

> The early authors of I Ching observed the stars and tides, the plants and animals and the cycles of all natural events. At the same time they observed the patterns of relationships in families and societies, the practice of business, the craft of government, the grim art of warfare, the eternal human drama of love, ambition, conflict and honour. They made no attempt to create a fixed chart of the cosmos, instead they organically grew a guide to the way things change.
>
> R. L. Wing

The I Ching does not present us with statements of prophecy denoting what will happen in our future. The wisdom behind the book does not see the future as fixed, but rather as a constantly shifting flux similar to the seasons, with which we can interact. It is almost as if the book is talking directly to your spirit. A consultation is like having a conversation with a wise and experienced friend, who through his wisdom points out that if you continue to take your present course within the situation as it stands, you might find yourself in a situation that is unfavourable; but if you take another approach, circumstances could change, and then you can act more forcefully and effectively.

When we ask for help in prayer, the whole of Heaven jumps to our aid. But we first have to ask. No self-realised being will interfere with our free will, no matter how much we might believe otherwise. Prayer is a means of connecting us into the holy ambience of the higher realms of existence. When we voluntarily open ourselves up to guidance, help and assistance, we will find that it is readily available. They (whoever *they* are in your world) are just waiting for us to ask.

Once there lived a village of creatures along the bottom of a great crystal river. The current of the water swept silently over them all – young and old, rich and poor, good and evil, the current going its own way, knowing only its own crystal self. Each creature in its own manner clung tightly to the things and rocks of the river bottom, for clinging was their way of life, and resisting the current was what each had learned from birth.

But one creature said at last, 'I am tired of clinging. Though I cannot see it with my eyes, I trust that the current knows where it is going. I shall let go, and let it take me where it will. Clinging, I shall die of boredom.'

The other creatures laughed and said, 'Fool, let go and that current you worship will throw you tumbled and smashed across the rocks and you will die quicker than from boredom!'

But the one heeded them not and taking a breath did let go, at once was tumbled and smashed by the current across the rocks. Yet in time, as the creature refused to cling again, the current lifted him free from the bottom and he was bruised and hurt no more.

And the creatures downstream, to whom he was a stranger, cried, 'See, a miracle! A creature like ourselves, yet he flies. See the Messiah come to save us all!' And the one carried in the current said, 'I am no more a Messiah than you. The river delights to lift us free, if only we dare to let go. Our true work is this voyage, this adventure.'

But they cried the more, 'Saviour!' all the while clinging to the rocks, and when they looked again he was gone and they were left alone making legends of a Saviour.

Richard Bach
Illusions: The Adventures of a Reluctant Messiah

Chapter 4

LETTING GO

Man cannot discover new oceans, unless he has the courage to lose sight of the shore.

André Gide (1869–1951)
French author and Nobel prize-winner

et go, move on...suck it up, Bubbles,' Marcos would say as I presented him with my existential angst about life and its ups and downs.

'How do I let go?' I asked.

'Like this,' he demonstrated, opening his hands as if letting go of an imaginary stick that he'd been holding. 'It's that simple. Make a decision, do something – anything; it doesn't matter, just let go.'

American poet Henry David Thoreau said, 'Happiness is like a butterfly, the more you chase it, the more it will elude you, but if you turn your attention to other things, it will come and sit softly on your shoulders.' I was always trying to force happiness in my life. When I understood that happiness was not about accumulating stuff or anything that was external to me, I tried desperately to change my thinking, change my outlook on life and learn to be grateful for the blessings I did have. But still that feeling of happiness only seemed to come in short bursts. Happiness is not something we can pursue, it unfolds within us, as the poet says, when we learn to let go.

Letting go is one of the most freeing aspects of life. Yet, like the creatures in the river who spend their lives clinging, it's one of the hardest things to do. I admit to being somewhat of a control freak for most of my life – a bit of a pointless pastime for a self-confessed idealist. When I was in control, when

361

money was flowing, when life was stable, I felt safe. But my path in life and the railroad tracks that I'd laid for myself meant that any security or material possessions I would gather around me would only be temporary. Some days my path was strewn with rose petals and another day with thorns. Success in my career came and went. One year money flowed, the next year it didn't. That's when I started to cling, grasping hold of whatever I could to keep my world from falling. Clinging brought me pain, but then again, so did the fear of letting go. Dealing with this dichotomy was such hard work that stress and anxiety were commonplace. I wasn't really succeeding with this 'letting go' idea.

We are a funny race, we humans. When we feel vulnerable and insecure, we grasp at anything that makes us feel secure: possessions, relationships, money, thoughts and ideas about ourselves, other people, the world and the way it operates. We become rigid and unbending, digging our heels in, hanging on and refusing to change even the smallest of notions in case it topples us entirely. Desperately we cling to anything that appears solid and unyielding, believing that it will provide us with the safety and security we lack, giving us shelter from the storm until it passes and we can emerge back into the world and carry on as before.

Life has a peculiar way of shaking us from our slumber. What we resist persists, and looking back, I can see that letting go was one of the things that I resisted with every fibre of my being. When things went wrong, I spent my time wishing for better days, as I strived even harder to get myself out of the mess I was in. Life became a battle – something to be survived and overcome rather than enjoyed. I became frustrated when I repeated many of the same mistakes and habitual patterns. No matter how hard I tried, I couldn't seem to master the art of dancing in the rain, preferring instead to avoid the storms or hunker down until they'd passed. It took me a long time to recognise that letting go is not something we do or have; it's not something that we can strive for, it's something we have to *be*. The river of life will eventually bring us to a point where we have no choice but to change, to yield and allow ourselves to get carried along by its current. When we learn the art of surrender without feeling that we've sacrificed a part of ourselves, we can realise the often illusive sense of togetherness and peace which provides us with an inner power to just *be*. I was reminded of this again recently.

I was feeling particularly anxious and uptight some months after moving to New Zealand. I'd had yet another fractious encounter with Steve as we tried to establish our natural rhythm together. So I decided to remove myself from the situation and find a way to deliberately unwind from the tension.

I am fortunate enough to live close to some of the most beautiful bush land and beaches in the world, where I can walk alone without concern for my safety. So I took a drive to Tawharanui Regional Park, set on a remote peninsula only twenty minutes drive from my front door. The park is an open sanctuary where native birds, including the rare kiwi, live and breed without fear of predators. It was my first visit, so I was astounded when I stepped out from the native forest and bush land onto this long, white sandy beach with shingled coves and beautiful cave and rock formations, sculpted by the ocean over centuries. As I explored, I walked within a few metres of several dotterel birds (whose chicks look like bumblebees on stilts). They eyed me nonchalantly before casually ambling away in their search for bugs. Clearly they had no fear whatsoever.

The whole area was swathed in a blanket of tranquillity, as if this secret cove had a special spirit which protected it from unwelcome intruders. The beach was almost deserted. Families were packing up their picnic baskets and children and making their way home. I was almost utterly alone. I closed my eyes, allowing myself to bask in that pleasure, and after several minutes I began to walk – not just for a few feet, but for kilometres. The tide was out and the wide sandy beach had few natural obstructions, so I was able to weave my way along without fear of gashing my big toe on a large rock or a sharp pebble. I am the clumsiest woman on the planet and if there is something to be tripped over, crashed into, dropped, smashed or broken, then I'll find it; but on this day, I didn't need to worry. It was probably quite a comical sight for the few remaining birdwatchers perched high on the rocks with their binoculars; I could imagine them nudging each other with wry smiles as they turned their attention to a different variety of bird, this crazy woman with the long red hair weaving her way across the beach as if she had just consumed several bottles of New Zealand's finest.

As I plucked up the courage to let go of this one sense – sight – the world took on a completely different perspective. All my other senses were instantly heightened in the absence of visual imagery to guide my path. I began to pay attention to other sounds and sensations that I would normally consider to be background interference. The roar of the ocean was now intense. I began to distinguish the different gravelly pitches, rumbles and rushing tones of each wave as it crashed against the shore. I could feel the vibration in the earth. I felt the different textures of the sand beneath my feet – the wet, the hard, the soft, the cold, the dry, together with the slightest of undulations, rivulets, and inclines. I felt the sun on my face, and after a while, when I became more practised, I was able to walk more or less in a straight line, guided by the terrain and by the sun, which I kept at a certain point beside my left eyelid. As I walked, I felt my spirits lifting, and I began to feel elated, light, free – almost as if my next step would be into thin air and I would find myself taking off, flying above the land.

I imagined I could. My spirits soared as I walked and walked, still with my eyes closed; opening them only now and again to make sure I wasn't actually going to fall off the end of the world. Letting go of one sense and just allowing myself to be out of control, I felt calm, grounded and at peace with everything.

Of course, we can't spend our entire life walking back and forth along Tawharanui beach with our eyes shut each time we feel the need to let go. We have to find more practical applications for everyday life. So here are some of the best practical ways that have worked for me. Sadly, they don't instantly open the door to happiness and inner peace and neither do they provide immediate feelings of calm and elation. However, the more we are aware of our clinging and let go of a few of the things that hold us back, the more we create space for life to flow. Eventually the dam walls give way and we find ourselves in the flow, learning to dance without really even trying.

LET GO OF 'OUGHTISM'

'Oughtism' refers to all the *oughts, shoulds* and *musts* we have about life, fuelled by our childhood conditioning – the yearning to fit in and the insatiable desires of the ego. Oughtism is driven by fear and guilt. For example, we keep visiting our in-laws, even though we dislike them, because in our family belief system it is the right thing to do; or we might fear the reactions of others if we don't somehow measure up to their standards. Or we might say to ourselves, 'I ought to be working right now instead of being a stay-at-home mum, because that would make me more accepted at dinner parties by all those out-there women who manage to juggle both a career and a baby. Besides, my mum did it, too, so what's wrong with me?' Or we may stick with a particular career path or way of life because we are afraid of being perceived as inadequate: 'I can't possibly go back to school at the age of 35 – I should have done this earlier in life, and besides, I can't afford to leave the corporate world now – what will people think of me?'

The ego will always cause us to doubt ourselves, to fear the future and feel guilty about the events of the past. When we learn to recognise how the ego plays out in our lives, we can start to let go of the things we believe we ought to be doing, must be doing or should be doing, and replace them with things that serve us.

LET GO OF JUDGEMENTS

As a species we like to label things. It gives us a sense of certainty and allows us to measure our position in relation to it. Science and the medical profession are great labellers – they conjure up all these wonderful names for aspects of existence and disease – the Big Bang, and the AIDS virus for example – but scientists and doctors are still very much at a loss to fully understand or explain these phenomena, how they came about or what they actually mean. Giving something a name doesn't mean that we understand it.

There is a saying in life that says: You can tell more about a person by what they say about others than you can by what others say about them. We all have our own ideas, thoughts, opinions and judgements about people and the scheme of things, and many of us are very quick to condemn others for their actions and deeds when they seemingly conflict with our own views. Our judgements about others allow us to put people into boxes to help establish with some degree of certainty whether the person in front of us is friend or foe. We give them labels like stupid, selfish, intelligent, clever or naive to help us identify what we *think* they might be, but these labels are not necessarily right. How often have you instantly formed an opinion of someone, only to change your mind some time later when you've got to know that person a little better? In my experience, people who judge (and I count myself among them) haven't really paid much attention to why they believe what they do, neither have they spent time evaluating it against their own 'original-thinking metre.'

When we sit in judgement of others, we are comparing our ideas about someone's good and bad points with our own. All too often, we judge people who are very different from us as inferior. For example, we might become irritated with those who are not as driven, focused, organised or together as we are. However, when we judge in this way, we are comparing our *perception* of their weaknesses to our *perception* of our own strengths. Our strengths were once weaknesses that we overcame in a previous life, which the other person may have yet to overcome. If you have acquired these skills, it's because you worked on them and became good at them. You turned them into power. Disorganised, unfocused individuals may have other talents that we don't have, their disorganisation might allow them the space to think in more abstract ways, considering options that our logical left-brain, organised thinking can't even conceive of. With every negative there is always a positive in existence somewhere.

LET GO OF THE NEED FOR APPROVAL

I was at a friend's dinner party recently, where the usual question arose about what everyone around the table did for a living. I listened as one wonderful woman in her mid-forties, who'd just gone through a painful divorce, said: 'Oh, I'm just a mother.' She then went on to justify in a five-minute discourse why that was. I'd seen it so many times before with women who have chosen to stay at home to take care of their children, how they feel like they need to justify themselves to others who are 'out there' with 'proper' jobs.

I silently recounted all the times that I'd done the same thing in an effort to fit in, to be understood, to please others or portray the image that I believed would make me more acceptable to those friends and family members who didn't understand me. The ego is the part of us that is concerned about what others may think as it constantly seeks approval and validation from external sources. We can never hope to control the thoughts and opinions of others. People are going to think what they are going to think regardless of what we say and do. Their opinions are based solely on their own level of understanding (or ignorance) about life, and how much they're affected by their own degree of oughtism and judgements. More often than not, people are too concerned about their own state of affairs to be concerned about our lives, anyway. I have found that most people who are quick to judge us and pass an opinion have no more idea about life and its complexities than we do. Their outlook is based on their degree of oughtism. If other people think you are stupid, let them. That is their judgment. If you believe they are worth listening to, then listen, but if they are not, ignore them – suck it up and move on, regardless of who they are. Even if they are right, you will come to the same inevitable conclusion in your own time. We are only answerable to two things in all of this creation: our own conscience, and God. So, a word of advice: The next time someone asks you what you do for a living, say, 'Nothing – I just live.'

LET GO OF THE NEED TO CONTROL

So often in life, usually with the people around us, and in particular our nearest and dearest, we find that the way they live their lives doesn't suit us. We become irritated and frustrated that our own agendas are not being met, that people don't say or do things in the way that we believe is right. But as warriors on the path of truth, we have an obligation to accept how other people apply their free will, no matter how much we disagree. Not even the Supreme Being himself will go against the free will of another human being. So if we deem it our duty to control others by interfering in their free will, we are placing our self higher than God and engaging in arrogance, which is incompatible with the scheme of things.

When I came to New Zealand, my partner, Steve, in the throes of his desire to impress me, told me that he wanted to get fit, lose weight, get healthy, eat properly, stop drinking and smoking, etc. And I, the new girlfriend, eager to show him how much I'd learned about stress management and health over the years, embraced this with gusto. With his permission, I tried to help him, making suggestions about his diet, nagging him about alcohol consumption, dragging him to spinning classes and engaging a personal trainer. I even made him lunches to take to work. Two months into it, he became difficult and testy, more so than he normally was. He stopped taking my lunches and got irritated when anyone talked about healthy eating. We fought more and more. In reality, he wasn't keen to make changes. So I stopped interfering and let him get on with his life. After all, it's his body, his health. If it doesn't matter to him, why should it matter to me? He is the one who has to live with the consequences of his choices. I realised that I was making myself uptight by trying to control what he was doing instead of focusing on my own diet and wellbeing, which was actually declining because of the added stress of trying to influence him.

Accepting the free will of other people is a very liberating precept. It's the quickest way to free ourselves from pain and worry. Going against the free will of others is like trying to push lead uphill and it's the easiest way to make karma.

LET GO OF THE NEED TO BE RIGHT

We like to cling to ideas, opinions and points of view that we have developed over time. They make us feel that we understand a thing or two about life, giving us a sense of security and grounding, which is why we cling to them fervently, often refusing to accept another's point of view, even when we know ours are outdated.

Clinging, however, causes a great degree of difficulty and worry. How many times have we replayed an argument or a conflict over and over in our head, perhaps for days or weeks after an event has happened, in an effort to prove our rightness? It serves no other purpose than to give us a sense of satisfaction and keep us locked in the problem, when we should have moved on a long time ago. Brooding over problems and difficulties is a function of the ego. It wants to be right and it wants others to know that it's right.

How often have you sat around the table at a dinner party and listened to the plethora of points of view that each guest has about a particular subject? Notice when someone is speaking, how others around the table are eager to interrupt and share their own opinions with a captive audience. They don't really listen to what the speaker has to say. Instead they become restless as he drones on and on. They drum their fingers on the table, squirm in their seats and maybe let out a heavy sigh or two, indicating their desire for an opportunity to impart their own pearls of wisdom. The air often becomes heavy with tension and indignation as people struggle to air their own points of view. I used to be the same – biting my lip, sitting on my hands and waiting with bated breath to dive right in and take the opportunity to deliver my little gem of insight that might overshadow others and make me the hero of the hour. We aren't really interested in what people have to say, we just want to let them know that we have something to say.

When our cup is overflowing with our own ideas, opinions, judgements and points of view, we cannot hope to discover anything new. The more we cling to our rightness, the more the ego is strengthened. If we let go of our opinions, the ego starts to weaken.

LET GO OF ATTACHMENTS

Our journey through life is often made more difficult because of our attachments. We are attached to all kinds of 'stuff', which we are often completely unaware of. Even though I am a little embarrassed to say this, I was so attached to my Mercedes that I cried when I had to sell it. It had defined me and my success after a turbulent period in my life, yet it was just a tin box on wheels. But attachment goes way deeper than feelings of sadness when we get rid of our car.

Attachment is about *desire, clinging* and subconscious *obsession,* and it doesn't just manifest in material things, it relates to *anything* in life that defines us or represents security. Attachment is the desire we have that things should never change. We can become attached to our partners, our children, friends or family members. We may call it love, but when it becomes attachment, it becomes a dependence. We can be attached to our bodies, our careers, an illness or disease, our thoughts, emotions and the events of our past – all the beliefs, mistakes and regrets we have that prevent us from moving forward. When we become attached to anything, it destroys our ability for freedom.

How do we know if we are attached? The true test comes when we can't bear to part with something or someone. How would you feel if someone crashed your car tomorrow or stole all your money? If the thought makes you feel sick, then you know you are attached. Perhaps we are attached to a thought or belief – for example, a belief that we are inferior in some way. We may tell ourselves that we don't have inferiority issues, but we only have to observe the patterns that unfold in our lives to believe otherwise. Any belief about ourselves that we are attached to serves us in some way. A belief about our inferiority stops us from having to really stretch ourselves or push ourselves out of our comfort zone, because we believe that we'll never succeed. Perhaps the beliefs we hold about ourselves and others stop us from asking for help or support – or from reaching out in compassion to help another. All attachments are functions of the ego, and to progress on the journey towards truth, we need to let them go.

I am not suggesting that we should overcome our attachments overnight; that's an impossible task. We need 'stuff' to survive: a roof over our heads, money in the bank to buy food, and a car to drive so that we can go to work. We also need our ideas and opinions about right or wrong, two co-ordinates in the scheme of things to help us understand where we are. Without them we would flounder. The danger comes when we refuse to let go of these ideas and opinions or any tethers to people, places, things and events. Non-attachment is a gradual process of unravelling ourselves from the clutches of *maya* and the spell that it weaves around us. It's a process of evolution, not revolution.

Those who have learned to stop worrying and start living are those who seek *freedom* and *liberty* above anything else. Ironically, we believe ourselves to be free, yet freedom is the one thing we fear the most. Our desires and attachments become our prison. If we were to sit and analyse what actually goes on in our heads most days, we would realise that it's full of garbage, full of the same old thoughts, ideas, impressions, opinions, fears and judgements that keep us stuck. We could compare ourselves to a convicted criminal who spends his days behind bars, surrounded by armed guards and high-tech security systems and yet believes himself to be free. But we are mistaken. Through attachment we become our own judge, jury and jailer. Whilst there may be no bars on the windows and doors of our prison cell, *we* define the parameters for what binds us and what liberates us in life, through our attachments.

Here's a little exercise: Make a list of all those things that you seek *ahead* of liberty. If you are striving for power, success, financial gain, the perfect relationship, the perfect body, revenge and getting even, then these attachments will bind you here to the reincarnation cycle forever. If you are tired of these pursuits, then let go of just one thing – one desire, one attachment, one wasted emotion. Only then are you taking a brave step towards true freedom.

LET GO OF YOUR RELIANCE ON OTHERS

Freedom and aloneness are synonymous. We are often too reliant on others for our happiness, fulfilment and joy – our families, friends, colleagues and groups to which we belong. It is only in our aloneness that we can find truth. Unless we are capable of being alone, our search for identity and truth will remain unending.

The ego has a deep need to be needed, accepted and valued, and when we are alone, our whole sense of meaning disappears. This is one of the reasons we can't bear to be alone. Without the constant attention of others, many of us feel discomfort, a sense of sadness or anxiety, perhaps because we confuse aloneness with loneliness. They are not the same.

Loneliness is a misunderstood aloneness. With loneliness there is a gap, like something is missing. Aloneness has a splendour, positivity and beauty. Loneliness is negative, dark and bleak, but in aloneness there is easiness and peace, release from the tensions and disturbances (vibration) of being around others. When we are alone, we are free from all the judgements, whims and desires of others who pull us this way and that and cause us to stifle our true feelings. The ego and the false personality grows in accordance with the demands society makes upon it, and the true self is relegated into the background.

We come into this world alone and we leave it alone. The relationships, friendships, children, partners, colleagues and fleeting acquaintances are all temporary. Yet so often we become attached to them and rely on them to provide us with the meaning we fear we will never find. We are brought up in a social network as a member of a family and a society, and we are educated and trained to fit into society in the best way we can. However, if we become too engrained in a particular group or culture, we lose ourselves, becoming a slave to the way of that society. It defines how we think, feel and behave, and ultimately how we live our life. Rarely do we ever find our own rhythm, because it's contaminated by those parts of society we have been involved in since birth.

To discover true freedom, we must learn to let go of our reliance on others and start to become comfortable with our aloneness. This does not mean going into isolation or hibernation, but it does mean learning to spend more and more time alone. In aloneness we find a place where love, silence and a relaxed coolness settles. It is in our aloneness that true bliss can unfold.

It was Lau Tzu who said, 'When I let go of what I am, I become what I might be.' Letting go is one of the most freeing concepts on the journey towards truth. When we let go of the old, we create space for the new. When we let go of what we have, we open ourselves up to receive what we need. But sometimes it means that we have to step off the edge for a little while and allow ourselves to be carried along by the ebb and flow of life without clinging to the rocks. Safety and security is not to be found outside of us, it is only found within. It's taken me a long time to understand that.

When we begin to understand that our attachments, our judgements, our need to be right, our ideas, worries and concerns are all as a result of the ego, the part of us we must eventually destroy, we start to relish the idea of spending longer and longer periods adrift in the current of life. Letting go is about *surrender*, *acceptance* and *allowing,* words that I couldn't even begin to entertain as part of my vocabulary many years ago. Letting go is also somewhat of a paradox. It means permitting life to unfold without being apathetic, without making it a mad rush to the finish line with everything figured out, labelled and placed neatly in little boxes. It means having goals and aspirations without being attached to the outcome. It means letting relationships just be, without trying so hard to make them work. It means recognising when we are clinging or becoming rigid so that we can allow ourselves to be carried by the tide to the next point on our journey. Many times, the journey is not what we might expect. Yet, when our expectations are shattered, by letting go we can practise an acceptance of how things *are* rather than how we *want* them to be. Most of our desires stem from how *we believe* our world should unfold rather than how it *is* unfolding.

Letting go means turning arrogance into humility, judgement into acceptance, loneliness into aloneness, fear into courage and self-doubt into a deep-rooted trust in ourselves and our divine nature. It means giving up the need to be perfect in the eyes of the world. The ideas we have about perfection, not being good enough, not knowing enough, not having enough, the fears and the anxieties we have about being wrong and looking small or stupid are driven by comparison with others and the needs of the ego. If we allow the ego to drive our existence, we need to accept that we are going to be here for a very, very, long time. As the tale of the cracked pots at the end of this chapter illustrates, it's within our imperfections that we unearth our unique gifts and talents. If we have the audacity to accept ourselves as we truly are – rather than what we think we are, or should be, or want others to think we are – we begin to experience an inner beauty, peace and tranquillity. Letting go is God's law. It is a process of *being in the mystery* and finding our own way to live the mystery. By doing so, we allow life to flow through us, unimpeded until the mystery opens the doorway to *all* understanding.

THE CRACKED POT

A water bearer in India had two large pots, one hung on each end of a pole that he carried across his neck. One of the pots had a crack in it. While the other pot was perfect, and always delivered a full portion of water at the end of the long walk from the stream to the mistress's house, the cracked pot arrived only half full.

For a full two years this went on daily, with the bearer delivering only one-and-a-half pots full of water to his mistress's house. The perfect pot was proud of its accomplishments, perfect to the ends for which it was made. But the poor cracked pot was ashamed of its own imperfection, and miserable that it was able to accomplish only half of what it had been fashioned to do.

After two years of what the cracked pot perceived to be a bitter failure, it spoke to the water bearer one day by the stream: 'I am ashamed of myself, and I want to apologize to you.'

'Why?' asked the bearer. 'What are you ashamed of?'

'I have been able, for these past two years, to deliver only half my load because this crack in my side causes water to leak out all the way back to your mistress's house. Because of my flaws, you have to do all of this work, and you don't get full value from your efforts,' the pot said.

The water bearer felt sorry for the old cracked pot, and in his compassion he said, 'As we return to the master's house, I want you to notice the beautiful flowers along the path.' Indeed, as they went up the hill, the old cracked pot took notice of the sun warming the beautiful wild flowers on the side of the path, and this cheered it some.

But at the end of the trail, it still felt bad because it had leaked out half its load, and so again it apologized to the bearer for its failure.

The bearer said to the pot, 'Did you notice that there were flowers only on your side of the path, but not on the other pot's side? That's because I have always known about your flaw, and I took advantage of it. I planted flower seeds on your side of the path, and every day while we walk back from the stream, you've watered them. For two years I have been able to pick these beautiful flowers to decorate my mistress's table. Without you being just the way you are, she would not have this beauty to grace her house.'

The Invitation

It doesn't interest me what you do for a living. I want to know what you ache for, and if you dare to dream of meeting your heart's longing. It doesn't interest me how old you are. I want to know if you will risk looking like a fool for love, for your dream, for the adventure of being alive. It doesn't interest me what planets are squaring your moon. I want to know if you have touched the centre of your own sorrow, if you have been opened by life's betrayals or have become shrivelled and closed from fear of further pain. I want to know if you can sit with pain, mine or your own, without moving to hide it or fade it, or fix it. I want to know if you can be with joy, mine or your own, if you can dance with wildness and let the ecstasy fill you to the tips of your fingers and toes without cautioning us to be careful, to be realistic, to remember the limitations of being human. It doesn't interest me if the story you are telling me is true. I want to know if you can disappoint another to be true to yourself; if you can bear the accusation of betrayal and not betray your own soul; if you can be faithless and therefore trustworthy. I want to know if you can see beauty even when it's not pretty, every day, and if you can source your own life from its presence. I want to know if you can live with failure, yours and mine, and still stand on the edge of the lake and shout to the silver of the full moon, "Yes!" It doesn't interest me to know where you live or how much money you have. I want to know if you can get up, after the night of grief and despair, weary and bruised to the bone, and do what needs to be done to feed the children. It doesn't interest me who you know or how you came to be here. I want to know if you will stand in the centre of the fire with me and not shrink back. It doesn't interest me where or what or with whom you have

studied. I want to know what sustains you, from the inside, when all else falls away. I want to know if you can be alone with yourself and if you truly like the company you keep in the empty moments.

Oriah Mountain Dreamer

Story-teller, author, and spiritual teacher

Chapter 5

LOOK INTO NOT AT

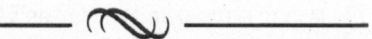

Watch with glittering eyes the whole world around you.
Because the greatest secrets are always hidden in the most unlikely places.
Those who don't believe in the magic will never find it.

Roald Dahl (1916–1990)
British author

have always found it difficult to make small talk. I never had a problem with deep and meaningful conversations about life, the universe and everything, but small talk just irritated me. In my corporate life, I really detested going to work-related functions, social gatherings, seminars, conferences or structured networking events where I had to strike up a conversation with people I didn't know – all in the aim of business and being nice. I always felt awkward and uncomfortable at the games people played to skirt around the real reason why they were having a conversation with me: to see if I could be useful in some way, if I might be able to get a letter to Richard Branson about a business idea they had, or – maybe to avoid standing there looking like a lonely lemon.

We have a standard, superficial repertoire when we meet people for the first time. It normally takes the form of seven questions, which go something like this: where do you work? what role do you perform there? where do you live? what car do you drive? are you married? what does your partner do? and, do you have children? When I mentioned I worked for Virgin, I would find myself surrounded by people all wishing to hear tales of Richard Branson and what he was like. When I left Virgin and worked for myself, it was a completely different story. Many times, when I connected with a person, after the superficial conversation dwindled, both of us found we had nothing left to say to each other. We would shuffle around uncomfortably, fiddling uneasily with our wine glasses or the buttons on our well-tailored suits, until one of us would politely find an excuse to move on and talk to someone else. Often being the 'deserted' and not the 'deserter', I would take it personally. It confirmed what I believed about myself: that I was a downright bore because I failed to present anyone with enough of a hook to keep them interested. It just added to the anxiety I already had about being at these events in the first place.

I came to realise that my own insecurities were built into my dislike of these events, and as I started to become more comfortable in my own skin, I would approach them with a certain amount of curiosity and amusement, rather than trepidation. I learned to observe the 'mating rituals' that took place between strangers as they endeavoured to establish some security with their surroundings, and I began to realise that I wasn't alone in my irritation. What we are party to in this ritual dialogue of the seven questions is the ego at work through the law of opposites and the concept of comparison. By asking the questions and comparing the responses with our definition of success, we superficially determine whether or not this casual acquaintance in front of us will be worthy of more time, effort and attention. From his responses, we establish ideas about his perceived standing in society, an estimate of his financial status, how successful we deem him to be in life and how valuable he might be to us. Most of us are incredibly shallow.

Most people look *at,* they don't look *into*. We see form and not content. We see what is on the surface and don't look deeper unless there is something in it for us. We see what we want to see and not what *is*. We are concerned only with outward appearances, social acceptability, or how useful someone or something might possibly be. People pride themselves on the size of their social networks, some even making businesses out of their long list of contacts. When I was part of the corporate world, I was exactly this way. In a world of constant pressure, with deadlines to meet and budgets to achieve, there was no time for anything else. We are generally only interested in those people that might benefit us in some way – add to our network, our social standing, or our capacity to get things done. Corporate life hasn't changed much in 2012, despite a recent global awakening of consciousness. As a human race, we have lost our ability to connect with, to have compassion for, to understand, not just our fellow human beings, but pretty well anything. It is without doubt one of the main reasons we are so stressed in life.

Shallow men believe in luck. Strong men believe in cause and effect.

Ralph Waldo Emerson (1803–1882)
American essayist, lecturer and poet

This ability to look deeper doesn't just relate to people; it relates to everything in life. Some people look, others see. Some people hear, others listen. Some people touch, others feel. One person drives past the golf course on his way to work and observes the autumn leaves on the road. But he thinks no more of it and drives on. He is busy with work, the meeting he has coming up, the new baby, his marital problems – why should he be thinking about autumn leaves? But another person looks at the leaves and asks why are all the colours the same? Why do the leaves need to change at all? It bothers him. So he thinks about it. He looks deeper, and when he does, he discovers the harmonious ways of nature. If leaves fall at the end of the season, they have to be reincorporated into the soil; nutrients have to go back into the earth. The leaf must be the colour of soil to be converted to soil, so the tree assists in this process, changing the leaf to the colour of the earth so that it will be of the same vibration, so that bacteria, earthworms and the whole of nature can now process this leaf and get it back into circulation as quickly as possible. If there was a build-up of leaves from season to season, in 200 years we wouldn't be able to drive past the golf course because it would be buried under kilometres of leaves. From this he can learn the axiomatic truth of living in harmony with nature and apply it to his own life. He learns to understand that there is a system, a flow, a natural scheme of things that we, too, are part of.

The difference between the ordinary man and the self-realised man is deep understanding. For what happens in the big picture can be found in the little picture, and vice versa. As above so below applies everywhere. Who would know that the keys to unlocking the secrets of the Universe are contained in a simple pack of playing cards?[11] That a termite mound holds the answers to many societal problems,[12] or that there is a mathematical formula that can be found in George Clooney's face, the Parthenon in Athens, the Egyptian Pyramids, plants, spirals in a snail shell, galaxies, musical notes, water crystals and the breeding cycle in rabbits which also applies to our own lives?[13] Everywhere we look, there is an opportunity to discover, but we walk around half blind, waiting for information to land in our laps neatly packaged and figured out so we don't have to think too much. We have become dulled to life.

An enlightening exercise to do (and a harsh one, for those of us who are life's know-it-alls) is to write down a list of all the things that it is possible to study in the Universe and rate yourself from one to ten on how much you know about each of the subjects – from aardvarks to zebras, from algebra to xenophobia. The list is endless and you will find that you know very little. I did. I had lots of zeros and ones against the things in my list. I was really embarrassed about how little I knew. After all, I went to school and college and studied hard. We seem to think that the only time we must learn is when we are at school. We get depressed and down in life because we are bored; we can't see the point of life after we have retired, lost our job or watched our children leave home. Depression is 'tired-mind syndrome' – we get tired of thinking, of rehashing life's problems and trivial matters. It's what makes us depressed. By making ourselves a list like this, and getting deliberate about learning, forcing the mind and the ego to focus on something different instead of life's problems, we can never be bored, *never*. There is a whole cosmic week's worth of things to get to know, and even then we probably won't be finished. God writes his message on the face of this round planet and everything in it. Yet because we are like machines, self-blind, we are unable to read it. So look for the patterns in life, look for the anomalies. They portray the natural rhythm and harmony of the Universe. There are formulas, patterns and reflections in everything, not just in our bathroom mirror.

We came here with a divine mission, which was to gather light through successive incarnations. We can't return unless we have that light, because then we have not fulfilled the promise we made to God. How do we gather light? We learn, we gather knowledge and wisdom. The more knowledge we gather, the more power we have over this illusion and the easier it becomes to liberate ourselves. The more we learn the more we can push the line between the possible and the impossible. What seems like absolute rubbish one day can propel us into another world of possibility the next. By learning to *look into not at*, we can learn to know God. It is impossible to understand or know the concept of the Supreme Being by meditating or reading the scriptures, even ones written by the most learned of sages. God is too vast, too paradoxical, too complex. If we want to know God, to love God, we can only do so by appreciating his handiwork.

So study *all* the things in this world with equal vigour. Don't just study spiritual subjects or subjects that you are interested in, like Madonna and the Cooking Channel; study *all* subjects: soap making, termites, forensic pathology, desert ecology, basket weaving, mathematics, blast furnaces, air conditioners, glaciers, volcanoes, human anatomy, quasars, earthworms, horses, book binding – everything under the sun and beyond. Pay particular attention to the beautiful things. Hermes Trismegistus says, 'For it is possible for the soul to also be deified while it lodgeth in the body of man if it contemplates the beauty of the good.' Just by broadening our interests and studying and contemplating the beauty of creation, we ourselves become a god. By appreciating beauty, we will raise our own vibration. It's also one of the quickest ways to alleviate stress. In this way at least we have a superficial understanding of the enormity of God and it will make us life's interesting people at dinner parties. (Maybe you will have better luck than I did at networking events, too.)

When we develop the ability to look into not at, it becomes easier to experience love and compassion for others. When we learn to know ourselves, we can learn to know others. In my corporate days, I believed the whole empathy and compassion thing to be somewhat wet. I wanted to get practical, real and tough, not wet. After all, that's what business was about. I was uncomfortable with the natural emotions I felt for others and didn't quite know how to incorporate them into my life as a leader and boss, so I suppressed them – there was no room for compassion unless you'd booked a sick day in advance.

Learning to look into not at means letting go of the judgements and opinions we have about another, some of which may have been formed over a very long time. It means letting go of the need to control or the need to be right. It means learning to visualise what someone is saying to us when they are speaking, instead of listening to the constant chatter of the ego in our head. It means letting go of the need to superficially define someone by his outward appearance or the title on his business card. When we start to look into not at, we start to learn to love – not a superficial love, which we have in many of our relationships and which is based on possessiveness, needs, wants or desires – but an all-encompassing love that knows no bounds; a love that is born out of beauty and curiosity; one that flows without effort or constraint. Even when we touch a rock or look at the trees, we can do so with love and an appreciation of the magic, fulfilment and joy that comes from looking at all of creation through a different-coloured lens.

The whole dynamic of creation is built on compassion. It is out of love and compassion that the Supreme Being, by creating a manifestation in which we could learn and grow, gave us the opportunity to brighten ourselves. He could have got practical and tough and wiped our names out of the Book of Life completely, as we weren't bright enough. By developing love and compassion for others, and for life itself, we move closer to liberation and we align ourselves with God and the scheme of things. The one who is full of love and compassion cannot deny even the lowliest of life forms. When you look at the hobo in the gutter, you are looking into the face of God – he is a divine fragment of the Supreme Being, just as we are. If we deny anything or anyone we are denying God himself.

MEDITATION – A PERSPECTIVE

When we develop a desire to look into not at, we start to have questions, perhaps hundreds of questions, about why things are the way they are. When we open ourselves up to the inexhaustible supply of knowledge out there, our world might appear to have been turned upside down. By developing the ability to meditate we can find answers to these questions.

The term *meditation* is used so frequently and in so many different ways in both Western and Eastern traditions, that I, for one, was confused as hell as to whether I was actually meditating or not. Meditation in the mind of the mystic is not about contacting your spirit guides and asking for help. That is a form of prayer. It's also not about visualising beautiful colours or chilling out after contorting yourself into a pretzel. That is relaxation. Neither is meditation about making the mind empty or focusing on the breath. That is concentration. However the exercise of stilling the mind and putting yourself into the present moment is an essential practice for those who want to lead a balanced life, develop spiritually and hear the voice of the true self.[14]

Meditation comes from the Latin word *meditatum*, which means 'to think or ponder'. It also comes from the word *meditatio*, which relates to any *scientifically* co-ordinated physical or mental exercise. In Eastern traditions it has been used to collectively describe a number of spiritual practices known as *dyana,* which translated means, 'to contemplate or meditate'. So meditation literally refers to any form of practice in which individuals can train their minds to enter, or self-induce, a specific mode of consciousness. Hypnosis is a form of meditation, or 'state induction', and so is prayer. So there are literally hundreds of styles of meditation practices. The key is understanding what you want to achieve and finding a system that works for you.[15]

The earliest source of meditation comes from the six *darshanas* – 'visions of reality'. The *darshanas* are Indian philosophies, or metaphysical systems, which share two axiomatic assumptions:

1. The doctrine of the endless cycle of rebirth, or reincarnation (which is associated with a cosmology of endless cosmic cycles);

2. The possibility of transcending phenomenal existence, of breaking free of the 'wheel of rebirth' and so attaining the state of eternal transcendent perfection (*moksha*, or release).

The darshanas are made up of *sutras*, or texts. One of the sutras is a yoga sutra, written by the sage Patanjali, which concentrates on an eight-fold path of Raja yoga, consisting of: *Yama* – observances; *niyama* – abstinences; *asana* – posture; *pranayama* - control of breath; *pratyahara* – control of senses; *dharana* – concentration; *dhyana* – meditation; *samadhi* – contemplation. (*Sama* means 'balance' and *adhi* means 'original' or 'ancient', a state in which we become attached to the divine reality.) Many meditative practices are based on these eight principles, or a combination of them.

Learning to meditate can only come about in stages. Anyone who has tried to meditate will know that the mind is never still. Many people give up the whole idea of meditating because the mind seemingly cannot be controlled, continuously hopping this way and that, and practice becomes too difficult. However, one way of learning to control the mind (and certainly not the only way) is by using the mind and its incessant activity as a way of meditating.

We are actually meditating or contemplating when we think deeply about any topic. In so doing, we are combining the skills of concentration and relaxation with meditation. As all things are connected with all other things, we can use the mind as a sort of 'mental librarian' to work out these connections and axiomatic principles. With practice, it can bring us the answers to any question we may have.

Meditation in this way can be a means of acquiring knowledge, which can make us independent of books and teachers. The mind becomes lazy when we allow the ego to take advantage of it. It spends its time thinking about errant thoughts and problems that serve little purpose other than to change our vibrational state and make us unhappy. By learning to make it work for a higher purpose, we can begin to use it as a valuable and powerful tool.

The first step in focusing the mind is to get our *mental librarian* to work by asking it questions: questions that it has to go and search for in the catalogues of our subconscious mind. Start with something simple that you'll be able to establish the answers to by normal means, *i.e.*, through a book or records. For example, what was the name of my second-grade teacher, or my best friend in first grade? Send it out to search for the answer and each time verify that it's correct, and it starts to give you confidence that the librarian is working. Later you can move on to more complex topics.

The second process is to use the mind in its natural way in response to more abstract questions. For example, how does the law of karma play out in your life? Sit in a comfortable position and watch where the mind goes. You'll notice that it will not slavishly obey you. If there is a sound or a distraction the mind will immediately focus on it. Perhaps you hear a car horn being sounded in the street. Instead of trying to ignore the sound and bring the mind back to a still point, ask yourself how the car horn relates to the question you posed. You might realise that the person behind the wheel of the car is impatient and uncomfortable. Someone is keeping him waiting, or there is someone in his way. Perhaps there are always people in their way. This is how his karma is operating in his life. Now, how does this apply to you? Perhaps you too are impatient, you don't like to wait an extra few seconds for anything, you don't like to stand in queues or experience delays, but it always seems that you are kept waiting for someone. This is perhaps your karma. You are kept waiting because you were impatient in your last life.

The next thing you hear might be a child having a tantrum in the neighbour's garden. What has this to do with you? You too cry when you experience pain, when your needs are not met or when you are disappointed. You lash out at others when you are unhappy or seek attention by sulking or withdrawing. Perhaps this is another clue as to how karma operates in your life. At the end of the session, the mind may have jumped to ten or more different things, but each time, instead of forcing the interruption away, you allow your mind to focus on it, allowing it to bring you an answer to your question, which brings karma into perspective for you.

By meditating in this way, we have made the ego work. It may cause the mind to jump around and focus on different things, but each time it makes an effort to escape, we force it to remain focused on the question in hand. If it wants to focus on the screaming child or the sound of the car horn, then let it, providing it brings back an answer. Eventually, after many battles, the mind submits and gradually becomes more disciplined. A disciplined mind is needed to do the deeper meditations that eventually result in *samadhi*.

Sometimes we won't find an answer because we don't yet have the insight or can't see the relationship between two abstract principles. But they begin to come in time. Even when our mind jumps to a topic that seems unconnected, there will always be a connection somewhere. The answers to our questions during meditation don't always come immediately; sometimes they come only much later, through a sudden flash of insight when all is still and quiet, or in a dream. I find that the answers to many of my questions come in that dreamy, half-waking-half-sleeping (theta) state first thing in the morning. The idea for this book came in a spinning class, when I was exercising like a demon and had stopped focusing on how to structure the content. During the year that I wrote this book, I found that I often benefited from taking a thirty-minute nap during the afternoon. When I awoke, some of the answers to my questions or dilemmas were resolved. In mythology, the answers to many of the heroes' problems come through dreams, visions or visitations from guides or messengers, which are forms of meditation. They indicate the location of the hero on his way down the spiritual path.

We can meditate in this way absolutely anywhere. We don't need a quiet sanctuary with candles and soft music to do so. In fact, it's probably better without them. We might need answers to our questions immediately, without waiting until the evening when we can sit quietly in our darkened room. By learning to meditate in any circumstances we build our resilience and expand the capacity of the mind as a valuable tool to be used when we need it.

Meditating in this way will ultimately help us to ascertain the truth about absolutely anything. By mastering our mind and the ego, we can start to receive answers, not only from our own subconscious, but also by tapping into higher and higher sources of knowledge on the mental plane.

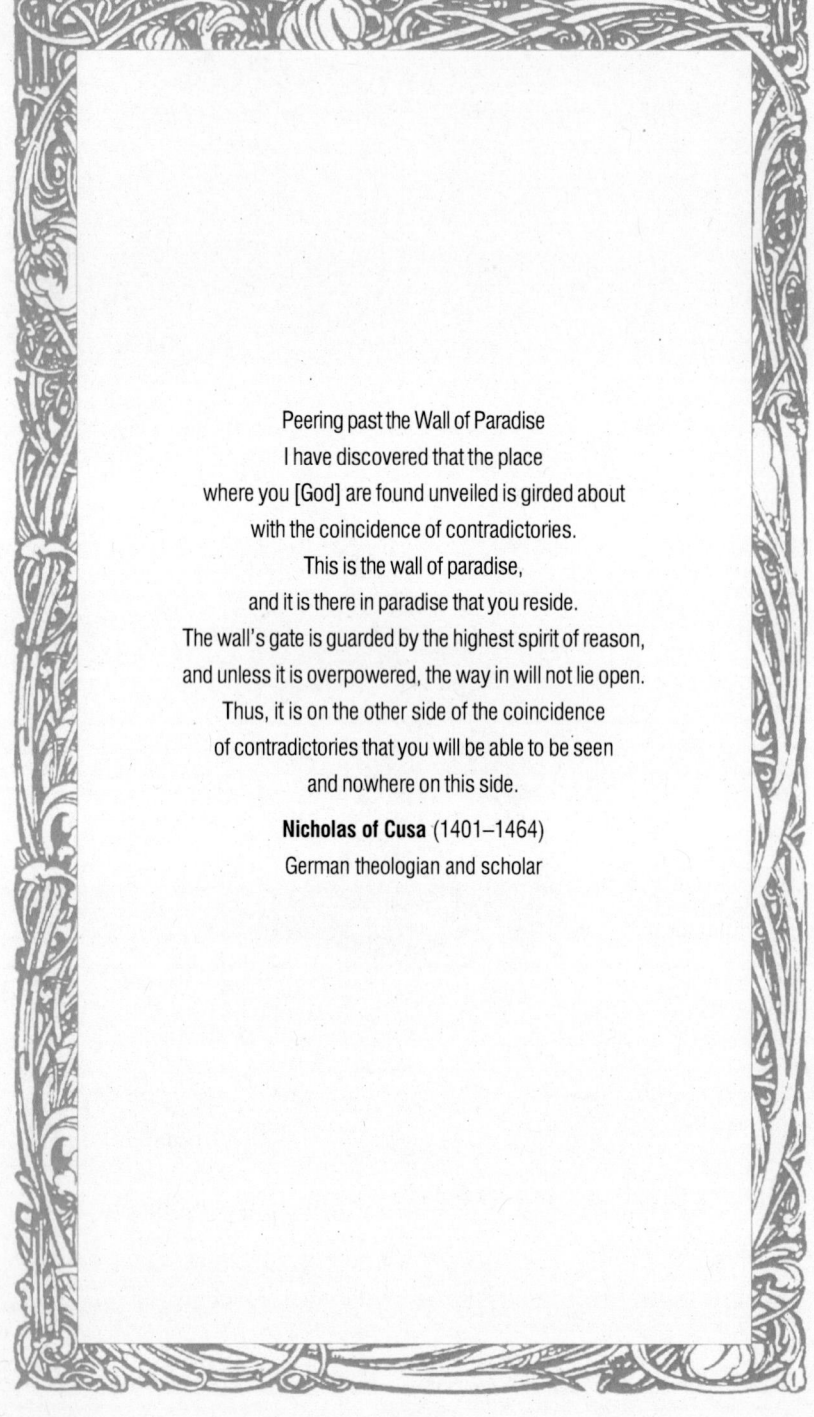

Peering past the Wall of Paradise
I have discovered that the place
where you [God] are found unveiled is girded about
with the coincidence of contradictories.
This is the wall of paradise,
and it is there in paradise that you reside.
The wall's gate is guarded by the highest spirit of reason,
and unless it is overpowered, the way in will not lie open.
Thus, it is on the other side of the coincidence
of contradictories that you will be able to be seen
and nowhere on this side.

Nicholas of Cusa (1401–1464)
German theologian and scholar

Chapter 6

CULTIVATE BALANCE

One who has control of the mind, is tranquil in heat and cold, in pleasure and pain, and in honour and dishonour, and is ever steadfast with the Supreme Self.

Bhagavad Gita

he journey of the spiritual warrior involves continuously striving for balance, not just a balance of the mind, but balance in all aspects of life, just as a tightrope walker traverses the small, thin wire between two poles on either side of a great ravine. So we can learn to do the same in life. This is why the spiritual path is often referred to as the 'narrow way'.

We are all at the behest of the ego and the dualistic nature of this universe – endlessly moving between the extremes of opposites: happiness and sadness, anger and passivity, confusion and stability. When we are balanced within, we are better able to cope, no matter what life throws at us. When we are in a state of imbalance, we experience frustration, stress, burnout, breakdowns, anxiety and depression. We get sick and we age quicker. This is why the spiritual warrior seeks balance above all things.

Balance applies to every aspect of our lives – physical, mental and emotional. It's not an overnight phenomenon. It can take years to cultivate, but it is the first step in the path of personal liberation and a stress-free life. The difference between the self-realised Adept and the rest of us, who are grovelling around here in the dust, is balance. Ultimately, when we are balanced we start to gain access to higher levels of consciousness, more than we can experience with our five senses alone. As we progress along the narrow path, our senses start to function in a heightened way, inwardly and outwardly, and our ego diminishes in equal proportion. As we become balanced, we start to recognise that rush-hour traffic doesn't irritate us as much, and we don't fly off the handle as quickly as we once did. People that exasperated us seem not to have the same infuriating ways. This state of balance is the prelude to experiencing what is known as the 'Ambrosia of the Gods', the 'Divine Intoxication', the 'Soundless Sound' of the Universe, which is the goal of all mystical practices around the world. Samadhi, nirvana and unio mystica are all transcended states where one's consciousness is exalted, becoming one with that of the Supreme Being. Achieving these states of ecstasy starts with simply seeking balance.

The more balanced we are within, the calmer and easier the journey through life becomes. Here are some ways that I have found that have helped:

ADOPT ANOTHER'S PHILOSOPHY UNTIL YOU FIND YOUR OWN

If the world seems chaotic and disordered out there, it's because there is chaos and disorder within. If there is nothing around you that seems dependable, it's because there is nothing dependable within. If the world seems like a hostile and difficult place, it's because there is hostility and difficulty within.

Without a personal philosophy in life, we are dragged through the streets by our emotions, inner conflicts and problems, lurching from one crisis to the next as life's worries and problems overtake us. Sadly, most of our philosophies about life are flawed in some way, fed to us or drummed into us by our parents, teachers, society or friends, all who are products of conditioned thinking. Quite often the philosophy that governs our lives is centuries old. We took them from our parents, who took them from their parents, who took them from our great-grandparents. Many of us go through life without challenging the foundation of the philosophy or beliefs we have, even when we know it comes from unreliable sources. That's fine, if it is working. If it's not, then we need to start questioning…everything. Don't just blindly accept things because they were passed to you from a perceived authority figure in your life or because it seems to be popular with 'the crowd'.

The Sufi poet Rumi said, 'It is easier to drag a mountain along by a hair than it is to emerge from the self by oneself.' We need a personal philosophy that makes sense to help us move on. If you are struggling in life, then find another philosophy that is perhaps completely different from the one you already have. Adopt that until you have challenged it enough to refine it into something that makes sense. This book, for example, might be a good place to start.

PAY ATTENTION TO YOUR BODY

Our own physical body possesses a wisdom which we who inhabit the body lack. We give it orders which make no sense.

Henry Miller

The answers to our problems in life can't always be found outside of us, but there are many clues which can be found within our own bodies. Most of us don't pay much attention to our bodies until we get sick. Sickness is an indication that things have gone too far. It's the body's way of telling us that there is something seriously wrong and that we are out of balance.

In my second bout of severe depression, I was at the end of my tether, physiologically. I couldn't sleep, I was constantly fatigued, moody and quick to anger, and found myself piling on the kilos again. I felt as if my body was continually 'wired'. When I should have been sleeping, I was wide awake, when I should have been wide awake, I wanted to sleep. My circadian rhythms were completely messed up. My only hope of getting some sleep was with high doses of sleeping pills, which sometimes didn't work – even if I took double or triple the dose. My GP couldn't help. My blood tests all registered 'normal'. He suggested that I enrol in a yoga class, continue with the anti-depressants and go to the gym, which I did. Eventually, in utter despair, I followed the advice of a friend to visit a stress and wellness practitioner named Laura McDermidt. She runs a health and wellness practice in Bryanston, Johannesburg, called All About Health, and it was she who introduced me to the SCIO machine.

The SCIO is designed to detect and treat the underlying causes of stress *before* they start to impact on the body's ability to cope. I, however, was already at breaking point. Laura immediately identified one of my reasons for being so debilitated as being due to severe adrenal fatigue (hypoadrenia) arising from prolonged stress and anxiety. The adrenal glands are responsible for secreting minute and precise steroid hormones, including adrenaline and cortisol, which assist in combating stress, into the body. When we are severely stressed for long periods of time, the constant demand that various stressors place on the adrenals weakens them considerably. Unless we treat them in a timely manner, they disrupt the entire hormone balance in our bodies, causing chronic fatigue, depression, mood swings, insomnia and the tendency to gain a lot of weight. I was astounded to know that many GPs don't recognise adrenal fatigue unless it's gone too far, in some cases becoming Addison's disease, which is life threatening. Instead many prescribe anti-depressants and sleeping pills when all we need to do is support our adrenals. I realised then that this was not the first time my adrenals had been 'shot' – they'd been running on empty for several years. Several treatments on the SCIO machine helped me to not only identify and remove the stressors that caused the imbalance, but also to take the correct supplements – naturopathic and homeopathic remedies that would encourage my body to heal and support the adrenals to function efficiently.

I learned a valuable lesson from this exercise about the terrible impact that stress has on our bodies. Most diseases are caused by stress of one kind or another. Even if we are not stressed now, the impact of previous stressful experiences – mental, emotional and physical – is stored in the cellular memory and, over time, weakens our bodies' ability to heal and function effectively. Adrenal fatigue is only one way in which the body responds to stress. We have been conditioned to listen to our bodies only when we get sick, only paying attention when we can't function effectively. Sickness is the body's last resort, forcing us to slow down so that it has time to recover. Just because we aren't sick, doesn't mean we are healthy.

Our body is changing all the time due to the different vibrations we experience every day – negative thinking, stress, toxic environments, poor quality food, lack of exercise, exposure to chemicals in our water, deodorants, sun creams, make-up, hair gels, etc. When we understand the concept of vibration and resonance, we learn that each cell in our body makes up our total IQ and vibration, and operates at a certain 'frequency'. As we interact with our environment daily, we experience changes in our moods and emotions as different waves of vibration push against us. Our cells work together to keep our body in balance; however, stress of any kind produces erratic vibrations that create imbalance, leading to disharmony, which is why we get sick. Viruses, bacteria, fungi and parasites all have resonant frequencies or vibrations. They multiply in environments where there is 'vibrational affinity', which is why we find that when our immune system is lowered, we are susceptible to attack by all kinds of pathogenic substances. Past traumas and experiences get stored in the body and often need to be treated before the body can heal. If we are not sensitive to our bodies, we may find ourselves out of balance far quicker than we think.

There are many ways to keep the mind body system in harmony and balance. However, I've found that monthly sessions on the SCIO, help me to subconsciously identify and treat what's happening in my body before I become consciously aware of it. Combined with a healthy diet and lifestyle, we can keep our body in balance. When our body is healthy, when our vibration is high, our thinking and emotions are more balanced.

BREATHE

When the breath wanders the mind also is unsteady. But when the breath is calmed the mind too will be still, and the yogi achieves long life. Therefore, one should learn to control the breath.

Yoga Swami Svatmarama (15th Century)

Author of *Hatha Yoga Pradipika*

Breathing is something we take for granted, something we do without thinking. Yet it is through consciously controlling our breathing that we can become calmer, more relaxed and more balanced.

We have a dualistic mind – one mind with two parts: the conscious and subconscious; the left and right hemispheres of the brain. The left brain – the conscious mind – is associated with thinking, reasoning, logic, and analytical and mathematical concerns, whilst the right brain is associated with the subconscious, artistic, creative, abstract concepts. In our current state of development, we can only use one part of our mind at one time. One of the goals of spiritual development is to integrate the two aspects of the mind so that we can use them harmoniously. By integrating the two aspects of our mind, our life automatically starts to become more balanced. Breathing exercises present us with an opportunity to do this.

When we sleep or are deeply engrossed in other things, the subconscious part of our mind keeps our body alive. It regulates our breathing, controls our heartbeat and adjusts the temperature changes in our body. When we are awake, we can consciously take over control of the breathing function from our subconscious. We can hold our breath, breathe more deeply, slow our breathing down, take an extra breath, stop breathing altogether. The subconscious part of our mind still controls our body temperature and heartbeat (although some mystical Adepts have been known to consciously control these functions, too), but we can control our breathing. It is the single aspect of our being that is controlled both consciously and subconsciously. This is why breathing exercises feature in many religious or mystical disciplines. Through breathing exercises, we can learn to forge a bond between the two different aspects of our mind and eventually integrate them. A mystical Adept is someone who has an integrated mind. When we are totally balanced in everything, including our mental capabilities, we can ultimately break free from the wheel of birth and death.

Most of us don't breathe properly, particularly when we are stressed. I don't – my breath is often shallow and infrequent, and I can find myself light-headed and lethargic as a result. Every cell in our body needs oxygen to survive, so if for no other reason than our health, a proper breathing exercise is a necessity. When you find yourself tense, stressed, anxious, fearful or upset, check your breathing and you will discover you are either shallow-breathing or holding your breath. By merely breathing deeply into your abdomen when you become aware of this, these negative emotions dissipate almost immediately.

Breathing exercises practiced daily for only ten minutes a day can result in a calm and focused mind. The more you practice, the more relaxed and focused you become, as energy is channelled rather than scattered. If I don't do my exercises in the morning I feel kind of adrift during the day. When you focus your attention on your breath for an extended period of time, your brain waves cycle down from the waking *beta* state (thirteen to forty cycles per second) to the *alpha* state (seven to fourteen cycles per second). This is the state we experience during sleep and hypnosis. In this receptive state, it is much easier to actually work with the subconscious mind and change negative emotions or behaviours.

Square, or rhythmic, breathing produces amazing positive results whenever you are feeling anxious, nervous, excited or fearful and you would like to calm yourself. It has also been reported as a way of loosening the astral body and building the intuition and psychic abilities. Some people may just feel calm and relaxed, others will have different experiences. I have on occasions felt a bit 'floaty', like I am falling forward towards the floor even though my body is sitting upright. Sometimes I have seen visions and faces as if I am dreaming while I am awake. This is perfectly normal. This exercise is also the first step to loosening the astral body from the physical body and integrating the subconscious and conscious minds. It's simple, and very effective. I use it daily as a discipline, in the morning and evening, for as long as I need to. In fact, it can be practised anywhere – I use it often while I am driving or watching TV, or to calm myself before speaking to a group or doing anything that I am nervous about. It works like this:

Breathe in through your nose to a count of five. Hold to a count of five. Breathe out through the nose to a count of five. Again hold to a count of five. Then repeat the same process over until you reach a calm state.

You can use any number you like to count – I use five. However, keep it consistent – the in-breath, the out-breath and holds need to be the same length. I find it helps to focus my mind if I imagine that I am creating a 'square' while I am breathing. The in- and out-breaths are the vertical lines, the holds are the horizontals ones. Work in a clockwise direction.

BECOME INDIFFERENT

If someone remarks what an excellent man you are and this pleases you more than his saying 'what a bad man you are,' know you are still a bad man.

Sufyan Ath Thawri (d. 778)

Sufi mystic

Travelling the Path of Love

Being indifferent does not mean becoming disinterested, apathetic or uncaring about life. Indifference is the equilibrium that comes from understanding – a product of balanced thinking and emotions and a solid personal philosophy. When we are indifferent things no longer bother us as they used to. We don't get upset any more. One of the ways to become indifferent is by focusing on the present and living in the *now*. It is only when our consciousness is in the present moment that we have the capacity to control the ego – the capacity to choose, and the capacity to act. In this way we can transcend the law of opposites and become masters of our own universe. Eventually, by practicing living in the *now*, we find that we actually have no other place to live. Yet, so often we allow our consciousness to slip into the past or the future when feelings of guilt and fear seemingly debilitate us.

I have lost count of the number of times that I've lain in bed, tossing and turning, wracked by guilt over the mistakes I've made. If you're anything like me, you will be familiar with the dialogue: 'Why did I do that, I should have been more careful, they must have thought I was absolutely stupid, what a dumb thing to say. If only I could change it.' On and on I go, until I am literally sick of the sound of my own voice. By rehashing the events of the past over and over in my head, I am actually participating in a fruitless pastime: seeking to exercise my power, my capacity to think, to feel and to act in a time that is already past.

There is nothing in the universe that is unconscious. Everything is in the process of evolving, moving from one state to the next. Nothing is bereft of consciousness. But if we have to find a definition for unconsciousness, then this is it: If we let the *now* slip into what *has happened*, we have become unconscious; if we let the *now* slip into what we fear *may happen*, we have become unconscious. And if we continue to carry these two burdens – fear of the future and guilt of the past – then we are going to get very tired and very sick and spend the rest of our days in misery. And when we die and do our triple review, we will remember reading this section in the book and slap ourselves hard on the forehead in frustration. Only then will we realise that we could have saved ourselves forty years of worrying and despair. What is done is done. Let it go.

I am not suggesting that by becoming indifferent we ignore what is done. Our job here is to learn, so, yes, we must learn from our mistakes. But we also need to accept that we can't change them. Every action we took was the sum total of everything we had available to us *then* – the sum total in terms of being awake inside, in terms of being conscious, the amount of insight we had into the situation, our level of understanding and wisdom. With all of this, we chose to do whatever it was that we chose to do. When we are angry, upset, afraid or depressed, we make decisions or take actions that we often regret. That is because we are not operating with our full quota of consciousness enabling us to consider carefully every aspect of the situation we are in. What we know with hindsight, to be right *now*, we didn't know *then*. However, whether the decision or action was good, bad, right or wrong is irrelevant. If we think we made a bad decision, it is only relatively bad by *comparison* to something else. By lying in bed and comparing our plight with what should be, could be, ought to be or must be means we are fighting a futile battle, a comparison with the law of opposites and the ego.

Knowledge and ignorance are degrees of consciousness, two poles of an opposite. Ignorance, or *avidya,* to use its Sanskrit term, is due to imbalance. If we move towards balance, we can gain greater levels of knowledge and understanding.

When we are balanced, we have greater access to the subconscious mind, which gives us a greater capacity to make the right choices using insight and intuition, and we will spend less time regretting them. Those who become balanced no longer fight, because they no longer compare where they were or where they think they should be to where they are now. They sail on the ebb and flow of life, not affected by either of the opposites. So stop fighting. It is going against the scheme of things. Stop comparing, become indifferent and live in the *now*.

When I have been uptight and anxious, fearful of what may happen, has happened or is happening, I have spent some time – often only a matter of seconds – quietly focusing on *open space* or the *space in between*. Even when life is hectic, and the world is pushing me to achieve deadlines and targets, when my world is abuzz with activity, by focusing on the space in between I can start to become indifferent.

The space in between is the nothingness (or seeming nothingness) between one physical object and another. The space between you and the screen of your computer, or you and the pages of this book. Wherever we look there is space: space between the words on this page, between your thumb and your index finger, or between you and the person that is yelling at you right now. Be aware of the space, the fact that you can distance yourself from whatever is happening physically, mentally and emotionally. It brings you back to the present moment, giving you a chance to collect rampant thoughts, stop tempestuous emotions, and choose how to respond. Most of all, it helps reduce stress and anxiety. The space in between brings an instant sense of calm. This exercise does not require effort. It is not about imagining distances or anything like that. It is about feeling and sensing, and it works.

SIMPLIFY YOUR LIFE

It is easier for a camel to pass through the eye of a needle than for a rich man to enter the kingdom of Heaven.

Mark 10: 25

If we become one of life's people-watchers we can learn a great deal about how to live our life, what to do and what not to do. Start paying attention to your friends and colleagues. Silently watch what they do and how they behave. Pay attention to their ethical and moral development and how the ego plays out in their interactions with others. Look at what motivates them and drives them. If you take time to observe the course of their lives, you will notice that they all have many things in common; that there is a certain human formula for existence.

They all have houses, they all have jobs, they all have children and holidays and bank accounts and money and cars and the gadgets and technology and they all want more – more money, bigger houses, more holidays, more expensive cars, the latest technology and equipment, more time watching sport, more evenings out at restaurants – more, more ,more, more, more. In all cultures across all civilisations, everyone wants more. It doesn't matter if your subject is a primitive Aborigine living in the Australian outback, or Bill Gates – they all want more. A rich man will never seek to be mediocre – he will strive hard to retain his riches and gain more. A poor man, too, will strive for riches because he no longer wants to be poor.

This 'more' formula doesn't seem to be working from a mystical development point of view, as there are many people still here in this world, including me, who have not made it back to Heaven. The Universe is sending us a BIG CLUE here: If your goal is to stop worrying and start living, and this model isn't working for you, then try something different. Even if you are not sure what to do, just make sure that it is not what everyone else is doing. Look at what other people are doing and be different from them.

Every possession and every happiness is but lent by chance for an uncertain time, and may therefore be demanded back the next hour.

Arthur Schopenhauer (1788–1860)

German philosopher

Abandoning the human formula is easier said than done. We all want the nice things in life and find it very difficult to be satisfied with the bare minimum. So we have to examine what it is that is driving our desires, because it is our desires that cause us to strive and worry. It is our desires that keep us coming back to this world again and again. More often than not, our desires are driven by the ego who will, through the act of comparison, have a good old look at what everyone else has, and want the same – or better.

We fool ourselves into believing that we need more. We don't. We need food, we need shelter, we need transport, we need a partner to share the load. What we *want* is the best wine and sushi every day, a mansion by the ocean in several countries around the world, a sports Mercedes and a 4x4, plus a whole heap of boyfriends and parties every year to keep us entertained! So we need to learn to pursue our needs and not our wants by gathering only the material things around us that are sufficient to fulfil our needs. This means learning to make our wants the same as our needs. If we want only the simple things in life, then we become very easily satisfied. Getting everything we want is an acquired taste.

Smoking is the same as getting everything we want. I hated the taste of my first cigarette. It made me dizzy, light-headed and nauseous. I had to work hard to learn to smoke (and work at it anew every time I decided to resume the habit after giving up). I didn't particularly want a cigarette when I started smoking, but try taking cigarettes away from me a few years down the line when I was in 'full smoking swing' and I would drive to the nearest garage at two o'clock just to get my fix. So if we acquire the taste for simple things, make our wants the same as our needs, we can become fulfilled even though we are getting by on less.

TAKE THE MIDDLE PATH

Life is like riding a bicycle - in order to keep your balance, you must keep moving.

Albert Einstein (1879–1955)

German physicist

Have you ever met those people in life who try to be too perfect? The ones who are fanatical about exercising, eating properly, thinking only happy thoughts, losing weight, being disciplined, sticking to a routine, and following the rules? They latch onto an idea and follow it through to its extreme conclusion, often trying to convince everyone else in the process that they should be following suit. Fanatical vegetarians are a good example. Besides not eating meat, they won't eat animal products such as eggs or butter. Then they take it one step further and decide they can't eat a certain vegetable, like a carrot, because it is taking the life of a plant. So they stick to eating fruit alone. Then they believe that the fruit doesn't belong to them, it belongs to God, and so they must be committing a sin if they take this beautiful apple from a tree – so now they live on fresh air and water.

I am exaggerating, of course, but I know from my own experience that sticking fanatically to an extreme regimen – the Atkins diet, for example – may produce some good results in terms of body shape and enable me to squeeze into the size 12s that I kept in my 'thin cupboard' for the odd occasion that they might still fit. But it eventually becomes really bad for my body and I start to get sick. So I revert back to my normal diet and pile on more weight than I needed to lose in the first place. Trying to be too good can eventually become bad, not to mention really irritating for others, and it's a product of imbalance.

Many think that the spiritual path is about asceticism, about giving up everything we like so that we can follow the path of truth. In the same way that the materialistic 'more' formula is unbalanced, so is the path of the ascetic. Materialism and spirituality are two extremes of the same scale. Think of them as the two wings of a bird; if one is missing, the bird cannot fly. The spiritual warrior seeks to balance the two extremes by allowing material values to go side by side with spiritual ones. Equal attention must be devoted to either side, provided that it does not become fanatical. Fanaticism too, is unbalanced. Both materialism and spirituality are instruments to help us achieve our ultimate goal, and we should not consider them to be goals in their own right. We can't focus on developing spiritually if we are worried about money and our future. And neither can we develop spiritually if we are totally focused on material gain. To achieve our ultimate goal in life we need to seek balance, and this means taking the middle path in everything.

By practicing moderation in everything we do, we can start to simplify our life and bring the material and spiritual together. So, don't eat too little or too much. Don't yell at your children every day but don't let them run around and become little monsters, either. Don't sleep too much or too little, don't work so hard that you have no time for other things. Don't become fanatical about your weight and your body shape like the size zeros in Hollywood, but don't allow yourself to become unhealthy and overweight, either. By all means have an opinion, but don't force it down other people's throats. Set boundaries and principles for yourself, but learn how to relax them when they are not really necessary. By practicing moderation and consciously bringing balance into our lives, our thinking becomes more balanced too. When our thinking is balanced, we can ultimately become calmer and more relaxed about life.

CULTIVATE TRANQUILLITY

Find a place inside where there is joy and the joy will burn out the pain.

Joseph Campbell

I spent a lot of time believing that peace of mind would somehow descend on me when I got everything else right in my life, when I'd earned enough money, found myself in the right country in the right profession with the right relationship. I quickly learned that it wasn't to be the case. We actively need to cultivate tranquillity in our lives by working at it ever day. Tranquillity means serenity, contentment and being even-tempered. These things result in balance and are the ideal platform from which to reduce anxiety and stress. If we can be balanced and serene and even-tempered in the most trying of circumstances, then our vibration will be much higher and we can rise above our problems and difficulties with ease. We can only do this by becoming indifferent, living in the now, simplifying our needs and becoming aware of our thoughts, emotions and desires.

We can, of course, cultivate tranquillity by ducking out of the world and living in a cave for the rest of our life, but I for one don't want to do that – the beds are too hard and I like some of the nice things that modern day living has to offer. Whatever we do, we can never duck out of life completely. Living as an ascetic or a monk removed from the world may be okay for awhile, but we always have to come back again at some point and start over. Ducking out, in whatever form it takes, is an extreme form of imbalance. Even suicide means we only go the astral plane to come back again to this physical world, probably with a heavier karmic load than when we left.

Cultivating tranquillity requires daily effort. It means being conscious of our vibrational state and actively taking time to keep our vibrations high. It means hanging out with people who lift us and don't bring us down. It means taking time out each day for our self, some time to be alone perhaps for a discipline or a spiritual practice, meditating, breathing, walking in nature, reading, playing music or any other activity that keeps our vibration high. By cultivating tranquillity in this way, we begin to get control of this 'illusion of life,' and not the other way around. Once we are in control of the illusion, we are very well positioned to get out of it.

THE KUNDALINI IN PRACTICE AND MYTHOLOGY

It is ultimately through balance, imagination, meditation and concentration that the *kundalini* energy, latent in all human beings, is released. The kundalini is an unconscious libidinal force, corporeal energy, or *shakti,* which lies coiled at the base of the spine. We feel this energy during orgasm. It is often depicted as a goddess or a sleeping serpent, hence many English references to the 'serpent power'. Kundalini means 'coiled'. When it is released, it travels upwards via the *nâdis* – meaning 'rivers' or 'flow', and is referred to in yoga as *ida, pingala* and *shushumna* – to reach the 'thousand-petalled lotus', or crown chakra. The nâdis sit on either side of the spine in the astral body and are associated with the left and right hemispheres of the brain. Ida is associated with the right side of the brain – female energy; pingala with the left side of the brain – male energy.

In mythology they are referred to as the 'twin pillars upon which all of creation rests' and are portrayed in the Hebrew scriptures as Boaz and Joachim, the two pillars in Solomon's temple. They are also depicted in the major arcana of the Ryder Waite tarot deck – the High Priestess (Card number 2) sits between two pillars. The Tree of Life glyph in kabbalah relates to the two pillars of severity and mercy and we find them as yin and yang in Chinese philosophy. Ultimately the twin pillars symbolise balance and the need for the mystic to travel the middle path between two pillars.

The three nadis also relate to the Caduceus of Hermes: the two snakes coiled around a staff symbolize the kundalini, or serpent-fire. The wings signify the power of conscious flight through higher planes. The myths also suggest that Hermes saw two serpents entwined in mortal combat and so separated them, bringing peace and harmony between them; thus, the Caduceus is often recognized as being a sign of peace and balance.

In alchemy, the two serpents are referred to as sulphur and mercury, sulphur (pingala) being red-hot and dry, likened to the sun, and the ida correlated with the moon and silvery mercury. The allegorical tale of the Chymical Wedding is symbolic of the merging of these male and female elements. It is through internal balance and inner and outer alchemical practices that the alchemist undertook the 'great work', the 'magnum opus' – the balanced mystical and spiritual state from which he created the philosopher's stone, symbolising enlightenment and heavenly bliss. From the stone, the alchemist could craft the 'elixir of life', or the ambrosia of the Gods, the nectar that rejuvenates and extends the life of any human being. The ambrosia was typically reserved for divine beings, ones who had trodden the thorny path of spiritual development and recognised their own divine nature. Hercules is given the ambrosia by Athena, while the hero Tydeus is denied the same thing when the goddess discovers him eating human brains, symbolic of his base, animal, egoic nature. One of the crimes that sent Tantalus to the underworld was his attempt to steal the ambrosia and give it to other mortals, once he had tasted some of the liquid himself.[16]

The different stages of the magnum opus related to rainbow colours that the mystic alchemist saw in his inner vision, expressing the inner alchemy, the fundamental change in his nature. This symbolism is illustrated in mythology by the rainbow. In Greek mythology, Iris is the goddess of the rainbow. The fairy Hope, in Pandora's box, had rainbow wings. In Norse mythology, Bifröst was the burning rainbow bridge between Midgard (the world) and Asgard, the realm of the gods.

With the rising of the kundalini, the seeker starts to experience an expanding extrasensory awareness. Empathy, intuition and psychism increase. It is the kundalini energy that propels the mystic to Nirvana. The kundalini is stimulated through different mystical practices, such as

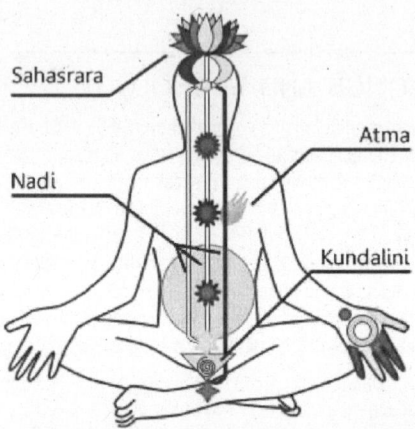

Pranayama, which involves alternate breathing through the left and right nostrils. Rhythmic breathing and other special breathing techniques influence the flow of these energetic currents through the chakras. (In Hindu mythology, each chakra is ruled by an incarnation of goddess Parashakti, also recognized as Brahma, the creator.) Every system of mysticism has a practice which stimulates kundalini. For example, it can be awakened by Pranayama, Asanas and Mudras through Hatha Yoga; by concentration and training of the mind by Raja Yoga. The exercises are generally only dispensed by a teacher when the pupil has reached an appropriate state of balance and absence of desire, and has control of his thoughts and emotions. Kundalini is no child's play, as Carl Jung describes:

One often hears and reads about the dangers of Yoga, particularly of the ill-reputed Kundalini Yoga. The deliberately induced psychotic state, which in certain unstable individuals might easily lead to a real psychosis, is a danger that needs to be taken very seriously indeed. These things really are dangerous and ought not to be meddled with in our typically Western way. It is a meddling with Fate, which strikes at the very roots of human existence and can let loose a flood of sufferings of which no sane person ever dreamed. These sufferings correspond to the hellish torments of the chönyid state....

C. G. Jung
introduction to *The Tibetan Book of the Dead*

Taking exercises from books to stimulate the kundalini can be dangerous and cause severe mental and emotional imbalances, which cannot be reversed. This is often referred to as the *kundalini syndrome*. Our samskaras, karma and experiences from our previous lives impact on how the kundalini energy unfolds within us. The practice of kundalini yoga can take upwards of fifteen to twenty years, but some modern day teachers report that they can help a pupil achieve it within six to eighteen months. As the process is associated with the nervous system, kundalini awakening causes a dumping of adrenaline into the body. 'Frying the system' then becomes a real possibility and danger. If the kundalini is awakened without suitable preparation and guidance, it can cause debilitation, insanity, a breakdown of the immune system, prolonged depression, anxiety, spiritual pain and suicide. Quite simply, playing with energy, any energy that we don't understand, is perilous and is openly discouraged by many spiritual disciplines.

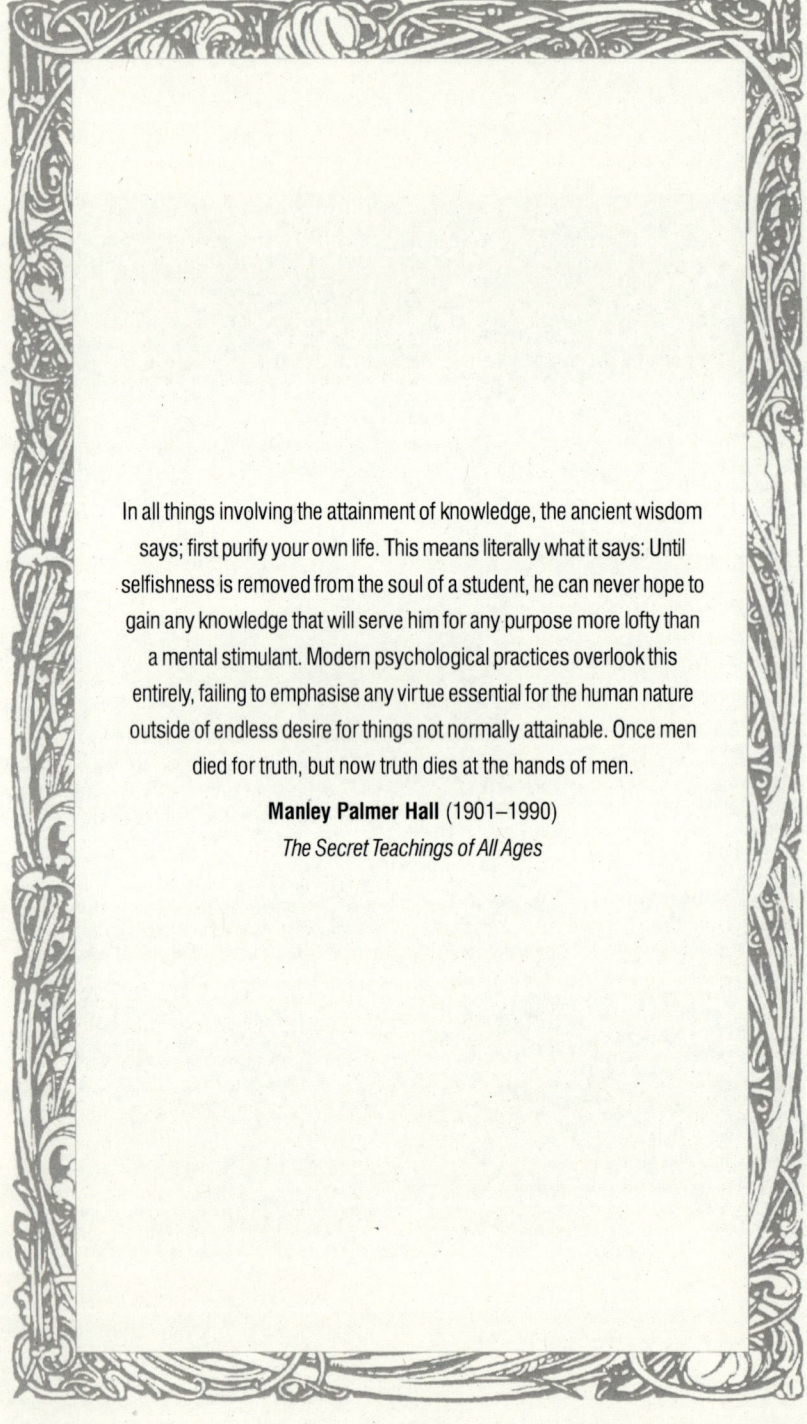

In all things involving the attainment of knowledge, the ancient wisdom says; first purify your own life. This means literally what it says: Until selfishness is removed from the soul of a student, he can never hope to gain any knowledge that will serve him for any purpose more lofty than a mental stimulant. Modern psychological practices overlook this entirely, failing to emphasise any virtue essential for the human nature outside of endless desire for things not normally attainable. Once men died for truth, but now truth dies at the hands of men.

Manley Palmer Hall (1901–1990)
The Secret Teachings of All Ages

Chapter 7

CHARACTERISTICS OF A SPIRITUAL WARRIOR

e often hear people describe themselves or others as being 'very spiritual', yet they are often at odds about what they mean by the term. Being spiritual generally refers to people who participate in some spiritual activity, who pray, or meditate, who read spiritual books, read the tarot cards, who go to *satsanghs* (spiritual assemblies), who chant or dance, heal or teach. Being labelled as spiritual indicates an interest in spiritual things: the mysterious, the unexplained, the secret and hidden. The term typically describes what people *do,* but not necessarily who they *are.* And this is where our difficulty starts: What are the characteristics of someone who is deemed to be spiritual? If spirituality is not about what we do – the religious, healing or spiritual practices we are involved in – how do we know if we are spiritual or not?

I have met many people who consider themselves to be spiritual, and yet use every opportunity to accuse others as wrong and to present themselves as right. They find ways to put others down, to lambaste others for their failings, to make others look small, so they can elevate their own importance. Some of these people have been self-appointed healers, counsellors, seasoned satsangh attendees or church goers. They may have some spiritual notions and ideas about the scheme of things, but within themselves, there is an unresolved anger, a sense of imbalance and a conflict with the world; a need to make everyone else wrong and themselves right; a need to pass along ideas, judgements and opinions in order that they can shine. Of course, we all have our dark shadows, our petty judgements, jealousies, imperfections, irritabilities and failings. I know I do. Even the greatest gurus and most seasoned meditators are not perfect. That's what makes us human, that's why we are here, to learn to smooth off the rough edges.

I believe that one *feels* the essence of spiritual individuals – we feel their soul through the subtle energy they emanate. They seem to light up a room when they enter it. You can sense their presence even when your back is turned, and when you look into their eyes, there is a depth, an understanding, a gentleness and sincerity which seems to know no bounds. We probably don't pay much attention to them at first, because they might indeed look to be quite ordinary. Yet they carry an air of complete calm, a quiet self-confidence that oozes from every pore. They aren't caught up in the bluster of life like we are, and are happy to blend into the background or stand in the limelight, whatever the task they assume demands of them. Yet these people may not have picked up a single scripture or uttered a single prayer in their lives.

The characteristics of a spiritual warrior are often to be found in the myths and legends, in the tales of gallantry and heroism. One example can be found in the tales of King Arthur and the Knights of the Round Table.

SIR GAWAIN AND THE GREEN KNIGHT

There was a time towards the end of the year in Arthur's court when all the knights had gathered together for a Christmas festival. As they set about their merrymaking, a gigantic man clothed in green rides into the middle of the great hall. He challenges the knights to behead him. Sir Gawain rises to the challenge and cuts off the head of this mysterious character in one blow. The Green Knight gathers up his head and climbs back on his horse, but before he leaves, he issues another challenge in the form of a prophecy: He says to Gawain, 'In one year and a day from today, you will come to my castle and I will behead you. I have offered myself to you willingly today and so you must do the same.' And with the challenge still resounding around the great hall, which had fallen into a deathly silence, he disappears into the night.

Now Gawain is in a spot of bother. He is a knight. He is courageous and does not shirk his duty. He has to find the castle of the Green Knight, and for a whole year and a day he searches in vain. Along the way, he meets many comrades. One of them, the beautiful wife of a king, is very hospitable but tries endlessly to seduce him with her beauty while her husband is away. Sir Gawain refuses. On the day he leaves her, the last day of his search, she presents him with a belt, a powerful talisman that she says will protect him from any misfortune. He initially takes the belt, feeling a little afraid of what is to befall him, but thinks better of it and refuses this too. He knows deep down, that this will give him an unfair advantage.

Eventually, with only hours to spare, he comes across the castle of the Green Knight where he presents himself on bended knee to meet his fate. The Green Knight makes as if he is going to kill Sir Gawain, but just before he is about to swing his sword down onto the knight's exposed neck, he stops, and smiles. 'This was a test,' he says. 'Because of your bravery, steadfastness and integrity, because you refused to give in to temptation, I spare your life, and set you free.'

In the few paragraphs below, I have tried to articulate the characteristics and qualities of a spiritual warrior as I see them. In addition to the weapons and tools we have discussed earlier in this section – letting go, balance, looking into not at – there are certain characteristics that we need to cultivate on this path if we are to make any progress. They are characteristics that I endeavour to master in my own life, although I don't always get them right. If we could learn to practice just one or two of them, maybe our world would be less fraught with anxiety.

CLEAR VALUES AND BOUNDARIES

Man is lost and is wandering in a jungle where real values have no meaning. Real values can have meaning to man only when he steps onto the spiritual path, a path where negative emotions have no use.

Sri Sathya Sai Baba (1926–2011)
Indian spiritual teacher

In life, we often get really bent out of shape when we believe people have insulted us or caused us pain. It's what causes us to worry and fret. But if we understand what we value and what our boundaries are and why, it helps us to make easier decisions when it comes to taking action and deciding what issues are going to occupy our minds and sap our energy.

In Johannesburg I owned a gun – a Glock 17 semi-automatic pistol. When one owns a gun, one has to know two things: The first is to know how to use it and use it well; and the second is to be certain that you can take a human life if the situation demands. When an intruder – sometimes several intruders – enter your house with a knife or a gun, threatening your life or the life of those you love, there is no time to get clear on your values or overcome the existential angst about taking the life of another. You don't have hours to write down a long discourse on whether or not what you are doing is right; when your life is in danger, you have to make a split-second decision and take action. Or not. It's quite often a choice of your life or his. The difference between those who live and those who die is the ability to know with absolute 100% certainty that their boundaries have been pushed and that they know what they will do when faced with those circumstances.

Not all of us will face life-threatening situations such as these, but all of us will come across many situations in life where our patience is tested and our buttons are pushed. The key to a stress-free life is to know what you will get upset about and what you won't. For example, if someone is talking behind your back or spreading rumours that simply aren't true, let them. There is nothing you can do about it, and if you know that you are innocent of all charges, why bother to fight? Spending time getting uptight and irritable is just draining your energy, not theirs. Is it worth the effort to clear your good name? And how important is their opinion, anyway? If your boss is a lazy good-for-nothing and takes the credit for all the good work that his team does without a word of thanks, then let him; he will have to pay the karma for it. Your only recourse is to do your best and know that if you were doing a bad job, you'd be the first to hear about it. (That's the way companies work, after all.) If it's really getting you down, vote with your feet and find another job.

In so many situations we spend time making our list of values, but we don't live them. Someone or something stops us from doing it, or the ego gets the better of us and we feel the need to bring any perpetrator to justice even though it's not going to change anything. If proving your rightness or innocence is your thing, then by all means, fight until the death. Just be sure that it was worth fighting for and paying the karma.

A list of values with well-intentioned words like *freedom, wisdom, health* or *family* is a waste of time unless we understand what we will and won't do to live them. An exercise of this nature can take many years and our values will change repeatedly as we grow in consciousness. However, if we understand our values and boundaries – the things we will tolerate and the things we won't – we can start to let go of the garbage that floats around in our head most days and better spend our energy on things that propel us forward rather than keep us stuck.

SILENCE

We need to find God, and he cannot be found in noise and restlenssness. God is the friend of silence. See how nature – trees, flowers, grass – grows in silence; see the stars, the moon and the sun, how they move in silence. We need silence to be able to touch souls.

Mother Teresa (1910–1997)
Roman Catholic Nun

Many years ago, a talented musician friend of mine shared a thought about silence that has remained with me until this day: 'It's in the silence that the music is made,' he said. 'The silence is more important than the note itself. It's only from the silence that the notes and rhythms emerge. It's the empty space between each note that literally allows the music to be music. If there are no spaces there is only continuous noise.' How right he was.

We talk too much. Some of us are obsessed with the sound of our own voice. Even when we're not talking, telling jokes, interrupting, moaning and groaning about our existential angst, we are obsessed with providing a jumble of obscure sound effects – oohs and ahhs, the tapping of feet or fingers, heavy sighs, sharp intakes of breath and many other exclamations that remind people we are still here paying attention or letting them know that they need to pay attention. For some, talking is a way of covering up nerves and anxiety, as it used to be for me. I'd often feel exhausted at the end of the day, being so busy talking and thinking about what I was going to say to avoid uncomfortable silences that I didn't pay attention to anything else around me. Yet it's only in silence that we can hear ourselves and others.

In *The Divine Pymander*, Hermes Trismegistus says, 'Above all other virtues entertain silence, and impart unto no man, O Son, the tradition of Regeneration, lest we be reputed calumniators.' In this sacred text, Hermes is saying: If you must speak, be careful who you speak to. Keep your thoughts to yourself, lest they be misinterpreted and lest we be branded as fools.

When we are talking, we are not listening; when we are not listening we are not learning. When we are not learning we are no longer fulfilling our prime directive for being here on this planet. If we are silent, we will learn more and we will wield a greater power. If we are silent, people will consider us as thinkers, and not propagators of 'white noise'. If we are silent, our enemies will write us off as insignificant, which is a good thing. There is a saying which goes something like this: 'When your enemy thinks you are far, be near; when your enemy thinks you are near, be far.' It puts us in a very powerful position if our enemies think we are so insignificant that they do not have to worry about us.

The need to talk is, of course, one of the wiles of the ego. If you think you are one of life's talkers, here's a little exercise to consider: Spend a day – or more, if you can stand it – not speaking. Unless someone comes up to you and greets you, don't speak. By all means, if someone greets you, greet them back, be polite, but say only the words that are necessary. If someone asks you a question, give them the answer. But then shut up. If you need to find something out, ask the question that needs to be asked then shut up. The ego hates silence and discipline, so it's a very difficult practice to apply.

HUMILITY

We must first develop within ourselves a true humility before we can know the liberating truth.

Paul Brunton (1898–1981)
The Secret Path

Humility is not something we value these days. It's often considered to be some sort of psychological malady that interferes with success and progress. We confuse humility with weakness and piety, something which the business world cannot tolerate. Although we might take steps to encourage humility as a leadership behaviour in our corporate performance management systems, everything else conflicts with this desire. In fact we are expected to be anything but humble. Business values those who are competitive, who know their stuff, who get it right first time and avoid mistakes. We are incentivised to be better than another, to have all the ideas, to win at all costs and to play the right political games that line up the shots for our next encounter. We value aggressiveness, assertiveness and arrogance, because these are the traits we have to demonstrate to get by.

Humility is often associated with the fictional character Uriah Heep in

Charles Dickens' novel, *David Copperfield*. Uriah Heep was infamous for his nauseating obsequiousness, blatant insincerity and sickly sweet talk. He made frequent references to his ability to be 'ever so humble', and yet everyone knew he was exactly the opposite. (I am sure we can find a few of these in our business world as well).

If we let our humility get to the point where we actually become proud of it, or if we put it on public display, then it's not humility but a function of the ego. Those who are humble are the last people to tell you about it. You won't find the humble man or woman spinning your wild stories about their accomplishments and achievements for outer show and self-aggrandisement. Neither will you find the humble man sitting quietly, willing you to ask about their achievements in order that he may have the chance to shine. People who've developed the quality of humility seem to have been liberated from the vexations of the ego.

The humble person is tolerant and even-tempered but quietly confident in himself. He has no need for constant affirmation of his abilities and strengths. He is secure within himself. He is unassuming and genuinely modest and may be somewhat of an enigma. The humble man, in the words of Stephen Covey, '...seeks first to understand before being understood.' Those with humility do not interfere or push their opinions on others. They have no interest in hogging the limelight or making themselves known for any reason. Yet if they need to take centre stage to accomplish a specific task, they do so in a quiet and unobtrusive way. People with humility are not shrinking violets, but they recognise their own talents and limitations and avoid pushing themselves into places where they are not wanted.

We often confuse humility with apathy, yet the humble man is not apathetic about life; he may be involved in a number of different pursuits, but he won't tell you about them unless you express a sincere interest. He gets on with life and what he has to achieve in a simple way without noise, bluster, fanfare or fuss. People may confuse the humble man with being a doormat – but he isn't. He has a quiet inner strength and resoluteness, strong principles and boundaries, and he doesn't let people walk all over him. When he needs to fight, he fights. Humility is indeed one of the hallmarks of a self realised leader.

INTEGRITY

So near is falsehood to truth that a wise man would do well not to trust himself on the narrow edge.

Cicero (106BC–43 BC)

Roman statesman, lawyer, political theorist and philosopher

Integrity is often confused with honesty, truthfulness and principles, but for me it goes way deeper than that. In his book, *Words to the Wise*, Manley Palmer Hall captures the profound essence of integrity in a beautifully simplistic way:

> In the eyes of the mystic, the word integrity goes much deeper than the ordinary word 'honesty'. Honesty is the acceptance of and obedience to standards of right and wrong. Integrity is honesty illuminated by inward realisation. It is the irresistible inward impulse to do that which is wise, noble and beautiful. It lifts the life above blind obedience to man-made law and establishes every thought and action upon the foundation of abiding justice. Integrity also implies perfect consistency between inward impulse and outward action. The outward life is dominated by inner conviction and there is no interval of difference between the beauty in the soul and the nobility in the outward deed. Integrity is the living of truth or nearest to the truth that he or she knows. A man who believes in fine spiritual principles and then lives a code of action inconsistent with these principles lacks integrity even though he may be honest in his weights and measures.

In my world, integrity is about ensuring that what we think, say and do are consistent, all the time. Our mental, emotional and physical practices have to be consistent. It sounds easy, but it's hard to fulfil in practice. How often do we flippantly agree to meet someone for lunch or dinner and never call them? How often do we meet someone on a vacation with whom we develop a really good rapport, and then say at the end of the holiday, 'Let's keep in touch,' instead of saying, 'It was nice to meet you, have a nice life'. We knew when we uttered these immortal words that we had no intention of fulfilling our promises, and hope to God that the other person didn't either.

It seems that living out of integrity, failing to keep our word, is par for the course these days. All too often, we give our word without thinking whether or not we can fulfil those obligations. The spiritual warrior understands that his word is his bond. He takes time to think about his decisions and does not give his word lightly. As he develops in consciousness, his conscience becomes more exacting and he pays a heavy price for reneging on promises. And so he learns to keep the ego in check. The ego loves to suddenly blurt out our agreement to do something that we don't really want to commit to. So many times, I found myself in hot water as I inadvertently agreed to participate in something that I wasn't really keen to do. I convinced myself that I'd feel better about my decision as the event loomed closer in my diary, but I never did. When the day finally arrived, I would drag myself along, trying to muster up all the enthusiasm I could, but I never once felt good about the decision I'd made. All it did was create a greater degree of stress and anxiety, because I was 'out of integrity' with myself.

The way I cured myself of this affliction, was to always make sure that I kept my word. As much as I didn't want to do something, I made sure that I went along anyway, no matter how much it hurt, instead of making some lame excuse. If my ego was going to get me into trouble, then it was going to have to suffer all the way through it anyway. I've noticed that my ego is a lot quieter these days when it comes to commitment.

VULNERABILITY

Except ye become as little children, ye shall not enter into the kingdom of heaven.

Matthew 18:3

This is a very misunderstood quotation. It does not mean that we need to become childish to get into Heaven, and neither does it mean that only children go to Heaven. It means that we need to develop childlike qualities before we can begin to experience the unseen realms – those attributes we had as children before the real world caught up with us and before the ways of damaged adults, parents and teachers made their mark.

If we remember our childhood, or watch how young children behave, we will notice how they demonstrate an innocence, a purity and vulnerability which is quite charming. When a child is scared or lonely, he won't think twice about heading up to the nearest child in the play park to ask, ' Can I be your friend?' When children fall down and hurt themselves, they cry and weep and wait for someone to comfort them. They don't mind demonstrating their weaknesses and how much they are in pain. Yet with adults it's a totally different story. When we fall and hurt ourselves, the ego immediately takes control. Even though we're in pain, we jump up quickly and furiously look around to see who might have seen us make a complete idiot of ourselves. We might be bleeding, bruised, limping and in obvious pain, yet we pretend not to be. The ego never wishes to show weakness.

In April, 2011, I was in Queenstown, New Zealand with my mum, who was vacationing with me. We were on the terrace of a small café overlooking beautiful Lake Wakatipu. A waitress had brought us some mugs of hot coffee which were sorely needed on this cold autumn morning. We'd just taken our first sip when we heard a large *whuumph!* behind us and an enormous clatter. We both turned around quickly to see the waitress sprawled across the floor, surrounded by several cups and plates, and pieces of uneaten cake that the pigeons were already delving into. I quickly got up to help the waitress, but she was on her feet, with blood dripping from her knees and elbows, her shirt ripped and stained from the wet cold concrete. Before I could utter any words at all, she brushed me aside, assuring me she was absolutely fine and hobbled off into the restaurant as quickly as she could, clearly embarrassed by what had happened. I felt her pain, both physically and emotionally, and it made me remember the times that I'd done the very same thing.

The spiritual warrior learns to develop childlike qualities. By learning to become, open, curious, detached and constantly expecting the unexpected without a hidden agenda, we develop an innocent quality and a vulnerability that makes us more approachable. When we can admit to our mistakes, no matter how bad they are, and share our vulnerabilities, we begin to create an environment of trust and harmony that everyone can relate to. It's from here that love can flourish.

COURAGE

Life shrinks or expands in proportion to one's courage.

Anaïs Nin (1903–1977)

French-Cuban author

We all want certainty in life. We search for somewhere we can belong, someone or something that we can rely on in life, some creed or ism to live by that can help us get through each day without too much pain or difficulty. We visit psychics, tarot card readers and gurus in the hope that they can provide us with insights that will make our lives more secure, more definite, more grounded; but then we might as well be an ostrich with our head in the sand. Life isn't a mechanical process, it's an unpredictable, unfolding mystery. Nobody knows what's going to happen in the next moment. God doesn't even know what's going to happen, because nothing is pre-destined. A spiritual warrior understands this. He knows that at times in his life, perhaps many times, he is going to feel insecure because that's just the way life is.

Having spent most of my life as an anxious individual, I am used to experiencing stomach butterflies before having to do something difficult or making a logical left brain decision, when I can't hear my intuition for the thunderous clatter of thoughts in my head. In the past, I'd always branded myself as someone who lacked courage because I always seemed to feel afraid. Yet the more I progressed along my path, I realised that to live a life of integrity requires tremendous courage. Following the road less travelled and finding our own truth, means going against the grain, against the commonly held belief, and constantly stepping into an unknown future.

Courage is not the absence of fear. Courage is about feeling the fear and doing it anyway. It's about navigating boldly through the butterflies, the light-headedness and the gnawing anxiety within, and carrying on regardless. In the final analysis, there are only two things we fear most: pain and death. If we can learn to overcome these two fears we can conquer *all* fears. Think about this: Our fear of spiders stems from the fear of the spider's bite. If it's poisonous we might die. If it runs in our hair and gets stuck (which is my fear), it's uncomfortable; I couldn't live with the uncertainty of not knowing where it was. Claustrophobia is also related to a fear of death. We are scared that if we go into a cupboard we won't be able to breathe, or that there might be a big monster lurking in the corner. Either way, we are going to die. If we are afraid of heights, we are afraid of falling; or, as some people have reported, we fear the overwhelming desire to throw ourselves off the building. Either way, it means we will die. We fear the pain of rejection when we are too frightened to ask someone out on a date. We'd rather be on our own and lonely than experience the emotional pain of being refused.

The goal of the spiritual warrior is to become fearless. The self-realised person, the mystical Adept, is fearless. It doesn't mean that he shows an absence of prudence or caution when it's necessary; indeed, he thinks deeply about all his actions. But he does not fear anything inside or outside of this world. Most of our fears are generated by the ego. So to begin conquering fear we need to accept that the stomach butterflies are going to be around all the time. We also feel them when we are excited about something, but we apply a pleasurable significance to these feelings, instead of experiencing them as painful.

How do we begin conquering our fear of pain and death? Firstly, we must accept pain as a way in which we can grow and become stronger, as the payment of a karmic debt that leads us much closer to a reunion with God. Once the pain is over, it never comes back again. It has passed forever. Instead of fearing death and only thinking about death when you are staring it in the face, try to figure out what happens when we die. Read books, talk to people and accept it as a natural part of existence. Start looking forward to your death as a release from this hard-school curriculum. Death signals the end of the school term and the start of the holiday season. We no longer have to work for a living or have to endure the limitations imposed by the physical world. Death is the beginning of a new and exciting phase of existence.

SELF-MOTIVATION

Liberty means responsibility. That is why most men dread it.

George Bernard Shaw

Most of us would describe ourselves as self-motivated. I did when I was in the corporate world – always leading the charge, solving problems. I had a reputation for getting things done. But after the initial excitement had worn off, I found that boredom soon set in. Getting up most mornings became drudgery, the security I craved became my prison. However, I carried on because I was afraid not to, because everyone else did it, because of what might become of me if I didn't. I waited for the next project or assignment to motivate me, to provide me with a purpose, a reason for spending my days this way, outside of earning a good salary. And I waited for my relationships to give me something to look forward to when my career didn't. If I wasn't in a relationship, I looked for the next exciting adventure or some way in which I could spend my hard-earned cash to give me a reason to keep getting out of bed every morning.

Our motivation to do anything in life comes from two things: the avoidance of pain, and the seeking of pleasure. Both are products of the law of opposites, the ego and comparison. We seek to do things that bring us rewards, good feelings, good times, financial gain, recognition and notoriety, we avoid doing the things that we dislike for fear of reprisal, or the fear of what may happen if we don't. Our life becomes all about likes and dislikes, happiness and sadness, joy and pain and avoiding the inevitable feelings of insecurity.

The spiritual warrior acts solely on the ability to do something because he can. He does it because it's the right thing to do, because he has a sense of duty to himself and the Supreme Being. He isn't motivated by like or dislike, happiness or sadness, pain or pleasure; they are the same to him. He doesn't need an external motivation and he isn't attached to the outcome of anything he does, because he elevates the most mundane task to its highest level of understanding.

It's easy to do things when we are motivated by those we love and respect – our families, our children, our friends – but often we have an expectation that our actions will provide us with something in return – greater affection, recognition, gratitude or whatever else we've attached to the reason for doing what we do. Quite often, when the rewards aren't forthcoming in the way we believe they should be, we get upset, we refuse to carry on, we become disillusioned and unhappy with our lot. For example: our boss doesn't praise us and recognise us in the way she should; the stepchildren don't show enough gratitude when we buy them new clothes; my partner doesn't sleep with me enough to make me feel valued, and my best friend doesn't show enough gratitude for the expensive piece of jewellery that I bought her for her birthday. We have lost the art of giving just because we *can*.

As we grow in consciousness, we begin to realise that there is no reward for what we are doing. Pleasure and pain become one. The spiritual warrior travels this path – not for what he can take from it, but because of a fulfilment of a promise – a promise that we made to ourselves (and the Creator) that we would brighten ourselves. We travel the spiritual path because it is the culmination of all our incarnations. We travel this path because we wish to discover the secrets of the Universe for their own sake and not so that we can have power and control over others, or get their respect and gratitude and affection. We travel this path not because our parents said we must, or because our preacher tells us that it's the right thing to do. We travel this path because at some point in our journey, a deep love and respect for ourselves and our role in the scheme of things starts to unfold. When it does we can begin to let go of our attachments to pleasure and pain, our likes and dislikes, happiness and sadness, and begin to settle into a natural rhythm. We can begin to enjoy life for life's sake and the promise of what we might one day become.

A SENSE OF ADVENTURE

Life is either a great adventure or nothing.

Helen Keller (1880–1968)
American author, political activist and lecturer

For the spiritual warrior, a sense of adventure doesn't mean that he should continuously be throwing himself off bridges attached to a long piece of elastic, scaling the highest mountains, diving to the bottom of the deepest oceans, or doing anything else that he might consider to be life-threatening or dangerous. Yet it does mean applying the same kind of spirit to everyday life that adventurers adopt when they place themselves in the jaws of danger. I know, from undertaking several potentially hazardous sports and activities myself, that I am always filled with a mixture of wonder and fear when I am involved in anything that is slightly off the beaten track: diving in an unfamiliar dive site, particularly at night; riding a horse that I am unsure of; or finding myself at the top of a steep ravine on an off-road driving track, knowing that once I allow the wheels to go over the edge, I have to free-wheel to the bottom using only the gears (and not the brakes), or the vehicle may roll. Whatever happens in this moment, one has to let go and trust the process.

Spiritual adventurers approach their craft or activity with a blend of wonder, imagination and aliveness as the adrenalin courses through their veins. Living with a propensity for adventure means getting out of bed in the morning with a sense of excited anticipation and a quiet feeling of joy and aliveness. They approach each day with curiosity without judging it or giving in to their own pre-conceived ideas about whether it will be good, bad or indifferent. Living with a sense of adventure means knowing that where you are is exactly where you are supposed to be, and the obstacles and windfalls you face are designed perfectly to help you learn in the moment. Of course, we can all decide that adopting this approach is a bit twee when we are feeling down and fed up, but like everything, our attitude is a choice, and I know which choice I'd prefer to make these days.

A SENSE OF HUMOUR

A day without laughter is a day wasted.

Charlie Chaplin (1889–1977)

Comic actor, film director and composer

People who follow the spiritual path tend to get very serious about life and assume that anything spiritual must be treated earnestly and with intensity. I know I do. This is true – our spiritual path is a serious thing, and those who wish to make progress can't do so unless they adopt a measure of sincerity and sobriety. But we can also do it with a sense of humour. If we can learn to lighten up, laugh at ourselves and the ridiculous circumstances we find ourselves in, our path will be a lot easier. When I find myself getting fed up and miserable about my situation, or with the people I encounter who are just impossible to deal with, I imagine what those who are 'on high' must be thinking about the way I am allowing myself to get all bent out of shape: 'Oh no, here she goes again with this whole seriousness thing. It's just a game, doesn't she get that yet? Let it go....' I can only imagine that God must be exasperated with us. He goes to all this trouble to create a universe so that we can brighten ourselves, and all we do is moan about it.

Find a way to laugh every day, even if it is at yourself. It doesn't always work, but I do find myself remembering to lighten up a lot more than I used to.

ENTHUSIASM FOR CHANGE

If you don't like how things are, change it! You're not a tree.

Jim Rohn (1930–2009)

American entrepreneur, author and motivational speaker

Our desire for security and the avoidance of pain keeps us stuck. We cling to things in an effort to avoid that feeling of falling, of being out of control – things like outdated ideas and notions about ourselves and others, our hard luck stories about the past and our fears for the future, our possessions, our money and anything we believe represents safety. We stay in relationships and jobs that are not working because we are afraid of the pain of change. Through rigorous dieting, exercise and plastic surgery, we fight to keep our bodies exactly the way they were in our twenties, to stave off the aging effect; and we don't quit smoking or drinking until our doctor gives us the 'live or die' speech because it's a habit we've become used to. We change course only when we are bludgeoned, pushed, cajoled and forced into a corner by external circumstances. Yet how often have we taken a brave step into a new world once we've seen the light, only to wish we'd done it sooner?

I remember Marcos giving a lecture to our class one evening when he was particularly frustrated with our progress. 'There is not one single person sitting in this room who is capable of succeeding on the spiritual path,' he said. 'Not one.'

I felt my heart sink when I heard that. 'Thanks for the motivation,' I thought.

'By the time you succeed on this path,' he continued, 'you will no longer be what you are now. Everything about you will have changed – your life will have changed, your circumstances will have changed, your friends will have changed, your health will have changed, the rate at which you age will have changed, your knowledge will have changed, your level of insight will have changed, your abilities and your habits will have changed. The end product of the spiritual journey is the Adept, or self-realised man, and that man is completely different from the one who started this journey. Change is the only way you can manage to go down this road. If you are fearful of change and avoid it, because you deem it to be too painful, you will fail.'

Need I say more?

Do one thing today that scares you, one thing that pushes you out of your comfort zone – go to a networking evening on your own and stand there like a lemon and allow the butterflies to whirl; give a speech in front of a group of people (supposedly the biggest fear most people have); learn to scuba dive to overcome your fear of deep water (like I did); learn to rock-climb to overcome your fear of heights (as my sister Suzanne did, but which I still don't have the guts for); enrol in a personal development programme that will push your buttons and compel you to face those parts of yourself that you don't like very much. If we step out of our comfort zone for just a moment, and continue to do so as often as we can, courage soon becomes a natural part of our existence.

However, if none of this appeals to you, then carry on as you were, because life will eventually force you to change – if not now, then at some time in a future lifetime. I am convinced that because this particular lifetime for *me* has been about nothing *except* change, I must have clung fervently to anything and everything that I could for several lifetimes in the past. By trying to stave off change, we are fighting a losing battle with existence, one we can never win. This constant flux and change in our Universe is the natural order of things.

EPILOGUE

LOOKING BACK ON THE JOURNEY

ITHACA

When you set out for Ithaca,
ask that the journey be long,
full of adventure, full of things to learn.
The Laestrygonians and the Cyclops, angry Poseidon –
Do not fear them.
Such as these you will never find in your path,
if you elevate your thoughts,
if choice emotions touch your spirit and your flesh.

The Laestrygonians and the Cyclops,
the fierce Poseidon you will not meet,
unless you carry them in your heart,
if your soul does not set them up before you.

Pray that the journey be long;
That there may be many summer mornings
When with what joy, what delight
you will enter into harbours you have not seen before;
and will stop at many Phoenician trading ports,
acquire beautiful merchandise,
mother-of-pearl, coral, amber and ebony,
and sensuous perfumes of all kinds,

as many sensuous perfumes as you can.

Visit many Egyptian cities,
to gather stores of knowledge from the learned.

Have Ithaca always in your mind.

To arrive there is your ultimate goal.
But do not hurry the journey in the least.

Better that it may last for many years,

that you cast anchor at the island when you are old,
rich with all you have gained on the way,
not expecting that Ithaca will offer you riches.

Ithaca gave you that splendid journey.
Without her you would have not have set out.
She has nothing more to offer.

And if you find her poor, Ithaca has not deceived you.
Wise as you have become, with so much experience,
you must already have understood what Ithaca means.

Constantine P. Cavafy (1911)

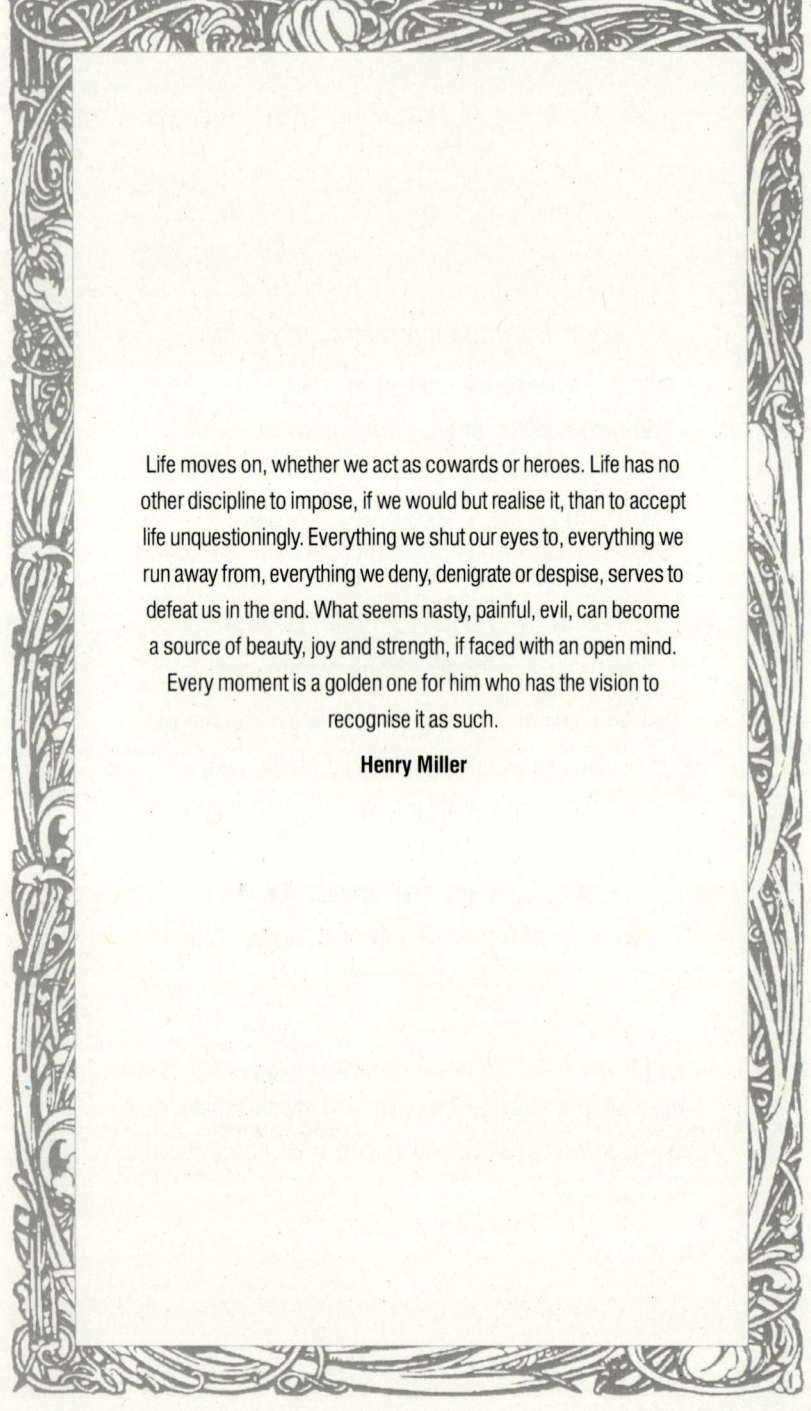

Life moves on, whether we act as cowards or heroes. Life has no other discipline to impose, if we would but realise it, than to accept life unquestioningly. Everything we shut our eyes to, everything we run away from, everything we deny, denigrate or despise, serves to defeat us in the end. What seems nasty, painful, evil, can become a source of beauty, joy and strength, if faced with an open mind. Every moment is a golden one for him who has the vision to recognise it as such.

Henry Miller

LOOKING BACK ON THE JOURNEY

Many people may doubt that finding God is the purpose of life; but everyone can accept the idea that the purpose of life is to find happiness. I say that God is Happiness. He is Bliss. He is Love. He is Joy that will never go away from your soul. So why shouldn't you try to acquire that Happiness? No one else can give it to you. You must continuously cultivate it yourself.

Parahamahansa Yogananda (1893–1952)

Self Realisation Fellowship

ver the course of my life, I've asked many people what they believe the purpose of life to be. I've had many answers: happiness, peace, fulfilment, joy, bliss, accomplishment, love, achievement, growth, wisdom, knowledge and a whole plethora of other explanations. Since I've been writing this book, I've had a lot of people ask me what I believe the purpose of life to be. To answer that I am going to share one last story.

In the middle of the last century, reconstruction work on the banks of the Chao Phraya River near Chinatown, Bangkok, required the destruction of an old abandoned temple that housed a stucco-painted clay statue of the Buddha. Despite the fact that the statue was less than attractive, the monks in one particular temple agreed that it couldn't be destroyed and should instead be moved to a temple of minor relevance at Wat Traimit, even though there was no building there big enough to house the statue. After it was moved, the statue was stored for twenty years under a simple tin roof until funds were made available for a new temple to be built. With the new building complete the monks decided to install the ordinary-looking statue inside. They hired a crane to move the giant figure carefully into its new resting place, but it was far heavier than anyone anticipated, and during the transition one of the main cables broke, causing the statue to fall to the ground. It was the rainy season in Thailand, and a terrible storm raged, which lasted the whole night, and so the statue was covered with a tarpaulin and left to weather the elements.

Just before dawn the following day, the abbot of the temple decided to evaluate the damage. He was walking around the huge clay figure that lay in the mud, shining his flashlight on all the cracks that had now appeared on the surface of the statue, when something bright and shining caught his eye. He returned his torch to the spot where he'd just shone the light and curiously began chipping away at the surface mud. As the crack widened, the monk gasped in amazement. Under the ordinary clay and terracotta surface was a statue made of solid gold!

Historians believed that the statue originally came from Ayatthuya, and that many centuries ago it was disguised under clay and plaster to hide it from an invading Burmese army. Unfortunately, none of the monks who guarded it at that time survived the army's onslaught to attest to its true beauty, and it was only 200 years later that it was discovered quite by accident. Today, the Golden Buddha is located in the temple of Wat Traimit, Bangkok. It's thought to be the largest solid gold statue in the world.

Inside every ordinary-looking individual, covered in layers of clay, is a golden Buddha, a unique fragment of a divine essence that is bursting to break free. Over many lives we've become bound and imprisoned by layers of *grossness*, which keeps our true essence hidden from the world. Babuji Maharaj of the Ram Chandra Mission described us as 'glass chimneys which have been coated with soot from the inside. The true essence of who we are is enshrouded in solidity and darkness. The lamp is still burning but there is no light coming out.' We have become spiritless machines – lost, wandering, trapped in a world which seems to make little sense, and from which we yearn for liberation. To find happiness, to find bliss, to seek wisdom or any other definition that we want to create for the purpose of life, we need to break free from those things that keep us mired in darkness. Whilst the purpose of existence may be learning, growth and consciousness, which are, after all the building blocks of the universe, the purpose of life – if we want to stop worrying and start living – is freedom.

The beauty of the hero's 'journey map' is that it not only describes patterns which can be found in myths and fairy tales, but it's also an accurate map of the path we must travel to become free and discover who we truly are. In mythological stories the hero or heroine sets out on an adventure to free the kingdom from the reign of a tyrant king, to free the princess from the tower, or to bring back the magical elixir that will once again bring life to the realm. The kingdom in the myth is symbolic of the ordinary world of the modern-day spiritual warrior who seeks freedom from those things that subjugate him and hold his kingdom for ransom. In search of freedom, he goes on a journey, one which might not make sense to the rest of the world. The path is often long and difficult, and along the way he falters and stumbles and slays many dragons. But as he looks back on the journey, he comes to realise that the fearsome beasts he encountered didn't really exist; the pressures he faced and difficulties he experienced were merely shadows within his own disoriented psyche. The obstacles he met were illusory, and the godly powers he sought and won were not to be found outside of himself, but were actually within his own heart all the time. The warrior's journey is ultimately an expedition into the dark forest of the subconscious, where the seeker may appear to have been swallowed entirely, lost to the world. Yet he emerges again, renewed; transformed; reborn. He sets out to seek himself only to lose himself and find himself again.

Although freedom may be the ultimate goal of the journey, and, for that matter, the ultimate goal of life, it is through the journey that the hero realises that freedom cannot be fought for, won or attained. Those who fight for freedom are never truly free because it's the fight that keeps them stuck. Freedom is a state of being which gradually unfolds in the hero as he opens his heart to the journey, learns to trust the path and surrender to life. This kind of freedom can only arise from love – a love that knows no fear, that has no attachments, no judgements and no boundaries. Those who operate from love forget about the fight. They forget about their problems and difficulties and the things that bind them in misery and illusion, not because they weren't important but because they no longer matter. Love has filled their hearts, and society and all its problems have simply disappeared. They have become irrelevant. It is from love that the spiritual warrior learns to live in the world whilst understanding that he belongs to it no more. As he begins to yield to the forces that carry him forward, his inner essence and true beauty start to shine.

With freedom, however, comes responsibility. Those who no longer fight and struggle realise that they are totally responsible for themselves, for the way they think and feel and for the choices they make in life. They no longer have to struggle with the old because they have broken free from its clutches by understanding the scheme of things and how it operates. They begin to realise that everything is as it's supposed to be and it is only possible to change themselves and not the world. Those who strive for freedom drop all conditioning, and look at life with fresh eyes. They become joyfully unpredictable because they themselves don't know what is going to happen next. Society no longer acts through them, love acts through them. Now there is nothing left to fight against. Those who travel this path realise that they need to channel their energies into creative exploits that allow them to make the world a little more beautiful. Those who are free find a definition of themselves that is true and authentic, one that cannot be contaminated by the ordinary world. Ultimately, the journey leads the seeker to desire more than liberation from the miseries and woes of life; he yearns to understand, to delve beneath the surface to merge with that harmonious force that somehow guided his journey. This is when he yearns to understand God.

As you will no doubt have gathered, the warrior's journey and the spiritual journey are one. True freedom is spiritual freedom and the two paths are inextricably entwined. Although the seeds of spiritual curiosity are embedded deeply within, many fail to set out on the journey, as the sacrifice seems too great. We're unsure that we'll find our way in the darkness, alone and unchaperoned through the plethora of religious doctrines, fake gurus and systems of belief that threaten to overwhelm us. Yet we do not need to give up our life in the ordinary world to travel this path. Spirituality is not the goal of life, it is a requirement of life. Both the ordinary world and the unseen world are essential for a balanced existence. We just need to find the right allies, guides and mentors to help us progress. Even though we might make a few false starts, take a few wrong turns and meet with less than savoury characters, nothing is in vain. If we are sincere in our quest, if our will is strong and our heart is open, we will find truth.

Those who succeed on the journey have adopted a philosophy that seems somewhat paradoxical: a 'Western mind and an Eastern heart'. The Western mind is wilful, determined, rebellious, creative, driven, always questioning, searching and needing to understand. Those with a Western mind are prepared to take risks, to be courageous, to go against the grain, even if it is for self-aggrandisement and recognition. When the Western mind finally learns to surrender to the path, the transformation is great. The Eastern heart, however, has already learned to surrender. It knows only of love. Love is both the question and the answer. It has a resounding faith in the ultimate, is comfortable to let go of the 'I' and to become one with the 'all', for there is nothing else left for it to do.

Those who adopt both a Western mind and an Eastern heart have discovered true freedom. They live life from their centre. They learn to truly be themselves, ready to face whatever life brings, ready to accept and live, but always alert, conscious, aware and mindful. Their questions continually propel the journey forward, but their continual surrender allows the realisations and insights to land softly in their heart. Those who balance East and West learn to continually release fragments of themselves until the true essence of who they are is finally revealed.

Never has there been a time when we have not been on a journey, for the path of the spiritual warrior is ultimately the path of life itself. It is only here, while we are in a physical body, that we can make progress, so whilst we may believe we have an eternity to set out on the adventure, why waste time? The possibility for liberation is now, in the present moment. One never knows what life has in store for us, how long we will be here, or when we will come back again, and under what circumstances. So any effort we put into our journey at this point will serve us well. We need to trust the path, trust ourselves, let go and step out.

And if we find ourselves lost, wandering and not knowing which way to turn, there are always the myths, the legends and the fairy tales to guide us. We do not need to risk the adventure alone, as the heroes of all time have gone before us. We have only to follow the thread of the hero's path to discover that where we thought we'd find danger, we'll find peace; where we thought we'd find anger, we'll find acceptance; and where we thought we'd travel outward, we'll come to the centre of our own existence. And where we thought to be alone, we shall find ourselves to be one with the entire world.

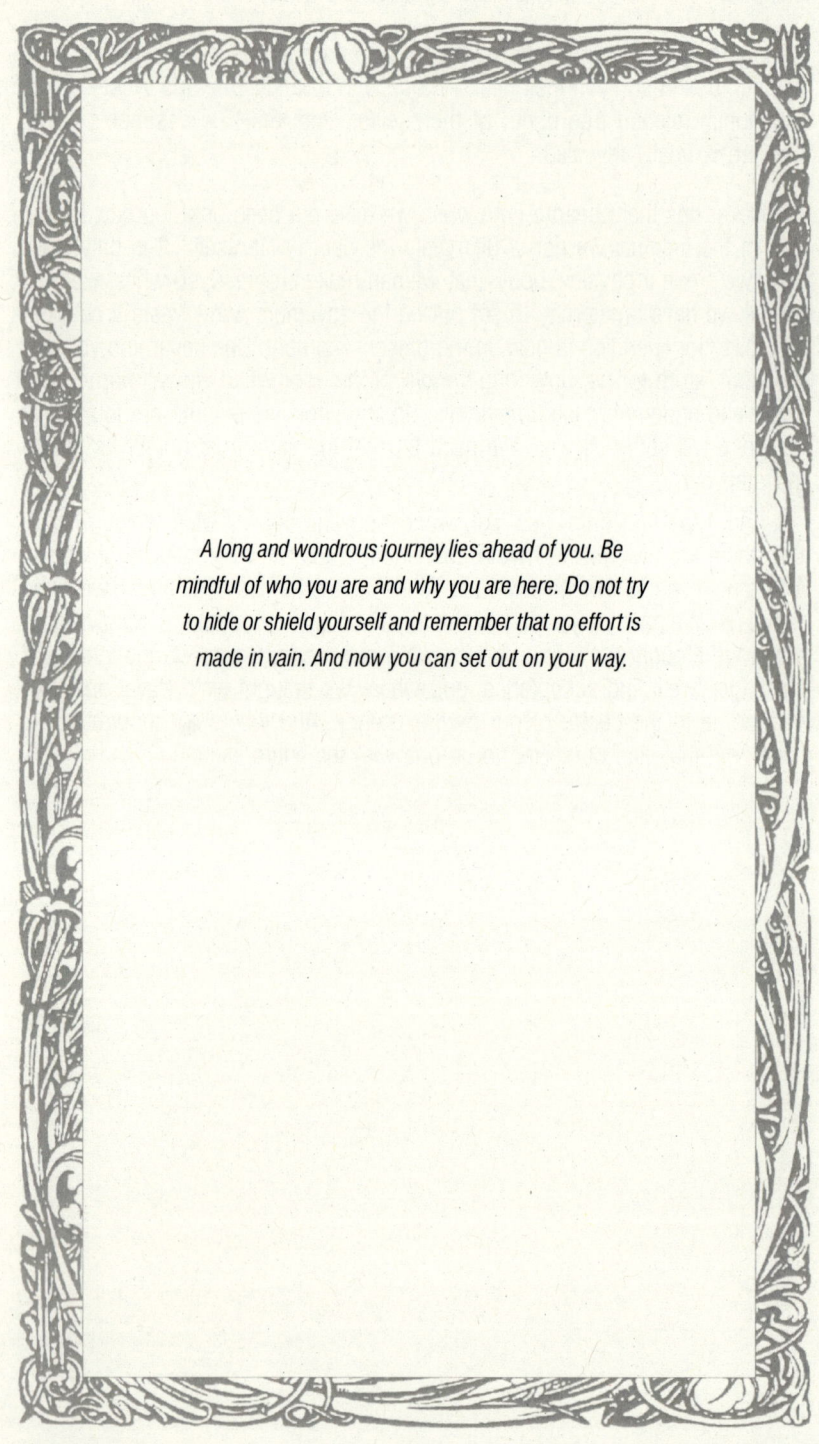

A long and wondrous journey lies ahead of you. Be mindful of who you are and why you are here. Do not try to hide or shield yourself and remember that no effort is made in vain. And now you can set out on your way.

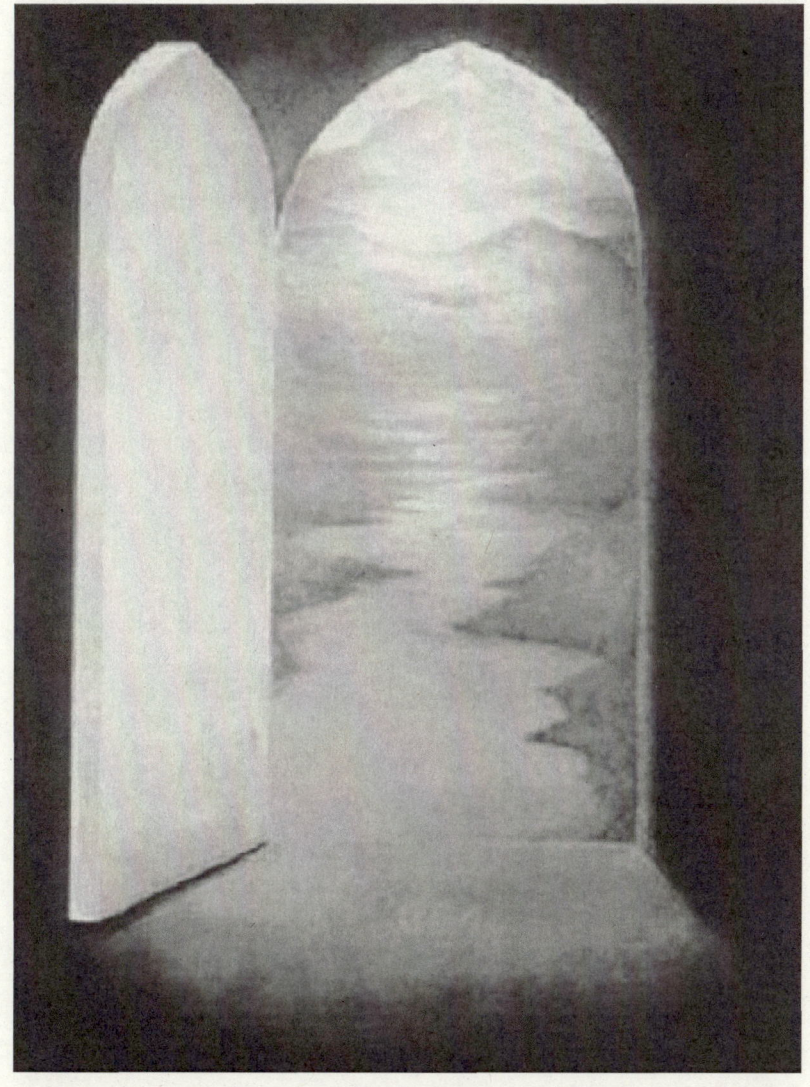

APPENDIX

Notes

BOOK I

1. Culture is immeasurable and poorly understood by many business leaders and MBA schools, simply because it is invisible, intangible and so all-encompassing. We don't identify its components as beliefs but think of them as simply the way things are. Everything we can conceive of has its own culture – a country, a family, a business, a school, a tennis club, a society, a musical group or even two friends meeting for dinner. In fact, the concept of culture itself sits more comfortably in the realm of metaphysics and group psychology than it does in the world of business, representing the collective unconscious, or subconscious mind of the organisation or group. We are never entirely free from the impact of culture; we leave one to join another, even though we may be unaware of it. Most of our actions in life are driven by culture from one source or another. We believe ourselves to be free. We are anything but.

2. The travel business is probably one of the most complicated businesses in the world. ACTE is a not-for-profit association established to provide executive-level global education and peer-to-peer networking opportunities. Membership spans all aspects of business travel, from corporate buyers to travel agencies and suppliers (aviation, hotel, car rental etc.). ACTE serves more than 6,000 members in over eighty countries and was formed in South Africa by Virgin Atlantic and Carlson WagonLits Travel. Its primary goal in South Africa was to create dialogue between travel agents and corporate buyers around the pending changes on the cards in the way in which air travel, primarily, was bought and sold. Historically, the airlines paid the travel agents to distribute their products; however, with the introduction of the Internet, spiralling fuel costs and greater competition, they sought during the latter part of the 1990s and the early 2000s to change outdated modes of distribution by ceasing these commission payments to agents entirely. To survive, agents sought remuneration from their corporate clients. This in turn forced the clients to actively manage T&E expenditure within their own organisations – generally the second largest expense after salaries. In 2000, few if any companies in South Africa had the expertise in-house to do this themselves and needed the advice of an unbiased, neutral advisor.

3. The frame exercise is the name given to a set of processes which affect the operation of the chakras and allow the kundalini to rise. All magico-mystical systems have the equivalent of this. One can achieve the same effect as the frame exercise by taking large doses of hallucinogenics to induce a permanent state of toxic psychosis. The latter course can be dangerous and

lead to insanity, especially if you don't know what you're doing. In tantra they use techniques involving sex as the font of the kundalini energy which they then shoot up the spine. In yoga there are certain asanas and disciplines which achieve a controlled ascendance of the genital fluid (aka shakti/kundalini). At some point in one's mystical or magical development, one has to switch on specific senses in order to operate in the higher realities. The jewel in the crown of these abilities, which everyone chases, is a fully functional third eye – the *ajna chakra*, which corresponds to the pineal gland. But stimulating the lower chakras also brings great power. The frame exercise is just one of many, many techniques to achieve this. The frame exercise itself is only one variant in a veritable ocean of techniques which fall under the heading 'buchstabenmagie'. There is no English word for it. Literally, it is 'letter magic' or 'alphabet magic'.

4. Viewpoint was the central hub of the order. It was a large rural property spanning many hectares in a farming community on the eastern side of Johannesburg. It had been donated to the order some years ago by a wealthy member and was considered prime development property. Several members, including Marcos, and their families lived there in some of the existing cottages. Viewpoint also contained the central office of the membership base, where a handful of members were employed in administrative and financial functions to support the lectures, projects and businesses, membership, and Marcos and Martin in their work. The outer-circle lecture halls, a nursery school and a temple with the most amazing atmosphere were also located there. The property was a continuous buzz of activity with people coming and going all day long, yet it had a sense of serenity and beauty about it, and given its size, one could always escape to a quiet corner somewhere. Plans were afoot to turn it into a full-fledged community, a natural and tranquil habitat for members wishing to seriously involve themselves in their spiritual studies, who wished to cluster together and share resources and insights and work towards the order's vision and mission.

5. In Hinduism, an avatar is a deliberate descent of a deity to earth, or a descent of the Supreme Being (i.e., Vishnu for Vaishnavites) and is mostly translated into English as 'incarnation', but more accurately as 'appearance' or 'manifestation'. The term is most often associated with Vishnu, though it has also come to be associated with other deities. Varying lists of avatars of Vishnu appear in Hindu scriptures, including the ten Dashavatara of the *Garuda Purana* and the twenty-two avatars in the *Bhagavata Purana*, though the latter adds that the incarnations of Vishnu are innumerable. The avatars of Vishnu are a primary component of Vaishnavism. An early reference to avatar, and to avatar *doctrine*, is in the Bhagavad Gita. (Source: Wikipedia)

6. Much of the information imparted in Martins organisation is *out there* in the world; one just has to know where to look, which books to read and what it actually means when one does encounter it. Sometimes it's so obscure, it's easy to overlook or disregard as a fanciful notion unless one has a solid platform of knowledge upon which to base their assumptions. In isolation, the different pieces of information mean very little; however, when combined into a single system of instruction, it becomes very powerful. In later years, the system of development I embarked upon which originated in India (yes, I finally got over myself about the Eastern way of teaching), made so much sense purely because of the teachings I'd already received as a member of the order. (All mystery schools or spiritual schools teach the same thing in a different way regardless of the culture or country in which they are imparted. It is the orthodox religions that are distorted.) This helped me to become more open to a different style of spiritual instruction using the platform of 'wisdom' I'd gained. However, much of the information that Father Rolfe had given freely to his pupils was withheld by Martin as a way of controlling his empire and ensuring that his pupils remained with him for many years in an attempt to uncover greater secrets at the revered 4th initiation. (Many initiates also reported that upon reaching 4th initiation, after spending 10 or 15 years in the order, that it was somewhat of a disappointment.) One can understand that an initiate has to prove their worth before obtaining the next level of teaching; any schooling system is like that. However, many sincere seekers were expelled from the order or refused access to certain knowledge or the next level of initiation if their face didn't fit or they hadn't contributed to the order in some way that Martin, or Marcos, deemed worthy. An 'out of control' guru can be a very dangerous person indeed.

7. Neuro-Linguistic Programming is an approach to communication, personal development, and psychotherapy created in the 1970s by Richard Bandler and John Grinder, which is capable of addressing problems such as phobias, depression, habit disorder, psychosomatic illnesses and learning disorders, and helps people attain fuller and richer lives. Bandler and Grinder claimed that if the effective patterns of behaviour of exceptional people could be modelled, then these patterns could be acquired by others. NLP has been adopted by private therapists, including hypnotherapists, psychologists and coaches.

BOOK II

8. There are many theories and interpretations of the Bible myth. However, it is widely believed that 'Adam' relates not to one individual, but to an early race of peoples known as the Adamites. The Old Testament often makes

reference to individuals when meaning an entire race. For example, Noah was from a race known as the *Noachs* (Hebrew) who were fisherman from the antediluvian (or pre-diluvian) period between the Creation of the Earth and the Great Flood. Noah's sons, Shem, Ham and Japheth, relate to the Semitic, Hamitic and Japhetic peoples (Indo-Europeans, Greek, Caucasians) from whom the earth's population is believed to have descended.

9. There is no time and space on the astral plane. Life is pleasant in comparison to what it is in the physical world. We make assumptions that the Garden of Eden was on the astral plane when we read in the tale of Pandora by Nathaniel Hawthorne (the equivalent of the story of Adam and Eve) that Epimethius was reported to 'never have a mother or a father and that life was very pleasant indeed.' We are only born to a mother and father when we are on the physical plane. The physical plane was not originally intended for all human life. It was a place for the animals, divine sparks with a lesser degree of light. Adam's job was to administer to the animals in the physical world. We can see this in the biblical reference of Genesis 2:19 and 20: 'And out of the ground the Lord God formed every beast of the field and every fowl of the air; and brought them unto Adam to see what he would call them and whatsoever Adam called every living creature that was the name thereof. And Adam gave names to all the cattle and to the fowl of the air, and to every beast of the field....' The same can be seen in the ancient Sumerian myths where the goddess Ninhursag created a beautiful garden full of lush vegetation and fruit trees, called Edinu, in Dilmun, the Sumerian version of Paradise. Ninhursag charged Enki with controlling the wild animals and tending the garden. It was only after the Fall of Man (depicted in Adam and Eve's exile from Paradise) that man came to the physical world.

10. Babel means 'gate to God'. In the Babylonian myth of the Tower of Babel, before the building of the Tower there was one language – one common form of speech for all people. The universal language of the astral plane is pictures and symbolism. When God discovered that the people of the Earth were trying to build a stairway to Heaven to make a name for themselves and to prevent their city from being scattered, he created confusion amongst them by causing them to 'speak in tongues', depicting their exile to the physical plane, where a verbal language through the use of the vocal chords was necessary.

BOOK III

11. Tarot cards are an ancient system of mystical instruction which date back into antiquity. They are believed to have been derived from the Book of

Thoth and are strongly linked to Hermetic kabbalah. The cards are replete with esoteric symbolism in accordance with kabbalistic principles which date back into antiquity. The idea of reducing the tarot system to cards was to make it portable so that secret teachings could still take place during the time of the early persecutions by the Church. The Rider-Waite-Smith tarot deck is believed to be the most popular and accurate depiction of these teachings. The images on the Rider-Waite deck were drawn by artist Pamela Colman Smith, according to the instructions of Christian mystic and occultist Arthur Edward Waite, and were originally published by the Rider Company in 1910. The keys to the tarot are each a kabbalistic teaching. In the tarot deck, the 'Major Arcana'(greater secrets), or trump cards, consists of twenty-two cards without suits that depict these teachings: The Magician, The High Priestess, The Empress, The Emperor, The Hierophant, The Lovers, The Chariot, Strength, The Hermit, Wheel of Fortune, Justice, The Hanged Man, Death, Temperance, The Devil, The Tower, The Star, The Moon, The Sun, Judgement, The World and The Fool. The 'Minor Arcana' (lesser secrets) consists of fifty-six cards, divided into four suits of fourteen cards each: ten numbered cards and four court cards. The court cards are the King, Queen, Knight and Page/Jack, in each of the four tarot suits. The traditional suits are swords, wands, pentacles, and cups, which became the very simplified version of the tarot in our modern-day playing cards. Swords became spades, wands became clubs, pentacles became diamonds and cups became hearts.

12. In his book, *The Soul of the White Ant,* naturalist and writer, Eugene Marais (1871–1936) studied the habits of the South African termite during investigations into animal psychology. His work revealed some extraordinary observations about the functioning of a group or community and its collective psyche, which Mr Marais depicted as being 'just as wonderful and mysterious as that of people.'

13. The mathematical formula refers to the 'Golden' section, also known as the golden mean, golden ratio and divine proportion. It is a ratio or proportion defined by the number *Phi* (1.618033988749895 – commonly rounded to 1.618). In the 12th century, Leonardo Fibonacci discovered a simple numerical series which formed the foundation of an incredible mathematical relationship between Phi and our entire planet. This ratio can be found in nature, architecture, the Great Pyramids of Egypt, the Parthenon in Athens, Notre Dame in Paris, Renaissance art, plants, crystals, snowflakes, the human body, trends on the stock exchange and even the breeding cycle in rabbits, indicating that there has to be a divine intelligence behind creation. (See the book *The Power of Limits* by Gyorgy Doczi.) The Fibonnaci series works in the following way: Starting with 0 and 1, each new number in the series is the sum of the two

before it – 0, 1, 1, 2, 3, 5, 8, 13, 21, 34, 55, 89, 144... As the numbers in the sequence get larger and larger, the ratio eventually becomes the same. That number is the golden ratio. The golden ratio is also an irrational number, meaning that it has an infinite number of decimal places and it never repeats itself! One more interesting thing about Phi is its reciprocal. If you take the ratio of any number in the Fibonacci sequence to the next number the ratio will approach the approximation 0.618. This is the reciprocal of Phi: $1/1.618 = 0.618$. It is highly unusual for the decimal integers of a number and its reciprocal to be exactly the same, which adds to the mystery of the Golden section.

14. In our modern day world, most of our time and effort is directed towards material well-being, and we often find our lives becoming overly complicated by multiple goals and priorities. Although we profess to follow the inner voice or our intuition, in reality it is often barely audible. We are so driven by our moods, emotions and attachments that we cannot hear the voice of the true self amid the clatter of the eight-lane highway of our minds. The ego, through the mind, often convinces us that it is the true self speaking, or the voice of our intuition; but it's not. Unless the mind is cleared of pollutions and brought into a state of peace and moderation, it can never reflect the inner voice of this higher intelligence. It is only through the continual practice of meditation that the true self can be heard. Meditation trains the mind to regulate itself, leading us beyond outer activity and bluster into the inner silence of our hearts, where we find ourselves connected to our divine essence. During meditation we develop a more balanced state of being in which we are less affected by the ups and downs of everyday life. It is only during meditation that our natural capacity for wisdom and right action begins to manifest, allowing us to better prioritize the conflicting demands of life. If one wants to truly develop spiritually, meditation is the only way.

15. I am reluctant to recommend in this book a spiritual practice that leads to enlightenment. Each one of us is different and I am certainly not a guru with all the right answers. The type of spiritual practice we choose is very personal, and I can only share my experiences of life and those practices that have worked for me. After leaving the order and trying many systems of development, I have found a system of meditation practice through *Sahaj Marg*, a system of Raja yoga, that contributes significantly to my spiritual and life goals. Sahaj Marg is a Sanskrit term meaning 'natural path'. While this system of meditation originated in India, its purpose is spiritual and universal, without religious or cultural bias. More information can be found at www.sahajmarg.org.

16. As you may recall from earlier chapters, in mythology, the ambrosia signals the ultimate achievement in spiritual development. It is earned through

the personal effort of the spiritual warrior upon the completion of the journey, a warrior who is totally balanced of mind, body and emotion. It is not intended for everyone. (Tydeus was denied the ambrosia because he was still mired in illusion and governed by the whims of the ego.) Spiritual growth is a gradual process, one that unfolds as the journey progresses. As one grows spiritually, so his vibration increases and subtle changes take place in the body's cellular, energetic and nervous system. The greater the vibration, the greater the capacity for wisdom and the more the body becomes ready for receiving higher energies of a more subtle nature. Not everyone is *ready* for truth. Although everyone may hunger for wisdom, few are ready to actually receive it. Each person has his specific rung on the ladder of the Tree of Life – his own path to walk, karmic debts to pay, dragons to slay and lessons to learn before he is *vibrationally* ready for such insight. No two men are equal. What is right for one is not right for the other. Those who attempt to steal the ambrosia and/or pass it to those who are undeserving are destined to be punished by the Gods for trying to shortcut the system of learning, interfering with the free will of another, disrupting the scheme of things and creating an imbalance in the system. Giving too much knowledge to those who are not ready is akin to handing a chainsaw to a four year old child or passing a high voltage electrical current through the body. It can damage an individual irrevocably and actually impede their spiritual progress in the long term and not enhance it. Those who attempt to steal the ambrosia, and/or pass it to those who are undeserving, are destined to be punished by the gods for trying to shortcut the system of learning, interfering in the free will of another, disrupting the scheme of things and creating an imbalance in the system. Stealing the ambrosia is symbolic of trying to gather too much knowledge too soon in the journey, of lifting all of the seven veils of Isis at once. This is also depicted in the biblical tale of Adam and Eve and the Greek myth of Pandora's box. By eating of the fruit of the Tree of Knowledge of Good and Evil in the Garden of Eden, Adam and Eve were trying to bypass the system of learning and were exiled to the physical plane from Paradise.

Bibliography

Book I

AESOP (1994) *Aesop's fables*. England: Wordsworth Editions.

ALIGHIERI, D. (2006) *Dantès divine comedy*. Arcturus Publishing.

ANDERSEN, H. C. (2009) *Complete Andersen's fairytales*. England: Wordsworth Editions.

AYTO, J. (2005) *Brewers dictionary of phrase and fable*. 17th Edition. Casell Publications.

BULWER LYTTON, SIR E. (2007) *Zanoni – A Rosicrucian tale*. Nu-Vision Publications.

BURGESS, T. (1997) *Great heroes of mythology*. Michael Friedman Publishing.

CAMPBELL, J. (1993) *The hero with a thousand faces*. Fontana Press.

CAMPBELL, J. (2001) *The power of myth*. Broadway Books.

CAMPBELL, J. (1973) *Myths to live by*. Souvenir Press.

COTTERELL, A. (1997) *Norse mythology*. Anness Publishing.

COTTERELL, A. (1996) *Encyclopedia of classic mythology*. Anness Publishing.

GODWIN, M. (1994) *The holy grail*. Bloomsbury Publishing.

GRIMM. (2009) *Complete Grimm's fairytales*. England: Wordsworth Editions.

ROSENCREUTZ, C. (1616) *The chymical wedding*. Rosicrucian Archive Library. (http://www.crcsite.org/wedding1.htm)

MILTON, J. (2000) *Paradise lost*. Penguin Books.

VOGLER, C. (1998) *The writer's journey*. Michael Wiese Productions.

WILMOT-BUXTON, E. M. (1908) *Told by the northmen: Stories from the eddas and sagas*. Gutenberg Press.

Book II

ARNTZ, W./CHASSE, B./VICENTE, M. (2005) *What the bleep do we know.* Captured Light Distribution LLC.

ATWATER, P.M.H. (2006) *We live forever*. Virginia, USA: A.R.E. Press.

BACH, R. (1997) *Illusions: The adventures of a reluctant messiah*. Mandarin Paperbacks.

BACH, R. (1970) *Johnathan Livingston Seagull*. Harper Collins.

BAILEY, A. (1997) *From intellect to intuition*. Lucis Trust.

BAILEY, A. (1996) *The soul and its mechanisms*. Lucis Trust.

BARDON, F. (2007) *Initiation into hermetics*. Merkur Publishing.

BARNSTONE, W./MEYER, M. (2003)*The gnostic bible*. Shambhala Publications.

BLAVATSKY H. (1998) *Isis unveiled*. Theosophical University Press.

BLAVATSKY, H. (1998) *The secret doctrine*. Theosophical University Press.

BODANIS, D. (2000) $E=mc^2$: *A biography of the world's most famous equation*. England: Walker Books.

BRABHUPADA, SWAMI A. C. (1984) *Coming back: The science of reincarnation*. International Society for Krishna Consciousness.

BRADEN, G. (2007) *The divine matrix*. Hay House Publishing.

BRUNTON, P. (1969) *The secret path*. London: Rider and Company.

BUTLER, S. (1944) *The odyssey of Homer*. New York: Walter J. Black Inc.

BUTLER, S. (1942) *The iliad of Homer*. New York: Walter J. Black Inc.

CAPRA, F. (1999) *The tao of physics*. Shambhala Publications.

CHANDRAJI, SRI RAM. (2010) *Reality at dawn*. Sri Ram Chandra Mission.

DAVIES, P. (1983) *God and the new physics*. New York: Simon and Schuster Paperbacks.

DOCZI, C. (1981) *The power of limits*. Shambhala Publications Inc.

EMOTO, M. (2001) *The hidden messages in water*. Beyond Words Publishing.

FORTUNE, D. (1995) *Esoteric orders and their work and the training of an initiate*. Thorsons Publishing.

FORTUNE, D. (2000) *The mystical qabalah*. Red Wheel/Weiser LLC.

FORTUNE, D. (2005) *Book of the dead*. Red Wheel/Weiser LLC.

FREKE. T./GANDY, P. (1997) *The hermetica: The lost wisdom of the pharaohs*. Judy Piatkus Ltd.

FREKE. T/GANDY, P. (1999) *The Jesus mysteries*. Three Rivers Press.

FRANKL, V. (2004) *Man's search for meaning*. Rider Publishing.

GUIRDHAM, DR. A (1970) *The Cathars and reincarnation*. Neville Spearman Publishers.

GRIBBIN, J. (1991) *In search of Schrödinger's cat*. Black Swan Books.

HANCOCK, G. (2001) *Fingerprints of the gods*. Century Books.

HESS, H. (1998) *Siddhartha*. Picador Books.

HEINDEL, M. (2008) *Ancient and modern initiation*. Kessinger Publishing.

JUNG, C. G. (1993) *Psychology and the occult*. England: Cox & Wyman Ltd.

Jung, C. G. (2009) *The archetypes and the collective unconscious*. England: Routledge and Kegan Paul Ltd.

KRISNA, G. (1970) *The evolutionary energy in man*. London: Vincent Stuart & John M Watkins Ltd.

MACKENZIE, D. A. (date unknown) *Indian myths and legends*. London: Gresham Publishing.

MACKENZIE. D. A. (date unknown) *Egyptian myth and legend*. London: Gresham Publishing.

MARAIS, E. (2009) *The soul of the white ant*. Australia: Review Press.

MASSEY, G. (2007) *Ancient Egypt: the light of the world*. Cosimo Books.

McTAGGART, L. (2003) *The field*. London: Element (Harper Collins).

OUSPENSKY, P. D. (1974) *The psychology of man's possible evolution*. Vintage Books.

OUSPENSKY, P. D. (1949) *In search of the miraculous*. Harcourt Inc.

PALMER- HALL, M. (2003) *The secret teachings of all ages*. Tarcher /Penguin Books.

PALMER-HALL, M. (2005) *Lectures on ancient philosophy*. Tarcher/Penguin Books.

PALMER-HALL, M. (1996) *Twelve world teachers*. Philosophical Research Society.

PALMER-HALL, M. (1963) *Words to the wise*. Philosophical Research Society.

RAJAGOPALACHARI, SHRI P. (2000) *Combined works of Chariji*. Shri Ram Chandra Mission.

REDFIELD, J. (1994) *The Celestine prophecy*. Bantam Books.

REICHENBACH, K. (2003) *Odic force or letters on od and magnetism*. Kessinger Publishing.

RIGARDIE, I. (1989) *The golden dawn*. Llewellyn Publications.

RIGARDIE, I. (2007) *The tree of life*. Llewellyn Publications.

RINPOCHE, S. (date unknown) *The Tibetan book of the dead*. www.holybooks.com.

SCHOLEM, G. (1963) *Zohar: The book of splendour*. Schocken Books.

SCOVEL-SHINN, F. (1998) *The game of life and how to play it*. England: C. W. Daniel Company Ltd..

SQUIRE, C. (date unknown) *Celtic myths and legends*. London: Gresham Publishing.

SHRODER, T. (1999) *Old souls: the scientific evidence for past lives*. Simon and Schuster.

STEWART, I. (1995) *Nature's numbers*. London: Weidenfield & Nicholson.

TOMPKINS, P./BIRD, C. (2002) *The secret life of plants*. Harper Collins.

TWEEDIE, I. (2006) *Daughter of fire*. The Golden Sufi Centre.

VAUGHAN-LEE, L. (1995) *Travelling the path of love*. The Golden Sufi Centre.

WATSON, L. (1973) *Supernature*. Sceptre Publishing.

WATSON, L. (1986) *Supernature II*. Sceptre Publishing.

WILSON, C. (2003) *The occult*. London: Watkins Publishing.

YUKTESWAR, SWAMI SRI (2010) *Holy science*. Self Realization Fellowship.

YOGANANDA, P. (1994) *Autobiography of a yogi*. Self Realization Fellowship.

YOGANANDA, P. (1995). *The bhagavad gita*. Self Realization Fellowship.

ZUKAV, G. (1980) *The dancing wu-li masters*. Bantam Books.

ZUKAV, G. (1990) *The seat of the soul*. Rider & Co.

Book III

BACH, DR. E. (1996) *Heal thyself*. C. W. Daniel Company.

CAMERON, J. (1994) *The artist's way*. Souvenir Press.

CHOQUETTE, S. (2007) *Trust your vibes*. Hay House Publishing.

DALAI LAMA/CUTLER, C. (2009) *The art of happiness*. England: Hodder and Stoughton.

FORD, D. (2001) *The dark side of the light chasers*. Hodder and Stoughton.

HAY, L. (2001) *You can heal your life*. South Africa: Creda Communications.

HOELLER, S. A. (2004) *The fool's pilgrimage*. Theosophical Publishing House.

HUDSON, R./ RISO, D. (1999) *The wisdom of the enneagram*. Bantam Books.

KATIE, B. (2002) *Loving what is*. Rider Publishing.

KEIRSEY, D./BATES, M. (1998) *Please understand me*. Prometheus Nemesis Book Company.

KORNFIELD, J. (2008) *The wise heart*. Rider Books.

LaBERGE, S. (2004) *Lucid dreaming*. Sounds True Inc.

LITTAUER, F. (1995) *Personality plus: the four temperaments*. Monarch Books.

MYSS, C. (2002) *Sacred Contracts*. Random House.

MCCOY, E. (2005) *Astral projection for beginners*. Llewellyn Publications.

McELROY, M. (2007) *Lucid dreaming for beginners*. Llewellyn Publications.

NAIMY, M. (1971) *The book of mirdad*. Penguin Books.

OKEN, A. (1988) *Complete astrology*. Bantam Books.

STONE, JD (1999) *Soul psychology. Keys to Ascension*. Random House.

TOLLE, E. (2001) *Practicing the power of now*. New World Library.

WILLIAMS, N. (2001) *The work we were born to do*. London: Element Books Ltd.

Recommended Websites

ALCHEMY GUILD: http://www.alchemyguild.memberlodge.org/

ANDERSEN FAIRY TALES: http://www.andersenfairytales.com/en/main

A COLLECTION OF THE WORLDS, FAIRY TALES: http://www.fairytalescollection.com/

CAROLINE MYSS: //www.myss.com/

ENNEAGRAM INSTITUTE. https//www.enneagraminstitute.com/

GOLDEN SUFI CENTRE: http://www.goldensufi.org/

GNOSTIC SOCIETY: http://gnosis.org/gnostsoc/gnostsoc.htm

GRIMM'S FAIRY TALES: http://www.cs.cmu.edu/~spok/grimmtmp/

GURDJIEFF SOCIETY: http://www.gurdjieff.com/

JOSEPH CAMPBELL FOUNDATION: http://www.jcf.org/

KEIRSEY TEMPERAMENT SORTER: http://www.keirsey.com/

LUCIDITY INSTITUTE: http://www.lucidity.com/

PHILOSOPHICAL RESEARCH SOCIETY. http://prs.org/wpcms/

PRACTICAL AND USEFUL INFORMATION IN OCCULTISM AND SPIRITUALITY: http://sharing-light.1134647.n2.nabble.com/

SAHAJ MARG. A SYSTEM OF RAJA YOGA MEDITATION. http://www.sahajmarg.org/homepage

Esoteric Orders and Their Work

By Dion Fortune

In all ages and among all races, there has existed a tradition concerning certain esoteric schools or fraternities, wherein a secret wisdom unknown to the generality of mankind might be learnt and to which admission was obtained by means of an initiation in which tests and ritual played their part. Whoever is familiar with the literature of folklore knows that this belief exists among primitive peoples, from the Eskimos of the Arctic Circle to the Digger Indians of the Tierra del Fuego. Whoever has also studied history knows that it has prevailed from the first dawn of human culture. Today, in the centres of the civilised world, this belief is still alive; and although it may be ridiculed by the orthodox-minded, an unprejudiced observer cannot fail to note that some of the noblest of men have been amongst its advocates and that the greatest creative intelligences have almost without exception born witness to a source of inspiration in the Unseen.

It is hard to believe that this rumour should be so widespread and so long lived if it were entirely without foundation; moreover, the fact that it has the same form among races who have had no intercourse with each other, such as the primitive Mexican and primitive Egyptian, is a further evidence in favour of its truth. It is not possible to demonstrate to those who are without the pale, the existence of the organisation to which we have referred because with the revelations of their secrets comes the obligation of silence. It is permissible, however, to give sufficient information to enable the earnest seeker to discern the path, whereby he may approach the entrance to one or another of these schools, and for that purpose, the following teaching concerning the esoteric orders and their functions is played before the reader, though the proofs of the statements therein contained must of necessity be withheld until he shall have entitled himself to receive them.

The different occult schools declare themselves to be the holders of a secret traditional science, communicated to them in the first place by divine founders, and enriched and revised from time to time by great teachers; this science concerns the study of the causes that lie behind observable phenomena and condition them. After preliminary tests as to the character and fitness, the occult fraternities are prepared to communicate the theory of this science to accepted candidates, and subsequently to convey the powers for its practical use by means of ritual initiations. These, briefly, are the claims made for the occult schools by those competent to speak on their behalf.

It is very frequently, and very reasonably, asked why it is that societies avowedly formed for the service of humanity, and having such valuable teachings to give, should not freely communicate it to all corners; should not, moreover, conduct active propaganda work in order to induce people to come and share in their wisdom, and not as they appear to be doing, hide themselves away as if seeking by every possible device to avoid observation and prevent themselves being discovered by those who learn from them.

The answer to this question will be found when the nature of occult science is understood. It concerns certain little known powers of the human mind and certain little understood aspects of nature. Were its researches into these subjects purely theoretical, there would be no need to guard their findings so carefully, but the knowledge of the facts thus discovered immediately reveals their practical applications; knowledge bestows power in this field of research, even more than in the fields explored by orthodox science, for the power thus rendered available is the power of the mind, and the effects of the use of this power are so far reaching, whether for good or for evil, that it is a thing not lightly to be trusted into the hands of any human being. Just as the Dangerous Drugs Acts restrict the purchase and administration of potent drugs, so do those who are the custodians of this ancient traditional knowledge seek to safeguard its use. Being of so subtle a nature, it is impossible to guard it from abuse at the hands of the unscrupulous, and therefore its custodians do all in their power to prevent such persons from gaining access to it. Hence the restrictions with which its teaching is hedged about. But the restrictions are no more severe than those which attend the practice of medicine, for which a five years onerous apprenticeship is required. We are so accustomed, however, to see spiritual teachings freely given, to hear the call, 'Ho, every one that thirsteth, come ye to the waters of life and drink freely,' that we cannot understand a policy which refuses any stream from this spring to those who are athirst.

The reason lies in the fact, which cannot be too clearly understood by its would-be neophytes, that occult science is a mental, not a spiritual thing, and is neither good nor bad in itself, but only as it is used. It is potent for good or for evil; it can save souls which no other means could approach, and it can, ever without evil intention, destroy them. It is no child's play, and few there be who are suited to that path to the heights. Nevertheless, for such as can adventure it, here is a noble quest for the soul, a true crusade against the Powers of Darkness and spiritual wickedness in high places. In the hidden places of the world, there is so much occult evil, little suspected by those who have not met it face to face, that men and women of courage, strength, and the necessary knowledge are needed to deal with it.

The training given in occult schools is designed to produce the adept, a human being who, by intensive training has raised himself or herself beyond the average development of humanity, and is dedicated to the service of God. Certain work in connection with evolution and the spiritual development and safeguarding of the nations is undertaken by highly trained men and women, though their work is never seen and the place of their training is never known. Their actual training, it may be said, is given on the Inner Planes, and only the preliminary training which fits them for the Inner Schools takes place on the physical planes. Consciousness is prepared for its Great Quest, and adventures alone into the Unseen. Not much can be told concerning this training, and not many are suitable for it, but enough has been said to give food for thought

The Riddle

By the Brothers Grimm

There was once a king's son who was seized with a desire to travel about the world, and took no one with him but a faithful servant. One day he came to a great forest, and when darkness overtook him he could find no shelter, and knew not where to pass the night. Then he saw a girl who was going towards a small house, and when he came nearer, he saw that the maiden was young and beautiful. He spoke to her, and said, 'Dear child, can I and my servant find shelter for the night in the little house?' 'Oh yes,' said the girl in a sad voice. 'That you certainly can, but I do not advise you to venture it. Do not go in.' 'Why not?' asked the King's son. The maiden sighed and said, 'My stepmother practices wicked arts; she is ill-disposed toward strangers.' Then he saw very well that he had come to the house of a witch, but as it was dark, and he could not go farther, and also was not afraid, he entered.

The old woman was sitting in an armchair by the fire, and looked at the stranger with her red eyes. 'Take a seat and rest yourselves.' She blew up the fire on which she was cooking something in a small pot. The daughter warned the two to be prudent, to eat nothing, and drink nothing, for the old woman brewed evil drinks. They slept quietly until early morning. When they were making ready for their departure and the King's son was already seated on his horse, the old woman said, 'Stop a moment, I will first hand you a parting draught.' Whilst she fetched it, the King's son rode away, and the servant who had to buckle his saddle tight, was the only one present when the wicked witch came with the drink. 'Take that to your master,' said she. But at that instant the glass broke and the poison spirited on the horse, and it was so strong that the animal immediately fell down dead. The servant ran after his master and told him what had happened, but would not leave his saddle behind him, and ran back to fetch it. When, however, he came to the dead horse, a raven was already sitting on it devouring it. 'Who knows whether we shall find anything better today?' said the servant, so he killed the raven, and took it with him. And now they journeyed onwards into the forest the whole day, but could not get out of it. By nightfall they found an inn and entered it. The servant gave the raven to the innkeeper to make ready for supper. They had, however, stumbled on a den of murderers, and during the darkness twelve of these came, intending to kill the strangers and rob them. Before they set about this work, they sat down to supper, and the innkeeper and the witch sat down with them, and together they ate a dish of soup in which was cut up the flesh of the raven. Hardly, however, had they swallowed a couple of mouthfuls before they all fell down dead for the raven had communicated to them the poison from the horseflesh. There was no one else left in the house but the inn keeper's daughter, who was honest, and had taken no part in their godless deeds. She opened all the doors to the stranger and showed him the heaped up treasure. But the King's son said she might keep everything, he would have none of it, and rode onwards with his servant.

After they had travelled about for a long time, they came to a town in which was a beautiful but proud princess, who had caused it to be proclaimed that whosoever should set her a riddle which she could not guess, that man should be her husband; but if she guessed it, his head must be cut off. She had three days in which to guess it in, but was so clever that she always found the answer to the riddle given her, before the appointed time. Nine suitors had already perished in this manner, when the King's son arrived, and blinded by her great beauty, was willing to stake his life for it. Then he went to her and laid his riddle before her. 'What is this?' said he. 'One slew none, and yet slew twelve.' She did not know what that was, she thought and thought, but she could not find out, she opened her riddle-books, but it was not in them – in short, her wisdom was at an end. As she did not know how to help herself, she ordered her maid to creep into the lord's sleeping chambers and listen to his dreams, and thinking that he would perhaps speak in his sleep and dis-cover the riddle. But the clever servant had placed himself in the bed instead of his master, and when the maid came there, he tore off from her the mantle in which she had wrapped herself and chased her out with rods. The second night the King's daughter sent her maid-in-waiting, who was to see if she could succeed better in listening, but the servant took her mantle also away from her, and hunted her out with rods. Now the master believed himself safe for the third night, and lay down in his own bed. Then came the princess herself, and she had put on a misty-grey mantle, and she seated herself near him. And when she thought that he was asleep and dreaming, she spoke to him, and hoped that he would answer in his sleep, as many do, but he was awake, and understood and heard everything quite well. Then she asked, 'One slew none, what is that?' He replied 'A raven, which ate of a dead and poisoned horse, and died of it.' She enquired further, 'And yet slew twelve, what is that?' He answered, 'That means twelve murderers who ate the raven and died of it.'

When she knew the answer to the riddle she wanted to steal away, but he held her mantle so fast that she was forced to leave it behind her. Next morning, the King's daughter announced that she had guessed the riddle, and sent for the twelve judges and expounded it before them. But the youth begged for a hearing and said, 'She stole into my room in the night and questioned me, otherwise she could not have discovered it.' The judges said, 'Bring us proof of this.' Then were the three mantles brought thither by the servant, and when the judges saw the misty-grey one which the King's daughter usually wore, they said, 'Let this mantle be embroidered with gold and silver, and then it will be your wedding-mantle.'

Source: *The Complete Fairy Tales of the Brothers Grimm*. Wordsworth Library Collection

Oedipus and the Sphinx
The outcome of the myth

Oedipus and Jocasta had four children: two sons, Eteocles and Polynices and two daughters, Antigone and Ismene.

Many years after the marriage of Oedipus and Jocasta, a plague of infertility struck the city of Thebes; crops no longer grew on the fields and women did not bear children. Oedipus, in his hubris, asserted that he would end the pestilence. He sent Creon, Jocasta's brother, to the Oracle at Delphi, seeking guidance. When Creon returned, Oedipus heard that the murderer of the former King Laius must be found and either be killed or exiled. Creon also suggested that they try to find the blind prophet, Tiresias. In a search for the identity of the killer, Oedipus followed Creon's suggestion and sent for Tiresias, who warned him not to seek Laius' killer. In a heated exchange, Tiresias was provoked into exposing Oedipus himself as the killer, and the fact that Oedipus was living in shame because he did not know who his true parents were. Oedipus angrily blamed Creon for the false accusations, and the two proceeded to argue fervently. Jocasta entered and tried to calm Oedipus by telling him the story of her first-born son and his supposed death. Oedipus became nervous as he realized that he may have murdered Laius and so brought about the plague. Suddenly, a messenger arrived from Corinth with the news that King Polybus had died. Oedipus was relieved concerning the prophecy for it could no longer be fulfilled if Polybus, whom he considered his birth father, was now dead.

Still, he knew that his mother remained alive and refused to attend the funeral at Corinth. To ease the tension, the messenger then said that Oedipus was, in fact, adopted. Jocasta, finally realizing that he was her son, begged him to stop his search for Laius' murderer. Oedipus misunderstood the motivation of her pleas, thinking that she was ashamed of him because he might have been born of a slave. Jocasta then went into the palace where she hanged herself. Oedipus sought verification of the messenger's story from the very same herdsman who was supposed to have left Oedipus to die as a baby. From the herdsman, Oedipus learned that the infant raised as the adopted son of Polybus and Merope was the son of Laius and Jocasta. Thus, Oedipus finally realized in great agony that so many years ago, at the place where the three roads met, he had killed his own father, King Laius, and subsequently married his mother, Jocasta.

Events after the revelation depend on the source. In Sophocles' plays, Oedipus went in search of Jocasta and found she had killed herself. Using the pin from a brooch he took off Jocasta's gown, Oedipus stabbed his own eyes out, and was then exiled. His daughter Antigone acted as his guide as he wandered blindly through the country, finally perishing at Colonus after being placed under the protection of Athens by King Theseus. However, in Euripides' plays on the subject, Jocasta did not kill herself upon learning of Oedipus' birth, and Oedipus was blinded by a servant of Laius. And the blinding of Oedipus does not appear in sources earlier than Aeschylus. Some older sources of the myth, including Homer, state that Oedipus continued to rule Thebes after the revelations and after Jocasta's death.

Oedipus' two sons, Eteocles and Polynices, arranged to share the kingdom, each taking an alternating one-year reign. However, Eteocles refused to cede his throne after his year as king. Polynices brought in an army to oust Eteocles from his position and a battle ensued. At the end of the battle the brothers killed each other after which Jocasta's brother, Creon, took the throne. He decided that Polynices was a traitor, and should not be given burial rites. Defying this edict, Antigone attempted to bury her brother. In Sophocles' *Antigone*, Creon had her buried in a rock cavern for defying him, whereupon she hanged herself. However, in Euripides' lost version of the story, it appears that Antigone survives.

Source Wikipedia

About the QXCI/SCIO
& Nelson Medicine

The stress of living in today's environmentally complicated world can lead to many pressures being placed upon the mind-body system. The stressors often result in a lowered immune system, chronic fatigue, pain, reduced performance, depression, insomnia and many emotional ups and downs.

The QXCI/SCIO can help balance the over-stressed body system by assessing and harmonising the body's stressors and imbalances and returning the body back to a state of well being. Designed by Professor William Nelson after twenty years of research, the QXCI/SCIO works naturopathically to stimulate and harness the tremendous capacity of the human system for self-healing.

The Quantum QXCI/SCIO scans the client's body much like a virus-scan on a computer, looking for everything from viruses, deficiencies, weaknesses, allergies, abnormalities and food sensitivities. The device gathers bio-energetic data from fifty five parameters on the body simultaneously at biological speed – 1/100th of a second for each stimulus – meaning that thousands of items can be screened for reaction from the body in only a few minutes.

The SCIO communicates with the body to determine what energy imbalances are most affecting the individual's health and translates the scanned data into useful information about the stressors affecting the person's physical, mental and spiritual wellness. It is calibrated to measure the body's subtle reactions to a database of thousands of electro-magnetic frequencies. The device is highly sophisticated and so finely tuned that it picks up the earliest signs of stress and distress.

Most causes of disease are beneath our conscious awareness. However, our subconscious is aware of the disease causing factors that come at us and reacts with subtle energetic changes in various electrical bodies which we come into contact with during our daily lives. The QXCI/SCIO is the first energetic medicine device to test energetic reactions to disease where both the therapist and the client cannot pre-empt what is being tested. The unconscious of the client causes the reaction which is displayed on the QXCI/SCIO device. Thus the QXCI/SCIO itself does not detect the reactions, but the subconscious of the client does. The QXCI/SCIO machine is a tool to make us aware of our unconscious and start to recognise the reaction patterns to disease and imbalance more easily. The QXCI/SCIO medical device is an Evoked Potential Biofeedback System designed to stimulate the conscious awareness of our unconscious processes. Our unconscious is aware of the initial interface in the flow of health and disease, thus we need to start our healing journey with an interface at this point.

What is Health?

Health is the ease of flow of items in and out of the body. As with everything in life, every day is a cycle of the absorption and excretion of various nutrients in and out of our body. We intake a whole host of nutrients: air, water, minerals, amino acids, fats, carbohydrates, thoughts, ideas, friendship, love, respect, mental stimulation, spiritual stimulation and a host of other nutrients. We also detox and excrete in a variety of different ways – via our breath, urine, stool, mucus, sweat, menses, bad feelings, fixations, addictions, coercions, intimidations, fetishes, manias, compulsions, spiritual doubts and a whole host of other things. Life is a cycle of intake, chew, absorb or reject, assimilate, produce toxins, detox and start anew. Add to this the need to reproduce and we can now see a very complex flow of energies (vibrations) which are continually taking place within the body.

An individual operates on many levels: body, mind, spirit, social and environmental. It is impossible to separate these and know where one starts and another stops. Thus these individual parts cannot be reduced or analyzed separately. When there is a flow of things in these levels, the person is in health. Health is the ease of flow.

The Flow of Disease

Disease starts when a stressor intrusion causes a disruption in the flow. The ease is now dis-ease. Hans Selye (1907–1982), the Hungarian endocrinologist, outlined a medical system (the 'general adaption syndrome') where disease comes into the body as some sort of stressor. This initially produces an ALARM reaction as the body tries to deal with the incoming stress. Thus the symptom is a sign of the ALARM reaction. If we fight the symptom and not the cause, we stop healing. So when our child is exposed to stress (like a bacteria from another child) a symptom becomes present – for example, a sore throat. The symptom is a sign of dis-ease in flow. The immune system then needs help. To fight the symptom is what an allopathic medical doctor (general practitioner) does by trying to block some other flow. He uses an antipyretic for fever, Monaimine Oxidase inhibitors (MAOIs) for depression, Serotonin uptake blockers for despair, calcium blockers for heart problems, etc.

So the child with the sore throat might have a toxin or a nutritional deficiency as the deeper cause of the sore throat. The sore throat is an indication that the body is attempting to detox and stimulate the immune system with the symptom. It's simply trying to cure itself. Everything would be alright, but, via a twist of fate, the child is taken to an allopath who spots the symptom right off and prescribes an antibiotic and an anti-inflammatory. The body's own attempts for healing and detox are thwarted and the disease is driven deeper into the system. The symptom goes away but the cause lingers and another disease, more insidious than the first, continues to develop.

As the stress continues, the body acclimates and goes into the ADAPTION phase. Here the symptoms start to become less familiar, but the disease progresses deeper. We now come to an ultra-important conclusion that might change medicine forever: BEING SYMPTOM-FREE IS NOT A SIGN OF HEALTH. In fact, you can be symptom-free and quite sick. Allopathy is for crisis intervention only.

If the stressor continues, the body now progresses from the ADAPTION phase to the EXHAUSTION phase. The first form of it is the FUNCTIONAL phase, where the organs dysfunction. They make either less or an excess amount of hormones, enzymes or others. After a while they slip into the ORGANIC phase, where the organ or organs will shrink (atrophy) or grow (hypertrophy). There is now a physical disease. If the stressor continues, the last phase results: DEATH. Cellular death, organ death, organ system death and finally organism death. The following diagram relates the flow of disease:

Stressor, toxin etc. →   Health

Adaption

Exhaustion

Functional

Organic

Death

The Causes of disease and possible stressors are:

Lack of Awareness	Toxicity
Trauma or Injury	Heredity
Allergies	Mental Factors
Perverse energy	Stress
Pathogens	Deficiency or excess of nutrients

When any of these enter the body, they disrupt the ease of flow. This produces the alarm symptom. Then the body adapts, symptoms go away, but if the cause continues, the disease continues. **Being symptom-free is not a sign of health**.

The ability to restore or heal the body is based on how much life *force* the body has. Life force has an electrical component and can be suppressed or obstructed by many things – smoking, diet, alcohol, environment, work pressures, stress levels, toxic substances, past traumas (mental emotional and physical). This is depicted in the SOC (the suppression and obstruction of cure index) indicated in the SCIO.

The QXCI/SCIO device and Nelson medicine is based on a different philosophy to allopathy. Its primary goal is to stimulate the body to heal itself. Symptom reduction is the fourth priority. We first try to prevent the disease from slipping further and encourage true healing and long-term symptom reduction. In Nelson medicine, the flow of treatment is as follows:

- Reduce or remove the cause of disease (reduce the SOC index).
- Repair the damaged organs resulting from the disease or stressor
- Unblock the blockages to the flow of energy in the body.
- Reduce the symptoms with natural methods and naturopathy.
- Deal with the constitutional make-up or tendencies of the patient.

The QXCI/SCIO device uses a cybernetic link to deal with the causes of disease. Thus, the device can zap pathogens, make us aware of nutritional problems, stimulate repair of injury, stimulate detox, desensitize allergies, reduce stress and more. However, the best use of the device is its use for clearing the blocks in flow. The SCIO can detect faults in the acupuncture meridian flow and correct them. It can find faults in the brain wave and correct them as well. Finally, the system can help in finding ways to reduce symptoms through other naturopathic means.

QXCI/SCIO Detects the following:

Allergens, Emotions, Meridians, Amino acids, Fatty acids, Minerals, Animal diseases, Flower Essences, Muscles, Aroma therapy oils, Foods, Organ sarcodes, Bacteria, Fungi, Parasites, Blood Chemistry, Geopathics, Physic Energies, Bones, Herbs, Prions, Candida, Homeopathics-Isodes, Spiritual Energies, Chakras, Homeopathics-Nosodes, Toxins, Chromosomes, Homeopathics-Classical, Urine chemistry, Dental diseases & products, Homeopathics-Combinations, Venoms, Digestion, Hormones, Viruses, Diseases, Ligaments Vitamins, Drugs, Miasmas, Worms, EEG, ECG, Brain wave.

QXCI/SCIO Therapies

Autofocus Therapies – Acupuncture, Chakra, Chiropractic, Color, Rife, Trivector (Bicom/ Mora), Spiritual Healing, Biofeedback. Specialist – Acupuncture, Craniosacral, Iridology, Brain wave, Allergen de-sensitization, Fat loss, TMJ, Eye, Hearing, Cholesterol, Sport, Beauty, Detoxification, Aging, Dental. Emotional & Mental – NLP Individual, NLP Group, NLP Family, Gestalt, Neuro-net Stabilization, Emotional Growth, Unconscious Reactivity, Electro-hypnosis. Stress – Music, Biofeedback. Focused – Degeneration, Injury, Pain, Metabolic Repair, Hormonal, Neurological,

Relaxation & Sleep, Digestive, Feel Good, Oxygenation, Muscle Building, Flexibility, Co-ordination, Immune Stimulation, Chronic Fatigue, Anti-inflammation, Fibrositis, Intellect Stim, Physic Abilities, Blood Sugar, Parasympathetic NS , Sympathetic NS, Autonomic NS. Testing – Test samples including hair, saliva, urine, skin, semen.

There are many key philosophies behind Nelson medicine. The first is responsibility. The client is encouraged to accept responsibility for his body and any disease or discomfort. The disease might have been caused by someone else or some outside imposition, but healing can only take place inside the body. Obsessing on someone else or blaming someone else is unproductive and sometimes damaging. Separation from a cause of disease is the responsibility of the diseased client. If there is a cause of disease in your environment, you can choose to change it or reduce the cause, move to a new environment or accept the conditions. Responsibility for healing is with the client.

Some patients are more aware of their unconscious processes. These patients are likely to feel the QXCI/SCIO device working and recognise the reaction patterns more easily. Others will take more time, but after several visits, they become more aware of their unconscious and feel the effects more readily. In Nelson medicine, the client and the therapist agree on a series of visits and a path of recovery that realises that you did not get sick in a day, but over a long period of time. Gentle, long-term healing and health can be yours as you and your unconscious merge as one force of healing, working for your well-being.

Source: Professor William Nelson/Nelson Medicine

QXCI – Quantum Xxriod Conscious Interface

SCIO – Scientific Consciousness Interface Operating System

Professor William Nelson – Biography

Born and raised in Ohio, Bill Nelson was identified as a genius from an early age. As a young man, his interest in quantum physics and electronic engineering led to his work on the navigation system for the Apollo space project. He turned his genius to the field of medicine and health after the birth of his first-born, a son. His son retreated into the world of autism – a result of an anti-nausea drug his wife took while pregnant. After devouring the information offered by a medical world, he turned to the world of alternative health. With natural remedies, he was successful in reversing many of the symptoms of his son's autism.

During his research, he was intrigued by a number of bio-electric devices being used in Germany – the Vega machine, the Voll, and the Mora unit – as well as biofeedback and cranial electrical stimulation (CES) units in the US. These units either measure the body's electrical response to help diagnose problems in the body, or they emit frequencies to treat problems. He also studied the body's subtle energy systems – acupuncture meridians, chakra energy, applied kinesiology or muscle testing, etc. The body's subtle energy system is an early-warning system. Imbalances in the body's subtle energies show up much earlier than disease symptoms. Bill Nelson decided to apply his genius to design an all-inclusive system, a computerized system that would both test and balance the body at the subtle energy level.

To develop this system, Bill Nelson has integrated the sciences of mathematics, quantum physics, electronics, naturopathy, homeopathy, chiropractic, energetic medicine and computer programming. He has also incorporated his knowledge of metaphysical subjects to bring a unique synergistic perspective to natural healing. He has studied homeopathy, naturopathy, science, business, computer science and international law. He has also mastered the difficulties of creating the software to integrate the many healing modalities he has programmed into the QXCI/SCIO system. His unique knowledge of esoteric subjects such as fractal dynamics, subspace theory, a tri-vector system and more has made this energetic feedback system possible.

Rather than deal with the politics of health in the US, Bill Nelson moved to Budapest in 1993. He has lectured at a college in Budapest on homeopathy as a science and healing modality. At present, in addition to offering training and regularly updating his computerized health system, Bill Nelson has started his own movie production company. One of his themes is, 'The politics of health'.

(Source: Wikipedia)

About the Author

Caroline Ravenall is a stress and wellness consultant based in Auckland, New Zealand. She is a qualified NLP Meta coach, hypnotherapist, a SCIO Biofeedback practitioner with a diploma in energy medicine, and is currently studying to be a naturopath. She is also a speaker and facilitator, and works with clients around the globe.

Caroline can be contacted at info@carolineravenall.com

Or you can visit her website www.carolineravenall.com